Tangled Loyalties

The problem of meaning confronts the individual in the passage of time. Judging ones own intentionality in a prior state is similar to judging the intentionality of another in the present moment.

↓ING COST OF CONFLICTS

AT LEAST 2 KEY ASPECTS

1. OVERALL LEGAL MANAGEMENT OF CONFLICTS
   - ENGAGEMENT LETTERS
   - WAIVERS
   - TYPES OF BUSINESS & CLIENTELE WILLING TO ACCEPT

VS.

2. MECHANICS OF IDENTIFYING & CLEARING PARTICULAR CONFLICTS.

ARRANGE TO FIND GOAL IN AN EFFICIENT MANNER.

CONFLICTS WISH LIST

Tangled Loyalties

Conflict of Interest in Legal Practice

Susan P. Shapiro

1) THEORY OF COLLECTIVE CLEARANCE

A METHOD WHEREBY CONFLICTS ARE AUTOMATICALLY RUN & AN INITIAL REPORT AUTOMATICALLY GENERATED. THE REPORT LISTS POTENTIAL PROBLEM AREAS & REQUIRES CERTAIN ~~[illegible]~~ LEVELS OF CONSENSUS FOR CLEARANCE/RESOLUTION.

A LEVEL 1 CAN BE CLEARED BY AN ANALYST
10 BY CONFLICTS ATTY(S) + RISK MANAGEMENT.

A CENTRAL ONLINE LOCATION WHERE ALL RELEVANT CONFLICTS INFO CAN BE ACCESSED.

Ann Arbor
THE UNIVERSITY OF MICHIGAN PRESS

2) GEOGRAPHY OF CONFLICTS

A WAY TO MAP THE LANDSCAPE & PULL OUT USEFUL INFO.

Published in the United States of America by
The Unversity of Michigan Press
Manufactured in the United States of America
♾ Printed on acid-free paper

2005 2004 2003 2002 4 3 2 1

A CIP catalog record for this book is available from the British Library.

Library of Congress Cataloging-in-Publication Data

Shapiro, Susan P.
Tangled loyalties : conflict of interest in legal practice / Susan P. Shapiro.
p. cm.
Includes bibliographical references and index.
ISBN 0-472-09801-2 (cloth : alk. paper) — ISBN 0-472-06801-6 (paper : alk. paper)
1. Practice of law—United States. 2. Lawyers—United States. 3. Conflict of interests—United States. I. Title.

KF300 .S43 2002
347.73'504—dc21 2002018714

Dedicated to the 1,994,200 American women diagnosed with breast cancer since I began this project.

Contents

Tables and Figures

TABLES

FIGURES

Preface

This book reports on an empirical study of conflict of interest in the private practice of law. Oftentimes, the kind of tunnel vision required to bring a large project to its conclusion leads to a distorted worldview. One sees one's subject hidden under every rock, lurking behind every shadow, the hidden agenda in all of life's dramas. Still, I was certainly not the only one to take notice when the U.S. Supreme Court, the consummate icon of objectivity and disinterestedness, selected the president of the United States in a stunning decision tainted by the conflicts of interest of two of its members. Mundane conflicts, by the way, that even the most undistinguished lawyer in my study would have recognized and eschewed. But, then, who watches the watchmen?

That conflict of interest was implicated in arguably the most significant political drama of the new millennium is a testament not only to my own myopia but also to the pervasive tentacles of conflict of interest throughout the social fabric—well beyond that secured by the weft of legal institutions.[1] This book brings a microscope to the myriad tangled loyalties that strangle the practice of law. But as I will

[1]And let's not forget the spiral of conflicts connecting the lesser players in this drama—from the candidate's brother/governor of the state in which the election was decided, to the state cochair of the presidential campaign/secretary of state who certified the vote of the state in which the election was decided, among so many others.

also show, fiduciaries of all stripes are buffeted by the conflicting interests of those they serve. And in the face of social and institutional change, the problem is only getting worse and the tangles increasingly difficult to unravel. Conflicts of interest do not merely lurk behind every shadow; they occupy center stage in the drama of life. Deafened by a cacophony of irreconcilable voices, the dramatis personae struggle to play their roles—some better than others, as we will see.

But who am I to cast such wide aspersions? What shadows threaten to darken these pages? I am certainly not immune from the conflicts of interest that roil the academic world, though I have tried to buffer myself from many of them.[2] Aside from my salary, I have not profited from this research. All presentations of my findings to interested groups of lawyers have been gratis, and my employer has paid my travel expenses. I have neither pursued nor been offered a consulting relationship related to this research. Any royalties that I receive from the sales of this book are unlikely to defray my own personal investments in the project. Aside from a blind pension fund, I have no investments. There are no lawyers in my immediate or extended family; though, as they say, some of my best friends are lawyers.

The costs of researching and writing this book have been supported by the National Science Foundation and the American Bar Foundation (ABF).[3] The American Bar Foundation is a nonprofit independent research institution. It receives income from a fund established by the American Bar Association (ABA) to advance research, regular contributions by the Fellows of the American Bar Foundation (a group of more than six thousand lawyers), research grants from government agencies and private foundations, and investment income from its own endowment. Although the ABF is independent of the ABA, its board is comprised entirely of lawyers, some of them officials of the ABA.

Despite its focus on lawyers' ethics or lack of them, this project has received fairly enthusiastic support, interest, and cooperation from the varied constituencies of the ABF. They seem delighted that, for once, they are supporting research that has some relevance to the bar and that investigates dilemmas that they actually struggle with in real-world practice. Though they are well aware that I could find skeletons in the closet of the legal profession, this downside risk is offset by the prospect that the research findings will teach them something useful, provoke policy reform, or improve the practice of law.

What if this book revealed that all lawyers are crooks? Most likely, it would never see the light of day, because it would never pass muster of disinterested scholarly peer review. But if peer reviewers pronounced the book balanced, methodologically rigorous, theoretically informed, and so on, would it be published? Yes. Would I be persona non grata with the ABF board? Probably with some members.

---

[2]See chapter 10 for more detail. Because I do not teach and am not on "soft money" and am not required to raise funds to support my research, I juggle fewer interests than most academics. Moreover, I have exploited the fact that because I am studying conflict of interest, I need to be "holier than thou" to extricate myself from varied sticky situations that continually dog scholars.

[3]Because I had served on the Law and Social Science panel of the National Science Foundation a few years earlier, my proposal was reviewed by a different independent peer review panel.

Would some benefactors terminate their relationship with the foundation? Probably; members of the ABA have quit over lesser insults, including the association's stand on abortion. Because the ABF does not tenure its researchers, I enjoy only limited academic freedom. Would my job security be at risk? The current ABF director assures me that it would not. Would I be more objective or courageous if I had tenure? Probably not (though I'd be a lot happier); at this stage in my life, I value my integrity and credibility more than my job. What if my book was effusively flattering to the legal profession? Not even lawyers would believe it.

To whom am I beholden? I am grateful for the financial support of the ABF and National Science Foundation, which helped ensure that this project could be conducted with depth and care as well as with disinterestedness.[4] I owe special thanks also to Sherri Lee, LaKesha Threats, and especially Benjamin Casper for research assistance; to Bryant Garth, Jack Heinz, Carrie Menkel-Meadow, M. Peter Moser, and many anonymous reviewers, colleagues, and commentators for their ongoing feedback and support; to Susan Messer and Jeremy Shine for editorial assistance; and most of all, to the lawyers who generously shared their time and experience with thoughtful reflection, colorful detail, and unusual candor. A stunning 92 percent of the law firms randomly selected for this study participated, contributing many tens of thousands of dollars worth of otherwise billable hours of their busiest and most senior partners. The extraordinary willingness of members of the legal profession to cast a light on their ethical practices—indeed, to an outsider—is something to be celebrated.

This project was conducted during a sacred time. Just two weeks before it was funded, I learned that I had breast cancer. I devoted what, for too many in the breast cancer sisterhood, turns out to be a lifetime in bringing the project to fruition. I dedicate this book to the memory of those women who didn't make it and to honor the rest of us who continue to struggle with this scourge. Not surprisingly, the project often paled in comparison with those poignant struggles, and the necessary perseverance to complete it was sometimes sorely tested by impatience and ambivalence. Though I am immeasurably grateful that this will not be my life's work, still I hope that those precious years were not squandered.

[4]NSF grant #SES-9223615. Of course, any opinions, findings, and conclusions or recommendations expressed in this book are those of the author and do not necessarily reflect the views of the National Science Foundation or American Bar Foundation.

Tangled Loyalties

> *Q. Why are scientists using lawyers instead of rats in medical experiments?*
>
> *A. There are more lawyers to begin with, they multiply faster, and laboratory personnel become less attached to lawyers than to rats. Then, too, lawyers will do many things rats won't.*
>
> *(Adler 1992, 136)*

The unending stream of lawyer jokes is but one indicator that attorneys are not held in the highest regard in many sectors of our society. A gaggle of public opinion surveys repeatedly finds resentment and disrespect for the legal profession, with the public regarding lawyers as unethical, dishonest, greedy, arrogant, and lacking in compassion (Hengstler 1993; Samborn 1993a, 1993b; "No Surprise" 1993). Even more disturbing, the harshest critics are those who interact most frequently with attorneys (Hengstler 1993). And surveys show that this anti-lawyer sentiment has grown over time (Klein 1997; "Public Confidence in Leaders" 1997).

Why are lawyers so reviled? In part, these trends have nothing at all to do with the legal profession, reflecting instead the declining public regard for most professions and social institutions (Lipset and Schneider 1983; Klein 1997; "Public Confidence in Leaders" 1997). But the disdain for lawyers derives from far more than generalized cynicism and distrust. The list of potential explanations is at least as long as the collection of indicators that document the declining image of the legal profession (Galanter 1994). They include the fact that lawyers often profit from the misery of others, a resentment of high legal fees and salaries, the adversarial and zero-sum quality of much legal work, the animosity of those who are destined to lose, lawyers' role in roiling unnecessary or frivolous litigation that ties up the court system, the negative impact of litigation on the economy and on the cost of doing business, offensive lawyer advertising, lawyer incivility and poor client relations, negative media coverage, and perhaps even the discomfort of knowing that attorneys often see people's dirtiest linen. Lawyers who defend the legal rights of criminal defendants are often blamed for the crime problem. And, as Marc Galanter has observed, negative attitudes—especially among elites—sometimes represent a "backlash against the use of the legal system to expand the rights of society's less privileged" and the "role of lawyers as agents of equalizing change in society" (Samborn 1993a, 22).

But why did I begin my book, which I hope to sell to lawyers, with a nasty lawyer joke and, indeed, an old one at that? Because the joke embodies yet another strand in the resilient shroud that cloaks the image of the American legal profession. Lawyers, it seems, will do many things that even the most odious creatures on earth will not. Ironically, at the same time that we revile lawyers as hired guns, as amoral champions of the often malevolent desires of their clients, opinion polls find that lawyers' most positive attribute in the eyes of the public is that they put "clients' interests first" (Samborn 1993a, 22) and act as their advocates (Hengstler 1993). We celebrate lawyers as unflagging, zealous champions at the same time that we resent and malign them for their indiscriminate advocacy and for the positions that they champion. Through one set of mirrors we see cultural icons, courageous defenders of the underdog, and valiant and uncompromising seekers of justice, and through another, teeming vermin. This intrinsic ambivalence, I would argue, lies at the root of much of the public's cynicism and disdain for the legal profession. And, unlike many of the sources of public disfavor that I have already cited, this one cannot be remedied. But perhaps it can be understood, maybe even appreciated.

This book explores what it means to be a hired gun, to act on behalf of another. Because we tend to see this unbridled loyalty (for a fee) as something suspect and disreputable, as a symbol of the eroding ethics of the legal profession, we often fail to recognize that maintaining such loyalty is itself embedded in ethical obligations. The following chapters will show that "putting clients' interests first" can be quite a daunting task—and not only because clients' interests sometimes compete with those of their lawyers. The simplistic imagery of the rat, eager to do anything for a few pellets, quickly gives way to one of a creature that is part visionary, part juggler, and part contortionist. Indeed, as we see how attorneys struggle to respect and champion the varied loyalties in which they are entangled, some of us may shrink in embarrassment at how much less vigilant and dexterous we are in fulfilling our own obligations to those on whose behalf we act. These struggles tell us not only about the practice of law but also about the difficulties of rendering trust in complex societies.

A PERSPECTIVE ON CONFLICT OF INTEREST

Conflict of interest is the central ethical problem of a profession, and indeed the problem that gives a profession its defining characteristic. By definition the function of a professional is to serve interests beyond the professional's own self-interest. The concept of "conflict of interest" is a reflexive definition of this fundamental characteristic, for it implicitly identifies those other interests that the professional must recognize. Accordingly, to analyze the problems of a profession's conflicts of interest is to probe the essence of the profession itself. (Hazard 1996, 85)

Though the term *attorney* "denotes an agent or substitute, or one who is appointed and authorized to act in the place or stead of another" (Black 1968, 164), lawyers by no means hold a monopoly of agency roles. Nor do professionals. Agency is simply the engine of the division of labor, insinuated in many social institutions and elaborated in many kinds of professional and nonprofessional work. Agents (1) offer differentiated labor markets, specialization, expertise, knowledge, and skill; (2) bridge physical, temporal, or social distance by providing contacts, intermediation, and brokering; and (3) collectivize (in labor unions, insurance, securities markets, retirement funds, etc.), thereby affording economies of scope and scale and protection from risk.

In classic agency relationships, principals "control and direct the activities of the agent" (Clark 1985, 56). But the very reasons to delegate responsibility to another suggest that principals often lack the expertise, access, or power to control their agents. Such asymmetries between principal and agent are labeled *fiduciary* or *impersonal trust* relationships (Shapiro 1987). Trust is not binary; it is located on a continuum defined by the degree of principal control in agency relationships. Some agency roles are more asymmetric or trust-like than others—say, conservatorships for the incompetent compared with the ties between a multinational corporation and the law firm that handles its litigation.

Relationships of impersonal trust are found in a variety of social and occupational roles: fiduciaries who manage other people's money (stockbrokers, bankers, accountants, mutual funds, insurance companies), public officials, parents, boards of directors, scientists, pharmacists, child-care workers, engineers, teachers, guardians, and of course, lawyers. The professions, characterized by control over recruitment, formal education and training, occupational credentialing and licensure, codes of ethics, self-regulation and assorted gatekeeping activities, represent one market strategy offered to control asymmetries of expertise and specialized knowledge (Abbott 1988, 15).[1] So professions figure prominently among the roster of positions of trust. But asymmetries are not merely occasioned by unequal knowledge or expertise; they arise from the separation of ownership and control over property and opportunity, unequal information, and social distance. So trustees embrace a far more diverse set of members than merely professionals and assorted money managers.

What these varied fiduciary or trust relationships share is that principals are "at the mercy of the other's discretion" (Weinrib 1975, 7). And therein lies the precariousness of trust. The structure of these asymmetric relationships creates a rich

[1]However, some critics charge that professionalization can also be understood as a "project of cartelization" (Gordon and Simon 1992, 231) to create market shelters through entry restrictions, monopolization of training and credentialing, thereby securing positions of privilege, prestige, and autonomy for would-be professionals. From this perspective, rhetorics about ethics, gatekeeping, self-regulation, and public service are merely used to support professional claims to market control (Abel 1981, 1989; Freidson 1975, 1986; Larson 1977).

array of temptations or opportunities for trustees to ignore principals, at best, and to indulge in unbridled self-interest, at worst (Shapiro 1987, 629–30; 1990; Cooter and Freedman 1991; Frankel 1995). Therefore, the bedrock principle of fiduciary obligation, the duty of loyalty, requires that trustees be disinterested, that they put the interests of those they act for or represent before their own or that of others. As Justice Stone observed some time ago, "The fiduciary principle, the precept as old as Holy Writ, [dictates] that 'a man [*sic*] cannot serve two masters'" (Stone 1934, 8).

But, of course, men and women serve many masters. The pursuit of self-interest—the fealty to ego over alter—represents only one of them and perhaps the easiest master to tame. Disinterested trustees who abjure varied opportunities for self-aggrandizement may still abrogate their fiduciary duties because of the multiple legitimate demands of others that emanate from the thicket of social roles they hold—past, present, and future. Moreover, the rule of disinterestedness—which provides clear, if simplistic, guidance about how to choose between self and other—is largely silent about how to negotiate among or disattend the diverse interests conveyed by the multiple masters that individuals and organizations in the real world serve. The choice between the first two masters (self and other) may be relatively straightforward; the choice among the rest is not. This thicket of tangled loyalties to self and countless others, otherwise known as *conflict of interest* in legal parlance or *role conflict* in the sociological vernacular, is the subject of this book.

The Sources of Role Conflict

How, then, are these multiple interests insinuated into the obligations of otherwise disinterested individual or organizational fiduciaries? At least five pathways seem common.

Multiple roles. First, individuals simultaneously and serially fill many different roles—some of them positions of trust—in their careers. In some jobs, trustees don multiple hats—as teacher/researcher/clinician, physician/gatekeeper, psychotherapist/forensic expert. Others hold several jobs at any one time or a primary position supplemented by part-time consulting, research, freelancing, or other moonlighting projects; entrepreneurial activity; or outside investments. Some hold positions that require or encourage honorific or representative participation in satellite organizations (e.g., the labor union president who also sits on the corporate or union pension fund board or the outside counsel who serves on the client's board of directors). And many others complement these pecuniary undertakings with voluntary work, some perhaps for the pure rush of altruism, others for the good will, advertising, or networking opportunities or potential quid pro quos to be exploited from their association with eleemosynary institutions. A good many of these part-time, voluntary, honorific, or constituency-representing roles demand fiduciary obligations or tend to recruit those holding fiduciary positions elsewhere. So there is undoubtedly a correlation between holding positions of trust and filling multiple roles; conversely, those structurally best able to be disinterested are least likely to need to be so.

Even those individuals more exclusive and single-minded in their vocational and avocational commitments at any point in time at best practice a kind of serial monogamy through their careers. Particular patterns of mobility are especially likely to create interest conflicts. These patterns include revolving-door career trajectories between public service and the private sector, golden-parachute deals, and leaves-of-absence or other arrangements to put careers on hold while role occupants pursue temporary opportunities to run for office or manage a political campaign, head a regulatory commission, or take a diplomatic post. These structures of mobility foster the multiplication of competing interests because of the typically incestuous patterns of movement, the inevitability of the transitions and therefore the prospective planning they stimulate, the tendency of trustees to ingratiate themselves with potential future employers, and the proprietary information and ongoing social and financial ties that actors typically carry from one position to the next.

Organizational growth. A second source of multiple and conflicted interest occurs with the diversification and growth of organizations. Regardless of whether firms diversify gradually and rationally fill out into related or complementary lines of business or change radically and haphazardly as the result of mergers and acquisitions, they take on a diverse set of new and often incompatible interests, clients, and obligations. Examples of routine diversification include accounting firms that provide both certified independent audits and tax or management consulting services or investment banking firms that underwrite securities while engaging in a retail stock brokerage business. Although individuals employed by these hulking organizations may maintain fidelity to a single role, the organizations often embrace many incompatible roles, sometimes even using one as a loss leader to market others.

Problems of conflicted interest are especially thorny when mergers suddenly concatenate a series of individual and organizational biographies, social networks, and clients—for example, where a newly constituted firm unexpectedly finds itself representing both sides of a contentious lawsuit, airing an inflammatory investigative series about the corporation that just took over the news organization, or developing advertising or political campaigns for head-to-head competitors. Fiduciaries who have been scrupulous in not taking on multiple roles (and interests) either simultaneously or serially may suddenly find themselves entangled in complicated interest conflicts by virtue of their unwanted association with new stepsiblings delivered by a corporate takeover.

Principals/clients. Multiple clients served by a single fiduciary role create a third and related source of conflict by forcing their representatives to choose among their competing interests or to serve one to the detriment of another.

Fiduciary organizations frequently serve many principals, whether because their very function is to collectivize discrete principals and thereby exploit economies of scale and opportunities to spread risk or to provide specialized professional services to a diverse clientele. Sometimes the interests of these varied principals are consistent, and dutifully serving one client means serving them all well. Often they are not, especially when resources are scarce or zero sum. The examples abound:

- stockbrokers give priority in the timing of orders and the allocation of limited-supply investments to institutional clients over individual ones
- criminal defense attorneys make "trade-outs," accepting "a guilty plea or a severe sentence for one client in exchange for a dismissal of charges or a lenient sentence for another" in a sequence of negotiated pleas (Alschuler 1975, 1210–11)
- health insurers provide coverage for treating some medical problems and not others, and managed care physicians must choose which among their patients are most deserving of a referral to a specialist
- parents make sacrifices or life-style changes to increase the opportunities for one child (e.g., a child prodigy or potential sports star, fashion model, or actor) at the expense of the other children

And some clients, of course, are adversaries, competitors, litigants, or ideological foes.

Moreover, many trustee roles provide intermediation, structurally drawing together divergent, often oppositional interests to which fiduciary loyalty is owed. Investment bankers, broker-dealers, commodities traders, real estate brokers, marriage or family counselors, or adoption agencies exemplify but a few of these agents charged with the intrinsically impossible task of arriving at a price or constellation of services that best serve buyer and seller, provider and recipient, or husband and wife. The ubiquitous conflict of maximizing the interests of both (frequently unequal) parties in what are often zero-sum transactions is further exacerbated in these trust relationships by transactional by-products that can introduce self-interest into the brokering relationship as well. For example, compensation arrangements for intermediation services may make one side of the transaction more attractive to trustees than the other (e.g., the preference for high prices on commission sales identifies agents with sellers), thereby disequilibrating the already precarious balance of fidelity.

Relational networks. A fourth pathway to conflict is relational. Fiduciaries take on conflicts of interest by participation in dense or intimate social networks. Nepotism represents one source of relational conflict. Friendships, professional school networks, and dual career families (especially those whose partners met and established relationships in professional training schools or on the job and who are therefore likely to encounter each other in the work force) exacerbate the structural impediments to disinterestedness. Instances of spouses or lovers in the position of referring business; making tenure, promotion, or partnership decisions about the other or a close associate of the other; or providing legal representation for or having proprietary information about adversaries or competitors have become increasingly common. On other occasions, the interests of clients conflict with those of intimates or the clients of intimates.

Joint ventures and interlocking directorates represent less intimate relationships that frequently create conflict as well. Examples of bank directors who participate in loan committee decisions affecting the interests of friends or business associates illustrate a piece of the problem. In a rather different setting, studies have found that peer review panels are significantly more likely to award grants to their own members than to nonmembers, even when the interested party disqualifies him- or herself from the deliberations (Alpern 1988; Cox and Munsinger 1985).

These dense social ties do not necessarily erode or atrophy when mobility transports network members into other vocations or organizational settings. Indeed, some role undertakings (such as government service or volunteer work for elite philanthropies) may represent forms of investment whereby actors attach themselves to social networks that they intend to exploit upon role exit.

Compensation arrangements. Finally, payment or compensation systems sometimes create conflicts of interest in otherwise disinterested relationships. Commission arrangements encourage trustees to execute many transactions and more costly ones; the former leads to problems of churning, the latter to excessive pricing.[2] Hourly pay or fee for service encourages excessive service. Capitation arrangements, where trustees receive a per capita fee regardless of need or service provided (e.g., tuition and some kinds of health insurance), create incentives for undertreatment or lesser service. Other compensation or incentive systems give fiduciaries ownership rights (equity shares or stock options) in the principals they serve, profit-sharing guarantees, or a percentage of civil damage awards or settlements (i.e., contingency fees)—arrangements that undermine disinterestedness as well.

Fiduciary services are increasingly compensated by systems of third-party payment. Government agencies, insurance companies, employers, charities, and parents—whose interests often diverge or collide with those of the principals or clients on whose behalf they pay—foot the bill for many fiduciary services. Because "he who pays the piper calls the tune," trustees are often encouraged or extorted to honor the preferences of these powerful repeat players on which their financial wherewithal depends rather than those of the individuals to whom they owe fidelity.

Other arrangements curiously require that fiduciaries be compensated for their services by the very firms from which they purport to be independent; these trustees include certified independent auditors, some bond-rating firms, kashruth inspectors (who ascertain that kosher foods have been prepared according to Jewish law), financial planners,[3] and investment banking firms that conduct due diligence reviews. Many critics have noted the difficulties of disinterested objectivity when future income—indeed, perhaps firm viability in the case of major clients—is endangered by the disclosure of bad news.

The coalescence of individual mobility, of organizational growth, and of the proliferation of clients, relational networks, and compensation systems exacerbates the conflict-of-interest problem. Large organizations amass huge numbers of employees, many of whom contribute a sizable collection of conflicted roles and relationships from their personal, vocational, and avocational biographies, thereby

[2]Churning by stock brokers involves constantly, needlessly, and gratuitously buying and selling their discretionary clients' securities holdings to thereby generate commissions on each trade.

[3]Who accept commissions or kickbacks from third parties for selling insurance or mutual funds to their clients rather than charging these clients a straight fee for their supposedly independent advice.

creating a multiplicative network of conflicts. Of course, only a subset of the nodes in this network pose a serious threat to disinterestedness. The tug of relational loyalties atrophies over time, trustees are capable of honoring and disattending confidences some of the time, fiduciaries cannot possibly communicate about every entrusted secret with all their colleagues in a large firm or have access to all discretionary decision making reposed throughout the organization, and so on. But the threat to disinterestedness persists.

The Attractions of Role Conflict

Even this partial list of the systemic sources of conflict of interest impugns the promise of disinterestedness. The variegated web of role conflicts does not arise accidentally, of course. What makes this ubiquitous tangle all the more interesting—and intractable as a social problem—is the ambivalence it arouses. The core precept of fiduciary obligation, that trustees cannot serve two masters, is particularly intriguing, not only because real-world trustees routinely serve many masters but also because their masters often want them to. Indeed, the paradox of conflict of interest is that it is at least as likely to be embraced as to be renounced. Seemingly, with every effort to ensure disinterestedness, antagonistic social forces propel fiduciaries toward even greater role conflict. As a result, the sacred norm of disinterestedness is often honored in the breach by institutions of trust, by principals, and by clients alike who discover that they are better served by fiduciaries most entangled in conflicts of interest. The impetus for further conflicts comes from at least four sources.

First, the impulse for organizations to grow, diversify, and swallow up the competition—and thereby take on more conflicts—is irresistible and frequently beneficial to some principals and clients. At least to a point, growth allows organizations to enjoy economies of scale. Economist Oliver Williamson (1975) argues that economic transactions that are recurrent and uncertain and that require substantial transaction-specific investments are likely to be internalized within hierarchically organized firms rather than performed by market processes across these firms.[4] Diversification into related lines of business or service may, therefore, spread or limit risk, minimize transaction costs, and create efficiencies. So clients tend to enjoy more efficient service and lower costs when large repeat-playing multiclient fiduciaries offer a fuller line of services. And the principals or owners of public corporations tend to enjoy greater profit and less risk as these firms grow horizontally and vertically.

Second, the attractions of political and human capital encourage the explosion of multiply held roles and incestuous patterns of mobility. Principals are best served by trustees with esoteric knowledge, extensive training, specialized skills, varied

[4]My reference to Williamson assumes that the choice of hierarchies over markets increases the potential for conflict of interest. This assumption may be wrong. Mark Granovetter's "embeddedness" project (1985) would argue that markets also create conflicts because of the overwhelming preference of exchange partners to exploit personal relationships and social connections in their transactions. This theme of social capital is the fourth source of the paradox.

hands-on experience, inside information, and social and political connections. As a result, principals with fiercely competing interests often vie for the same trustees. Because fiduciary work typically requires technical mastery and specialized expertise, principals generally favor revolving doors, interfirm mobility, and the use of part-time consultants over on-the-job training of promising candidates notable for their short résumés and clean biographical slates. The most able and experienced individual and organizational candidates for positions of trust arrive freighted with considerable baggage; independence often comes at the price of inexperience. If we wanted "clean," inexperienced, truly disinterested trustees to perform these delicate, complex tasks, we would probably do some of them ourselves.

Third, the need for financial capital also undermines the goal of disinterestedness. Curiously, many fiduciary roles and organizations are underfunded by design: candidates for political office must raise most of their own campaign funds; academic researchers must seek outside funding for the scholarly research without which they would "perish" from their university appointments; universities, in order to meet operating expenses, must campaign alumni and local businesses for contributions to the endowment; nonprofits generally—religious organizations, charities, museums, performing arts organizations, and so on—must continually seek donations and volunteer labor. But because these beneficiaries of charitable largess are fiduciaries, donors hold no ownership rights in these organizations or legitimate claims on the exercise of fiduciary obligation. And therein lies the conflict. At best, trust organizations dependent on a continuing stream of funds, contributions, donations, or gifts experience "golden goose" problems; they must ingratiate themselves with past and future donors or, at least, not overtly antagonize the geese who lay the golden eggs. At worst, trustees become vulnerable to illegitimate demands for quid pro quos or other special favors from their benefactors.[5]

The value of social capital—embodied in personal relationships, social networks, prestige, reputation, or reciprocal obligations—provides a fourth impetus for conflict of interest. Because of the inherent asymmetries of fiduciary relationships, principals strive to minimize their vulnerabilities to abuse by searching for trustworthy agents to act on their behalf, would-be trustees to reassure principals about their fidelity. Social capital, by creating the reality or pretense of "personalized" trust (Shapiro 1987), provides the common denominator between their projects. As Mark Granovetter (1985) and many others have demonstrated, principals gravitate to the familiar, to members of their social networks with whom they have ongoing relationships, whose integrity has been tested in the past and is readily subject to surveillance in the future and for whom a potent array of informal sanctions are available to encourage fidelity and to deter misconduct. For their part, trustee organizations load up on community leaders and notables on their boards of directors and choose mainstream banks and law firms, Big 5 accounting firms, and Wall

[5]For example, to give the organization's investment, banking, legal counsel, or insurance business to firms with which benefactors are identified; to intervene in or seek to influence regulatory matters involving individuals who have made substantial political campaign contributions; or to support management in proxy battles involving corporate securities donated by these managers.

Street investment banking firms as symbolic signals of familiarity, legitimacy, or fidelity. Moreover, fiduciaries—including wayward ones (Shapiro 1984)—recruit clients and principals by exploiting social, religious, ethnic, familial, professional, and neighborhood networks and ties that provide reassurance to would-be principals that fiduciaries are honest and trustworthy. Universities, museums, opera companies, disease-fighting foundations, and other charitable organizations enlist prominent elites to join their boards in order to take advantage of their appended social networks and reciprocal obligations with others in the world of philanthropy for purposes of fund-raising.

These forms of social capital, then, provide fiduciaries access to principals, clients, and benefactors and guide principals to seemingly trustworthy representatives. But the impetus on both sides to rely on personal relationships and social connection profoundly undermines the goal of disinterestedness.[6] Trustees and principals and other principals and other trustees are all enmeshed in multiplex relationships.[7] Hence, the impulse to draw on social capital increases the likelihood of role conflict.

In a system not unlike that of natural selection, fiduciary organizations evolve by assuming or orchestrating greater conflicts. The fittest survive by growing, diversifying, and swallowing up the competition and by recruiting experienced employees who have diverse and complex career trajectories and who, like benefactors, come from central nodes in large well-heeled social networks. Principals and clients gravitate to these tangled webs where they find more trustworthy agents, greater expertise and talent, vicarious access to positions of power and influence, economies of scale, greater profit, protection from risk, and all manner of exceptional service. The attractions of role conflict on both sides of the fiduciary relationship are quite compelling.

Managing Conflicts

Fiduciary organizations and their principals, therefore, face a curious dilemma. On the one hand, trustees serving many masters have considerable opportunity, incentive, and even necessity to shirk, ignore, or abuse their duty of loyalty. On the other hand, these same role entanglements often make them most attractive to principals. Principals and agents, then, choreograph a delicate balance. Trustees demonstrate that despite varied relationships and the tug of other interests, principals can be assured of their absolute fidelity and undivided loyalty. Principals, for their part, seek out disinterested trustees, structure incentives to maximize their allegiance, strive

---

[6]To take, perhaps, an extreme example, who would you be more inclined to trust with the excruciating decision to cut off life support—in the event that you were comatose or incompetent—than a loved one? Yet loved ones generally have the most to gain by your passing—not only a financial share of your estate (which will be larger the quicker you die) but also an end to often punishing medical costs, to the responsibility of caretaking, and to the anguish of seeing you suffer.

[7]In multiplex relationships, actors are joined together by a network of intersecting roles based on kinship, work, community, ethnic, religious, or political ties (Gluckman 1967).

to negotiate or police their loyalty, or rely on yet other trustees to do so for them (Shapiro 1987). In short, the providers and consumers of trust devise strategies to exploit the desirable features of conflicted interest while searching out more disinterested trustees or at least disabling the persistent temptations of those who are not. And they turn to the punitive sanctions or compensatory arrangements provided by law and insurance when their precarious balancing act topples.

This choreography draws on steps to renounce, limit, select, divest, conceal, silence, disclose, align, or balance interests. And when they are unavailable, unattractive, or ineffective, those with tangled loyalties recuse themselves from the exercise of trust or shift responsibility to third parties. Some of these varied measures are taken at the initiative of the trustees themselves, who hope to attract principals and minimize liability, and others are implemented to satisfy the demands of clients, third parties who pay for fiduciary services, government regulators, or liability insurers.

Trustees strategically limit the interests that they agree to champion, forgoing new roles, clients, financial interests, and relationships. Some renounce multiple roles, resisting community service or consulting, freelancing, or moonlighting opportunities, or participation in political, ideological, corporate, or nonprofit organizations or social movements. Indeed, some organizations place limits on outside income or how much time employees may devote to ancillary roles. Other organizations limit mobility or the interests that are transported through the job market, opting for entry-level over lateral hiring, and they slow or lock revolving doors by placing restrictions on employment transitions (forbidding accountants from taking a job with a client, for example) or mandating waiting periods before fiduciaries are allowed to take on certain kinds of work or certain clients. Other fiduciaries turn away principals whose interests are likely to conflict with those of actual or would-be clients or constituents.

Nepotism rules, civil service requirements, regulations that uncouple interlocking directorates, and other relational bars seek to eradicate relational conflicts of interest. Some fiduciary organizations forbid trustees from developing personal, sexual, or financial relationships with clients. Vows of celibacy in the priesthood represent an extreme example of rules that bar particularistic relationships that undermine disinterestedness. And fiduciary organizations that offer independence services rotate personnel (auditors, beat reporters, police officers) to extinguish particularistic ties that typically develop between trustees and those from whom they must maintain independence.

Other trustees strive to eliminate the conflicts created by compensation systems and capital requirements. Vows of poverty represent one such device. So, too, are regulations that cap gratuities or contributions at a de minimus level, restrict contributions from particular sources or refuse them altogether, or blind or launder the identity of donors or funds in order to leave fiduciaries in the dark about the location of their conflicts.

Alternatively, fiduciaries jettison or divest themselves of conflicted roles, relationships, clientele, lines of business, or financial interests. Or, when compromised by a particular role conflict, they eradicate conflict temporarily by recusing or disqualifying themselves from the exercise of discretion in that particular instance.

The problem with the former response, as I noted earlier, is that even when such radical divestiture is possible, the mere fact of exit does not necessarily or immediately sever ties or end a chain of reciprocal obligations. The problem with the latter response is that even when trustees recognize the subtle pull of other masters and know to recuse themselves from deliberations, their dense, ongoing relationships with fellow fiduciaries often create a bias in favor of their interests that operates even in their absence (Welles 1980; Cox and Munsinger 1985).[8]

Other fiduciary organizations seek to silence or conceal interests, especially those that are often unintentionally acquired by lateral mobility, diversification, or organizational growth. They erect walls to screen, segregate, or barricade individuals tainted with conflicting interests and confidences who have entered through revolving doors or to block the flow of information between independent operating divisions (e.g., investment banking and retail stock brokerage divisions in securities firms). Or interests may be silenced by structural guarantees of autonomy, for example, granting lifetime tenure to federal judges and university professors so that their pursuit of truth or justice is untainted by the interests of those to whom they would be otherwise accountable.

Varied fiduciary organizations seek to conceal interests—even self-interests—by blinding them. Peer reviewers and others exercising discretion receive manuscripts and applications in which identities and affiliations have been stripped. Medical experimentation relies on placebos and double-blind trials. Other fiduciaries can sometimes avoid divesting their interests by instead blinding themselves to them. They place investments and other interests in blind trusts, subject to the discretion of independent third parties. Not knowing what their interests are, they cannot be conflicted by them.

Where walls are routinely breached and regulations or structural contrivances to eradicate conflicts are unrealistic, unsuccessful, or impair the exercise of fiduciary duty in some other way, trustees may rely on the less permeable walls that separate them from the outside world, turning to third parties for independence and disinterestedness (Heimer 1985). Some third-party arrangements are mobilized at particular crises of disinterestedness, as in the appointment of special prosecutors, public guardians (in right-to-die or surrogate mothering disputes), or receiverships (upon charges of mob influence in a labor union or in the face of massive fraud in a publicly held corporation). Others are routinized and ongoing—the use of outside certified independent auditors, pharmaceutical testing laboratories, self-regulatory organization inspectors, and the like. The vulnerability of ongoing third-party oversight to emerging conflicts of interest (from the development of financial and relational ties between subjects and overseers), of course, threatens these arrangements.

A different and much simpler regulatory strategy requires that trustees disclose their competing interests up front—at least to the extent that disclosures do not

[8]It is for that reason, for example, that the proposal for this conflict-of-interest research was not reviewed by the National Science Foundation panel on which I had served two years earlier but was assigned to a different—somewhat less substantively appropriate—panel comprised of strangers. (The downside, of course, was that expertise was sacrificed for disinterestedness.)

breach confidences of other principals. Principals are then theoretically able to exit from the fiduciary relationship, decline to join in the first place, or waive or consent to (or not) their trustee undertaking a conflicted role or exercising self-interest.

A different approach to the inevitability of conflicts and the difficulty of eradicating them involves abandoning the goal of disinterestedness and instead strategically selecting, creating, or orchestrating conflicts. Principals may recruit trustees whose interests coincide with their own so that as trustees unabashedly pursue self-interest, they will also be furthering the interest of their principals (Frankel 1983, 811). Where interests do not naturally coincide, parties may manipulate incentive structures—devising performance fees, profit-sharing plans, contingency fees, compensation or joint ownership arrangements, and the like—that artificially couple the interests of principals and trustee and thereby give the trustee a stake in the outcome (Jensen and Meckling 1976, 308; Frankel 1983, 811; Moe 1984, 763; Pratt and Zeckhauser 1985).[9] Alternatively, they may seek to balance persistent conflicts by stocking fiduciary bodies with representatives of diverse interests in the perhaps naive hope that active but antagonistic interests will somehow cancel each other out and thereby collectively constitute disinterestedness.

Finally, when these prospective normative and regulatory arrangements fail, legal and compensatory measures may provide some relief after the fact. Principals may attempt to recoup their losses from conflict of interest or construct a more disinterested arrangement for the future through shareholder's derivative suits and other private litigation. Directors' and officers' liability, fiduciary, or malpractice insurance policies or surety bonds may provide compensation in some instances as well. Administrative or self-regulatory agencies or professional disciplinary bodies may suspend or revoke charters or licenses or disbar errant trustees. Regulatory or other law enforcement agencies may respond with administrative, civil, or criminal action. Civil sanctions may enjoin fiduciaries from interest conflicts, order disgorgement or restitution, or require that firms divest conflicting interests, purge errant managers, erect walls, or introduce other structural arrangements to eradicate sources of conflict. And criminal actions provide additional sanctions and moral opprobrium for those culpable of abuse of trust.

As I (and many others) have written elsewhere, the problem with some of these regulatory strategies is that they tend to make matters worse—increasing the transaction costs of trust relationships, creating moral hazard problems, constraining the exercise of discretion, and limiting the efficiency, information, access, and experience that trustees require to maximize their return to principals (Shapiro 1987). Principals would be best served if they could eschew regulation and simply trust their fiduciaries to ignore all other masters. But they can't. So they equivocate,

[9]Though, even here, it is difficult to match precisely the interests of principal and agent. Contingency-fee lawyers, for example, may have a different orientation toward time than do their clients. Those lawyers with an immediate need for cash may settle a case at a substantial discount (and far less effort) rather than go to trial. Attorneys with a financial cushion and who expect a windfall in a jury verdict many years down the pike may push to go to trial even though the client is severely injured or dying and in immediate need of income—even discounted income.

hoping that trustees will not take the regulations too literally while simultaneously fearing that they will not. This paradox of regulation is not unlike the paradox of conflict of interest itself, which impels principals to simultaneously embrace and renounce it.

CONFLICT OF INTEREST IN THE PRACTICE OF LAW

Relationships of trust are found virtually everywhere and conflict of interest threatens nearly all of them.[10] But perhaps nowhere is the conflict-of-interest tangle more extensive or stubborn, the inherent structures of duplicity and the temptations and tensions they provoke more prevalent or persistent, than in the private practice of law. Structures of professional mobility; multiple commitments; patterns of law firm growth, diversification, and specialization; relationships with clients and colleagues; compensation arrangements; and the like—especially as they are exacerbated by economic changes roiling the profession—portray near perfect prototypes of the five sources of role conflict described earlier. Conflict of interest arises in the most fundamental components of legal practice and legal career: the ability to serve more than one client, to acquire new clients, to represent complex organizations and their functionaries, to broker and consummate deals or resolve disputes, to grow their firms and diversify their practice, to market their expertise, to recruit experienced or well-connected colleagues, to change jobs, to do pro bono work or lend legal expertise to voluntary organizations, to secure compensation, to solicit clients in ways compatible with ethical standards, and so forth. Conflict of interest inevitably touches the practice of law and confounds careers, especially of the most active and successful practitioners and firms.

Moreover, like many other fiduciary roles, this potential for conflicts among legal practitioners provokes ambivalence in their clients. Fearing disloyalty or abuse, some clients search out disinterested lawyers. Yet, hoping to exploit economies of scale or human, social, or financial capital, others enthusiastically embrace—if not demand—opportunities to retain legal representatives entangled in role conflicts. The attractions of role conflict for both lawyers and clients are irresistible. Taken literally, the duty of loyalty would shackle the practice of law and ill serve those who must rely on it. But without such an obligation, admittance to the bar would provide a license for some to steal. Lawyers must deftly navigate, then, between the shoals of paralysis and duplicity. They do so by fashioning mechanisms, like those

---

[10] Unfortunately, few of these settings have received sustained empirical attention. One can unearth the occasional study that undertakes cartographic excursions into conflict of interest discerned from public records—mapping out chains of interlocking directorates (Allen 1974; Useem 1979; and many others), the stops of the revolving door between the public and private sectors, government employees' statements of financial interest cross-matched with lists of companies affected by their official duties (Kneier 1976), or routine disclosures by officials of publicly and privately held corporations of their (near universal) conflicts of interest (Barnard 1988). The Twentieth Century Fund (1980) study of conflicts of interest in the securities markets and Marc Rodwin's (1993) study of conflicts in the medical profession represent rare exceptions in this otherwise sparse terrain; unfortunately even those studies provide less systematic data than one would have hoped for.

described previously, to eschew, jettison, disclose, neutralize, or blind interests and to regulate disinterestedness. It is this voyage that this book will chronicle.

Conflict of interest is not only commonplace but especially visible in the world of legal practice. Law is heavily shrouded in normative rhetoric, ethical canons, and judicial opinions about conflict of interest. The issue is repeatedly revisited in the law school classroom, the courtroom, the trade press, allegations of legal malpractice, and debates about legal ethics and the future of the legal profession. Because conflicts often arise as firms grow and prosper, attorneys talk easily about them. Moreover, concern for conflict of interest among lawyers is not simply a matter of ethical scruples or a desire to maintain the appearance of propriety. Conflicts sometimes carry high stakes: loss of major clients or significant business (when firms are "conflicted out" of a matter or favor one set of loyalties to the detriment of another), disqualification in ongoing litigation, steep malpractice judgments and deductibles, and sometimes divisive discord among colleagues. With so much at stake, it is no coincidence that law firms typically delegate conflicts oversight to their most senior partners.

The world of legal practice, then, offers a window on a multitude of relatively public stages on which conflicts of interest are enacted in a varied array of relationships of trust. But what is most compelling about the window is not its unusual clarity but rather the panoramic view it reveals. Private legal practice offers a rich site in which to examine conflict of interest because its extraordinarily diverse settings vary both in the conditions under which conflicts arise and the opportunities or impediments to ameliorating or controlling them.

Lawyers practice alone or with thousands of colleagues, in single offices or quarters shared with other solo practitioners or in branch offices proliferating across the globe. Some have the only shingle in town or, indeed, for miles around, whereas others practice in communities with dozens or hundreds of other competing law firms. Some firms grow slowly, hiring new colleagues fresh out of law school, some develop instant expertise by "cherry picking" specialists from competing firms through lateral hires, and others explode haphazardly through acquisitions of groups of lawyers or mergers with other firms. Some firms have deep roots in their community that go back into the last century and serve multiple generations of families, whereas others are not even a decade old. Some offer a general practice to clients, whereas others focus on a narrow set of specialized areas or concentrate in a single boutique practice. Some represent individuals; others, small businesses or corporations with their own in-house legal departments that can dwarf the number of lawyers in the firm; some serve one-shotters, and others, repeat players. Some receive a significant proportion of their business from a handful of major clients with longstanding ties to the firm, whereas others derive less than 1 percent of their income from any one client. Some are paid by an hourly or preset fee; others fund their operations with contingency fees, taking a fixed percentage of civil awards that they win for their clients. Some divide their profits based on billable hours or seniority, and others do so proportionately to the amount of business that the lawyer brought into the firm. Some attorneys in private practice also work part-time as public defenders, government lawyers, or public officials. Some participate financially in the enterprises of their clients or nurture private business interests on the side.

But this static vision of the legal profession is only part of the picture. Political, social, and particularly economic change over the past two decades, and especially in the years preceding this study, roiled varied sectors of the legal profession, inciting even greater differentiation in the social organization of legal practice and giving rise to ever more thorny conflicts of interest. These developments include:

- historic numbers of new law school graduates, increasing numbers of attorneys, and declining ratios of lawyers per capita
- the growth of large law firms and an increasing number of multioffice firms
- growing numbers of law firm mergers and acquisitions
- increasing substantive and geographic diversification of large firms
- greater job mobility among lawyers
- a more competitive market for legal services
- increasing business litigation
- the growth of corporate in-house legal departments
- greater sophistication of in-house counsel staff and their increasing role in calling the shots, shopping for lawyers, and spreading their business across many firms
- long-term general counsel relationships with a single law firm on retainer giving way to clients retaining firms for specific matters[11]

By the early 1990s, law firms faced a severe recession, resulting in a buyer's market, record rates of attorney unemployment, firm downsizing and even dissolution, and greater competition among firms, which began to pick off the most profitable lawyers and clients of the other and to take cases they might not have in the past.[12]

The Demise of the Professional Role?

Twenty years ago, before many of these trends had even begun to take root, scholars of the legal profession were already questioning a defining characteristic of professional status, namely autonomy from client control. In their pioneering study of Chicago lawyers conducted in the mid-1970s, Heinz and Laumann (1982) found

[11]See, for example, Sander and Williams 1989; Gilson 1990; Galanter and Palay 1991; Galanter and Rogers 1991; Garth 1993; Nelson 1994; Dezalay and Garth 1996. The legal landscape experienced many other significant changes as well, for example, in the racial, ethnic, and gender composition of the bar (Menkel-Meadow 1994; Nelson 1994; Wilkins and Gulati 1996); increasing economic stratification within the bar (Nelson 1994); the introduction of lawyer advertising; new kinds of legal service organizations (Van Hoy 1997; Seron 1992, 1996); and the like. This list simply details those developments with greatest impact on the proliferation of conflicts of interest.

[12]Though the profession had largely recovered from this nadir by the end of the decade, only to confront new economic threats and challenges a few years later, such was the state of affairs when I entered the field. Of course, the market for legal services is cyclical, tracking to some extent the robustness of the overall economy. With each new boom and downturn, the impetus for, nature of, and response to conflicts of interest change.

the bar divided into two hemispheres, one serving individuals and small businesses and the other serving corporations and large organizations. Ironically, the researchers found that

> . . . lawyers are likely to have greater freedom of action, greater control over how they practice law, if their clients are individuals rather than corporations or other large organizations. . . . the lawyers who serve the more powerful, corporate clients are likely to be less "professional" in this respect than those who serve the less powerful clients, individuals. (323)

The turbulent social change in the social organization of legal practice of the past two decades widened the chasm that Heinz and Laumann had observed. In an intriguing economic analysis, Gilson (1990) has argued that the traditional long-term relationship between clients and large full-service law firms—still fairly prevalent when Heinz and Laumann conducted their research (1982, 42–46)—arose as a response to information asymmetries. Without technical knowledge, traditional clients were unable to identify what kind of legal expertise, if any, they actually needed or which lawyers were best qualified to meet their needs. Moreover, because legal outcomes are influenced by an array of factors beyond the caliber of the lawyering, clients were unable to evaluate the quality of legal services they had bought simply from the outcomes their lawyers achieved. Once clients found a firm that they felt offered high-quality service and that knew their unique characteristics and special legal needs, the price of switching was very costly. So clients were locked into a long-term relationship with a particular firm. And that security conferred market power on their lawyers to engage in what Gilson calls "gatekeeping"—the ability to say no to clients (what others would call "autonomy")—which is the distinguishing feature of law as a profession (as opposed to law as a business), according to Gilson.

Information asymmetries in the market for legal services, then, gave lawyers control over and autonomy from their clients. Transformations over the past decade or two in the legal job market changed all that. With the influx of sophisticated lawyers, many of them former partners in large corporate law firms, into corporate legal departments, the asymmetry broke down. These in-house lawyers could internalize for clients the functions they formerly provided as outside counsel. They were able to assess their corporation's legal needs, select the appropriate lawyers, monitor their work, and evaluate quality. The value of a long-term commitment to a full-service firm was substantially reduced, as were the costs of switching firms (Gilson 1990). With a credible threat of exit, an oversupply of lawyers, and fierce competition among firms in a recessionary market, clients wielded the potent sanction of pulling their business from noncompliant lawyers. Outside counsel lost market power and, thereby, the clout to say no to clients.

In the past decade, lawyers located in the corporate hemisphere of legal practice faced more substantial incursions on their professional autonomy by some corporate clients who were emboldened by their new market power and were now better able to exit and take their business elsewhere when outside counsel resisted their demands. My interviews of practicing lawyers are laced with annoyance, frustration, indignation, anger, and even angst about the profound impact these uppity clients have had on their practice, indeed, on their professionalism.

These developments in the practice of law, echoed in other professions—the impact of managed care on the independence of physicians, for example—led some scholars to advance arguments about the decline of professionalism, or what Gilson (1990) called the "devolution" of the profession.[13]

But what is deprofessionalization really but the flip side of trust? Agents who offer expert knowledge are considered professionals when they are unconstrained by their principals. Trust relationships emerge when principals cannot control their agents. In Gilson's analysis, for example, lawyers' ability to say no—their professionalism—conferred by market power is a byproduct of the asymmetries between lawyer and client. As the balance of power between principal and agent—which is a central feature of the definition both of a profession and of trust—starts to teeter, some observers begin to pronounce the demise of professionalism. Professionals lose autonomy by the assertion of client control, and thereby, the continuum tips from trust to agency.

And when the continuum tips, some policymakers begin to question whether the creeping equilibrium justifies the onerous and inflexible ethical obligations and costly legal and regulatory edifice erected to protect more vulnerable relationships of trust. For example, at a different site on the fiduciary landscape—the corporation—legal academics have been debating for some time now whether fiduciary obligations should be mandatory rules or whether trustees and principals should be permitted to opt out of standard, off-the-rack fiduciary duties and negotiate their own private contracts to specify the obligations owed by trustees.[14] This argument, of course, only makes sense when parties have relatively equal information and bargaining power, clearly the exception more than the rule when it comes to relationships of trust. Still, we might extend the argument to the relationship between lawyers and sophisticated repeat-playing clients who wield substantial market power and ask whether particularistic contracts to regulate their mutual obligations—say, regarding conflict of interest—could be fashioned to replace standard fiduciary duties. Or we might query whether regulatory regimes other than fiduciary law are more appropriate where the relationship between principals and trustees is more symmetric or, at least, whether fiduciary obligations should be relaxed under those conditions. From

---

[13]See, for example, American Bar Association 1986; Nelson, Trubek, and Solomon 1992. In contrast to traditional accounts for the decline of professionalism that blame the lawyers, Gilson (1990) argues that

> the threat to professionalism comes from the demand side, not the supply side. The good news for lawyers is that economic analysis of legal professionalism provides some solace—the devolution of the profession may not be our fault. The bad news is that, for precisely the same reason, there may be very real limits on what the profession alone can do to arrest the decline. (872)

[14]Selected representatives of the so-called contractarians and anticontractarians include Easterbrook and Fischel (1983), Butler and Ribstein (1990), Coffee (1988), Brudney (1985), and Frankel (1995).

a less normative perspective, we might ask, empirically, whether fiduciaries are, in fact, policed differently where relationships are more or less symmetric.

But we are way ahead of ourselves. The teeter-totter may have teetered a bit, but it has not reached equilibrium by any means. The costs of monitoring and switching lawyers may have declined for sophisticated institutional clients, but they are far from zero. Though monopolies of knowledge and expertise have been broken and imbalances of control have righted somewhat, the asymmetries between lawyer and client have not disappeared, even for powerful sophisticated clients. Lawyers' obligations of confidentiality ensure that asymmetries of information will always persist. No matter how powerful they are, clients cannot extract information about their lawyer's relationships with or obligations to other clients—information that may be essential to their analysis of whether these loyalties to others compromise their lawyer's ability to zealously champion their own interests.

Moreover, these trends, which profoundly restructured sectors of the legal market, did not penetrate the entire profession. Many law firms—especially those serving unsophisticated, one-shot clients and located in underserved and less competitive markets—are barely touched by these developments. You could still visit old established law firms and find the same stolid furniture, the same nineteenth-century canvases portraying distinguished jurists on the wall, the same governance structure and social organization of the workplace, and the same client base as when the senior partner's grandfather ran the firm. You could still visit small communities in which clients remained loyal to their legal counselors and lawyers toiled in the same firms from law school until they died. Some of the smaller firms located in or near more competitive markets may have felt some residual effects of the changes buffeting their larger neighbors. Some encountered more competition for business from the mass of underemployed lawyers and from larger, economically strapped firms that diversified into new markets that they once considered beneath them. Others found their business flourished as large-firm clients sought them out for their lower fees and more personalized attention. But their autonomy was barely threatened by these developments. In a few large urban law firms, the teeter-totter trembled and slowly began to right itself as big fat clients hurled themselves on board. But vast numbers of practitioners remained firmly in control, their clients precariously straddling seesaws suspended high off the ground with little hope of getting off and seeking a new game, finding a different partner, or bargaining for different rules.

The legal profession, then, does not provide some monolithic, ideal type of trust. Lawyers' relationships to clients range from trust to agency, from profoundly asymmetric to more balanced, and from more to less professional, again standing in for the broad continuum of ties between principals and agents in other social institutions and sectors of social life.

Selected Themes

Whatever impact these differences in lawyer-client relationships had on the professional status of lawyers writ large, they had a significant effect on how law firms experience and respond to conflicts of interest. Heinz and Laumann's finding (1982) that the kind of client that attorneys serve influences the social organization of their work is replicated in firm practices surrounding conflicts. The relationship between client size, type, sophistication, amount of repeat business, ongoing ties to the law firm and conflicts of interest represents a major theme percolating through this book.

A second theme concerns firm size. Because large law firms tend to represent bigger, sophisticated, repeat-playing clients, we might assume that differences by firm size in the incidence and control of conflicts of interest are spurious. But the variability across firms is not merely an artifact of their client base. As I noted earlier, as organizations grow, they accrue ever more interests, some of which inevitably collide. Conflicts of interest multiply rapidly as law firms expand.

Because much theoretical literature on the fiduciary role anthropomorphizes the fiduciary (and often the principal as well), we often fail to recognize the collateral ethical conundra that arise when trust is delivered by huge, complex, differentiated, multisite organizations. The whole is often far greater than the sum of its parts. Conflicts of interest, for example, are not mere tangles in which individual trustees are snared (except in the rare occasions in which they work alone). They are attributes of organizations, formidable convoluted knots, intertwined and woven together from the tangled loyalties of all their members. Not only do megafirms face the challenge of a continual swelling stream of conflicts, but they must also devise a means of ensuring that largely independent practitioners, who are aligned with at most a handful of interests at any one time, are apprised of all the interests being championed elsewhere in the firm that they must also respect. And firms must then implement a package of procedures, incentives, or sanctions to ensure that those practitioners do respect these other interests. Moreover, economies of scale afford these larger firms resources to meet this ethical conundrum in ways that would be impractical or very expensive to replicate in much smaller firms. Large and small firms, then, tend to respond very differently to potential conflicts of interest.

Another virtue of locating an inquiry about conflict of interest in the practice of law, then, is the extraordinary variability it offers to tease out these and other theoretical questions regarding the social organization and control of conflicts. Unfortunately, the rich legacy of empirical work on the legal profession has been built in quite narrow increments. Most studies have been restricted to some combination of (1) a geographic site—a big city (Carlin 1966; Heinz and Laumann 1982; Heinz et al. 1997), a medium-sized city (Handler 1967), the country (Landon 1990), Wall Street (Smigel 1964), Silicon Valley (Suchman 1994); (2) a type of law firm organization or practice—large firms (Spangler 1986; Nelson 1988), small firms or solo practice (Carlin 1962, 1994; Seron 1992, 1996), franchise legal clinics (Van Hoy 1997); or (3) a substantive specialization—legal aid lawyers (Katz 1982), personal injury lawyers (Rosenthal 1974), divorce lawyers (Sarat and Felstiner 1995), criminal defense attorneys (Blumberg 1967), the white-collar crime defense bar (Mann 1985).

Because these inquiries were animated by very different theoretical questions than my own, their narrow focus was largely appropriate. Such is not the case in the world of conflict of interest (Shapiro 1999). A study of a single community would be unable to examine how the market for legal services and the number, mobility, expertise, and competitiveness of local practitioners affect the incidence of and response to conflicts of interest. A study limited to solo practitioners or mega-firms would be blinded to the powerful relationship between conflicts and organizational size and type. A focus on a single area of practice would usually limit variability in types of clients (e.g., only individuals or only one-shotters or only clients with inside counsel), thereby obscuring our appreciation for the impact of clients on how lawyers experience and deal with conflicts. Moreover, it would be impossible to examine how substantive diversification exacerbates conflict of interest.

The research reported in this book instead draws on interviews in a broad and diverse sample of law firms. The firms were selected randomly but stratified by size and location to ensure that a variety of practice types, clients, and markets were represented. I traveled almost ten thousand miles, from urban ethnic enclaves to small town squares in which only one law firm shingle could be found; from mammoth general practices to boutiques that specialize in a single area of law; from firms where lawyers work alone to those where attorneys wouldn't even recognize some of their colleagues in a lineup; from practices built more than a century ago to those just established; from offices where lawyers were still unpacking from their move to larger quarters to those where partners were still reeling from recent downsizing; from firms with opulent expansive lobbies to those with plastic and vinyl and standing room only even early on a Saturday morning; from firms whose partners told me they were inundated with conflicts of interest to others who said I would be wasting my time talking to them about the subject. In drawing a sample, I set only two limits: because legal ethics rules vary somewhat from state to state, to stay within a single jurisdiction (Illinois) and to study only private practitioners.[15] Chapter 2 and the appendix will tell you much more about my journey and its method.

Beyond the Legal Profession

Although lawyers are often held up as the poster children of fiduciary and professional roles, there is no ideal type. Trustee roles are enacted in families, banks, universities, churches, newsrooms, and hospitals and on drawing boards, balance sheets, and prospectuses. No one fiduciary could possibly stand in for them all. Because of the highly differentiated social organization of the legal profession, especially as it has been roiled by social and economic change, particular legal practice settings, client relationships, and versions of trust have remarkably similar counterparts in many other nooks and crannies of the fiduciary world. In its extraordinary variability, its chameleon-like facility to blend into other roles, the legal profession offers a fertile site from which to learn about conflict of interest.

[15]Almost three-quarters of lawyers nationwide (78 percent if you exclude those retired or inactive) are private practitioners. The remainder work in private businesses, government, the judiciary, or educational institutions (Carson 1999, 24).

But lawyers are also unique in ways that do not make them such attractive exemplars of the world of trust. First, law is frequently adversarial and zero-sum (what is good for one party is bad for another) or distributive (e.g., securing a patent for one precludes all others from reaping financial reward from similar technologies). As a result, the likelihood that interests will conflict is much higher in law than in other fiduciary relationships. A doctor's patients, for example, sometimes have competing interests—those on the waiting list for a new kidney or heart transplant or casualties being assigned priorities for care in triage. But, generally, what a physician does for one patient has no impact on another or has a positive impact, as when it contributes to greater skill or technical proficiency.

Second, law is normative; services performed for one party can have huge ripple effects when they create legal precedent that applies to others. Our lives have been profoundly changed, for better or worse, by the lawyers representing Linda Brown (the Topeka third grader in *Brown v. Board of Education*), Allan Bakke, Ernesto Miranda, Norma McCorvey (aka Jane Roe of *Roe v. Wade*), and Karen Ann Quinlan, among so many others. Few other mundane acts of fiduciary responsibility have the power to touch, to advance or undermine the interests of so many strangers so profoundly. So, even as the story of conflict of interest in the practice of law casts a mirror on many other kinds of trustees, it also conveys a picture that will remain unique and in some ways remarkable. I will return to this theme in chapter 10.

THE STRUCTURE OF THE BOOK

> You know, if we were absolutely pristine and followed the academic literature, we wouldn't be in business. [26Ch100+][16]

Thousands of books and articles have been written about conflict of interest in the practice of law. They fill the academic law reviews, trade and bar association journals, shelves of legal case books, legal tabloids, and commission reports, not to mention the occasional best-selling novel. They range from the general and mundane to the esoteric and arcane. Their pages overflow with doctrinal analysis, commentary, reviews of current developments, cases and ethics opinions, and gossip concerning ethical breaches among prominent lawyers and firms. Much of what they disclose is groundbreaking, precedent setting, exceptional, or particularly egregious.

Unfortunately, rarely do these disclosures rest on a solid empirical foundation and report on how or whether representative real-world lawyers, day in and day

---

[16]All quoted materials from the interviews are identified in the following way:

- a sequential number (from 1–128) that identifies the interview
- the location of the firm (Ch = Chicago, CC = collar county, DSL = downstate large city, DSM = downstate medium-sized city, DSS = downstate small town)
- firm size

So this quote comes from the twenty-sixth interview, conducted in a Chicago firm with more than one hundred lawyers.

out, encounter, avoid, and resolve conflicts of interest in their work. The literature may share the most nuanced exegeses of law on the books and regale us with cutting-edge rules and interpretations, but it is largely silent about law in action. It does not tell us whether the latest legal scholarship even penetrates into legal practice, indeed, how practitioners understand, interpret, and use conventional legal rules or perhaps misunderstand, misinterpret, or misuse them.

Practicing lawyers do not have very much positive to say about this prodigious literature, though they can usually cite one or two publications they have found useful. The quote reproduced at the beginning of this section is typical. It reflects a common sentiment among my informants that the literature is sometimes naive and frequently out of touch with what happens in legal practice day to day. Many others expressed disappointment and frustration at how often they are unable to extract from the literature any practical guidance about how to deal with the difficult conflicts they face. Interviewees often asked me how others answered a particular question or dealt with a difficult problem, and many nervously queried how their firm compared to others. Keep in mind that I interviewed conflicts mavens, those with greatest responsibility over conflicts of interest in their firms and who presumably have the most expertise in legal ethics and professional responsibility.

So what could one more volume possibly contribute? A few things, I hope. First, the book tries to honor my informants' curiosity and respond to their queries about what is going on in other law firms and how their own compares. It takes readers where only the most mobile of lawyers have ever gone before—behind the closed doors of scores of law firms—to expose the tangled loyalties and self-regulatory efforts aimed at avoiding or unknotting some of the snarls. Second, the book ventures to right the balance, if ever so slightly, between the doctrinal and empirical, the precedential and commonplace, between the preoccupation with big, powerful, cutting-edge firms and attention to those in the center that rarely receive notice. Third, it discloses what practitioners actually think and do, not what the experts say they should do. In the process, perhaps some of the empirical data will even force theorists and policymakers to recast their formulations, rethink their conclusions, revise their recommendations, or—best of all—imagine and ask different questions.

In the spirit of righting the balance, the subsequent chapters will cite almost none of the conventional legal literature on conflict of interest unless necessary to explain or credit a concept or to share relevant data. The practitioners' estimation of that literature notwithstanding, you don't need me to be your Sherpa up that Everest. With several of the very best on-line data bases offering complex, sophisticated searches of the legal literature and with the most prodigious footnoting conventions ever to hit the academic world, legal scholarship is very easy to find and extraordinarily accessible. Moreover, you don't need me—a nonlawyer—to analyze, interpret, or synthesize the subtle legal points mined in those tomes. The authors do a superb job on their own.

But as unfamiliar as these conventions will be for those trained in law, so too will they be for many social scientists. If I'm bothering to take you behind closed doors, why sterilize the account with the searing heat of sociological verbiage and abstraction? It makes much more sense to share an authentic flavor for how law firms experience conflicts of interest, especially when the firsthand accounts are as thoughtful, nuanced, and articulate as those of lawyers tend to be. Though I gathered the materials and will structure and analyze them through the eyes of a sociologist, I tell the story as much as possible in the words of the lawyers themselves.

I've defined my role as that of constructing an elaborate jigsaw puzzle. I methodically and systematically collected and selected thousands of pieces of narrative and assembled them in what I found to be the most cohesive configuration.[17] Once assembled, I consider my role to be to display the puzzle, not to describe it. The duet in the following chapters between the words of the lawyers and my own is not like that between an orator and simultaneous translator or sign-language interpreter. I have ceded much of my authorial role to the lawyers. When I quote extended passages from the interviews, they are not meant to simply bolster my argument but to make the argument. It is through their words that you will learn about conflict of interest. You may be tempted to skip all the quoted material and listen only to my voice. But you would miss a lot.

Viewing a puzzle requires far more trust in the artist or assembler than, say, reading the results of a scientific survey shored up with tallies, distributions, summary statistics, significance tests, and the like. More trust is required because the puzzle does not use all the pieces.[18] How can you know what was left out; whether the pieces selected were representative or simply colorful; whether the assembler overrelied on a particular source because these pieces were more compatible with the others; whether some pieces had to be pried and jammed into place or even trimmed to fit; whether some pieces were jettisoned because they would have changed the entire shape and aesthetic sensibility of part of the puzzle?

These informational asymmetries between viewer and assembler are real. Mostly, you have to trust me—though who better to trust than someone who has devoted her career to studying trust, those who abuse it, and how institutions try to bolster it? Still, I've tried to balance the asymmetries between us. I labored to assemble the puzzle responsibly by selecting representative quotes and by identifying distinctive or unusual ones. Unfortunately, in an effort to shorten the manuscript, the edifice of corroboration, redundancy, and nuance had to be dismantled and its pieces discarded.[19] To keep my selections honest and to provide some context,

---

[17] The quotations from the interviews are as literal as possible. I cut the "ah's," "uh's," "um's," "you know's," and stuttered repetitions of words or phrases, but I've done nothing else to clean up the narrative. When the quotations included identifying information, I replaced it with brackets containing more generic descriptions. Very rarely, when a gendered expression would identify the respondent, I degendered the language (*spouse* instead of *husband*, *sibling* instead of *sister*, use of plurals) and, when that didn't work, once or twice actually gave a respondent a linguistic sex-change operation. When the speaker stopped or trailed off midsentence or midword, the phrase ends with ellipses enclosed in brackets. Ellipses without brackets indicate that I deleted some prior text to remove unnecessary identifying information, an aside, or extraneous or redundant information or to shorten or simplify the text. L, of course, refers to the lawyer respondent. When I interview more than one lawyer in the firm, they are denoted L1 and L2. MP is the managing partner. Nonlawyer respondents are R. I am S.

[18] Nor does a quantitative study, but the omissions are far less obvious.

[19] Though I am happy to share a view of the cutting-room floor. Just ask.

quotes are always accompanied by identifying information: the chronological number of the interview (so you can judge whether I overrely on some respondents at the expense of others),[20] the location of the interview (Chicago, a so-called collar county encircling Chicago, or a large, medium, or small downstate city or town), and the size of the firm.

After introducing you to the setting, the first half of the book depicts how loyalties get tangled, and it traces the varied twisted pathways along which conflicts of interest arise. The second half of the book portrays how diverse law firms avoid, abort, or respond to these conflicts. The book ends by returning to the real world and examining the conflicts of interest that beset many of the rest of us, as mirrored through the window on the legal profession.

---

[20] I do, because some interviews were far longer, more complex, and more reflective than others, but I try to do so as little as possible.

The Scene

Imagine, if you will, all of the roughly fifty thousand lawyers in Illinois, county by county, stacked in a prone position, one on top of the other. Each lawyer occupies a foot of vertical space. Such a map of most of Illinois would look pretty much the same as the standard topographical map of the state—profoundly and uniformly flat. On our legal map, four-fifths of the state's counties are dwarfed by a mature elm tree.[1] The county containing the state's capital stands as high as the Eiffel Tower (1,000 feet). Counties housing the larger cities stretch a bit taller than the pyramids (450 feet), medium-sized cities tower like redwood trees (300 feet), and the Illinois counties across the Mississippi River from St. Louis collectively approach the height of the Empire State Building (1,250 feet). The so-called collar counties that surround Chicago's Cook County range from the Washington Monument (555 feet) to almost twice the height of the Sears Tower (2,800 feet). The cities that immediately encircle Chicago rise as high as the depth of the Grand Canyon (5,700 feet). The city itself stands level with Mount Everest (29,000 feet). Figure 2.1 conveys the same information about the distribution of Illinois lawyers, this time plotted in two-dimensional

[1]Because Illinois has 102 counties, many of them very small, countywide lawyer populations of four or six or thirteen are perhaps less surprising.

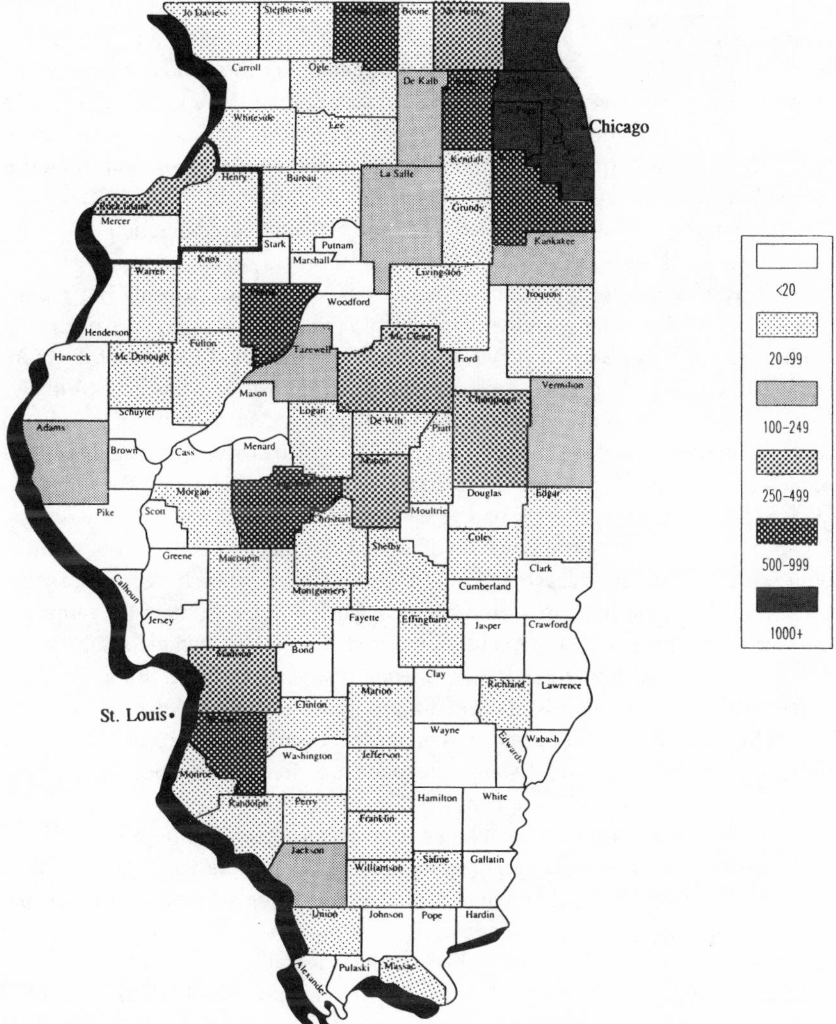

Fig. 2.1. Lawyer Density in Illinois

space, with counties shaded increasingly darker as their lawyer population grows.[2]

The legal communities of Illinois are perhaps as dissimilar as the world's highest mountain and a speed bump. Though it would be more efficient to hang out atop the former—the roughly square mile near my office that houses almost two-

[2]Numbers of registered attorneys are derived from Attorney Registration and Disciplinary Commission of the Supreme Court of Illinois (1994, 5–6) with projections about the proportion of Cook County attorneys practicing in Chicago derived from analyses of the Martindale-Hubbell Law Directory CD-ROM data base (1995).

fifths of the state's lawyers—the view from this elevated perch would be terribly unrepresentative of the rest of the legal landscape. So I undertook a journey that extended beyond Chicago across almost ten thousand miles throughout the state. The journey took me to law firms overlooking lakes and rivers, cornfields and strip malls, grain silos and drilling rigs, storefronts and historic landmarks, seedy neighborhoods and town squares, courthouses and residential neighborhoods, deteriorating downtown areas and glittering high rises.

In planning my journey, I wanted to ensure adequate representation of the full range of the legal landscape. If I had selected my destinations randomly—say from a list of registered lawyers in the state—I would have spent most (roughly 70 percent) of my time in Cook County and with either solo practitioners or lawyers practicing in larger firms, because that is how lawyers in Illinois cluster.[3] But some of the more significant conflict-of-interest problems arise in medium-sized firms and in smaller towns with fewer lawyers among whom to spread the potential conflicts. In order to secure representation of the panoply of settings in which lawyers practice, I sampled randomly within clusters of law firms, stratified by size and location. The appendix elaborates the sampling strategy and research design. Table 2.1 depicts the results.

Some of the entries in the two boldface rows in the table fall short of my goal of at least ten firms in Chicago and ten firms downstate for each size category because fewer than ten firms exist in certain categories. Some strata in the sample—the largest law firms in Chicago and the largest downstate—include a substantial proportion of all existing firms; others reflect a very small fraction.[4] But in order to differentiate between what is idiosyncratic to a given firm and what features are shared by firms of similar size and setting, it is necessary to have at least five to ten firms in each category, even if some categories are virtual populations and others mere slivers of their constituent members.

Because of this stratified sampling design, the sample is not representative of the population of Illinois lawyers. However, the firms were selected randomly; those in a given cluster had an equal probability of being selected. Moreover, because an astounding 92 percent of the firms sampled actually participated in the study, concerns about nonresponse bias or the possibility that firms that participated in the study were atypical (for example, had less to hide about their conflict-of-interest experience) are minimal. The sampled firms, then, do typify the population of firms in the clusters from which they were drawn.

Although the 128 law firms in the sample represent fewer than 1 percent of the law firms in the state, they do encompass a much more sizable number of practitioners. About a fifth of the lawyers in Illinois work in firms included in the sample.[5] So despite the small size of the overall sample, the findings bear on the experience of a sizable proportion of private legal practitioners in Illinois.

---

[3]Attorney Registration and Disciplinary Commission (1994, 5) and Curran and Carson (1994, 83). According to Curran and Carson's 1991 data, 43 percent of Illinois's lawyers are solo practitioners and 26 percent practice in firms with more than fifty lawyers.

[4]The sample includes almost three-quarters of Chicago law firms with more than one hundred lawyers, close to 100 percent of downstate firms larger than twenty lawyers, and less than 1 percent of Illinois firms of less than ten attorneys.

[5]Another reflection of the high proportion of larger firms included in the sample.

TABLE 2.1. THE FIRMS

	Number of Lawyers					
	1–9	10–19	20–49	50–99	100+	(*N*)
Chicago	**14**	**12**	**18**	**18**	**24**	**(86)**
Downtown	9	12	18	18	24	(81)
Neighborhood	5	0	0	0	0	(5)
Downstate	**20**	**13**	**9**	**0**	**0**	**(42)**
Collar county (50,000–100,000)	3	4	0	0	0	(7)
Cities >100,000	4	1	8	0	0	(13)
Cities 30,000–100,000	3	4	1	0	0	(8)
Cities <30,000	10	4	0	0	0	(14)
Total	(34)	(25)	(27)	(18)	(24)	(128)

In the following pages, I share some snapshots from my road trip through Illinois to provide a feel for the terrain, the local color, the varied settings and markets in which lawyers practice, the individual and organizational clients for which they work, the nature of that work, and the scale and structure of their workplaces. Like many travelogues, mine may also seem unduly detailed. But the information I present is not merely obligatory background. As the book unfolds, you will learn that these differences in the social organization of legal practice profoundly affect if, when, and how lawyers and law firms encounter and respond to conflicts of interest. As you listen to the respondents recount their experiences with conflict of interest, these snapshots provide a recurring backdrop.

CHICAGO

Just as Illinois lawyers cluster disproportionately in some regions, so, too, do Chicago's lawyers, most of whom work in a section of downtown Chicago known as the Loop. This area, just a bit more than a square mile in size, received its name in the late nineteenth century from the old cable car tracks that encircled the downtown business district, later to be replaced by the elevated train tracks that add eerie shadows and a constant screech and rumble to the urban landscape.

Figure 2.2 displays a legal map of Chicago—or, more properly, of Illinois's 102 largest law firms, 96 of which are located in Chicago. The firms are denoted with white numbers, which indicate a ranking based on the total number of lawyers worldwide who are affiliated with the firm.[6] Number 1, located slightly to the right of center, is Baker & McKenzie, the world's largest law firm in the late 1990s with more than 2,300 attorneys worldwide (Oster 1998), though not even 200 of them

[6]The bird's-eye map was designed by Pierson Graphics (1988) Copyright-MAPSCO, INC. (Dallas, Texas) LCR-01–004. Rankings, which are superimposed on the map, come from data presented in Andersen (1998). Repetitive numbers arise because some firms are of equal size and therefore tied on rank. That's also why there are 102 law firms in the top 100.

Fig. 2.2. Legal Map of Chicago. (Adapted from Pierson Graphics, copyright MAPSCO, Inc. [Dallas], LCR-01-004.)

practice in Illinois (Andersen 1998, 21). Chicago's largest truly indigenous law firm, Sidley & Austin (number 5), with more than four hundred lawyers in Chicago and more than eight hundred worldwide in the late 1990s, is situated to the left of center.[7] The four smallest firms in the top 100 each employ 26 lawyers.

Virtually all Chicago's largest firms and three-quarters of its lawyers practice within a few blocks of the Loop. Indeed, all but one of the fifty largest law firms in Illinois are located here. More lawyers work in the Sears Tower[8] than in all but 5 percent of the counties in Illinois.

Chicago is the birthplace of the skyscraper as well as home to as many as a quarter of the world's tallest buildings. As depicted on the map, many of them house the city's law firms, which tend to inhabit their upper stories. Law firms literally tower over the city. The Mount Everest imagery is just right; we can easily envision Chicago lawyers as a tightly clustered band floating high atop Chicago's center of business and industry, a kind of Goodyear blimp of legal services.

Because of their lofty perch, these large law firm offices are airy and flooded with light, rarely darkened by the shadows of el tracks or nearby skyscrapers. Their expansive windows offer spectacular panoramic views of the city. Unlike the law firms frequently encountered in other cities, whose dark woods, carpets, fabrics, and early American furniture and art offer the image of a stolid, old-line, conservative connection to traditional centers of power, money, and respectability, most large Chicago firms present a more modern and bright ambiance. Vacillating between ostentatious and understated elegance, they offer cavernous lobbies, expanses of glass, abstract and sometimes quirky art, inviting modern furniture, and upscale reading materials. A smaller number of law firm domiciles are a bit older and dingier, their overstuffed offices bursting with documents and files, their worn furnishings and Formica surfaces conveying a seemingly cultivated ambiance of restraint and frugality.

Large Firms

The large Chicago firms comprise the biggest cluster in the sample.[9] As noted in table 2.1, the sample includes twenty-four downtown Chicago law firms employing one hundred or more attorneys. Because no firms elsewhere in the state approach this size, I oversampled Chicago firms to have enough cases from which to generalize. The median-size firm in this cluster employs roughly 275 lawyers. Most of

---

[7]A merger in 2001 changed Sidley's name to Sidley Austin Brown & Wood and added a substantial number of lawyers to its ranks. Firms ranked second through fourth (with between 950 and 1,275 lawyers practicing worldwide) are headquartered in Cleveland, New York, and Los Angeles, respectively. Each has roughly one hundred lawyers working in their Chicago office.

[8]Left side of the map, technically a block outside the Loop, housing seven firms whose ranks range from fourth to seventy-eighth.

[9]Data on law firm size presented in this section are derived from counts of entries in the annual *Martindale-Hubbell Law Directories.* Unless specifically noted, data pertain to the firms at the time that the research was conducted. Law firm founding dates were derived either from *Martindale-Hubbell Directories,* the *Law Firms Yellow Book,* or the *Directory of Legal Employers* published by the National Association for Law Placement. Medians are generally reported over means or ranges.

these firms have more than one office; four of them are branch offices of firms headquartered out of state. The median firm in the large-firm cluster has three other offices. For almost all the firms, at least one of these offices is located out of state—most often in the District of Columbia, metropolitan New York, or California, with smaller numbers of branch offices located in nearby Midwestern states, Texas, or Florida, and scattered offices elsewhere. Almost a third of the firms have one or more offices in other cities in Illinois—generally in the collar counties surrounding Chicago or in the three or four largest cities in the state. A quarter have one or more offices outside the United States—most often in the major cities of Western Europe but also in Asia, Eastern Europe, South America, the Middle East, and Canada.[10]

Chicago's large law firms are venerable institutions, a quarter of them more than one hundred years old and half in existence for more than eighty years. The very youngest in the sample came into existence during the baby boom generation. These firms have undergone considerable change over the years, adding new offices, merging with other firms, spinning off practice groups or individuals who established new law firms, and of course, growing. Thirty years before I undertook the study, not a single large firm in the sample had more than seventy-five lawyers, and five out of six worked out of a single office. Half the firms employed fewer than thirty-two attorneys, and several had not even ten. Generally, the older firms are the larger firms; almost all the larger-than-average firms were founded before the Second World War. Over the next thirty years, the firms grew tenfold on average, with rates of growth increasing over time, culminating in a big growth spurt between 1983 and 1988 and then tapering off.

Firms are continually in flux. Of the seventy-five largest law firms in Illinois at the beginning of the study, five are now defunct and four are now so small that they are no longer listed among the state's one hundred largest law firms. Many others, remnants of which remain on the top-100 list ("The Illinois 100" 1992), have split into two or more law firms; merged with another; experienced the defection of one or more name partners (often along with other colleagues), practice groups, or clusters of partners; or otherwise downsized.

Specialization. Figure 2.3 displays the areas of practice of the firms in the sample.[11] The gray bars show the proportion of all the firms—large and small, urban and rural—that specialize in a given area. As depicted in the figure, most law firms practice real estate, corporate law, litigation, and estate law; very few practice in the areas on the right side of the figure: collections, entertainment law, legislative law, construction law, and public finance. But firms vary considerably in the nature

[10]The pace of globalization among the large law firms has accelerated since the research was conducted. Half now have offices outside the United States.

[11]Figure 2.3 draws on data from several sources published during the period in which the interviews were conducted:

(1) listings by law firms of their substantive specializations published in the *Martindale-Hubbell Law Directory* (95 percent of the firms in the sample had such listings)

(2) "The Illinois 100 Largest Law Firms" in *Merrill's Illinois Legal Times* (this listing—which includes 44 percent of the firms in the sample—is based on a survey of law

of their practice—both in the extent to which they are generalists or specialists and in the kinds of specialties to which they commit most of their resources. Some of these differences vary by firm size and setting.

The jagged line mostly on the top of figure 2.3 plots the distribution of expertise only for the large Chicago law firms that employ one hundred or more lawyers. It is immediately apparent from the figure that the large firms evince more special expertise than smaller firms do. Much higher proportions of large firms than smaller ones specialize in all but seven of the practice areas displayed in the figure. Indeed, although large firms on average indicate expertise in more than half the practice areas (twenty-two of forty-three), firms of less than eleven lawyers specialize in only seven areas; firms with eleven to twenty-five lawyers, in nine areas; and firms with twenty-six to ninety-nine lawyers, in fourteen. Though these rather dramatic differences are probably exaggerated slightly by the more thorough data available for large firms (see the previous note), their source is obvious. With more personnel, it is easier for firms to structure a complex division of labor and expertise. Moreover, large law firms diversify in order to accommodate the divergent legal needs of large corporate clients. So large firms are more likely (71 percent) than smaller ones (28 percent) to claim a general practice; indeed, this is true of 92 percent of the very largest firms (with more than 300 lawyers) in the sample.

Of course, listing an area of specialization in a law directory or setting up a department—the criteria for figure 2.3—do not a major specialization make. For the larger firms, data are also available from *Merrill's Illinois Legal Times,* in which firms were asked to estimate the percentage of attorney time devoted to a smaller set of common specializations. These data are presented in figure 2.4. The gray bars in the figure simply repeat the information displayed in the line in figure 2.3; they depict the percentage of firms with one hundred or more lawyers that indicate expertise in an area. The solid black bars demonstrate the disparity between announcing a field of expertise and allocating substantial resources to it by showing the median percentage of attorney time devoted to a field across these large firms. For example, though all large firms specialize in litigation, only 23 percent of their

---

firms conducted by Ernst & Young in which firms are asked to compute the percentage of attorney time devoted to an array of practice areas)

(3) *The Law Firms Yellow Book,* a directory of about six hundred of the largest corporate law firms in the nation, which lists the departments and practice areas of each firm (27 percent of the firms in the sample are included in this directory)

(4) the directory of the National Association of Law Placement, an annual data base of large law firms prepared for law school graduates, which specifies the number of attorneys in the firm assigned to various areas of practice; the data base also includes narratives supplied by the firms that specify other substantive specializations (21 percent of the firms in the sample are listed in this data base)

(5) Chicago's twenty-five largest law firms, published annually in *Crain's Chicago Business,* which specifies the number of partners in each firm engaged in an array of various specialties (only 13 percent of the firms in the sample are included in this listing)

These sources obviously provide more information on larger firms than smaller ones. For the smaller firms, I also included any areas of specialization of practice disclosed during the interviews. Information culled from these diverse data sources were coded into forty-three different areas of specialization, and firms were credited with expertise in an area if any one of these sources (including my interviews for the smaller firms) disclosed such specialization.

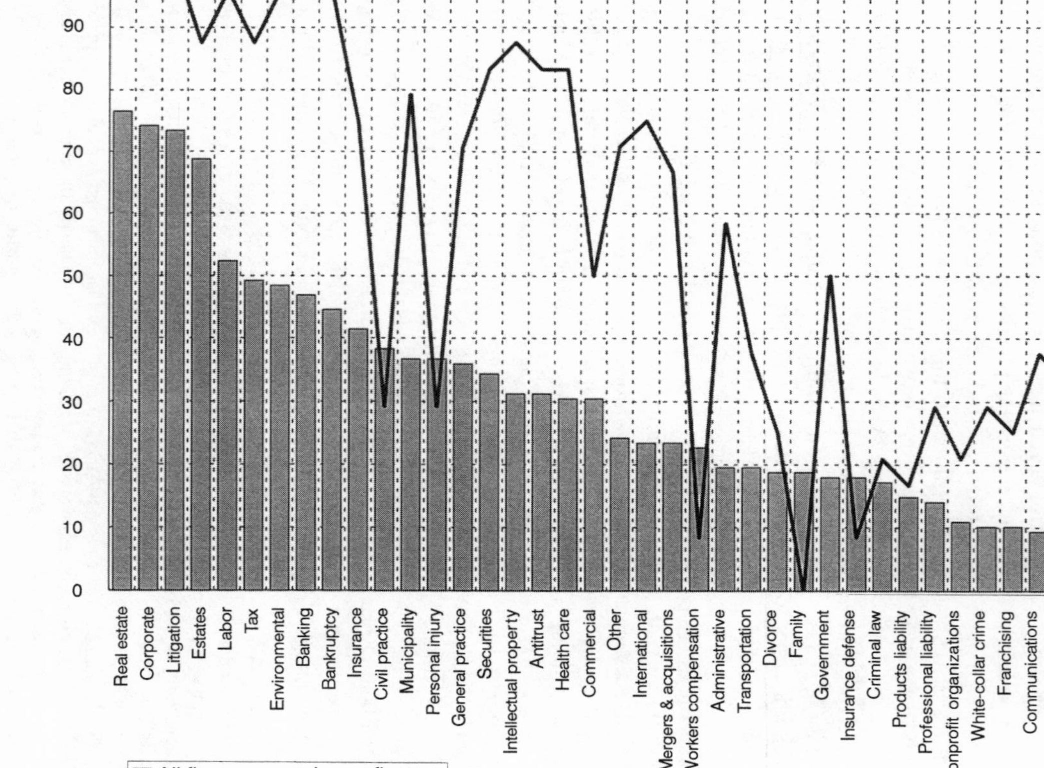
Percentage of firms with this specialization
100
90
80
70
60
50
40
30
20
10
0
Real estate
Corporate
Litigation
Estates
Labor
Tax
Environmental
Banking
Bankruptcy
Insurance
Civil practice
Municipality
Personal injury
General practice
Securities
Intellectual property
Antitrust
Health care
Commercial
Other
International
Mergers & acquisitions
Workers compensation
Administrative
Transportation
Divorce
Family
Government
Insurance defense
Criminal law
Products liability
Professional liability
Nonprofit organizations
White-collar crime
Franchising
Communications
Public utilities
Civil rights
Public finance
Construction
Legislative
Entertainment
Collections
All firms
Large firms

Fig. 2.3. Areas of Practice

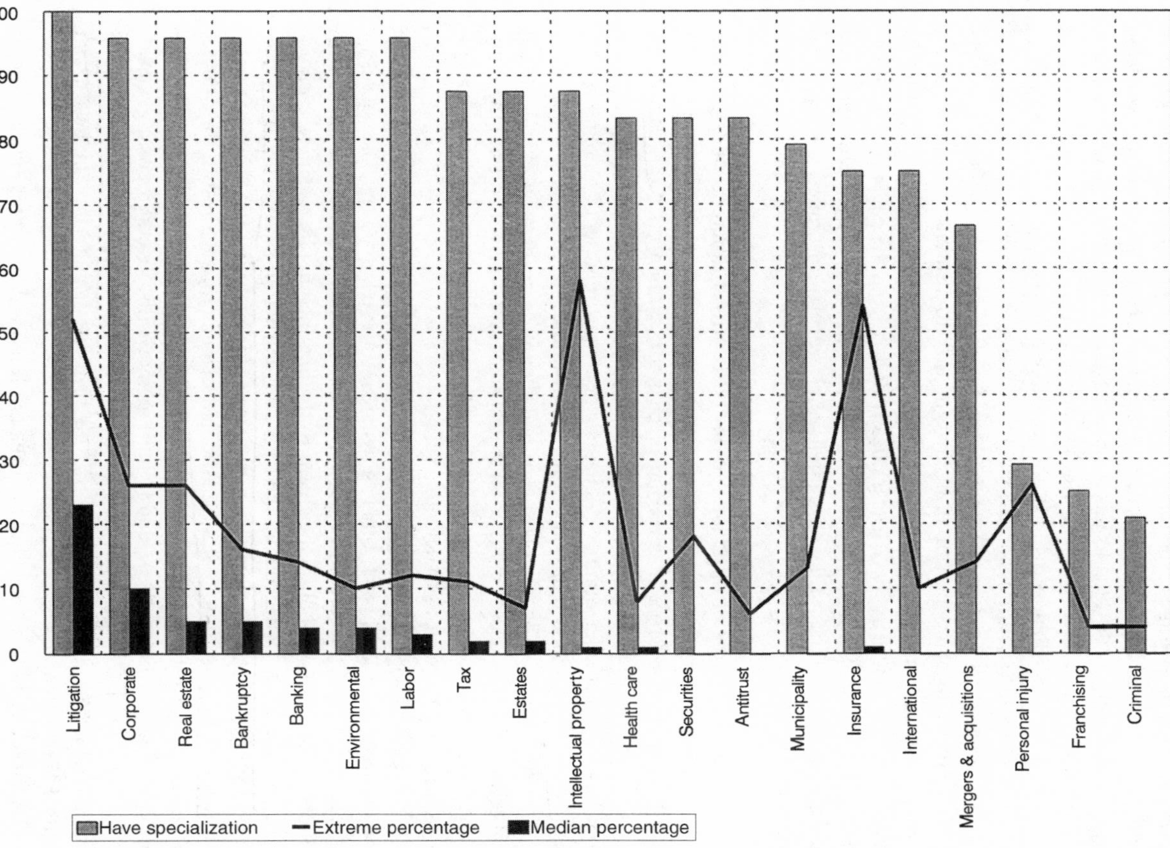

Fig. 2.4. Large-Firm Specialization

attorneys' time on average is spent litigating. More dramatic, although almost nine-tenths of the firms have expertise in intellectual property law, only 1 percent of their lawyers' time is devoted to this area; not even a full percentage of legal labor is allocated to many other fields in which a majority of the firms specialize.

The solid bars, then, provide statistical support to the notion that most large firms are generalists, but not all. The solid line in figure 2.4 displays the average of the two most extreme values of firm legal staffing. For example, although the average large firm allocates 1 percent of its lawyers' time to insurance work, two of the firms allocate more than half of attorney time. The spikes in the solid line plotted in figure 2.4—where at least two firms radically depart from the general trend—represent some of the fields in which firms are most likely to specialize in what are called boutique practices: litigation, intellectual property, insurance, and personal injury law.

Clients. Firms of different size obviously attract different kinds of clientele, but there is some variation even among the largest firms. Firms that specialize in litigation serve a broader spectrum of clients but often on a one-shot basis, whereas firms with a diversified transactional practice tend to have ongoing relationships with a smaller number of clients, sometimes representing them on hundreds of matters. Firms that concentrate on insurance defense work often count their major clients on one or two hands and then correct themselves and explain that technically (i.e., according to legal ethical standards) their clients are the thousands of insureds they represent rather than the handful of huge insurance institutions who send them cases to defend.

Some firms serve as general counsel for one or more corporations, doing the lion's share of their legal work; others gravitate mostly to limited special counsel assignments. One of the latter firms reports, for example, that no one client contributes more than one-half of 1 percent to its total income. Increasingly, corporations are spurning such general counsel arrangements and spreading their legal work around to a larger number of law firms, often setting up beauty contests through which firms compete for a particular assignment. As a result, the number of clients per firm has increased over the past decade, even controlling for firm growth. Large law firms, then, tend to have many clients, several reporting considerably more than ten thousand active clients; others opening hundreds of new matters, often for new clients, every month. Still, firms vary significantly in the size and volume of new matters.

A survey of Illinois's largest law firms (with more than twenty-five attorneys) found that, overall, 83 percent of their business comes from corporations, 11 percent from individuals, and 6 percent from government entities (Andersen 1998, 19). The largest law firms traditionally represent the largest institutions and corporations in the United States and many of them abroad as well. Many large firms also handle the personal legal business of individuals they have gotten to know in their corporate capacities. Some firms—especially those that are somewhat smaller—gravitate to smaller companies or wealthy individuals or families. Firms that have grown rapidly may continue traditions of serving largely individuals and smaller businesses. Law firms with special expertise may represent at one time or another all companies in a certain industrial sector—banks, municipalities, insurance companies, construction companies and contractors, for example—or every major corporation with respect to a specific area of law—for example, real estate or international trade. For others, an exclusive relationship with a particular bank, manufacturer, or retailer may preclude representation of all competitors. Many large institutional clients have in-house legal staffs that rival in size and sophistication their outside counsel. Relationships with emerging companies and wealthy families may be much more personal and clients far less sophisticated.

Economics. The 1980s were a golden age for large law firms in the United States. Their unprecedented growth was accompanied by economic prosperity as law firms amassed huge revenues, compensation skyrocketed, and client demand outstripped supply. As summarized in Nelson (1994), legal service revenues grew 480 percent between 1977 and 1989, about twice the rate of the gross national product, and the annual income of law firm partners increased from less than $50,000 to almost $130,000 (345, 395). The boom fizzled in 1990 when a roughly three-year recession hit the legal profession. Large firms faced greater competition, downsized, cut back numbers of and compensation to partners and associates, and instituted cost-cutting measures to satisfy the demands of newly assertive clients emboldened by an oversupply of lawyers.

It was into this economic environment that I launched my study. Still, the picture was not terribly bleak by more conventional standards. During the period of the study, thirteen of the eighteen largest indigenous Chicago law firms were listed in the AM LAW 100, *The American Lawyer's* compilation of the 100 most profitable law firms in the United States. The profits per partner of these thirteen most profitable firms ranged from $240,000 to $710,000, with gross revenues ranging from $68,500,000 to $477,500,000 ("The AM LAW 100" 1992, 20, 45).

Malpractice insurance. All but two law firms in the study carry some kind of professional liability insurance.[12] Both exceptions are solo practitioners, one exclusively defending criminals, the other serving the poorest population in the sample. The smaller firms tend to be insured by a mutual insurance company pool formed in 1988 by the Illinois State Bar Association or by one of a small number of private carriers that reduced their premiums to remain competitive after the state bar program was instituted and cut skyrocketing commercial premium rates by 30 percent (Illinois State Bar Association 1999a). A few of the larger boutique law firms with more idiosyncratic risk profiles have secured malpractice policies packaged by their specialty practice associations, for example, for insurance defense counsel or for intellectual property practitioners. And a few firms buy their liability insurance from their own insurance clients.

But the large firms are different. Because of their diversified practice—especially specialization in corporate law, securities, and banking, where most malpractice claims occur—and because of the sheer number and magnitude of cases, their vulnerability to significant liability is much greater. Up until the late 1970s, most large law firms were insured by Lloyds of London, and a few still are. But as their

[12]Because type of malpractice insurer has a significant effect on law firm self-regulatory practices, I delve into greater detail here than would otherwise seem justified.

premiums continued to rise, several firms explored the possibility of creating a mutual insurance company that, through strict selection criteria and loss prevention activities, might keep insurance premiums below that in the for-profit insurance market. The Attorneys' Liability Assurance Society (ALAS) was founded in 1979 by thirty-five large U.S. law firms and was headquartered in Chicago. At the time of my study, 375 law firms and 50,000 lawyers from around the country were covered by this mutual company. A crude comparison of the ALAS membership roster with the *National Law Journal* list of the 250 largest U.S. law firms (with more than 130 attorneys) during this period suggests that roughly two-thirds of the firms eligible to join ALAS had done so (Attorneys' Liability Assurance Society 1991; Weisenhaus 1991). The percentage is higher for Chicago firms (79 percent), probably because ALAS is headquartered here.

This mutual insurance company has a vigorous loss prevention program, a significant component of which concerns avoiding conflicts of interest, which tend to swell the size of malpractice awards. Member firms are required to have one or more loss prevention partners to serve as liaison with ALAS and, along with other colleagues, are required to attend one or more seminars or conferences each year. ALAS publishes and annually updates a weighty loss prevention manual and also circulates to all insured lawyers a loss prevention journal three times a year with reviews of new cases and ethics opinions and other guidance on how to minimize liability risks. At the time of my research, three ALAS loss prevention counsel visited member firms, conducted loss prevention audits, and provided in-firm seminars as well as day-to-day guidance to lawyers who called with difficult professional-responsibility questions; that number has since grown to seven.[13]

ALAS makes many recommendations regarding law firm structure and procedures. Firms are encouraged to form new business screening committees, to appoint ethics partners, and to refrain from serving on the boards of directors of clients. Because so many large law firms are subject to this active loss prevention program, their self-regulatory practices are likely to be more homogeneous than those of smaller firms, which are insured by a larger complement of insurance providers, few of which provide any loss prevention program at all.[14]

The varied reasons for selecting professional liability insurance significantly confound the ability to disentangle the effect of self-regulatory practices on firm conduct. For example, if ALAS firms have a much better ethical track record than non-ALAS firms, is that because of their considerable loss prevention activities and the self-regulatory practices ALAS firms typically adopt? Or is it because ALAS

---

[13]ALAS loss prevention counsel receive 2,000 phone calls a year on conflicts of interest alone (Attorneys' Liability Assurance Society 1999).

[14]In the last few years—after my research—the Illinois State Bar Association Mutual Insurance Company began a loss prevention program that emulates that of ALAS—with a newsletter, articles and written materials, and free in-house loss prevention seminars and telephone consultations as well as a web site and discussion groups (which ALAS has instituted as well) (Illinois State Bar Association 1999b). Some of the commercial insurance carriers also provide seminars and give premium credits to attorneys who attend them. But at the time of my research, virtually none of my respondents insured commercially or by the ISBA knew or took advantage of any support or loss prevention program provided by their insurer aside from seminars or newsletter columns.

will not underwrite bad firms? If the track record of ALAS firms is no better or even worse than other firms, is that because low-risk firms are discouraged from joining because they can get much lower premiums from private insurers? In other words, do the high premiums and lack of experience-rating characteristic of this mutual insurance pool select for the more high-risk firms? Would the track records of ALAS firms look considerably worse if they did not benefit from their insurer's loss prevention activities?[15] Fortunately, these largely unanswerable questions do not lie at the core of the inquiry. But to get a better sense of this potential "ALAS effect," I did oversample large firms that are not ALAS members.

Smaller Firms

A little more than half the smaller Chicago firms (one to ninety-nine lawyers) in the sample are in the twenty-five to ninety-nine range.[16] Ninety-two percent of the smaller firms are located in the downtown area of the city. This percentage actually probably underrepresents the predominance of the Loop in the legal landscape of the city. Only one firm in the original random sample was located out of the Loop. After visiting the firm and discovering how different it was from the others, I randomly selected four more firms situated on the outskirts of the city (more on them in the next section). Almost four out of five of the small Chicago firms work out of a single office, though this is much more common for the smallest firms (84 percent) than for those employing fifty to ninety-nine lawyers (61 percent). More than half their branch offices are located in counties surrounding Chicago, another 16 percent in Washington, D.C., and the remainder spread across nearby cities and those located in warmer climes.[17] Many of these branch offices are very small, staffed by one or two attorneys or comprised of shared office space to be used to meet with more distant clients.

Almost one in ten of these law firms—each of them employing more than thirty lawyers—trace their origins to the nineteenth century. A quarter were created between the end of the Second World War and the 1970s, and almost a third were born during the 1970s and early 1980s. More than a quarter were founded within five years of the study.

These figures may create the erroneous impression that the birth of law firms can be marked as precisely as the birth of lawyers themselves. But the circumstances under which law firms are conceived are considerably more varied than those for lawyers, even in this age of diverse reproductive technologies. A significant number of conceptions arose from practice groups that were spun off or groups of lawyers that split off or defected from larger, sometimes ailing or fractious firms

[15]Since the time of my interviews, the professional liability insurance market has softened and become more competitive (Chanen 1999), affording firms more insurance options and probably reducing this selection bias.

[16]Again, note that this sample is a stratified random one, not a representative one. These proportions do not reflect the distribution of all lawyers in Chicago. Indeed, in all of Illinois, there are about seven times more law firms comprised of a single lawyer than the total number of law firms employing two or more attorneys (Carson 1999, 83–84).

[17]The predominance of Washington, D.C., probably reflects the importance, for intellectual property boutiques, of having an office near the U.S. Patent Office.

that eventually dissolved. Many of these separations were amicable, and the new firm thrived in its early years on referrals of business from the parent firm—especially cases that created conflicts of interest for the latter. Other firms were created by partners or associates affiliated with several large law firms who joined to start their own practice. Many of the smaller firms and solo practices were created by lawyers who had practiced elsewhere—in firms (where they were not made partner or from which they sought more autonomy or to strike out on their own), in the public sector (a state's attorney's office, attorney general's office, public defender's office, or a municipal agency), in legal aid, and so on.

Many of the firms have grown substantially in the last ten years or so—doubling, even quintupling in size—a few by mergers with other firms, others by entry-level and lateral hiring. But several of the firms are actually losing lawyers through defections or attrition.

About half the firms in this cluster share much of the ambiance of the larger firms—if writ on a somewhat smaller scale and from a lower perch—with spectacular, elegant lobbies; attractive, sometimes ostentatious furnishings; eccentric art; flowers; and the like. The others, especially the smaller of these firms, sometimes resemble a dentist's office more than a law firm. They have smaller lobbies or none at all—simply a chair or two near the receptionist. The furnishings are spare, nondescript, serviceable, sometimes a bit worn. The computers are older or absent. The interiors are often metal and plastic rather than wood and are cluttered, with boxes piled in the hallways and files strewn about tables and floors. The attire—of secretaries, receptionists, lawyers, people waiting in the lobby—is more casual: sweat clothes, jeans, shorts, shirts that won't accommodate a tie. As for the reading material in the lobby, the *Wall Street Journal* and *Forbes* give way to *People, Sports Illustrated,* and *Modern Maturity.*

These firms occupy different physical niches as well—on the wrong side of and often very near the el tracks (the trains' periodic rumbles and squeals drowning out our conversation), closer to the local courthouse, on lower floors of Loop high-rises, overlooking the less picturesque side of town. They share the floor of their office building with small business offices, other law firms, doctors, dentists, and the like. Many actually share interior space or a suite of offices with other lawyers or law firms. In a few cases, a firm comprised of a dozen or more lawyers rents space to one or more solo practitioners or a much smaller firm. In other cases, a number of small independent one- or two-lawyer practices share a floor as well as a receptionist, pool of secretaries, office equipment, and so on. In still other cases, the occupants of the suite of offices are more connected and their relationship more long-term; they often refer cases back and forth.

Specialization. Figure 2.5 displays the distribution of practice fields for the Chicago law firms that employ fewer than one hundred lawyers, contrasted with all lawyers in the sample (the gray bars). The distributions are very similar, in part because the small Chicago law firm category is the largest in the study ($N = 62$) and, therefore, heavily weights the total distribution. Litigation is the most common area of practice among these small firms, followed by real estate and corporate law, true of larger firms as well.

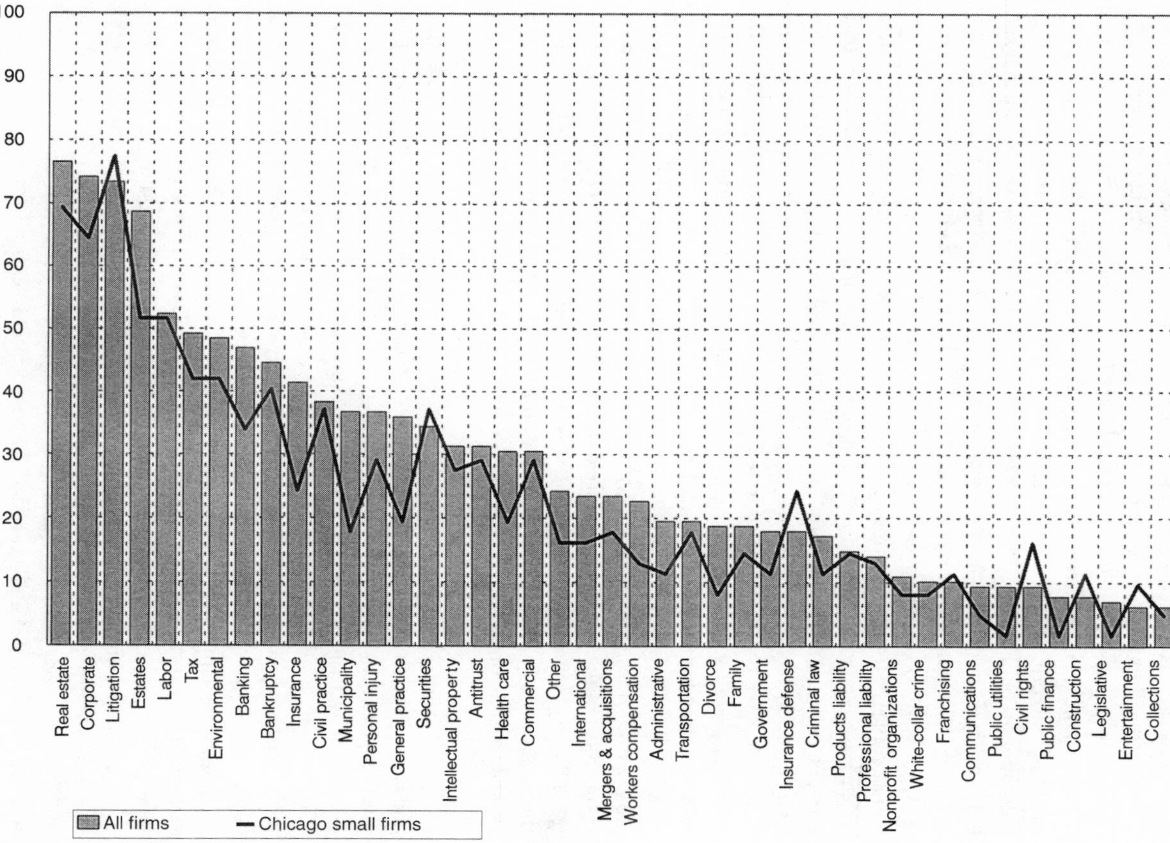

Fig. 2.5. Chicago Small-Firm Practice

A few of the medium-sized firms model the large general practice firms, offering expertise in civil litigation, corporate law, real estate, tax, labor, securities, finance, banking, estates, bankruptcy, and the like. However, this cluster of firms (in the one to ninety-nine lawyer range) is the least likely of any other constellation in the sample to offer a general practice of law; large firms are more than three and a half times more likely, and even downstate firms of comparable size (or smaller) are twice as likely to have a general practice. Smaller Chicago firms, then, are able to occupy a more specialized niche, with their larger neighbors developing both more esoteric kinds of expertise as well as more general coverage. These small-firm niches conform to a few patterns. A number of firms specialize in civil litigation, the larger ones usually defending claims for personal injury, products liability, toxic torts, or professional liability, the smaller ones asserting as well as defending these claims. Another cluster of firms predominantly litigate but also offer expertise in basic fields like real estate, corporate law, or estates. A number of the others offer boutique practices in a single area of law, specializing in plaintiffs' personal injury litigation, intellectual property, worker's compensation, labor and employment, disability and discrimination, criminal law, or collections. Two small firms in the sample are each house counsel (i.e., on the payroll) for an insurance company, undertaking most of the insurance defense caseload of their parent.[18] The very smallest of the Chicago firms—those with ten attorneys at most—look quite different from their counterparts with eleven to ninety-nine lawyers. They are much more likely to specialize in divorce, criminal law, collections, personal injury, and family law.

Clients. Because of these differences in fields of practice, diversification, and specialization as well as in the number of lawyers who can be mobilized for a given engagement, large and small Chicago firms tend to have different kinds of clientele. Law firms in the one to ninety-nine lawyer range usually represent smaller corporations, local businesses, second-tier insurance companies rather than those with household names, entrepreneurial or newly emerging companies, closely held corporations or smaller subsidiaries, partnerships, nonprofit institutions, government entities, family businesses, and of course, individuals. The largest client of some of these firms may, indeed, be an individual, something unheard of in the largest Chicago firms. Clients served by this cluster of firms tend to be less wealthy as a rule, and some may be financing their representation with contingency fees.

Some of the specialized boutiques do offer particularistic expertise, though: intellectual property firms, for example, will represent large institutional clients as well as multinational and Fortune 500 corporations. Other firms will represent a single large company—a major retailer, for example—or concentrate in a single industry whose players may be quite large. In some of these instances, the number of in-house counsel working for the client may dramatically overshadow the size of the outside law firm.

Many of these firms market themselves as being large enough to offer a full complement of services and mega-firm expertise but small enough to hold down

---

[18]Because those firms had typical law firm names, I did not know when drawing the sample that they were not traditional private law firms. (If I had known, I would have excluded them.)

costs and give prompt personalized attention to client needs. Relationships with clients tend to be more personal and long-term. Interpersonal dynamics change when lawyers work directly with the individuals whose personal wealth is on the line (rather than with the in-house counsel more common in large-firm practice), and issues of institutional loyalty or taking slights personally figure more prominently in these dynamics. The size of the caseload among these firms is quite variable. Some of the bigger firms in this cluster serve a limited number of clients or cases, concentrating instead on what they call "big ticket items." Others, especially the smaller firms, have a very high volume of clients and a huge number of cases. Whereas one firm in this cluster concentrates on about ten big cases a year, another will not take a trial that lasts more than ten minutes.

Economics. Law firms in this cluster also vary in their profitability. Some of the smaller firms have found it easier to adapt to the recession in legal services than the big firms have. Many still turn a great deal of business away. Some boutiques with little diversification have been affected by downturns in the industries or markets they serve. Law firms with substantial real estate practices, for example, have been challenged by the recession in the real estate market. Insurance defense firms have watched their markets become more competitive, saturated, and less profitable, even as their adversaries on the plaintiff's side are enjoying extraordinarily lucrative awards. Some of the small firms and solo practices are having a harder time; respondents express worry about paying their rent or making a payroll.

Non-Loop Firms

The Chicago sample includes five law firms located outside the Loop. The first, a two-lawyer firm, is located on the north side of Chicago in an ethnically diverse area. Another two-lawyer firm resides a few miles north of the Loop and just west of a white yuppie neighborhood that is also home to the Chicago Cubs. The third firm of four lawyers makes its home on the northwest side of Chicago near a major freeway in an area that combines a Polish and Asian residential community with many commercial businesses. The fourth, a solo practitioner, has practiced on the far west side, within a mile of the Chicago border, for twenty years. The neighborhood is very white, with few traces of ethnicity and comprised of large homes and small restaurants, shops, and strip malls housing chain stores that sell basic consumer goods. The fifth firm, also a solo practice, is located on the south side of Chicago in a stable—though not especially prosperous—African American neighborhood.

Four of the firms largely serve neighborhood clientele, although several respondents commented that clients do not like to go downtown and pay for parking to see their lawyers and, as a result, their firms also draw from well beyond the immediate neighborhood. The fifth firm, largely a collections practice that doesn't require face-to-face meetings with clients, is located away from the Loop presumably to enjoy the lower rent. Three of the firms represent ethnic communities—one African American, one Korean, another Indian. Two of the firms are among the few in the sample that coexist precariously on the economic margins. One solo practitioner schedules formal office hours twelve hours each day and on weekends and had a lobby filled with waiting clients when our interview ended a bit after 9 A.M.

on a Saturday morning. The respondent complained that many clients do not pay their bills and instead refer new clients who also don't pay their bills. A respondent in the other marginal firm complained that they can't afford to hire any other attorneys and that his legal options were limited when clients arrive with $300 in their pockets.

These five firms distinguish themselves in their legal specializations as well. One solo practitioner advertises more than thirty specialties—starting with adoptions and ending at wills. This lawyer enjoys a high-volume practice generated by a large ad in the yellow pages and spends a good deal of time in court. Another lawyer, with a high-volume collections practice, schedules all his downtown court appearances for one day each week. A third respondent concentrates on a neighborhood-oriented transactional caseload that includes real estate, banking for local financial institutions, and corporate law for neighborhood businesses. The other two neighborhood firms concentrate on real estate, personal injury, and general business law, one also handling minor criminal cases and the other wills and divorces.

DOWNSTATE

Figure 2.6 displays a map of Illinois, noting its four largest cities; its 102 counties, including the collar counties around Chicago (darkened); and the towns that support a single lawyer or firm (small hearts). As is obvious from the map, Illinois counties are extraordinarily small.[19] In a burst of eighteenth-century public spiritedness, Illinois counties were carved up so that all residents could visit the county seat by horseback and return home the same day (Clayton 1970, 26). Though this criterion is still just about right for the clogged and congested arteries of Cook County, one can seemingly traverse an entire rural county on the interstate while listening to the same song on the car radio. Each county supports and maintains an independent judicial system, including courthouses, jails, sheriffs, state's attorneys, and public defenders, even though two-fifths of them—even at the end of the twentieth century—did not have even twenty lawyers (Attorney Registration and Disciplinary Commission 1994, 6). (These are the counties that are colored white in figure 2.1.)

In all, I conducted forty-two interviews in twenty-two downstate communities, ranging in size from seven hundred to more than one hundred thousand residents.[20] In order to maintain the anonymity of respondents, these communities will not be named. My journey extended from the Wisconsin border in the north to the beautiful hills and far less attractive oil fields near Kentucky to the south, and from the endless miles of pungent farmland along the eastern Indiana border to the sandbagged Mississippi River slicing through Iowa and Missouri to the west. Actually, pungent farmland was omnipresent through most of the journey.

---

[19]Except for Cook County, which contains Chicago and more than one hundred other communities and is the second most populous county in the United States.

[20]See the appendix for detail on the stratified random sampling design by which these firms were selected. Because of this sampling strategy, the sample is not representative; it profoundly overrepresents large downstate firms, none of which, on odds alone, would likely make it into a small unstratified sample. But the sample includes exemplars of many settings in which lawyers practice.

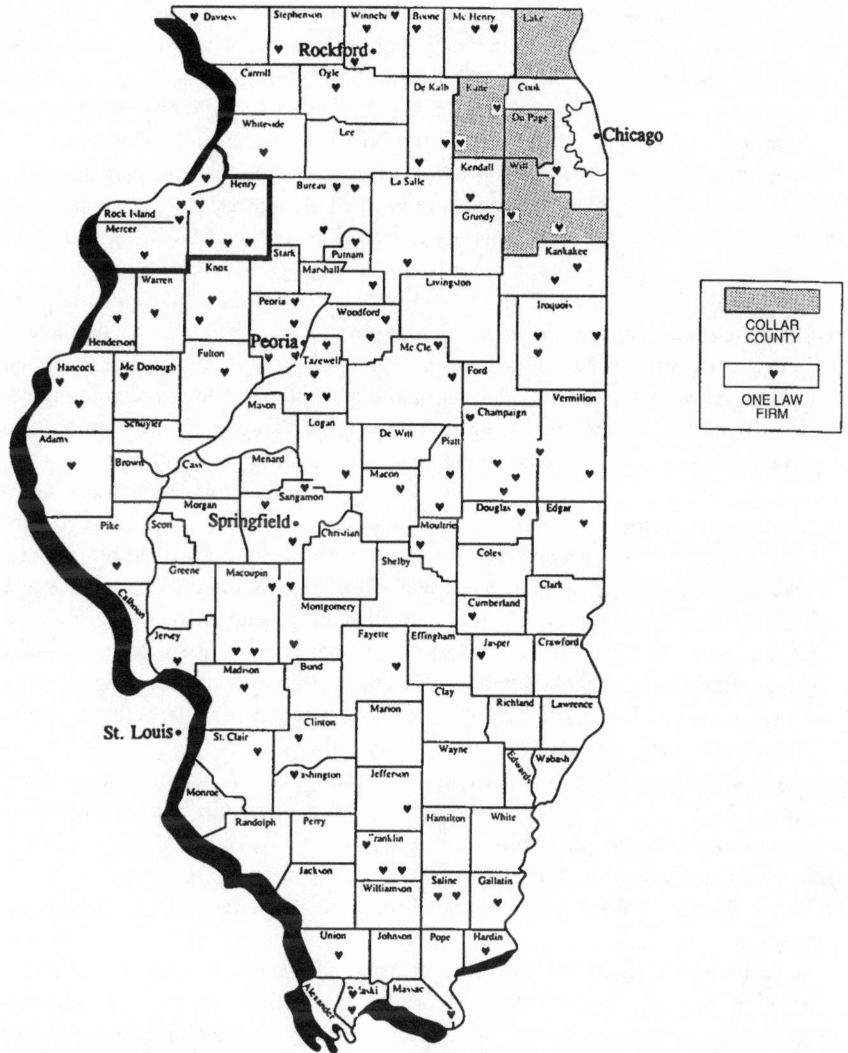

Fig. 2.6. Downstate Illinois

Collar Counties

Collar counties (darkened in figure 2.6) extend roughly fifty miles around Chicago and house bedroom communities of commuters who work in Chicago; autonomous cities and towns with little connection to the city; commercial neighborhoods with few residents but expansive office campuses, corporate headquarters, and high-rise office towers at the intersections of major interstate highways; and—on their outskirts—farmland and communities revitalized by riverboat gambling operations. These extended Chicago suburbs are home to roughly six thousand attorneys, many working in indigenous law firms, others in branch offices of Chicago firms (Attorney Registration and Disciplinary Commission 1994, 6). A little more than one hundred cities and towns in these four counties boast one or more law firms.[21] I conducted seven interviews in three of those communities with relatively large lawyer populations.

The major law firm meccas in the collar counties are cities with several tens of thousands of inhabitants (many with 50,000 to 100,000), making them larger than almost all of Illinois's freestanding cities. Most are more than 90 percent white (though for several, as many as a quarter to a third of their residents are nonwhite); median 1990 family incomes generally exceed $35,000 or $40,000; and median housing values exceed (sometimes very substantially) $120,000 (*1990 Census Snapshot for all U.S. Places* 1992, 114–45). These communities have an air of prosperity, renewal, and economic vitality unusual in much of urban downstate Illinois.

I visited law firms that ranged in size from a solo practitioner to more than ten lawyers. The firms represent widely disparate generations, one founded many decades ago, most others within the last two decades. Collar county law firms tend to be younger on average (twelve years) than their counterparts either in Chicago (thirty-seven years) or in other downstate communities (forty-nine years)—undoubtedly a reflection of more recent population movements to the Chicago suburbs. Some collar county firms are housed in professional office buildings; others, in old houses in or near the center of town. They variably share the ambiance of a dentist's office, a small upscale Chicago law firm, or a social science department in an old college town. Some of their legal personnel grew up there or in a nearby Chicago suburb, and others migrated from Chicago in hopes of becoming a "country" lawyer, a lifestyle described by more than one respondent in the collar counties. Many received their legal education in Chicago.

The Chicago legal community and opportunities to practice in Chicago come up in many of these interviews, not only as a point of comparison for what respondents consider their far superior lifestyle. Chicago law firms have made inroads into the collar counties, setting up branch offices and attempting to skim off some of the cream of the legal business. At the time of the study, 15 percent of the Chicago law firms in my sample had twenty-six branch offices in the collar counties, a market penetration relatively constant for several years. Although many of the indigenous lawyers in the study note the presence of these branch offices and some acknowledge that Chicago firms have had an impact on their practice—especially in the insurance defense area—many others find their impact limited. Chicago firms, they explain, charge more; staff their offices with young, inexperienced associates; and haven't achieved much visibility or name recognition among suburban clients. Indeed, several collar county lawyers indicate that they even represent small Chicago businesses—referred to them by Chicago law firms—to which they provide more experienced lawyers, quicker response time, and lower fees than are typical of large Chicago law firms. Many respondents do note, though, the increase in sharp practices and incivility in the courthouse, and attribute much of it to the arrival of Chicago lawyers. Respondents further downstate complain about the same trend.

---

[21]In addition, Cook County includes over one hundred towns and cities outside Chicago that are also home to legal practices (*Illinois Legal Directory* 1995). Technically, these are not considered collar county communities.

Bigger Cities

I conducted twenty-one interviews in eight cities with more than thirty thousand inhabitants, about two-thirds of them in cities with more than one hundred thousand residents. The list includes many of the largest cities in the state outside Cook and the collar counties. Most are located in the northern and central portions of the state, but several are situated to the west, near the Mississippi River. Most of the communities have median 1990 household incomes in the mid to high $20,000s; median home values cluster in the high $50,000 to mid $60,000 range, though several are much lower. For most of these cities, nonwhite residents comprise roughly 10 to 20 percent of the population, again with some notable exceptions in both directions (*1990 Census Snapshot for all U.S. Places* 1992, 114–45). The downtown areas of a good number of these communities have seen better days and appear depressed, run-down, and bedraggled, with some empty buildings and others in need of rehabilitation.

Law firms are more conspicuous in the urban landscape downstate than they are in Chicago. Many structures are adorned with large striking signs that name the firm or firms inside and often all their lawyers as well. The downtown streets of some of these communities are littered with these signs, usually outside the nicer structures. Downstate law firms make their homes in high-rise—often bank—buildings, storefronts, big old houses, rehabbed warehouses, and self-standing structures in or near downtown. As in Chicago, the larger structures often house several law firms along with other professionals, insurance agencies, and the like. Interiors vary, much as they do in smaller law firms in Chicago and the collar counties. A few are modern and airy with beautiful new furnishings; others betray their nineteenth-century origins with massive antique furniture, traditional rugs and draperies, and old portraits on the walls. Others could be mistaken for dentists' or doctors' offices. And some are a bit dingy, lacking even a glimmer of ostentation. Coffee and end tables are stocked with *Reader's Digest, Ladies' Home Journal, House Beautiful, Highlights for Children,* and children's books, few of which would be found in their Chicago counterparts.

The firms I visited range in size from solo practices to those of several dozen attorneys. Half the firms have been in existence for more than seventy-four years, a quarter of them dating back to the nineteenth century. Some firm histories include great grandfathers, grandfathers, fathers, and sons, many of whom still practice together. A little more than a quarter of these firms have one or more branch offices, usually in nearby communities. Six percent of the Chicago firms in the sample have branch offices in one of these cities; several St. Louis firms do as well.

Many of the firms characterize their practice as regional—covering at least a one-hundred-mile radius—necessitated, in part, by conflicts of interest that can disqualify all the lawyers in particular specialties in a given town. The firms in this cluster represent the full range of clients: individuals, professionals, farmers, banks, municipalities, family businesses, large corporations, and insurance companies. Unlike the big Chicago firms with a very diversified client base, several of these firms indicate that they have only a handful of major clients that together account for as much as three-quarters of their business.

Conversations with lawyers in these large and medium-sized cities as well as those in the collar counties often turn to the precious value of one's reputation.

> You know, we survive in downstate communities by reputation. This won't sound good—it'll sound terribly provincial—but there's a lot of stuff that goes on up in the Chicago area . . . practices that down here, if you did anything like that, you could forget it. You, you'd be done. Your business would dry up and it would go away—in a flash. . . . But I think that there's an awful lot of people out there who are in one-, two-, three-, four-man shops up there in the Chicago area who have no sense, particularly, of the fact that there's a continuity to this business. And they're never going to see anybody from that same firm again—in all probability. It would be as freaky as running into the same guy twice on the highway. It just doesn't happen. . . . But I can absolutely guarantee you that, if I have a case with Joe down here, I'm going to have another case with Joe and I'm going to have yet another case with Joe. And if I don't play square with Joe, then it's going to get around. And it's going to be a subject of conversation. And, before long, no one's going to be trusting you. [68DSM10–19]

Small Towns

Finally, I conducted fourteen interviews in eleven small Illinois towns with fewer than thirty thousand inhabitants. The smallest of them has 700 residents, the median, roughly ten thousand. These towns cover the entire state; none are near Chicago. Three of the towns are county seats. The four smallest ones were purposely chosen because they host only a single law firm (the full complement of such firms from which these were randomly selected are denoted by a heart on the map in figure 2.6). A little more than a quarter of the sampled firms in this cluster are solo practices; half employ more than five attorneys. Most of these firms were founded after the Second World War, though several have been in existence for more than seven decades; one firm began just three years before I visited.

The seven larger towns in this cluster are home to several law firms. Typically one or two of them has six or more attorneys, and the remaining firms have one, two, or three lawyers. Depending on the size of the town, the lawyer population might reach several dozen. These towns typically cover five to ten square miles. Those communities closer to an interstate highway might support a mall or two or a thriving retail business sector. Others offer a lovely town square, antique shops, and nice old houses. Average 1990 household incomes in these towns range from $15,000 to $25,000; housing, from $20,000 to $55,000. Housing stock is frequently mixed, suggesting significant class stratification, with old, small, frame houses on small lots among very, very large brick homes. Many of these smaller towns convey an air of prosperity and revitalization less common in the bigger downstate cities. The economic significance of agriculture is obvious from the surrounding landscape as well as the local news, which devotes several sections or segments to agriculture and lots of advertising for tractors, livestock, and the like.

Several respondents in larger towns explained the fundamental axiom of establishing a legal practice: "One lawyer in town starves. Two make a mint. That's the basic rule." [125DSS<10] Nonetheless, Illinois has about 120 communities that contain only a single law firm or lawyer.[22] Though the four with whom I spoke

---

[22]This statistic comes from eyeballing the more than 200-page listing, city by city, in the *Sullivan's Law Directory* of all attorneys in Illinois outside Cook County.

may not be making a mint, they are not starving either; indeed, they seemed quite busy. These one-law-firm towns typically have several hundred to a couple thousand residents living on a square mile or two. The towns are surrounded by farmland and occasionally abut a major highway. A one- or two-block downtown area shades into residential streets that simply end abruptly at a parcel of farmland. The housing stock includes small, worn houses of clapboard or aluminum siding with a few large brick homes on the outskirts of town. Many towns boast "century" farms and churches. A visitor typically also encounters a silo, post office, library, VFW hall, gas station, video store, John Deere distributor, and school. In some, the gas station is the sole local food vendor. Often the law firm is the only professional office in town.

Not quite half the small-town respondents grew up there or in a nearby town, though many of the others have lived in this community for a number of years. The homegrown lawyers do not consider this attribute much of an asset. One told me that, in an ideal world, lawyers would live at least one hundred miles from their offices. Others described how much easier it was to practice law before they moved back home. Another is looking for work in surrounding counties, where the impediments of familiarity and social connection are not so endemic. However deep their local roots, nearly all these small-town lawyers speak at length of the difficulties of being entangled in disputes involving lifelong friends, neighbors, the parents of their children's friends, the members of their church, divorcing spouses—at an individual level—and—at an institutional level—those involving the city and other municipal institutions, the local bank, the local newspaper, the hospital, the doctors, the major businesses, many or all of which they represent.

These difficulties are compounded by the fact that small-town lawyers seem to play a larger role in local business, eleemosynary, and community organizations than do their big-city counterparts (Landon 1990). Several of these respondents described local banks and other business enterprises that their families own or in which they have a substantial financial stake. Many more describe community or nonprofit boards on which they serve—the local hospital, a mental health agency, a religious organization, the Little League or Boy Scouts or Big Brothers, the YMCA, the zoning or library board. They serve in part because these commitments provide a good networking device, in part because they feel an obligation to the communities in which they live, and in part because their clients expect them to serve.

This embeddedness in the social networks of clients and adversaries is not unique to small-town life, of course. Chicago lawyers occasionally talk of the difficulties of being asked to handle the divorce of their children's pediatrician's spouse or to sue their synagogue; this pattern is even more common among Chicago lawyers whose clientele come from narrow ethnic communities. But the ubiquity of the problem is clearly unique to small-town life, as are the difficulties that result from the fact that lawyers are more likely to be embedded in the social networks of their clients and clients are more likely to be embedded in the social networks of other clients.

Happily, at least as lawyers tell it, few clients feel bounded by local legal communities and readily travel to other towns to find more detached lawyers and greater anonymity and privacy. Indeed, because they must leave many of these towns anyway to see a doctor, buy clothing, or even go grocery shopping, consulting with out-of-town attorneys is not perceived as particularly burdensome. Small-town lawyers often describe their legal "community" or reference group as crossing not only municipal boundaries but even county and occasionally state lines as well.

Specialization

Figure 2.7 displays the now-familiar contrast between the distribution of fields of practice among all lawyers in the sample (gray bars) and those who practice outside Chicago (black lines). Downstate lawyers are most likely to practice in the areas of estate law, real estate, and corporate work, followed by litigation and personal injury law. They are more likely to be generalists than are lawyers practicing in firms of comparable size in Chicago. Generalists are especially found in the larger firms, which have a hand in such community institutions as municipal government, the local bank, and the major businesses.

Though only a few of the downstate communities are large enough to support specialized boutique law firms, several of the firms tend to concentrate in one or two areas of law, typically civil litigation, insurance defense, collections, criminal law, family and divorce law, or personal injury plaintiff's law. The Illinois counties near St. Louis have a long-standing history of generous jury awards to personal injury plaintiffs. As a result, the area is thick with lawyers in general (see figure 2.1) and personal injury plaintiff's firms and insurance defense firms in particular. Several of the lawyers in other regions play quasi-public roles, serving part-time as city attorney or counsel to the city or public defender for the county. Although attorneys in the one-firm towns describe their practice as a general one because they must handle much of the legal business of the area, a significant portion of their workload tends to be concentrated in a few areas, especially family and divorce law, criminal defense, estates, and real estate.

THE LAWYERS

For each firm in the sample, I wrote the managing or most senior partner and asked him or her to identify the partner in the firm with greatest authority over conflict-of-interest matters. Depending on the size of the firm, interviewees come from managerial positions in the firm (62 percent)—managing or senior partner, member of the executive or management committee, or the head of a practice group—or from committees dealing with conflicts, ethics, or professional responsibility (almost a third).[23] In 13 percent of the firms, I interviewed more than one individual.

More than half the respondents are litigators, and a large number of the others specialize in areas that routinely entail litigation—insurance defense, personal injury,

[23]Three percent of the respondents working in firms of less than twenty-five lawyers served on a committee with responsibility for conflict-of-interest issues; this was true of 55 percent of the respondents in firms of 25 to 249 lawyers and 81 percent of those in firms of 250 or more lawyers. Similarly, eleven times more respondents from Chicago (44 percent) served on committees than did respondents working downstate (4 percent).

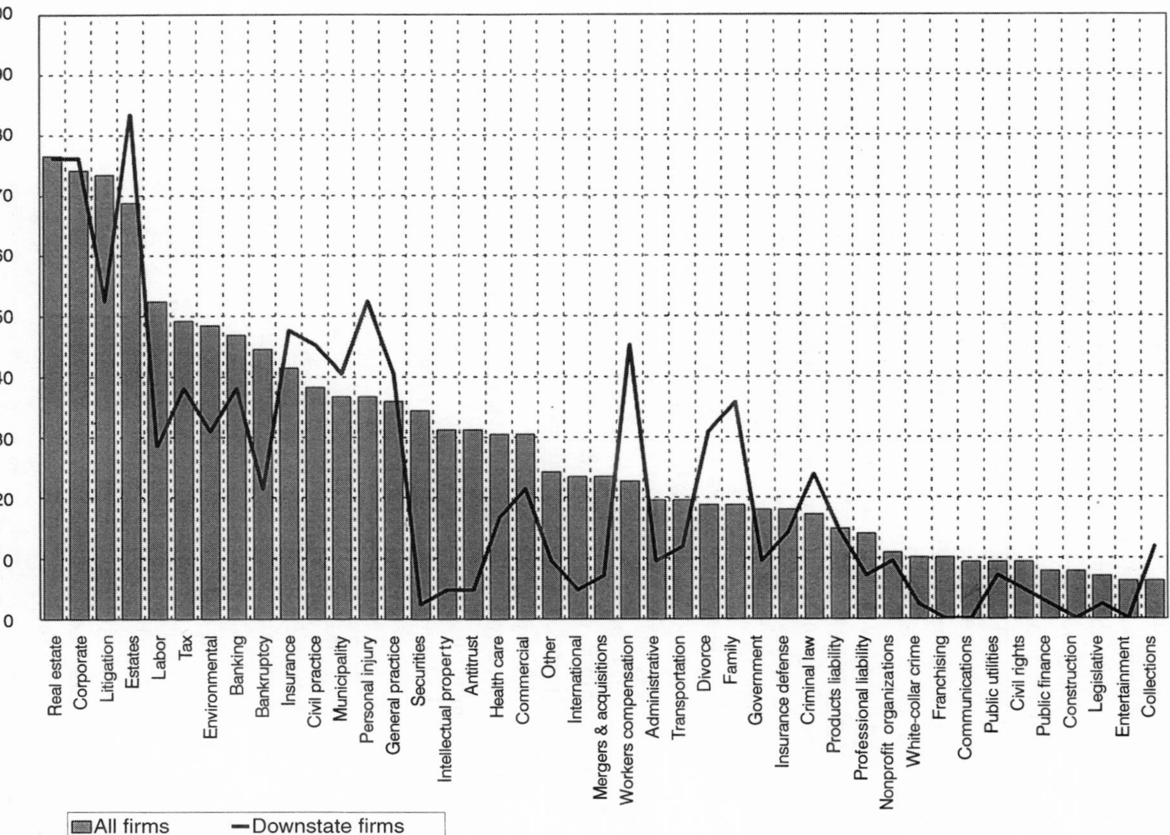

Fig. 2.7. Downstate Practice

professional liability, intellectual property, or environmental law. More than a third of the respondents practice in the area of personal injury or professional or products liability, most of them on the defense side, often representing insurance carriers. Almost a quarter practice in areas related to corporate law, about 15 percent in a cluster of family, divorce, or estate law; 12 percent, real estate law; and 9 percent, a cluster of finance, including securities, banking, public finance, venture capital, and the like.

Litigators are overrepresented in the ranks of the law firm conflicts experts because—as will be described in later chapters—conflict-of-interest issues tend to be most straightforward and visible and mistaken calls most costly in this area of legal practice. Serving as head of the firm's litigation department often becomes a trajectory for taking on firmwide responsibility for conflicts of interest. In particular, litigators who specialize in defending professional liability, malpractice, or professional responsibility cases often chair ethics or conflicts committees within their firm, mobilizing their inside information on how lawyers in other firms get themselves into trouble and devising risk management policies for their own firm. Several other respondents in the study have been personally involved in a conflict-of-interest case. Having learned the ropes firsthand, many are called on for guidance or leadership as changing rules of professional responsibility in the last decade or requirements imposed by malpractice insurers have demanded greater regulatory oversight by the firm. A few others have developed an interest in ethics and professional responsibility and have welcomed committee work in the hope of cultivating a niche as the firm ethics czar. These conflict-of-interest experts are more likely to be found in the larger firms whose division of labor permits such specialization.

The largest number of respondents (18 percent) received their legal training at the University of Illinois; the second largest (11 percent), at Harvard. Almost half the respondents were trained in Chicago: 9 percent at the University of Chicago, 9 percent at Northwestern, and the rest at local law schools including De Paul, Kent, Loyola, and John Marshall. More than twice the proportion of Chicago lawyers (55 percent) attended law school in Chicago than did those downstate (25 percent), while almost twelve times more downstate attorneys studied law at the University of Illinois (47 percent)[24] than did those who practice in Chicago (4 percent). More than twice as many Chicago lawyers (31 percent) attended elite law schools than did their downstate counterparts (13 percent), a difference not explained by a greater likelihood of the former to be educated at the University of Chicago.[25]

The respondents are overwhelmingly male—94 percent of them—reflecting in part gender stratification in the profession and in part the seniority and clout necessary to govern a law firm or chair a major committee that sees its share of discord

[24] Located in Champaign-Urbana, almost 150 miles south of Chicago.

[25] In their classic "Chicago Lawyers" study, Heinz and Laumann classified Chicago, Columbia, Harvard, Michigan, Stanford, and Yale as elite law schools (1982, 445). In their 1995 replication of that study, about 14 percent of the Chicago lawyers in private practice attended elite law schools; this was true of 21 percent of those practicing in firms with more than fifty lawyers (Schnorr et al. 1995).

and often dictates which cases the firm can and cannot take.[26] Three-quarters of the female respondents are in firms of one or two attorneys. One of the women, a solo practitioner, has a general practice that serves a relatively impoverished clientele. The others are more specialized, often concentrating in areas consistent with ideological preferences or prior careers—family law, discrimination, disability, labor, criminal law, or pro bono work. These female respondents come from Chicago as well as downstate Illinois.

Respondents range in age from the late twenties to the late seventies, though only 6 percent are under age forty and 9 percent over age sixty-five. The average age (both means and medians) is roughly fifty.[27] Respondent age varies neither by firm size nor location. Age seems to make a significant difference in how respondents think about conflict of interest and the extent to which it affects their legal practice. As I will develop in later chapters, older lawyers generally find conflicts most problematic and disruptive. Many factors account for this perception. First, the rules of professional responsibility have changed several times in the careers of the older lawyers, redefining and reconfiguring conflicts of interest and lawyers' obligations regarding them. Many younger lawyers have grown up with these new rules, practices, and procedures, never having known professional life to be otherwise. Second, as they have aged and taken on greater responsibility for law firm governance, older attorneys have become more aware of the organizational difficulties and costs imposed by conflict of interest. Third, the exponential growth of law firms in the lifetimes of older lawyers and profound changes in the relationships between law firms and clients have increased the incidence of conflicts of interest. Fourth, conflicts of interest have played a greater role in the increasing adversariness of legal practice.

But, most interesting, older practitioners, especially transactional lawyers, actually have more profound conflicts to contend with than do their younger colleagues. In their years of practice, these lawyers have amassed enduring multiplex relationships with multiple generations of families and family businesses, corporations and their managers, and small companies that have evolved into massive conglomerates. These lawyers have stockpiled not only complicated loyalties but also proprietary information, secrets, and confidences that they are obliged to protect and honor. Because loyalties, confidences, and obligations desist slowly, older lawyers are tangled and often strangled in a dense web through which they must negotiate every new potential commitment. Conflicts often serve as a symbolic touchstone in older lawyers' remorse about the evolution of legal practice from a hallowed profession to a mere business.

[26]Though women are underrepresented in the legal profession overall, the 6 percent in my study is still low. Curran and Carson's 1991 representative data for the United States finds that women comprise about a fifth of all lawyers in private practice and about a tenth of law firm partners (1994, 10). A study of a representative sample of Chicago lawyers in 1995 also reports that roughly a fifth are female (Schnorr et al. 1995).

[27]My sample is somewhat older than general estimates for lawyers in private practice. Most likely this difference reflects the greater seniority attached to the role that landed these respondents in my study. The mean age of lawyers in private practice in the 1995 Chicago Lawyers Study, based on a representative sample, is forty-one (Schnorr et al. 1995). Figures for the entire United States in 1991 indicate a median age of forty-three for solo practitioners, forty-two for law firm partners, and thirty-one for law firm associates (Curran and Carson 1994, 11).

THREE
Adversity

Once upon a time there was a young orphan, Lawrence Lexman. Lawrence had been born into a wealthy family and spent a good part of his early life in tortured soul-searching, struggling to find a worthy vocation in which to channel his energy, skill, ambition, and values. He eventually settled on law and dug into his ample trust fund to pay for his legal education, spending his summers jet-setting around the globe. Three years later, he passed the bar and, having never worked a day in his life, began the process of setting up a legal practice. He scouted out a beautiful office, hung up his shingle, and settled in. A few days later, his first potential client stumbled into the office. The young man was distraught, clutching a dog-eared copy of a subpoena that he had just received from the IRS. Lawrence immediately identified with this young man who, like Lawrence, was all alone in the world, single, and self-employed. Lawrence examined the subpoena and realized that the IRS had opened a criminal investigation of tax fraud against this young man whose entrepreneurial dreams had apparently gone bust. Lawrence salivated at the prospect of taking on the IRS in his very first case, the government agency more responsible than any other for threatening his own quality of life. He explained to the potential client that he was a bit of a tax buff, would be delighted to take the case, and would do so pro bono, as he did not need the money and looked forward to the prospect of saving a compatriot from the greedy clutches of the IRS.

He noted that his practice was still young and that he would have plenty of time to devote to the case, indeed that he intended to set all other work aside until the young man's tribulations were resolved. As he signed the engagement letter, tears welled up in the young man's eyes at Lawrence's generosity and the passion he brought to the case.

Lawrence Lexman is the poster boy of disinterestedness. Indeed, his life story provides a caricature of what it takes to stay clear of the rules regarding conflict of interest. He has had only one client in his life and no other legal positions in which he might have obtained confidential information about or amassed obligations toward others. His client is an individual, a single man filing an individual tax return, conducting business alone. Any problems he has with the IRS involve him alone. He has approached Lawrence on a one-shot matter, with no prospect of an ongoing relationship in the future. The client is adverse to a government agency that never has been and never will be a client of Lawrence Lexman; at most, it will always be on the opposing side. Because of his financial independence, Lawrence is willing to handle the case pro bono and, therefore, has no interest in amassing legal fees that is at odds with his client's interest in minimizing them. Because Lawrence has no other cases, the client need not worry that the pro bono matter might play second fiddle to other engagements. Because of Lawrence's suspicions of and animus toward the IRS, his passion for the case and ideological interests are perfectly allied with those of his client.[1] Because Lawrence works alone and has no family, the confidences, fiduciary obligations, or financial interests of potential partners, colleagues, or intimates have no impact on his freedom to undertake legal responsibilities.

In short, neither the interests of Lawrence Lexman nor those of any past, present, or future client are at odds with those of his new client. To paraphrase from the *Model Rules of Professional Conduct* (American Bar Association 1983), which specify lawyers' ethical responsibilities, the representation of this new client will neither directly and adversely affect Lawrence's relationship with another client nor be materially limited by Lawrence's responsibilities to another client, to a third person, or by his own interests. Lawrence is free and clear.

Obviously the rules surrounding conflict of interest are not quite so narrow nor so unbending. If they were, no one would be practicing law at all or at least for very long. But the tale of Lawrence Lexman incorporates many assumptions that lie at the core of the rules about conflict of interest. Once Lawrence's clientele includes other individuals and organizations likely to be affected by the tax fraud investigation and once Lawrence develops a richer life with a family, prior jobs, other clients, partners and other colleagues, a more diversified practice, ongoing relationships with clients, engagements that are not as adversarial as the tax case, financial interdependence between his firm and its clients, the need for a future income stream, and so forth, maneuvering free and clear of the conflicts rules becomes both more dizzying and more difficult. In the next few chapters, I gradually depart from the simplifying assumptions that shroud Lawrence's life to understand how

---

[1]Though Lawrence must be wary that his ire does not, at some point, get in the way of reaching a settlement with the IRS that would best serve his client.

the social organization of legal life and practice gives rise to conflicts of interest, indeed makes them ubiquitous features of the legal landscape.

THE RULES

Rules designed to regulate lawyers' conflicts of interest are found in the major codes of professional conduct, documents drafted by lawyers and adopted by state supreme courts.[2] These normative texts predicate lawyers' duty to avoid conflicts on the basic obligations of lawyers to their clients, which require competence and diligence, communication, and especially loyalty and confidentiality (American Bar Association 1969; American Bar Association 1983; Wolfram 1986; Hazard and Hodes 1990, 1; American Law Institute 1990–92). The fundamental tenet regarding conflict of interest is stated in Rule 1.7 of the *Model Rules of Professional Conduct* (American Bar Association 1983):

> (a) A lawyer shall not represent a client if the representation of that client will be directly adverse to another client, unless:
> (1) The lawyer reasonably believes the representation will not adversely affect the relationship with the other client; and
> (2) Each client consents after consultation.
>
> (b) A lawyer shall not represent a client if the representation of that client may be materially limited by the lawyer's responsibilities to another client or to a third person, or by the lawyer's own interests, unless:
> (1) The lawyer reasonably believes the representation will not be adversely affected; and
> (2) The client consents after consultation. When representation of multiple clients in a single matter is undertaken, the consultation shall include ex-

[2]Either the *Model Rules of Professional Conduct* (American Bar Association 1983, Rules 1.7–1.13), adopted in most states, or the earlier *Model Code of Professional Responsibility* (American Bar Association 1969, Canon 5). Differences across states in conflict-of-interest rules also result from different caseloads and court opinions in various jurisdictions as well as ethics rules and opinions issued by state bar associations. The House of Delegates of the American Bar Association is in the process of debating its Ethics 2000 report (American Bar Association 2001), which offers amendments to some of the 1983 *Model Rules of Professional Conduct.* This process is still ongoing, and initial votes are subject to further amendment and even possibly reversal over the course of a year or more. And, of course, there is no guarantee that the revised rules enacted by the ABA House of Delegates will be adopted by the state courts. Although Ethics 2000 will eventually result in changes to the conflict-of-interest rules, they will largely clarify the rules, provide better guidance to their application, or formalize current practices governed by court opinions, ethics committees, or state ethics rules. Indeed, much of the commentary in the Ethics 2000 report about proposed revisions indicates that no change in substance is intended. In the text, I refer to the rules in effect during the period of the empirical research, before the Ethics 2000 project began. Where significant substantive changes in a particular rule or procedure seem likely (based on my observation of the debate), I will note them. Copies of the Ethics 2000 report and commentary, proposed amendments, and updated summaries of the actions of the ABA House of Delegates can be found at http://www.abanet.org/cpr/ethics2k.html.

planation of the implications of the common representation and the advantages and risks involved.[3]

At the core of these conflict-of-interest and other ethical rules, of course, is the question: Who is a client, that is, to whom are these duties owed? Lexman has a simple answer: the young man who stumbled into his office, clutching the IRS subpoena. Few lawyers can answer so easily. Lawrence is one of an ephemeral cohort of attorneys who, for a fleeting moment, stand at the threshold of their careers, having never before served a single client nor closed a single case. Their client is the first person who crosses the threshold.

The who-is-a-client question is more complex than it seems because it has a curious temporal component that means that lawyers cannot simply identify their clients by reviewing billing statements or a cabinet of open files. Because of confidentiality rules, lawyers have fiduciary obligations, not only to parties they are currently representing. They also have duties to former clients and even to *potential* clients—parties who consulted them about a possible representation (often along with a number of other law firms in so-called beauty contests), divulged a few secrets, and decided to go with another firm instead, as well as parties whose potential representation the attorney declined. These duties to current, former, and potential clients have no statutes of limitations, no formula whereby responsibilities desist. They can continue long after the lawyer-client relationship has ended. As long as lawyers possess relevant confidential information regarding a client, they are precluded from using it for the benefit of another. So the list of clients whose interests must be weighed in a conflict-of-interest analysis may include many remote, unlikely, or forgotten candidates.

A second complication to the who-is-a-client question comes from the fact that responsibilities to clients are biographical as well as positional; lawyers carry obligations from job to job. Just as duties of loyalty and confidentiality do not cease when a lawyer terminates a relationship with a client, they do not cease when a lawyer leaves the firm that continues to represent that client. As lawyers navigate through the job market, passing in and out of revolving doors and from firm to firm, they accumulate weightier and weightier baggage.

Making matters worse, these obligations extend not only to a lawyer's own clients or even to law firm clients with whom the lawyer has had only the most remote contact. Ethical norms treat obligations as collective. The duties of any one lawyer in a law firm—no matter how large the firm or how far-flung its offices—are imputed to all lawyers in the firm, regardless of whether they have had any contact with the particular client or were privy to any of its confidences. The law assumes that confidences will be shared among colleagues and, therefore, distributes ethical obligations toward clients to all attorneys in the firm.[4]

[3]The proposed Ethics 2000 amendments to the *Model Rules of Professional Conduct* substantially reword the original Model Rule 1.7 and commentary, require that informed consent be in writing, and explicitly state that some conflicts are nonconsentable (American Bar Association 2001).

[4]See chapter 7 for further elaboration of the impact of this "imputed disqualification rule" on conflicts of interest.

In short, the analysis of whether the representation of a new client will be adverse to that of another is complex. In amassing a roster of clients whose interests must be inventoried and given priority over those of the potential new client, lawyers must scour their histories, biographies, and collegial networks as well as their computers, appointment books, and file cabinets. They must consider current, former, and potential clients, those of all members of their firm, and those of all their former employers or former employers of their colleagues. These complexities will be addressed in greater detail in the next four chapters. In this chapter, I consider the central issue in conflict of interest—that of adversity—noting, for the time being, simply that analysis of adversity is so problematic largely because the salient interests subject to analysis can be so numerous and so remote.

ADVERSITY

> When I was young . . . if a law firm—or in those days, really, a lawyer—had two important clients that got into a dispute, the most natural thing for them to do would be both of them would go in, see their lawyer and hash it out with them. . . . And they'd reach an agreement. Maybe it would be worked out in writing, maybe it was a handshake. We can sit back and say, "How unethical that guy was! Here he is collecting a fee from two people who had adverse interests. It's cutting across lines of loyalty and duty and everything else." But that's not how it was viewed in the '40s and '50s and maybe even into the early '60s. It was: they went to their lawyer; their lawyer is a professional; he's an ethical man; he understands his obligations to both sides, and he can be trusted in that situation. And I think the change that you see is today, what we are saying is, "No, nobody can be trusted in that situation! . . . People have a right to independent counsel. People have a right to have a lawyer that's just thinking about their best interests. You know, the adversary system, hooray, hooray!" [11Ch100+]

Litigation

Though adversity is the cornerstone of conflict of interest, the ethical rules never operationally define adversity nor specify its dimensions.[5] Instead, the rules leave to lawyer interpretation whether a representation will adversely affect another. Respondents and legal commentators alike do share a narrow but clean ideal type of direct adversity: an attorney representing both sides in a litigated matter. Few would disagree that it is forbidden; indeed, the rare exceptions that prove the rule arouse gossip, amusement, and embarrassment.

> L1: I'll tell you the best conflict I ever had. There was a case filed in—I believe it was before the Peoria federal court—for a TRO [temporary restraining order]. And it was all happening like in hours. . . . So that a client that was

[5]However, the commentary to the proposed Ethics 2000 amendments to the *Model Rules of Professional Conduct* reflects a bit more on the nature of adversity than did the original *Model Rules* (American Bar Association 2001).

> the plaintiff goes to its law firm, gets them to prepare this . . . petition for TRO. . . . And they call up the opponent and tell 'em they're going to be in federal court at two o'clock on the TRO. So [. . .] the defendant calls up its law firm and its law firm goes charging down to the Peoria District Court to defend against this TRO. And it is us. We're on both sides. . . . There was no time. Everything was happening within a matter of hours and the petitioner for the TRO was us and when [. . .] the opponent contacted its lawyer, its lawyer was us. . . . They both go charging into the courtroom and it's we!
>
> L2: We won. [laughter]
>
> L1: . . . we had to get out of it. [6Ch100+]

Though attorneys agree that they cannot represent *both* adversaries in litigation, what role can they play when two clients have a dispute? Can they represent one of the parties in litigation if the other is represented by a different firm? Does it make a difference if they act for the plaintiff or defendant? Does it make a difference if the law firm played no role in the underlying dispute—say, over a contract or bank loan or real estate transaction that was undertaken by the parties themselves or with the assistance of another law firm? Does it matter if the underlying dispute is minor or repetitive? Does it matter if the dispute has not yet reached the point of litigation? Can the law firm advise one client about whether a lawsuit against another client is appropriate and then assist the first client in securing outside counsel? Or can it mediate between the two disputants? In short, what are the circumstances, if any, under which the firm can counsel both clients or even one of them?

As respondents reflect on the conflicts of interest that arise in their practice, they speak with greatest clarity and assurance about instances in which clients or potential clients are engaged in head-to-head conflict. Though their responses varied, their ease of response did not. Many of the respondents indicate that disputes among clients or potential clients constitute the most mundane, day-to-day kind of conflict of interest faced by their firm.

> Sure, probably the most classic one is suing a client. That comes up all the time. And especially as the firm grows, we find that [. . .] I'll bet that probably once a week, we're invited to get into a situation where we'd be adverse to a current client. [7Ch100+]

I asked respondents how they would evaluate the opportunity to represent an ongoing client in litigation against another ongoing client (with independent legal counsel) over a matter in which their law firm played no role or had any confidential information. Few embraced this opportunity—however unhappy most are to turn away any business—though the reasons for and degree of their ambivalence varied considerably. A few responded sternly, referring immediately to legal doctrine:

> L: [describing a conversation between two colleagues] Well, [one] would say, . . . "that's an active client of the firm. You're asking me if you can sue them. The answer is no, you can't sue an active client."
>
> S: And is that a firm policy?

L: The Canons mandate it.
S: Even if it's on an unrelated [. . .]
L: Can't sue an active client on an unrelated matter. [17Ch100+]

Many respondents made no reference to the ethical rules in rejecting the opportunity; their paramount concern was the possibility that it might impair or rupture ongoing relationships with clients. Indeed, several explicitly dismissed the significance of the rules in their reluctance to take a position adverse to a client.

> I am not sure that whether or not the conflict rule is there . . . really would have much impact on how I conducted myself. Because, especially today, where it's so hard to get the business and keep the business, I want my clients to think I'm loyal to them. [18Ch100+]

Respondents elaborated on the business risk in representing one of the clients, some with abstract reasoning:

> If two clients are fighting, we try to stay out. . . . We're just going to lose. . . . if we represent somebody who's really adverse to another client, we're guaranteed to lose that other client. I mean, it's like no question! Because if you do as good a job as you can possibly do for the client you're staying with, you're just going to tick the other side off. So, that's a no-brainer; no-win situation. [10Ch100+]

Others regretfully cited real-world examples:

> We would generally step out of both sides. I can think of an instance once, where one of our clients said, "Go ahead. We'd just as soon have you as someone else." The client made a very generous gesture and then ended up really ticked off. As the litigation proceeded, some very bad facts surfaced that led to a very nasty result. Our generous client didn't like it one bit. Would I do it again? I still might have gone ahead. I'm enough of a realist. But things can go sour on you. [14Ch100+]

Other respondents reflected on circumstances under which they would (or did) entertain suing a client, if able to secure the client's consent. Some looked at the significance of the litigation and its potential impact on the client in making this judgment.

> You just don't sue your own clients, unless, as I said, very peripherally related. If someone is really there, but they're indemnified by someone else and they don't really care about it. Or they're a minor party in all of this and have very little at stake. But, if they're really a major party, you would not sue. [28Ch50–99]

Most referred to their ethical duties, reasoning about their ability to ensure loyalty and especially confidentiality in these circumstances. They offered examples of very narrow representations unrelated to the present litigation, often involving different groups of lawyers in their firm.

> Well, I think big firms are able to do that. I mean, I think the duty of loyalty is not impaired . . . because we are using different—invariably—using different lawyers. In terms of the standard of whether we're able to do it—whether we can fulfill our responsibilities—I think the answer is we can. So, typically, we would certainly ask for a waiver. I think the only instances we wouldn't would be if we knew we wouldn't get it and it would annoy the client for us to do it. Or it would hurt the ability to get future work. But I think we're perfectly capable of not breaching our duty of loyalty. So, lawyers A—you know, A group—will do the litigation and B group, somewhere else, is doing the corporate work. [26Ch100+]

Some expressed surprise that their clients did not respond to these opportunities quite the same way that they had:

> I faced one that I found to be very surprising. Did some work for a bank in a smaller town in Illinois—for their trust department. We had a client in the firm that wanted to sue that bank with regard to mishandling of a commercial loan. It had nothing to do with their trust department. This bank is represented by every lawyer in town—not in Chicago—but in their town. So that, from the point of view of finding someone to defend them, they had no legitimate gripe. From the point of view of my knowing anything that would have any bearing upon this suit, they had no legitimate gripe. We thought it would be nice to ask them anyway. And they said no, that they absolutely did not want us representing anybody who was suing them. Probably as a conflicts matter—as an ethical matter—we probably still could have maintained the suit. We chose not to. But, that was a very surprising reaction. [51Ch20–49]

Adversariness is a bit of a catch-22, unfortunately. Clearly the representation of one client in a dispute with another client holds great potential for adversely affecting the latter (and, when attorneys pull their punches, sometimes the former as well). Fearing "ethics slaps" or the business consequences of antagonizing loyal clients, it is only with the greatest sensitivity and forethought that lawyers broach this possibility with their clients. But refusing clients' overtures for representation often comes at considerable cost as well. Ongoing clients may feel abandoned by their trusted counsel in their hour of need. From the clients' perspective, the refusal means having to pay an unfamiliar new law firm more money to get up to speed on their particularistic needs, resulting in likely delay in the legal proceedings and all the additional costs and risks associated with securing trust, loyalty, and expertise from newly engaged fiduciaries.[6] Indeed, both sets of clients may feel this way and even wish that their attorneys at least represent their adversary, if not themselves, in the interest of resolving the dispute, they hope, more expeditiously and amicably. (Cynics, of course, might point instead to the cost—not to the clients but to the law

---

[6]Of course, large corporations may have ongoing relationships with a slew of relatively interchangeable law firms to which they can easily turn when conflicted out by one. Though even here, not all these firms may have the specialized expertise or prior knowledge of the firm that faces the conflict.

firm of the lost business of both clients, coupled with the risk that the clients will find a comfortable home in the replacement firm and never return.)

In a perverse twist on the conflict-of-interest rules, from this perspective, *failing* to take on an engagement may be even more adverse to another client than taking it. As a result, a good number of respondents reflect on the impulse—and risks—to stay in the dispute as long as they can in the hope of resolving it short of litigation. For them, the adversity implicit in choosing sides or abandoning sides can be minimized by providing a safe haven for both sides to try to resolve their differences outside of court. Two extended examples, one from a small firm in a small town, the other from a large multioffice Chicago firm, illustrate the issues:

> Our client is a local investor service. And they sold a particular investment to another client of ours. . . . This transaction was done without us involved in it at all. They just get together and do it. As it turns out, investor becomes very unhappy with the investment he has purchased, and they are trying to work out the problem. . . . Both clients saying "however, we want you people. We trust you. You do all of our work. We want you to be involved." "But, you understand, we can't be involved in an adversary [. . .] " "Well, what can you do?" So, we ended up sitting in our conference room with both of the attorneys and both of the clients and trying to, I guess, mediate it, you might say. "Well, this is what's going to happen if litigation occurs. This is what the costs of litigation are going to be." I mean, these are two very sophisticated people. . . . I don't know if I'd try that with less [. . .] . . . After that, the clients then went off and talked with one another, and worked out a compromise . . . But so far, they both seem very happy. . . . And we sort of acted as, I guess, lawyers for the situation, facilitators. It seems to have worked. I guess that's an example of where you can be involved in a potentially adversary [. . .] I, I guess you can, I suppose that's ethical. It seems to me it was. It was with full disclosures, sophisticated clients, etc., etc. . . . So, I guess we have to use some common sense [. . .] [97DSS<10]

> . . . there was a client for whom we did work in Washington office (and we did this discrete kind of work for the client) was being sued by a client here in Chicago where we were not involved. We were not representing the client here. It was being done in-house. And the client in Chicago decided to bring us into the litigation. Now, that was a direct conflict. So [. . .] called the client and said—the client in the branch office—and said, "Look, obviously we're not going to get involved in this matter. But if you would like, . . . we'd be happy to try to use our good office and see if we can mediate this dispute or bring it together. . . . If you think it would be of any help. But obviously we wouldn't get involved in a litigation." And the clients out east [. . .] came back to us a couple of days later and said, "Look, we'd really appreciate [. . .] We'll be happy to waive the conflict. We think that it would be helpful to the whole process if they did have representation from an outside firm that we knew and were comfortable with. Not comfortable in the sense that we'd get a better deal but that at least people we knew [. . .] And we would be happy to waive the conflict." And then explained the whole situation to the client that wanted to come in here and they said "We think that would be a

> good idea." So, we got all these waivers, got involved in the lawsuit, and sure enough, the lawsuit immediately turned fairly nasty. Fortunately it was able to be resolved and it wound up being settled in the way that it should have been settled and everybody was happy, but [. . .] You know, I thought there was a great lesson from that. . . . And it seemed to work out well, but, having done this once, I'd be real skeptical about doing it the second time. [9Ch100+]

Transactions

> Lawyers are getting more sensitive to the fact that you don't have to be in court now to be adverse to a client in another context. [4Ch100+]

If disputes among clients, especially those that have escalated to the point of litigation, epitomize adversity to most respondents, what about the other occasions in which clients seek legal counsel? Does adversity begin and end somewhere on a continuum of contentious clients? What about the so-called transactional side of the practice, the win-win matters that some respondents distinguish from the win-lose intrinsic in litigation? As one attorney queries:

> Now, everybody's preaching win-win negotiations. So we can't hardly call ourselves adversaries if we're representing negotiating parties, because adversaries—that connotates a win-lose, doesn't it? [97DSS<10]

Respondents evince less consensus about whether clients undertaking deals, sales, contracts, mergers, loans, and the like face adversities of interest and whether their firm can represent both or even one of these clients in finalizing these transactions. Indeed, even members of the same firm disagree. I elicited the following dialogue between the senior partner (L1) and a new associate (L2) in a two-person law firm in the smallest town in the study. Both seemed a bit surprised by the practices of the other:

> L1: Well, we've got one now with—it was a sale of a restaurant. And done a lot of work for the fellow that owned the restaurant and was selling it. And I don't know where he got the buyer from, but he came in with the buyer and they wanted a contract. And I said, "Okay, we'll do a contract." And I had never seen this other guy before. And the long and the short of it is the deal fell through. The seller [. . .] doesn't want to give back any of the earnest money. And now the buyer has gone to a different attorney and filed a lawsuit against the seller to get his money back. I'm not sure how we could have avoided that. Looking back at it, I guess I wish [. . .] the other guy had an attorney from the beginning. Maybe it would have been better. But he was on a shoestring and everything was going fine until the bank wouldn't loan the money. So you kind of learn by experience I guess.
>
> L2: All of mine have involved two attorneys just from the very beginning.
>
> S: . . . [to L2] Now, when you say there are always two attorneys, is that because you've insisted on it?

L2: Yes. Right off the bat. The most recent thing that I did for my brother-in-law ... was a sale of assets of a business. And the gentleman that he's buying it from is getting ready to retire ... and he says, "well, [brother-in-law], I trust you, I trust you, I trust you. We don't need to get another attorney. We'll just let [L2] do all this for us." And at the end of my first conversation with [brother-in-law] as to what we were going to do, I said, "he's got to get another attorney. He needs to understand that he's got a lot to lose here. And I don't care if he trusts you and if he trusts me or whatever. He still has a lot to lose." And so he did get an attorney. And we had attorney[s] all the way through.

S: Now, if they came to you and said, "we've already worked out the deal. All we want you to do is write it up [. . .]"

L2: No. [128DSS<10]

Differences among colleagues on the adversities inherent in transactions are not unique to small towns or small firms. The dismayed observations of a litigator and chair of his firm's professional standards committee about some of his transactional colleagues were echoed by other large-firm litigators in the study:

> Because sometimes people [other lawyers in the firm] again, will come in and say "Well, this isn't really a conflict is it?" That's my most common question in my committee work here is, "This isn't really a conflict? We're representing the buyer and the seller, but it really isn't a conflict because they both want to do the deal." You know, people will say that. [whispering] Yes, it's really a conflict! [36Ch100+]

This view of conflicts, attributed mostly to transactional lawyers, resonates with practices of generations past. Echoing the reflections of the respondent first quoted in this chapter, who reminisced about his youth, many of the older respondents in the study recall that in their early years of practice, attorneys often, if not routinely, would represent both sides in a transaction or negotiation.

> When I first started practicing, it was very common for one partner to represent A and the other partner to represent B. I mean, there was a consent. They'd be sitting there arguing with themselves. Well, I mean, come on now! Today we aren't doing that. [53DSL20–49]

Some still do.

So how is it that some attorneys today consider win-win negotiations adversarial? The dismayed litigator quoted earlier might explain that although both parties are eager to "do the deal," they may still have different preferences about its terms—the price or interest rate, the valuation of assets or property for tax purposes, the penalty for noncompliance, and so forth.

> ... a cleaner example of that is where we have two parties who come in and just want to use one lawyer for a property transaction. And I think that's almost impossible to do without conflicts. Although people ask you to do it all the time....

> But it's to the seller's benefit to pro-rate taxes at the current levels. Or the buyer's benefit to pro-rate taxes at an estimated 110 percent level off previous taxes. Inspection clauses, who's going to pay for repairs if they're required? All that kind of thing where there's just absolutely no way you can—aggressively, anyway—represent both sides. You always have to kind of compromise in the middle. And I think that's a real, real conflict. [116Ch<10]

In some instances, then, there is actually more at stake and more variation in the potential outcome of a deal than in a routine piece of litigation that is settled before trial. To consider the interests of the parties in the latter adverse and not in the former is mere artifice.

In short, these parties have conflicting interests. Though few negotiations have quite the winner-take-all quality of litigation that goes to trial, the magnitude of the gains for one side in so-called win-win negotiations may vary considerably from negotiator to negotiator. Lawyer A may negotiate a better deal for the buyer than Lawyer B could. The conflict-of-interest question is whether Lawyer C—who also happens to represent the seller—can negotiate as good a deal for the buyer as even lawyer B could. What makes the question interesting is that some—lawyers and clients alike—assert that Lawyer C can actually negotiate a better deal for the buyer than even Lawyer A could. They argue that features of the lawyer-client relationship—expertise, familiarity with the needs of both clients, trust, reasonableness, good will, ease in moving back and forth between the parties, and so on—and the speed and lower cost in using fewer lawyers allow for better results for *both* clients by relying on Lawyer C, who is mired in conflicts. But how do we reconcile a potentially better result with the fact that it comes at the price of adversity? Or that the better result for one party, because of its relationship to the lawyer doing the deal, is quite a bit better than the better result for the other?

I asked respondents to reflect on how their firm reacted when two current clients ask them to represent them both in a transaction. Downstate lawyers, especially those in small towns, spoke mostly about real estate transactions; Chicago lawyers and those from larger downstate communities rarely did, reflecting instead on purchases of businesses, leasing and lending transactions, mergers, negotiating insurance contracts, and the like.

More respondents referred to the ethical rules in reflecting on my question about client transactions than they did when I asked about litigation, though they sometimes came to different conclusions about the rules.

> But we've had instances where people have wanted us to represent both sides of the transaction. Even where it's a relatively friendly transaction . . . we will simply not be on both sides of the transaction. It doesn't matter whether everyone's consented. As far as we can tell, that's just prohibited by the rules no matter what. [28Ch50–99]

> I think we shouldn't do it. And there's some Illinois ethics opinions (that I'm sure you know) that are old that say you have to. There's some stuff in the new code of professional responsibility that says you can do it. So we do it. [2Ch100+]

And many others explicitly commented on their ethical duties of loyalty and confidentiality to their clients as they framed their response:

> . . . what we do there is we ask the lawyers to tell us whether or not they think they can satisfy their duty of loyalty. We want to know something about the clients because, at least in my view, you can't even think about doing that unless you're sure you're not compromising your duty of loyalty to each one [. . .] It doesn't matter whether they're willing to do it. It's your independent obligation. [7Ch100+]

> Clearly you can't represent both. With the representation of one, we would make a determination: Are we privy to any confidential information that would preclude the representation of one? If we are, then it's "no." [58Ch50–99]

Clearly, the rules don't offer too much guidance.

> L1: It's handling a porcupine.
>
> L2: There are no formulas on how to deal with that situation. I mean, the only possible formula would be to say no in all cases. Being frail humans, we don't necessarily do that. We try and figure out whether it'll work or whether it is handling a porcupine. . . . frequently it's not just the bilateral deal. It's more a buyer and a seller, a lender and a borrower. It's a multisided deal. So, it is more difficult to assess where the differences of interest are. . . . You don't foresee that at the outset of the negotiation where the differences will be. [5Ch100+]

Though few of the attorneys embrace the opportunity of representing two ongoing clients in a transactional matter, some grudgingly will, under the right circumstances, usually after trying to talk the clients out of it. For the kinds of transactions envisioned by the Chicago lawyers, the right circumstances include two sophisticated institutional clients, preferably with in-house legal departments and with relatively equal bargaining positions. The transaction involves a routine matter and not a lot of money. The parties have their own procedure for negotiating the terms of the agreement and struck the deal before the lawyers ever got involved. The transaction does not require due diligence to be performed by the law firm. Preferably, the two parties have known each other for a long time and know more about the business issues involved than the lawyer ever could (e.g., a long-time partner with a 50 percent interest in a partnership buys out the other 50 percent partner). The lawyers are to participate in documenting and drafting the agreement only—to act as "scriveners" of the deal. They are not to advise on the business terms of the transaction. Both parties are fully informed of the risks to dual representation and advised to consult with independent counsel about whether they really want the law firm to represent both of them. Finally, the parties are informed, usually in an elaborate letter that they are asked to sign that, should a dispute arise between them, the law firm will withdraw from representing either one of them.

> We had two trade associations which we represented for many, many years—both . . . representing different aspects of the same profession. They chose to merge.

> First, from the standpoint of economy, they perceived it made sense to see if we . . . could handle the whole thing. Our concern was to identify up front to what extent there would be issues as to conflict between them and to have identified within the separate associations the mechanism for resolving them, so that we would basically not become advocates for either side, but rather, scrivener of the issues as they would be resolved. Because of the dynamics of this particular merger there were no real conflicts requiring separate legal representation. And there was built in a separate procedure, where each side had their own committee that could address issues that required negotiation, if you will. And I think, in some instance, individuals may have sought outside counsel. So our—as I say—our role was really one of putting together the deal, upon agreement, rather than participating in the negotiations of agreement. And that was all defined before we went into it. [49DSL20–49]

> It's happened once in the last ten years—that I'm aware of—with a very closely held company, family-owned business. The owners were getting up in years. Two of them wanted out, two of them wanted to buy—I guess it was their brothers or their father and one of their brothers—out of the business. And they came to us and said, "Look, we don't want to pay two law firms and inflate it. Can you represent all of us?" I said, "If all of you agree that we do so, we can—provided you work out your deal amongst yourselves. And we'll just play scrivener." That I don't have difficulty with, but for the fact that we had represented them all for many, many years. It was not a deal that involved a lot of money. And it was a deal where they had come to us and said, "We've already worked it out. Just write it up." I didn't see that as being a real big issue. [79Ch20–49]

Though the parties and circumstances are quite different in small-town real estate transactions, the rationale for representing the buyer and seller and bank—which attorneys from many of the smallest towns in the sample generally do—is basically the same as it is in corporate transactions in Chicago. Lawyers find a comfort level by refusing to be negotiators. They observe that real estate brokers negotiate the price and terms of the sale. And banks set interest rates on mortgages; buyers can take them or leave them—there is little negotiation there. So the deal is struck before the lawyer is ever called in to document the negotiations and complete the paperwork—sometimes on behalf of all *three* parties to the transaction: the seller, the buyer, and the bank.

> We are by far the largest firm in this small community. As a result of which, even on a routine residential real estate transaction, we will often find ourselves representing—or being asked to represent—both the buyer and the seller. . . . We represent lending institutions as well. And so, again, in a real estate context, if you represent—on an ongoing basis—[names local bank], and they're the lender, can you represent the borrower? . . . On the residential real estate, we do disclosure and the waiver. And that's not usually a problem. . . . I can't ever remember getting into a dispute with a lender. That's always, pretty much, cut and dried. The borrower has signed the documents that the lender wants him to sign, or they won't

> make the loan. . . . If I'm representing the borrower, I tell them quite frankly, "Here's the deal. These are the bank's documents. This is not negotiable. You either sign them or you go somewhere else and get a loan." So, you don't get into a dispute with the bank. At least, I never have. [87DSS10–19]

Lawyers who agree to participate in these dual representations similarly try to stand on the sidelines while the negotiations proceed. They explain that they participate only as innocuous "scriveners of the deal"—perhaps the most common piece of archaic jargon recorded repeatedly in the interview transcripts and clearly a linguistic resource that empowered some to take on this role. Of course, if attorneys truly serve as mere scriveners, most of the benefits that accrue from using one set of negotiators (aside from cost and speed)—expertise, familiarity, trust, and so on—are lost to both parties.

So some attorneys are able to represent two or more parties to a transaction by resolving or dispensing with the adversarial elements prior to their participation—or at least believing that they have done so. Still, a somewhat greater number of respondents indicate that they will not represent two clients on a transactional matter than say they will. Citing numerous examples, they argue, first, that there is no such thing as a fair or friendly deal, a truly neutral legal agreement, or a mechanism for balancing loyalty.

> . . . how can you sit down and write a lease that's fair? There's no such thing as a fair lease. No one ever wrote one. No one knows how. [2Ch100+]

> I had represented a professional practice, on the one hand—did all their work. On the other hand, I represented another business practice. The professional practice was about to combine with the business practice. They were going to rent space from them; they were going to use their facilities; they were going to use their personnel. I didn't think that I could do a fair job of representing both of them because there was too much—as I viewed it—there was too much potential for conflict. "How much should they charge? Should it be higher, should it be lower? How much worth of clerical help will they get? How much time would they get? What kind of priorities would they have?" I don't think I could have resolved that between the two of them. And so I told the professional practice to seek independent counsel. [77Ch10–19]

Second, with ongoing clients, law firms often have confidential information about the parties that could be used to the advantage or disadvantage of another.

> Well, the thing I worry about, obviously, is the confidential information situation, where one client, let's say, . . . knows something about the deal and doesn't convey it to the other one, but conveys it to us. I mean, that's the one thing I worry about—that there be secrets later on that turn out. Although, in every case, I've been assured that "no, there aren't any secrets." I mean, that's the one I worry about besides the fact—the obvious one—that if they ever get into a dispute, that we're out of it. You know, we're not going to take on either side. [26Ch100+]

These respondents also identify the third and most common reason to stay out of transactions. Deals go sour all the time; something inevitably goes wrong or becomes adversarial, and the law firm is blamed for favoring one client over another.

> L2: You're going to become the insurer of the deal.
>
> L1: Guarantor of the deal. . . . Let's do lender-borrower. If the borrower has a failed venture; if the lender doesn't get paid back; if anything goes wrong in that deal; then some expert witness will testify against the firm about exactly what it was that should have been disclosed but wasn't in getting this consent which, if the parties had known about it, would have caused them to get separate counsel. So that is out of the question. [6Ch100+]

Because of this third reason, a few firms will not even agree to represent *one* of the clients in the transaction. They fear that the client they *did* represent may suspect that their lawyers did not negotiate as vigorously as they might have if the other party did not have an ongoing relationship to the firm.

> Probably the most conservative approach is everything is adversarial, because it has the potential of becoming adversarial. [5Ch100+]

Just as some lawyers refuse to represent two clients in litigation, they refuse to advise either client when the clients seek to make a deal together. Many other lawyers consider the odds that a deal will go sour rather remote and agree to participate in the transaction with the caveat that they will withdraw entirely if a dispute develops. And still other attorneys who refuse to deal with either party in a litigated matter will represent one of them in a transaction with the other.

As a gross rule of thumb, though, many attorneys will represent one client more in a transaction than they will in a dispute. This generalization suggests that lawyers see some potential for adversity in transactions but less than in head-to-head disputes among clients. In articulating these decision rules, respondents seem more mindful of the risk that the deal will go sour than that clients will get the shorter end of the stick because of the lawyers' ties to other parties to the transaction. Respondents think about transactional adversity, then, as a kind of incipient form of direct adversity. As the downstate respondent (who earlier asked how win-win negotiations could be adversarial) explained:

> So, I guess, hopefully, look at our role as—more and more—as facilitators rather than adversaries. But then capable of seeing when the adversarial role now supersedes the facilitation role. And say, "Stop, this has become adversarial." [97DSS<10]

It is the transformative character of a deal as a protolawsuit that gives it adversarial potential, not the fact that transacting parties have different preferences and that some dealmakers are better at securing these preferences than others are.

THE ECOLOGY OF ADVERSARINESS

Features of the structure and ecology of practice predispose certain kinds of law firms to more frequent encounters with disputing or transacting groups of clients than others. It is no coincidence that it was a Chicago solo practitioner who was most unsure about whether it's okay to sue a client. With a fairly general practice and little specialization, largely one-shot relationships with clients, and a small caseload drawn from a population of millions, the odds of attracting both adversaries in a dispute are relatively small. It's just not something he had to face before. As the downstate lawyer quoted in the last chapter commented about the differences between his legal community and that of Chicago, "it would be as freaky as running into the same guy twice on the highway."

Firm Size

Because ethics rules impute obligations toward any one client to all lawyers in the firm, large law firms provide a major locus of client adversity. Respondents in the larger firms cite estimates of thousands of active clients and hundreds of matters open for many of these clients. And, of course, as I noted at the beginning of this chapter, because ethical obligations to a client do not end when the relationship ends, the increased probability of client adversities occasioned by opening new cases is not necessarily offset by those that are closed. So tens of thousands of former clients must also be added to the probability-of-adversity function. Moreover, many disputes are not dyadic—they may aggregate hundreds or even thousands of coplaintiffs or codefendants—and many deals are multisided rather than bilateral.

Of course, with a potential client population in Cook County of more than five million individuals and more than one hundred twenty thousand businesses (Slater and Hall 1995, 146, 152), the mathematical odds of head-to-head adversity contained within a given law firm with thousands or tens of thousands of clients don't seem all that daunting. But large law firms do not draw randomly from these populations. They tend to serve the larger companies with repetitive legal business and few of the individuals. Moreover, they tend to have ongoing relationships with these companies, such that their interests in a new matter must be considered even if the firm is not engaged in an active case on their behalf at that very moment.

For reasons of history, firm culture, and substantive specialization, large law firms vary in their caseload and ratio of clients per lawyer. Some derive a relatively high proportion of their income from a small number of clients; others have vast numbers of one-shot clients for whom they handle smaller matters. The latter firms with higher caseloads, of course, are more vulnerable to adversities among their clients.

But because of changes in the structure of the legal profession and the consumption of legal services, which I spelled out in the first chapter, virtually all large law firms face many more client adversities than they did in the past. First of all, firms are considerably larger, thereby amassing more lawyers, more clients, and still more potential adversities. Second, large-firm lawyers today are more mobile than those of generations past. No longer casting their lot with a single law firm from cradle to grave, they move laterally from firm to firm as new opportunities emerge or partnership prospects dissolve. As they travel, these mobile attorneys transport a growing collection of confidences of and duties toward former clients, some of whom must be added to the already swollen ranks of clients of their latest pit stop from which probabilities of adversity are computed.

Most important, clients are less likely today to invest exclusive loyalty in a single law firm, but instead they spread their business across the legal community, often at the conclusion of a series of beauty contests with competing law firms (each of which may learn enough about the potential matter to conflict out all the losers of the beauty contest from representing the other side) (Gilson 1990; Nelson 1994).[7] Law firms contribute to this trend as they go after the clients of their competitors more aggressively in recessionary times. Respondents explain that no one law firm is counsel to the major corporations on everything any more. They note that some corporations utilize as many as a thousand different law firms across the country and have picked off all the largest law firms in Chicago—sometimes intentionally to conflict them out from representing their adversaries. The implications of the disaggregation and proliferation of legal business are profound: large law firms will often find themselves on both sides of disputes or transactions embroiling major corporations. Indeed, it may be difficult to find a large firm that is not conflicted out in this way.

Large law firms are the most obvious site of client adversities simply because of the gross odds of a match when client pools are so large. Even small correlations are statistically significant in large samples. But the odds of adversity do not require large numbers. If the correlation is large enough, even small samples can yield statistically significant results. If clients are not allocated randomly across firms but instead gravitate to particular ones for particular problems, correlations will be high and conflicts abundant. Client adversities tend to cluster in law firms, regardless of their size, that enjoy geographic, substantive, or social network monopolies—where fighting neighbors, competitors, or colleagues and associates, respectively, seek assistance from the same law firm.

Geographic Monopoly

A classic instance of geographic monopoly is found in small towns that host only one or a small number of lawyers to service the legal needs of the entire community. With a small pool of attorneys to begin with, further limited by specialization (e.g., only one firm does corporate or criminal work) or stratification (one firm represents all the elite individuals and large businesses), clients on both sides of transactions or disputes often race to the same law office for representation. Two examples of quite different problems from distinctive downstate communities illustrate some of the issues. The first respondent, a solo practitioner and the only lawyer in a town of roughly three thousand, is also one of the only criminal defense lawyers in the region:

---

[7]Since the time of my interviews, it appears that corporations are beginning to reduce the number of outside law firms to which they send work (Committee on Lawyer Business Ethics 1998, 180–81; Neil 2000a).

> I was trying a murder case here. And, on the eve of trial, two of my clients that I had represented previously—. . . they'd been sentenced or were scheduled to be taken to the Department of Corrections—made statements against a third client of mine in the murder case. . . . I really found myself in quite a dilemma. . . . Now, in the scheme of things, I guess I had mixed loyalties there. Because, on the one hand, I'm still in active representation of a client who's charged with murder, and that's a real serious concern for me. But, on the other hand, these guys are making statements—and they're headed to the Department of Corrections—that, if they make 'em, the likelihood of them coming out of the Department of Corrections alive is not great. And, obviously, law enforcement's not telling them that. But I was almost in a catch-22 situation. I couldn't get to them to say, "Guys, it's probably not in your interest to say this." And then I almost have a conflict by saying that, because I'm really trying to help my other client. [126DSS<10]

The second respondent, a partner in the largest law firm in a community of less than twenty thousand, reflects on the inherent difficulties of representing the major and most contentious institutions in town:

> One of our regular clients is the local newspaper. Another one of our regular clients is the city of [names firm city], and another one is the local school board. The newspaper doesn't always say nice things about the city and the school board. . . . They want to sue the school board or the city over some Freedom of Information issue. I have a developing issue—on the newspaper—where a policeman interfered with a photographer at an accident scene—hit him. And I don't know quite how all that will, that one will wash out. There are opinions out that our representation of the city as utility counsel does not preclude our being adverse to them on nonutility and nonbonding matters. That sounds great, but it's the same mayor. . . . I met with the mayor on behalf of the paper last week. . . . I don't know how far I'll go with that. You know, is that a conflict question? I don't know. . . . My real concern is [. . .] I'm not genuinely dull. . . . I'm worried about pulling my punches a little bit, because I don't want to make the mayor mad. [70DSS10–19]

Substantive Monopoly

Law firms acquire substantive monopolies when they specialize in facilitating an esoteric transaction or asserting or defending against a particular kind of legal action or when the nature of their expertise attracts diverse entities from the same industry. Particular firms in the sample concentrated in the representation of brokerage firms, athletes, transportation providers, road contractors, municipalities, utility companies, supermarkets, and the like, many of them head-to-head competitors. Competitors are frequently attracted to the same law firm because of its track record and varied hands-on experience; its extensive knowledge of industry practices and the arcane bodies of operative law; the cost savings in not having to pay to get its lawyers up to speed on a common industry problem; the firm's political capital and ties to regulators, politicians, prosecutors, judges, expert witnesses, financiers, and industry insiders; the value of a united front on industrywide concerns;

the opportunity to free ride off the investments of other firm clients; and even the firm's confidential inside information on the practices and problems of competitors that are also represented by the firm.

Although many of the specialized services supplied to clients clustered in a given industry pertain to intraorganizational issues—taxation, labor, zoning, finance, property or contract matters, and so on—that have no bearing on industry competitors and, therefore, pose no adversities of interest for these clients, occasionally they spill over. Employees in a given industry may move from client company to client company—provoking disputes about trade secrets, intellectual property, or employment issues.

> Because we represent a lot of broker-dealers in the securities industry, and because . . . financial advisers or brokers are a pretty mobile group, we can find that one can leave one client and go to another client. And if there's an employment problem, that can create a potential conflict. Or, if there's a recruiting matter, where one firm recruits an account executive from another firm, and we have a dual representation. Or—because brokerage firms sometimes have different relationships in investment banking situations or underwriting situations, and disputes can arise—we can find that two of our clients are in opposite positions in a dispute, which could create a conflict for us. [108Ch10–19]

Negotiations with labor unions, suppliers, or truckers on behalf of one client company may have consequences for another client company whose employees are represented by the same union or who use the same suppliers or truckers.

> The same holds true for celebrities and athletes. Conflicts can arise in that field—although it has not arisen with me—where you represent more than one, for instance, player on an athletic team. And one player's contract is about to be up. Or a couple, multiple players' contracts, that you represent, are about to be up. And the club tries to use leverage with one player—in terms of money and terms—to the detriment of the other player. And I've not personally experienced that. But I've seen that occur. . . . But I have seen, in my own experience, management working with an agent to corral a couple players, with one of the players, maybe, not getting as good a deal as if he had been separately represented. . . . that's just a serious way to get a conflict of interest in representing athletes: you play off one against the other. Manager makes out, the agent makes out, the player who is of lesser value does not. [105Ch<10]

Dangerous production processes employed industrywide may lead to environmental or product liability claims against more than one client. Or an effort to exonerate the manufacturer of one component of a faulty piece of equipment may result in the blame being shifted to another client responsible for producing a related component. A zoning change in one municipality may cause traffic congestion or excessive noise or crime to spill over to adjacent communities, all of them clients of the law firm.

And, of course, companies in the same industry do have many direct legal disputes or deals with each other. They bid for the same work; compete for rights to the same property; vie for the same labor; make and break agreements with each other; lobby the same legislators; fix prices or restrain trade; try to use the regulatory process to thwart the expansion, innovation, or production processes of the other; and so on—all of which pose clear, direct conflicts of interest for their law firm.

> . . . we represent the four or five major road contractors in this area. . . . And, believe me, they don't like it. And so we tread very, very carefully in those things. Now, they don't get adverse to each other very often. The most common situation they get adverse to each other in is bidding [. . .] You know, they submit all their bids to the State of Illinois. And one of them feels there was a defect in the bidding process. . . . And they come in and they want to contest the bidding process. Or "So-and-So cheated in the bidding process." . . . That doesn't happen all that often, but these guys are sensitive enough to the fact [. . .] We've told them for twenty years that we don't, we're not going to get involved in those conflicts between them. And now they don't bring them to us anymore. They go someplace else. There are other more subtle problems. . . . We know how they're all doing and they each want to know how the other is doing. And I'm used to being pried for information on the golf course about So-and-So, what they're doing and that kind of stuff. But, you know, we're sensitive to those issues. [70DSS10–19]

A different kind of substantive monopoly is specialty based rather than industry based. Here boutique law firms or practices are known for a rare specialized expertise needed at one time or another by clients from all sorts of industries. The conflicts arise because parties on both ends of the transaction or dispute seek that specialized expertise from the same firm. Three very different examples cited by respondents illustrate the range of difficulties here. The first was offered as an apocryphal story by several lawyers in the study—of the unique skills of the mergers and acquisitions specialists at Skadden Arps Slate Meagher & Flom in New York, who struck terror in the minds of corporate executives presiding over what they feared might be potential takeover targets. So apprehensive were they and so eager to immunize themselves from a possible attack by a Skadden Arps client, they conflicted out the law firm by giving it some business—any business—thereby creating a direct adversity between their company and any potential client that might engage the firm to go after them.

Major corporations are not the only ones needlessly engaging law firms in order to strategically conflict out a firm possessed of rare expertise that might be used against them. Several respondents in the study noted that even unsophisticated individuals are known to do the same thing when they face the demise of their marriages. The goal in the big city is to conflict out all the best, most aggressive, most cut-throat divorce lawyers in town so that one's spouse will be limited to a less effective or less aggressive advocate.

> And I think one of the reasons—in the divorce area—is that there are people who deliberately shop around for lawyers, in order to create conflicts so that their spouses can't hire those lawyers. And there are lawyers who will send people around to do that. . . . Obviously, I think it's unethical. . . . And there are also liti-

> gants and people have been through a divorce and who are familiar with the process who, I am told, will encourage friends of theirs—people going through a divorce—to "go see five, six lawyers before you . . . sign with the one who you intend to sign with, so that your husband can't, or your wife can't, see those lawyers." So, that's why we have to be real careful in dealing with the issue of conflicts in divorce. [94Ch10–19]

The small-town version is to conflict out *all* the divorce specialists in town, forcing one's spouse either to hire a local lawyer with less expertise or to pay the cost (both financial and social) of hiring an out-of-town specialist for representation.

> There are a limited number of lawyers in the divorce field, especially in a small county [. . .] Now a wife seeking a divorce . . . may go and see lawyer A and B and C and D. She will talk to each one and maybe even pay a small retainer. She selects lawyer E. Then she will raise the issue in court when lawyer A represents her husband. The courts will decline to let lawyer A represent the spouse. [90Ch20–49]

A third example, from intellectual property practice, is perhaps most daunting, because the monopolies lie in the nature of the legal issues themselves rather than in the strategic behavior or demand curve of clients.

> In a patent firm, you are not interested in the client "name," but in the "product." If you are applying for a patent for a color television, you want to ensure that no one else can produce a color television or get a patent for a color television. You are trying to cover everyone else in the world; they are our enemy. [42Ch20–49]

Patents provide winner-take-all licenses. As a result, the direct adversity in a patent application is not between the finite number of parties on both sides of a traditional transaction or dispute; it is between the prospective winner and all others. Because the goal of a patent firm is to exclude all companies but one's client access to a particular technology, the adversities quickly snowball. They also are often difficult to identify.

Of course, when intellectual property firms specialize in particular kinds of esoteric emerging technologies, the kinds of substantive monopolies I've just described—every company that is developing a more potent computer chip trying to engage the same specialized law firm—further exacerbate the conflicts of interest imposed by winner-take-all advocacy. Even a more general practice, however, has its own difficulties.

In the color television example, it is clear that the patent firm could not represent a second company seeking a patent on a color television. But what if that second company had engaged the firm, not for its color television process but for its compact disc player? The direct adversity between client 1 and client 2 over the color television patent still remains—just as a direct adversity exists between Skadden Arps client A who engaged the firm strategically on a labor matter and Skadden Arps client B who wanted to engage the firm to launch a hostile takeover of client A.

And what if client 2 had engaged the firm, not for its expertise in intellectual property at all but for its real estate or tax expertise? Again, the adversity between the two clients remains. Because of the inexorable mathematics of winner-take-all adversities in a corporate world comprised of huge conglomerates producing vast arrays of unrelated products seeking patent protection, several respondents insist that intellectual property law must be practiced in relatively small boutiques.

S: How are larger firms—say of 200 lawyers—able to avoid these conflicts?
L: They can't. Two hundred lawyer firms are not in our business. The very largest patent law firm will have 75 lawyers—and they mostly do litigation, which does not pose as great a conflicts problem. Our firm does a lot of patents prosecution . . . which poses a lot more conflicts problems. . . . There is a practical limit to how much a patent law firm can grow; I would say not more than 50 lawyers.
S: Is this due to conflicts of interest or are there certain economies of scale that make 50 an upper limit?
L: Oh, absolutely, size is a constraint solely because of conflicts. . . . Take a 700-lawyer or even a 300+-lawyer firm with an intellectual property department. It is impossible to do it. I don't believe it can happen. Take the law firm of Shearman and Sterling in New York. Say they get only one patent application. That patent application covers everyone in the world. It necessarily poses conflicts for many of the firm's corporate clients. And it's likely that an intellectual property department of that size will file one hundred patent applications in a year. It is just unbelievable. [42Ch20–49]

Network Monopoly

Adverse clients cluster in the same law firm not only because the firm is the only game in town or the only specialist around. Social networks that feed into a particular law firm may create virtual monopolies as well. The interviews are laced with examples of adversities of interest among clients that arise from their membership in common social networks.

> For example, let's say, we set up a program for a franchiser, okay? We set up their franchise disclosure statement or something like that. And then we also happen to represent one of their franchisees in another matter unrelated to getting the franchise. Maybe the franchisee was buying the ground for his location. And then, ultimately, there was litigation between the franchiser and the franchisee. Well, the franchiser . . . would definitely want us to represent them because we had prepared the franchise disclosure statement and were very familiar with it and knew the ins and outs of it and had done all the litigation against other franchisees. And now there's a problem with this franchisee: "Sue this franchisee, okay?" I don't think we would be able to avoid that. [10Ch100+]

Perhaps even more common, the dispute embroils a company, for which the law firm does corporate work, and its employees, who have ongoing relationships with the firm for personal financial or estate planning, divorce, or real estate matters.

> I represented one of the . . . largest . . . medical clinics—in this state. . . . I draw up a contract, which says, basically, "In the event you leave this clinic, you cannot compete with us or open up an office within a given distance for a period of years." If I also represent that doctor, when he's going to leave, I cannot represent him. And it makes it extremely awkward for me to decide . . . whether it would be proper that I continue to . . . serve the clinic in that particular instance. Basically, I shudder when that happens, and consider that on an individual basis. It's happened. And I've brought suits . . . by the clinic against doctors, and won. And fortunately, up to now, they haven't been doctors I represent. [110DSM<10]

More thorny conflicts of interest arise in the practices of lawyers who concentrate in serving members of particular social networks—ethnic groups, for example—many of whom live together, cluster in the same industries, transact business together, socialize together, and intermarry. Hence, the potential for disputes between ethnic group members is quite high. Where the supply of lawyers of similar ethnicity is low, monopolies develop that ensure that these attorneys will face an inordinate share of conflicts of interest. A few Chicago respondents, serving various ethnic communities, explained how true adversities of interest were made even more difficult by engagements that threatened merely social rather than fiduciary ties, rigid conceptions among clients of loyalty and exclusivity, and the high visibility of their practice to ethnic group members.

> But, in the [ethnic group] community, it's a small close-knit community of businessmen. . . . It happens, probably four or five times a year, at least, that we have existing clients doing business with each other. And, generally, the clientele we have is very insulted if we even suggest that they seek another lawyer. . . . And we usually end up referring them out if there's going to be a real conflict. . . . Sometimes, they just refuse to get other lawyers. . . . And they try to count on us to be fair, which is not something we ever want to try to do. But, it's an unusual situation. I don't think many other lawyers have that problem in their practice.
>
> . . . I'll give you a story [. . .] Just so you can have a kind of [. . .] a little bit of an insight as to how they think—how the [ethnicity]-American businessmen think. I represent a guy I went to high school with who was born in [country of ethnicity] . . . He buys out his partner in a restaurant. There is some fraud involved in concealing certain debts in the restaurant. The partner that he buys out, his daughter is a dentist. She and her husband are my clients. She is a good friend of my wife's. The two partners—the two brothers that eventually buy this other gentleman out—come to me and want to sue the withdrawing partner, the withdrawing shareholder. I tell them I really can't do it, because I felt I had a conflict because of the close relationship I have with that gentleman's daughter being a client and because of the amount of times I see him socially during the course of a year. Well, they went to another lawyer who eventually referred them to a person that's of counsel to our firm, who has the office next door. He went on vacation one time, and some emergency matter came up, and I went—even though there was no technical conflict—I went to court to help him out. My name appeared on the other

> firm's billing statement to the client. The client saw my name, told his daughter and his son-in-law that their lawyer was trying to hurt them by hurting him. And it created a little bit of a tense situation with existing clients. Eventually the of-counsel lawyer came to odds with the two clients he had. They came back to me looking for me to get involved in the case. To which, for the second time, I invested another three or four hours explaining why I couldn't. To which they were very unhappy with me. [121Ch<10]

Finally, lawyers themselves may be responsible for creating social ties among their clients. Steeped in inside information on the business activities of their clients, they are often the first to learn of opportunities that arise that might be of interest to another client. On some occasions, they serve as matchmaker; on others, they facilitate or lubricate transactions among strangers who trust them. Indeed, some clients are attracted to the law firm in the first place because they view it as a node in a coveted social network. But once a firm has brought two clients together, is the firm able to represent either of them when it comes time to consummate the deal? Certainly the potential for adversity looms.

> . . . a partner joined the firm and brought with him a client that was in precarious financial condition. And talking to another partner who realized that we had another client that might well be interested in acquiring his business. They were looking for this kind of business. . . . And they started to put this marriage together, but we didn't know whether the client in bad financial straits was going to tell the truth to the client that was thinking of doing the acquisition. And we couldn't tell the client the truth. . . . They were talking off by themselves and we just didn't know what to do [. . .] [2Ch100+]

HANDLING A PORCUPINE

Though disputes and transactions between clients may represent the most common source of conflicts of interest for many law firms, the ubiquity of adversity and responses to it will vary by firm size, location, substantive specialization, client base, and its locus in diverse social networks. One respondent who was quoted earlier in this chapter analogized the encounter to handling a porcupine—invariably a dangerous task in which one can easily be skewered regardless of how one approaches the beast. To mix metaphors, one can be skewered by failing to recognize the perilous rapids downstream from what appears to be a placid, gentle pool or by anticipating peril at every turn and refusing to ever stick a toe in the water. One can be skewered by seeming disloyal to clients through abandoning them in their hour of need or through staying by their side but not achieving the hoped-for result (clients suspect out of loyalty to another) or through choosing to represent one client over another. Many of the sharpest needles pierce one's skin not by breaching the ethical rules but by angering clients while pursuing one's ethical responsibilities or options.

The difficulty with a requirement that relationships can be forged only after assessing whether they will adversely affect (or be affected) by the representation of another is that it requires an aptitude for fortune-telling and a psychological insight that eludes even the most sagacious lawyer. Becaues lawyers are unable to predict with any certitude the twists and turns of a long, complex, and arduous course, it is not surprising that they tend to rely on more formulaic criteria in forging or forgoing relationships—or at least they respond to abstract hypotheticals in this fashion.

I have sketched the matter of adversity with very broad strokes somewhat stripped from the context of legal practice. The ethical issues underlying conflict of interest are even more complex because they also depend on conceptions of who is the client, on how far the ripples of adversity travel, on temporal issues, and on the practices of law firms and lawyers themselves. These additional sources of conflict of interest are the subjects of the next four chapters.

FOUR

Who Is the Client?

In a firm like ours, where we represent people on an ongoing basis—corporations and family members—and we are at a point in our growth now where we're representing . . . more than one generation in one family, there are a lot of potential conflicts of interest. We live with them every day. And, for the most part, we can work through them. Occasionally, we can't. But, I think it was Brandeis who was questioned by the United States Senate when he was nominated for the Supreme Court. One of the senators posed a question to him regarding a transaction that he had been involved in. And he said, "Well, let's see, you represented the estate and you represented the decedent and you represented the shareholders and you represented the heirs. And Brandeis said, "That's correct." And the senator—I think the quote's accurate—he said, "Well, who exactly did you represent in this case?" And, he [Brandeis] said, "I was the attorney for the situation." We have a lot of those situations in this office, just by the nature of our practice. [122CC<10]

Two or three apocryphal stories or lawyer jokes reappeared throughout the interviews. One was about Abraham Lincoln (not terribly surprising in a study in Illinois). Another was some version of this story about Louis Brandeis.[1] The Brandeis story is compelling for many respondents because it gives voice to the often per-

[1]For a more scholarly discussion, see Dzienkowski 1992 or Spillenger 1996.

plexing questions they also face about who is their client, especially when many parties simultaneously vie for their loyalty. Were it possible to represent situations rather than clients, one of their most difficult conflict-of-interest conundra would be resolved. Unfortunately, few respondents see the Brandeis solution as a viable option.

We return to this theme at the conclusion of the chapter. First, we need to explore the conundrum. Lawrence Lexman, of course, is no Louis Brandeis. Nor did he face such a conundrum. He could easily identify his client: the first and only person ever to cross his office threshold, the young man who stumbled into the office clutching an IRS subpoena. The who-is-a-client question is more difficult for most of Lexman's counterparts because few clients are truly autonomous solitary individuals like Lawrence's first client. As expounded in evolutionary social theory, such "natural persons" as the basic units of social action have increasingly been supplanted by organizational forms—families, states, churches, associations, organizations, and corporations—that collectivize natural persons or, indeed, other organizations (Coleman 1990). This societal trend is exacerbated in law, which, because of its role as organizational progenitor, midwife, regulator, referee, and mortician and as facilitator of collective action, becomes a magnet to organizational clients. Not surprisingly, we find much higher rates of participation by natural persons in other social institutions (medicine, education, religion, and the like) than in legal ones. Moreover, the dominance of organizational over individual clients in legal arenas is increasing. An array of social indicators—law firm demographics, the growth of in-house corporate legal departments, court dockets, census data on law firm receipts, and survey data on public use of lawyers—document the growing share of legal services purchased by organizations in the last two decades (Nelson 1994; Galanter and Palay 1991; Galanter and Rogers 1991; Sander and Williams 1989; Curran 1977, 1989).[2]

Unlike natural persons, organizations cannot act on their own. Who in these often massive, structurally complex, far-flung collections of natural and corporate persons is the client? The organizational agents with whom the lawyer interacts? The members of the organization? The partners? The owners or shareholders? The officers and directors? The managers? The subsidiaries, divisions, or branch offices of the organization? And how do lawyers stay apprised of all these often changing parties and shifting interests and ensure that none are abrogated?

FAMILIES

The difficulties of serving organizational clients, compounded by the indeterminate temporal sweep of lawyer-client relationships, is illustrated by the simplest of organizations, what Coleman (1991) considers a "primordial" form of social organization, an inchoate precursor to more complex constructed organizations: the family.

[2]Indeed, much of the legal business attributed to individuals or the "personal client hemisphere" (Heinz and Laumann 1982) is actually organizational as well, because it concerns the representation of families (e.g., estates, real estate acquisition, and the like) and not persons (Curran 1977, 1989).

> Years ago, it never bothered me that, if there was a family dispute—even a husband and wife dispute—it never bothered me if the two of them came in the office and I tried to resolve it. It never bothered me that two brothers owned a business and they were having troubles within themselves, that I wouldn't pull them into the office and try to knock heads and get the thing resolved. And it might even end up drafting some type of an agreement between the two of them. And I never worried about their not being represented by another attorney. That just didn't even come into my head. This was the job [knocks desk for emphasis] . . . that I had to do. I didn't have a conflict. I was trying to resolve differences between people. But, today, if that came into the office, . . . I'd start to think, "Whose side am I on? And shouldn't that other person be represented?" That, to me, is the biggest difference. In a certain sense, I feel it's extremely unfortunate. I think that I could avoid a lot of the litigation that's going on. But somebody might say, "But, maybe at the expense of somebody." . . . in the past, you were always looked at as the family attorney, as the attorney for the business. The kids got in trouble, why, you always were called and you found a way of taking care of this and that and the conflicts and everything else. And you could sit in the shareholder meetings and let 'em holler at each other. And you could make the decision for 'em and everything else and not feel that you were getting into some kind of a conflict. It's difficult now. . . . I think that that's part of my responsibility in having gotten to that point with the family. But, in today's world, it's [. . .] With the concept of the development of some of the conflict of interests, the smartest thing would be just to wash your hands and walk away from it. I have a hard time doing that. [54DSL20–49]

This melancholy reflection from one of the oldest respondents in the study on the changing nature of his practice suggests some of the difficulties in representing families. Families pose conflicts of interest for their lawyers in at least three ways. First, as this respondent noted, family representations tend to snowball—they lurch from one legal problem to the next, rarely waiting for one to reach closure before another begins, respecting few boundaries, amassing new confidentialities, and frequently collecting different constellations or additional members of family networks with each revolution. As I noted in the last chapter, even when prior representations have concluded, the strictures of confidentiality require that the interests of former family member clients be honored and given priority over those of potential new family member clients dragged in by the ever enlarging snowball. So plucking out new clients from the nodes of dense social networks, such as those in many families, exacerbates the threat of conflict of interest.

This impetus for legal business to snowball through families comes from many sources. Clients develop trust in their lawyers. They have entrusted their lawyers with their financial wherewithal, their dreams, vulnerabilities, or most embarrassing secrets and have not been betrayed, maybe even feel well served. Their lawyers know them, their histories, their business operations, and their values and preferences. Clients have paid to bring their attorneys up to speed and now hope to bank on this investment in future legal skirmishes or opportunities. Clients happily reuse these rare resources and willingly share them with members of their social networks in need (Curran 1977). And even if none of this is true, some legal problems are dire emergencies; when the call from the police awakens the CEO at two in the morning, there may be only one lawyer he knows to call.

Law firms nurture this networking phenomenon as well. Some eschew advertising or explicit marketing of their services and rely on referrals from current or former clients to stay in business. Large firms increasingly diversify to offer expertise in the areas to which corporate client snowballs typically roll, frequently establishing estate planning or matrimonial departments, for example, to meet the personal needs of many of the corporate officials with whom they work.

Second, these snowballs often produce confounding unit-of-analysis questions, in which some engagements pertain to a single family member, some to spouses, some to households, some to family businesses, some to children or siblings or cousins, some to heirs, and some crossing several generations. And the shoots of even relatively simple engagements for a single natural person—a grandfather's will whose tentacles reach across nuclear families and generations, for example—can grow, eventually becoming hopelessly entwined throughout the family tree.

Finally, law is especially invoked at times of or in planning for family transition—birth (e.g., adoption or estate planning), marriage (e.g., prenuptial agreements), divorce, remarriage, financial crisis (i.e., bankruptcy), retirement, incapacity, and death—the very points at which fault lines emerge and chasms develop as the interests and alliances of family members shift, clash, and reconfigure. But because of popular stereotypes of families as safe, loving, harmonious, nurturant havens, the festering disputes and grievances and the structurally irreconcilable interests are less likely to be recognized or acknowledged than in other organizational settings.

Whether the proper imagery is that of being buried under a runaway avalanche of relatives or snarled in the underbrush of a family tree, the picture is clear: families are uncomfortable places to practice law. And it is the older respondents in the study, whose relationships with families and family businesses have continued long enough to go through many of these transitions, who express the most discomfort and have the greatest difficulty ascertaining who is their client.

Adversariness

Because ongoing relationships with clients give rise to many complexities, I begin with the easiest conflict-of-interest question—a one-shot encounter between an attorney and a couple with clearly adverse interests. They have decided to end their marriage, and they appear together at their first meeting with the lawyer, where they explain that their divorce will be amicable and that they have already agreed to a settlement and do not want to pay for two lawyers but simply want the lawyer to formalize their agreement. After joking that there is no such thing as an amicable divorce, respondents reminisce that, in days gone by, most lawyers would take on this engagement. Few, if any, of them will today, though the difference may be more one of artifice than substance—they simply designate one of the two as the client.[3] The following response is typical:

> One person will come in and will actually hire you. And that's the person that is my client. And what I usually do is meet with that person and determine the issues. And explain to him that I will be glad to meet with the other person, but they have to be aware that I am not their attorney, that I am your attorney and that I will be coming at this from your best interest. And, generally, that's explained to the other person before they come in. But if it's not, it's the first thing I do. I sit across from them and say, "As far as I'm concerned, you're your own attorney. And I'm not here to give you legal advice. And I am not here to tell you what you're doing is right or wrong. I am here looking out for his or her best interest, and that's how I will be proceeding." And I always inform that, if they feel that I'm taking advantage of them or they feel that this is not an adequate settlement agreement, they are free to hire an attorney at any time in the proceedings. And if they want to stop the meeting, I will stop it at any time. I've never had a problem with it. [112DSS<10]

Some respondents will strongly encourage the designated unrepresented or so-called pro se party to consult another attorney, citing numerous examples of issues—child support, child custody, and the like—for which his or her interests may substantially diverge from those of the represented spouse. And at least one respondent refuses to take such cases if the unrepresented client does not consult with an attorney concerning the settlement agreement:

> L: Once we prepare a settlement agreement and a dissolution, then I will always recommend to the other party an attorney whom I trust, and who will basically look it over—. . . at a reasonable fee—and advise the client one way or another if it's fair or not fair, that type of thing. And then I usually request then that that attorney at least sign the settlement agreement. If they don't want to do that because they feel that they haven't done a lot of consultation, at least the client will sign it in front of them—or the adverse party, I should say[4]—would sign it in front of them.
>
> S: Is it common, when you recommend that, that the other party will say, "No, I don't want to do that"?
>
> L: I've occasionally had that, but I refuse to go through with one, quite frankly, unless I know they've seen somebody else. . . . I just absolutely, positively will not get myself into a situation where one of the parties who has something to lose will not seek outside help—at least with regards to the settlement agreement itself. [128DSS<10]

---

[3]Although lawyers increasingly serve as mediators or third-party neutrals in marital as well as many other kinds of disputes. Because the disputing parties are not *represented* by the mediators and are not clients (to whom lawyers owe loyalty), third-party neutrals do not face conflicts between the often adverse interests of those subject to alternative dispute resolution. (On the ethics of alternative dispute resolution, see, for example, Menkel-Meadow 1997.)

[4]A not surprising Freudian slip, given the machinations involved.

But there is a flip side to this acknowledged risk that the interests of the pro se party will not be advanced. Receiving far less attention is the more subtle risk that the interests of the true client will be less vigorously championed in an effort to ensure a more level playing field. The attorney, perhaps even unconsciously, compromises his or her undivided loyalty to the designated client because of some attenuated sense of obligation to a third party. Indeed, although the pro se party will often enjoy full disclosure of the assorted ways in which he might be disadvantaged by his lack of representation, it is unlikely that his counterpart, the designated client, will be apprised of the subtle losses that may arise because her representative sparred with one hand tied behind his back.

Still, these cases are the easy ones. One reason families provide such an intriguing setting for exploring conflicts of interest is that adversariness is so much less palpable or predictable as it undulates in and out of relationships over time and from one episode to the next. Many families coexist in a never-never land of virtual harmony, the differences and acrimony simmering below the surface. When family members are in denial about their discord, lawyers may inadvertently stumble into conflicts of interest when these differences ultimately surface.

So now consider a less adversarial one-shot encounter between the attorney and the couple, perhaps a few years earlier, when they sought counsel in planning their estate and preparing their wills, the most common occasion for Americans to consult with lawyers (Curran 1977, 135). Until recently, attorneys never questioned the appropriateness of representing both spouses in estate planning, and most of my respondents still don't. But of late, professional association and malpractice insurance company seminars are beginning to chronicle the ethical conundra that arise from this practice. Several respondents who specialize in estate planning echo these concerns, describing scenarios in which the interests of husband and wife diverge:

> Obviously, on the whole, the more nuclear the family is . . . the more "Ozzie and Harriet" the family is, the less likelihood there is for a conflict. That is to say, both husband and wife are parents of the same children, and more often than not, they have the same goals and ends and attitudes in mind. Even then, there is the potential for conflict. . . . Well, this nuclear family has assets—whose name might the assets be registered in when they come to see you? Quite often, they're in joint tenancy. Estate planning oftentimes requires that the couple break up their joint tenancies. Now the question is: okay, fine, whose name do we register it in? And how might that—theoretically—develop in the future? That is to say, you put the house in your wife's name and then you get divorced, where are we now? [81Ch10–19]

> You represent the husband, okay? The husband runs a business and the husband and wife come in, want a will. And you go through the litany with them. The husband calls back later and says, "I'd like to make a little change in the will. And I want to take a little less from my wife and give it to [. . .]" whatever, girlfriend, what not. The problem is, who do you represent? You have situations where you've got to do something. You should have an obligation—I think—to at least

> disclose the change to the wife, because she is also a client at this point. I don't know how that situation would end up getting resolved. [74DSL<10]

> Because of the nature of doing a particular estate plan, one spouse may be doing something to restrict the other spouse from having free access to monies or other properties during the surviving spouse's lifetime. To use a cliché, preventing the second spouse or the second husband or second wife, as the case may be, from getting access to that. And that's something that you have to deal with. And we've been telling husbands and wives that come to us that one or the other should also consider getting their own counsel. [123Ch<10]

Spouses planning their futures together and arranging for their separation only after "death do they part" certainly have fewer incompatibilities than marriages ending long before the death of one. Still, their secrets and different values, priorities, and predilections pose difficult problems for their legal representatives. Can one lawyer really advise two partners on how to maximize their interests when these interests profoundly diverge and when the adviser is gagged by confidences of one partner? Why the problem? Divorcing spouses do not want to pay two lawyers, and neither do outwardly committed, loving spouses who cannot fathom how their interests might be fundamentally opposed. Indeed, the need to pay two separate lawyers may defeat the economic rationality of preparing an estate plan in the first place:

> And you'll go to seminars on estate planning and you'll have some guy say, "Well, you really should tell her she's got a right to get her own attorney, if he came to you first. Or, vice versa." And again, I say, "Okay, what you do there, is you take estate planning, and you move it to the realm of the tremendously expensive and almost unaffordable." . . . You know, you start figuring out time value of money. And is it worth you spending $8,000 today to save them $240,000? If you're thirty years old and you have a life expectancy of ninety? I don't know. [122CC<10]

Continuing Relationships

As I noted earlier in this chapter, legal representations snowball. The attorney may have had a prior or continuing relationship with one or both spouses. Frequently a long-standing relationship is forged between the attorney and one spouse who works for a business that is represented by the firm. When a personal legal matter, such as estate planning or divorce, arises, the spouse often turns to this trusted familiar lawyer for representation, an impulse supported by the practice of law firms to diversify into specialties catering to the personal legal needs of corporate executives. Now the commonplace divergence among spouses in one-shot matters is further imbalanced by the greater loyalty of the attorney to one spouse over the other. And it is exacerbated further by the possibility that the future stream of all corporate business is at risk if the lawyer antagonizes the long-standing client-spouse by insisting on evenhandedness or on disclosing confidentialities or by even refusing to take the engagement at all because of the inherent conflicts of interest. Though respondents acknowledge this risk, not surprisingly they do not admit to succumbing to the pressure. Most continue to take on these engagements, though some meet alone with the business client to outline the issues of dual representation before agreeing to represent both spouses.

> If the husband is the business client, . . . when he calls and says, "I'm thinking about a will" or I call him and say, "Isn't it time you think about a will," I might say to him, "Do you want your wife to come with you in our first meeting—or not?" And I might give him an idea of why [. . .] he might or might not want her there. And, then—depending on how that works—I can be more or less free to run through this whole scenario. But, one way or another, I really have to broach the subject. . . . And sometimes they have to go home and discuss this and then they come up with a marital decision as to how this is going to work. So, again, the conflict exists. But, I tend to address that conflict by educating both spouses on the area—if you will, a mini-course on estate planning. [81Ch10–19]

In other instances, the attorney previously represented both spouses—in estate planning or the purchase or sale of real estate, for example—who now seek representation in a more adversarial matter such as their divorce. Here respondents are less comfortable taking on the engagement. Many suggest that they played a role in acquiring the property that may be subject to dispute and feel that their personal interest or confidential inside information will become further entangled in the already contentious thicket of interests. Others feel loyalty to both parties and refuse to take sides, even with the consent of one to represent the other, fearing perhaps that their advocacy might be less vigorous as a result of these ties or that it might be difficult to disattend inside information secured from prior representations that could be used against the other. That both parties may be significantly disadvantaged by their trusted lawyer's insistence on extricating him- or herself from their potential conflict of interest is suggested in this account from one interview:

> I had a very successful client. He and his wife were friends [of mine]. Did their estate planning, the whole route, long-term relationship with them. They lived down in Hilton Head. In their . . . later mid-life, decided they wanted to get divorced. And they called up and they said, "We'd like you to recommend some attorneys. So, I recommended to each of them two members from the American Academy of Matrimonial Lawyers. . . . Guys with very good reputations. I checked them out with two local members of the academy, who said, "Hey, these guys are top-notch." Sent two names to each of them. They each got an attorney. Didn't hear anything about it for about a year and a half. I came back from vacation to find that my secretary had scheduled a meeting with both of them in my conference room the morning I came back from vacation. . . . And their story was, basically, "We've had it with these two lawyers. We know what they're doing. They're milking us. We want to settle our divorce with you." I said, "Uh, gee, I wonder if I have a conflict here, you know?" [laughs] So I told them I would try to act as a mediator. I would not make recommendations, but I would talk through issues

> with them and see if the two of them could reach an agreement which we would then memorialize and send to their attorneys. And I tried to stick to that very hard. And if I went back and we taped—like we are here—everything that I said, maybe I always just wasn't the sounding board on every point. But basically, I think, what they did was used me as a sounding board to try to come up with what they thought was fair. . . . they put together an agreement which they asked me to draft and send to their attorneys to resolve the case. I wrote them and their attorneys and said, "I'm a mediator. I'm not taking a side." Was I in a potential conflict of interest? Absolutely. Was I in a real conflict of interest? Absolutely. Did the clients get the job done the way they wanted it done and avoid a lot of pain and suffering for them and their family? I'd like to think so. And amazingly, I told them, I said, "You know, when this is all over, either one or both of you are going to hate me. This is a lose-lose for me. There's no way I can win here." And they said, "Please do it." And amazingly, they're both still friends. But how do you deal with that situation with the rules on conflicts of interest? How do mediators deal with the conflicts of interest? And what should I [. . .] I suppose, if they reported me to ARDC [Attorney Registration and Disciplinary Commission], I would be in trouble. I suppose that I would have a hell of a time explaining that to a hearing panel. But I think I got the job done for the client. [122CC<10]

Crossing Hierarchies and Generations

The imbalances between parties in the scenarios described in the previous section were limited somewhat by the fact that the parties are spouses, occupying lateral positions in the family tree. But often subsequent legal needs pop up all over the family tree, crossing nuclear families, generations, and relationships. Here greater disparities in power, claims of confidentiality, and preexisting loyalties significantly threaten the lawyer's ability to champion the interests of the newest client, given his or her prior or ongoing relationships with other family members. A classic example of the long-standing client dragging his elderly father to his attorney's office and pleading with the lawyer to prepare a will for Dad illustrates the tension and trade-offs.

> L: Children bring in their father, their mother. They draw up a will. The children kind of tell you what would be a good plan. You kind of have a discussion. You kind of draw the will. It turns out four years later there's a dispute in the family—children against parents and so forth. I'm involved in a dramatic case involving that now, where everything was fine when Mom died, and Dad went in and made his will leaving everything to the children. And then he decided to remarry. And now there's all kinds of problems. I think that those things are virtually insoluble. I think that for you to say, "I'm sorry. I can't draw a will for your father because I've represented you and you might have some conflict with your fa [. . .] " Nobody would understand that. . . . Well, you're going to do it, and you'll face the consequences of it later if there are any.
>
> S: And if you were to say to the father, "You know, maybe you should talk to someone else," the children—who are your client—would be [. . .] ?

L: They've been beating him up for the last seven years to see a lawyer at all because he's afraid, if he makes a will, he's going to die. And they finally hauled him down here [. . .] Or, sometimes, they've hauled me out to his house. "Please, please, you've got to talk to my dad." He doesn't want to talk. "I don't want to die, I don't want to tell you anything." Or, "Come on, Dad, you gotta! You gotta do this." . . . And then I come up with, "Oh, by the way, sir, there might be a conflict of interest here. I really think you ought to get a lawyer who's totally independent of your children." Who am I serving? Anybody? I mean, I'm not serving anything or anybody. I'm just playing a game which is theoretical in nature and so on and so forth. I'm protecting my ass at the expense of doing something good for somebody. [51Ch20–49]

True enough, the only way the children might be able to convince Dad to write a will is by exploiting the social capital—and patience—of the trusted family attorney. But it is also true that this major corporate client imploring his lawyer to prepare Dad's will is one of the potential heirs to his father's estate. Given the son's corporate role as conduit to considerable law firm business unrelated to these personal family matters, the lawyer may have qualms following Dad's instructions to prepare a will that leaves all his substantial assets to the other siblings or to Dad's eighteen-year-old girlfriend or to an evangelical preacher on late-night television. Might not the lawyer be more tempted than usual to try to convince Dad to rethink the allocation of his estate?

Or, to take another classic example, what about the CEO who calls his corporate counsel at two in the morning to bail out his son who has been arrested on a DUI or drug charge? Might not the father's interest in securing a plea agreement for his son that includes extended residential treatment, rehabilitation, and counseling conflict with the son's interest in securing the most lenient punishment (preferably one that allows him continued access to the friends and intoxicating substances of which his father disapproves)? Can the lawyer unequivocally champion the interests of the elderly father who lacks a will or the substance-abusing son, given how profoundly these interests oppose those of the ongoing original client?

Family Businesses

L: I had a business where I represented them for, why, I'll bet you thirty, forty, fifty years. The principal stockholder wrote his will and rewrote his will, and everything else. And we worked up a way that the employees could buy out the business as they went along. And the man died. And it ends up that the executor decides we have a conflict, and they retain another lawyer. And when we try to represent the business, why, they say that we've got a conflict because we know too much about it, and so forth. So we withdraw. We end up no longer having the estate nor representing the business. And everybody on both sides are angry at us, because we haven't completed what we had done along the way. And you have a sense of, "Gosh, it's a shame!" . . . And it was a matter where—over the past two years—the principal had been in the hospital thinking

> that he was dying and calling me up on the phone. And, "[names himself], I want to change my will. And I want to be sure that this is done." And we're rushing up to the hospital to get his information and getting a codicil executed and that type of thing. And holding his hand and doing the whole thing. And then—there it's gone. . . . You see, that's the type of business that the lawyer could very well fall into in a community of this size—if you do represent a small business and you know the family and they look to you. You're their counselor. They tell the other members of the family, "There's a question? Call [names self]." It's just that simple.
>
> S: And were you to say—when they call—"I can't talk to you because I'm not wearing that hat?"
>
> L: They'd be shocked. "You can't do that!" [54DSL20–49]

Representation of family businesses often entails the most complex negotiation among divergent interests because families typically amass so many of the structural features that give rise to conflicts of interest: ongoing relationships with lawyers, adversarial intertwined with compatible interests, denial of or distaste for controversy, snowballing engagements, and so forth.

Frequently a single lawyer or firm handles the plethora of disputes, transactions, negotiations, and crises that arise in family businesses as well as in the personal affairs of their members. This reliance on a sole legal representative reflects matters of trust, knowledge of business operations, expertise, timing, and the economic realities of small businesses. Because this practice exacerbates the potential for conflicts of interest, it requires not only an intricate choreography and considerable finesse to maneuver through the many minefields embedded in the organizational structure but also the ability to withstand the risk that an explosion might sever the law firm's relationship to the business and its principals entirely—as befell the downstate respondent who represented the dying patriarch. It also requires that lawyers frequently back off entirely in moments of crisis, leaving clients to fend for themselves or find independent lawyers.

A systemic conflict in the life cycle of a family business—succession planning—epitomizes the complex choreography: What happens when the founders or owners retire or die? How is the business handed down to other family members, employees, or outsiders? In particular, can the interests of the children working in the family business who hope to succeed their fathers or mothers be maximized by the same attorney who represents their parents and, often, the business as well? Or on the flip side, because the parent is on the way out and the child will soon control the purse strings and decisions about who will provide legal counsel to the business, can the parent count on the lawyer to be a dedicated advocate of his interests, given the lawyer's need to ingratiate herself with the child? Most respondents say yes. The following two commentaries illustrate the issues, the limits, and the rationalizations:

> Father, a founder or whatever [. . .] owner of the business. Child comes in. Definitely, potential for conflict. As a matter of fact, oftentimes the conflict there can be greater than the husband and wife conflict. . . . Again, you get different genera-

tions, you've got different contributions. There definitely is a potential for conflict. The reality there, however, is . . . that the business is the father's. The child has little clout. It's not as if he is in a true bargaining position to get more from Dad than Dad is giving him to begin with. It can be, however, circumstances where the son—if you will, daughter—. . . at some point down the road . . . is at least as important to the future of this company than the father is any longer. The clout, if you will, might shift. . . . Now, the child has the ability to come to the table and demand certain things and negotiate for them. As opposed to, "Dad, I really think it would be fair if I had more of a long-term commitment here." "Dad, I really don't want to deal with Mom when you're gone." And there is the conflict between Mom and child. Who does Dad leave the stock to? The child that's going to run the company, or Mom who was at his side—more or less—whatever he was doing there? And [. . .] what might she garner from the business? Is he just going to leave it to the child? Or is the child going to have to wait for Mom to die? Or does the child have to wait until Stepmom dies? Okay? So there's all sorts of potentials there. . . . The father and the son might very well work it out in their own context. And if they come back with instructions to us how to draft it, fine. Again, that was when we educated them on their problem. . . . Now, we would probably tell the son, "You know, if you want somebody else to look at it, go right ahead." [81Ch10–19]

The minority shareholder's son negotiating to buy the company from the widowed mother. . . . I mean [. . .] that's a real conflict. You can't represent both sides of that one—I don't think. . . . But, very often, father and son walk in here and say, "Okay, help us in succession planning. How do I transfer the company to my son?" There's a potential conflict there. In fact, there's no real conflict, because these people have the same goal: How do I get this company down to my kids, at the lowest cost in tax dollars possible? And the other issue is, how does the company reimburse Dad? And that's usually a function of economics. It's not Dad saying, "I want a hundred and fifty a year" and the son saying, " . . . I want to give you fifty a year; you can live on that." It's a function of what the company can bear and still keep going. And the two of them [. . .] literally, can run the numbers. And if they agree on the numbers, they'll say, "Okay. Yeah, Dad, the company can afford to pay you seventy-five thousand dollars a year. That's it." . . . there's no real conflict. . . . If these two people are running down the same road, parallel, and they can get the job done with one lawyer, it doesn't have to become an adversary for either one of them. Isn't it better for them to get the job accomplished that way? Because a lot of the potential conflicts are issues that are going to be resolved without the involvement of the attorney. . . . They go to an accountant and he runs the numbers. And you know and I know, accountants can play games and the numbers will come out different. But for some reason, in their profession, it's not a conflict of interest. But that's the number they're both going to live with. And they're going to come back to us and say, "It's going to be a hundred thousand dollars a year." We in no way impacted the result of what was a potential conflict of interest. And so why should we be telling these guys, "Oh, you'll both have to go get different lawyers," when it's this accountant over here—who

> doesn't have a conflicts problem because his profession says he isn't in a conflict—who's really making the decision for him? . . . And I think a lawyer who says, "Oh, geez, con [. . .] potential conflict of interest. Send him off to other lawyers"—which is what we get at a lot of seminars—are doing the clients disservices. They're not analyzing the situation, not saying, "Hey, do I really have a problem here? Because it's going to cost my client a tremendous amount of money and time and grief if I have to send them off to a bunch of other lawyers." Because, really, one lawyer can solve a problem, five lawyers will turn it into a federal case. Rule of common sense. And there's got to be common sense brought to these situations. Clients are not best served by five partners each having their own attorney at a meeting, I don't believe. [122CC<10]

Notice that both respondents echo the sentiments of the transactional lawyers, described in the last chapter, who minimize the potential for conflicts of interest by standing on the sidelines while the parties negotiate and resolve the issues on their own and then return as scriveners of the agreement.

These two reflections on succession planning, however upbeat from the lawyers' perspective, also make significant simplifying assumptions. Dad owns the business. Apparently he has only one child and that child works in the business. There is the issue of Mom, seemingly ignored but whose interests lurk in the background. Still, we are dealing with only two generations and two parties with direct involvement in the business, and a negotiation that occurs at a single point in time. Now look at a more complex family business—with three generations, multiple siblings, in-laws, and cousins, some in the business and some not—with different needs and life-styles, and a single lawyer who has been serving the business and various members of the family, day to day, for almost forty years.

> L: I have lots of conflicts when I represent family businesses and every member of the family. And they're all shareholders and sometimes two or three generations. And their interests are different. They're not really technically adverse, but occasionally they get to be adverse. . . . if there develops a real hostile situation, then I can't represent anybody. But, normally, I'm a sort of "godfather" and everybody knows that I'm representing the grandfather and the grandchildren and the business and so forth. And there's nothing very formal about it. I haven't had much trouble with it, mainly because there's been peace. Occasionally I'm put into family situations because there's a conflict—and I'm totally neutral. But, more often, it's a business that I've represented for thirty-five to forty years. Just perforce they turn to me, and occasionally conflicts. If it's ever a real conflict—in the sense of hostility—I don't serve anybody. I just say, "I'll represent the business if you want me to. You guys go get separate lawyers." It hasn't happened often.
>
> . . . I represent one company where I represent every member of the family, I'm trustee of shares in a trust under a will, I'm trustee of a voting trust. I really am—for all practical purposes—control of the company. And I've never exercised it. And if they have a fight, then it gets resolved that I'm representing the

company. But their interests aren't all the same. Because when you get down a generation, some of them need money, some don't need money. Some are rich, some are poor. Some want to see the company grow, some want more money out of the company. . . . Those are relatively hard situations. But I just simply don't act. I let them sort it out and work it out. . . . The members of the family are a mother and five daughters. The husband of one of the daughters runs the business. The amount of his salary and bonus is an inherent conflict because the more he gets, the less there is left for the others. In fact, that's how I first got hired. They were in a fight over his employment contract—whether to pay dividends or leave the money in the business. It was a conflict in the sense that people have different needs. . . . Well, originally, they resolved it with a whole bunch of lawyers. And then they made peace and there's been peace ever since. When the mother dies and the "girls"—as I call them; they're all over sixty [. . .] fifties and sixties—become the real parties in interest, they may have a fight. Some may want to sell out. Should the corporation buy? Should other shareholders buy? Some may think, "Well, we'll get our best money by selling the whole business to somebody else." The husband of the one daughter who runs the business now has his son in the business and none of the cousins is in. There could be some tension. I don't know if there will be conflict.

S: And who would be your client at that point?

L: Well, my client, perforce—just by time—is the business and the son-in-law who runs it . . . and his son. 'Cause those are the people I deal with every day—every day. I could end up with no client. I'm sufficiently conflicted. And if any of the daughters object to my continuing to represent the company—because I'm really the president's lawyer [. . .] (He had a separate lawyer till about three years ago, four years ago. He did all his personal stuff.) But I'm terribly identified with him at this point, because I work for him. . . . When the mother dies—this is the goose that lays the golden egg—for the first time, the girls will have significant income—which now goes to the mother mostly. And, that cures lots of things. You know, a schoolteacher will have fifty, sixty, seventy thousand dollars in additional income. Chances are, she's going to be pleased. But they may not. They may decide, "Well, the other guy gets salary first. It should come out of his piece or her piece." It's easy to have problems. I'm hopeful we don't. . . . The problem with the business—it's kind of interesting—is the son-in-law—the head of the business—was brought in by his father-in-law. The father-in-law ran a [describes business] [. . .] almost a junk business. This guy has converted the thing to a [describes business]. Huge success. It has no relationship to what the father-in-law started. His reality is he made this business. The girls' reality is he fell into this business. Her father set him up in the business, and but for that, he wouldn't amount to anything. That's a conflict. And it surfaces all the time. I happened to be at a eightieth birthday party of the mother-in-law of one of the girls—who happens to be a client of mine—unrelated to this. And I'm very friendly with this daughter and her husband. So I said to her, "Is it more peaceful than it used to be?" (It clearly is.) And she said, "Well, there's never going to be peace as long as he—the president—gets so much more than we get." . . .

> So that conflict is not my conflict. But as long as I'm sitting there, I could be conflicted if they get into a fight. If this girl, for instance, said to me, "Well, you represent the president. I really don't want you in this argument," I'd have to get out. No question about that. Whether I should on my own initiative [. . .] It just seems to me it's working so well. It's crazy. But I'm very, very conscious of that kind of conflict. [80Ch10–19]

Death

> There's something in the nature of death that opens up old wounds. Whether it's family members or people who have been very close. . . . And so, I think . . . you start walking very gingerly and looking at people in the eyes very carefully. 'Cause that's when fights start. More so than almost anything else. [122CC<10]

As much of this chapter has illustrated, many of the most spirited and perplexing conflicts of interest in families arise at times of or in planning for transition—marriage, divorce, entering the work force, retirement—when interests shift, disagreements erupt, and coalitions change. Death, of course, is the ultimate transition at which lawyers, who have been able to maneuver deftly around the many family conflicts for so many years, finally get caught in the thicket of conflicted interests. The respondent quoted at the end of the last section speculated about changes in the family business and the relationship among siblings that may follow the death of the family matriarch and the possibility that he may be forced out of his forty-year representation of the family business as a result. That, of course, is exactly what happened to the respondent quoted at the beginning of the last section.

Death, then, provides the ultimate venue for potential conflicts of interest to actualize and for new ones to develop. Death often brings to light the multiple roles that the lawyer has somewhat invisibly played in the family. Death tends to liberate property and thereby stir up new interests and adversities among potential heirs that were quiescent or nonexistent when the decedent was alive and the property firmly in his or her grasp.

> I, at least, tell everybody and make it pretty clear at the beginning of an estate settlement—where, especially, conflict's more apt to arise on the death of a second spouse—that we're representing the executor and we're not representing the individual beneficiaries of the estate and, if they really have problems, they should get their own counsel. Nobody ever listens to that. It just goes over their head. Everybody's feeling fairly good about each other and what a wonderful family they are and how nice they support each other. They haven't started to deal with fighting over the money yet. And a few months later, they've all decided that they don't like each other after all and they're fighting over the money. And, we start to really get [. . .] be asked to be in the middle of those problems and referee those problems. Well, I'm very sensitive to the fact they exist. And I do tend to go so far. And then I . . . sit down with the executor, reach what we think is a fair resolution, and then throw it out to everybody and tell them, if they don't like it, to go get their own attorneys. Usually that shuts everybody up and they sign. [70DSS10–19]

Death often forges bridges across generations, stepfamilies, and disbanded nuclear families that had been unconnected and isolated during life. It creates new legal entities—estates—and roles—executors and beneficiaries—who often require legal counsel and turn to the conflicted lawyer. And, given gender-based actuarial tables and the greater proclivity of family patriarchs than of matriarchs to have ties with lawyers, death often creates lawyerless widows with unexpected legal problems, desperate to find someone trusted and familiar to help them in their time of grief. Widows, then, often join the other new entities and roles born in death in seeking representation from the family-business lawyer already mired in all the other family, business, and estate problems.

> We had one very visible fight . . . in the probate court against another firm our size—maybe a little bigger [. . .] In our view, they basically ignored what were pretty blatant conflicts. They wanted the business. It was a very good piece of business for them and it was an important client for them. It evolved around an estate. And they had represented some of the trustees in the estate. And they had been corporate lawyers with respect to some of the transactions that led to the purchase of the various assets. And then when the decedent died, they decided they were going to represent the widow—adverse to the trustees in fighting over some of the assets that they had played a role in purchasing. And to us, it was pretty blatant. And we filed a motion to disqualify, which they fought vigorously instead of admitting. And the judge slammed them pretty bad in both the disqualification and the subsequent sanctions. I think we learned from that lesson. [39Ch50–99]

The Tangle of Family Loyalties

This brief survey of the most common scenarios in which conflicts of interest arise in the representation of families highlights variations on the generic theme of "who is the client?" When the lawyer is representing organizational entities (the family business, the marital unit) as well as the individuals who compose these entities, when the lawyer is representing husbands and wives, brothers and sisters, parents and children, grandparents and grandchildren, estates and executors, heirs and benefactors, widows, cousins, stepfamilies, businesspersons and their spouses or children or parents, majority and minority owners of the family business—on matters related and unrelated, contentious and less adversarial, concurrently or sequentially, sporadically or repeatedly—who is the client at any one moment? What interests or confidences of former clients may be unexpectedly aroused by the latest legal problem of one of their relatives or in-laws? And how can the lawyer ensure that the representation of any one of these parties will not adversely affect his or her relationship with any of the others or be limited by the confidences of or obligations to any of these others, as the rules of professional responsibility ordain, given their intertwining lives?

Lawyers could avoid these conundra by braking the snowball as it first begins to roll, thereby stanching the inevitable avalanche. But this defensive strategy is as unwelcome to most clients as it is incompatible with the lawyer's own pecuniary interests. Clients seek out conflicted lawyers, for their expertise, inside information, trustworthiness, accessibility, or social contacts; because clients cannot admit their adversities with loved ones; or, if for no other reason, because they cannot afford another lawyer. There are, of course, situations in which, despite the entreaties and pressure to take the case, lawyers just say no, and other situations in which lawyers devise an artifice to maneuver around the conflicts. But as the respondent who agonized over his role in preparing "Dad's" will acknowledged, "Well, you're going to do it, and you'll face the consequences of it later if there are any."

ORGANIZATIONS

These themes in the representation of families foreshadow the structural sources of conflict of interest in constructed or more complex social organizations. The theme of adversariness, for example, an awkward undercurrent in the representation of families, is often cleaner in corporate or formal organizational settings. Here there is no dishonor in acknowledging differences, and simmering rivalries and competition between divisions or departments or tiers in the hierarchy are commonplace and de rigueur. So corporate lawyers need not tread lightly, gently suggesting to clients that their apparent harmony may be transitory or even illusory, as they sometimes must in families. Nor is it quite as likely that these lawyers will find themselves snarled in a conflict of interest some time into an engagement when the seeming unity explodes to reveal irreconcilable differences that they had not sensed at the outset.

The phenomenon I have referred to as snowballing is also less significant in formal organizational settings than it is in families. Organizations are more likely than families to be repeat players in the legal arena. They have repetitive legal needs that require special expertise, and they develop ongoing relationships with lawyers or firms (often many of them) that routinely provide these services. Separate product or geographic divisions or subsidiaries within the corporation may well have secured their own independent legal counsel and do not raid the stables of their corporate siblings or cousins when legal needs arise. Moreover, when unprecedented legal problems materialize, organizations tend to be better able to find appropriate counsel and better able to afford bringing a second lawyer up to speed, when necessary, than their family counterparts are. So the impetus to share one's lawyer with all the nodes in one's social network is more limited in corporate organizations than in family ones. This sweeping generalization should not blind us, however, to the "embeddedness" (Granovetter 1985) of the relationships of complex organizations to their lawyers—and the importance of trust, familiarity, and inside knowledge in selecting legal representatives—nor to the extent to which law firms market their practice and structure their expertise to facilitate and exploit corporate snowballs, thereby keeping all the client's legal business within the firm.

The greater clarity of adversariness and the diversity of legal talent characteristic of formal organizations brings into even sharper focus the other themes identified with family organizations: confounding questions about what is the unit of analysis and who is the client, the centrality of law in times of transition, and temporal features of lawyer-client relationships.

Partnerships

> But, I think, twenty-five years ago or thirty years ago, lawyers didn't even think about the conflict in representing people who were forming a partnership. Now, at least, I think they think about it and probably advise the clients of the possible conflict. I think there's probably a lot more disclosing of possible conflicts now. [46Ch20–49]

Partnerships represent the organizational form most akin to that of the family. They are relatively small, their structure flatter than that of most corporations, with the distribution of authority and responsibility not unlike that in a nuclear family. And as in families, law is central to the creation, transformation, and breakup of partnerships. Not surprisingly, they face some similar tensions surrounding conflicts of interest. For example, the impetus to minimize cost, complexity, and discord often results in reliance on a single lawyer to formalize partnership agreements.

> First of all, nobody wants to pay attorney's fees. They certainly don't want to pay two or three attorneys' fees. So, when they come into the firm—within the context of creating the company—they perceive that they have the deal worked out. And they don't each want to get their own attorney and pay all these different guys. They also perceive—rightly or wrongly—. . . that, the more attorneys you get involved, the more likely that there will be for conflict. (That is, conflict among them, not conflict like we're talking about.) And, to some extent, . . . they're correct. That is, lawyers tend to raise all the negatives. And it's only when faced with all the negatives, will people try to solve all the theoretical possibilities up front [. . .] most of which are never going to occur anyway. You never know which ones are going to occur, and that's the problem with being a lawyer. So they really—generally speaking, more often than not—want you to create that company. Just, "Yeah, we know. But don't bother us. Just let's get done with it." [81Ch10–19]

Though the process of drafting partnership agreements may be smoother and cheaper with one lawyer involved, the issue of transactional adversity, raised in the last chapter—whether it is possible to negotiate a fair deal or a neutral partnership agreement—remains.

> And the real problem is for me to [. . .], say, drafting a partnership agreement or something. How you draft it could [. . .] make a difference also, as far as whether you want to protect one party over another or if one party's bringing in more of the money. There might be certain things that you want in the agreement that would benefit one side, but not necessarily the other. . . . I mean, I think you can come up with a fair agreement. But I think people have to realize [. . .] I mean, we have to give advice on both sides. Basically, you have to play devil's advocate against ourselves, also with people. And I always think it's better in [. . .] some sort of a situation like that, if [. . .] each party has their own lawyer. But they don't want to pay the cost of a lawyer. So, yeah, I think it's a fairly common kind of thing. . . . They don't want to pay for two lawyers. [116Ch<10]

But the conundra raised by partnerships are not limited to this question of transactional adversity and whether a sole lawyer or firm can provide disinterested counsel to parties with potentially adverse interests. They also encompass intriguing puzzles about who is the client. Partnerships contain many entities, of course: the partnership itself, the general partners, the limited partners, all the partners. When an attorney creates and then serves a partnership, which of these entities is the client? And is the lawyer's understanding about who is the client shared by the varied entities?

> When you take three promoters of a business and then you incorporate it and then they become shareholders and now you had a corporation. Who's your client? Okay? And what lawyers don't understand is the relationship is consensual. You have to agree to be a lawyer. Now, who are you going to be a lawyer for? The company? Because if that's your decision, then having made it, stick to it. Now you're not representing those shareholders. And when they get into a fight or when they want to buy-sell, when they want to adjust their rights inter se, then they got to go somewhere else, okay? Because you are the corporate lawyer. . . . For example, if you wanted to really do it right [. . .] And you take these three guys and you make 'em shareholders, equal shareholders. And the next thing should be, "Okay, gentlemen, you are now a corporation. I no longer represent any of you. I represent ABC company." And then you bill ABC company and then you don't undertake to represent one or more of them in any battle with the third. You don't do it. The problem is that lawyers do. See, they let the relationship become ambiguous. [6Ch100+]

This mystery about who the client is in a partnership is compounded by the typical trajectory along which partnerships are conceived and brought to life. Frequently the lawyer who formalizes the partnership is not some anonymous agent plucked out of the blue and asked to balance the interests of multiple parties and entities. Rather, the attorney often has some preexisting relationship with one or more of these parties.

> I would say [the toughest conflict situation] comes when you represent a person and that person decides to form a partnership or a corporation and brings in a few investors. And then you begin doing work for the corporation. And then there's a dispute. And these other people are saying, "You represent the corporation; you represent the partnership. You must do what's best for the corporation. And we, of course, know what's best for the corporation. And it's not what your former client—who's now the president and fifty percent shareholder—wants to be done." . . . I think that's a tremendously difficult problem. [51Ch20–49]

Despite the expectations of the new partners, the lawyer may feel more abiding loyalty to the original (and often ongoing) client than to any of the other partners or to the partnership itself.

> Well, I have a case right now where we represent a joint venture that owns some trademarks. And one of the joint venture partners is a regular client of our firm

> and the other one is not. . . . We told the other joint venture partner that if a conflict developed between the two of them during the course of litigation, we might have to withdraw as representing the joint venture and just represent our original client. And their initial reaction was, "Well, I don't like this at all! We might get halfway through it." And we said, "That's right, we might get halfway through it. But we do represent client A. And now you—client B—and client A are asking us to represent joint venture C. And we'll be happy to do it, but we do have a higher loyalty to this guy." They finally signed off on it because when we talked about it we said, "The risks are probably pretty slim that there is going to be an adverse problem between us." But we had to let them know. And so they probably [. . .] decided, "Well, if we don't do it, maybe we're going to wind up having two sets of lawyers in here. And it's going to be twice as expensive to run the litigation, so why bother?" [18Ch100+]

Even more problematic than the situation in which the lawyer has a preexisting relationship with one of the parties to a partnership is that in which various parties, with different roles and stakes in the partnership, all have prior or ongoing ties to the lawyer.

> More normal is the situation where you have two clients who want to form a corporation and [. . .] then you represent both of them in the formation of the corporation and in a shareholder's agreement, okay? Or where you represent a joint venture [. . .] or an investment partnership, where an individual you represent is the general partner of a partnership. And you bring in limited partners as investors, because they're your clients. And he says, "Well, do you know anybody who'd be interested in investing in the deal?" Well, sure I know somebody [. . .] You know, it's a good deal. I'm an investor in the deal. "Sure." So I got the role being the investor, which is a limited partner; I represent the joint venture; I represent the general partner; and I represent individual investors in the deal who are other limited partners. And we've got a bunch of those. And if you think they aren't full of conflicts of interests? Absolutely. And does everybody know we have conflicts? Absolutely. And if there's litigation, would we be involved? Absolutely. [10Ch100+]

These examples suggest that, despite the intrinsic adversities of interest, attorneys seemingly wear many hats in their representation of partnerships and the various entities that comprise them. Several respondents, though, do specify limits.

> . . . you can have situations where a sixty-five-year-old potential shareholder comes in with a thirty-five-year-old potential shareholder—quote, "partners," if you will. And, therefore, one is more likely to die than the other. One is more likely to retire sooner than the other. And, therefore—within the context of buy-sell agreements, etc.—when you're drafting it, there would be a—depending on what you write, what form it takes—there is an advantage for the older or an advantage for the younger. And, within that context, sometimes you have to somehow make it very clear to everybody, get all the options out on the table. . . . If they don't want that

> second attorney, then you have to tell them both, "Well, if we do it this way, there's an advantage for the older. If we do it the other way, there's an advantage for the younger," or whatever the circumstance might be. So, you're kind of advising [. . .] You're giving them a course on corporate law—okay?—as opposed to tailoring their advice to the individual. . . . But, oftentimes, what occurs is two guys in their mid-thirties, whatever, well, two people of similar age will come together to form a business. So now you've no idea . . . what the future will hold. And, therefore, when you create that document, you don't know—nobody knows—who it might benefit, who's going to take greater advantage of it. [81Ch10–19]

Other respondents, who indicate a willingness to preside over the creation of a partnership, are reluctant to play a role in a subsequent transition—whether a dispute among partners, changes in ownership, or the demise of the partnership—in which the adversity of interests is more palpable.

> I happen to . . . be involved right now in a dispute between two of my clients who have been partners for fifteen years—buying and selling businesses and all that kind of stuff. And I've told them, "I'm happy to represent their businesses. I'm happy to represent them each in things that they're doing. But I am not going to represent them in connection with their dispute with each other. And furthermore, gentlemen, it may interest you to know that nothing you have said to me about your affairs with each other as partners is privileged any more. It's all discoverable. Because I've represented you jointly." And then I said, "I want you each to get your own lawyers." [51Ch20–49]

Complex Organizations

Answering the who-is-the-client question becomes more challenging in organizational forms that are comprised of far more complex structures than partnerships are—structures with multiple tiers, diverse roles and entities, and varied connections or affiliations among the entities. In such instances, the determination of who is and who is not a client may turn on considerable detail about the particularistic characteristics of the structures, relationships, and networks involved, information about which lawyers may not be especially knowledgeable.

> . . . there is simply no easy way to get [information on corporate structure]. Even annual reports only list major corporate affiliates. And so those are very tough to find. And we've had, on occasion, I can tell you, where someone says, "You can't do this, because you represent us." We say, "We don't represent you." And they say, "Oh yes, we're a remote subsidiary of So-and-So Corporation." Well, we didn't know that [. . .] [28Ch50–99]

> Before we were done, the partner responsible for the potential third-party defendant's parent pulled out an organizational chart. And it had looked like a lesson in Chinese algebra. . . . And this particular company probably has—on their organizational chart—thirty subsidiaries. [44Ch20–49]

Even if attorneys are able to find or reconstruct a complete organizational chart, the information contained therein does not stay accurate for very long. Because mega-corporations are constantly gobbling up other organizations; jettisoning various appendages; and making, breaking, and restructuring alliances, lawyers have a difficult time keeping apprised of the salient units and affiliations.

> But right now, it's pretty difficult. I mean, you really do have to know who's who. And with some of these corporations, they're buying and selling companies all the time. And so, all of a sudden, they've bought somebody that you didn't know anything about . . . because you weren't involved in the deal. Somebody'll call up and say, "Hey, your guy just sued our guy! What the hell?" "That's not in our system." "Well, we bought them last year." Well, how am I supposed to know? Am I supposed to read the paper and go through it every day? That's physically impossible. [18Ch100+]

Once attorneys map the shifting, undulating terrain, the next challenge becomes figuring out how to navigate through these complex structures.

> You're talking about a general partner of a limited partnership in which the limited partnership is a general partner of, indeed, another limited partnership, which is the limited partner of another partnership which is a general partner of a joint venture. And you have to just figure out who's who and what's what and who are we representing? And sometimes the very simple question, "Who are we representing?" is not capable of an immediate answer. [11Ch100+]

> But what about a case involving client XYZ? XYZ is a wholly owned subsidiary of ABC. ABC is in a joint venture with DEF. The law firm is suing officers and directors of DEF. There certainly is a direct possibility of conflict. [40Ch20–49]

In thinking about who is a client and the potential for conflicts, respondents distinguish between whether they are traveling up, down, or across organizational hierarchies as well as how attenuated the links are among corporate parents, children, siblings, half siblings, or former spouses. If the firm represents a parent, is one of its subsidiaries also a client, or vice versa?

> . . . a well-known Chicago retailer—not Sears . . . —another well-known Chicago retailer. For years, we have spent money on promotion, wining and dining—nothing. And it turned out that we got, on a reservation of rights from an insurance company, a lawn mower case. Someone had [. . .] purchased a lawn mower. And we got involved in litigation against a subsidiary of this retailer that—at the time we filed the lawsuit—we didn't know that they were a wholly-owned subsidiary. We just didn't know that. It was a small little branch. We got involved in a contract dispute. And inside counsel for this retailer—well known retailer—called me and pointed out that we couldn't [. . .] This guy, we wined and dined him. And I can't tell you what I told him, but I hung up the phone. . . . I said, "This is outrageous! First of all, we didn't know. We didn't know you owned this." And I

> said, "Yeah, that's a conflict, you got it." And I said, "We didn't know the subsidiary was yours. And we've got this stinkin' lawn mower case, and that's why you think we're your lawyers." I said, "We're not your lawyers. The hell with you." And I hung up the phone on him. And I've never heard from the guy again. Now, that was unusual, and I probably shouldn't have done that [. . .] [16Ch100+]

If the firm represents a subsidiary, is a sibling or half sibling subsidiary a client as well?

> For instance, we have represented [names a major corporation]. They're owned by [names a Fortune 500 conglomerate]. [The Fortune 500 conglomerate] also owns [names a major brokerage firm]. A while back someone asked us to look into filing a claim against [the brokerage firm], and when we saw the relationship, we didn't pursue it, even though the [brokerage firm] people and the [first corporation] people never see each other. [47Ch20–49]

If the firm represents a branch office of an organization, are other branch offices also considered clients? If a client organization splits apart, are all the various remnants to be considered clients?

> I think this case [. . .] is the toughest one we've had to resolve. Because it's such a unique situation, where, basically, you have a company that splits in two. And we represent the company. . . . And there's an agreement as to the split-up and the purchase price. A third party is coming in and buying the split-off party. And the question is, did we really represent both companies; do we have confidential information that works to a disadvantage to the split-off company? That was a very complicated one. We even got outside help on that one from [names a national ethics expert]. . . . after the split-off, you've got company A and company B. And company B is taking a position, "Hey, listen, you really represented us too—because B kept the name of old . . . single company—and you really represented us." The briefs are this thick on that one [. . .] I mean, we've got probably two or three of the best ethics guys in the country on affidavits saying what we did was perfectly all right and there's no conflict involved. But it was tough to decide because we knew it was going to be a big problem. . . . I mean, we gave a lot of thought to not doing the case. [18Ch100+]

Are there any conditions under which the firm can take an adverse position against this "relational or affiliational" client? Respondents indicated that these questions required some of the toughest calls they've had to make and complain that ethics rules and cases do not provide sufficient guidance.[5] Many respondents do not con-

[5]Shortly after I completed my interviews, the American Bar Association's Standing Committee on Ethics and Professional Responsibility issued a controversial nonbinding opinion on "whether a lawyer who represents a corporate client may undertake a representation that is adverse to a corporate affiliate of the client in an unrelated matter without obtaining the

sider the siblings and appendages of organizational clients to be clients and—with much soul-searching—have taken on cases adverse to the sibling's interests that do not compromise the firm's relationship with the original client. But because these judgments potentially threaten business relationships at least as much as they do ethical principles, attorneys make them cautiously and with much consultation.

Natural Persons

> But the old question: "Who do you represent? Do you represent the entity? Do you represent its owners? Do you represent its management?" . . . You ask yourself the question in a couple of different ways, for different reasons. The first is, "Who is responsible for paying the fee?" To a large extent, that will dictate who your client is. Because if you're going to send the bill to XYZ Corporation, that's who you are representing. [79Ch20–49]

Subsidiaries, branches, parents, and the like are not the only corporate entities about which attorneys must be cognizant in efforts to negotiate around conflicts of interest. Organizations, of course, aggregate the assets and act on behalf of many others—owners, shareholders, partners, and so on—who may assume or assert client status along with the organization itself. Moreover, as I noted at the beginning of this chapter, organizations cannot act on their own. They require the contribution of natural persons—officers, managers, employees, and others—who act as their agents. Although the latter may not assert client status, they often become synonymous with the corporate client in the minds of the lawyers who work with them and take direction from them, day after day and year after year. Organizations, then, not only serve as an umbrella of various ancillary organizational forms. They also collect a vast assortment of natural persons—owners, constituents, and agents—some of whom may hold client status as well and many of whom will have adverse interests on particular matters. Which of them are clients? And how do the interests of natural persons embedded in organizational structures create conflicts of interest for corporate lawyers?

> Transaction work, I think, is very difficult because I find a lot of the lawyers there don't know who their clients are and they identify with an individual when, in

---

client's consent" (American Bar Association, Standing Committee on Ethics and Professional Responsibility 1995). A slim majority opined that the lawyer may do so. Securing consent, it argued, is often prudent but is required only in circumstances in which the affiliate should also be considered a client, in which the client has instructed the lawyer to avoid representations adverse to its affiliates, or in which the lawyer's obligation to the corporate client or the new client adverse to the affiliate would materially limit his or her representation of the other. Critics lamented that the opinion shifted the burden of protecting the client under the conflict-of-interest rules from lawyers to clients, who must now instruct their lawyers to treat their affiliates as clients. (See also Romansic 1998.) Proposed revisions incorporated in the ABA Ethics 2000 report, if adopted, draw on this opinion, although the reporter for Ethics 2000 notes that "the Commission believes that there will be more situations in which the lawyer will be prohibited from undertaking representation than may have been reflected in that opinion" (American Bar Association 2001, Rule 1.7, comment 34; American Bar Association 2001, Model Rule 1.7, Reporter's Explanation of Changes, comment 34).

> fact, the client's the corporation. And then they may represent multiple corporations and individuals. They tend to put them all in the same pot when they do have competing interests. . . . where you have problems develop is where they thought they could sort all these interests out. But it wasn't up to them to do it. . . . [For example, you represent] a small corporation and its owners and then maybe the corporation gets sold to an acquiring company. Now you're representing owners of the former corporation, a buyer and a seller. They're now on opposite sides and you really haven't thought your way through that, because you're thinking of Don as your client. And so, as that evolves, and you want to hold onto all the business, now you really are representing diverse interests. And corporate lawyers think of themselves more, I think, of being brokers and people who can put together competing interests, where litigators don't look at it that way. [7Ch100+]

Even when attorneys can clearly identify which entity is the client, they face a second question regarding which of the multiple organizational officials and agents speaks for the organization:

> . . . representing municipalities, . . . you just wear a striped shirt and carry a whistle to the meetings. . . . And it was just a terrible situation. And the mayor would turn to you and say, "Well, who are you representing—me or the city council?" And the city council would say, "Well, who are you representing?" I think the city attorneys are placed in terribly compromising situations almost on an ongoing basis. And probably the best advice I ever received in that regard was from a person who had done some work for a long time in that regard and he says, "The best thing I can tell you is never give them an answer on the day you're asked it. Tell them you'll have to research and get back." He says, "Three-fourths of the time, it'll never come up again." And he said, "On the other fourth, you'll at least have time to prepare." [126DSS<10]

In other instances, attorneys explicitly act only on behalf of the organizational entity, but principals or shareholders assert that they are clients as well:

> What happened was we were doing corporate work for the XYZ Corporation. And Mr. Jones was the owner—the sole owner—of the XYZ Corporation. Mr. Jones then files a lawsuit against Mr. Brown—totally unrelated. . . . Is the client the XYZ Corporation or Mr. Jones? And so we had concluded that we represented the XYZ Corporation and that we were free to take the case . . . on behalf of Mr. Brown. . . . And it was a personal injury action that he had brought against Mr. Brown. And so it had nothing to do with the corporation. [Respondent then comments that he doesn't know whether the firm will continue to get the corporate work from XYZ Corporation any more.] [45DSL20–49]

Less problematic from a legal perspective, but more so from an interpersonal one, are the often inevitable scenarios in which the interests of the organizational agent with whom the lawyer has worked and taken his or her orders diverge from those of the organizational client. Though the attorney clearly owes fiduciary loyalty to the organization, the tugs of personal loyalty to the agent pull in the opposite direction. This dissonance is compounded because abrogating that personal loyalty in favor of institutional loyalty sometimes threatens the ongoing business relationship between the corporation and the law firm that is controlled by the agent:

> You could have a situation where an employee—top employee—is doing things that are deleterious to the operation of the company, to the detriment of shareholders or partners or closely held stock ownership. And yet you represent the entity, but at the same time, you have a close personal relationship with that person. Or . . . if you bring that up, you may lose the business. [105Ch<10]

Finally, whether because of the trust and intimacy that develops between corporate officials and lawyers or because law firms explicitly use snowball strategies to market other firm specialties to these individuals, lawyers often handle or are asked to handle personal matters for corporate agents. Some of these engagements are clearly adverse to corporate interests.

> We have a situation now where a senior employee, a CEO, is negotiating the actual purchase of that business from the ownership. That individual wanted to use us in his negotiations for the purchase of the business. We told him we were unable to perform that duty because we were already representing the corporation as a whole. And we had to decline that representation. . . . the [CEO] comes to us because they've dealt with us and wants us to represent them. And we have to make a decision as to who can we represent in that transaction, if anyone. And generally speaking, under those circumstances, since our representation is from the corporate position, we feel that if we are to continue in any role, it has to remain in the corporate role—even if it is likely that we'll end up representing [. . .] continue to represent this entity upon the completion of the purchase. We can't shift loyalties midstream. [108Ch10–19]

Other engagements that seem absolutely unrelated to corporate interests may eventually develop unforeseen adversities with the corporate client.

> Most of the large law firms that do a lot of corporate stuff have added matrimonial lawyers to their staff because, if they have very highly successful businessmen who want divorces, they don't want to miss that business. And they're quite frank about that. . . . if it's a closely held business and there's an issue of who owns the business in that dissolution [. . .] I can't imagine a situation in which that would not be an issue in the dissolution. I don't think that that makes sense. I think you're dealing with a lot of conflict there and that firm ought to keep the business [. . .] represent the business as such. 'Cause the business may be brought in—very often is brought in—as a third-party defendant in some of the financial issues. And I see that happen all the time. And I'm real concerned about it. Ultimately, they may end up disqualifying themselves when they get the business brought in as the third party. But I think that is way too late. If there's a divorce involving

shareholders in a closely held corporation, I think you have to send it out—the divorce out. And that is rarely done. And they'll tell you that "We've brought So-and-So into our firm because we kept seeing all these big divorce fees go and we didn't want to lose them." And I think that's wrong. Now, there's a sort of in-between area, where you might represent a businessman in a large corporation which is not closely held. And you might also want his divorce business because he's so successful and there's a lot there. . . . I think ultimately you can still get in a conflict. Because even though it's not closely held, his pension benefits may be involved in the divorce. . . . for sure, you'll have to [. . .] answer to subpoenas for his records. And I think, once the corporation receives a subpoena for his financial records, you've got a conflict. And you can see it coming. And I just [. . .] I know it's done. . . . I know it's happened. And I think, from day one, it's a conflict. Even if it's an amicable divorce, it's a conflict. If there is such a thing as an amicable divorce. [103Ch<10]

MULTIPLE CLIENTS

Inside Organizations

Conflicts of interest also arise in organizations when more than one natural person, and sometimes the organization itself as well, are named as defendants in a civil or criminal investigation or law suit. Because of the nature of collective action, many parties within organizational structures may be culpable or responsible—or alleged to be—for corporate harms, misdeeds, or malfeasance. A broad assortment of employees, supervisors, managers, accountants, and the like conspire in or contribute (sometimes unwittingly) to corporate fraud, price fixing, environmental pollution, medical malpractice, faulty products, industrial accidents, and other occasions for litigation. In other instances, organizations and their high-level officials may be held responsible for the misdeeds of or failure to impede or control the misdeeds of their employees—be it sexual harassment, police brutality, computer software piracy, copyright violations, or corporate bribery.

Because many corporate offenses or wrongs are hidden within corporate suites and complex organizational structures and then further obscured by elaborate cover-up schemes, investigations or lawsuits may initially name many more suspected wrongdoers, conspirators, or facilitators than were actually involved. This scattershot approach assumes that, ultimately, the true culprits will be culled from the pool, that the more innocent among them will identify or testify against those less so, or that charges will also stick against those with deeper pockets or greater ability to abort such misconduct in the future—the organization itself or its leaders. Of course, this assemblage of variously blameworthy parties needs legal representation. In many of these skirmishes, a single law firm will be solicited to represent the entire collection.

The impetus to rely on a single firm comes from a variety of sources. First, charges are often more successfully defended when a single law firm coordinates the defense and can demonstrate a united front among codefendants.

> You could take a position of saying, "Well, the simple way is [. . .] with every party, have a different lawyer." But there's two problems with that. First of all, . . . it causes litigation costs to just skyrocket, if you take that position all the time. And, secondly, it really—if there is no conflict—it is a much smarter thing, I believe, to have one attorney representing all the parties. Because . . . it's much easier if that attorney has everybody that he's preparing, working with for the trial, to keep everything in a control and make sure it's presented in a way that that unanimity gets emphasized. Once you get more than one attorney involved representing, you get the problem of the fact that you don't coordinate as well. [33Ch50–99]

Second, as this respondent noted, use of a single law firm obviously maximizes economies of scale. Joint representation minimizes defense costs for organizations, individuals, and insurers. Third, many insurance policies contain monetary caps from which both defense costs and judgments are paid; joint defense leaves more money available to cover judgments or settlements.

> But the securities claim has a common interest in defense too. And the problem that the directors and officers face, if you have to go out and hire counsel for every one of them, is that the insurance coverage for that will have a cap. And it includes defense costs. So that, as a group, their interest is to have one counsel, to make sure that they have enough insurance money there to pay a judgment. Because, if they all have different counsel, you can use up all of the insurance money just on defense costs. [47Ch20–49]

The interviews are filled with examples in which lawyers were asked to represent various constellations of parties within organizations:

> Now the employee, obviously, can potentially have a separate liability from the corporation. Normally, it's not a big problem because you have a coinsurer and it's—in all probability—going to be within the limits [of insurance coverage]. And no one gives a lot of thought to those. The tough ones come where you know that there's a potential to go over the limit. And the interests of the corporation can be significantly different than the interests of the individual. You don't always identify those at the outset. . . . I can think of—within the last week—an instance in which we started representing both the corporation and an individual. . . . And it was just an automobile accident. But it involved a large vehicle and there were serious injuries. And there is potential for it to go over the policy. We got into discovery, met with the individual, and—in the course of doing that—he said, "Well, you know, the brakes failed." Now, in this particular case, one could question whether or not that's accurate, given the fact that the bus that was involved was tested after the incident and no problem was found. Nonetheless, that's this man's story. And it obviously deserves to be heard, if he feels it should be heard. But what that presents is the potential for a claim against the employer saying, "You failed to maintain your bus properly." [68DSM10–19]

> Well, let's say—in an employment piece of litigation—you can have a situation where a supervisor and a company are both named. Typically, what we do is immediately go to the client that retains us—which is typically the corporation—and say, "We can represent you." Then they'll ask us, "Can you also represent our supervisor?" We'll say, "Yes, as long as you and the supervisor understand that, at some point, there may be [. . .] It may be in the corporation's benefit to point the finger at the supervisor, by saying whatever occurred was outside the scope of employment, etc." And, in that situation, obviously, we will want some kind of a written waiver from both the company and the supervisor. That's kind of an obvious example. Other than that, I guess, you just have to look at the facts that are alleged and look at the various legal theories that are possible to be asserted and try to see if there's ever going to be a point where one defendant would benefit by shifting all the blame or the liability to the other. . . . Once you get to that situation, obviously, you've got to raise the issue with the client. [82Ch10–19]

> . . . invariably, if it's a malpractice action, then they sue the clinic as an entity and they'll sue, say, the doctor. They may sue the hospital, as an entity, sue nurses, individually, who are employees of the hospital. They might sue an anesthesiologist who's independent contractor. And, boy, you get all of them in together. . . . And we're asked to represent all of 'em. Well, then, let's say [one] doctor . . . thinks that the first doctor was the one who really screwed up. And the first doctor thinks that "No, it wasn't me; it was the second doctor." We've had that situation come up. And we have talked with the doctors and said, "Now this is where the plaintiff is coming from. He's blaming both of you. And you think that, between you, that there should be some separation as to culpability or degree of culpability." And we have encouraged them that they should try to keep a united front, for example, and not get fighting among themselves if that's possible. If it is not possible—if they insist or if they think that this is where the error really is—then they'll have to get another lawyer. We've had that come up. . . . Then we'll contact the insurance carrier and say, "It looks like doctors A and B are feuding among themselves and we cannot represent both of them." . . . It gets into a problem where one of the doctors—two have been sued—one wants to settle, because he sees the potential exposure, he doesn't want the publicity—whatever reason—and the other one doesn't want to settle. And we get that. And we just sweat those out, to tell ya the truth. And we explain to the doctor, "Well, it's your choice. If you want to go to trial, we'll do it, if this one wants to settle." And we get that situation. . . . Well the problem there is, usually, the plaintiff won't settle with just one. And then you [. . .] Ughhh! Then you drink a lot of coffee and do a lot of talking to try to get the damn thing worked out somehow. The clouds open and the sun shines and then, "Hey! It went away! What's the next one?" It just gets to be real difficult at times. [67DSM10–19]

These examples also suggest some of the risks of adversity that inhere in such joint representation—the inability to maintain confidentiality across the codefendants, the likelihood that one party will point a finger at or seek to shift the blame to another, and the possibility that codefendants will have different preferences as to settling or litigating the charges. A perhaps more profound challenge posed by the opportunity to represent constellations of intraorganizational defendants involves determining the adversities of interest at the outset, so that potential conflicts can be identified and avoided. If the underlying conduct subject to litigation is complex and has developed over a period of time, such an assessment may be difficult. In light of these difficulties, a few respondents indicated that their firm routinely refuses to represent more than one party from within the organization. Most others, though, agree to do so when no definite adversities of interest are apparent at the outset.

Multiple Defendants

The examples cited in the previous section describe allegations of harm or misconduct committed by various parties *within* a given organization—a hospital, a trucking company, a publicly traded corporation. But harm or misconduct also arises from collective action *between* organizations or natural persons. Often the multiple parties named in civil and criminal charges come from different organizations that allegedly conspired in misconduct or collectively contributed to injury or harm—a score of chemical companies whose effluents polluted a river, a host of asbestos manufacturers whose products injured shipbuilders and their families, a group of friends who stuck up a liquor store. Though the impetus for defendants to seek legal counsel from the same firm may be less automatic here than in the intraorganizational context, many of the attractions are the same: economies of scale, significantly lower defense costs, the opportunity to present a united front. Respondents in firms of all sizes explain that the opportunity to counsel more than one codefendant represents one of the most common sources of potential conflicts of interest for their firm, arising as often as once a month or more.

Environmental and toxic tort litigation, such as that involving asbestos or Superfund, perhaps best illustrates the attractions of joint representation for multiple defendants. Many of these matters name large numbers of defendants, or what in Superfund litigation are called "potentially responsible parties" (PRPs). Respondents described a Superfund toxic waste site in Connecticut with 1,200 PRPs and another in Indiana whose 200 to 300 PRPs have depleted the entire population of environmental lawyers in the state. Such large numbers of codefendants pose many challenges for the legal system.

First, as evident in the Indiana example, the pool of defendants may exceed the number of experts qualified to defend them. The problem is exacerbated by the fact that Superfund dump sites are generally situated some distance from the upscale urban neighborhoods that house major law firms, even further limiting available local legal talent. The same can hold true in asbestos cases.

> Because, a lot of times you're sued in some small city and there's literally not enough lawyers to go around for all the asbestos defendants. So you have one lawyer representing two or three or more asbestos defendants. And there's full disclosure back and forth. And you say, "Fine, you know, no big deal." [73CC10–19]

Second, given the regional basis of legal practice and the fact that toxic waste dumps are generally filled by nearby companies, codefendants often have ongoing relationships with the same—usually small—set of local law firms that have served them on their routine legal needs and to which they naturally turn when named as a Superfund PRP. As a result, those firms may be conflicted out of representing any of these ongoing clients with respect to their Superfund problems.

> I do some environmental work as well. Potential conflicts come up in those cases fairly frequently. If we get a Superfund site that's, say, in the area—by that I mean, Gary, Indiana, Rockford, Illinois, sometimes Kansas City, Missouri—the waste trail seems to have included many local manufacturing plants. So they all get named as PRPs. . . . So we may have five or six local clients who—back in the '60s or '70s —generated a particular waste. And, unbeknownst to each other, they all ended up at the same site. Can we, then, represent more than one of those companies at the site? [87DSS10–19]

Joint representation is often compelling for the law firms as well, which don't want to risk losing all these clients forever to another law firm to which they were driven because of the conflicts of interest that arose over Superfund litigation.

> And it makes more sense for us because we're also keeping control of our different companies in the sense that we're doing the work for them rather than another law firm. And we hope that we're going to get a good result. Presuming we do, it's going to be us that gets it for them rather than some other attorney. [33Ch50–99]

Third, with so many defendants, defense costs often dwarf those of the cleanup itself and deplete the funds available for the latter (Acton and Dixon 1992).

> As we know from the Mansville bankruptcy and stuff, the defense costs are outrageous, compared to what goes out to the claimants. . . . under those circumstances, you have a heavy obligation to avoid big defense costs and stuff. So, I think—as a practical matter—you have to do that and try to keep some money left over for the poor injured folks out there. [73CC10–19]

Fourth, companies named in one Superfund site or one asbestos case are likely to be named in many others—one company described by a respondent was named in 20,000 asbestos cases—for which they will also need legal representation. Many of these thousands of other toxic tort cases will be populated with the same cast of defendant characters—though sometimes occupying slightly different positions in the hierarchy of culpability or responsibility or share of the effluents dumped—all seeking representation, often from the same cast of law firms with expertise in this area.

Fifth, for a given case, much of the necessary discovery and other legal work undertaken by each defense firm is repetitive or redundant and needlessly taxes the legal system, government officials, witnesses, victims, and others. There is no reason that depositions need be taken 1,200 times for the Connecticut Superfund site.

Much time and expense can be saved by aggregating or sharing some of the defense responsibilities and costs. Moreover, with a united front and the finest repeat-playing lawyers who can now finance full-out warfare with their larger base of paying clients, defendants increase their probability of vindication or at least reduce the magnitude of loss.

Of course, mass toxic torts such as asbestos and Superfund are the extreme cases—exceptions, perhaps, that do not prove the rule. Respondents suggest as much when they observe how conflicts rules are sometimes flouted or disregarded in this arena or when they suggest that the rules ought to be modified for these exceptional cases:

> The rule on that is there is no such thing as conflicts between asbestos defendants. Seriously, I think that's the universally accepted rule. [73CC10–19]

> And the dump sites, the Superfund sites, every time we represent a client in a new site, the thing just carries with it a whole baggage of other problems. . . . It just goes on and on. And they take a lot of time to resolve, and I sometimes wonder if the profession shouldn't develop a new set of conflict rules for those kinds of cases because they're just fraught with trouble. If you look at it from conventional conflicts rules, it's just almost endless and you try and identify them as you get into [. . .] It's tough. It gets to be very difficult. [pilot interview #6]

Joint representation is particularly compelling in these areas in which the numbers of defendants can be staggering, parties have relatively consistent interests, the legal costs overwhelm the potential liability, and codefendants are insured by the same company. Other examples offered by the respondents concern construction accidents:

> Often you'll find an insurance company that is suing everybody known to man in a construction accident. Often there will be forty different defendants involved. Our firm will be asked to represent three of the forty defendants in the case. If they don't have a beef with each other or a contract of some sort and are unlikely to become involved in pointing a finger at each other, then we go to the three defendants and say, "Here is the story. What do you want to do?" Generally, they will want to be represented. [12Ch100+]

In contrast, if the number of defendants is relatively small and the potential stakes high, defendants and their lawyers generally spurn multiple representation.

> . . . multiple representation in any kind of a litigation matter that's bigger than a bread box is a dumb idea. And you don't have to be a genius to convince people of that. . . . Yeah, it costs more, but the risk you run . . . is that you get to a week before trial and people start snarling at one another. [36Ch100+]

> We represent [names a major insurance company] in litigation involving tax shelters. The plaintiff sued [the insurance company]; they sued [a large securities

> firm]. [Securities firm] settled for twenty-five million dollars. We didn't settle. The judge just threw the case out. Now if we represented both of them—[securities firm] wanted to settle, [insurance company] did not want to settle—we'd have just a devil of a time. That's why we represented one defendant, one defendant. [Securities firm] did their silly things. We did our thing. And I didn't have to torture myself. It's too difficult, by and large, to represent multiple defendants. [30Ch100+]

Here, the modest cost savings from sharing legal fees among a couple of clients do not offset the potentially dire outcomes that might result if lawyers must temper their advocacy somewhat to accommodate the preferences of multiple clients or if they have to withdraw from the case in the eleventh hour when the seeming harmony and coincidence of interests vaporizes.

Criminal cases—with relatively small numbers of codefendants and potentially dire consequences—sometimes depart from this pattern. The departure is explained by less sophisticated clients, their desire to present a united front, and especially their inability to pay for separate attorneys.

> Probably most of my conflicts, if they develop, develop in the situation of codefendant situations. It's not unusual at all for us to get three or four defendants together in a codefendant situation. . . . And then it's not unusual at all for me, in those situations, I'll interview the first person, and . . . I'll explain the situation and the potential conflicts. . . . And typically at the most, it's—"Well, I didn't do quite as much as the other guy"—but they're all pointing fingers at one another. And they think it's going to make a vast difference. But, in reality, it really doesn't from the nature and extent of the statements. And they're acting in concert anyway. So, typically, when I talk to these people and advise them of the nature of the conflict, and so forth, I ask them also, "Do you want me to represent you only or do you have any problem with me representing the other people?" And I will give them that same explanation. And I find that, oftentimes, that they're far more comfortable with me representing either two or three in that situation. They actually, I believe, prefer it . . . They have one person working toward a common goal. I find also that the state likes it, if for nothing else than the economy of not having to deal with half a dozen different people too. [126DSS<10]

Though a Chicago solo practitioner who defends minor criminal charges disagrees:

> L: Take a barroom fight. There are two defendants charged with aggravated battery. Defendant A struck this person and there are allegations that defendant B also struck this person. Both say they didn't do it. I will pass on one of them.
>
> S: What happens when the defendants complain that they can't afford two lawyers?
>
> L: They can't afford to be represented by only one. [120Ch<10]

Balanced against the list of what, for many cases, are compelling reasons for joint representation, however, are the downside risks to which some of the previous quotes alluded, most of them versions of potential conflicts of interest. What are the prior relationships between the law firm and the various codefendant clients? Are some relationships more long-term, more lucrative, more important to powerful partners in the firm? In short, do some clients command more loyalty than others? And how will the legal fees be allocated among the various codefendants? How does the lawyer identify the interests of these multiple clients? Who speaks for them, especially if disputes develop among the group?

Of course, the most obvious and fundamental of the potential conflicts of interest faced by multiple defendants represented by the same lawyer arise because, as one respondent put it, "Basically, to the extent I'm trying to minimize my liability, I may be maximizing yours" [87DSS10–19]. Opportunities to minimize the costs to one codefendant, possibly at the expense of others, arise throughout the engagement. How attorneys structure and pace their case will affect some defendants differently than others. An extended example illustrates the differential impact on defendants of trial strategy, allegedly influenced by a conflict of interest, that resulted in a life sentence for an unlucky codefendant:

> And I was sent [for appeal] this record of two brothers, [names the brothers, here given the aliases "Tom" and "Joe"], who had been tried in a bench trial in front of Judge [names judge]. One lawyer represented both of them on a retain basis. And the state's case basically was that they had information that [Joe] was selling PCP out of the front door of this apartment. They went and made a controlled buy, did their little tests, and then went back to arrest. And [Joe] was arrested, found to have money, be in close proximity of the drugs by the door. And [Tom], who is his brother, was at a table with two or three other people, and according to the police testimony, he picked up two packets and handed it to a girl who stuck it under her sweater, or whatever. And it turned out to be Class X amounts of PCP. The trial was very strange to me because the lawyer represented both clients. He had [Tom], who had two prior felony convictions, get on the stand and basically deny that any of this had happened. [Joe] never testified. And judge found them both guilty and found [Tom] guilty of possession with intent to deliver, which made it a Class X. Otherwise, it was just a Class 1. [Joe] got ten years. And [Tom] got natural life, because it was his third felony. . . . Well, they send this record over to me and I made a motion to the appellate court to appoint separate counsel for [Joe] on the basis that I had a conflict in defending both of them on appeal—which usually, as you're probably aware, it's less likely you're going to have a conflict on appeal than a trial. . . . The appellate court citing said there is just simply not enough in this record to say there was a conflict of interest and that the lawyer couldn't give an effective assistance to [Tom]. And this is where it gets subtle. My argument was that, had a lawyer representing [Tom]'s interest only said, "Hey, obviously the evidence is [Joe] is a seller of drugs. [Tom] is his brother and all [Tom] was trying to do was to conceal the evidence from the raid, from the police entering the building. So this is not an intent to deliver—possession with intent to deliver—this is a possession with intent to conceal to help your brother out." Which would have brought it down to a Class 1 and which would have voided the mandatory life sentence. Well, the appellate court in their opinion . . . basically

said, "Sorry, you can't speculate on what somebody would have done." . . . But it, to me, this lawyer went in there, and there was only so much money and he wasn't going to share it and he went ahead and represented both of them. I thought it was just outrageous. . . . I sit there as an experienced criminal defense lawyer and say, you've got to be crazy to try this case, with the word of a convicted felon against three police officers, and think you're going to win on a bench trial. . . . And the defense, to me, was obvious—that you should say, "Yeah, he possessed the stuff." . . . And it didn't seem to me the lawyer was looking out after [Tom]'s interest. And if [Joe] really was the drug dealer, probably [Joe] was the paying client. . . . I mean, I'm saying, "[Tom], you told me this guy never talked to you about you having separate counsel or explored the possibility of defending on the basis of agreeing with the cops?" And he said, "No, he never talked to me at all. He talked to my brother. And then, suddenly we're in court and we're on trial." [113Ch<10]

Even more thorny than questions about trial strategy are those issues that develop further down the road regarding pleas, settlements, offers of immunity, monetary judgments, and the like. These potential adversities of interest among codefendants arise from different degrees of culpability or responsibility for the alleged injuries or misconduct, different amounts or kinds of insurance coverage to pay for legal fees or for judgments or settlements, different net worths or other assets to fall back on, cleaner or dirtier criminal records, varying degrees of risk aversion, concern for reputation, or tastes for conflict or conciliation—which make some deals more attractive to some defendants than to others. Prosecutors and plaintiffs sometimes exploit or exacerbate these potential adversities by employing divide-and-conquer strategies toward codefendants represented by the same attorney. For example, they offer settlements or plea bargains to some defendants but not to others:

I represented multiple business entities as defendants. And the plaintiff's lawyer offered to settle the case with some of my clients and not the others. That was after the case had been pending like four years and we were a year away from the trial. You can see that, on the surface, if I'd accepted that offer without thinking about it—because I thought it might have been a good thing for those who were being offered a settlement—I'd be funding the fight to continue against my other clients. So I—not alone, but with two other lawyers—dug into the facts and the law and the rules of ethics and decided that it was not in the best interest of those offered a settlement to take it. That was both a legal and a factual thing. I then disclosed to everybody what had happened and told those who had been offered the settlement that, if they disagreed, to let me know. And I gave the reasons why I thought it wasn't a good settlement. That was very difficult. And we did have a letter, by the way, which I had drafted at the beginning that, if there were conflicts, that I could withdraw from, as I remember it, from some, but not the others. But if I had concluded that it would have been in the best interest of those who had been offered the settlement to get out, I certainly could not have continued in that representation of the whole group. . . . That one stuck in my memory as the most troublesome one because it took us, maybe it was four or five days before we could really feel

> comfortable with the rules of ethics and the facts in the law that our conclusion was correct. I happened to have been vindicated because the case did go to a jury and all of the defendants were found "not guilty." But . . . you don't know what's going to happen when you're making that decision. [4Ch100+]

Or they make the offer contingent on all defendants accepting it:

> One guy wanted to plead and could get a good deal, and the other guy didn't want to plead. And there were times when [the prosecutors] said they wouldn't take a plea without everybody pleading. And they had enormous power. I mean, at that time, armed robbery was probationable or could be one to life. So here's somebody charged with an armed robbery. And says, "Hell, I'm not stupid. I'm not going to take a chance on twenty years in the penitentiary. I'll plead if they give me probation." And they got a weak case. And the other guy says, "Screw you. I didn't do anything. I'm not going to plead." And the prosecutor is saying, "No, I'm not going to take one without the other." And that's a huge conflict of interest for a defense lawyer because then you've got to put pressure on one. And I'll tell you very honestly, I pressured a lot of people to plead guilty in those days, because they were dead bang on the evidence. I had a judge who would give away the building for a plea—especially if it was a good golf day—and who, if you went to trial, would add ten, fifteen years to your sentence. I mean, the most commonly punished offense in those days was the offense of jury trial. [113Ch<10]

Or they offer immunity from prosecution to some in exchange for their testimony against the others.

Once a settlement is reached or a judgment imposed, codefendants must resolve how to allocate costs among themselves—another stress point in the delicate fabric of their union. When these defendants begin filing third-party complaints or cross claiming for contribution against each other, formerly abstract adversities of interest become real and the law firm representing them all faces a potentially serious conflict of interest.

> PRPs may be adverse with respect to the allocation formula—is one really responsible for 1 percent and another for 20 percent of the waste? It is hard to represent more than one company on allocation disputes. [38Ch50–99]

With the clear, twenty-twenty vision of hindsight, many of us probably read through these examples and clucked our tongues that the attorneys should have known better and turned away these requests or opportunities to represent more than one defendant. The problem is that many of these differences among the clients that ultimately posed significant conflicts of interest for their attorneys were not at all apparent at the outset.

> L1: . . . the problem can arise when there are multiple defendants who you think are aligned on the same side. And, as the case develops, they turn on each other and [. . .]

MP: And frequently, that's x number of years down the road. . . . and exiting at that point is enormously difficult. Because one client has already invested a lot of time and effort in getting us up to speed, paid us a lot of fees, etc.

L1: . . . usually, when these cases start out, everyone wants to present a united front and not let another defendant know that, "If worse comes to worse and we lose, it's really their fault. They're 90 percent to blame and we're going to [go] after them." No one likes to think of those things. They're all gung-ho to beat up on the plaintiff, if they're all defendants. And these issues sometimes are not addressed as quickly as they should be. Or no one can foresee the facts as they develop. Everyone may think that, if we take down defendant A, defendant B really was a passive bystander in this whole process. And we don't understand why they were even joined by the plaintiff as a defendant, and maybe they don't either. But a year goes by and, in discovery, smoking guns come out of the woodwork, and they're clearly to blame, . . . and all hell breaks loose. [5Ch100+]

Respondents identify several simmering adversities in the interests of multiple defendants that emerge over time: it may become apparent that some are much more responsible for the harm than others, that the apparent esprit de corps was illusory from the beginning or broke down under the strain of litigation as coclients begin pointing fingers at each other. When, belatedly, lawyers make these discoveries, they face conflicts of interest that may force their firm to withdraw from representing some or all the parties. Other firms, believing that such conflicts are inevitable, refuse to get involved in the first place.

So how, then, can defendants enjoy the advantages of collectivizing under the counsel of a single law firm while minimizing the risks that such conflicts of interest will develop and sabotage their representation? The interviews contain several examples of repeat-playing clients that band together and work out in advance how they will allocate legal fees and deal with the various adversities of interest that are likely to develop as the case evolves—thereby insulating their lawyers from becoming embroiled in their conflicts and potentially forced to withdraw from the engagement.

> We are involved with one client right now—whom we have represented in a lot of litigation—whereby . . . the clients, among themselves, have banded together and selected one firm—our firm—to represent them. And they have—we're advised—written understandings and agreements among themselves that they won't counterclaim back and forth against one another . . . and that they will share the common defense. And so that's an agreement that was reached among themselves. And then that group of defendants—banded together like that—came out and hired us. So that was all taken care of when we were hired. We had the understanding up front—when we were hired—that, "Look, don't worry. . . . we have this agreement among ourselves. And you're going to represent all of us. And there'll be no counterclaims; there'll be nothing. And you go ahead." [45DSL20–49]

In other instances, these coalitions are constructed by the separate law firms that represent each defendant and that can handle any disputes that arise among the codefendants in the future. This arrangement thereby buffers the law firm representing the collectivity from involvement in intramural disputes among the coparties:

> But the PRPs have many issues in common. A group of them may be sued by two dozen plaintiffs. They argue in common that the plaintiffs are not entitled to any recovery, that the claim is not consistent with what they are entitled to. Each of these defendants will be represented by their own law firm. And the defendants and law firms will elect to have our firm represent them all on these common issues as well as to serve as liaison in the litigation—to distribute the forms, to ensure that only one voice is speaking in court, to trek up to Rockford to make court appearances, etc. In this instance, we got a stipulation from each of the defendants regarding exactly what our role was and what common issues we were representing and that we wouldn't be conflicted out on unrelated matters. And then we got everybody—including the law firms—to sign off on it. [38Ch50–99]

Often these coalitions will formalize a structure for identifying the interests of the group:

> Typically, what we have tried to do is to have the group identify a committee that will speak for the group and that we are bound by what the committee says, not what any one individual may say. And that is part of the understanding when we get into the client relationship. Sometimes where that hasn't been in place and an individual was unhappy with the group representation, we have just let them engage their own separate counsel. [49DSL20–49]

And they will determine how members will deal with future disputes about apportioning liability. Multiple insurers providing coverage for a single defendant may make similar arrangements.

Multiple Plaintiffs

Just as more than one organization or actor may be collectively responsible for crime or injury, multiple parties may be harmed by the actions of others—whether because they were all together at the time of the incident (e.g., a plane crash); because they were all exposed to the same product (e.g., asbestos or silicone breast implants); or were all creditors, customers, or victims of a bankrupt, negligent, or disreputable business or professional. Multiple plaintiffs have some of the same incentives as multiple defendants to collectively seek representation from the same lawyer. They enjoy economies of scale. They can split legal fees and thereby afford a better lawyer or mount a more vigorous case. Their sheer numbers may evince credibility or have evidentiary value, implicitly suggesting to jurors that the injury did not result from a fluke but from more systemic negligence or misconduct. And the magnitude of their collective injuries may be so high as to induce defendants to settle rather than contest the charges.

When the legal costs of asserting a claim overwhelm the size of the potential award, plaintiffs, like defendents, are more likely to collectivize. But there is one wrinkle on the plaintiff side not found on that of their adversaries. Many personal injury lawsuits are taken on a contingency fee basis. Here, unsuccessful plaintiffs do not have to pay legal fees; the attorneys of successful ones take a fixed percentage of their awards. As a result, an accident victim awarded $100,000 will pay legal fees of, say, $30,000 regardless of whether he had his own attorney or shared one with five other victims of the same accident. He saves no money by joint representation with other plaintiffs.

So why collectivize in a contingency fee regime? First, the likelihood that the claim would be successful may be so low or the expected award so small that few lawyers would be willing to take the case on a contingency basis. By aggregating a number of similar but modest claims, the overall expected judgment may be high enough to induce a skilled attorney to invest the requisite effort to prepare and argue the case. Second, collectivization may be necessary to balance the talents and war chests of the two sets of adversaries. Plaintiffs frequently face repeat-playing defendants whose experienced attorneys have contested similar claims many times before and who have deep pockets and hefty insurance policies to finance such litigation. By joining together, plaintiffs may better equalize or advance their position relative to that of their adversaries (Galanter 1974). Third, given the social ecology of injury or victimization, some multiple plaintiffs are members of the same social network—families, neighbors, coworkers—and wish to draw on their solidarity, trust, and mutual support to navigate through the sometimes arduous civil litigation process together with the same lawyer. And, of course, not all civil litigation is funded by contingency fee arrangements; some potential plaintiffs pay by the hour, bills that are substantially reduced when split with fellow plaintiffs.

So—like defendants—plaintiffs with certain kinds of claims enjoy considerable advantage by joining with others. And, like defendants who band together, they create conflicts of interest for their lawyers. The following engagement letter, sent by an attorney to two coworkers charging their employer with racial harassment, details many of the pros and cons of joint representation:

> "Dear Blank and Blank. This letter is intended to set forth the impact and potential conflicts of interest that could arise, since you have both decided to retain me to represent you together. There are both advantages and disadvantages of this arrangement, of which I believe you should be aware. The advantages include your strength in numbers. Your cases are similar, in that you both have been subjected to racial harassment by the same party. While one of you versus the company becomes a credibility contest, where there are two of you, there is suggested a pattern. Moreover, there is something about the two of you each explaining what really happened, that I find very compelling, and I expect a jury would see the same way. Additionally, dividing most of the hourly rates by two makes this matter significantly less expensive than if you each had to bear the cost yourself. And, since much of the same discovery will need to be done for you both, I believe the litigation process itself will be more efficient. The potential disadvantages are, first, as among the two of you and your lawyers, there can be no confidential communication. Everything that each of you tells us may be shared among all of us, even though it is confidential and privileged as to any third-party—that is, an out-

sider. This requires a commitment to candor and to working together towards a common goal. Second, while your cases are very similar, there are always differences personal to each of your own experiences. For example, Blank has received a poor annual evaluation and, to date, Blank has not. Furthermore, your employment histories at the company are distinct and you are not earning exactly the same salary. Consequently, if an offer of settlement is made, you each will probably have different losses and, thus, may be entitled to a different percentage of a settlement amount, if a total amount is offered to settle the two cases. The same is true with regard to each of your cases before a jury. Each will be slightly different and may result in a different damage award, should your case go to trial. Occasionally, defense counsel will try to divide and conquer by offering to settle one claim and not others. Other unforeseeable things relating to life situations can happen causing, for example, one of you to need a continuance, while the other is ready to go to trial. In each of these scenarios, including a great number of other possibilities, we would have to evaluate whether the potential conflict of interest has turned into a real conflict. It is possible to go ahead and settle one person's case and not another without conflict. But, if there is an insoluble or irreconcilable conflict, we may have to withdraw from representation of one or both of you, if it becomes apparent that we can't represent you both to our fullest extent. It is really the last point that is the key. All of us need to feel confident that I can represent each of you in such a manner that our loyalty and efforts for one of you do not interfere with our loyalty to and efforts for the other. Having said all this, we would not even consider representing you both, if we did not believe that it is likely the advantages outweigh the disadvantages. Please give me a call to discuss this letter before you sign below, confirming that you are aware of the potential problems and you agree to this joint representation." [118Ch<10]

The rhythms and junctures in an evolving civil case at which conflicts of interest among multiple plaintiffs become problematic parallel those described for defendants who band together. Just as codefendants bring to the case different degrees of culpability or responsibility for the injury or misconduct, coplaintiffs may also have played different roles in the injury or victimization that befell them. One classic example was offered repeatedly in the interviews:

A situation, say, where one client is driving and the other is a passenger and they're involved in an accident and there's some question about who was at fault. The passenger has a cause of action against the driver, under the guest statute. And frequently both parties will come to the same lawyer to seek representation against the driver of the other vehicle, say. And, yeah, we definitely let people know then that there's a potential conflict, because what's best for one party may not be best for another. . . . we had a situation where our client was riding a motorcycle. She was a passenger on a motorcycle. . . . And they were involved in an accident. And liability did not look good against the other party. It looked like it may have been the motorcycle driver's fault. And, I mean, I pushed very strongly for us not to represent the motorcycle driver because I thought that the passenger's best bet was against the guy whose motorcycle she was on and not against the other party that they were involved in the accident with. So that gets me to not represent the driver. [116Ch<10]

The same kind of adversity among plaintiffs arises in other scenarios in which the conduct of one plaintiff may have contributed to or precipitated the injury to others.

We're involved in a case that's assigned in a multidistrict litigation panel on the east coast. And there are a lot of plaintiffs and a handful of defendants. And, although we are one of the plaintiffs, we have elected not to go into the plaintiffs' group. It's not a class case. But there's a plaintiffs' discovery group that we are not part of because the principal plaintiff in that group has a claim that we feel is tainted by his own conduct. And, ultimately, we really are adverse to them because their claim is so big and, we believe, so tainted, that, in the end, it ought to be knocked out—make the pot bigger for everybody else. And to cooperate a whole lot with that particular party is problematic in some respects. You don't want to be in a situation where you, you know, lawyer to lawyer talking about your theory of the case and divulge a work product, where you've got really adverse positions—even though you're both plaintiffs. [104Ch10–19]

Plaintiffs' interests may be adverse not only because of differences in fault, negligence, or contribution among them but also because some plaintiffs have priorities in compensation over others. Here, bankruptcy cases—sometimes with thousands of creditors—are the classic exemplars.[6]

Well, you have to make sure that they have the same interests. And if they have the same interests, I think that that's not a problem. But, say, in a bankruptcy situation where one of the firm's clients is a senior lender and another of the firm's clients is an equity holder—so that they're at different places in the capital structure of a bankrupt estate. We wouldn't feel comfortable without a lot of disclosure and a lot of formal waivers, I think, representing those kinds of adverse interests in a bankruptcy. [17Ch100+]

The most palpable conflicts in joint representation of plaintiffs (as was true for defendants) arise around the resolution of the case—whether to settle or go to trial and how to divvy up the pot among the multiple plaintiffs. When defendants proffer a settlement offer, will plaintiffs agree about whether to accept it or, rather, to persist with litigation? Plaintiffs are likely to differ in the significance of their injury or harm, in how quickly they need to be compensated or their ability to withstand (physically or economically) a protracted trial, in their risk aversion, in their psychic need for a public trial and vindication or a retributive outcome, or in their desire for immediate closure, such that some plaintiffs may value an expedient settle-

[6]Though they came up infrequently in my interviews, so, too, are mass tort class action settlements—where attorneys can represent tens of thousands of parties with different injuries (some not yet even realized), legal preferences, and interests. See, for example, Menkel-Meadow 1995.

ment much more than others. Some may place priority on cutting their losses, whereas others will spare no cost for a psychic victory. A downstate lawyer reflected on this dilemma when investors of very different backgrounds lose their shirts on a failed oil drilling venture.

> Well, the problem always is going to arise, though, is, "Who's in charge of the ship and do we want to go ahead and pay a lawyer a bunch more money to win this case? Or should we take the amount that's on the table and go away and just cut our losses? Or are we going to force somebody into bankruptcy?" . . . that's what I would see when you're trying to represent a bunch of people—especially a bunch of investors from all over. And some are going to be mad and some are going to be sophisticated and want to cut their losses and others are going to want blood on the table. And that's where you'd have a problem. [63DSS<10]

Even more thorny conflicts of interest arise when plaintiffs' lawyers secure a lump sum settlement or award and face the prospect of dividing it up among multiple clients.

> Generally, the parties' interests only come to any divergent stage during settlement. And it depends on who you're dealing with. And it depends on the parties. And it depends on the types of offers that the defendants make. Some defendants try to put you at odds with your clients and try to cause you to have a conflict. Other defendants aren't quite as devious, and make an honest, legitimate offer separately to each of the plaintiffs on the case. It depends. We've had both situations happen here. [121Ch<10]

Both plaintiffs and defense attorneys interviewed in the study disparaged the conduct of other plaintiffs lawyers around these allocation issues.

> I mean, we see conflicts all the time. . . . I've got a case right now where the plaintiffs lawyer has sued [a] railroad on behalf of fourteen hearing-loss plaintiffs. And it is not uncommon in those settings to sit down with the plaintiffs lawyer and say, "Let's settle all these cases." And if you do that and if you arrive at a figure for all fourteen cases, he's got a horrible conflicts problem. How is he going to divvy up the money among his clients? That happens all the time. Or he sits down and he says, "Look, Client A—I can get by with five grand for him. But Client B is a hard-nosed guy, and I need twenty-five for him." In effect, he's letting me settle cheap on some, so he'll pay more on others. I mean, those kinds of situations are fraught with all kinds of conflict problems. In a perfect world, every client would have his own lawyer. But then, if that happened, we'd need even more lawyers then we got now. And that's not a very good idea. [106Ch20–49]

Triangular Relationships

When lawyers represent multiple plaintiffs or defendants, the who-is-the-client question is easy to answer: *everyone*. The difficult tasks involve ensuring that the interests of these myriad clients remain compatible through the course of the engagement and resolving how best to serve them all when they do not. The question is much more problematic, however, in a special case of joint representation—sometimes labeled "triangular lawyer relationships" (Hazard 1987) or "the eternal triangle" (Wunnicke 1989)—in which, generally, the party who pays the legal fees is different from the party in need of representation. Such triangles are most common in situations in which insurance policies provide for the defense of liability claims against policyholders, but they are also found when employers pay for the representation of their employees or family members for their children or relatives (recall the example of the teenager arrested on DUI charges) or where litigation is supported by a public interest group. The tension that surges through the triangle, between the interests of those who pay the lawyer's bill and those whom the lawyer actually represents, was illustrated earlier in this chapter in the case of the two brothers convicted of drug charges, with the nonpaying free rider brother now spending his natural life in prison. An even cleaner example is provided by a murder trial in a small town in downstate Illinois:

> I had another one—it was a murder trial. . . . Murder trials are rare around here, by the way [laughter]—one a year. . . . The public defender was representing the defendant. And the defendant's mother came to the public defender and said, well, they wanted to hire another attorney . . . and she might be able to scrape the money up. And the public defender talked her into giving him the money and he would represent them privately and so on and so forth. And the public defender did not bother—the appointed counsel—did not bother to tell the court about this. It's very clear to me why he didn't bother to tell the court about it. Because he could charge all of his expenses—the copying, deposition expenses, and everything else—to the county and not have to have to take those out of his fee. But the interesting thing to me was that the mother was potentially a beneficial witness to the defendant in the case, but what she had to say was incriminating to her. And the defense coun [. . .] the appointed counsel did not have the mother testify. I wondered about the fact that she had . . . paid the fee—$25,000 or whatever it was—might have had something to do with the fact [. . .] It seemed like it. Anyway, . . . at the sentencing hearing, the defendant got up—for, really, unrelated reasons to all of what I've told you—and said he wanted to fire his attorney—after he had been convicted. And the court said, "You can't, he's appointed." And the defendant said, "Oh no, he's not." And so it all came out. Then I was—while I was on vacation—was appointed to represent the defendant, and did, and found all this out, and brought it to the court's attention. And it's in the nature of the same kind of conflict . . . I was asking to have the verdict overturned, though. [70DSS10–19]

Ironically, here, as in the drug case, the appellate court was not persuaded that the conflict of interest in which the defense lawyer was entangled and that arguably affected his trial strategy to the detriment of the client was sufficient grounds to overturn the conviction or to order a new trial. Nonetheless the tension is there: the mother's interest in paying the bill but not in testifying was antagonistic to the interests of the client, whose mother's testimony might have resulted in an acquittal. We will never know whether the first attorney was influenced by the interests of the mother. Nonetheless, perched on the tip of the triangle formed by mother and son, he faced a clear conflict of interest.

Because about a fifth of the law firms in the sample have an insurance defense practice and because many other respondents routinely represent plaintiffs who sue these insureds, many of the interviews contained lively discussions about the ethical conundra created by the much more common triangles that connect insurance companies, their insureds, and their lawyers. Who is the client in these eternal triangles? Though some attorneys might argue that both the insurer and the insured are clients (Hazard and Hodes 1990, 245), most lawyers—including those in my study—would answer only the latter. Often, though, in the same sentence or paragraph in which these respondents expressed their exclusive fiduciary obligation to the insured, they would unwittingly commit the Freudian slip of calling the insurance company a client. The mistake is understandable. Law firms usually have one-shot dealings with the parties they defend under liability insurance policies but have long-term relationships with the insurers who assign them this ongoing stream of business and to whom the lawyers often feel beholden.

> It's an easy issue. A lawyer's obligation is to the insured, not the insurance company. However, we make it clear, if there is a problem [. . .] And I'll tell you how exactly these come up, because it comes up all the time—I mean, *all the time!* We make it clear to the insured: "Hey, look it. I'm your lawyer. My primary obligation is to you. But let's not lose sight of the fact that I'm going to represent you in one case, but I've got a hundred cases for that insurance company. You can certainly feel uneasy and say, 'Why is this lawyer really serving me? When I'm long gone, he's got to make the insurance company happy.' " I said, "I feel strongly about my obligation to you. But it's more important how you perceive it. And, therefore, if you are uneasy at all, you should seek separate counsel—at your own expense—and talk it out with him and have that lawyer call me to express your views, if you feel that those views need to be expressed." [76Ch10–19]

Respondents concede that these obligations to insurers reflect business and not ethical considerations. But the former can significantly compromise their ethical obligations to their real client—the insureds—whose interests in resolving their alleged liability swiftly and with no added risk or cost to their reputation or pocketbook often collides with those of their insurer. Recall, from the last chapter, that lawyers are deemed to have conflicts of interest when their representation of a client is materially limited by their responsibilities to a third party. Clearly, the stage is set for conflicts of interest within these triangles.

Potential conflicts among the interests of insurers, insureds, and lawyers surface at several junctures in the defense of a liability claim: (1) disputes about insurance coverage, (2) disputes about the expenditure of funds for the defense of the insured defendant, and (3) disputes about litigating or settling the charges, especially when the claim exceeds the amount of coverage. A fourth kind of conflict of interest arises when the insurance defense law firm makes a claim against an insured of an insurance company "client" that routinely sends the firm unrelated business.

> I have terrific conceptual problems with insurance defense-type cases—terrific problems. I may have a problem of how far I can go in pressing the insured's interest against the party who is paying my bill. A problem of how far can I hammer another insurance company that I also represent. Taking plaintiffs cases against defendants who I know are going to be represented by insurance companies that I represent. Professionally, I can divorce those questions pretty easily because I know what the law is. It is the gray area. When you get in that gray area, that's when it becomes a tough question. And, obviously, you just do the best you can and you probably err on the side of staying away from the—what even may appear to be—the conflict. Just because you just don't want the hassle. You don't want the problem. I don't want the problem. [54DSL20–49]

Coverage. Not all forms of liability are covered by a particular insurance policy. The harm or injury might have been inflicted outside the period of coverage. It might have resulted from intentional or "willful and wanton" conduct—not covered—rather than from stupid or negligent acts, which are. The defendant or policyholder might have done something to void the insurance contract. And so on. Many of these temporal or behavioral subtleties that void coverage are only apparent upon close examination, perhaps uncovered as the defense lawyer questions his or her client in preparing the case or in the process of pretrial discovery. At this moment—when the lawyer has obtained information of potentially great interest to the insurer, which hopes to limit its liability, but damning to the insured—the third corner of the triangle begins to pull. Middle-aged and older respondents in the study reminisced that, in the early years of their legal practice, practitioners routinely attended to that tug.

> Good Lord, thirty-four years ago, one of the first cases in that was where the attorney representing the individual, deliberately—at his own client's deposition—asked some questions which, in effect, voided his coverage. And then told the insurance carrier and they disclaimed coverage. And nobody saw that as a conflict until that time. Well, obviously, it is. [66Ch20–49]

The law has since changed on that score:

> First of all, in the area of insurance, since I've been practicing here in Illinois, the law has changed to make it crystal clear to lawyers, they can't be double-dealing when they've been retained by an insurance company to represent one of their insureds. Because there were lawyers that were ferreting out the information necessary to eliminate coverage at the same time they were representing the insured. And that was not an unstandard practice. And then the Supreme Court came out with some cases and just slammed some lawyers and, basically, stopped that practice. [105Ch<10]

Though the proper procedures for managing a potential coverage dispute are now formalized and the issue is now considered unproblematic by most respondents, the tension still remains:

> Maybe there's a coverage question, and rather than just denying coverage to the insured, the insurance company sends it down for us to represent the insured. In the meantime, they send a letter to the insured saying, "We're reserving our rights under the policy, because of so-and-so. If it proves that this is the case—that there is no coverage—then you won't have any additional paid defense. Nor will you get any indemnity if you get hit." Well, that presents a problem, because I'm investigating the case on behalf of the insured. And I could accumulate facts which might, eventually, help the insurance company defeat coverage. So that becomes a sticky wicket. . . . I never talk to the insurance company about coverage problems. . . . if they want that kind of information, they have do what is ordinarily done in acquiring that information. That's generally filing a declaratory judgment action; hiring another set of attorneys to investigate it. . . . The law has evolved pretty clear in that area. . . . Believe me, there's still a lot of hanky-panky that goes on. But there's no question that law has evolved in that area. And the rules are pretty specific. It's just a question of whether the lawyer—who has a vested interest in being paid by an insurance company and may have a number of cases with them—is going to follow his conscience in representing his insured to the best of his ability, potentially, to the detriment of his best client—from a money standpoint. [102Ch10–19]

Expenditure of funds. Most of the other sources of tension in the triangle between insurer, insured, and defense attorney have not been as well resolved by legal interpretation. Even as conflicts of interest surrounding coverage disputes have waned, one controversy that has taken on greater importance—in this age of belt-tightening and cost controls in legal services—concerns the expenditure of funds in preparing the defense.

> But, where you get into a problem . . . is when the insurance companies—because they're so cost conscious—will send you a file and they'll say, "Protect the interest of the insured. Follow the appropriate pleadings, motion, whatever." And the next sentence says, "Do not start any discovery until we notify you." Or they'll say, "Minimize the amount of discovery." . . . I know they're looking at the cost side of it. Well, that puts you in a real box because your duty is owed to the client, not to the insurance company at that point. And yet, if you send a bill, say, to the insurance company and you show, say, a thousand dollars of interrogatories, some paper chase or some depositions, and you aren't authorized to do it, but yet you feel you have to do it to learn things about the case, that can cause a conflict. And we've just gone ahead and did it. We just go ahead and do what we think has to be done. We get these letters and I look at them and say, "That's interesting, but I'm the one to be sued [for malpractice], not the insurance company." So that's what we do. . . . I mean, that causes, in a way, a conflict between your client—the

> insured—and the insurance carrier. . . . I'm sure any lawyer that does defense work has gotten these letters from insurance companies. "Cut down costs, cut down costs." And things like, "Don't use any more than ten hours of legal research." Right. . . . And we'll send a bill in. And somebody up in never-never land—with a red pencil—goes through these—he will audit my statements—and says, "Ah ha! I see ten point five hours of legal research. We're going to dock you for point five hours." [laughter] So you think, "Geez, you know, come on!" . . . Yeah, that's a conflict. You owe your duty to your client to do as much as you can, what you think is appropriate. And someone else is trying to put a dollar bill on that and say, "Don't do it." So, yeah, that comes up with clients sometimes. [67DSM10–19]

Though a Chicago large-firm lawyer, commenting on his experience, disagrees:

> I've heard a lot of talk about this business of an insurance company telling defense counsel, for example, to do this or not to do that. I have. I have never seen any good insurance company try to do that. I've heard about it, but in any case I've ever handled or my department's ever handled, I've never seen it yet. Because carriers are actually pretty reasonable. And . . . if it's reasonable to get an expert, for example, or to go to California and do a "dep," then they go along with it. They play ball with that. [6Ch100+]

Settlement. Potential conflicts between insured and insurer surrounding the decision about whether to settle or litigate charges resemble situations in which lawyers represent multiple plaintiffs or defendants. But there are some significant differences in the insurance triangle. Insurer and insured did not play mutual or contributory roles in the liability—they don't both have reputations at stake or mutual losses, nor can one accuse the other of greater blame or responsibility for the liability. Nor do they share autonomy over decision making concerning the course of the engagement, as do joint plaintiffs or defendants. Most insurance contracts vest the insurer with the right to control the litigation—to select the defense lawyer and to decide whether to litigate the matter or offer a settlement and for how much.

> We get a lot of situations where the people we represent as defendants will find out a case is settled. And they call up and they are boiling mad. They can't believe the insurance company paid any money. They don't want the case settled; they want to go to trial. . . . They think it's going to go on their permanent record somewhere—that they were in an accident and somebody had to pay and, therefore, it's an admission—of some type—that they're at fault, even though the releases specifically say that it is not an admission. So some people are extremely mad like that. However, actually, I think settling a case within the terms of the policy limits is definitely within the assured's best interest. Because, if it were to go to trial and if it were one of those one-in-a-million shots where there was an excess verdict, the assured would be—I'm sure—extremely irritated that it didn't settle within their policy limits. [102Ch10–19]

This last comment is critical. The really serious point of conflict occurs when the injury is so severe that the claim far exceeds the amount of insurance coverage. In that instance, the insurance company's strategy about settlement can have profound implications for how much personal exposure the insured faces. In these instances, policyholders may be much more sanguine about settling charges. Often their insurers differ.

> But they also have to be careful when—and we do too—about excess situations, where the claim or the exposure is more than the amount of the insurance coverage. Then there's a little conflict there—it's between the insurance company and the client. And the insurance company has one possible interest—they'd like to defend the case. They have a limit of, say, $300,000 on their policy. And, rather than pay $250 and settle it, they'd rather take a chance and try the case, because the most they can lose is another $50,000, or $100,000, or whatever it is. Whereas, . . . they're really gambling with the insured's money. And we're representing the insured. So that gets kind of tricky. What do you, as a lawyer, do with regard to trying to settle that case? Are you looking out for the best interests of the insured or the best interests of the insurance company—which is really your regular client? Although you're representing the insured in name (the insured is really your client), but the insurance company is paying the bills. So that gets very, very tricky. [62DSM10–19]

The respondent here characterizes this conflict as between the insurance company and the insured. But, of course, he is in the middle; the conflict of interest is his own. The nonclient, the third-party insurer who pays his bill, is ordering him to go to trial. His true client, the insured, is ordering him to try to settle within the policy limits. The lawyer must submit to the will of the third party against the best interests of his client—a classic conflict of interest. So what does he do?

> Our role . . . is to advise our client, the insured, that he or she should retain their own attorney to address this problem and make the appropriate demands upon their insurance carrier to settle the case. And we usually do that in writing to the insured client and carbon copy that to the insurance carrier. They know we're doing it. Because we do have a conflict at that point. We have two clients, really. [66Ch20–49]

This advice, then, obviously signifies that the insurance defense lawyer has been rendered impotent, entangled by his allegiances to both parties and unable to vigorously champion the interests of his client. The formulaic dance that attempts to neutralize the conflict goes like this:

> Now, where that comes up, every day of our lives [. . .] Classic situation: case sitting right there that I'm going to trial on week after next. X amount of dollars in insurance—let's say, a hundred thousand dollar policy. A death case—as that one is. A case that's worth, conceivably, several million dollars. If the case goes to trial and the jury comes back with several million dollars verdict, the insurance company

> only has to pay a hundred thousand dollars. The insured is then liable for everything above that—I mean, his personal assets. Let's say the insured doctor says, "Hey, I didn't do anything wrong, but I'm not about to put my whole life in this kind of position." So he says, "I want you to settle that case." I convey that information out to the insurance company and the insurance company says, "No, we want to defend this case." I tell the doctor, "Doctor, we're going to defend this case." I think that he said, "I think that's unfair. You guys only have a hundred thousand dollars in it (by "you guys," meaning the insurance company). I've got twelve million dollars and four kids and a garage and, you know, whatever. What can I do?" I said, "Well, I can't tell you what to do, but you might want to get separate counsel to advise you, of course." Well, what happens, he goes to a lawyer—of course. And the lawyer writes a letter, which is a relatively, well spelled-out letter by the case law saying, "Dear Insurance Company, I represent Dr. Jones. You have been made aware of the circumstances of the case. If, in fact, you do not settle this case within the policy limits, we will consider you to be acting in bad faith"—that's the term of art—"and you may very well be held liable for any judgment entered over that hundred thousand dollars." Okay? So that's the classic bad-faith letter that the insurance companies have to deal with all the time. And what the law clearly says is that an insurance company has to take into account the insured's own personal situation as well as theirs. So if the insurance companies say, "Hey, we want to save a hundred thousand dollars," if to save that hundred thousand dollars, they're jeopardizing two million dollars, you know, that's very unequal. So, those are the conflict situations that arise all the time. [76Ch10–19]

The comments cited thus far pertain to the inherent tensions between the interests of major reputable insurance companies, their policyholders, and the private law firms hired to defend liability claims against them. The conflicts are even more profound when defense lawyers are not independent of the insurance companies whose policyholders they represent. Some work in "house firms," whose sole client is the insurance company, which pays their salaries and benefits. Others represent—and sometimes have ownership interests in—what are known as "substandard" insurance companies, which write automobile insurance policies for people who have a hard time getting insurance elsewhere. Here the triangle is even more distorted, undermining the necessary loyalty of lawyer to client. Respondents charge that these insurers impose more severe restrictions on pretrial expenditures and exert even greater undue influence on the settlement process—pressures that these lawyers have more difficulty resisting because of their lack of independence.

> There's a law firm called [names a Chicago firm], which represents some of the worst insurance companies in Illinois. And I've always heard—I don't know if it's true or not—but that the partners in the firm are the owners or have ownership interest in the companies. And they will universally try cases and get verdicts in excess of the insurance coverage against their insureds. And all they write are the little twenty-forty policies. And you can have a claim that's worth a hundred grand, and they won't pay anything to settle. When you try the case and you get

a verdict for a hundred grand, they've got a twenty thousand policy. Then they'll finally pay the twenty. But, if they would have paid the twenty in the first place, you wouldn't have tried the case and they wouldn't have exposed their client to that excess burden. [73CC10–19][7]

Suing an insured of an insurance client. A fourth kind of conflict of interest that arises in an insurance defense practice falls outside the triangular relationship. Here the law firm is taking action on behalf of a client which is adverse to a policyholder of an insurance company that routinely sends the firm business. The law firm client may be a plaintiff who is suing the policyholder or a codefendant who is seeking contribution from another codefendant who happens to be insured by the insurance company. This scenario has become more common in recent years as insurance companies have begun to pursue subrogation claims against parties responsible for the losses for which they have compensated their insureds.[8]

Because, according to the ethics rules, the insurance company is not a true client of the law firm, these scenarios do not pose the classic conflict of interest that arises from directly adverse interests between two clients. The adversity is between the client and policyholder being sued; the insurer is a third party. So the situation poses neither triangular nor classic direct adversity conflicts. However, several other potential conflicts of interest can surface in this scenario. First, there is the business conflict (though not a true ethical conflict): the lawyer does not want to antagonize a major source of business by vigorously advancing a significant liability claim that the insurer must pay. Most respondents indicate that in assessing whether they face a significant business conflict, they evaluate the nature and solidity of their relationship with the insurance carrier on the other side, the amount of business it gives the firm, and its likely reaction to learning that the firm is suing one of its insureds. Many indicate that the carriers they work with are not especially troubled.

Second, there is the problem of confidentiality: by virtue of representing so many of the insurance company's policyholders in the past, the law firm has amassed a considerable amount of inside information about the insurer (about settlement strategy, etc.), which the lawyer may be tempted to exploit for the benefit of his new client. Again, because the insurer is not a client, the confidentiality concern is more of a business problem than an ethical one.

Third, there is the true ethical conflict: the lawyer may restrain (perhaps even unconsciously) his otherwise vigorous advocacy of his new client because he does not want to jeopardize a lucrative ongoing relationship with an insurer he hopes to be a significant source of future law firm revenue. Indeed, the fact that insurers say they prefer that their long-standing insurance defense firm take the case against their insured provides an indirect clue that they anticipate somewhat better treatment than they expect to receive from an independent and disinterested firm.

---

[7]Though the managing partner of one of the house firms in the sample disputed the stereotype of less-than-vigorous lawyers in the pockets of the insurers who pay their salaries.

[8]*Subrogation* refers to the substitution of the insurance company in place of the insured to pursue a claim of the latter against a third party.

> Now you get to the practical side. Does that insurer want to deal in the handling of that lawsuit and the possible settlement of that lawsuit—and most of them do get settled—would they rather cope with [our firm] or would they rather we turn the case down that goes to Phil Corboy, who would try to cut them to pieces, whereas we might deal with them in a more genteel, civilized manner? They may decide—from their side—that they can work with us better in the case than they can if it goes to some big-time plaintiff's lawyer who has no interest in doing anything but rendering them insolvent. [19Ch50–99]

> . . . when push comes to shove, and you're representing a client who's an individual plaintiff, and the carrier whom you're really trying to play—push to the wall and get them to pay their whole policy, for example—is a good client of yours, you might find yourself, unconsciously, having a conflict, I mean, not doing the job. So we wouldn't take a serious plaintiff's case. Run-of-the-mill stuff, it's just as easy to deal with them. And they'd rather have us than [. . .] I mean, they know it will be handled right and there's no problem. . . . As long as everyone knows who is involved, it's not a real conflict. But I wouldn't want to handle a "leg-off" case against one of my good insurance company clients. [66Ch20–49]

Because of these business and ethical conflicts, many insurance defense boutiques and other firms with significant insurance defense business find it difficult to represent plaintiffs at all, because they are invariably adverse to the insureds of one of the firm's important insurance "clients." The struggle continues, though, because:

> You get a million-dollar fee from one of those [plaintiffs] cases. Why, it takes a lot of hundred-dollar-an-hour [defense] cases to get that kind of money. So, from a practical standpoint, you would look at it. But, we do turn them down [. . .] [100DSS10–19]

LAWYERS FOR THE SITUATION

We return, finally, to Louis Brandeis. In hindsight, the scenario about which his Senate interrogators questioned him sounds far less outlandish and his entanglement in such a complex web far less reckless or irresponsible than might have seemed on first blush. The last two chapters have documented, through countless variations, the insistent impulse for lawyers to represent more than one party simultaneously or serially, whether on the same or opposite sides of a dispute, whether parties to an agreement or transaction, whether relatives, colleagues, friends, partners, or neighbors. Clients demand dual, joint, or multiple representation for a host of compelling reasons. It allows them to turn to lawyers they trust, who are familiar with their background, business, problems, and needs. They can enjoy access to legal expertise and take advantage of the social and political capital of lawyers in specialized niches, drawing on their special knowledge, social contacts, and inside information. They don't want to have to pay two sets of lawyers, especially in order to get strangers up to speed; indeed, some may not be able to afford two sets of lawyers and would be precluded from any legal representation at all if that is required. They can enjoy economies of scale and save money on legal fees, the costs of discovery, experts, and the like. Collectively, they can better finance their case, afford better lawyers or more aggressive advocacy. Their cases can proceed more expeditiously and with greater speed. They can present a united front to the opposition and collectively garner greater credibility or believability than they could on their own. Collectively, they can force a settlement or at least equalize the preexisting advantage of the repeat players on the other side. By limiting the number of lawyers involved, they believe they can minimize the possibility of discord or that the dispute will escalate. Moreover, they expect that an attorney who knows all the parties involved will better facilitate conciliation and maximize the likelihood of finding a fair and palatable compromise. And, of course, like their clients, lawyers embrace such arrangements because it means turning away less business and minimizing the risk that a long-term client will be lost forever to another law firm as well as the risk that they might offend or anger clients by abandoning them in their hour of need.

This chapter has also documented the inevitable and thorny conflicts of interest that arise when lawyers accede to clients' wishes to join together or when they ignore or disregard the often murky boundaries that separate one party from another. Some attorneys try to finesse the potential conflicts by compartmentalizing their representation: they agree to handle the engagement to the point of litigation or open hostilities among the parties. They agree to handle the consensual elements of the case but insist that the adversarial elements be handled by other lawyers, by an arbitrator, or by the parties themselves. Others radically limit the kinds of legal services they will offer to clients. They will serve as a sounding board but offer no advice; they will lay out options but refuse to assist in deciding among them; they will offer their good offices to bring the parties together but do nothing to help them resolve the dispute; they will act as scrivener but play no role in negotiating or forging the agreement. Still others will officially represent one designated party and allow the other to act pro se, perhaps with the lawyers' unstated protection or restraint.

Of course, all these contrivances impair the quality, range, and continuity of legal services that the attorney can offer to clients. If only the attorney could represent situations rather than parties, the dilemmas raised in this chapter would effortlessly vanish. Many try. Prior examples cited in this chapter and the previous one described a collar county attorney acting as a mediator in the failed efforts of the pricey lawyers of a Hilton Head couple to settle their divorce, a small-town downstate firm that tried to mediate a dispute between two clients (an investor service and an investor), and a large Chicago firm that offered to mediate a dispute—that immediately turned nasty—between a Chicago client and a client of its Washington office. Though very mindful of his conflicts, a small-town attorney who had represented a bank and one of its officers in an employment dispute also celebrated his contribution as facilitator:

> I was having a good conversation with [my father] at lunch the other day. And, of course, all this—in a small town—gets involved in a lot of gossip. . . . he was a little

> upset because he was getting a lot of feedback about how badly it had all been handled. And I'm being a little paranoid there. And I said, "Look," I said, "you've given me a list of everybody on both sides and they all sound a little bit unhappy. They're not all a lot unhappy. It sounds to me like it was a splendid resolution of the problem." . . . At least that's the view I like to have of it myself—is the self-congratulatory view, is, "Nobody else could have gotten it to where it got. Because it was a facilitator role to a large extent. And, if it would have turned into a very nasty, ugly lawsuit, it wouldn't have been good for anybody." [70DSS10–19]

Examples of lawyers attempting to act for the situation occur in other contexts as well:

> L: We do a hell of a lot of bankruptcy. There's a lot of conflict potentials there. Especially when I wipe out the people that I've been representing . . .
>
> S: You mean where some of the creditors are also clients?
>
> L: Yeah. I'll go and talk to 'em and tell 'em. Sometimes, I've actually felt that, by my representing both sides in the past, I've been able to get some money out of my client, or for [. . .] from my client in a way that he's happy. And they both know it, both sides know it. . . . I mean, I'm not pulling the wool over anybody's eyes. But I tell 'em, I say, "Hey, I'll work with ya. I'll work with ya." And the absence of litigation means that both sides are happy. They're getting their money. And they're saving legal costs. But they know it. I mean, I've told 'em that I've got him and he's bankrupt and I'll try to get what I can. I just did a big business bankruptcy like that recently. And risked getting my—the main guy that I do my collections for—get him mad. But this went on for so long, and I just kept telling him. I said, " . . . this guy's got no money. He's just absolute rock bottom. There's nothing there. The wife with a hundred thousand dollars in medical bills. IRS after him for sixty thousand bucks. I mean . . . handwriting's on the wall. There's nothing there. You're never gonna get your money. I don't care what lawyer you go to." So, I tell him that. [125DSS<10]

"Lawyering for the situation" arrangements described by the respondents are intricate and precarious as attorneys try to balance their responsibility to advocate aggressively the interests of their clients with their obligation not to abandon them or contribute to the escalation of their difficulties. Centered in the eye of a storm with incompatible responsibilities to diverse clients, they opt for a different kind of lawyering—often more detached and undirected.

> Now, if I withdraw from everybody, and everybody has to go get their own attorney and we don't work this out, it's going to cost everybody about three times as much money. And these people may end up suing each other. We do have egos. We feel we're pretty good facilitators, pretty good negotiators, and we can probably bring these guys to a comfortable settlement among each other. But, if they go out and get some of those hard-asses out there—their hardball litigators—they may end up in court for years. I mean, is that something we are to consider as lawyers? I guess maybe it's an expansion of our classic role as adversaries and the adversarial

> system. . . . I suppose the idea becoming more prevalent . . . is something we've probably considered on an ad hoc basis of the lawyer as facilitator. . . . Just because there are two parties involved . . . and that there may be a dispute, doesn't necessarily mean that, initially, that it's an adversarial situation. . . . But, I guess, with all of the emphasis on alternate dispute resolution-type things, it seems to me to downplay the adversarial nature more, and maybe says that there is more room for you to be a facilitator, a mediator. The idea of win-win negotiating I think [. . .] If I'm negotiating a deal with you, we should try to both come out of this with making the pie bigger, rather than splitting the pie up. If I'm splitting the pie, then my duty for my client is to absolutely make sure he gets the biggest piece of pie there is. But, if I look at it in the bigger picture and say, "I can make this pie bigger." If I can use my skills as a lawyer—which go far beyond just being a litigator—if I can use those skills to increase the benefit, then isn't it my duty . . . less adversarial and more facilitator-wise, the more creative problem solving, I guess, maybe. . . . I think it's much easier, but less pleasant, just to be an absolute advocate. . . . One of the great stresses of our profession is . . our view of ourselves as strict advocates. And the way the system, perhaps, looks at our role and says, "We don't trust you. . . . You can't be involved in this deal and have the best interests of all parties involved." Because it looks at the system as an all-or-nothing situation or as a zero-sum game. There's only one hundred points here, and if this guy gets sixty, this guy's got to get forty. Whereas . . . we know that, in human relationships, that's not the case. . . . I think the stress on lawyers arises a lot out of our fact that, morning til night, we view our role and we view our system's role as adversarial. [97DSS<10]

The interviews are filled with tales of lawyers' efforts to be there for their clients and maintain relative impartiality as well as their fears that this impartiality may lead clients to take actions that are not in their best interests.

Amid these exquisite accounts of rationalization and soul-searching, we also find the skeptics, usually from large Chicago law firms that have the somewhat greater luxury of sending their client away when the tangle becomes too convoluted:

> I have literally had several instances where, after a person explains the transaction to me, I will say, "Well, who are you representing?" And they'll say, "Well, I'm sort of counsel to the deal." And I say, "Well, [laughing] that's kind of a dumb way to explain this to you, but you can't do that." . . . There's sort of this sense of, "Oh, well, we're all trying to get to the same goal and it's really to make the deal and all that." . . . It's very hard to sometimes convince transactional lawyers there are things such as conflicts.
>
> . . . There are very few lawyers any more like Edward Bennett Williams, who regarded himself as "counsel to the situation." . . . Some lawyers feel that they are so capable and so able to serve all interests and everyone will be happier because of their brilliance and their skill, that when everyone goes away—because he was representing everybody or trying to work things out for everybody—the situation is better. And we just try to convince people that that's a mistake. [11Ch100+]

Other Clients

The Ripples of Adversity

The last two chapters have woven together two tangled webs: one, the many subtle variations on the theme of adversity; the other, the complex structures of natural persons, organizations, social networks, generations, and triangles. Any legal matter will feature one or more nodes within these tangled webs. Where these diverse webs are located, where the nodal boundaries are drawn (i.e., who is the client?), how the nodes are implicated in the matter, and who is chosen to represent them will determine the kinds of conflicts of interest, if any, that lawyers will face.

Only a finite number of nodes in these vast expanding webs directly participate in a given matter, of course—one or more plaintiffs, defendants, buyers, sellers, creditors, insurers, inventors, heirs, and so on. But the webs in which these parties are embedded still exist. And, because of their connections and interdependencies, many network neighbors of the direct participants are affected as well—sometimes profoundly—by the outcome of the case, in general, and the activities of the lawyers, in particular. The ripples of adversity occasioned by a legal engagement can extend far beyond the original point of impact.

This proximate victimization poses no ethical problem for the lawyers handling the case, of course, unless these neighbors happen to be their clients as well. Unfortunately, because of the social ecology of the legal marketplace—and sometimes sheer coincidence—neighbors often are. They had engaged, on some *unrelated* matter, the very law firm that has now—perhaps unknowingly and inadvertently—betrayed their interests or contributed to their injury. As I elaborated in chapter 3, lawyers have ethical obligations to decline representations that will adversely affect another client or that will be materially limited by responsibilities to other clients. The adversities of interest here between client participants and client neighbors and bystanders are less direct than those described in the last two chapters and the conflicts of interest more attenuated. As a result, lawyers' ethical obligations are considerably murkier.

Because of the dearth of ethical guidance for these indirect conflicts of interest, we find far more variability among law firms in how they struggle over what to do about the possible harm their advocacy will cause. Moreover, other powerful influences—such as business and financial considerations, the proprietary stake that particular law firm partners have in particular clients, and the stratification of power within law firms—play a greater role in resolving conflicts questions when the ethical course is less clear. Consequently, as we follow out the ripples of adversity, we find a somewhat different landscape than we observed at the epicenter.

In this chapter, we will "surf the web." We begin at the epicenter of legal transactions and disputes and follow the centrifugal movement of the ripples of adversity.

COPARTIES

Whether because of the tensions and intrinsic adversities of interest that simmer and sometimes detonate among multiple plaintiffs or defendants represented by the same law firm or for other economic, instrumental, or strategic reasons, coparties sometimes seek exclusive, independent representation in multiparty litigation (not uncommonly, at the insistence of their lawyers). Rather than seeking joint representation, coparties B, C, and D, all regular clients of law firm 1, engage law firms 2, 3, and 4 on a particular piece of litigation, while law firm 1 continues to represent coparty A. Though some of the direct adversities of interest confronting firm 1's lawyers are thereby neutralized, the conflicts of interest are not necessarily entirely eradicated. Clients B, C, and D still have a stake in the litigation. Firm 1's lawyers may have confidential information about the business practices and financial exigencies of B, C, and D or merely have finely honed experiential knowledge about their risk aversion, patience, vindictiveness, or settlement practices that could be used to the advantage of coparty A. And even if the lawyers have no such useful inside information, their advocacy on behalf of A may result in harm to B, C, or D. Where coparties are victims or plaintiffs, monies extracted for one coparty—in a zero-sum world of finite resources—leave less for the others. Where coparties are defendants, attorneys' efforts to exculpate their immediate client may require shifting the blame to other codefendants; where these efforts fail, lawyers strive to minimize costs to their immediate client by seeking greater contribution to the penalty or judgment from codefendants. And of course, mindful of possibly harming or angering B, C, or D, law firm 1 may champion the interests of A with somewhat less vigor, thereby disadvantaging A.

Because adversities are less direct here, conflicts of interest fall on a continuum—from the occasional clearly proscribed engagement, to situations in which clients can consent to waive the apparent conflicts, to mere business conflicts in which lawyers risk antagonizing important clients who demand exclusivity or greater loyalty. Though the latter may not breach ethical norms, they threaten significant relationships and financial interests and may be more difficult and painful to resolve than the former. Attorneys must weigh situational factors and particularities of the parties as they negotiate the murky ethical and relational boundaries in such cases.

By refusing to represent more than one party in multiparty litigation, lawyers do not necessarily dodge the inherent conflicts of interest; they just nudge them a bit further along the continuum. At the extremes of the continuum, respondents evince considerably less consensus about whether they face true conflicts of interest and what to do about them.

> But I would say that the most common situation is . . . where we are coparties, codefendants with a client. I don't consider that a situation that raises much heat, because . . . that frequently happens and there is no adversity. There is no real risk. But that comes up. . . . And there's no question there is a continuum in those cases. There are cases in which you feel very comfortable that nothing—till hell freezes over—there will not be a problem between these defendants. Then there are the circumstances where trouble is brewing constantly. There is no conflict; there is no reason not to take the case. But there is an uneasy truce between these people. And if things went bad, they would start to turn on each other. I would say we have a fair amount of that. But in general, we do not get excited about that at the outset. . . . But there have been times where things got out of hand and, all of a sudden, there was some fighting. . . . There have been situations like that where we've sort of gone along, keeping our fingers crossed a little bit that nothing will happen, recognizing that we might have a real problem if it turned into warfare. But, I think, usually I view those as not a conflict situation, simply a potential-for-conflict situation. And we don't get too excited about it. [44Ch20–49]

The structural conditions that contribute to the likelihood that law firms will encounter numerous clients in the ranks of the coparties on a given case include many of those cited in the last chapter as the impetus for multiple parties to seek joint representation in the first place. Some kinds of litigation implicate such a vast collection of parties that law firms should expect many clients to be involved by sheer mathematical odds alone.

> We have a thriving environmental practice. . . . Firms with huge environmental practices, I think, go pretty well nuts about this subject. Because, in a Superfund case, the government is after hundreds of companies for contribution to the commonweal. And each of them wants to minimize its percentage interest and blame it on somebody else. And big firms may only be retained or usually are only retained by one of those companies. But there are lots of your other clients in there. And those just seem to get worked out as these matters go along. There's no sensible, easy way to handle it. [5Ch100+]

Substantive or technological expertise provides another potent magnet to attract clients from related industries that often harm collectively—by dumping pollutants in the same place, producing dangerous products with related or integrated components, constructing precarious edifices together—and are accused collectively.

> But we do do a lot of products liability defense. . . . For example, we have some clients that . . . make multiple components of certain product systems. Well, there are other people making some of those components too. And so you can enter into the litigation wearing one hat or the other hat for this client. And in one piece of litigation, you may be worried or recognizing "Well, there's a potential to dump on this other component supplier." But you may be in exactly that position in another case. You may be having that component and another manufacturer with the component you had in the last case. And what kind of problems are you creating? [44Ch20–49]

Regional specializations pose the same difficulties. Law firms that defend parties implicated in construction accidents, for example, face the same local cast of characters from accident to accident but often defend different parties from one case to the next. Because large-scale construction projects—especially on the scale of Chicago-style architecture—require the contribution of so many tradespeople and contractors, an accident will typically collect a host of potentially responsible parties, many of whom are long-time clients of a specialist defense firm. The social structure of construction projects creates repetitive and thorny conflicts for defense specialists.

> One of the things I do in my products work is I represent a lot of different construction companies. And I represented a company in a number of actions, where stuff that they had put on buildings had fallen off. One building collapsed, another building was in the process. . . . And I firmly believe that our job is to represent our clients' positions as best we can. But the deeper I got into . . . one of the cases for them, the more I recognized that there was really [. . .] Just from my standpoint, this was not a client that I was happy with the way they had done this. . . . It was clear to me that their work was substandard, to say the least. The attorney on the other side was maybe not the brightest person in the world, maybe not even the best lawyer. And, because of some technical mistakes that he made really during the trial, . . . we ended up paying nothing. . . . And so the company was very happy. I did not want to represent these people again. The more I looked at it, the more I became convinced that there really were some, if not criminal wrongdoing, it was very close. I didn't think it was my position—I was representing this client—to go into details about this and start doing investigations into [. . .] That was somebody else's job. But I didn't want to represent them again. Well, a case came down the road—a similar type of construction—and one of the subs [i.e., subcontractors] wanted me to represent them. I got involved. At the same time this company again asked me to represent them and I refused. . . . Because I had so much information on them as far as their erection methods, they felt that that applied to all cases in the future. I did not. I mean, to me, when you [put] up a building, each building is different and [. . .] However, we got into quite a little fight over that. . . . And first they tried to get me back involved in the case for them. Then they were willing to take—if I represented the other people, if I would

> represent them as well—they were willing to waive any potential problem there. And then, when I said I just simply didn't want to do it any more, then they got a lawyer and tried to disqualify me from the other, representing other people. I refused to withdraw in that case for a lot of different reasons. And we got into quite a little fight over that. Those kinds of things can be difficult, particularly when you've decided you sort of reached the end of representing a client. Does that mean you're not going to represent anybody again in litigation that involves them? Particularly in the kind of work we do [. . .] Construction cases, it's all the same people, over and over again. . . . And that can be a problem. [33Ch50–99]

RELATIONSHIPS WITH ADVERSARIES

Further along the continuum, clients cease to be adversaries or coparties in a particular transaction or lawsuit and their direct stake in its outcome attenuates. So do the direct adversities of interest among clients and the clarity of potential conflicts of interest faced by their lawyers. Though no longer direct participants in the case, these clients can still be affected—sometimes significantly—by its outcome.

Clients can have relationships with adversaries of other law firm clients. Though ethical norms generally forbid attorneys from taking an adverse position against a client, what about when clients are merely affiliated with or somehow connected to these adversaries? This is not a who-is-the-client question; the adverse parties involved are *not* clients. But how close can adverse parties and clients become—and in what sorts of structural relationships—before the ethical rules about adversely affecting or causing harm to a client kick in? Take two examples, in which respondents think differently about potential conflicts:

> The most recent one I can remember is we [brought] a suit against an owner of a building which was managed by a client. And the lawyer who represents the management company raised the question of conflict—I think, primarily, because of his client relationship and politics. And I just ruled that . . . it's not a conflict. The party in interest was the owner. And nothing suggesting that the managing company was in any way involved. I said, "That's just baloney." . . . Analytically, there simply was no conflict. A was suing B and B had an agent nonemployee that we represented. But he was not involved in the litigation in any way. So that seems to me a no-conflict thing. [80Ch10–19]

> . . . the firm represents the RTC (Resolution Trust Corporation) on professional liability work. Often on a case, we will get a list of potential people who might be named in a S and L [Savings and Loan] case. And the list tends to be extremely long. We really have to be careful. We are especially attuned to the related-party issues. For example, we take on a [case for the RTC]. There are no direct conflicts. Then it turns out that a client has an interest in a partnership which is a potential defendant in the case. [56Ch20–49]

Clients sometimes become entangled with law firm adversaries when they are called as witnesses for the other side or when their own experts and witnesses have adverse relationships with their lawyers. Attorneys, whose specialized work taps into dense social networks of repeat players, confront this quandary most often. Most examples offered by respondents illuminate the worlds of medical malpractice, personal injury litigation, and crime. Personal injury and medical malpractice litigation rely on the testimony of medical experts as well as of regular doctors, known as "treating physicians," who provide care for injured plaintiffs. Potential conflicts of interest arise when law firms bring medical malpractice charges against these physicians who are testifying on behalf of other clients in unrelated cases. The risk to these clients is that the physician's willingness to testify or the quality of the testimony may be compromised by the anger or malice the doctor feels toward the lawyers suing him or her.

> I think the key one would be a medical expert. We get calls from the lawyers . . . about bringing an action against a particular doctor or to review a case against a particular doctor. And if it is someone that we have used or use in cases, we obviously feel we cannot and won't do it—regardless of the nature of the case. . . . It happens that these same people have been or are experts for us. When they are experts, you obviously can't do it. Because, in that type of a situation, if you alienate your own expert [. . .] I mean, you may make money on that, but you do a disservice to your client—and where he is your expert—because either he'll withdraw or he will not be too enamored with your position. And so I look at it that you have to first look to the client you represent, not to the case you can get from someone else or against one of the people that you now are using. [60Ch20–49]

In the social worlds of crime, the conflict arises from the complicity and social connections among recidivist criminals and the fact that state prosecutors have turned or "flipped" one law firm client into a witness against another. The dilemma for defense lawyers is whether, in the service of a second client, they can aggressively cross-examine one of their own clients and, indeed, use damning—often confidential—information about their criminal or life histories in order to undermine their credibility. This scenario is most common in downstate Illinois, which has smaller criminal networks and fewer defense attorneys who have repeated contacts with many of their members.

> L: So, if I have represented a person who is later listed as a witness against another person that I'm representing, I always withdraw on those. 'Cause that's a conflict. Because if the former client is called as a witness, I'm in a position to cross-examine him and to undermine his credibility—which would entail me using the evidence or my knowledge of him from the former relationship. And so I'm precluded from representing the new person because of my prior representation.
>
> S: And does that happen a fair amount?
>
> L: A lot. That's how I get the majority of my appointments from the public defender's office. Because he's represented Joe in this case, and Joe's now a witness against Sam. So he'll withdraw on Sam's case. And I'll get Sam. And then there's always the possibility that, when I get him, I may have represented one

> or two of his witnesses. So it'll keep going until they find an attorney that hasn't represented anybody involved in it. [112DSS<10]

Respondents differ over the likelihood that client witnesses provoke conflicts that require them to withdraw from the case.

COMPETITORS

> A typical problem that arises involves an instance in which an actual or potential competitor of an ongoing client approaches the firm for counsel. This is very likely, since we have developed expertise in particular areas and competitors are attracted by our expertise. Now there may be no ethical prohibition from taking the new matter. But there is a potential business conflict if your client does not want you representing the competition. [69Ch20–49]

As this respondent observes, because of specialized knowledge of industry practices and sometimes arcane bodies of law, extensive experience, demonstrated track records, political and social capital, and inside information, law firms often attract clients from the same industries, many of which are competitors. Despite these attractions, the downside, of course, is that ethics and conflict-of-interest rules limit the range of services these firms can offer industry competitors. Firms cannot represent either client when litigation erupts between them, nor can they draw on confidential information about one for the benefit of the other. And as previous materials suggest, lawyers face both business and ethical constraints in the extent to which they can play a role in transactions between the two or in litigation in which they are coparties.

But what about legal representation in matters in which competitors do not directly figure? Can law firms secure patents, negotiate union contracts, bid on new business, or defend against hostile takeovers for one client while other clients develop related intellectual property, negotiate with the same unions, bid on the same business opportunities, and are vulnerable to hostile takeovers as well? How about if the second client does not enlist the law firm for assistance on these sorts of matters for which the firm is representing the first—perhaps using the firm only for its expertise in taxation or corporate finance? The answer, according to the respondents, is "sometimes" or "within limits" or "depending on the clients":

> We have a major client with a given scope of matters that we represent them in—as, for example, a public utility in proceedings before the Commerce Commission. We now have another client who wants us to represent them in proceedings before the Commerce Commission. And we say to them, "We have this other client with an existing relationship [. . .] We can serve you in your requirements, but we will not serve you on any issues that pertain to these defined subject matters or these specific areas of regulation." In other words, at the front end of establishing the client relationship, we build the wall around that relationship, so that everyone with a new client knows going in that our services can extend only in certain defined areas. [49DSL20–49]

> We represent two very large [retail] chains here in Chicago. One of them, we've represented for a number of years; the other came in fairly recently—about two years ago. When [the second chain] came in, obviously, we saw a very strong potential conflict, but talked to our contacts at the first retail chain. And they said, "As long as you create a Chinese wall in your firm, we can live with it."[1] And the new client coming in could live with that as well. And it's worked fine for a couple of years now. It really hasn't been a problem. . . . We get involved in—at least, for the one chain—with their collective bargaining. . . . That's the one area where there's some sensitivity as to confidentiality—in terms of wages, job security, things of that nature. . . . It's more on the labor relations end that we have to be a little bit careful. . . . With the two chains, obviously [. . .] I mean, it's the same unions; their stores are within blocks of each other; basically the same methods of operations; a lot of the same suppliers. . . . There has to be absolute silence where you don't . . . even talk about that issue—at all. . . . But, again, a lot of it is client trust. If they didn't trust us, it would never work. Because it's not like the client can come here and monitor whether or not we're keeping our promise. . . . We also represent the trucking company that brings the product to the chains. And then we represent the [product] producer that provides [product] to both of the [retail] chains. So it's somewhat incestuous. But everybody knows about it. And we're trusted enough that information that we may have on the distributor is not going to be divulged to the [product] producer nor to the [retail] chains. And it's worked; it's worked. We even had some situations where the chain and the distributor and the producer were sued, and we represented all three. . . . I think the biggest thing is that you just be very up-front with the clients that you currently represent, if the new business opportunities present themselves. And, I think, if your client trusts you enough, it can work. [82Ch10–19]

This last example suggests that a critical element in the representation of competitors involves managing and protecting the inevitable storehouse of proprietary or confidential information, of considerable value to a competitor, that a law firm amasses in the course of a long-term and varied relationship with a client. Though breaches of confidentiality pose serious ethical violations for lawyers, the client-relations challenge of how to cultivate and fortify trust in the face of temptation or simply lack of vigilance is usually more salient.

> . . . if you do a lot of work for a company in one particular technical area, they might not want you to represent competitors, even if there is no conflict with respect to a certain matter, because . . . we've become very educated in their technology and in their trade secrets and their confidential information. . . . I've had clients that have been concerned that, if you represent a competitor—even though the subject matter isn't a conflict in the technical sense—if you learn about their technology, there's a chance that some of the information—through you—will kind of seep through. Some clients are very concerned about that; some aren't

[1]More about Chinese walls or ethical screens in chapter 9.

> concerned at all. But it's something you have to always be cognizant of, depending on what you're doing. If you have a client that's a major enough client—important enough—that feels a concern over this, you probably [. . .] Well, we certainly have passed up work that would create more of a client relations problem than an ethical conflict. [41Ch50–99]

Clients worry about more than the possible seepage of confidential information when their lawyers represent competitors. Many cannot fathom how their trusted lawyers could do anything to promote or protect the business interests of their fiercest competitors and archenemies, even if the legal services have nothing to do with their own interests or business operations. Indeed, some cutthroat competitors intentionally seek to foreclose rivals from access to the best lawyers by spreading around small amounts of legal business among the topflight specialists, thereby conflicting out these firms from representing the competition.

> We have had a client for some time. One of our partners is approached with the possibility of representing a competitor of this client. There is no ethical conflict. We could undertake the representation of both without violating the ethical rules. But the existing client may be keen to be represented by a law firm that doesn't represent any competitor. . . . Some clients are pretty sophisticated and it doesn't bother them. Or the representations of the two clients may involve different product lines that do not overlap—especially if the product lines involve independent profit centers in the corporation. In these instances they don't care. But big sophisticated companies can also be the most jealous. Indeed, some corporations will try to retain all the expert law firms in the area to impede their competitors. [69Ch20–49]

> Sometimes you will have two companies that are fearsome competitors. Their products don't conflict, and you might be asked to do a land deal or something that won't pose a problem. We got a call from Tel Aviv from a potential new client to file a new lawsuit—a likely $1.5 million job. We have worked for a German company—which is a fearsome competitor—for many years. We approached the German company and explained that the lawsuit did not involve them. But they asked us not to take the matter. So we didn't. [42Ch20–49]

In a variation on the same theme, a respondent describes the case of a regulatory agency and one of its most reviled enforcement targets, both represented by the same law firm on unrelated matters:

> A regulatory agency hires lots of lawyers to sue people responsible for the demise of savings and loans. "A law firm" is defending someone who is accused of malfeasance in a matter not involving the regulators, but shareholders. The matter is completely unrelated to any work that the firm has done for the regulatory agency. This is an egregious case; just a notch below a Milken kind of case. This case was a thorn to the regulatory agency. They will waive all other conflicts, but not this one. It was like World War I; they simply would not retreat. . . . There's

not much you can do; the risk is that you won't get any more business from the regulatory agency. [8Ch100+]

As these examples attest, many of the difficulties in representing competitors involve the potential for emerging business conflicts rather than for true conflicts of interest. The consequences are no less real or costly.

I think the toughest one involved the communications industry where we had two clients who were close to being equally worthy. And we had to decide which client we were going to keep and which we were going to send away, . . . because there was no way we could continue to represent both. They were turning into direct competitors and they made it fairly clear we had to choose. And that involved partners who had strong feelings about, obviously, their own clients. And so it turned out, I think, to be more of the application of business judgment than strict conflicts rules. But those are where it's the most difficult. [7Ch100+]

COMPETING FOR THE SAME POT

As noted in the last chapter, when law firms represent coplaintiffs, they face the inherent conflict that, in a zero-sum world, their clients are competing for the same finite resources. This kind of structural conflict of interest is not limited to litigated cases or other discrete matters in which clients are formally linked as coparties. Legal action on behalf of one client may deplete the assets of a target against which another client, for unrelated reasons, has a valid claim.

We have a case where we are representing a woman in a divorce case. And she and her husband either own or owned a building. And we also have a . . . client of the corporate department who had brought a lawsuit against the woman's husband—not my client, against the husband—to recover something in connection with the building. So I guess, technically, if our corporate client were to recover, it could reduce the marital estate—or the nonmarital estate, whichever the case would be—and thereby affect our client. And there was one instance, I think, where our client just waived the conflict. . . . If they didn't do it, somebody else would do it. . . . She was more concerned with us representing her in the divorce, than in whether or not this lawsuit against her husband was successful. [94Ch10–19]

This scenario is especially common in the social worlds of credit, where several clients may be lenders or creditors of a vulnerable debtor.

The minute you have more than one client, you can conceive of undertaking something for client A that's going to be adverse to the interests of client B. Situations where—[1] a client may come in to have a trademark recorded; [2] and then, subsequently, that client decides to ship merchandise to an entity that goes into bankruptcy, an entity who'd been borrowing money from a bank that the firm represents; [3] a bank that might have some security interest in assets of the

> bankrupt—which would include the property that was shipped in by this client for whom you did the trademark work—[This] can present some very interesting problems in adversity of interest. [23Ch100+]

Although these examples appear to be unfortunate random coincidences, the social ecology of law firm practice exacerbates the potential for such conflicts. Obviously, law firms with specialized expertise or niches in representing financial institutions are more likely to find competing creditors among the roster of their clients. The problem is compounded because attorneys often serve as brokers, bringing clients together—buyers and sellers, lenders and borrowers, investors and those in need of capital, retirees and would-be successors.

> By way of further background, the bulk of our clientele are closely held businesses. The nature of our practice is such that we develop close business relationships with our clients. We act as business advisers as well as lawyers. There are often succession considerations where someone is nearing retirement age and no longer wants to be that involved in the business. They come to us asking for assistance. And, in finding someone to acquire their business, we often look at our own existing universe or pool of clients for possible buyers. And, obviously, that's rife with potential for conflicts. We typically find, try to find, or do find independent counsel for one of the two parties. We generally also, though, try to find a way to be involved in the transaction and represent the buyer of the business. In those instances, we do obtain consents. We're sensitive to the potential for problems there, and frankly, it causes us some discomfort and we try to be very careful in those situations. That there's an economic imperative, very frankly, to try to find a buyer, a friendly buyer, a buyer we already represent, so that, in sort of losing a client, we maintain a client. . . . I can recall at least two occasions where I've been at cocktail parties with investment bankers from [this city] where they joke—but only halfheartedly—that they viewed us as their principal competition in this game in terms of investment bankers. [pilot interview #3]

When these deals go sour, lawyers find themselves in the middle, beset by thorny conflicts of interest.

ON THE SIDELINES

Respondents report myriad situations in which clients hover along the sidelines—detached but not disinterested and often oblivious—of another client's legal case. The first client may be a victim in need of protection or compensation, a codefendant or coconspirator that was not charged or sued, a guarantor of the transaction or insurer of the injury, an investor or funder of a venture, a coplayer in a regulated market—someone who could feel the consequences of the resolution of the case or benefit from information generated by it but with no direct stake in the matter and no right to intervene or listen in. The lawyers, however, may feel torn, especially when they have a preexisting relationship with the client on the sidelines. Indeed, often the lawyers were swept unwittingly into representing the second client, with no way of knowing at the outset that the first client was situated along the sidelines with some marginal interest or involvement in the matter. These lawyers may, therefore, feel compelled to protect the original client's interests as well as those of the second, to share relevant information, to temper a settlement or minimize the precedential consequences of an opinion to lessen the impact on the original client—all formula for flirting with conflicts of interest on both sides.

These conflict-ripe scenarios arise for familiar reasons—expertise that draws clients from related industries and with similar legal needs to the same law firm, regional monopolies that ensure that many parties to a local dispute will have longstanding relationships with the same attorneys, the social networks from which law firm clientele are plucked, and the like. A few of the diverse examples offered by the respondents illustrate the range of settings in which clients, straddling the sidelines, get touched by the legal undertakings of fellow clients:

- When the resolution of a dispute among two parties will have a financial impact on another client:

  In the antitrust area, you may have two companies that are at a point of disagreement. And when you do a market analysis or a share analysis of product—that sort of thing—you find that you've got another client that has got some part of that market or that will be affected by the resolution of your case. They're not a direct participant and so you don't see the conflict. But they are impacted at a ripple point by the resolution. And you get that sort of conflict. [9Ch100+]

- When taking on an engagement to represent one client may result in limiting the rights and opportunities of a second:

  Because we are trying to protect intellectual property and you're trying to get as broad a protection as you can get in your client's behalf. When we are doing, for example, prosecution work in the patent area for a client, and we're involved in a certain subject matter area and somebody else comes to us with work in that subject matter area closely aligned. The two ideas or inventions might [not] be very close to one another, in which case the attorney prosecuting the one could still get as broad a protection as possible for the client's interest without having any conflict with the protection that you might have to get for the other client. On the other hand, they might be so closely related that you conclude that you couldn't [. . .] that there would be an overlap in the breadth of the protection if you did the best you could for both of them. So you're looking at subject matter in that instance. And it's not always easy to do. Because when you first get it in, you just have a general idea of what you're dealing with. You don't have the details, so you don't know how much potential for conflict there is. So we're always concerned if two clients ask us to work in closely aligned subject matter. And, depending upon the circumstances, we might consult with a client before taking it on or not. [41Ch50–99]

- When small-town lawyers, in representing many of the major institutions in town, find themselves on all sides of a local dispute and discover implicated clients stacked up along the margins:

> Woman had defrauded local company's pension plan and then also defrauded several local banks. Now here's a conflict situation, okay. . . . Well, we're on retainer to the local company. We're on retainer to the bank that was also defrauded. We are concerned that Local Company be released from all liability, but we're also concerned that the person doesn't, for example, turn around and sue the bank for some reason or another. . . . and we have, by the way, been consulted by both of these people with regard to this, and have told both of these people, "We represent them. They represent you. You guys could be suing each other in this case. And we don't know what we're going to do. We're going to have to withdraw, if it comes to that." . . . So Company says, "Prepare a release for us to get signed." . . . Well, the guy calls this morning and says, "The employee won't sign your release, says it's too complicated, says it's too long, and says it releases everybody." And I said, "That's right, it does release both you and the bank." And Client kind of laughs, and says, "You want to make sure everybody gets taken care of." I said, "Look, if that guy sues the bank—yeah, we're concerned that the bank gets released also—but if that guy sues the bank, the bank's going to turn around and sue you. . . . I want to release everybody. Don't you want to release everybody, because you also deal with these banks all the time?" He said, "Well, I'm glad you're up-front about all this." And I said, "Well, I hope I'm up-front." . . . I guess there are some potential conflicts in there that, if the guy won't sign the release for my client company if it releases also the bank, . . . what are my duties there? Now, if I withdraw from everybody, and everybody has to go get their own attorney, and we don't work this out, it's going to cost everybody about three times as much money. And these people may end up suing each other. [97DSS<10]

- When law firms are solicited to represent a defendant in a case in which other clients are complicit but not formally charged:

> I handled a case once. It was a catastrophic accident—an oil refinery explosion where about twenty people were killed. And a suit was filed against multidefendants. . . . the refinery . . . we had represented in some other litigation, maybe a half a dozen different cases. . . . Now [we're] being asked to represent one of the principal defendants in the lawsuit. And the plaintiff couldn't sue the employer [the refinery] because a compact bars that from happening. So I took that case for that principal defendant and always was worried sick that the employer—who had a stake in the lawsuit—would blow the whistle on our firm over half a dozen little cases that may have not produced more than fifty thousand dollars worth of income in the past. But, instead, I took this case that generated a couple million dollars worth of income over a period of about four or five years. I was always worried sick. [laughter] . . . I think when we took the case in, if we had had a half a dozen different matters for the refinery

> owner, maybe they were down to about two matters. And they were relatively minor matters. And I told the attorneys handling those things, "Get rid of those cases. Get them off the books." And I didn't ask for consent. I wasn't about to ask for consent in that case. I mean, I knew I was going to handle a huge case versus somebody disqualifying me because I was handling a couple of minor cases. Well, it had a happy ending. I did handle it for four or five years and nobody ever sought to disqualify our firm. And we hadn't learned anything about the operations of the refinery that were going to be in derogation of their interest during the handling of the lawsuit. So that's the way that worked out. [19Ch50–99]

POSITIONAL OR ISSUE CONFLICTS

> Abraham Lincoln was arguing a case in front of the Illinois Supreme Court. And he was arguing that, on a given set of facts, the law should be A. And that afternoon he was back in front of the Illinois Supreme Court on a similar set of facts—this is in Carl Sandburg's biography of Lincoln—and he was arguing on this very similar set of facts that the law should be B. And the chief justice said, "Mr. Lincoln, weren't you here this morning arguing that the law should be A?" And he says, "Well, yeah, I was, but I've learned a lot since then." [6Ch100+]

Variations on the Abraham Lincoln story—though not always attributed to Lincoln and with somewhat different endings—reverberate throughout the interviews. The Lincoln saga illustrates yet another indirect conflict of interest, variously labeled "positional" or "issue" conflicts, in which lawyers advance a position in the representation of a client that is inconsistent with the interests of other clients who are neither parties to the case nor have any stake in it whatsoever (Dzienkowski 1993). Positional conflicts move us even further out the continuum of direct adversity, in that other law firm clients did not play even a remote role in the events in contention, nor do they have any interest in or relationship to any of the parties involved, the property or business opportunity sought, the assets to be divided, or the markets at play. Their interest is in the law itself. Because of the precedential force of case law, if lawyers succeed in altering legal doctrine while advancing the interests of one client, they may hurt other clients whose defense requires a radically different interpretation of the law.

Did Lincoln face an ethical dilemma when, on the same set of facts, he argued that the law should be A for one client and B for another? Respondents disagree. Those who invoked the tale of "honest Abe," America's consummately sympathetic legal role model, would say no. Indeed, as we will see, they celebrate the legend as the essence of what it means to be a good—and ethical—lawyer. Many other respondents differ, though a good number of them do so on a technicality, invoking a comment to the *Model Rules of Professional Conduct* that allows lawyers to advocate antagonistic positions in different cases, making an exception only for cases that are "pending at the same time in an appellate court" (American Bar Association

1983, Model Rule 1.7, comment, paragraph 9).[2] In other words, had Lincoln brought the two cases in different jurisdictions, in trial courts instead of an appellate court, at different times, had they been transactions rather than litigation, had he been lobbying in a legislature or pontificating in a law review rather than in a court, these lawyers would find Lincoln's conduct unproblematic.

Other respondents quibble with the narrow loophole. They acknowledge that although it may be easier to create adverse precedent through appellate litigation, a whole host of other less visible forms of advocacy on behalf of one client do impair others. Still others note that, whatever the ethical status of positional conflicts, they are world-class business conflicts. Clients generally fail to understand, appreciate, or sympathize with the nuances and loopholes of the conflict-of-interest rules that bind their lawyers. But they have clear conceptions and expectations of loyalty. They may not care whether their lawyers advocated a position adverse to their interests in an appellate court, a trial court, *Harvard Law Review,* or congressional testimony, nor may they care whether the Rules of Professional Conduct permitted or even required such advocacy. All these activities may violate *their* sense of loyalty, and many redistribute their legal business accordingly. Even if the ethical requirements and nuances do not grab them, many law firms are acutely concerned about positional or issue conflicts because the business consequences can be so severe.

Positional conflicts provide an intriguing window on the social worlds of law firms and on lawyering itself. They expose the core conceptions of what it means to be a lawyer as well as an effective and honest advocate or counselor. But the variations among law firms in their response to positional conflicts have structural as well as philosophical or ideological roots.

A Case Study in Positional Conflicts: Insurance Coverage Disputes

> We will not try to advance certain theories in a tax court, because we know that there will be adverse reaction—I mean, adverse impact—on lots of clients. . . . In the antitrust area, . . . we wouldn't, probably, like to challenge too many mergers, because we do a lot of mergers and acquisitions. We might not like to go in and try to make new law in the antitrust area to expand the reaches of the antitrust laws, because it would impact, probably, a lot more clients than the one that we're helping. The same way in the securities law. You wouldn't want to necessarily try to make new law that would be adverse to, quote, "corporate America"—just because it's cutting off your nose. I mean, everybody sits up and says, "You mean,

[2]The proposed Ethics 2000 revision of the *Model Rules* deletes paragraph 9, the reporter indicating that it makes "too much of a distinction between trial and appellate courts" (American Bar Association 2001, Rule 1.7, Reporter's Explanation of Changes, paragraph 24). Rather, it substitutes a new paragraph that suggests that positional conflicts be evaluated according to whether there is "a significant risk that a lawyer's action on behalf of one client will materially limit the lawyer's effectiveness in representing another client in a different case." The comment then suggests a list of factors to evaluate (American Bar Association 2001, Rule 1.7, comment 24). This proposed revision accords with the judgments of many of the respondents in my study.

> [this firm] is representing that guy in that stupid case?" So, but nothing quite as dramatic as the insurance area. I mean, there you just have to be on one side or the other. I mean, that's just 'cuz it is a war. I mean, the insurance companies just view it as a war. You can't represent both sides. [18Ch100+]

The interviews are laced with other examples of the arenas in which client preferences have been most fierce, the sides most clearly drawn, and the boundaries inviolate. The most common include professional liability (especially medical malpractice), employment law, bankruptcy, and banking and lender liability. Nothing comes close, though, to the discord over insurance coverage for liability for environmental pollution that erupted in the late 1980s.

> We had a major reinsurer who had sent us a good deal of coverage-related opinion work relating to environmental problems—where they had insured people and maybe the U.S. EPA or the Illinois EPA had made claims against their insured for allegedly spoiling the environment in some way, you know, dumping something in a river stream or burying barrels of some toxic substance or whatever it might be. And they, in turn, go back to their insurer and they say, "Well that's what we've got insurance for. You insure us." And the insurance company says, "Well, the provisions of our policy exempt that from coverage, so we're not going to defend you on it." And so then the insured sues its own insurer seeking a declaration that it is in fact covered for this claim. . . . So we had a lot of business . . . having to do with coverage opinions and defending them in declaratory judgment suits over these claims by the insured to be indemnified against the claims of the government. [19Ch50–99]

These coverage disputes produced wrenching positional conflicts, especially for large law firms. These firms, of course, represent large corporations and institutions. Many count both insurance companies and major manufacturers among their clients. In the nascent stirrings of the environmental law movement, these firms represented their diverse clients variously implicated in environmental cases. At the behest of their insurance company "clients," they defended insureds charged with liability for pollution or other environmental disasters. They represented corporate clients in disputes with their insurers over coverage for increasingly massive liability claims. They also represented insurance company clients sued for denying such coverage. They, of course, declined cases that involved disputes between their own clients. But they would litigate against nonclient insurers and defend against nonclient insureds. In so doing, they espoused positions that would be devastating if used against their own clients.

> Our firm represents the insurance industry. The firm was beginning to represent corporate America on Superfund environmental issues. It took a while for the bell to ring. . . . There has developed a war between corporate America and insurance companies over environmental coverage issues. It's a multi-billion-dollar issue. . . . There's no legal conflict, but a business conflict. We had lots of discussion about this within the [New Business] Committee and eventually the process crystallized.

> The firm decided not to take Superfund cases. Period. As a result, a group of lawyers left the firm. . . . This was by far one of the thorniest issues in my experience. We had to remove ourselves from these cases and that was hard to do. These were huge cases. [22Ch100+]

Losing lawyers over conflicts of interest is less common than losing money.

> One place where that comes up is in the environmental practice, where you represent either the insurer or the insured. And it's very hard to do both. . . . We happen to represent insurers. . . . It would be very unusual that we would represent an insured asserting a theory contrary to one of our existing clients. . . . It's very difficult to deal with. They are thought through very carefully. It's enormously time consuming. It takes days and weeks, at times, to resolve the issues, to—first of all—to get understanding of what the economic risks are and what's really at issue, what the interests of our clients are. And we spend an awful lot of time on that issue. Now, that may be kind of a bad example, because I think we now have that resolved. But getting to the conclusion that I just stated to you was not self-evident at the time we started the process. It was only through weeks and weeks and weeks of work that we finally got to that conclusion. . . . That generates an enormous loss of business. That's why . . . getting it resolved was so difficult—because the economic consequences were so draconian. [17Ch100+]

A third large law firm underwent the same difficult process of choosing sides, though it came out on the side of representing insureds.

> We have certain policies of people we will not represent, like insurance companies that are in the casualty business, because we do a lot of environmental coverage work where we're suing insurance companies. So our policy generally is not to represent casualty insurance carriers, although we make exceptions if they're just . . . hired for a tax matter, and they'll give us a waiver. . . . the decision not to represent insurance companies came out of [. . .] We saw our environmental practice booming nationwide. And we just concluded we couldn't be on both sides of that issue. We couldn't one day sue the carriers for hundreds of millions of dollars and then try to represent them. So that policy developed out of a decision that came up through the Environmental Department to the Executive Committee, and was published as a policy. And it irritates some people, because they might know somebody at Travelers or CNA or something. And they think that they have a chance to get, you know, $500,000 worth of business a year. But, when you're talking about possibly giving up your environmental practice, you have to make those decisions. [18Ch100+]

Though the process was seemingly most agonizing for the largest of firms, somewhat smaller ones have struggled with the same issues.

> That's a huge positional conflict in this firm—huge. We handle it by never taking on coverage representation for insureds—never. That is a straight-up positional

> conflict that we have made a policy decision on and have decided that it's a brick wall that will never be violated. [27Ch50–99]

Others continue to struggle over these issues.

The Case for Positional Conflicts

True proponents of the positional conflict notion do not belabor the slender reed of contemporaneous appellate jurisdiction on which it technically hangs. First of all, it's not so easy, when initially evaluating whether to take an engagement, to predict whether some day, in the distant future, it will end up on an appellate docket. Too many unforeseen contingencies in the life of the case—many controlled by adversaries—determine that trajectory. Moreover, so little is known about the case at the outset that even if they were guaranteed that the case would be appealed, attorneys would have difficulty predicting on what grounds the case would be appealed and whether those grounds would be adverse or even matter to fellow clients. However difficult these predictions may be, the regulatory exception further requires lawyers to predict that the firm will have a *second* case—in the same appellate court, at the same time, advancing an incompatible position—in order to determine whether they face a potential positional conflict in the technical sense. Lawyers may respond to the quandary by throwing up their hands and playing the odds (i.e., doing nothing) or by treating all cases as though they may end up in appellate court.

> You never know that when the case comes in. . . . You ardently represent somebody, and if that were to ultimately result in some change in the law that worked against your interests when you were defending lawsuits, then I guess that's the way it would be. But you don't know that when you take the case in. It would be very rare if you did. [19Ch50–99]

Why struggle to make these difficult predictions at the outset? Why not merely wait to see what happens? Because ethics rules prohibit dropping clients like a hot potato, when the going gets tough (more about this in the next chapter). Moreover, even if ethically permissible, withdrawing from a case in the eleventh hour may impose severe financial costs when it necessitates returning or forgoing fees for work already performed, giving up the law firm's share of a hefty award in a contingent fee case, or rupturing a relationship with a valued client.

So most respondents are sensitive to the possibility that they might put their clients at risk by advocating or facilitating adverse positions whether or not they ever set foot in an appellate court.

> The problem being, if we take it to litigation—from the plaintiff's point of view—we're going to push as far as we can. And, then, we might create new law which would adversely affect our other clients. . . . And our view is that it's just not the way to approach it—not only from a business perspective, but ethically as well. You don't want to be in a situation where you're trying to create new law on behalf of one client that's going to adversely affect so many others. [82Ch10–19]

> Well, sure, I mean, you know who your major clients are. And there are some things that you wouldn't do because you know that, if you won, you would be killing that client. And that's an issue that would be very sensitive to them and you just wouldn't do it. Now, is there any formal prohibition, any rule? No. [28Ch50–99]

For many respondents, concern for positional conflicts means they will not represent or will not sue certain industries or niches within industries, whether for fear of creating "bad law" for their regular clients or simply out of a concern for maintaining the appearance of loyalty.

Of course, conflicts of interest are insidious, and not only because they threaten potential harm to other clients unconnected to the case. As I noted repeatedly in the last two chapters, conflicts may also impair the representation of the client who has engaged the attorney. Because of abiding loyalties toward long-standing clients whose interests and positions are antagonistic to those of the new client, lawyers—perhaps subconsciously—shortchange the latter. They pull their punches, refrain from pulling out all the stops. A few respondents note that they avoid positional conflicts as much for these new clients with the adverse position as for their long-standing ones.

> Let's say we defend a number of clients on RICO [Racketeer Influenced and Corrupt Organizations Act] charges. One day, a potential new client comes to us and asks us to represent it as a plaintiff in a RICO case. Now the law on RICO is still potentially ambiguous. In order to vigorously advocate on behalf of the plaintiff, it may be necessary for the firm to take a position inconsistent with that which we have been making on behalf of our defendant clients. Where do you draw the line? You need to step back and look at the issues. We would refer the plaintiff to someone else. We can't say to the potential plaintiff client, "Look, we'd be glad to take your case as long as we don't include any RICO claims." That's not in the best interest of this client. It ought to be represented by someone else who can be vigorous on its behalf. . . . It may not be fair for a particular law firm to argue on both sides. Now some lawyers will say that is what the practice of law is all about; we can be vigorous advocates on all sides of a debate on behalf of particular clients. But I don't believe that that is exclusively our right. Arguing on both sides may have an adverse impact on our client. Take a statute of limitations question—the position that you advocate on behalf of one side is clearly adverse to that on the other. How do you look yourself in the face when you do that? [40Ch20–49]

Positional conflicts are not always so attenuated. The adverse interests of franchisers and franchisees, insurers and insureds, brokers and investors, lenders and borrowers are not limited to their conflicting interpretations of the laws that regulate their activities. The Lincoln sympathizers who perilously traverse the tightrope back and forth across the chasm of positional loyalties sometimes encounter direct adversities of interest among their clients. This is a particular problem in areas where parties tend to be repeat players, whereby a client in one case regularly turns up as an adversary in another.

> No, we'd lose too much money if we started defending in accident cases. . . . You can't do that. There's one or two lawyers in the plaintiff's work that, every now and then, handle a small insurance company. But, in the main, you simply can't do it because—good God—what if you had one client come in with a million dollar brain injury? And it's going to be against a company that it might take you ten years to make a million dollars from. . . . You wouldn't want to turn down that million dollar fee case. So, for that reason, it doesn't happen. I don't know of any plaintiff's lawyer around here that represents any insurance company or does any defense work. [65DSM20–49]

So another rationale for respecting the boundaries of positional conflicts is that they function like a set of blinders, shutting out the distraction and temptation of enticing matters that are likely to create serious conflicts for the lawyer. By maintaining rigid positional loyalties—essentially severing the tightrope—attorneys limit the number of occasions in which they are conflicted out of taking on attractive cases because of direct adversities with other clients.

Yet another rationale for honoring positional boundaries is that some clients demand it. As demonstrated in the case of insurance coverage disputes, clients are not shrinking violets.

> L: The hardest ones are when they're not really conflicts, but they're institutional conflict issues. What cases should we not get into, or should we get into, what sides of issues? And this has just arisen the last three or four years—what I would call "issues" conflicts, institutional policies, not taking certain types of cases. That's not our tradition. Our tradition is we're cowboys—whoever wants to hire us to shoot, that's what we do. And this is very much counterculture to us.
>
> S: And what accounts for the change?
>
> L: Well, because the nature of the practice changes, and as we represent larger and larger institutions, corporations, we are more identified with the establishment. And, therefore, antiestablishment types of lawsuits are bad for us. For example, taking a high-profile case before the United States Supreme Court in favor of punitive damages—that's very much against the interests of most of our clients. . . . to have the constitutionality of punitive damages sustained by the United States Supreme Court is very bad for [that corporation] and all the manufacturers. They don't like it. Certain rules relating to expert witnesses: the more loose the rules are as to who's an expert and on what subject, that's bad for defendants—and we represent defendants. So that would be a bad institutional issue. Telling corporations they can't cut down trees is bad. . . . Well, you lose clients, I mean, you just lose clients. . . . That's the thing that's vexing us. . . . It won't be the Wild West anymore. It'll be sad. But there you are. . . . I think it hurts us. But it's reality. [30Ch100+]

Several respondents described clients that insist—as a condition of the engagement—that the firm refrain from taking certain positions or representing certain kinds of clients or industries. Tobacco companies will not allow representation of asbestos manufacturers; certain banks won't allow representation of debtors in bankruptcy; bank regulators won't countenance defense of officers or directors of troubled banks. And other respondents offered examples in which clients threatened to pull their business if the firm took a disfavored position or represented the other side:

> Now if you talk about medical malpractice, like, we do [gives acronym for a medical insurer]. . . . They tell you to "[acronym] out of it." And, of course, they're the biggest insurer positions in the state. If we sued somebody in Galena—which is about as far away as you can get from here—they would have a major cow. They just wouldn't [. . .] I mean, they'd say, "Sorry. Good luck in your lawsuit, but we're not sending you any more ever again." I'm pretty sure that's their position. [63DSS<10]

Still others speculate about all the business they don't even know they lost because potential clients—unhappy with the positions the firm has taken—never even approached them.

> What business are we not getting because we're doing all this coverage work? I mean, that is really the conflict issue for us. And it's amorphous. It's hard. We don't know that, in fact, we've been passed over. We just think we have. . . . The problem is it's starting to become acrimonious. . . . Yeah, what some people [in the firm] say is, "Gee, we're losing a lot that isn't even [. . .] We're not even being considered, because of our position on other stuff." . . . The breast implant stuff, for example, is a situation where we would have thought we might have gotten some of that business. But we've defended—in coverage cases—involving that. So, we think we're conflicted out and that we'll never even know it, but we just [. . .] we'll never be considered. [24Ch50–99]

At least one respondent considers this array of economic sanctions available to clients to keep their lawyers in ideological line so potent that bar regulators need not worry about articulating and enforcing ethical standards regarding positional conflicts.

> The reality there is, if someone is having their bread buttered by a particular insurance company—or an insurer of a particular type—they are not going to [laughter] espouse something that would come into conflict with their income. It's not going to happen. . . . So, I don't view that as—truly—an area that is generating conflicts. . . . Phil Corboy [prominent Chicago personal injury lawyer]—is he going to represent Allstate [laughter] or Illinois Medical? I mean, this isn't going to happen. [laughter] And is he going to espouse . . . a position that is in conflict with [his] very being? [laughter] No! We don't have to worry about that one. [86CC<10]

Of course, not all clients insist on such positional orthodoxy. And other clients undoubtedly care about positional fidelity but lack the clout to demand it of their lawyers. The availability and potency of these sanctions vary by area of practice, type of client, and nature of the lawyer-client relationship. As a result, some types of practice are heavily regulated and others are not. That is to say, in some practices, notions of issue conflicts are well articulated, and in others, they are not.

The Social Ecology of Positional Conflicts

Positional conflicts are not distributed evenly or randomly across the legal landscape. How firms respond to the positional conflicts they do face often varies by the communities in which they are situated and the kinds of clients they serve.

The role of clients. Not all clients equally wield incentives to shape the positions a law firm champions and to ensure that it adheres to the party line. The influence of a particular client or constellation of clients is greatest when they exert great economic power over a firm. Such clout is more likely when one or more like-minded clients are responsible for a sizable proportion of the firm's business. It is more likely during a legal recession, when there are more lawyers available than there is work to occupy them. It is more likely in a competitive buyers' market, where many other law firms provide the same specialized services to which the clients can turn. It is more likely in routinized areas of legal practice or for clients that already distribute similar work to a number of other law firms, so that the start-up costs of reallocating business and bringing replacement firms up to speed are minimal. It is less likely for law firms that are heavily diversified than for more specialized boutiques. It is more likely when clients have access to legal intelligence and are able to oversee the positions taken by their lawyers on cases in which they are not involved. It is probably more likely when powerful partners—or "gorillas," as some call them—in the law firm are responsible for and whose compensation depends on bringing in that particular stream of business that is at risk. Firms that have many of these features generally pay greater attention to positional conflicts and are more likely to respect positional boundaries than firms with greater autonomy over a given client or cluster of clients.

A related way to think about the impact of the structure of client relationships on a firm's response to positional conflicts is suggested by Marc Galanter's (1974) typology of one-shotters and repeat players in legal institutions and his analysis of the myriad and profound advantages that the latter have over the former. On the one hand, repeat players have the incentives to shape and enforce positional boundaries because they have a stake in the substance and interpretation of the law itself, as they regularly advance the same interests in case after case. Galanter describes this commitment as "playing for the rules." Repeat players will invest vast resources in an important test case; they will flood the courts with amicus curiae briefs; and they may even be willing to sacrifice a few cases—settling weak cases out of court or refusing to appeal unfavorable trial court verdicts—in order to ensure that the evolution of common law favors their side. On the other hand, their continual stream of business gives repeat players the financial clout to influence and enforce the positions taken by their legal advocates. They have both the will and the means, then, to articulate and enforce positional commitments.

Not surprisingly, those areas of practice in which positional conflicts have been most fiercely contested and most reverently respected are those in which at least one of the parties is a repeat player. Indeed, positional boundaries are perhaps most inviolate in insurance coverage disputes in which two repeat players (insurance companies and corporations alleged to have polluted the environment) confront each other. In contrast, positional conflicts rarely, if ever, evolve in areas of practice that regulate the relationships among one-shotters—family law, divorce, real estate, and the like. Here lawyers tend to represent all sides to transactions or disputes from one case to the next.

So the composition of a law firm's clients affects its preoccupation with and response to positional conflicts. Firms with a large number of clients, few of which contribute a substantial share of business, report fewer concerns over these conflicts.

> ... there have been times where we have taken positions that—positionally—will benefit one group of clients or the other.... It's not like we represent a major Fortune 500 company, where we're living off of them. And, obviously, if we were, we're not going to be running around and suing other similar corporations and creating legal precedents that are going to really hurt our company. You know, a relatively small firm of [under 20] lawyers can't afford ... to decline all business ... that might—in some way—ultimately, adversely affect some present or future client.... We have some clients ... where that might be a more important consideration. But, many of them just, we really can't worry about it—I don't think. [94Ch10–19]

> We say, "We're trying to earn a living. If you'd send more business in, we wouldn't have to take plaintiff's cases." [laugher] And there are just some practical considerations here. We just can't be obedient to people's notion of what we ought to take, particularly if they're just sending in a modicum of work.... We've got two floors of a building here and we have to pay our expenses and pay our lawyers. And we require a flow of incoming work. [19Ch50–99]

Law firm size. Firm size represents another feature of the ecology of positional conflicts. Large firms are the site of these conflicts for a number of reasons. First, repeat players typically gravitate to large law firms, if for no other reason than they have the staffing and resources necessary to support large-scale repetitive transactions and litigation. Recall the former "cowboy" who lamented the issue conflicts that have beset his firm and constrained its choices as it has grown and come to represent major institutions with rigid vested interests, on whose business it now depends.

The diversification characteristic of most large law firms provides another structural opportunity for positional contests within the firm. Coverage disputes, in which the interests of clients of the firm's environmental department or corporate department collide with those of the firm's litigation or insurance departments, provide one example. An even more systemic controversy in large firms arises between its transactional lawyers and litigators. Many of the professionals and institutions—accountants, bankers, investment bankers, financial institutions—needed to facilitate major transactions pursued by the firm's deal makers are often the very targets of the firm's litigators. Because these parties are facilitators and not clients, of course, the firm faces no direct adversity and no true conflict of interest in suing them. But the scenario parallels the examples offered earlier in the chapter in which witnesses in one case are being sued in another. Taking an adverse position in an unrelated case against those facilitating a deal risks undermining the facilitators' goodwill and cooperation in the transaction.

> We don't sue accounting firms, for example. That's a policy matter, just because we work so much with accounting firms in transactional work and all that, that we just feel that it's not that much to be gained by turning around and suing Price Waterhouse when, two weeks from now, we'll have to work out a deal with them. [18Ch100+]

Diversification, of course, is a strategy for hedging against risk and fluctuating markets. It protects a firm from the dominance of a single constellation of clients characteristic of some kinds of boutique practice and lessens significantly the impact of those clients' economic threats to yank their business from firms that breech their positional boundaries. But diversifying clients also diversifies interests, positions, roles, and ideologies. It thereby multiplies considerably the number of occasions in which lawyers must choose between fidelity to the positional interests of one set of clients over the conflicting demands of another.

Areas of practice. Substantive specialization represents a third feature of the ecology of positional conflicts. Litigators, for example, face more positional conflicts than transactional lawyers do. The positions attorneys advocate are more visible in trials than in deals, the issues are more contentious, the adversities more apparent, and as I have already noted, litigated cases are more likely to shape legal precedent and affect the rules by which everyone else must play.

Respondents also describe areas of practice in which the legal principles are well established and litigation tends to focus on disputes about the facts of the case rather than about applicable legal doctrine. Here lawyers rarely feel troubled or constrained by issue conflicts.

> But most of the work we do is fairly fact-specific; it rarely rises to a positional conflict. With respect to litigation, our firm tends to be defense oriented—roughly about sixty-forty. We do work on restrictive covenants; this tends to be very fact-specific. One day you are on one side, the next you are on the other; the first case has no impact on the next. The way you argue the case depends on the nature of the agreements made in the first place and the facts of the case rather than some more generic positions. [34Ch50–99]

Location. Finally, although positional conflicts are found everywhere, firms respond differently in disparate communities, and positional commitments are much more likely to be honored in Chicago than elsewhere in the state. Take, for example, two relatively small firms, one in Chicago and one downstate:

> . . . I tend to specialize in an area of law where I don't run into the opportunity to be on the other side of the same kind of case too often—which is where the more obvious conflicts lie. So, for an example, if you contrast my practice with, let's say, someone in Kankakee, that is not uncommon for even the small firms in the smaller communities, to represent both sides of an issue. It's accepted and very commonplace. Not so in downtown Chicago. By and large, I always represent plaintiffs, who are individuals. And I'm always suing corporations and/or health care providers. [92Ch10–19]

> We do, for example, in personal injury work—we handle plaintiffs' cases as well as defense of those cases. We represent injured parties as well as insurance companies. And other civil matters, we'll represent corporations that are being sued for sexual discrimination or harassment. . . . And we've also represented parties that brought actions against them. . . . The implication was, it's not technically a conflict. But do we tend to stay away from certain types of work? The answer is no—other than certain types of work we don't handle on a regular basis. [64DSS10–19]

But this correlation between firm location and the incidence of positional conflicts is largely spurious, explained by features of legal practice already entertained. The large law firms, most beholden to positional demands, are all found in Chicago. Powerful repeat-playing clients and major institutions tend to be located in Chicago and to recruit city firms. Threats by clients to yank their business and allocate it to another firm are more credible in a big city with many hungry competing firms offering the same high-quality specialized expertise. So client sanctions against positional infidelity are probably more potent in Chicago and yield higher rates of compliance. Moreover, urban clients have easy visibility of the positions taken by their lawyers; indeed, Chicagoans can rely on a daily law journal to supplement other forms of gossip and surveillance. Though small towns are stereotyped as fishbowls, their attorneys may actually enjoy more privacy than their big-city counterparts do. Small-town lawyers must often travel some distance to the nearest county or federal court to ply their trade, where their activities are less likely to be seen by locals. And others avoid the appearance of positional conflicts by taking unpopular positions only for clients in distant communities.

But most important, downstate lawyers can rarely afford to specialize; the legal marketplace simply does not permit it. There are exceptions, of course. A few of the largest downstate firms devote a sizable niche of their practice to insurance defense litigation over local accidents, injuries, and malpractice. And a few firms on the Illinois side of the Mississippi River near St. Louis specialize in personal injury litigation exclusively on the plaintiff or defense side.[3] But most downstate at-

---

[3]The counties in southwestern Illinois contiguous to St. Louis have a reputation for providing union-sympathizing, working-class, pro-plaintiff jurors. As a result, a good deal of tort litigation, especially related to railroad accidents, has gravitated to that venue, supporting the viability of a few boutique legal practices in the area.

torneys must be generalists. With a diversified clientele and diversified practice, small-town lawyers are generally spared the demands for rigid positional fidelity.

> I've never had a client say, "You can have our business provided you do not take this type of business that would be adverse to our type of business. Although it may not be adverse to us directly, it would be adverse to our industry. We wouldn't want you to handle that type of work." I haven't come across that. . . . it's just a matter of reality in southern Illinois. Nobody, I think, can earn a living doing only what I call "one-sided defense," so to speak—doing nothing but plaintiff's work or doing nothing but insurance defense work. Oh, I take that back. . . . I can think of one or two firms that do predominantly personal, plaintiff's personal injury work. And what's interesting—as an aside—is I saw in one ad recently, when the Yellow Pages came out—which is great comic relief when you look at the [. . .] "We do not represent insurance companies." It's put in the ad. It's put in the ad. So I guess that's a form of advertising. But, if somebody comes in to us and we want to handle their case—and I think we can do as good a job, if not better, than any other plaintiff's attorney firm down here—and if the client would say, "Well, have you ever represented insurance companies?" "Yeah, I do it all the time." He may say, "Well, I'd rather not have you do my loan. It's nothing personal." But we've never had any pressure that I'm aware of, of clients specifically saying, "You can handle our work but don't handle this other work." [64DSS10–19]

A respondent from a relatively large insurance defense firm located in one of Chicago's collar counties explained that he would happily concentrate on the defense side. But that positional stance has become increasingly difficult in recent years, with the recession in legal business.

> But we don't have much of a choice. There are firms in Chicago that handle nothing but insurance defense. But, downstate, you can't survive only on defense work. Indeed, many of the defense cases here are being handled by Chicago firms. They are setting up offices out here. [78CC10–19]

Responding to the Temptations

Because of the sometimes powerful influence of client preferences, positional conflicts raise business questions as much as ethical ones for attorneys and their firms. Some firms have been largely reactive in the evolution of their positional commitments, allowing the boundaries to emerge by the accretion of new cases as much as by conscious design.

> We have a fairly young practice. And I've been doing this now for [less than 15] years. And our practice is shaped more by financial realities than it is by an overall scheme of how we want things to be or how we want to position ourselves. If CNA Insurance were to come here tomorrow and say, "We want to let you do all the defense work on our medical negligence cases," we would start doing that work, and we'd withdraw from any case we had a conflict at currently. We just

> happen to get a lot of plaintiff's cases. And we happen to want to pursue cases against doctors. And we'll probably continue to do that unless something pretty astronomical happens to the contrary or would make it financially advantageous for us to change our position. [121Ch<10]

Other firms are more proactive, honing their positional commitments to advance—or at least not sabotage—the ways in which they are marketing their firm.

> At one point, we did more medical-mal defense work than we do now, because the carriers that we represent—and still represent—wrote that kind of coverage. They don't do that now. So we've had an interest in trying to acquire clients—insurance companies—. . . in the medical-mal field. And because of that, we have—for a period of years—declined to take plaintiff's medical-mal cases. . . . It was really a matter of marketing, if that's the right word. We were trying to break in with some of these insurance carriers and get on their list to represent them or their insureds or doctors. And so we didn't want to be perceived as a plaintiff's medical-mal firm. . . . I mean, there's no conflict as such, but from just a strategy point of view, you might decline. [66Ch20–49]

In recent years, many attorneys have found this conscious strategy to specialize in a positional niche sorely tested by the changing economics of law practice.

> We turn away a very small percentage—mainly plaintiff's cases that we have to decline from a business standpoint. We discuss potential conflicts maybe three or four times a month—usually these are discussions over opportunities to take a plaintiff's case. . . . Oh, we moan and groan about it. The area—the defense side—has become really developed and overbuilt. The insurance defense field has become incredibly competitive. But we have worked so hard to develop a base and expertise on the defense side, that it would be throwing away too much. [89Ch20–49]

> Particularly, in the last five years or so, with the expansion of remedies—under both federal statutes and then under state common law—awards in [the labor] area are running, probably, $300,000, $400,000 for a successful plaintiff. And, on a contingency basis, that's a nice pay day. And they go a lot higher. There have been some major awards. And, yeah, at times [. . .] time to time, you sit back and you go, "maybe we're on the wrong side of the fence." Obviously, we know a lot of plaintiff's attorneys in this area who are making a ton of money. And you go, "Well, maybe we just switch our allegiance." [laughter] But, I don't know, a lot of it is your own philosophical bent. In our view, you can't do it both ways. You really can't. Now, I know other firms in the city that do work both sides of the fence. I don't know how they do it. We just don't think it's the right way to go. And, yes, from time to time, though, you go, "Oh, my God! [snicker] That was a good case." But we just, we have made that decision not to do it. [82Ch10–19]

So how do firms respond to the temptations to represent the other side? Some of those with the strictest policies about honoring rigid positional boundaries try to eke out limited exceptions that honor the spirit of their principles, if not the letter of them. For example, they agree to render opinions or advice, educate or investigate, help negotiate a settlement or a termination agreement for those traditionally their adversaries—but only to the point of litigation. None will participate in a trial. Many disclose to prospective clients that, if the matter about which they have agreed to provide counsel escalates to the point of litigation, they will withdraw from the case.

> I could never take on a medical malpractice case directly, . . . because I'm so much involved with the plaintiffs in that. On the other hand, I have been involved as a private counsel to physicians. But I would not appear in the court. In other words, . . . some of the people that are our experts or close friends that have been sued. And they've come to me for advice and I've talked to their lawyers that have been appointed by the insurance company to defend them—but only to give my opinion as to what the nature of the case is, the likelihood of success—to the extent they want me involved—but never in the courtroom. . . . Because I really don't feel that I could do a good job in the courtroom for someone that is being sued, when this is what I do all the time. And I always have the fear that my personal alignment with the victim might not produce the type of defense that I should. And so I stay out of that. [60Ch20–49]

Other lawyers with firm positional commitments seemingly require greater justification to make even such a limited exception, indicating that they will represent the other side—short of litigation, of course—when they feel it furthers the same abstract goal for which they traditionally represent their adversaries.

> I have been retained by a company in a sexual harassment case because I was a plaintiff's attorney. And what I said is, "Look, I'll do the investigation for you. And I will advise you as to what I think. And you can take my advice. And if you choose not to take it, get yourself another attorney." But, I mean, my goal is to have fair employment practices. So if I do it through prevention or solution of problems that arise, okay. I mean, my heart is in plaintiff's law. But, on the other hand, I mean, hey, if a company will retain me under those circumstances, I'm accomplishing the same goal. And, in that case—it was a sexual harassment case—I settled it. 'Cause I told them I thought the case should be settled. And it was for a figure that the plaintiff and the plaintiff's attorney felt were reasonable. So, I didn't see a problem. . . . I might have a problem litigating that case. I don't think I would have done that. But I didn't have a problem investigating it. And I didn't have a problem advising them about it. . . . And if it was. . . . a company with terrible, with practices that I thought were awful, and they really were really retaining me to clean 'em up, I mean, I'd see it as a wonderful opportunity. [118Ch<10]

These respondents offer a conception of law as a tool to achieve a valued social outcome that ought to be wielded to prevent victimization and not only to provide compensation to victims after the fact. Few respondents spoke of their role in such terms. For these unusual lawyers, traversing the ideologically charged tightrope between adversarial camps represents a "wonderful opportunity" rather than an ethically or financially perilous journey. This perspective requires a much more nuanced and subtle interpretation of positional conflicts than we traditionally find in legal discourse. (And probably one-shot individual clients rather than institutional ones.)

Respondents, tantalized by the temptation to represent the other side but concerned about antagonizing clients by advancing adversarial positions, will make exceptions on low-visibility cases in which their clients would be unlikely to find out. Low-visibility litigation opportunities are more rare, available mostly to small-town, downstate law firms. Several downstate attorneys, who would never sue a local doctor, hospital, or employer, will do so outside the community.[4]

> We do labor work and we represent management. And so we would not—as a general policy—do any union representation or take on a labor matter against a company.... It's not prohibited.... We would never represent a union because of our ties to companies. Would we ever represent an individual against a company on a matter that we normally defend? Well, we may.... If it's a low-profile matter and, say, it's out of town and it's just a company thing and there's no conflict—it's just a matter of do we want to do it?—that will normally be resolved among the people who handle that type of business.... "Do you think this would create a problem with our clients if I represented John Smith in a discrimination claim against Jones Corporation over in Arapin, Ottawa?" And if they say, "No, I don't think that's a problem. Go ahead and do it," that would be the end of it. If it's something that may be higher profile and it would be publicity—something may hit the newspapers or the other clients are definitely going to know about—then, oftentimes, that will come to a partnership meeting and say, "Well, I'm considering this. It's not a conflict, but do you think it's going to create a problem with our clients—a perception problem?" [50DSL20–49]

Other respondents indicate that they manage the temptation or necessity to represent varied positions by discussing these positional issues at the inception of a relationship with a new client and negotiating the terms of the engagement.

> You try to arrive at an understanding with the client about what you will and will not do.... I mean, for example, let's assume you have an insurance company client for whom you're doing some financing work. You may arrive at an understanding with that client that you will not assert against it whether a particular insurance policy that it has issued covers a spill. But you will also work out with

[4]Well, let's say that there was no problem with the insurance company and that we could sue ... somebody here in town. We probably wouldn't do it. We represent enough of 'em that they would be upset with us. The physicians—for the most part—view someone who sues another physician as a pariah, a bad guy, a bloodsucker, and all those terms we hear. And so often we have to rely on physicians in our regular personal injury cases.... I would think it would be a bad idea to sue someone in your own neighborhood.... I would say you'll never see an attorney in [this city] who does medical malpractice sue a physician in [this city].... That doesn't get into conflicts so much. And you don't shit in your own backyard is the phrase, I guess. [63DSS<10]

> that client that that is an issue that you might be asserting against another insurance company, even though it deals with the same language in another policy. But these are the kinds of things that, when you sit down, in the very beginning of a relationship, you can work out often. If you don't do it then, it becomes very difficult to work it out. [23Ch100+]

Or they may refuse to handle that aspect of the prospective engagement that requires advancing positions that would be unpopular with other clients. They chisel off a chunk of the legal work with which they are comfortable and send the rest off to another law firm.

> We represented a steel manufacturer in an environmental case, where they were being sued by another steel manufacturer for contribution under CERCLA [Superfund]—all kinds of environmental loss. Now, when we were first retained, as far as doing that matter, there was no problem. But we also told them that, "You're being sued in an environmental area, which means you should look to see if you have insurance to cover it." Now, they also requested that we do that for them and do the insurance aspects of it. Well, that's where we had to tell them, "No, we couldn't do it," because we represent insurance companies. . . . So that the insurance side of it, which we're not involved in, is entirely handled by a different firm. We don't even know what's going on. [47Ch20–49]

Ultimately, of course, decisions about positional conflicts are matters of discretion. Firms obviously weigh client preferences, the potency of the sanctions available to them, and their willingness to impose these sanctions for what they consider positional infidelities. But aside from assessments of which client's ox will be gored by advancing a particular position, some cases and some positions are clearly worse than others in how significantly they threaten the overall interests of the clientele of the firm. Positional conflicts are not dichotomies of good or bad, appropriate or inappropriate. They are arrayed on endless continua that differentiate the impact that these cases will have on client interests. Firms assess each opportunity and how likely it will offend clients, harm them, or make the achievement of their interests easier or more difficult—rejecting some opportunities and embracing others. As a matter of policy, law firms neither categorically avoid positional conflicts nor ignore or even embrace them; they exercise discretion. Some temptations are worth the risk; others are not.

> You know, there are some people who will not take a lender-liability case against some banks; but they will take disputes against banks. I mean, that's a gradation. In other words, we'll never sue a bank if there's a claim of lender liability because we don't want ever [to] make lender-liability law, okay? But we will sue as to whether or not there was a fraudulent guarantee. We will defend a case on that basis. I mean, there's all kinds of gradations. But we've talked about this at great length. . . . let's think about whether or not we want to represent somebody in this particular situation. Look at this situation and say, "This is probably not a good one for us to do. Because it's just going to open up a whole can of worms as to

whether or not banks are acting properly in certain ways that we know our other clients are acting." [10Ch100+]

A small-town respondent explained that his firm deals with the temptation to represent all positions by doing just that. Firm clients include both plaintiffs and defendants. But attorneys within the firm tend to advocate one position or the other.

> To date, we have never concluded that we had to turn down work because it would be, kind of, philosophically contrary to a position we have taken in a totally unrelated matter. I have been practicing for [almost twenty] years. Early on in my practice, I did a majority of insurance defense work. So I was on the defense side of things and would take an occasional plaintiff's case as it came along. Probably three, four, five years ago, I made a conscious decision that I was not going to do any of the firm's insurance defense work any more. I'm going to do it from the plaintiff's side. That's a personal choice of mine, because I felt an internal conflict—not a legal conflict—between advocating for the injured party on Monday and trying to whittle down the injured party's claim on Tuesday when I was defending the client. So in our office, we have attorneys who do primarily all the defense work and the others who do primarily plaintiffs' work, just to, kind of, avoid that internal conflict. I must say, though, I find it very helpful—in my plaintiff's practice—to have my defense partner across here. Because I can go get a different perspective on the case. . . . So, it's useful to have both, but it's hard for the same attorney to do both, I think. [87DSS10–19]

Taking All Comers: Dismissing Positional Dogma

And then there are the hired guns who assert that there is no discretion to be exercised. They take all comers and do so happily. Indeed, many invoke an ethical obligation to do so.

> This is not a problem. I believe that you have an obligation to do the very best for the client. You can't worry about the effect of this case on your other clients. [111DSM<10]

> I've never [. . .] Maybe I'm naive and behind the times. I don't view that as a conflict. I mean, I think that's one of the arts of being a good lawyer. I ought to be able to take any side of an issue. [66Ch20–49]

Moreover, they argue, taking all comers, embracing all positions, makes them better lawyers and more valuable to their clients.

> More problematical is our continued representation of debtors and borrowers against financial service industry clients, where we have played both sides and

> continue to play both sides. And I think it benefits our clients because we play both sides and we know the law on both sides.... We have a glass wall in front of us, instead of a brick wall, which we can see through the other side. So we know their arguments; we know the weaknesses and strengths on both sides. And our lawyers, I think, are better trained by being on both sides. But it's getting harder and harder. Because, what happens if you make terrible law against banks? They're not going to like you a lot. [10Ch100+]

These respondents concede that their firms do advocate incompatible positions for different clients and sometimes even contribute to the creation of legal precedent that hurts some subset of them. But, they rationalize, if they didn't do it, some other law firm would.

> ... I mean, we've taken some positions in the insurance cases where, I guess, it ... affected personal injury rights or things like that. But that's, I mean, that's just things you work around. I mean, if you win a case that construes a contractual statute of limitations in an insurance policy, ... —it might be a restrictive interpretation—so, now the personal injury department has to comply with that law. And, as I said, if we didn't do that, someone else would do it. And that's the position we took.... I mean, I've won cases in the Illinois Supreme Court that have established precedents that our insurance clients didn't like. But, if I didn't do it, somebody else would have done it. I mean, it wasn't that I was just such a genius. I happened to have the case that went there. And that's just, you know, that's just life. [94Ch10–19]

> As far as I know, lawyers just forge ahead with their cases, make their arguments, and if they're adverse to a position that one of their partners made in another case six months earlier, it just happens.... I'm not aware of clients complaining about it and I'm not aware of our losing business because of it. And I'm not aware of a lawyer, in any way, changing his position because we took a different position six months ago. The most active recent one that I'm aware of ... is the statute of limitations for securities actions under 10(b)(5). Are you familiar with this at all, where the Supreme Court came down and developed a one-year–three-year statute? And then Congress tried to overrule the Supreme Court's opinion? And there's been a lot of fighting in the courts about what was the proper interpretation of the congressional override statute and so on. And it became relevant to every single pending securities case. And, at the time the opinion came down, we had 50 percent defense work in securities and 50 percent [...] [plaintiff's work]. And I worked on briefs saying, "This is what the case means and what Congress intended," and other cases saying the exact opposite. And until the Supreme Court decides, both positions are reasonable to advocate. I've often taken a plaintiff's brief and handed it over to a defense lawyer and said, "... This is what I perceive to be the best arguments on that side." ... I mean, if I was in court arguing that ... the statute of limitations should be four years, and the other lawyer pulled out a brief that my partner filed in Minnesota six months ago

and said, "Ah ha! The [names his firm] firm argued the exact opposite point six mon [. . .]" I think the judge would say, "Counsel, you know what? . . . If you're so enamored of the brief they filed in Minnesota, white out their name on the front and stamp your name on it. Step up and make your arguments. But the fact that they happened to represent the other position in another unrelated matter is of no interest to me." And I'm very confident that that's the position a court would take. [39Ch50–99]

We've come full circle to honest Abe. This last respondent supplies a modern-day ending to the Lincoln saga. The judge would never take Lincoln to task for his inconsistent positions, he predicts, because the judge wouldn't care. We turn, finally, to the last variation on the Lincoln story. This version offers yet another ending, one that blames the judge for mistaken judgment rather than the unnamed Lincoln and that celebrates this positional agnosticism as the essence of honest, effective, ethical lawyering. Note, once more, that this impassioned critique of positional dogma, celebration of lawyers as hired guns, and plea for blind unbridled advocacy comes from another small-firm lawyer.

> Oh, I think [positional conflicts] are absurd, myself. . . . I have no problem arguing one thing in front of a judge one day and arguing the exact opposite in front of the judge the next day. Any client that doesn't understand that, I don't think understands what lawyers are all about. There's the old joke about, where the lawyer's in front of the judge. And the judge says, "Well now, counsel, weren't you just in front of me yesterday, arguing the opposite side of the same issue?" And the lawyer says, "Well, yeah, I was." And the judge says, "Well, counsel, didn't I rule in favor of you yesterday? And now you're asking me to rule the exact opposite? How can you argue that?" And the lawyer says, "Well, judge, obviously, yesterday you were mistaken." [laughter] I mean it's a funny joke, but I think that's the essence of what we do. Anybody that can't argue alternative, inconsistent theories shouldn't be a lawyer. . . . I think, if we had a case in the appellate court, . . . and we were advocating a position that was contrary to a position of an existing client in a trial court level, I don't think we'd have any obligation whatsoever to do anything except try to win both cases. And if making law in one hurts us in the other, well, so be it. I don't see any problem with that at all. . . . I think anybody—also—that doesn't believe that, hasn't read the code of ethics. Because the number one code of ethics is to represent your client zealously. It doesn't say do it lukewarm because you got another client who pays you more. I mean, if a lawyer can't separate the concepts for each client individually and do the best they can for that client, they shouldn't be a lawyer. So, I mean, positional or issue conflicts—to me—are ludicrous. And I think they're contrary to the concept of being a lawyer. [73CC10–19]

PRO BONO CASES

Sometimes the positional conflicts become even more attenuated when law firms advocate positions that deeply offend religious, political, moral, or ideological beliefs and values embraced by important clients of the firm. Occasionally, these ideological conflicts are triggered by solicitations from paying clients.

> We were asked to become counsel for the [political candidate] campaign. One of the people that was put in charge of it has been a long-term client of the firm and he wanted to use us as general counsel for the [candidate] campaign. Now, despite whatever philosophical feelings I might have about [the candidate], . . . my attitude is "business is business," as long as it doesn't conflict with anything. However, we have a client who is very involved with [another political party] in Illinois. Now, we don't do work for the [political party]. We're not a political firm, so we normally don't get involved in any of that. I tried to do a lot of work with partners to determine whether that could present a problem. And, interestingly enough, it would have. [33Ch50–99]

More often, such conflicts arise from opportunities to take on a pro bono case.

> Well, one that we worry about is where a lawyer would take on a representation of a client where the client would be so abhorrent to either other clients of the firm or other lawyers of the firm, as to cause a problem. Now, that's not a conflict in the legal sense, but a conflict that we have to sort out. And we typically resolve that by permitting lawyers to represent whoever they want to represent. Although there probably are some limits on—just as a matter of a community that we operate in [. . .] It comes up in abortion cases; it comes up in Nazi cases—the two where we've felt it most strongly. [17Ch100+]

> And I suppose if I had clients that felt very, very strongly—say, for example, about gun control, and I was representing Remington. I haven't seen instances where a client would feel so upset about that, that they would necessarily pull the business. Although, I think Skadden Arps took some heat when they jumped in on behalf of Phelan [Cook County Board president] on a pro bono on the issue of abortion [reinstating abortions at Cook County Hospital]. . . . I had heard that there were clients where, higher up in that company, they basically said, "We don't want Skadden doing our work any more because we're so offended by positions that they've taken now." . . . I haven't seen that happen to us too often. But if you jump out in front on an issue that's very controversial, I can see where that has the possibility of happening. [59Ch50–99]

> Classic case down here, too, is with our courthouse sign. It's in federal court right now. [Quotes the sign's reference to God]. I mean, there's no way that we would agree to represent the plaintiffs in that action, even though we may agree with the ACLU argument. . . . I can't imagine [any] of us agreeing to take that. . . . That would be professional suicide. [128DSS<10]

The fact that these ideological rifts largely explode over pro bono cases makes them no less wrenching or acrimonious. Obviously, though, they are easier to resolve when lucrative fees are not at stake and when the firm does not risk antagonizing a loyal paying client by declining a matter near and dear to its heart (as the first firm with the political problem might have).

The heat generated by these disputes does demystify, though, the underlying rationale for less attenuated positional controversies and fidelities. Few of these ideological antagonisms challenge legal or ethical principles. Lawyers are not ethically compelled to decline these pro bono cases. Clients who privately delight in the proliferation of semiautomatic weapons or recoil every time the state executes a felon have no valid claim on the positions championed by their lawyers—as long as they have never engaged them on a gun control or death penalty case—though they are certainly entitled to yank their business. These disputes over pro bono cases are not about fiduciary obligation or fidelity; they are about crass business conflicts and the raw power of clients to influence the substantive agendas of their lawyers. For many firms wrangling over more legally and ethically salient positions, this power struggle is what issue conflicts are all about.

Of course, the positional conflicts triggered by pro bono cases are not always so attenuated. In many of them, law firms represent indigent, powerless underdogs making claims on society's most powerful institutions, which have ignored, discriminated against, or injured them—institutions such as banks, insurance companies, real estate companies, hospitals, employers, government agencies—the very lifeblood of the legal profession and the interests it holds sacred. Some pro bono cases require lawyers to advance positions that *are* adverse to the legal interests of these powerful long-standing clients. And some of the most famous, of course, have concluded in a Supreme Court decision that, in granting rights to the underclass, have imposed costs and constraints on the institutional constituencies of many law firms.

> We've had some situations on occasion, where we . . . had opportunities to represent—the Chicago [. . .] I forget what it's called now. It's an AIDS group. . . . And we have done some work helping them out on occasion, patients who needed some assistance to kind of cut through some red tape. And then it was no problem. But I do remember one instance where they wanted to sue either a hospital or a pharmaceutical company to demand certain types of treatment. And we just could not take the case. [59Ch50–99]

As with all other conflicts of interest, taking on such pro bono engagements threatens not only the interests of these institutional clients but also those of the pro bono client as well. Such powerful entanglements with major institutions may compromise the zealousness with which lawyers go after them on behalf of an indigent client.

> We're bond counsel for the [names government entity]. And you get a pro bono criminal case where [names government entity] versus Joe Schmedlap. And I guess we take most of those. But it has always troubled me that the individual—the pro bono client—if he loses, could be in a very good position to come back and say, "The [government entity] pays the firm that represented me $500,000 a year. They threw my case." [3Ch100+]

CONCLUSION

The ripples of adversity that emanate from the epicenter of legal transactions and disputes serve as a kind of Rorschach test with which to understand how respondents view their roles, responsibilities, relationships, and revenue. With more degrees of freedom to respond to indirect conflicts of interest and less ethical guidance, other influences—business and marketing concerns, power dynamics within the firm, lay notions of loyalty and fidelity, client pressure, personal moral values—figure into the exercise of discretion. With a broader range of frames in which to conceive a potential conflict of interest and legitimate options to resolve it, respondents elucidate and justify their choices. The peripheral ripples, then, break the silence of justification and embellish the uniformity of response found at the epicenter of direct adversity. They expose some of the tensions that conflicts of interest embed in the practice of law that remain hidden in those more central sites where the tension seemingly pulls in only one direction.

And so we hear about zealous advocacy and pulling punches, hypocrisy and loyalty, trust and revenge, fidelity and harm, persona non grata and counseling short of litigation, and perhaps most of all, that universal technique of neutralization resurrected when confronted with temptation: “If we didn’t do it, someone else would.” But as we listen to the dissonant choir, we realize that the clashing melodies come not only from the lawyers themselves but also from the social structures in which they practice. These Rorschach tests reveal not the lawyers’ psyches but their social worlds. Some practice in dense, vast, intricate webs; others in small, attenuated, disconnected ones. Some must deal with ripples of adversity that emanate throughout their practice; others rarely encounter a ripple at all.

Are lawyers hired guns, championing one position today and its antithesis tomorrow? Yes, they are, if those who do the hiring are—excuse the pun—one-shotters. When clients come and go and are not expected to return, their advocates, with pistols blazing, can boldly saunter into the gunfight, undaunted by the fear that a stray bullet may graze an innocent bystander. Their marksmanship does not require the finesse of those cowboy-advocates who practice in dense, populated networks where clients keep returning and otherwise hover on the sidelines, observing their every shot and vulnerable to stray bullets.

As Time Goes By

. . . You have to be sensitive to the fact that a conflicts search is really only a snapshot and, as time goes forward, things can change. [7Ch100+]

So many things are said to improve or ease with time: fine wine, riding a bike, mastery of technical skills of all sorts, Stradivarii, grief, love, wisdom, bad haircuts, teenagers. Not so with conflicts of interest. Because time allows relationships to accrete and transform, conflicts of interest involving ongoing clients almost always get worse over time because interests change and new ones blossom. The three previous chapters have offered a kind of photo album of conflicts of interest shot in their natural habitats—families, organizations, relationships, markets and industries, dump sites, prisons, small towns and big cities, disputes, transactions, and agreements. Some photos even captured the role of law at times of momentous transition—the end of a career, a marriage, a life, a company—when lawyers are especially sought.

But these still shots, however complex and intricate, oversimplify. They conceal the difficulties that come from the unremitting, unremarkable passage of time and all the microtransitions in the life of a client and the social webs in which that client is embedded—many of which lawyers cannot possibly be aware of—that reconfigure interests and provide new ones. (Not to mention the difficulties caused by changes in the lives and practices of the lawyers themselves, which is the subject of the next chapter.)

But the interest in the dynamic over the static is not merely one of greater appreciation, bigger thrills, or even better or more nuanced understanding. Temporal concerns figure explicitly in the rules of professional responsibility that govern how relationships between lawyers and clients begin and end and that differentiate the priority of interests of and obligations lawyers have to prospective, current, and former clients. Time is not merely a canvas upon which new conflicts of interest unfold; it is also a regulatory occasion. Ethical rules provide guidance and constraints in how attorneys respond to the histories that evolve in their practice. Even if lawyers did not find all the permutations in the lives of their clients momentous and ripe for new conflicts of interest, the ethics rules tell them to look again.

So in this chapter, I briefly drag out the motion pictures that depict the significant epochs and turning points in the history of a legal matter and in the evolving relationship with a client that typically generate new conflicts of interest. These moving pictures will not be entirely unfamiliar, because many of the tensions described in the last chapters arose at points of transition. Here I revisit the major themes and systematically add the overlay of time. What happens when clients, their structures, and their boundaries change? What happens as the relationships among the assorted parties evolve? What happens in the course of an engagement as the attorneys learn more about the matter, unearth new evidence, and sometimes discover additional interested parties? What happens as the case, moving through the legal system, reaches various transition points—settlements, pleas, verdicts, judgments—that reconfigure the interests of the diverse parties with a direct or indirect stake in the case? What happens when engagements end?

DISPUTE TRANSFORMATION

"Through No Fault of Our Own": Client Changes

Answering the question "who is a client?" is by no means a simple task, especially in complex organizations, be they extended families or multidivisional, multinational corporations. Chapter 4 provided an overview of the complexities, particularly when organizational clients have ongoing relationships with their lawyers and bring a steady stream of varied legal problems, each involving different combinations of parties, units, roles, and entities within the organizational structure. It's like shuffling a deck of cards over and over again, dealing a random number of cards at each iteration, and then returning them to the deck to be shuffled and potentially dealt yet again. As the snowball of legal engagements lurches from matter to matter, lawyers must continually reassess. Which subset of natural persons and organizational units constitute the client this time around? Are their interests all compatible? Are any of their interests adverse to those of other subsets of organizational parties implicated in previous or other ongoing cases?

But the overlay of time is not merely the occasion for reshuffling the deck. As time goes by, cards are dropped and added to the deck. Large organizations continually hire and fire personnel; add or lose members or partners or offices; change their owners and directors; expand or downsize; raid the competition; gobble up other organizations or get gobbled up themselves; make, break, and restructure alliances. With time, the total number of cards can actually shrink or grow; the deck can thereby end up with duplicate cards or lose an entire suit or just a random card here or there. Once the size and composition of the deck changes, lawyers must also be attentive to the possible importation of interests from other organizations or exportation of interests, confidences, and clients to other organizations. But because only the face of the cards is readily apparent, attorneys cannot easily see that the king they are dealing with, for example, actually came from another deck.

Which of the imported and exported cards, now shuffled into unmatched decks, are to be construed as clients? And how can lawyers possibly keep track of the changing boundaries, migrations, and interests? One respondent, quoted in chapter 4, complained:

> I mean, you really do have to know who's who. And with some of these corporations, they're buying and selling companies all the time. And so, all of a sudden, they've bought somebody that you didn't know anything about . . . because you weren't involved in the deal. Somebody'll call up and say, "Hey, your guy just sued our guy! What the hell?" "That's not in our system." "Well, we bought them last year." Well, how am I supposed to know? Am I supposed to read the paper and go through it every day? That's physically impossible. [18Ch100+][1]

The element of surprise is the least of the problem. Even when mindful of organizational changes, law firms may be stymied about how to resolve the often unintended conflicts of interest that follow in their wake.

> And that actually segues to the other area which is very difficult, where at the outset, . . . you have no conflict. And through nothing that you as a firm have done—or nothing inappropriate—you get hired by the party on the other side on an unrelated matter or whatever or there's a corporate reorganization, acquisition, divestiture. All of a sudden you find yourself in a conflict position. And, as innocent as we may feel that this was just sprung upon us, it can be very difficult to sort out what the appropriate thing to do is with the clients. [5Ch100+]

This was the one section of the interview where the mantra "through no fault of our own" was echoed repeatedly—and rightly so. Most other conflicts of interest described in this book arise from choices made by the law firms themselves—to

[1]Of course, as this respondent notes, lawyers are less likely to be in the dark when they play a role in the deal. Firms that serve, more or less, as general counsel for their client will be apprised of corporate changes because they were their midwives—helping to consummate a hostile takeover or merger, a bankruptcy, or a divorce. Because corporations have been backing away from general counsel relationships in recent years and spreading their legal workload across a broader swathe of law firms, this problem of tracking organizational change has grown.

take on a new client, to institute or defend a lawsuit, to represent multiple parties, to broker a deal or implement a transaction. But these conflicts in which the deck changes because of choices the clients make are more like drive-by shootings, with lawyers grazed and sometimes mortally wounded by stray bullets being discharged by their clients acting independently. It comes with the territory, with hanging out in these volatile neighborhoods. And though some clients might be more sympathetic or indulgent about the wounds they inflict on their own lawyers than they are about the wounds the lawyers inflict on themselves, the conflicts are no less real or serious. And not all clients are so indulgent.

> Last year, we had to . . . turn down a long-standing client of the firm—an ongoing matter—seek replacement of counsel. . . . This was a three- to four-month negotiation process between two long-standing clients of the firm . . . on a specific matter, where we've been representing one client in connection with a contract negotiation—basically with a contract which was falling apart. There was a potential for litigation. There was another corporate client on the other side. Wasn't originally on the other side, but acquired the company with which we were dealing. And . . . suddenly a conflict arose a year and a half into the engagement. . . . We contacted the corporate client on the other side. They said, "Absolutely not. We will not waive this conflict. Too bad!" They used conflict as a sword. Our representation of the two clients was totally unrelated . . . We attempted to negotiate something on the lines of "Well, we will only represent this client up to the point we go to litigation. If you go to litigation, we refer it out." They wouldn't do it. The client on the other side just had a policy, "We will not let any law firm that represents us be adverse to us. Period." Did we really have to withdraw in the representation? As an ethical matter, I can't say that we did. We, in fact, consulted with [an ethics expert outside the firm], got his views on it. He said, "Well, technically, you probably could proceed with this. This is more of a business question." Well, we ended up withdrawing. We ended up replacing counsel in connection with the side we'd been representing through this. . . . We cut our fees, and in fact, we wrote off a substantial amount of our fees and brought somebody new in to represent the existing client. . . . I personally met—even though I had no involvement with either client—personally met with both clients, discussed the matter with them. It was a very difficult situation with two long-standing clients of the firm, where the conflict had arisen after the fact. That was the worst conflict situation, because you were balancing internal politics between two very highly respected partners of the firm, two long-standing clients of the firm, an ongoing relationship with one client. Fees being written off. Everybody being unhappy with the result internally. The clients not being harmed, but being distracted by a conflict issue. [1Ch100+][2]

The probability of facing continual—and sometimes imperceptible—structural changes among organizational clients is greatest for large law firms, which are

[2]In a second interview, the chair of the firm's new business committee lamented that they spent maybe fifty to one hundred hours trying to resolve the conflict.

more likely than smaller firms to represent these hulking, volatile corporations. Still, respondents throughout the state, in firms of all sizes, cited examples in which changes in their clients that developed in the course of an engagement created difficult conflicts of interest for their firms. The name partner of a largish downstate firm described the same corporate-acquisition conflict that his counterpart in Chicago did.

> Now, one case I had recently was where I had the client for some time. I was suing the [names bank]. And the [commercial] department [of the firm] represented a bank that took over the [bank being sued]. It bought out the [bank being sued], so to speak, during the course of my representation. So there the conflict arose. And the commercial department and I had to decide, "Well, who's going to withdraw?" . . . In that instance, I withdrew from representing the client—the individual. And the [commercial department] kept representing the bank. And I assisted [the client] in having the other firm and made no charge for the time that I put in. [65DSM20–49]

So time is often the catalyst that turns what I called "other clients" in the last chapter into adverse parties. Law firms must superimpose over an adversity analysis a who-is-the-client analysis of each new organizational chart—and each subsequent version or iteration thereof. The analysis must consider not only the nature of the new affiliation but also what has actually changed about the client. Was the client swallowed whole? Did a mere individual or division within the client move elsewhere, leaving behind a still viable company that the law firm continues to represent? Had the law firm performed work for that now-mobile person or entity; does it have confidential information regarding its operations that can be used to the advantage of another client? Does absorbing a defector turn an adversary into a client?

Sometimes changes in "other clients" create new adversities, but less direct ones. The other client may have acquired a new company that is a direct competitor of another valued client. Or it may experience internal change, redirecting its scientists, chemists, and engineers to work on the development of a new AIDS drug or pollution abatement process or smaller computer chip. These low-visibility, nonstructural changes may create conflicts of interest for the company's law firm, whose intellectual property specialists have been trying to secure exclusive patents in these areas for another client.

On the flip side, conflicts of interest can arise from changes in the client the firm is currently representing. The conundrum here is not about how these changes ripple out to infect the representation of other clients but rather how the lawyers continue to serve the transformed client itself. Organizations often fracture as marriages fail and partners retire or die. When they do, which pieces of the wreckage, if any, are clients, and how does the law firm continue to serve any or all of them? Many examples offered in chapter 4 consider how law firms plan for the probability or inevitability of organizational demise (e.g., in estate planning) and how they deal with the legal problems occasioned by the breakup itself. But often the breakup or its possibility is incidental to the matter for which the lawyers have been engaged. The entire partnership or marriage may be the plaintiff or defendant in a lawsuit. Given the long delay in civil cases in Cook County, many rocky marriages—often further strained by the injuries sustained or legal problems faced—fail by the time the case goes to trial. Who does the law firm then represent?

> And I've had a number of cases where I have a husband and wife who then get divorced, cases where there's cosigners on a loan. And I've got to be very careful as to how I'm representing each of the individual plaintiffs. . . . We have one right now, where a husband and wife got divorced and are very bitter. And I think I'm going to have to withdraw from the case entirely. The case pended for two years. And then they got a divorce. And it's very bitter. I don't see how I can represent either one of them. [84CC<10]

Other organizations remain intact over time, but change their ownership or control. What happens in a corporate takeover, especially when corporate officials with whom the lawyers have worked are forced out?

> I just had one recently, where a long-standing client of mine—about two years ago—was bought out by a much larger corporation. And, basically, through the force of my contacts at the smaller corporation, we continued to represent that corporation. (Because the big corporation, obviously, wanted their in-house legal counsel to take over and things like that.) Well, as it happens a lot of times in these corporate takeovers, ultimately the existing management is kind of told to leave because they don't fit the corporate culture. And my good friend was just told to leave. And that's an awkward situation. Because he called me and—to his credit—said, "I don't want to put you in an uncomfortable spot. Can you deal with me on this?" And I said, "There's no way I can do it." Because even though I may not represent that company if he ever sued them—given the fact that they want to use their in-house people—. . . that just would put me in a very awkward situation. And I think it would pose a conflict—ethically—in terms of talking to him about his situation and still—ostensibly—representing this corporation. So we've had that situation occur a number of times. And, typically, the best we can do is tell the person, "We can't do anything for you" and let it go at that. [82Ch10–19]

New Evidence

> The problem, though, is that every day that you work on a case, you learn more about it. It's an ongoing thing. You really don't know what a case is about when you first take it. So it is likely that problems will emerge that were difficult to identify at the outset. [69Ch20–49]

As this respondent observes, lawyers invariably learn more about their clients and their cases as time goes by. They've met with and interviewed their clients, colleagues, and associates. They've studied complaints, pleadings, or indictments. They've examined records and documents. They've conducted depositions and discovery. They've inspected physical evidence. They've questioned witnesses and experts. Where they have ongoing relationships with clients and represent them in repetitive transactions or litigation, they learn more about their clients' business practices and their relationships with other parties. They may, thereby, get a better perspective on whether the issues alleged in a particular case are an isolated incident or whether they reflect a pattern of conduct or negligence.[3] A similar intelligence opportunity arises in situations in which cases and clients snowball or in which law firms represent dense social networks—families, industries, corporations and their employees, business associates, and so on. Over time, the representation of proximate parties in the network may unearth information about related clients or matters as well—though, of course, the use of some of these data may be limited by confidentiality rules.

Sometimes conflicts of interest arise because lawyers fail to gather all the relevant facts before taking on a new engagement. Respondents cite numerous examples in which they were misinformed or underinformed about the matter by prospective clients:

> And sometimes you're not aware of the conflict in some of these cases until the day it gets called. A lot of these, my clients are not real good about coming forward with their witnesses and telling you much about what your defense is going to be until their feet are actually right at the fire—in other words, a day or so before we have to go to court. [91DSL<10]

> We were approached to represent a corporation in an action arising from a water pollution situation. Our understanding was that we would represent the corporation in a CERCLA [Superfund] action by the government for the cleanup. And the information that was transmitted to the partner postured the case that way. The underlying facts were transmitted in a phone conversation to that partner, the details of the engagement and the representation were to follow by correspondence. The partner took pretty detailed notes of the phone conversation—which is typical—and opened a . . . general file for the client, who we had not done work for in the past. Work got to us by referral from another lawyer. We opened the file—that is, we created a repository and billing codes and all those kinds of things—and waited for the correspondence to come in. What came in was a fairly large package of information which the partner who took the phone call went through and found out that, in fact, the underlying Superfund case, while going on, was not what we were being engaged for. We were being engaged to represent the corporate interest against other potentially responsible parties, one of whom was one of our clients. This action was intended to be brought quickly and quietly. And we were now in a pickle. . . . We had to just decline the representation. The trouble was conversations—engagement conversations—never tend to go one way. And so I had to

[3]Recall the litigator in the previous chapter who described a construction company he defended for erecting buildings that collapsed or from which "stuff" was falling off. Over a series of several lawsuits involving construction accidents at different sites, he began to realize that the company's work was substandard and perhaps even reflected criminal wrongdoing—and chose to cease representing the client on future cases.

> interrogate—almost like on deposition—my partner as to what he said to them. I was convinced he hadn't disclosed anything to the existing clients adversely. And then I told them that we would have to send this back and we wouldn't be able to take it on the other side. . . . Then had to go back to the other client and nicely tell them that they had inadvertently misrepresented the engagement to us, but had put us in a conflict situation and we could not take the case. And then had to document the fact that the knowledge in our possession would be never disclosed and send everything back to them with assurances that no copies had been made. We then did get the call on the other side a few weeks later and told them we could not take it—without comment—just couldn't take it. They were not happy and suspected that we had something to do with the other side. And I thought we could not even disclose to them what those conversations were. We simply had to say that there was a conflict situation. Over time it got smoother. But it was not that smooth at the beginning. They were not satisfied with the answer, "We can't take on their representation." Because the question was "Why?" And the pressure, it got—it built. It went higher in the company and higher and finally the general counsel said, "Why can't you do this?" And the other partner and I had a conference call and said, "Because it would put, potentially put us into a conflict situation with you which we think we need to avoid. Period." [27Ch50–99]

As the last example illustrates, frequently what lawyers fail to learn at the outset is that there are additional parties implicated in the matter—parties that are also clients of their firm and whose interests they have an obligation to honor. Somewhere in the pesky web, an unexpected client has become entangled. Indeed, the discovery of additional evidence is the primary trajectory along which so-called other clients, the subject of the last chapter, are brought into the case. The interviews are laden with such examples;

- Lawyers representing two codefendants later discover inculpatory evidence suggesting that one of them is more guilty than the other:

  > And a lot of times, you don't know there's a conflict until you get in the middle of the damn case. Suddenly some witness is on the stand, saying very favorable things about one defendant and very unfavorable things about another defendant. . . . If you started out and looked at the case in terms of the police reports and the discovery material and said there is no conflict here, you could end up in the situation where, during the trial, a conflict arises. How do I cross-examine this person effectively when his testimony has been beneficial to one of my clients and detrimental to another of my clients? Do I try to impeach his credibility? Well, obviously, that'd be hurting one client to help the other. [113Ch<10]

- Lawyers representing a client discover, after some inquiry, that the party responsible for the problem happens to be another client:

  > If you get into the case . . . and, all of a sudden, the doctors say, "Well, gee, the nurse didn't [. . .]" or we discover the nurse didn't follow the medication orders

> and you're going to stick it to the nurse [. . .] That actually happened in a case we had. And the hospital [liable for mistakes by its nursing staff] got very angry at us because we represented the doctors. And one of our paralegals—she did a great job—she noticed that the . . . nurses do not follow the doctor's orders—orders of the doctor being sued. . . . I don't think the plaintiff realized that he had a good claim against the hospital—which it was. So he was just pushing against the doctors. And then our investigation revealed, "Hey, it's the nurses screwed up." And so we shifted all our defense—in the discovery depositions—against the hospital. Which, of course, the plaintiff was real happy about. And our doctor, he was happy we found out it wasn't his fault, really. But then the hospital was kind of, "How come the law firm that we have used in the past—and might use in the future—is going to stick us for big bucks?" [laughter] We laughed about it years later. But at the time, it was a little bit delicate. [67DSM10–19]

- Lawyers representing one or more defendants discover additional victims—unfortunately, clients in an unrelated matter—who were harmed.
- Lawyers discover triangular relationships involving third parties—especially insurers—that were unknown when they took on the engagement:

> A client and friend owns a rental house. There is a fire. People are killed. Four or five insurance companies are involved. There are brokers and agents involved, with their own insurance policies. We represent one of the insurance companies. We won't take the case because the lawyer must be able to represent the client to the fullest extent. And you can't if an insurance client is likely to be harmed by your advocacy. In this instance, we didn't determine that initially. We agreed to take the case. Then we began to contact the brokers and the agents and discovered the insurance conflicts. [71DSL10–19]

Transactions may grow as well with time, as additional investors, lenders, guarantors, underwriters, bidders, subcontractors, and the like join or help to shore up the deal.

> I can think of one where we were representing somebody in a bankruptcy court action. . . . We had one client who's trying to purchase the assets out of bankruptcy. And, lo and behold, another client—not with us, but with another a law firm, and somebody who we didn't realize until after the fact that they were a client—filed some papers against the purchase. And we filed pleadings, opposing that petition. And all of a sudden, it developed [. . .] that was a client of the firm that we had filed a petition against. And it's something that you really don't think of. Here were lawyers who were involved in a transaction, and somebody else comes in and opposes a complete different set of lawyers and they weren't familiar with this other client. And a conflict came up in midstream. I mean, those are the types of things that it's very hard to spot. [1Ch100+]

Some of the ancillary parties or witnesses, recruited or dragged into the case at the eleventh hour by other people's lawyers, will be clients of the original firm, whose interests must be considered and honored. Matters that were conflict-free as a result of the careful scrutiny, diligence, and occasional sacrifice by the firm suddenly explode down the road—again, "through no fault of their own"—when other people's lawyers—sometimes strategically to conflict their adversaries out—bring new parties into the case.

> . . . we began representing one software company in some major litigation on the West Coast. And we represented them and we sued another company. And [the other company] brought in—as a cross-defendant—another client of ours. And that client retained other counsel to represent them and then found out we were in the case. They've moved to disqualify us. . . . So that's been a real tough one for us. We do tax work for one; we do intellectual property work for the other—out of the same office in [names western state]. . . . And the rules, particularly the rules in [that state], are rather strict with respect to withdrawal. And there's fairly harsh penalties. We've got one saying, "I won't let you withdraw," and the other is saying, "You've got to withdraw." [16Ch100+]

The conflicts of interest here are even more insidious and frustrating because firms have no control over the ancillary parties that others add to the soup. So lawyers may try to anticipate the cast of characters that might join or that other lawyers might bring into the case.

> There had been an explosion, and we were asked to represent one party who was a primary defendant. And there was some possibility that, down the line—if some unlikely events had occurred—there could have been a potential claim against the utility that we also represented. It's real hard to flag that. . . . It's not a conflict. They're not a party. They're not reasonably a predictable party. But one can create a potential that they could become a party three or four steps down the way that would create a problem. . . . It seemed unlikely. They wouldn't waive. They were a sufficiently large, long-term, established client that had made the representation of the new client really impossible. But it was not a conflict that on paper showed as a real direct conflict. And so that created some touch. [9Ch100+]

Turning Points

As matters unfold, the relationships among parties evolve and interests may begin to collide. When more than one party is a client of the firm (whether or not the firm is representing more than one of them simultaneously in the particular matter), the collision may paralyze lawyers who cannot champion all of what have become incompatible interests. The collisions can occur at any point along the way. At any moment—though perhaps precipitated by external shocks or unanticipated complications—a harmonious, consensual deal may turn bitter and acrimonious.

> We are a major financial firm representing a lot of banks. We're also a major corporate firm. Corporations are frequently borrowers, many times from our banking clients—unrelated matters. When you're doing a new deal, everyone's very happy to see you on, say, the borrower's side when ordinarily you're on the bank side or vice versa. Because everyone wants the deal to go through. The conflicts are rather easily waived. If the deal sours, if economic times become harder, if there's a difference of opinion that develops between the borrower and the lender, we then find ourselves in a situation where one side or the other may be increasingly uncomfortable with having us be there. [5Ch100+]

The passage of time almost never heals these incipient wounds; rather, it helps them fester. It can do no less. Because the legal process is so protracted, it provides a cushion of time in which the needs, priorities, resources, and interests of various parties diverge. Because a complex matter has myriad junctures requiring the exercise of discretion, it continually tests unanimity and consensus. Because reputations and fortunes embedded in tangled webs of collaborators are at stake, paranoia and disunity loom under the surface. Because outcomes are zero-sum, they are inherently divisive. Because costs or awards must be split, they provide an opportunity to fracture alliances yet again. Time creates a kind of repeated Prisoner's Dilemma game writ large—if all the parties stay cooperative and altruistic throughout, they all do better; if one defects, they all do worse. So conflicts of interest are by no means inevitable; Prisoner's Dilemma games do sometimes end positively. But at each turning point in the evolution of a case, interests get pummeled and stretched. And some, ultimately, cannot withstand the stress.

BECOMING A CLIENT

Now we move from conflicts of interest that arise in relationships with longstanding clients to the extremes of the time line—as candidates initiate contact with a law firm and as that contact ends—epochs in client or potential client histories that are also covered by legal ethics rules.

Law is one of the few institutions with statutes of limitations—universalistic prespecified temporal frames after which disputes or claims lose their legal validity, a kind of no-fault forgiveness. But conflict-of-interest rules have no such safety valve, no statute of limitations beyond which a lawyer's obligations to respect and champion the interests of a client—even a former client—finally desist. Though, as we will see, these responsibilities lessen when relationships formally end, they never disappear entirely. The reason is that confidentiality rules have no statute of limitations. A lawyer's obligation to protect the secrets of a client is eternal. As long as attorneys possess relevant confidential information regarding a client, they are precluded from using it for the benefit of another.

> I'm in litigation today whereby a deed my father drew for a client in 1948 is being questioned. . . . He drew a deed that created a trust. . . . And this is what's there. And it's set. Now this deed was drawn for a lady who had been a long-time client. The beneficiary was her daughter. Her daughter recently died. And the question

> now is whether the next generation—the next daughter—takes or whether she has only has a life interest. The daughter who is now questioning this—who never [. . .] I guess she met her grandmother, but that was it—is saying that, because my father then represented her mother following the grandmother's death—and we had continued to represent the trust—that there's obviously some conflict of interest. We obviously violated some fiduciary duty etc., etc. [53DSL20–49]

Client secrets and their associated interests, then, have a kind of perpetuity that may persist long after the legal engagement concludes; indeed, as in the last example, they may extend even from the grave. The lasting grip of confidences provides yet another reason why conflicts of interest get worse with the passage of time. Interests do not desist as rapidly as they are created; over time law firms amass ever more interests that must be respected and around which lawyers must gingerly navigate. Recall from chapter 2 that a quarter of the large Chicago firms in the sample have been in existence for more than a hundred years and half for more than eighty. And the problem is not restricted to large firms.

> My older partners—[first partner] is [over 70] and [second partner] is [late 60s]—so they've represented probably thousands of people in the [city] area over the years in real estate transactions and wills and trusts and that kind of stuff. . . . So they've been practicing law for a real long time. Yeah, you get into lawsuits over real estate a lot of times. And it turns out that you represented the person when he bought the farm twenty years ago or something. Or you did somebody's divorce twenty years ago or something crazy like that. In those situations [. . .] I mean, those are the only situations I can think of, where we have said, "Yeah, there's a conflict in the sense that we represented you a million years ago." But we're not going to think that's a significant conflict to get out of the case. And we've had a couple of those type of situations where it had to be brought to the attention of the court. And the court had to tell us if we could stay in the case or get out. And we've had it go both ways. The court has said, "You've got to get out." And there's some where the court agreed with us that there is no conflict and we could stay in. [73CC10–19]

These firms, thus, are the repository of long client histories, some pieces of which they must be mindful and continue to respect, interests that can place a stranglehold on the firm's course well into the future.

It is the receipt of confidential information and not the agreement to take on a client or an engagement that triggers fiduciary obligations.

> . . . another example involves a unified defense with a codefendant—where your firm works very closely with their lawyers and their witnesses, etc. to present a united front. Subsequently, you are asked to sue this codefendant on a similar issue down the road. If confidences had been divulged in the original unified defense, the firm might be disqualified in the subsequent litigation. I've thought about this. . . . If this ever happened, we would have to treat them as our own client for conflicts purposes. [48Ch20–49]

That is why, as I noted in chapter 3, firms cannot simply identify the clients whose interests they must consider and respect by reviewing billing statements or a cabinet of open files. They may face conflicts of interest from idle chatter on the golf course; from wining and dining a prospective client in an elegant restaurant; from free legal advice elicited in a supermarket line; from a telephone call to the law firm receptionist; from prospective clients whose engagement the law firm declined or who decide, after an initial conversation, to take their business elsewhere; and from former clients who haven't received a bill from the law firm in more than a decade. Because of this long legacy of client confidences, some firms proceed delicately in initiating potential new relationships, cautiously in framing them, and judiciously in ending them.

The manner in which Lawrence Lexman back in chapter 3 quickly and unequivocally embraced his first and only client was perhaps a bit misleading. In truth, interacting with and sifting through the pool of prospective clients requires sagacity, delicacy, and circumspection. The tension by now should be obvious. On the one hand, lawyers fear becoming captives of confidences that bind them indefinitely to unwanted clients or even nonclients. Though receipt of confidential information cannot compel the firm to represent the disclosing party, it can preclude its lawyers from representing anyone else—even long-standing clients—in the case or in related cases.[4] On the other hand, lawyers need massive amounts of constantly changing information—about parties, coparties, adverse parties, third parties, partners, evolving organizational or family structures, social networks, alliances, and so on—if they are not to be snared at some point down the road by conflict-of-interest booby traps embedded in the social structure of the case.

Attorneys require, then, both omniscience and thick blinders. What makes the tension more than theoretical, of course, is that honoring both of those instincts—as well as declining prospective engagements because of the lack of sufficient information or discomfort about getting too much information—would bankrupt the practice of law. The minuet between lawyers and prospective clients can, therefore, be quite intricate. It is performed in chapter 8.

Beauty Contests

So-called beauty contests, in which a prospective client will interview a number of firms before selecting legal counsel, pose special risks.

> Let's say you're being interviewed by Mobil and Mobil doesn't hire you. And then Atlantic Richfield comes along and . . . you say "Hire us." And they say, "Okay." And then Mobil says, "Whoa, wait a second. We told you all this stuff during our interview about what our position was going to be and we asked you for your theories and everything else." Well, that's a big problem. . . . Because, unless we know we're being hired, there's a potential that ARCO is going to hire us. [10Ch100+]

---

[4]And taking on the engagement may foreclose lucrative future opportunities to represent parties directly adverse to the interests of the new client, even on unrelated matters.

Lawyers have even greater incentives to securely fasten their blinders before starting down the runway in a beauty contest. First of all, given all the gorgeous contestants, the odds of getting the business are lower than when prospective clients solicit one firm at a time. Second, these matters tend to be big and lucrative; prospective clients wouldn't bother holding a beauty contest otherwise. So getting shut out of the case entirely—unable to the represent the client staging the contest or any co-parties or adversaries (some of whom may turn out to be long-standing clients of the firm)—by a few stray confidences can be costly indeed. Because of these risks, law firms have become increasingly cautious in entering beauty contests.

> . . . you should advise the client in the beginning that, before they give you any information—or a potential client—that they should give you no confidential information, that you are not yet their attorney. It may not be covered by the attorney-client privilege. Or, if you're not willing to take that risk—because you're afraid the client won't give you enough information or won't even want to interview you then, and you can't make a good judgment as to what his needs are and what you can offer that client—then you'd better understand that, when he gives you that confidential information, in order for you to make your judgments and give him the judgments to see if he wants to hire you, then you may be conflicted out of representing the other side. And that's just tough! [11Ch100+]

But without confidential information, attorneys may be unable to assess whether to take the case or whether conflicts loom below the surface. Nor may they have enough information to convince clients that they deserve the grand prize. So lawyers are damned if they do (receive the confidences and get conflicted out) and damned if they don't (refuse the confidences and lose the case). As the respondent so aptly concluded, "That's just tough!" Another catch-22 of the world of conflicts of interest.

Beauty contests are not merely benign exercises in just how much to stay blind to and how much to peek. They have a more sinister side as well. They give savvy contest holders the opportunity to kill off the other contestants—what one respondent called "neutralizing the experts."

> . . . potential clients can take advantage of lawyers by . . . having a so-called beauty contest and going to the law firms and saying, "Well, we're considering hiring you in this particular matter." . . . And disclosing enough information that you can't accept the other side of that dispute because you heard in confidence, as you were being considered for representation. And that can be abused and lawyers have to be aware that they—before they hear too much from a new client—they better make sure that there are no conflicts with existing clients. Because what could happen is you couldn't represent, in that dispute, a client you've been representing for fifteen years, because you suddenly were approached by somebody who was neutralizing the experts in the field at a certain location. . . . I think it's just generally communicated that you have to be careful—and that's true almost of every piece of new business—that you really should be searching for potential conflicts before you hear too much. Or else you may end up not being able to defend an existing client. [4Ch100+]

Some clients orchestrate de facto beauty contests when they meet with and confide in a number of attorneys before selecting legal counsel. Sometimes their motives are pure; they are simply searching for the best fit and someone they can trust. Other times, as examples of divorcing spouses in chapter 3 revealed, their motives are not. They intentionally shop around, sharing confidences with lawyers in different firms in order to conflict out—depending on the size of the legal marketplace—all the lawyers in town, or all the experts, or all the best or most cut-throat ones.

> A woman knew that she was going to be filing for divorce. And she called around to a number of different attorneys' offices and said just enough to these attorneys about her case and about what she wanted to do that she disqualified most of the attorneys in town from representing her husband. There were specific attorneys that she didn't like. And she didn't want to have to deal with them. So she made a point of calling those offices and saying enough to disqualify the attorneys. That was really a clever thing to do. [85DSM<10]

Unlike acknowledged beauty contests, in these de facto competitions, lawyers are not told that they are one of a number of contestants. And because the clients are smaller and the matters more limited, firms are unlikely to learn about the beauty contests through the grapevine or from someone other than the prospective client. Being unwitting, attorneys may, therefore, be less cautious in interacting with these clients than they are in aboveboard beauty contests. So they inadvertently learn some confidences and, to the delight of the prospective client, get snared.

Conflicted Out!

Despite the fears and rumors, few respondents report that their firm was actually snared by a strategic aboveboard beauty contest. Big companies don't use beauty contests to conflict a firm out, some respondents argued; to do that, they simply give the firm business:

> I believe that people don't do that. I believe people hire people to do that. I believe they actually do hire you to keep you off of other people's backs. I know that some large companies will hire ten firms in a city to do some individual matters for them so that, in effect, when something else comes along, they are conflicted out of handling all of them. You know, like somebody'll spread the work to Kirkland, Sidley, Mayer Brown, Skadden, Keck, Winston, whatever. Everybody'll do some little thing for them, okay? So that then when something else comes along, they can control whether or not that firm does work or not. Because they'll always have an active matter going on at those institutions. [10Ch100+]

Of course, clients need to have lots of legal business or lots of money to pick off all the major firms in a market as large as that of Chicago.

> . . . if you were in a small town and there were two good law firms in town and nobody else but individual practitioners. And you hired one firm to do your bidding and you wanted to seek to disqualify another firm, because you knock out the only other good firm in town. And if you can knock 'em out, that client is left with the remains—which aren't very good. That's different. But in a major metropolitan area like Chicago, what real advantage does it have for a client to knock you out from representing somebody when there's two dozen wonderful law firms, I think, that could represent them with just as much vigor and interest? [19Ch50–99]

But the tactical opportunity is not as limited or expensive as appears on first blush. I described in chapter 3 how conflicts of interest tend to cluster in geographic, substantive, and social network monopolies, clusters that may not contain all that many firms. A client need not be quite so rich or litigious to conflict out the significant law firms in a small town or small market or the firms that offer specialized expertise:

> . . . there are no other firms [that] do this kind of stuff. . . . I've been asked to represent a few [specialized retailers], including guys that I've sued and gotten punitive damages. Obviously, they would much rather have me on their side, so nobody would sue them. They'd get away with what they're doing. . . . My ego says they want to do it because I'm a real good trial lawyer. The fact is, they want to do it so that nobody can sue them. And I wouldn't hesitate to give the opinion that these guys would hire me, fire me the next day.[5] . . . And then I'm sure they'll come into court with their next lawyer saying, "Ah ha! you can't sue us. You represented us for two days." [84CC<10]

So the making of law firm clients is not merely about organizational intelligence or information management and the trade-offs between amassing enough information to make a reasoned judgment about a potential engagement and shutting out confidences that may conflict out the firm. It's not even about outsmarting strategic clients too willing to share secrets or business in an effort to neutralize the firm from ever opposing them. All cases and confidences—not only strategic ones placed by manipulative adversaries—have long trajectories. Even the most innocent of conversations can conflict out the firm:

> Dog bite case in [this town]. The individual who owned a dog was renting a house. The dog was put in a cage—a pit bull. Chewed his way through a metal cage, attacked a neighbor, and bit off like two of his fingers. The kid came into our office right away and talked to one of my partners and said, "I may be sued over this. What do I do?" And one of my partners talked to him, got all the facts, etc. . . . Later on, a lawsuit is brought by the plaintiff, who was injured. . . . We then were contacted to represent one of the codefendants and also, perhaps, bring

---

[5]Another way to cut the cost of strategically conflicting out all the experts.

> a countercomplaint against the college student for failure to keep control of the dog, etc. We ran a conflicts check. And when it came up, I went down the hall and said, "What do you know about this?" My partner says, "You can't [. . .] we can't represent him." "Why?" "I've talked to him already." Although he never retained us, we've talked to him. . . . We lost out on defending a case because we had talked to a kid for a few minutes on just some, basically, free legal advice. [64DSS10–19]

Perhaps the most difficult task in assessing prospective clients and matters, then, is predicting their trajectory well beyond the case at hand.

> Here's another example that came up recently. [Industrial company] is . . . one of the largest employers in our community. Historically, we have done very little work for them. They've used Chicago counsel or New York or Pittsburgh, wherever. They've gone to a larger firm. Recently, we were approached to do some work for them—certainly not all that they have, but some. If we accept those assignments, can we take workers' compensation cases on behalf of their injured employees or any other types of cases that might be adverse to [the company]? So we discussed that at some length. And we try to make a judgment, how much work are we going to be getting from [the company] versus what work will that preclude us from taking for other clients? Sometimes we're right, sometimes we're not so right. [87DSS10–19]

Though the trajectories certainly carry ethical conflicts, they often preclude future business opportunities, as these examples suggest. How law firms try to predict the future and assess the trade-off between birds in the hand and flocks in the bush is the subject of chapter 9.

ENDINGS

Premature Endings

For all the reasons enumerated in the first half of this chapter, matters that were conflict-free at the outset can explode with conflicts of interest after the engagement is underway: clients, their structures, and their boundaries change; lawyers unearth new evidence; additional parties are implicated in the case; transition points in the case expose incompatible interests and tear alliances apart; and so forth. Many of these downstream conflicts could not have been anticipated by the lawyers and occurred "through no fault of their own." Some were possible, but the attorneys took the calculated risk that they would not materialize. Others were clearly foreseen, but the parties chose to proceed nonetheless and deal with the conflicts if or when they developed. And others occurred because someone made a mistake, as when the prospective client mischaracterized the engagement in the Superfund case.

In several examples offered in the first half of the chapter, when these unforeseen conflicts detonated, law firms offered to withdraw from the case. Withdrawal is the conciliatory solution to downstream conflicts. Conflicted firms step out of the case and are replaced by a disinterested other.[6] The process is quite a bit more complicated than a simple, congenial parting of the ways, however. Many complex questions and negotiations remain:

- Does the withdrawing firm get paid for its aborted labors, and if so, how much?
- Does the withdrawing firm assist its client in finding a replacement, turn over its files and records to the new counsel, and help subsidize the transition? (Where firms are conflicted out because they had access to confidential information concerning the other side, such cooperation—however much irate clients expect it—may be ethically proscribed.)
- Does the law firm that represented multiple parties have to withdraw from all parties, or can it withdraw from the representation of some (for example, those who want to settle the case) but continue to represent others (those who want to litigate the matter)? And if it can stay in the case, which of the others will it continue to represent?

When attorneys anticipate a downstream conflict, they may negotiate or specify in advance how these issues will be resolved—a kind of lawyer-client prenuptial agreement. Many do not, for the same reason that lovers decry prenuptial agreements: they represent a rather distrustful, pessimistic beginning to a relationship, at best, and may scare off prospective partners, at worst.

Though withdrawals are by no means costless—frequently expending time, precious resources, goodwill, reputation, and harmony within the law firm—they still represent a welcome escape hatch when a firm is snared by a conflict of interest. Why ever worry, then, about downstream conflicts? Why bother peering into crystal balls and struggling with the excruciating trade-offs suggested in the last section? Why ever decline a prospective engagement that has a worrisome trajectory? Why not always take the first matter in the door and, if something better comes along in the future, simply withdraw from the first one?

Aside from the fact that such wanton disloyalty and opportunism may not attract many clients, withdrawing from such entanglements is not the great panacea because the ethics rules say lawyers can't. The so-called hot-potato rule, enunciated in a series of state and federal court opinions, directs that "a firm may not drop a client like a hot potato, especially if it is to keep happy a far more lucrative client" and that conflicts of interest cannot be cured by severing the relationship with the preexisting or less favored client.[7]

The temptation to dump inconvenient clients in order to resolve conflicts of interest is not unfamiliar to the respondents.

---

[6]Respondents report that withdrawals sometimes accelerate the resolution of the dispute. Parties, unwilling to start all over with a new firm, settle the case instead.

[7]The first quote came from *Picker Int'l., Inc. v. Varian Assocs., Inc.,* 670 F. Supp. 1363, 1365 (N.D. Ohio 1987), *aff'd.* 869 F. 2d 578 (Fed. Cir. 1989). See also *Truck Ins. Exch. v. Fireman's Fund Ins. Co.,* 6 Cal. App. 4th 1050, 1057 (Cal. Ct. App. 1992) and *Flatt v. Superior Court,* 885 P. 2d 950, 957–59 (Cal. 1994), among others.

> A client—last year—with relatively modest billings—not a significant client to the firm at all. Involved in a matter. Another client came in that, you know, huge multinational corporation, with a potential for huge billings. And there was a conflict and we couldn't take it. Now the guy who had a potential of bringing business in was madder than hell about it. But that's life. We have the conflict, and we couldn't just say "The old one is gone and bring the new one in." I think, potentially, we could have had a serious conflict and the clients would have been mad. And the bottom line is, you have to consider the type of damage that you do to the firm and its reputation if you just are ignoring your ethical obligations. [1Ch100+]

Not all hot-potato impulses arise from the desire to take in lucrative business; sometimes it's the opportunity to hire a new lawyer.

> S: What would you describe as—say, in the last year—the most challenging, the most difficult kind of conflict call that you felt you had to make?
>
> MP: Well, there's one that I'm aware of that had to do with a possible opportunity to hire a lateral. We had lengthy discussions with this individual and thought that there was going to be a real opportunity to put together a deal with this person. And kind of at the eleventh hour, he made it known to us that his client—his principal client that he was going to bring into our firm—had some very ongoing, bitter litigation with another company that we were doing some pretty minor work for. And so we talked about that and we said, "Well, we don't know that we see this as a problem." Well, he did and said he thought maybe the only way we could get it resolved was not through the consent route, but rather we might have to consider turning back the work that we already had. And we looked at that and thought that we would possibly be subject to criticism for doing that. 'Cause this was business already in the firm. And there's a couple of cases that seem to suggest that you just can't willy-nilly dump work back in order to favor your firm with more lucrative stuff. So as a result, we lost this lateral opportunity, because of what appeared [. . .] I guess it was a legitimate conflict. But it was fairly minor—minor in terms of the small amount of work our firm was doing for this other company. That was a call that our executive committee, I think, had to make. And we just said, "We just can't do that." So that deal fell apart for us. [15Ch100+]

And other respondents recall instances in which clients of the firm asked that their lawyers dump other clients with whom they had developed an indirect adversity.

Whether or not they call it by name, many respondents seem to know about the hot-potato doctrine. Some refer to it directly:

> Because we definitely will not dump a client because we want to take some other matter. You have to make that going in. You don't undertake the representation. Once you undertake the representation, that is your client, you have to stick with it. You don't say, "Hey, we can make more money on another matter, and there-

fore, let's dump this case and take that case." That doesn't work. That's prohibited. You have to make that determination going in, of course, if possible. [50DSL20–49]

Some respondents acknowledge the rule by describing how they try to get around it. And others—after underscoring the confidentiality of the interview—suggest how their preemptive maneuvers sometimes bump against or cross the ethical line.

> But—there's always a "but"—let's assume somebody sends in a case, calls in a case, and they don't send in an awful lot of business. And now, a week later, a much better client calls in and wants you to represent one of their insureds. And, in fact, it looks like the second defendant would be more directly involved in the lawsuit than the first one. . . . There have been times when we've dumped the one in favor [of] the second. And what we do then is, we have to call back the first defendant insurer and claim a mistake had been made, that our docket department screwed up and we already had the case in for somebody else. And that's something I'd like to keep completely confidential. [laughter] . . . But, where we actually take in a case, and we're not representing anybody, and we write an acknowledgment letter, and we start the ball rolling, and now, two weeks later, we get a late assignment from somebody else that we wish we had instead, we're just sort of stuck with it. I mean, we're not going to risk injuring feelings by formally taking a case and then dumping it. But we can dump it before we acknowledge receipt of it. [laughter][8]

In this example of skirting hot-potato problems in multiparty litigation, the period of omniscience is relatively circumscribed—perhaps a few days or weeks. The firm is asked to represent one of several defendants in the case, and the worry is that one of the other parties might be more desirable. The hot-potato temptation is not terribly great here. The lawyers did, after all, get some piece of the action. And they can play for time, to some extent. The list of defendants is known, the summonses go out more or less simultaneously, firms can use their bureaucratic intake procedures as a delaying tactic, they can use their contacts with insurers as a buffer between clients, and so on. And the conflict, if there is one, erupts at the beginning of the case. In other areas of practice, the hot-potato temptation is much greater because the roster of more compelling future clients is unknown and because conflicts involve unrelated cases, with their own time frames and momentum, and can erupt at any moment over many years. It's not a matter of stalling for a few days to pick the best of several known options. It's a matter of taking or declining an engagement in light of a possibility of the most remote of unknowable future prospects.

So, maneuvering around the hot-potato rule is quite a bit more difficult here. One strategy respondents describe is to anticipate future opportunities and, over the long run, phase out business that is likely to get in the way—to drop clients slowly and ambivalently like a bad habit rather than like a hot potato.

---

[8]Because of the respondent's expressed confidentiality concern, I have not indicated here the identification code for this Chicago firm.

> That's a management problem and it's a big problem, particularly when you find that, with the way technology advances, one industry that may be booming today, may become technologically obsolete in the future. And there's another competing industry that may take the lead in the future. And if you have clients that are in the old group that are thriving now, but you know in five years they're going to be out of business. And there's another group coming in. They're at odds with each other. How do you deal with that? There's no good answer. The problem is you can't drop the old clients like a hot potato—they call it the "hot-potato doctrine," whatever—and it's frankly just a difficult problem. Basically, our view has been to date that, if we have a client in-house, that's where our loyalties have to be. And even if there's a potential in the future to have tremendous business develop from a new set of clients, if they're adverse to our existing clients, we generally will not take their business. We view it as our ethical obligation to keep the existing clients. That's not to say that if we honestly see that there's a limited business potential, that we may not taper off our business development with the old set of clients, taper down our business, and subsequently phase in representing the group. . . . Management ends up sitting down with department chairmen and the billing attorneys involved and saying, "We have this problem. We have these people who want to develop this business. We have these people at this business." And say to the group that wants to develop it, "You're going to have to hold off. We just simply can't do it because of the conflict." And talk to the other group and say, "We don't see that the future potential is here. And we'd rather not have you be mining this group of clients in developing a lot more business. You've got to continue your existing representation, but it might be a good idea to wind it up." [1Ch100+]

Another strategy is to wait for the opportunity to arise and then try to clear the underbrush very quickly (perhaps sometimes too quickly)—in the words of one respondent, to "juggle" the hot potato, rather than either dropping it or waiting for it to cool off:

> I think what would happen is that, if a major client came in the door and a conflicts check was put out and there was a conflict. And the guy who was about to bring in the big piece of business said, "Wait a second. Are you telling me we've got to turn away a million dollars of business 'cause we represent someone that's going to generate a ten thousand dollars in fees over the next five years?" That person would, in all likelihood, go to the executive committee . . . and says, "We really need to evaluate this thing. We really need to think about this situation. We really need to talk to Partner B about letting go of their client," and so on and so forth. . . . I think the place that I sort of remember this occurring is in our representation of the FDIC and the RTC, where conflicts were identified. And it might be a situation in which some juggling did go on in order to make sure our plate—our conflict plate—was clean so we could take on some long-term FDIC-RTC representation. . . . And I know that conflicts have been worked out—have occurred and have been worked out. Whether it's through disclosure and waiver, or whether it's through telling the client that we were going to take the business and

that they were free to go elsewhere—I hope that hasn't happened, but it may have. [39Ch50–99]

The hot-potato impulse, because it zeros in on the greatest temptations to defy or obfuscate the conflict-of-interest rules, represents a kind of organizational seismograph, monitoring and exposing fault lines within law firms. On any given matter, the hot-potato impulse is not necessarily shared by all members of the firm; it is often dreamed up by one to be used against the clients of another. These examples expose internal law firm politics that erupt when one partner's client is asking for priority over that of another or when a lawyer bringing in a huge piece of business is paralyzed by the paltry case of a colleague. Hot-potato solutions are conceived, then, to deal with other people's clients; therefore, they inevitably expose or create fissures in the social fabric of the firm.

Former Clients

Legitimate withdrawals go only so far, of course, in curing conflicts of interest. They do not eradicate open-ended obligations to maintain client confidences or proscriptions against using secrets obtained from a client for the benefit of another. However, lawyers' obligations do ease after their representation of the client has ended—whether prematurely, through withdrawal, or from natural causes. For former clients, the proscription against taking a matter directly adverse to client interests is limited only to new matters that are substantially related to those for which the firm originally represented that client.[9] If I defended Dow Corning on breast implant litigation, for example, I cannot turn around at the conclusion of the case and bring an implant plaintiff's lawsuit against the company. The likelihood that my litigation strategy would draw on confidential information I obtained while defending the implant maker would simply be too great. But I might be able to sue the former client for employment discrimination, something that would have been prohibited while the original implant case was underway.

> We have a case against a major nationwide company. And we wrote the first letter and said we think you ought to pay our clients. And came back the answer from their attorneys, "Our company advises that your firm has, in the past, done legal work for them and considers it a conflict of interest for you to be involved." We had done our initial search and hadn't found anything. I did a second search and still found nothing. And finally, one of my partners said, "Well, I vaguely remember that maybe ten, fifteen years ago, we may have done a small lien foreclosure for them or something." Well, it's my understanding that they're not a current client. And if I did past work, then I have to evaluate whether or not that past

---

[9]Rule 1.9(a) of the *Model Rules of Professional Conduct* (American Bar Association 1983) states: "A lawyer who has formerly represented a client in a matter shall not thereafter represent another person in the same or a substantially related matter in which that person's interests are materially adverse to the interests of the former client unless the former client consents after consultation."

> work in any way—has any information gathered from that representation—affects this case and could adversely affect their position in this case. Well, in that case, obviously, we couldn't find anything. [97DSS<10]

If ethics rules prohibited adversity between law firms and ex-clients forever, a single minor engagement would buy a law firm's loyalty for all time. The lower conflict-of-interest standard for former clients, then, provides a narrow escape hatch without which law firms would eventually be conflicted out of practically everything—especially as clients increasingly spread their business around to many firms.

What's a former client? Thus, in order to maximize their freedom to take on new matters, law firms need to transform current clients into former clients. But what exactly is a "former" client?

> Ours is primarily a transactional practice. A client may call you up to do one thing. It is completed. The firm continues to send a newsletter to the client. Lawyers occasionally make a sales call to them. How does this fit into the assessment of whether someone is a former client? [34Ch50–99]

> We take the position—in terms of determining when a client is a former client—is "Have we fully discharged the assignment?" And if we have, if the client is waiting for nothing further from us, that's a former client. . . . I think of all law firms on the face of the earth, we probably have the narrowest starting point in determining "Is XYZ a client?" We move as quickly as we can into thinking, " . . . they paid us fees yesterday, but now they're a former client." And then we get into . . . the business side of it: . . . "Should we be treating them as a former client?" [16Ch100+]

Not all law firm respondents find their colleagues as eager to recognize or facilitate this transformation of temporal status as the large firm informant who was just quoted.

> A lawyer likes to think that, if he did a good job, that client's going to come back if they have another problem. . . . A lawyer's reluctant to say, "It's a former client." I'm hoping they're going to send me more business, because I did such a good job for them. [4Ch100+]

> One of our partners brought in a deal from [a large national insurance company]—never represented them before. . . . Now he did that deal. He hoped to get more deals. He was told he was going to get more deals. Is that a former client when that deal was over? Is it a current client? When does it become a former client? Do you think that anyone in their right mind is going to now send a letter to that client saying, "It was a pleasure working for you. We don't work for you any more. We consider our relationship terminated. Very truly yours?" No. They might send a letter—which I would recommend sending—saying, "It's been a pleasure handling this deal. We look forward to working with you again."—whatever.

> But the concept of a termination of the relationship in that situation is very difficult from a practical situation. Nor do I know that it is terminated. For example, would they not regard you as their lawyer if there was problem on that deal in a month or two months? Would it not be reasonable for them to regard you as their lawyer on that deal? Would it be unreasonable to think that you were the lawyer for that deal if they never gave you any more business and two years later they called you up because there was a problem. If you said then, "But wait a minute, we've got a lawsuit against you. You've never said anything about that. Now you want us to [. . .] " "Well, we always thought you were our lawyer on this transaction." I think that would be unreasonable on the part of the clients. So there is a time frame within which, I think, a client becomes a former client. [11Ch100+]

As this respondent explains, the disinclination to treat clients as former clients is not merely a matter of ego or financial self-preservation or even the often reasonable expectation in long-term relationships that future business looms just around the bend. The concept is a slippery one because legal disputes and agreements do not necessarily conform to fixed temporal boundaries, opening and closing like an on-off switch. Cases that appear quite dead—in which assignments have been fully discharged and bills fully paid—can become resurrected down the road as problems arise, misunderstandings become apparent, and simmering disputes flare.

> L: I'm representing a gentleman in a personal injury case. The potential defendant—although no lawsuit is yet filed—the potential defendant happens to be his ex-brother-in-law, also an ex-client of this firm. This firm handled his dissolution—the potential defendant's dissolution—five or six years ago. When I accepted the new plaintiff's case, we had absolutely no ongoing matters for the potential defendant. I had heard of him. We're a small enough town that you know a large number of the people. So I opened the file for my client. . . . About two months later, a file was opened for [defendant]—post-dissolution matter. Okay? When I saw that opened, I immediately had a discussion with the attorneys involved in representing [defendant]. . . . There was adequate insurance coverage for [defendant]—we already knew that—so that his personal assets probably were not going to be involved in the resolution of the personal injury matter. Nevertheless, it clearly was a conflict. . . . Our decision, then, was either to simply reject the post-dissolution work or to ask for the waiver of conflicts. I wanted just to reject the post-dissolution out of hand because I didn't want to irritate my plaintiffs at all. . . . I first said to my partner, "[Partner], hey, it's a post-dissolution matter. It's going to be a headache anyway. We don't want it." He says, "Well, I see this guy socially all the time. And it would be uncomfortable for me just to tell him, 'We're not going to do your work.' He's not going to understand that because he knows that your plaintiff is suing him and it doesn't bother him at all." I said, "Well, just tell him that we won't take his case." So he had a conversation with him—which he reported back to me that the guy is really upset. "We represented him in a divorce. And now we're just dumping him on the street. And he had been with us before Mr. Plaintiff walked in the door. Why doesn't he get first dibs?" And then you have

> to explain, "His matter was completely concluded. It was closed. There was no ongoing representation." . . . And that's why we eventually [. . .] [partner] persuaded me, "Well, talk to your plaintiff guy and see if he'll waive it in writing." Which I did, which irritated him as well.
>
> S: And he ultimately did?
>
> L: No, he ultimately did not. [87DSS10–19]

Given the on-again, off-again quality of legal matters, how do attorneys ascertain which of the off-again parties are truly former clients?

> There are cases in which a law firm has gone for years without any contact with a client and the court has ruled that these are current clients. [34Ch50–99]

So how long does a lawyer—or ought a lawyer—wait to ensure that inactive clients remain inactive, that dormant volcanoes do not again erupt? What is the time frame within which a client becomes a former client? Or, as one respondent asked, "What's the appropriate cooling-off period?" And how does the cooling-off period vary by the type of case, the substance of the dispute or transaction, the characteristics of the parties, and the nature of the firm's relationship with the client?

> It was very difficult—had to do with whether or not an (in quotes) "client" was a former client. It was a client for which we had done a minimal amount of work on a specific issue. But it was fairly current. And a client that we had represented for many, many years wanted to sue that former client. And the issue had to do with whether it really was a former client. And that was wrestled with by our professional practice committee and with meetings with the lawyers that were involved on both sides, but primarily the lawyer for the one that had done the work fairly recently for this other client, but not on a regular basis. [4Ch100+]

The question is even more difficult to answer in situations in which clients have casual long-standing relationships with law firms but no longer use them as general counsel, instead sending business sporadically on a range of matters over the years. Are they to be considered current clients throughout, or does their current-former status oscillate over time?

> For multinational companies, we may . . . handle a major acquisition first in the U.S.—fine. Three years later, there's a divestiture in Canada. A couple of years later, we register a string of trademarks in South America. Are [we their] lawyers? It's a different answer at different times in the course of those four or five years. Those are the things that we end up having to face. But we try and start with looking at people, looking at entities as former clients as quickly as we possibly can—as a starting point. . . . We may get a couple of assignments one year and maybe one the following year, maybe nothing the year after that, then three. . . . We're truly not general counsel for many companies. So that's a particular problem for us. . . . We're not pushing the envelope ethically. But, because we're special coun-

> sel, I can have a client come in and have me do something for them, and I won't see them for ten years. That's just the nature of what we do. And I think what you will see is . . . more and more special counsel. The notion of general counsel is fading. Even large, sophisticated clients are breaking up their legal work and sending it around to different parts of the United States. . . . And I think more and more firms will move toward where we draw that line. [16Ch100+]

As monogamous general counsel relationships are increasingly being transformed into promiscuous one-night stands with special counsel, law firms can ill afford to shelter their uncommitted paramours from the former-client category. As many respondents observe, they face both potential ethical and financial consequences when they consider one-shot patrons former clients and financial consequences when they do not.

When are two cases substantially related? Ascertaining whether a client is truly a former client and assessing the business risks of making such a designation are not the only obstacles to enjoying the lower conflict-of-interest standards for former clients. Determining whether two matters are not substantially related and, therefore, eligible for this standard presents an even higher hurdle. Because clients do not select legal counsel randomly but gravitate to those with special expertise and social and political capital, new matters often are related to old ones. The hypothetical breast implant plaintiff chose my firm precisely because of our expertise in the technical and arcane field of implant litigation, our ties to the relevant parties, and any inside information we had acquired about Dow Corning's practices and closeted skeletons. So matters often are related, sometimes even substantially. Some determinations, like the implant one, are straightforward, even easy. But many are not. Notwithstanding varied case law that define and explicate the so-called substantial relationship test, many respondents, even those with the greatest expertise in professional responsibility law, found insufficient guidance for the harder calls.[10]

> Once in a while, I guess, on the [Model Rule] 1.9 situations—where you have a former client—it is occasionally very challenging. Now that I'm babbling about this, I guess that the trickiest ones are figuring out what's substantially related. Because, with substantially related, sometimes it's obvious, but usually it's not. And, as you know, you never know until it's too late. [36Ch100+]

This last observation is underscored by the number of respondents who shared troubling memories of instances in which they guessed wrong and were disqualified from a matter that a judge considered substantially related to a prior representation of a former client:

---

[10]Indeed, the proposed Ethics 2000 amendments to the *Model Rules of Professional Conduct* add a new paragraph to the commentary on duties to former clients that clarifies and provides examples of the application of the substantial relationship test (American Bar Association 2001, Rule 1.9, comment 3).

> This is a personal one that I agonized over—actually "agonized" is too strong a word—concerned me the most. There was a pharmaceutical company located out of state. It was represented as outside counsel by the premier law firm in its home state; my cousin is a partner in that firm. The pharmaceutical company was involved in some litigation in Illinois and my cousin referred the matter to me and we did a bang-up job. Years later, there was an unrelated commercial suit on the East Coast between the pharmaceutical company and another company that retained a partner in our firm to represent them. The partner came to me and asked whether I had a problem with it. He was sure that there was no technical conflict. And they had done the research and determined that it was slam dunk that, if there was a motion to disqualify [because of a conflict of interest], they would lose. I called my cousin, not to get a waiver—which we didn't think was needed, since there was no conflict—but simply to be decent and inform him. I explained that there was no technical conflict. I joked that we were returning the favor—they had given us business and now we were giving them business of having to defend this unrelated lawsuit. My cousin saw no humor in it, and he and the client saw a technical conflict here. We'd already invested lots of time in researching the matter, and the client had invested in a lot of start-up costs. So we proceeded. The pharmaceutical company moved to disqualify us in the litigation in the eastern state; and the judge agreed. To this day, I am certain that the judge was wrong. I guess we could have appealed his decision. But our client did not want to pay for us to prove a principle and got a firm in that east coast state to represent them.[11]

And for every anecdote in which judges rejected the firm's analysis that two matters were not substantially related, I heard others with quite similar features in which the outcome was different—either because the former clients did not notice or object or because the judge shared the firm's interpretation.

Some respondents described how they searched in vain for a reliably predictive formula by which to classify matters as related or unrelated. Indeed, some complained about the shifting sands and what they perceived as a broadening of the concept in recent court opinions, as it is being used strategically as a litigation tactic.

> Another tough area is determining whether you can sue a former client or defend against a former client when, increasingly, former clients are talking about the developing area, which still is probably wrongfully called the "substantial relationship test." . . . A law firm knows so much about the inner workings of that particular company that judges will say, "Maybe this case has nothing to do with any of the work you did for that former client. But you were so close to that client and you defended so many cases that had issues that were touched on this, that you just got into their skin and bones. And until more time has passed, you can't be an adversary." Those are tough issues, and former clients are taking judges' words and decisions out of context and throwing them up as kind of a smokescreen to play this disqualification game. [5Ch100+]

[11]Because the respondent expressed special concern about confidentiality when he shared this story, I have not included the identification code for this Chicago firm.

TURNING BACK THE HANDS OF TIME

This chapter has traced how conflicts of interest undulate with the passage of time. The seeds of some conflicts are planted even before the law firm takes on an engagement. Other engagements proceed smoothly until an unforeseen conflict explodes well into the case. Some conflicts lie dormant most of the time and flare at classic transition points. Some are detonated by the actions of clients or adversaries, far removed from the lawyers, and others by the actions of the lawyers themselves. Some conflicts of interest are aborted when lawyers withdraw prematurely, others abate when the matter reaches its natural conclusion, and others remain active long after the case has ended. And—to mix the metaphors of botany, geology, and warfare one last time—some never blossom at all. There are no hard and fast rules or blueprint of trajectories by which conflicts of interest develop, detonate, and desist. The only generalization is that time is a catalyst, that conflicts almost always worsen with time—at least until a case has concluded or relationship ends.

Time collects a series of benign, serene snapshots and assembles some into dull documentaries and others into suspenseful horror films—and you can rarely tell which is which from the opening reel. It is no wonder, then, that stills are preferred over motion pictures; it's just too hard to control or predict the endings. But because of the power of time to derail cases and destroy relationships, some law firms try to do just that. They seek to edit motion pictures into short features, to stunt the trajectory of a case, to turn back the hands of time. Some firms do so at the front end, weeding out prospective engagements with worrisome trajectories, carving up a case and proceeding incrementally, or contracting with clients in advance about how they will proceed if a land mine detonates down the road. Others manipulate the back end, taking care to conclude cases or terminate relationships as quickly as possible, thereby transforming current into former clients. The strategies that firms devise to manipulate the temporal dimension of their caseload are examined in more detail in chapter 9.

Through Some Fault of Their Own

How Lawyers Beget Their Own Conflicts of Interest

Many of the conflicts of interest reported in the previous chapter arose through no fault of the lawyers but, rather, from actions taken or transitions sustained by clients that their counselors could never have anticipated or averted. This chapter considers the flip side: conflicts of the lawyers' own making. Lawyers beget their own conflicts of interest in myriad ways: where they work and how often they change jobs, how they "grow" and structure their firm, whom they hire, where they locate their practice, how they get compensated, which roles they play outside the firm, where they invest their money, how they structure their free time, and with whom they establish intimate relationships. This chapter collects a large assortment of seemingly unrelated professional and life-style choices regarding practice, career, money, community, and family. In making them, lawyers beget or avoid still other conflicts of interest.

MOBILITY

> What a different world we've created. The "good old days" (whether good or bad) are but a distant memory. Back then, the traditional firms had just one office, comfortably ensconced in a pre-Depression office building, complete with linoleum floors and patched green carpeting. Associates were hired right out of law school, given genuine promises that if they stayed out of trouble for six years,

> partnership would be their reward, and they fully expected to retire from the firm 40 years later. . . . Now a blue-chip firm may have 1,000 lawyers, a dozen trendy offices in as many states, plus two outposts overseas and an affiliation with a firm in Budapest. Associates come and go like United flights at O'Hare. And partners with books of business think nothing of switching firms or forming boutiques on their own. (Fox 1993, 41–42)

> . . . there is a high velocity of movement in the marketplace right now, with lawyers going everywhere . . . and splits and mergers and everything else. That in itself is a big problem. I myself can't reconcile the amount of movement that there has been at the partnership level in this legal community and not have serious conflict problems. [27Ch50–99]

Lateral Hiring

That lawyers display less firm loyalty—that they no longer cast their lot with a single law firm from "cradle to grave" but rather move laterally from job to job as firms fail or downsize, new opportunities emerge, or partnership prospects dissolve—became a basic fact of life by the 1980s (Galanter and Palay 1991, 54–55; Weidlich 1993). This trend in lateral hiring continued or even accelerated in some sectors in the 1990s. The National Association for Law Placement, reflecting on their own employment data, pronounced that "the lateral market is hot," indeed, that "there is a strong nationwide movement toward hiring more laterals and fewer entry-level associates" (Patton 1996, C4).

The explanations for this transformation in the career mobility patterns of lawyers are varied. The standard ones range from blaming the lawyers to blaming the economy. The former include observations about the demise of professionalism and the alleged opportunism and erosion of values or sense of loyalty among the most recent cohorts of lawyers. The latter point to greater competition among law firms that induced them to "cherry pick" or raid each other's stables of lawyers or practice groups in order to develop instant expertise or substantive or geographic diversification. Accounts also cite the recession of the early 1990s, which jolted the legal marketplace, already bloated with record numbers of new law school graduates. The recession resulted in higher rates of unemployment and in firm downsizing and even dissolution that left hordes of experienced attorneys out on the street looking for work along with the newly minted lawyers.

Other explanations suggest that clients, newly empowered by the oversupply of lawyers, were also responsible for the explosion in lateral hiring. The founder of a legal placement firm explains:

> There has [*sic*] been continued pressures on the firm which didn't exist ten years ago. Clients are seeking premium pricing. And there is a concern that clients do not like the process of throwing young bodies in on their matters. They resent paying inexperienced people at high rates. There is a greater value of getting experienced people. . . . It is difficult for small- to-mid-sized firms to bring people up through the ranks. I would presume those pressures to have cost-effective lawyers

would continue to pressure law firms to not hire more entry-level people than lateral. (Papanastasiou 1996, B1)

Moreover, more senior lateral hires often bring business as well as experience to their new partnership. The *National Law Journal* survey of the late 1980s and early 1990s found that "when the firms go headhunting for individual attorneys, they are more likely to bring in lateral partners, because of the clients who will follow them, than to sign on associates from the outside" (Weidlich 1993, 1).

Even conflicts of interest themselves have accelerated the movement of lawyers through the marketplace. When adversities develop between firm clients that require that the firm decline the representation of one or both, the affiliated lawyers, whose compensation often depends on the business of these clients, sometimes depart along with the client.

> I remember a firm that I used to be with, where, in an asbestos case, the codefendants were already suing one another. And we had one lawyer in the firm who represented one client and had, gosh, he almost had like a hundred different files for them. Another more senior partner had the opportunity to represent another company. Maybe not quite the volume, but to him it was going to be important. And they basically just made the decision—it was more of a power play—that the younger lawyer could not represent that company that he had 100 files for. As a result, he ended up leaving and taking that client with him. [59Ch50–99]

As firms grow and diversify, the conflicts of interest can become more systemic. They arise not from the mere coincidence of clients but from areas of specialization that consistently foster or undermine particular interests. Attorneys practicing in these specialized areas find themselves increasingly conflicted out of significant cases by the commitments of their colleagues.

> I can think of a lawyer who left the firm because of this kind of conflicts problem. This lawyer did a lot of transactional work representing banks. And the litigation side of the firm was suing these entities. He felt that it was necessary to turn away too much of his business because of these conflicts, so he left. [31Ch50–99][1]

Positional conflicts also create systemic tensions that can fracture a law firm. Recall from chapter 5 the firm beset by conflicts of interest between its Superfund defense work on behalf of corporate America and its representation of insurance companies that sought to deny Superfund coverage. When the firm decided to resolve the positional conflict by jettisoning its environmental practice, a group of lawyers left the firm.

The legal press sizzles with frequent rumors and occasional notices of such defections. A significant chapter in the genealogy of the births, deaths, marriages, di-

[1]Though some respondents wonder whether this is the actual reason for the departure:

> . . . who knows if it's true; perhaps it's just a cosmetic gloss to explain a much more troubled or contentious departure. [8Ch100+]

vorces, and offspring of Chicago law firms would have to be devoted to the systemic conflicts of interest that made it more profitable for certain specialists to split off—often amicably—from the parent firm than to negotiate around the increasing collisions of interest with other practitioners. My random sample encountered a number of these parents and offspring that parted ways largely because of irreconcilable or increasingly costly conflicts of interest.

Whatever these mobility trends bode for the employment prospects, wealth, or job stability of lawyers or for the expertise or quality of services that law firms now offer their clients, they have created an ethical quagmire. Professional responsibilities are biographical as well as positional; lawyers carry them from job to job. Confidentiality rules apply across physical as well as temporal space. Just as duties of loyalty and confidentiality do not end when attorneys terminate a relationship with a client, they do not cease when attorneys leave the firm that represents that client. As lawyers navigate through the job market, passing from firm to firm, they accumulate weightier and weightier baggage that collects the duties owed to the clients they encounter along the way. Career mobility multiplies their conflicts of interest. And, as it turns out, it also multiplies the conflicts of interest faced by everyone they affiliate with along the way.

Imputed disqualification. Conflicts of interest multiply for new colleagues because duties of loyalty and confidentiality do not apply only to the mobile lawyer. The rules of professional responsibility treat them collectively. The conflicts of any one lawyer in a law firm—no matter how large the firm or how far-flung its offices—are imputed to all lawyers in the firm, regardless of whether they have had any contact with the particular client or were privy to any of its confidences. This so-called imputed disqualification rule states that

> . . . while lawyers are associated in a firm, none of them shall knowingly represent a client when any one of them practicing alone would be prohibited from doing so . . . (American Bar Association 1983, Rule 1.10)

Without such a rule, conflicts of interest could be resolved by simply turning over problematic cases to a colleague in the firm. The rationale for prohibiting such a solution, as Hazard and Hodes (1990, 324) explain, is that "[l]awyers in a firm . . . in fact normally function more or less as a single unit. They consult each other, have access to each other's files, overhear conversations with clients, and have a mutual financial interest in their clients' cases" (see also Wolfram 1986, 391; American Law Institute 1995, ch. 8, 38). Whether or not this is always true or even structurally possible—especially in very large and geographically dispersed law firms—the ethical rules assume that confidences and revenues will be shared among colleagues and, therefore, distribute ethical obligations toward clients to all attorneys in the firm. It is because the conflicts of interest of any one lawyer are imputed to all of his or her associates that large law firms tend to be so much more beleaguered than smaller ones.

It is no wonder that the literature frequently refers to mobile lawyers as "tainted," "infected," or "Typhoid Marys," because, with imputed disqualification, a single attorney can conflict out thousands of his or her colleagues. The more contemporary AIDS metaphor, that unprotected sex is like sleeping with everyone your partner ever slept with, is especially apt. If mobile lawyers have *actual* knowledge of the confidences of a former client in their former firm, then they are personally barred from taking an adverse position against that client, and correlatively, that knowledge is imputed to all their new colleagues in the second firm, who are also barred.[2] However, the rules of professional responsibility do not impose a subsequent imputation as lawyers "carry" imputed knowledge from job to job. Imputed confidences, ascribed merely by virtue of membership in the first firm, do not bar either the mobile lawyer or his or her new colleagues from taking on a matter adverse to a client of the first firm.[3] So the impediments of mobility are constrained somewhat; lateral lawyers carry their own infections, not those of their former colleagues. Were it not the case, job mobility, especially across large firms, would be virtually impossible.

The study. Illinois firms in the study seem to reflect national trends in lawyer mobility. That is to say, their hiring patterns are all over the map. In the early 1990s, the period reflected in my interviews, roughly a fifth to a tenth of the smaller firms employing fewer than twenty lawyers—both in Chicago and downstate—were not hiring at all. Informants in these firms report either stability in their work force or economic stresses that precluded hiring additional lawyers or that even required downsizing. Among the firms that were hiring during this period, those with fewer than twenty attorneys were much less likely to hire laterally than were their larger counterparts. About a fifth of the Chicago law firms with twenty lawyers or more—that were hiring—rarely if ever took on lateral attorneys; this was true for a third of the firms employing ten to nineteen attorneys and a bit more than half of those employing fewer than ten lawyers. The corresponding percentages for downstate firms are 50, 64, and 88.

As these figures show, lateral hiring was much more common in Chicago than in downstate communities, even controlling for firm size: overall, about three-quarters of the Chicago firms hired at least some lateral attorneys, compared with not quite half that proportion downstate. Still, the phenomenon is not as rare as many non-Chicagoans believe. Indeed, a tenth of the downstate respondents—in small towns as well as bigger cities—reported that their firms did a lot of lateral hiring. In one instance, the firm was located in a city in which respondents in other firms told me that lateral movement was virtually nonexistent locally. The same percentage of Chicago firms—all employing somewhere between ten and seventy-

[2]One strategy to avoid the imputation of confidences is to erect an ethical screen or so-called Chinese wall around the tainted new lawyer—a solution that is available only for former government attorneys and for private practitioners in selected jurisdictions (Illinois being one of them). The use of screening devices to resolve conflicts of interest is considered later in this chapter in the section on paralysis and in greater detail in chapter 9.

[3]The difficulty, of course, is ascertaining and proving whether or not the mobile lawyer had any actual knowledge, however minuscule, of the affairs of the client. That is why a per se imputed disqualification rule within—if not between—law firms exists in the first place. The burdens of proof would be otherwise overwhelming.

five lawyers—also reported significant lateral hiring. A few of these firms had been recently founded, and virtually all their attorneys came laterally from other firms. Others had grown rapidly and relied on lateral hires to facilitate expansion; a few of the others preferred to hire young lawyers with some experience.

A more consistent feature of the legal marketplace nationwide that predates the explosion in lateral hiring across private law firms is the ubiquitous revolving door between the public and private sectors.[4] My informants report some lateral hiring from government positions. Firms of all sizes and locations hire the occasional judicial clerk or former prosecutor; the odd Chicago firm will report a lateral hire from an environmental, tax, labor, patent, or banking agency. But many more do not. The revolving door seemed remarkably still in Illinois.

My interviews were conducted during the aftermath of the legal recession of the early 1990s, so respondents were probably reporting on hiring programs that were somewhat less active than usual. And perhaps trends in lateral hiring from government positions were also depressed by the sheer absence of open slots and the keen competition government lawyers received from unemployed practitioners in the private sector. Still, the fact that three-quarters of the Chicago firms and even 35 percent of those downstate report lateral hiring from either sector suggests that many firms were confronted with the potential conflicts of interest stimulated by lawyer mobility.

The key word, though, is *potential.* Lateral hires do not inevitably produce conflicts of interest. They arise when laterals bring along to their new firm flesh-and-blood clients or confidences of former clients whose interests are adverse to those already served by their new colleagues. Many career transitions, fortunately, do not fit this model, as one downstate respondent illustrates:

> [Colleague 1] was a lateral hire, but he came from the state's attorney's office and any conflicts there went away within months. [Colleague 2] was a lateral hire from a law firm in Kansas. That was no problem. [Colleague 3] was a lateral hire from the state's attorney's office. That was no problem. We've just hired a young man from [a southern state] and I don't foresee that to be a problem. . . . We've just associated with [colleague 5], who . . . has been an attorney in [city on the east coast] and he's had quite a practice up there. . . . How we're going to handle conflicts there? I don't know. There probably won't be any because his practice is mostly in the EPA area and national-type firms. [100DSS10–19]

---

[4]Though conflicts of interest arise from lateral mobility here as well, the ethics rules are somewhat more hospitable toward transitions from the public to private sector than within the private sector itself (see Rule 1.11 of the *Model Rules of Professional Conduct*). Government lawyers are, of course, prohibited from drawing on confidential information acquired from their government posts in the representation of private clients. However, the imputation rules are more lenient in that if these lateral lawyers—barred from working on matters substantially related to their government service—are screened, the bar is not automatically imputed to their new colleagues (as it is in most jurisdictions for lateral hires across the private sector). Moreover, this bar is not open-ended; many government agencies allow for a cooling-off period of a number of years, after which their former attorneys can take matters adverse to the agency. The rationale for greater leniency in this particular turn of the revolving door is the public policy goal of attracting the most able lawyers to government service and the concern that restrictions on their future employment may deter recruitment efforts.

The mobility patterns of this small-town firm illustrate pathways that minimize the accretion of conflicts of interest. First, more common for downstate than for Chicago firms, lateral moves sometimes span considerable geographic distance beyond the reach of clients, their networks, or their interests. Some attorneys move out of the area when local markets are depressed; a few downsized Chicago lawyers have even relocated to the collar counties or beyond in search of more secure or lucrative work. Some laterals move to follow a spouse; others are driven out of town because the conflicts of interest created by a spouse or relatives preclude finding work (more on this at the end of this chapter). Some return to their hometown, after beginning their career elsewhere, to assist elderly parents, start a family, or set down roots. Others decide to strike out on their own and identify an underserved area several counties away as a fertile site for a fledgling practice. Still others flee their Chicago practice to realize their dream of becoming a country lawyer.

Few of the clients of these highly mobile lawyers are fellow travelers or have personal or business interests in these often remote locations. So their lawyers can make the journey unencumbered by the baggage that usually inflames conflicts of interest. Of course, this scenario is more likely with individuals and small corporate clients than with the large national and multinational companies typically served by larger law firms. It is hard to imagine a locality in which General Motors or McDonalds would not have an interest.

Second, many lateral candidates are relatively young. Few have collected a loyal stable of clients that will follow them from firm to firm. Rather, in their first job, they provided often routine services for the clients of senior colleagues who will remain with the firm. Few—especially those working in large law firms—have had much client contact or been entrusted with any confidences that could be imputed to their new partnerships. They too leave unencumbered.

> . . . I had no access to confidential corporate information. I was like the low end of the team. So what I did is work on, for example, drafting interrogatories or reviewing documents with regard to a particular case. I was never in a position then where I had access to either confidential information regarding the corporate structure . . . and I didn't talk to who would be considered the control group. So I had very limited potential exposure. [118Ch<10]

Third, transitions often impose or provide an opportunity for transformations in the structure of practice. Many young laterals were formerly prosecutors in U.S. attorneys' or state's attorneys' offices. Though they hope to draw on their litigation experience, most eschew criminal work and join civil practices where their case-specific confidential baggage will have no value. Other laterals discard the experiential baggage altogether, switching firms intentionally because they have tired of their specialized niche and hope to start afresh.

> We did have an attorney that was with the state's attorney's office as a[n] assistant state's attorney. And then he came on board doing basically insurance defense work. But he never handled any criminal matters because he said that's the reason [laughter] he got out of the criminal end of it. [95CC10–19]

Other laterals make the transition of necessity; downsized lawyers often join smaller firms serving an entirely different client base with few opportunities for adversity with their former firm's clients.

> I mean, they're usually two, three, four years out or they're from very large firms. Like we've got an attorney here from [one of the largest Chicago firms] and who's he worked on? He's worked on—he was telling me—Union Pacific, Baxter, you know [. . .] There's not a chance [laughter] in the world that we would have worked on that kind of business. . . . Generally, it's not been a problem. Because they either have worked on very, very large clients, or they've worked on a bunch of small clients. [77Ch10–19]

Finally, as I noted earlier, some firms hire laterally to create instant expertise in substantive areas previously wanting. Some of these new recruits bring new clients, new interests, and new secrets totally unrelated to those of the traditional clientele of the firm and, therefore, pose few conflicts. On the other hand, as prior chapters have amply documented, diversification of practice more often sets the stage for escalating conflicts of interest. Acquiring a boutique of intellectual property lawyers or an insurance practice, for example, is likely to set off the conflicts Geiger counter in a corporate law firm. So in assessing the risk of exacerbating conflicts, attorneys must look carefully at the sorts of clients, positions, and interests imported to the firm by the new specialists.

These features of lawyers' career mobility patterns identify narrow pockets of immunity from conflict of interest. Generally, if lawyers make a lateral move before being entrusted with significant client confidences or start afresh, eschewing their expertise, inside knowledge, and social connections, or move to a faraway world of strangers, they can travel through the legal marketplace unencumbered by conflict-of-interest baggage. The downside of this strategy, of course, is that employment prospects shrink as aspirants cast off all their social capital. Lateral candidates who arrive without a so-called book of business, with no special expertise or contacts, will not compare favorably with often cheaper, entry-level law school graduates. Indeed, as the legal consultants quoted earlier in this chapter suggest, it is precisely the value of the social capital brought by lateral candidates that accounts for the recent trend away from entry-level hiring. So the very qualities that make a lateral candidate attractive also exacerbate conflicts of interest. The pockets of immunity are, therefore, narrow and exceptional.

> Well, as I told you, conflicts are maybe taking an hour a month. And probably fifty-five minutes of that hour are laterals. . . . So, I mean it's maybe once every six months that a conflict issue is gonna come to me that it doesn't relate to a lateral. [61Ch20–49]

Though this respondent is unusual in the extent to which he attributes the conflict-of-interest burden to lateral hiring, this growth strategy is problematic for many law firms. The interviews contain considerably more discussion of the ethical difficulties wrought by lateral hiring than of the ease of recruiting more senior lawyers who travel along these narrow pathways of immunity. Conflicts arise both from the clients that move with lateral hires and from those they leave behind.

> And we bring in lateral partners every year and that brings in problems. He's got a bag of business that he wants to bring. And there are cases where you have to leave some things behind and other cases where he's too heavily involved in the matter, where you have to get waivers. The problems are monumental in nationwide law firms. [18Ch100+]

Traveling cases and clients, just like new matters, may pose direct or indirect adversities of interest with current or former clients of the host firm, or they may arrive conflict-free but preclude taking on lucrative business in the future. The most blatant conflicts of interest arise when the mobile lawyer is suing a client of the host firm, a circumstance that may kill or postpone the hire:

> Suppose you're bringing in a corporate partner who has annual billings of two million dollars. You've had a lot of discussions. And then, when it comes time, and he tells you who his client is (although, if it's that important, you probably should have known ahead of time), and this is somebody we're in a lawsuit with! Well, then, that's a deal breaker. I mean, you can't expect him to give up his major client for the honor and glory of joining this firm. [11Ch100+]

Adversities between host clients and lateral clients can even blossom before the ink is dry on the employment contract—in the few days between the hire and the lateral's actual move:

> It turns out that, until last Monday, we did no work for a client—a specific company. We did not represent that company. We just brought in an attorney . . . last Monday, who represents that company. . . . And she had not even opened up any files yet. Last week, an existing client of ours called us up and said, "We've got a problem with Such-and-Such, okay? Will you take care of it?" So [a colleague] wrote a letter last Thursday, okay, the day the file came in. You know, conflicts check right away. Nothing popped. Okay? No problem. We don't represent them. . . . But on Friday, when it came through . . . on the daily diary sheet, up pops our client—opposing party, this credit company. That credit company happens to be this [newly hired] person's client—who will never waive a conflict. That's it. Never . . . they just said, "We will not waive any conflicts. So, if you choose to represent someone who is opposed to us, then you will lose our representation." That's just their attitude. Fine! [said with high inflection], okay? Well, the letter was already written. . . . So I don't know what's going to happen. [10Ch100+]

Although ongoing disputes between major clients traveling with the lateral candidate and those of the host firm would seem to be relatively easy to identify and assess, several respondents note that the secretive and intricate courtship of a prospective partner often clouds the potential conflicts stirred up by a lateral hire.

The result can be employment negotiations that get aborted in the eleventh hour or embarrassment when firms find themselves on both sides of a dispute:

> . . . the real problem is when someone comes laterally with business. Those negotiations are almost always secret. The people involved in the negotiations will, of course, find out who that person's major clients are. And those people we would know right away whether we had a problem with, in general. That is, "Oh, you can't represent these people because we're always suing them." But they won't actually do a conflict check. And so you won't know whether affiliated and related parties or there are minor conflicts around. And there won't be a complete check of all of the client list until the person is willing to announce that he's leaving. Well, at that point, it's basically too late. That may be only a day or two before they actually leave another firm and move and may turn out to be very unhappy to find conflicts at that point. Now, in theory, you're supposed to have done that check before the negotiations got serious. Because you are supposed to have alerted your clients if, in fact, you are negotiating. There's actually a bar association statement on that. And it's just impossible. You can't do it. . . . He doesn't want to tell his firm that he's negotiating to leave. And he certainly doesn't want to tell his clients yet, because then he may be in conflict with some provision in his partnership agreement that he won't try to solicit clients for another firm. That he doesn't really want to tell his clients anything till after he's made the move so that he's not accused of trying to take work for the other firm before he left. And you don't even know whether it's going to go through. You don't want to announce to the world, "Well, I'm negotiating with someone," and then find out. So those are impossible. I don't know how anyone expects that works. . . . I, certainly, I don't see how it works. [28Ch50–99]

Still, these are the easy cases. Mobile and host clients often have no ongoing disputes at the time the transition is being negotiated, but the potential for future adversities looms. Perhaps the two sets of clients are fierce competitors:

> For example, our firm represents [large retailer]. A group of lawyers joined us from another firm that had represented a particular division of a head-to-head competitor, [second large retailer]. Both companies told us that they did not want to be represented by the same law firm no matter how tangential the matters. Most of these sorts of potential future conflicts occur after a lateral move of lawyers to the firm. [56Ch20–49]

Or the two clients periodically do transactions together that might turn acrimonious. Or the clients are coparties with complementary interests in ongoing litigation that unexpectedly changes course:

> We represented a client in a case where—this was a hospital—and we represented them in the case and got them dismissed from the case. We then had [. . .] another group of attorneys joined us from another firm. They were in the case—in that

> same case—for another client. We looked at that and didn't feel there was a conflict because we were already out of the case. And there was no problem. However, as luck would have it, the client that we got out of the case had doctors involved, where depositions were needed. And they got the deposition notices, called us up, and said, "We want you to represent the doctors," and then said, "Wait a minute, it's your name on the deposition notice." And that represented a potential problem as to, had we created a conflict and now, in essence, deposing our former client? Potentially we had. [33Ch50–99]

More subtle conflicts of interest are triggered by former clients and cases that the mobile lawyer does *not* bring to the new firm. Because of ethical obligations of confidentiality that bar the use of information regarding even a former client for the benefit of others, compounded with imputed disqualification rules that imprint these confidences on the entire host firm, business left behind can become a noose strangling the livelihood of lateral hires and their new partners. So the legacy of a lateral attorney does not end at the moment of hire; his or her biographical tentacles reach far into the future because the new firm is repeatedly at risk of being conflicted out by the past confidences and loyalties of their new member.

Baggage left behind is far more insidious because it is harder to inventory (and remember) everything on which the lateral hire actively worked, in which he or she was only tangentially involved, or that he or she inadvertently overheard.

> And when the firm started to grow . . . is when we started worrying about conflicts. Because we would bring lawyers in from other firms. The institutional memory is quite good. But when you have a lawyer who comes in from another firm, I don't know his clients. I don't know his practice—because I've never worked on them. [79Ch20–49]

Because the burden of proof of ignorance is on the mobile lawyer and the new firm, even matters about which the lateral was truly clueless can be problematic:

> One of our lateral hires used to be an in-house counsel for a corporation that we represent. And a lawsuit was filed against that corporation. That attorney was not involved with working on the case internally, but plaintiff's counsel brought a motion to disqualify the firm based on her former employment. Fortunately, the timing was such that she had left before any of this came up. So the court did not disqualify us. [82Ch10–19]

Other respondents described more problematic situations in which the lateral hire did have some connection to a matter in the former firm that is adverse to the interests of a client in the host firm. That connection might be financial:

> We've had the situation . . . where a lawyer at another big firm brought in—while that lawyer was at this big firm—brought in a plaintiff's case that was worth about four hundred thousand dollars. So this big firm was plaintiff's counsel on a four-hundred-thousand-dollar case. That lawyer wasn't even handling it at the firm,

> okay? It was a lady. She came in and joined [our firm]. Unknowingly, [our firm] had been defense counsel all along. Now, because she brought the business into that other firm, while she was at that other firm, she was entitled to half the fee, which was something like fifty grand or something like that. But, in the process of joining [our firm], we were never informed that she had 50 percent of that fee. So we never knew. So we never put into place any of these screening mechanisms, in the absence of which, it is presumed that there's been the spillage of confidential information. So she couldn't take the fee. Very unhappy. I don't blame her. [6Ch100+]

Or the connection could be informational:

> We ran into one this year, that we fortunately spotted in time, where we weren't in *Jones v. Day*. . . . we're not in that lawsuit that that lawyer worked for in that firm. . . . But we were in *Pale v. Day,* which was a related case. And the lawyer was about to bring with him knowledge of the same issues on behalf of the other side in the case we were handling that would have tainted us in a god-awful way. [5Ch100+]

Or the lateral attorney may have actually worked on the opposing side before leaving the firm:

> We have a lateral partner now that we were not able to hire for a year because he was, at that time, handling a large matter against one of our clients. He wasn't the only one handling it; he was one of a team of lawyers [. . .] And we made an informal inquiry to the client, saying, "We're talking to this person. Would that make you uncomfortable?" And the client said, "You know, we'd rather you wouldn't do it." So we didn't. . . . It was a one-shot matter; it wasn't like, it wasn't a continuing thing. And we didn't talk to him further until that matter was done with. [106Ch20–49]

Sometimes lateral attorneys in their new firm work on matters adverse to the interests of clients of their former firm, a clear conflict of interest if there is evidence that they worked on or had knowledge of the case before they left:

> [Describing a disqualification motion] In that instance, the other firm had a prior involvement with our client. Now that's not fair! In theory, there never should be a disqualification. I don't think the other firm cared. It was a lateral hiring situation. They brought in a lawyer who had contact with our client while working for another firm. There was no question that his expertise would have been beneficial to their case. They claimed that the lawyer had been screened. But it became clear to us—by looking at various records in the case—that he had not been screened; indeed he played a role in the development of their case. [40Ch20–49]

Several firms in the sample encountered the flip side of lateral mobility, when attorneys in their own firms made lateral moves. In some instances, respondents felt comfortable that departing colleagues honored their promises to avoid matters on which they had worked in their former firms.

> And we've also had associates in our firm, that have had access to our files, . . . go and work with a plaintiff's lawyer. So that is a problem. . . . can he handle cases that he's had access to in our office? We would insist, of course, that he not do that. And, generally, that's the way it works. . . . We had one of our associates—oh, maybe five years ago—that went to one of the larger plaintiff's firms. But that worked out very well. We had an understanding with him. And there were no hard feelings or anything. And he just did not work on any matters that he was handling while he was here. And then after a year or two, there were no files still pending that he had worked on. So, it didn't give us any problems or, really, didn't give his other firm any problem either, because they had plenty of other stuff he could work on. [62DSM10–19]

In other instances, partners felt less comfortable that their former colleagues had honored their obligations to maintain confidentiality, and moved—not always successfully—to disqualify their new firm.

> We had an attorney leave our firm and go to work for another firm. And he had been involved in this particular file. And then he went over to this other firm and they were involved in the file. And we even went before the judge on it—it was kind of determined that they set up this proverbial China wall [. . .] But you're working in the same law firm with somebody. I thought that was a serious conflict of interest on their part and that they should have withdrawn from representing the . . . other insured in the case. But I felt that he was privy to our theory and all of that information. And he's estopped from saying anything to anybody else. But I thought it was very inappropriate and improper. There's nothing we could do about it, because we presented it to the judge and the judge said, "Set up the China wall and he's not supposed to talk to anybody about it." . . . They said they did. And they said, "He's not going to work on the file." Come on! That's what you work with associates and partners with, is to discuss things and bounce things off of them. But I'm not saying that they didn't, but, I mean, I think there was strong evidence a impropriety could have existed there. [95CC10–19]

Several firms in the sample, burned by the betrayal of defecting lawyers who switched sides and carried client confidences with them, responded by instituting procedures to apprise departing colleagues of their ethical responsibilities and the conflict-of-interest implications of their move. Generally, though, respondents seemed more mindful of potential conflicts when they were on the receiving end of a lateral hire than when they lost mobile lawyers.[5]

[5]The impact of mobility on conflicts of interest is not limited to legal professionals. Lateral moves of paralegals, law student clerks, secretaries, and other staff from firm to firm provide opportunities for the leakage of client confidentialities as well. Indeed, the potential for conflicts of interest here may be more significant than in the movement of junior lawyers. Though

Mergers

> The dramatic expansion of many law firms through mergers and acquisitions was one of the most striking developments in the legal profession in the 1980s. (Whitfield 1996, 8)

In the extreme case of lateral hiring, of course, an entire firm, department, or practice group joins another firm through merger or acquisition, a growth strategy that also took off in the 1980s (Galanter and Palay 1991, 54; Weidlich 1993). The explosion of merger activity was more short-lived than were more limited law firm growth patterns based on acquisitions or lateral hiring, which continued well into the 1990s (Howard and Remly 1995). Analysts explained that firms had become more cautious, turning “away from wholesale mergers in favor of carefully targeted acquisitions designed either to broaden their practice areas or strengthen their positions in particular geographical regions” (Weidlich 1993, 1).

These trends are reflected in my Illinois sample. More than two-thirds of the large Chicago firms reported one or more mergers or acquisitions in the prior decade, and several of those that did not described serious courtships that ultimately fell through. This was true of more than half the Chicago firms employing fifty to ninety-nine lawyers at the time of the study and a substantial number of those with twenty to forty-nine lawyers. Indeed, mergers and acquisitions accounted for the explosive growth spurt of many of the medium-sized firms during this period. At least a third of the largest downstate firms grew through mergers and acquisitions, and a handful of firms with fewer than twenty attorneys did as well. Like their counterparts nationwide, most of the firms seemed less enamored of mergers at the time of the study than they had in the decade past.

Though a handful of respondents reported mergers of two solo practices or two small firms, most marriage partners were of unequal size, mirroring national trends. Large firms swallowed smaller ones to open a branch office in another city, or to expand their client base.

> . . . there was a period of a year or two when we associated with a [town about twelve miles away] firm. . . . it wasn't a merger; I'd call it an association. We actually hired them on a[n] agreed basis to provide so much work and then we would provide the other background. The idea was that there would be an orderly transition of that firm into this firm. . . . And his particular clientele was a [nearby

secretaries and especially paralegals may be much more privy to client secrets and the particularities of a case than a clerk or young associate is, these nonlawyers have not been inculcated in legal ethics or bound by the rules of professional responsibility that regulate their legally trained colleagues. Nor is there much guidance about how to protect the confidences these nonlawyers may carry through the job market. The interviews suggest that law firms muddle through. Some avoid hiring lateral staff entirely. Some hire only the seemingly most discreet and judicious. Others shield their lateral secretaries or paralegals behind the same ethical screens or Chinese walls in which they segregate laterally hired attorneys. And on occasion, a firm will seek to disqualify an adversary that hired a former paralegal, secretary, typist, or proofreader.

town]-oriented clientele. And one of the things we wanted to do was break in, get a stronger foothold in the [that town] market. So that was one of the advantages to us of employing them. [87DSS10–19]

Or they wished to enlarge their resources in order to take on more significant transactions or litigation.

The theory of the merger between [current firm] and [former firm]—my old firm—was that [former firm partner] had the contacts to do much bigger deals than he was doing. And what happened is that, within five years, he went from doing deals, where a really big deal was ten million dollars, to doing a . . . leverage buy-out which was a billion dollar deal. You just need a lot more people to do bigger deals. There are more pieces of paper to look at. Due diligence is more complicated. And I think that was a big factor in growth. [2Ch100+]

Or they sought to acquire the instant expertise of a boutique practice or build an area of specialization.

And the particular merger—like I say, their experience is labor law, which fit in well to our client base. Labor law is not something we offered. And, really, no one except for these two in the [area] do much of it. And since we represent a lot of private interests and so forth, that was a nice mix. In short, they were doing labor work for some of their clients, but their clients were using other attorneys for the nonlabor work, because they didn't have any expertise in it. And we're having to refer out labor matters. Well, that worked very well—that client mix. [72DSM10–19]

Few mergers among firms in the sample coupled two large firms. So mergers frequently did not look all that different from acquisitions; the difference was whether the marriage partner was a small firm or an entire department or cluster of specialists in a large firm.

If lateral hiring creates an ethical quagmire, mergers and acquisitions are accomplished on an ethical minefield.

There was a big rumor a few years back that Katten Muchin was exploring a merger with Winston and Strawn and Jenner and Block [among the six largest law firms in Illinois]. It would have been the merger of all time, with more than fifteen hundred lawyers. The merger fell apart, the rumor goes, because the conflicts problems were just too hideous. [8Ch100+]

As the number of lawyers, clients, and confidences that move to the new partnership increases, the potential for conflicts of interest grows. Moreover, as the collection of mobile lawyers increases in diversity, the number of traveling confidences imputed to them gets weightier. A team of specialists who work together on the same cases may not bring much more inside knowledge of client secrets than a lateral traveling alone; when an entire firm makes the trip, the imputed confidences projected onto their new colleagues will be vast indeed. This is why acquisitions are more common than outright mergers and why mega-mergers of two or more large firms occur so infrequently.

Mergers and acquisitions, then, represent lateral hiring writ very large. Potential marriages percolate through much the same delayed, awkward, indirect courtship as lateral hires, where disclosures of client lists are withheld until the very last minute when it is more certain the match will actually be made. Yet the economic rationale for the partnership may hinge on the very book of business that may, of necessity, be abridged by adversities of interest among clients of the two firms. When the cover is finally cracked and the contents assayed, the rationale for the marriage may instantly vanish, as lucrative chapters must be jettisoned in order to neutralize the conflicts. So conflicts of interest kill mergers and acquisitions as they do lateral hires, but often not until a good deal of effort has been expended exploring the promise of partnership. Many a lateral hire has been consummated with no book of business at all, when mobile lawyers instead offer their hosts needed labor or expertise or social connection. But mergers require mobile business and are, therefore, far more vulnerable to conflicts of interest.

> And we have done one of those, where we brought a number of partners and associates over from the [large Chicago firm] to join us. There, what we did is try to determine roughly what they thought. Obviously, there's always a problem there, because they can't contact the clients before they make the determination they're going to leave. But we also—from our standpoint—had to make a determination as to whether this is going to work before . . . they say they're going to leave. It's sort of a catch-22. So what they do is an estimate, is the best guess on what they think would go with them. We run our conflicts checks to see what percentage of our cases would be in conflict. Which is why you sort of tend to look for people who—it doesn't make a lot of sense to merge with firms that are doing work for the same clients that you're doing work for—you tend to look for people with different client bases. Generally, then, those conflicts are pretty much held to a minimum. [33Ch50–99]

Outcomes

> Confidentially, the firm is actually in the process of conducting merger talks with another firm, even as we speak. So far, the conflicts issues that are arising are business ones and not ethical ones. We're still talking. I don't know what will ultimately happen. I do know that one of us has a big client which is a competitor of a smaller client of the other—which is known to be jealous. So you have the normal conflicts in the ongoing operation of a law firm in a more stable state. And then you have the conflicts that arise when you add lawyers to the firm by hiring or mergers. [69Ch20–49]

This collection of mobility tales offers radically different endings. Several respondents reported incipient mergers abandoned when the parties discovered significant adversities of interest between clients of the two firms.

> I can think of one major acquisition that we had with a litigation group at another big firm, where we were involved in a major case where, not only did they—that firm—have the client, but those particular litigators were involved in that very same case. We just decided there was absolutely no way—no matter how we could structure it—for us to have them come here. We would have involved, literally, both firms pulling out of the lawsuit. And we had responsibilities to our own clients that would not have permitted us to do it. So the deal fell through. [59Ch50–99]

Similarly, many lateral hires were forgone because the amount of business that had to be jettisoned to avoid conflicts of interest no longer made the marriage attractive.

> L: I had a guy the other day . . . great practice in the bankruptcy area. But he's always on a side that we're always on the other side of. And I just told him, I said, "You're just not going to survive here because these classes of people that we normally represent are the ones that we want to represent. They pay the bills and all that. . . . It's not going to work." We have people who we've talked to and keep talking to for years, because they've been in a matter directly adverse. And we say, "If this matter ever gets resolved, we'd like to have you join us." But sometimes a matter drags on so long, that he loses interest or you lose interest.
>
> S: So it sounds like a fair number of potential hires don't work out because of conflicts?
>
> L: . . . Oh yeah, easily 80 percent don't work out. [18Ch100+]

Other marriages were consummated because mobile lawyers or one or both courting firms—sometimes flirting with hot-potato violations—withdrew from or declined problematic engagements or sent clients elsewhere.

> Actually, we didn't have to kill the hire. What we did is—basically—told that person that we couldn't hire them if they were going to continue to represent such-and-such a client. And the person decided to come with us and then helped find other counsel for that one client. . . . it worked out fairly well. But, some other attorney got a good piece of business because of it. [82Ch10–19]

And some mergers proceeded only after particular lawyers were also jettisoned from one or both firms in order to neutralize significant conflicts.

> . . . when we were in merger discussions several years ago, we had some lawyers in the firm say, "I know who the major clients of that firm are, and if they come, I'm going to have to leave." . . . It's very complicated and I think you can assume that, if you merge, you're going to lose . . . a number of people and clients through conflicts. Because you just can't do it. [1Ch100+]

Other partners departed quickly thereafter when they found themselves consistently conflicted out of lucrative cases by the interests of new clients brought to the marriage:

> Well, at [former firm], we had a partner with a big P.I. [personal injury] practice. He joined [current firm] in the merger. He had several cases—good cases—he had to turn down for conflicts reasons and left the firm. He said it was just for the conflicts reasons. I think there were some, certainly, other reasons. But that was an important factor. [2Ch100+]

Most often, mobile lawyers made their transition to the new firm, some with the consent of former clients and firms, some shielded by ethical screens from imputing conflicts to their new colleagues, some wearing blinders and muzzles to stanch the leakage of confidential information, and others cavalierly going about their business without much awareness of the baggage that trailed them. Given the circuitous route of the courtship process, it comes as no surprise that some firms in the sample discovered significant conflicts of interest immediately after the honeymoon.

> . . . we were representing the RTC [Resolution Trust Corporation] with respect to a particular institution. When the lawyers from another firm joined our firm, their prior firm was representing a holding company that was a target of a claim by the RTC which we had been asked to review. Now when these new people were contemplating joining the firm, we looked at a client list so that we would have cleared the potential conflicts when they walked in the door. This was not picked up because it was not a direct conflict. But their client was the real guy who was responsible. To make sure, we set up a Chinese wall in which there was no talking among groups of lawyers. Then we farmed out the RTC claim to another firm. [56Ch20–49]

These different outcomes obviously reflect the varied baggage that follows mobile lawyers. Some bags contained significant confidential information and clear and present adversity; others did not. Some contained important clients and major cases that could not be jeopardized, and others contained trivial, one-shot matters. Some clients were paranoid and uncompromising, others were trusting and flexible. Some laterals or firms brought expertise and a book of business that would consistently threaten the client base and caseload of their new colleagues; others simply had one immediate knotty problem; still others brought social capital that complemented that of their new partners. And some of the variability in outcome reminds us that some law firms are simply more risk averse than others.

Paralysis?

> You know, the biggest, single biggest problem is the imputation rule—that there's a lawyer in Chicago; does work for that client; that means the whole firm is tainted. That's the single biggest, biggest problem. Firms are just not going to be able to grow. I mean there's a whole set of practice areas that they're just not going to be able to go into. [26Ch100+]

Conflicts of interest no doubt chill lawyers' mobility. Many medium and large firms in the sample—situated in Chicago and downstate—reported hires, acquisitions, and mergers that were abandoned because the conflicts could not be resolved or because the sacrifices needed to neutralize the conflicts made the marriages no longer attractive. Several respondents complained about being imprisoned in a firm because conflicts of interest restricted their own movement. Indeed, several empathized with the unemployed lawyers from a recently disbanded firm who found that conflicts of interest severely limited their ability to find another job.

> . . . Pope Ballard just dissolved, and that's primarily employment law. And I was talking to a couple of the attorneys there, and they're telling me it's a nightmare, just a nightmare—how many firms they can't go to because of the potential conflicts. [118Ch<10]

Other respondents noted that they had earned the title of conflicts expert in their firm after weathering a disqualification motion provoked by their own lateral movement to the new firm.

Respondents in other firms—even large ones—conceded that conflicts of interest complicate hires or mergers, but do not preclude them.

> S: Do you find that it's . . . becoming prohibitive to merge because of all the conflicts that come up?
>
> L: I wouldn't say it's prohibitive, but it's difficult. It's very difficult. . . . If you've got people who've been active at all, it takes a long time and a lot of effort. And sometimes, very often, the lateral lawyer has to give up some business, unless they have a reasonable, understanding client. [36Ch100+]

In short, many large-firm respondents echoed the following sentiments:

> Have potential hires been aborted because of conflicts problems? Sure. [14Ch100+]

Still, other respondents in seemingly similar firms disagreed.

> You can always solve it. Maybe they'll have to drop a client. Maybe there'll have to be some substitutions of counsel. Really, the only time that we had an obstacle to a merger was when the senior partners of the firm to be merged with just made too damn much money and we wouldn't pay 'em. [laughter] [6Ch100+]

Lawyers, especially in large diversified firms serving clients that are increasingly disaggregating their business and spreading it around, do experience somewhat limited mobility but clearly not paralysis. Indeed, what is most striking about the interviews in large and medium-sized firms, where conflicts are more likely to slow or jam the revolving door, is the relative absence of the hand-wringing that the legal literature had led me to expect.

This disparity between what I heard and what I read was worrisome. Illinois is one of few states that allow conflicts of interest that arise from lateral hiring between private firms to be removed by merely erecting ethical screens.[6] Could the response of these Illinois respondents be attributed to this device? Perhaps the literature was echoing the paralysis that besets lawyers practicing in most other states, who can proceed with a tainted lateral hire or problematic merger only with the consent of the affected clients.

I explored this hypothesis by examining a handful of pilot interviews that I had conducted in large firms in another state, where rules of professional responsibility do not permit ethical screens to cure these conflicts. Moreover, I distinguished the large Chicago firms in my sample with headquarters or significant branch offices in states without these Chinese-wall provisions to see whether their spokespersons complained of greater difficulty in hiring than did indigenous Illinois firms. Admittedly, this sample is a limited one. But this subset of multistate and out-of-state firms did not look particularly different from those that practice only in Illinois. I found many that had grown rapidly and had undertaken a good number of lateral hires and an occasional merger or acquisition. Some of these respondents explained that their firm had abandoned an isolated merger or lateral hire because the conflicts of interest could not be surmounted, though roughly the same proportion of informants within this subset as in the sample as a whole could not think of a deal that was killed by a conflict. Like their Illinois counterparts, some complained that conflicts of interest slow or complicate the process of growing, but few, if any, found them debilitating.

> L: Well, we've acquired small groups, as I mentioned; we have not been involved in a large merger. . . . And we haven't contemplated a large merger. That would create very difficult conflicts problems.
> S: And that's the reason why you pursued the strategy of smaller groups?
> L: No. The decision about that has nothing to do with conflicts. [pilot interview #1]

> Oh, I think there is a disinclination for that reason. But I don't think it's one of the two or three most important. I think it's just recognized that these days, at least, that if one firm merged with another one, there would be a tremendous likelihood of possibilities for conflicts, at least if they're in the same city. [pilot interview #12]

> S: Does it become a deterrent for the firm to grow [through mergers and acquisitions], because of the conflicts problems?
> L: No, not in my experience. [Chicago branch office of a large firm headquartered in another state]

Though one respondent in the pilot indicated that he didn't really know how a Chinese wall worked, many of his counterparts in other pilot firms were very conversant with ethical screens and indicated that they used them frequently to help neutralize conflicts of interest. Several of these respondents indicated that offering to shelter lateral hires with ethical screens facilitated securing the necessary consent from clients.

---

[6]See chapter 9 for detail on the origins, structure, incidence, and efficacy of ethical screens.

> People are willing to consent to the conflict, but in fact they're only willing to consent to it or we are only comfortable in doing it in a situation in which we can generate an effective Chinese wall. We have done that. . . . I don't think it's common, but it is certainly, I mean there are probably Chinese wall situations around here at all times. [pilot interview #10]

So jurisdictions with and without provisions for automatic ethical screens may not necessarily look all that different on the surface. The difference is whether lawyers must also secure the consent of affected clients. That difference is certainly not trivial.

> We had one very bad situation in [branch office] where a conflict for whatever reason did not show up and it was an enormous problem and the clients didn't want to consent and they threatened malpractice suits and we ended up getting limited consent letters and the client . . . fired us and said they'd never use us again. That was the best we could do. . . . it happened right after the merger was consummated. We have a daily green sheet that comes around with all new matters. And when someone joins the firm, all their matters eventually get listed on the green sheet. And here was this glaring *X v. Y*, where we were representing X . . . and Y went ballistic. So, as I say, we got consents, but the client down in [branch office] said they'd never use us again. [pilot interview #2]

But rules that permit ethical screens to resolve conflicts of interest that arise from lawyer mobility do not neutralize client-relations problems. Undoubtedly some Illinois clients also "went ballistic" when mergers and lateral hires brought into the firm lawyers who represented competitors and adversaries. Undoubtedly many of them also fired their lawyers or took their business elsewhere, though perhaps more silently, given that their consent was not sought. The fact that their Illinois lawyers were not breaching the rules of professional responsibility in extending offers to these tainted lawyers probably smoothed the ruffled feathers of few clients. As the managing partner of a large law firm observed back in chapter 3 in a slightly different context,

> If that were a rule that I could sue a subsidiary of General Instruments and not have to worry about getting an ethics slap, my client's still going to be mad at me. . . . I am not sure that whether or not the conflict rule is there or not really would have much impact on how I conducted myself. Because, especially today, where it's so hard to get the business and keep the business, I want my clients to think I'm loyal to them. [18Ch100+]

These rules are for lawyers, not for clients; they do not ameliorate client-relations problems, nor do they address lawyers' ever-present business concerns. It is probably for this reason that the mobility patterns and the merger and hiring practices of Illinois and out-of-state firms do not look all that different. Mobility is difficult because it threatens clients. Ethical screens may reassure some of them. But reassurance comes with consultation and consent, a client-relations strategy that is available to lawyers practicing in all states. Illinois lawyers who, by undertaking a merger or lateral hire, risk losing significant clients will usually abandon the endeavor—just like their counterparts in other jurisdictions.

WHAT IS A FIRM?

Remember Lawrence Lexman, the solo practitioner from chapter 3? As his practice matured, Lawrence discovered the downside of practicing alone. He could not share the costs of personnel, office space and equipment, of building a library, or of marketing his practice, nor could he enjoy the other economies of scale available to larger groups of practitioners. He lacked the personnel to take on major cases and had difficulty juggling the ones he had. He did not have the expertise to serve all the diverse legal needs of his clients. As a result, he was unable to attract wealthier, repeat-playing clients and risked losing the ones he had when they had to go elsewhere for specialized legal services. Unable to diversify his practice, he felt constantly buffeted by the feasts and famines in the limited markets he served. Moreover, he found that with no one to cover for him, he even had to forgo the carefree, jet-set life-style that he so enjoyed as a law student. Lawrence began to understand the impetus to grow. But he also recognized that because of the imputation rules, he would pay a significant price to practice in a firm. Instead of losing clients because he didn't have the resources to serve them, he would lose them because their interests conflicted with those of a client of one of his partners. He privately gloated as he listened to his law school buddies whine about all the lucrative cases they had to turn away because some faceless colleague in Manila had conflicted them out with some insignificant piece of business. Happily, this was not Lawrence's fate. If only he could have it all—enjoy the benefits of collectivizing without the associated constraints imposed by the imputation rules. If only he could neutralize conflicts of interest by simply turning problematic cases over to an associate.

It turns out he can. The strategy is to simulate a firm but eschew those elements that create fiduciary obligation, namely, shared confidences and financial interests. The ersatz "firm" can enjoy economies of scale by collecting many practitioners who share overhead, office space, support staff, library resources, and the like. It can diversify practice by amassing under one roof a broad range of autonomous specialists. Alternatively, it can imitate a boutique firm by collecting independent lawyers who specialize in the same area. Yet, when conflicts of interest arise, these independent practitioners can pass would-be clients with adverse interests back and forth without fear that conflicts of one will be imputed to the other. To help smooth the inevitable fluctuations in workload or ensure that there is someone to cover for them, they can develop "of counsel" relationships with lawyers who are neither partners nor employees of the firm, some of whom share office space, others who practice elsewhere. Affiliations with lawyers of counsel can also be used to diversify the practice or provide a continuing stream of case referrals. To achieve the geographic coverage available to multisite firms, they can affiliate with local counsel in distant locations.

Office Sharing

My Illinois sample contains a number of small law firms—mostly in Chicago—that undertook one or more of these kinds of loose affiliations. Most often, they simply shared office space in order to spread overhead costs. I'd call the firm to set up an interview and would be greeted by a receptionist intoning "Law Office" rather than the long string of surnames that greets a caller to a traditional law firm. When I would arrive for the interview, the office would lack that distinctive, usually understated (in Chicago) law firm moniker or shingle that defines and marks its territory. Rather, the firm would share a generic unmarked lobby, suite of offices, receptionist, bank of secretaries, and office equipment with a handful of other firms or, less frequently, would be housed within a much larger law firm from which it rented space.

I visited one of these communal law offices located several miles from the Loop and was confused when the solo practitioner kept referring to "we" as he described his policies and practice. I asked whether he had other partners.

> We are all practicing as individuals, but refer cases to each other. For example, one of us does nothing but divorce work. I don't do divorces. So when a client comes in with a divorce matter, I refer the case to him or suggest that he is one person that the client might wish to see on the case. . . . There was a time where we almost became a firm. But then I got involved in another business, so I wasn't available to join the firm. And, nowadays, I go out and get business. Another guy doesn't. So it wouldn't work out between us as a partnership. But we refer cases between us. We like to keep them in the building. [120Ch<10]

Another solo practitioner working in an ersatz criminal defense boutique was more explicit about the economic rationale for the arrangement.

> L: [Office Mate] is my—I can't even say partner, 'cause he's not—for [more than ten] years. And we intentionally are simply an association of people sharing space. Because if we were a partnership, we couldn't represent people on conflicts. . . . And what'll happen, if two or three people come in to see [Office Mate], he'll go get [another office mate] for one and me for another [. . .]
>
> S: And is your decision not to become partners primarily one of not wanting to preclude your ability to take cases because of conflicts?
>
> L: That's a very large consideration, sure. . . . when I looked for a place to start my private practice, I selected [Office Mate] because of his [expertise]. . . . At that time, [Office Mate] was renting space from civil lawyers. And the lead person there died . . . and [Office Mate] and I basically became the managing tenants, I guess you'd call. We had a suite of [several] offices that . . . were filled by various lawyers. So [Office Mate] and I would go on the lease and then sublease office space. And, hell, let's face it, a very large consideration in my mind and in his was to make sure the other made a good living. Because, otherwise, the rent didn't get paid. . . . So there was a huge economic pressure. People have a misconception about what private criminal lawyers make.

> 'Cause they don't make that kind of big money. And so, sure, if I got two clients in on a case and they were each going to pay a ten-thousand-dollar fee, damn right I wanted [Office Mate] representing the other one. 'Cause I wanted to make sure he had money in his pocket to pay the rent—to help me pay the rent. Plus the fact that it's a hell of a lot easier to work with a lawyer who is in the office right down the hall from you than somebody who is over in the other side of the Loop. For instance, in this [case that I just finished], the discovery material which they made the defendants pay for the copying for was two file cabinets. I had a minor defendant, so my stuff was maybe a foot long. And so [Office Mate] ordered one set of it and paid for it. And then I simply worked off his file. Whereas, if we'd been in separate offices, that would have been an additional eight or nine hundred dollars of copying that would have been a problem. . . . I think it's a very major thing that we try to make sure each other make a good living if we're sharing expenses.
>
> S: Do you think that's a common pattern among criminal defense attorneys?
>
> L: I think so, sure. I mean, hell, why would I expect somebody from another office to call me on a case? I mean, it happens, it certainly happens. But not from lawyers who have two or three other lawyers in their office. Because why would they do that? It's a business as much as a profession, let's face it. [113Ch<10]

So this boutique arrangement provides a constant source of case referrals among the office mates and a way to share not only overhead costs but case-specific litigation expenses as well. Moreover, it solves the conflict-of-interest problem that arises when multiple defendants have clearly adverse interests. Attorneys can take the ethical high road and disaggregate the representation of coparties. And by farming out the various parties to office mates—and promising defendants a better coordinated and less costly defense—they keep the fees within the office, thereby lowering their own financial risks and overhead.

As long as office mates do not share confidences or fee income, their simulated organization does not constitute a firm according to the rules of professional responsibility; the conflicts of one are not imputed to the others. However, these examples suggest how easily ersatz can cross over to genuine. First, as the previous respondent described, because of the shared responsibility for meeting office expenses, the independence of income streams among cotenants may be more theoretical than real. Second, confidentiality is at risk when office mates share secretaries, phone lines, conference rooms, and file cabinets and leave reams of documents strewn across desks and piled along common corridors. The preservation of confidences and independence is even more precarious when office mates disaggregate cases, representing codefendants and sharing records, witnesses, and the like.

> Well, we're certainly not going to surprise each other in the courtroom. On the other hand, if I've got a witness that I have to call for the benefit of my client, I certainly have never—and I'm sure he's never—considered withholding that witness if it hurt his client. But you sure as hell tell the person that you're going to do it so that they can prepare and mitigate the effect on their client. [113Ch<10]

Of Counsel

An alternative office-sharing arrangement reflects even greater involvement among office mates in the lives of their mutual clients. Here independent office mates may occasionally serve the same set of clients, perhaps on different problems. Rather than disaggregating parties on a one-shot matter, office mates disaggregate legal needs in ongoing representation of a single party. For example, one firm in the sample shares a kind of boutique office with other independent practitioners who represent families of children with special needs:

> I share a suite with another group of attorneys. And I am of counsel to one of the firms and one of their people is to me. . . . they do some of what we do. . . . They take the same position we do. . . . They tend to represent a slightly different client base. . . . We've been together for so many years. . . . In fact we share many clients. They do more of the estate planning than I do. And I do more of the special education than they do. So very often we're handling different aspects for the same client. But it's really much more cooperative. . . . At one point, we were in the same firm. And then each of us left at separate times. . . . We formed our own firm since we moved into here. But it's done more for tax and . . . other issues than it is for separation. [103Ch<10]

This example is different from the others in that a member of each firm is of counsel to the other.[7] Many of the firms in the sample, even the large ones, have affiliations with lawyers of counsel.[8] Many of these lawyers are independent practitioners, providing occasional labor, expertise, referral networks, or coverage and feedback for lawyers practicing alone.

Not all respondents characterize these arrangements or affiliations as "of counsel," nor do all the corresponding firms acknowledge this role on their letterhead. Some of counsels have offices in the affiliated firm; others do not, often working dozens, hundreds, or even thousands of miles away. Though some of counsels seem like faceless tenants or boarders exploiting opportunistic relationships, many have enduring connections with their affiliates. Some are former partners or colleagues; some, friends or spouses. They chose a more impermanent connection for any number of reasons. One acknowledged tax implications. Some only practice law part-time. Others note that their temperaments, work ethics, or rainmaking abilities make them incompatible partners. But some office mates, like col-

---

[7]*Of counsel* denotes a rather heterogeneous category of attorneys that includes retiring law firm partners who seek a less active role in the firm, part-time lawyers pursuing a second career (often former judges, politicians, public or corporate officials, law professors, etc.), probationary partners-to-be (often lateral hires), and former associates who were not made partner but who seek permanent status within the firm. The last status has begun to account for a growing proportion of lawyers in this category, especially in large law firms.

[8]On average, Illinois firms with more than one hundred lawyers worldwide employ seven lawyers of counsel in their Illinois office(s) alone. The number ranges from zero to eighteen lawyers (Fox 1995, 22).

lege roommates, become trusted lifelong confidants whose professional lives sporadically intersect.

These intersections are ripe for conflicts of interest. Indeed, because of counsel lawyers enjoy greater financial interdependence with the firm and have greater access to the confidences of its clients than do mere office mates, imputation rules generally extend to the former, even as they ordinarily do not to the latter. Larger firms may treat the baggage of these affiliated lawyers the same way they do any of their permanent or prospective hires or, indeed, any potential new business:

> And it turns out that, even before a decision was made on whether we can [establish an of counsel relationship], we looked at the issue of conflicts of interest. And it turns out that they represent a partner in an accounting firm that we are suing for malpractice on behalf of a client. And they are not representing that gentleman in connection with his professional life at all. It just happens to be that his job is to be a partner in the accounting firm that we're suing. And I hit my palm on my forehead and said, "Got to be kidding me. You know, how, how could? What a coincidence!" But that's what it's about. And, with an of counsel relationship—notwithstanding whatever ethical opinions there are and the propriety of doing it—it's still all subject to conflict-of-interest rules. . . . everyone has to be treated as the same law firm for conflicts purposes. . . . And we haven't decided what we're going to do. [104Ch10–19]

Smaller firms may not be so thorough. Many firms and of counsels do not have a clue about the caseload of their counterpart.

> S: I noticed a rather large number of of counsels [almost twice as many of counsels as partners and associates] listed on the front door of the office [. . .]
>
> L: Well, the of counsels are not doing any litigation . . . We do a lot of litigation. Indeed, our relationship with them is that they will often hand over their work that spills into litigation—their personal injury, divorce, etc. Most of the of counsel are one-person stands; some will also be working for some company. Their cases that involve litigation will go to us. They tend to work in real estate, probate, unemployment compensation. I don't know how it works. One of the lawyers does 100 percent unemployment compensation cases brought before arbitrators. We don't do unemployment compensation, so there's no problem.
>
> S: Is it possible that he could be bringing an unemployment case against one of your clients?
>
> L: I have no idea if their cases are against our clients. [90Ch20–49]

Respondents in other firms whose affiliated lawyers practice in areas distinct from their own substantive niche also seem unaware of the of counsels' caseload; they simply assume the practices do not intersect. Where practices are more likely to intersect—either because of counsels handle related aspects of the legal needs of many of the same clients or because they provide labor or expertise to the firm—parties may be more vigilant about potential conflicts:

> So we always do a check back and forth—when somebody comes in—to make sure. Sometimes we know directly where it came from and we know what the story is. And we know that they haven't been in. But when there is somebody who might have seen someone else before—there might have been some involvement before—we do that. . . . Most of it is verbal, and if we can't make an immediate verbal contact, then it's a letter. . . . I just go next door and ask, 'cause we're a few feet away. I would say, "Have you ever seen this case?" . . . And if they haven't, fine. If they have, either find out what their record is [. . .] I also have access to their records, if I want to. And if for some reason they're not in while I am doing the interview, then I can leave a letter or a note saying, "Do you know So-and-So? Do you have any record on this person?" And get a response back right away. [103Ch<10]

Local Counsel

An even more impermanent affiliation materializes to span the geographic scope of a given case. Law firms, big and small, often receive requests to serve as local counsel on behalf of a distant law firm that finds it necessary to litigate a case, make a court appearance, question witnesses, take depositions, or file legal papers in the former's own backyard. Local counsel may be used to save travel costs or to exploit the expertise and social capital local attorneys have cultivated with other lawyers, prosecutors, regulators, judges, witnesses, or jurors. These temporary alliances, even when repetitive, certainly do not simulate a merger of the two firms but, like some of the other ersatz firm structures, may have implications for engendering new conflicts of interest. Though imputation rules do not apply across the two firms (in what is called *double imputation*)—one firm can still represent adversaries of the other on unrelated cases—local counsel do sustain fiduciary obligations. When they act on behalf of a client of another firm—even in a circumscribed way—they accrue long-standing obligations of loyalty and confidentiality to the client as if it were their own. Recall the example from chapter 6 in which a Chicago firm, acting as local counsel for a pharmaceutical company embroiled in litigation in Illinois, was disqualified years later when the firm brought an unrelated commercial suit against the company. It is for this reason that many firms are reluctant to take on the role of local counsel because of its potential to conflict them out of more lucrative future engagements.

> If I get a call from Dewey Ballantine [a New York law firm] saying, "Would you be our local counsel in this case?" And it's a one-shot deal. I will say, "Yeah, but I don't want this used as a [. . .]" And, if they won't [sign a waiver indicating that they will not use this as grounds for disqualification in the future], we won't take on the case. I mean, why be—you're a fifteen-hundred-dollar mail drop. I'm really doing it as a favor to Dewey Ballantine, not really for his client. And if he says, "No, our client won't sign it," I say, "Fine, go hire Mike Coffield [prominent Chicago litigator], or somebody you know." [18Ch100+]

Moreover, firms acting as local counsel must ensure that their actions on behalf of the clients of another firm are not adverse to the interests of their own clients. Respondents cited numerous examples in which requests to act as local counsel inflamed adversities with their own current or former clients.

> We are one of the few strange firms that believe in ethics. I see things that I just can't believe that other firms do. We had a situation involving a large West Coast law firm that was serving as local counsel [for us] on a matter involving a huge corporation. We were suing that company on antitrust and fraud. This company was a client of that law firm. I asked them how they thought they could take that case. The lawyer responded that he thought every law firm in the country represented this company in some capacity. He had no qualms in taking this matter. [42Ch20–49]

Branch Offices

Law firms also establish branch offices to increase their geographic reach. Some send partners from their headquarters to establish satellite offices from the ground up, others merge with indigenous firms, and others recruit laterally from existing local firms. As I noted in chapter 2, many firms in the sample have one or sometimes many more branch offices. Overall, 38 percent of the firms in the sample have at least one other office. The proliferation of multioffice law firms accelerated in the 1980s, shadowing the geographic expansion of corporate clients, the emergence of new markets, and the increasing globalization of the economy. Firms typically establish branches in the collar counties surrounding Chicago, in large downstate communities, and in major or emerging legal markets across the country or the globe.

The transition from local counsel to branch offices as a way to respond to the geographic dispersion of clients and cases comes with an ethical price tag. Just as other ersatz versions of law firm structures enjoy some relief from the conflict-of-interest rules, so do these transitory makeshift branch offices. Although local counsel are permitted to take an unrelated matter adverse to the interests of some other client of the affiliated firm, branch offices cannot. When local affiliates are swallowed as permanent fixtures of law firm structure, these branch offices become part of the firm and are subject to the same imputation rules as any other member of the firm. The conflicts of any attorney situated anywhere in the firm are imputed to colleagues everywhere.

Branch offices contribute to the conflict-of-interest profile of a law firm in often contradictory ways. If a firm is committed to growth, it may be safer—from a conflict-of-interest perspective—to add lawyers off-site than on. Very large law firms struggle to find work in saturated markets. As they develop long-term relationships with local clients and become known for championing particular positions, they increasingly find themselves conflicted out of representing opposing positions, adversaries or competitors of major clients, and sometimes entire industries. As they survey the social networks in which they are embedded, they find themselves increasingly surrounded by contaminated nodes and pathways they cannot touch. The more work they find to support their swollen ranks, the more they must turn away. By establishing a base elsewhere, the firm taps into a different social network with fewer contaminated nodes and greater opportunity to make inroads into the network without detonating new conflicts of interest. They begin afresh without the entanglements that conflicted them out of so many business opportunities in their home office. Of course, the extent to which a firm can find relatively uncontaminated social networks in distant sites is a function of their clientele. Large law firms that represent vast multinational corporations, insurance companies, corporate chains, franchisers, and the like may discover these clients have relationships, disputes, and interests practically everywhere. But law firms that represent entities with relatively circumscribed interests and relationships may uncover almost unlimited opportunities when they open an office in a new location.

But distributing a firm's lawyers across many far-flung offices also magnifies the difficulties of keeping track of potential conflicts and resolving them. Previous chapters have described the circuitous evolution of many conflicts of interest. The adverse interests may be held by parties with substantial ties to a client, by third parties, by clients without a direct stake in the matter, or by potential or former clients rather than current ones. Or the constellation of interests may shift so that what begins with a consensus of interests ends with profoundly incompatible ones. Conflicts arise through what is not happening, but might—who is not involved but could be. To anticipate these more indirect conflicts, lawyers in distant outposts need extraordinarily fine-grained information about the evolving activities of their colleagues and clients situated elsewhere. They need access to a kind of institutional memory and intuition about the future from which they are structurally foreclosed. They must know their colleagues' clientele well enough to discern who is and who is not a client as well as the identities of all their affiliated parties. They must know their colleagues' clients' interests well enough to recognize which positional or issue conflicts on unrelated cases would deeply offend them.

> We represented some municipalities in . . . a municipal antitrust . . . case, in which we got shellacked. . . . But, at the same time, somebody out of our [branch] office was representing a developer that was in a position of suing the municipality on essentially the same theories that had been advanced against our clients in the litigation up here. And the question was, was there an issue conflict? And I think we felt that there was. [44Ch20–49]

Lawyers must be sufficiently informed about their colleagues' rainmaking activities to know that they are courting a prospective client or that a given matter will conflict the firm out of ever representing the potential client in the future.

> A partner in Chicago had been working pretty actively and for a long period of time to develop a relationship with a new client for whom he had not done work. Had gotten access to some information. Had seen some documents by way of: "This is our business and this is how we operate"—not really in a meaningful way, but at least was generically aware of some documents. And that company was a partner in a venture that was a defendant in a lawsuit that a client in a different office, for whom we had done work, wanted to bring. So again, it was hard to balance a lot of competing interests. We took the litigation in the branch office, since

> we were not doing work. Sealed off everything that we had here. But the partner who had spent a lot of time trying to develop a client relationship was not real happy about it. But . . . what are you going to do? [9Ch100+]

They must know the twists and turns of an ongoing case well enough to realize that the configuration of interests has been or will surely be transformed. This kind of institutional memory, intuition, and organizational intelligence suffers as law offices proliferate around the globe. Out of sight, out of mind.

Resolving conflicts across branch offices can be as great a challenge as identifying them. Chapter 9 will consider the tensions within law firms when the client of one partner conflicts out the client of another; when business must be declined; or when a lawyer seemingly abandons, antagonizes, or betrays a client because of conflicts that have erupted elsewhere in the firm. Peacemaking is never easy. But resolution and conciliation are far more difficult when fault lines track geographic borders, when lawyers must make sacrifices for faceless, unknown partners (rather than for colleagues whom they know and respect, with whom they work side by side, who have made similar sacrifices for them in the past, and whose fees eventually trickle down into a common compensation pot).

HAT TRICK

The first part of this chapter described conflicts that law firms beget or evade as they grow, structure, and situate their practice. But individuals beget conflicts of interest as well. They arise when lawyers don too many hats, playing multiple roles on behalf of a client or taking on various positions outside the firm.[9] In chapters 3 through 6, the interests of their clients collided; here the duties of their assorted roles and obligations collide.

Part-Time Public Employment

Chapter 2 described the historical traditions that carved the Illinois map into more than one hundred very small counties, so small that not even twenty attorneys can be found in two-fifths of them (Attorney Registration and Disciplinary Commission 1994, 6). Yet each county supports an independent local judicial system with courthouses and jails, staffed by judges, sheriffs, state's attorneys, and public defenders—many of whom are lawyers. Indeed, in some counties, after filling these requisite positions in the public sector, there would be no private lawyers left to represent clients in

---

[9]A common example of role proliferation is dubbed the "lawyer-witness" or "advocate-witness rule," which prohibits attorneys from appearing as witnesses in cases they are also litigating. Ethicists provide many arguments for the rule, but the most important is the potential for conflicts of interest—that the lawyer's testimony may be adverse to his or her client, especially when called as a witness by the opposing side, or when "the lawyer's own interest in maintaining a reputation as a truthful person may 'materially limit' his [*sic*] ability to function as an effective advocate" (Hazard and Hodes 1990, 685; see also Tuite 1992). Attorneys who foresee being called as a witness in a trial are expected, in most instances, to withdraw or face disqualification by opposing counsel. Disqualification is not imputed to their firm, however.

the courthouses or spar with state's attorneys and judges. And that's just at the county level; the legal needs of Illinois's thousands of municipalities multiply the demand for legal talent many times over. The solution to the dearth of public-sector lawyers, coupled with limited funds and workload in small towns and counties, is to hire private practitioners to work part-time. Other jurisdictions, including state government and the city of Chicago, with greater financial resources and an adequate pool of lawyers to fill public-sector jobs, occasionally elicit specialized expertise from the private sector. They, too, fashion special temporary roles for lawyers in private practice.[10]

To fill these varied legal needs, some private practitioners—solo proprietors as well as firm lawyers—devote some portion of their practice to public-sector lawyering. Several small-town respondents in the study couple firm practice with employment as the city attorney. Others serve state government as special attorneys general or as hearing officers for regulatory agencies. Some handle litigation for government departments. And still others act as part-time public defenders. In the seven smallest towns in the sample, all with populations of less than twelve thousand residents, four respondents reported serving as city attorney for their own or a neighboring community and four served as public defender. (Two of the attorneys did both at one time or another.)

Many respondents have been juggling their two careers for more than a decade, some since graduating from law school. This is especially true of public defenders and city attorneys, who devote anywhere from a third to two-fifths of their time to their public responsibilities. Many of these lawyers indicate that they couldn't afford the public-sector work unless supplemented by fees from private clients. Others note that the extra income from their public role provides the financial cushion that allows them to practice on their own. Most report that they are salaried as independent contractors, but a few are or were employed by the city or county and continue to receive employee benefits. Some of these attorneys work alone in their part-time role; others have assistants (usually to handle the conflicts of interest) and, in the larger counties, may share the role with several other part-time practitioners.

But however nice the supplemental income, acting in a public capacity can potentially wreak havoc on the private side of a lawyer's practice. These part-time practitioners face conflicts of interest when they represent private clients with interests adverse to the public entity. City attorneys, for example, cannot represent criminal defendants arrested by police officers employed by the city—a particular problem for those who serve as both city attorney and public defender.[11] Nor can they represent private citizens with claims against the city.

---

[10]Many law firms count government entities among their clients. They represent towns and villages, municipal bonding agencies, bank regulators, school districts, county hospitals, public utilities, fire districts, libraries, and the like, sometimes even pro bono. Others are occasionally assigned cases by the court to act as public defenders for indigent parties. Here we consider something different, situations in which attorneys actually hold government or public-sector positions, whether on a temporary or ongoing basis.

[11]Only one respondent explained that he was required to resign from his position as city attorney before he could accept the offer of public defender for the county. Several other respondents held both roles simultaneously, instead declining cases in which arresting officers were employed by the city.

Attorneys serving in other public capacities also report that their private clients or those of their colleagues have cases adverse to these public entities, often on matters remote or unrelated to their public service. Sometimes it is necessary to turn down the business and step out of the public role; sometimes both sides will give the lawyers waivers to stay in the matter on behalf of the private client.

> I sued the county years ago in a traffic accident case. The kid's mother had been on a criminal jury of mine the week before he was paralyzed by running off a little county road. . . . I ended up suing the county and the town—that particular township—and a contractor. And made quite a bit of money. That, in fact, that was the—probably will be the biggest civil case I'll ever handle and ended up getting paid quite a bit of money by the settling out the county. And I remember discussing that at the time with my boss, as public defender. And I think I talked to somebody else about it and they said, "Hey, don't, you know, as long as your client knows that you're a public defender and that doesn't bother your client, who cares? You're not going to get fired for suing the county, even though the county pays your public defender checks." But that would be the only time that I . . . in fact, I think that's the only claim I've ever, ever raised against the county on behalf of a private client. [91DSL<10]

The conflict-of-interest problem tends to be ubiquitous among attorneys wearing several hats because these part-time public officials often secure their positions either because of special expertise or because they serve communities with few other lawyers. As a result, they likely will already serve or attract potential clients who are on the opposing side of matters they take on behalf of government entities. For example, being one of the few lawyers in town, a part-time public official may be counsel to the local real estate company, which has an occasional zoning problem with the city. As one city attorney explains:

> Or if a client—and you're in real estate—petitions for or wants a zoning change or something like that, we still advise [the client] to appoint independent counsel. And also, we don't handle it neither [for the city]. . . . I do that pretty frequently—not frequently, but I would say, probably five, six times a year I tell the city to appoint independent counsel. [117DSS<10]

Or these attorneys have represented individuals in the community on a variety of legal matters, individuals who are subsequently victimized by parties that the lawyers are obliged to represent in their role as public defender. This dual role results in lawyers cross-examining or seeking to undermine the credibility of other clients. Often, as public defenders, they negotiate restitution or a plea bargain—deals in which the criminal client's interest is to secure a light sentence or limited restitution and the victim/other client's interest is for greater restitution or a more punitive sentence—thereby entangling the lawyer in a wrenching conflict of interest.

> The more difficult one is when the victims of the crimes are my clients in the community—burglar victim, theft victims. . . . It's when there's a lot of victims that are

> my friends, real long-time clients, that type thing—that I don't want to tick off—then I'll just get my assistant to do 'em. . . . Because a lot of times, . . . these are property crimes where the penalty involves restitution to the victim, where the defendant's got to pay back the value of the merchandise stolen and not recovered or damaged. . . . Obviously we [. . .] for the defendants, you don't want to have to pay it back. But the other extreme is that you don't want to get your clients mad at you either. Have them show up and see you there representing the other guy. I had one here that I probably maybe could have got out of. I didn't. It was an aggravated battery. The guy went to the Department [of Corrections]. He was happy with the penalty, actually. He only got—[asks his secretary, "What'd [defendant] get, forty months?" Secretary: "Yes."]—and the state was asking for like eight, ten years. But he beat his girlfriend up real bad, big time. Went to the hospital. And I had done work for the girlfriend's mother. And she was a nice lady, super nice. She patted my arm in the courthouse after it was all over and said, "I understand you're doing your job." . . . So, I could have got out of that one. And some of it's a feel for what you have. They know you got to do your job in those situations. And you don't shirk it. Otherwise, we'd wind up sometimes having to appoint separate counsel—not in my office, not my assistant, who's on salary as well—and that's when the cost really mounts. 'Cause then those private attorneys charge by the hour. [125DSS<10]

This respondent's observation about the financial pressures to hold onto problematic cases is not unique. The fact that many counties have few public defenders and limited funds to pay appointed counsel (when the former are conflicted out) exacerbates the already ample share of conflicts of interest these lawyers face. Given the rather limited criminal element in small-town Illinois, the defendants, witnesses, and sometimes even victims tend to be the same cast of characters, alternating roles from escapade to escapade and often co-offending together. Public defenders working alone often face the prospect of representing codefendants—with, as I pointed out in chapter 4, enormous potential for conflict of interest—or having to aggressively cross-examine and discredit former, present, and future clients who witnessed the crime. The lawyers' instinct to cure the conflicts of interest by declining the case altogether or referring coparties to other counsel butts up against the considerable cost to the county of doing so, money squandered if the case is ultimately settled before trial.

Other Roles

Attorneys collect and sport still other hats, taking on additional positions outside the firm that sometimes conflict with interests of firm clients. They serve as bankruptcy trustees or arbitrators:[12]

---

[12]Though there were few examples among lawyers in my sample, conflicts of interest arise in all sorts of alternative dispute resolution, including arbitration and mediation. See, for example, Feerick et al. 1995.

> Because I have a lot of former judges [in this firm]—a lot?—[less than five]. They become arbitrators—what have you. So I try to get them to get the parties to agree in advance that we will not be conflicted out on a subsequent matter. Because they, you know, it's sort of a pro bono public-duty thing. And then it can be very irritating to me if they're being paid whatever their hourly rate is—it doesn't matter, it's not leveraged. And so maybe they'll get a fee of ten, twenty thousand dollars. And because they're arbitrating a matter between, let's say, General Electric and Illinois Bell, you know. . . . Either Illinois Bell or General Electric wants to hire me. Because I've got somebody arbitrating that, I'd be disqualified. That would be irritating. [30Ch100+]

Others serve as lobbyists, which sometimes aggravates positional or issue conflicts:

> We represent a horseman's association. . . . They pay us a modest annual retainer to lobby on their behalf. This costs us lots of business from casinos and the like. Their interests are adverse with practically everyone. We've lost a lot of business by serving in this capacity. I don't know why we do it. It's crazy. . . . We have two lawyers who engage in the lobbying practice. For example, they lobby on behalf of beer distributors. Now, I represent, in a corporate capacity, a wine and spirits producer. Their interests are not necessarily consistent. [71DSL10–19]

Quite a few hold elective office, serving on municipal and county boards and occasionally in the legislature:

> My son [and a partner in the firm] is the president of the [suburban] village board. . . . We won't represent anything at all involving the village—not even a traffic ticket. I had a client who was arrested on a DUI in another suburb. We told her to go to court and ask for a continuance. (You want to get a continuance, because you want to get a chance to review the police report before you develop the defense. They all say they only had one drink when you first speak with them.) The client didn't want to go to court. We insisted; we told her to take a cab, to do whatever was necessary to get to court. Well, she didn't go, and the city issued a warrant for her arrest. The warrant was sent to [village where son is president of the board], and they arrested her. What do we do? We told the [village] police to "deliver the goods" and then got out of the case. [90Ch20–49]

The conflicts go in both directions. It's mostly a matter of timing. In some instances, client interests preclude taking on these varied roles. In others, the outside activities create adversities of interest that force the firm to turn away clients or new business, as reflected in the arbitration case and the lobbying example. In others, whether because of inadvertence or the twists and turns in an ongoing case, the firm becomes embroiled in an actual conflict of interest between role commitments, on the one hand, and the interests of a client, on the other—as in the DUI case. Because these outside roles rarely bring much income into the firm, they can become a flash point for discord among colleagues when lucrative business must be declined because of potential conflicts of interest created by the role. The previous comments about arbitration—which has the distinction of infecting two opposing positions in one fell swoop—allude to this intrafirm tension.

Board Memberships

Even more frequently—in at least 80 percent of the firms—lawyers take on the role of officer and especially director of for-profit and nonprofit organizations, some of which are clients, some of which they hope will become clients, and some of which they hope will not. Board service holds many attractions. First, it provides a mechanism for marketing and business generation, particularly attractive in decades past when ethical rules prohibited lawyers from advertising. Board service exposes the lawyer to other board members from the corporate world and other social elites from whom the lawyer hopes to attract new business to the firm (Landon 1990).[13]

> Lawyers do use service on nonprofit boards as a marketing tool—they can hang out with what they consider to be other movers and shakers and give them an opportunity to learn about them and the firm. [40Ch20–49]

And serving on the board of a client gives lawyers the first shot at directing the client's business to their firm.[14]

> Because, from the standpoint of business getting, being on a board, the board hears first what's going on. And if I'm on the board of a corporation and I can say to the general counsel, "You know, my partner So-and-So is an expert in this area; I'd really like you to give us a shot at it." You hate to not do those boards, but [. . .] There are some firms that I [. . .] That's one area where I think they just wink. They just figure it's too important. And Howard Trienans has been on so many boards at Sidley [one of the largest Chicago firms]. . . . And he's been in big positions. I don't know how the hell he could—when he was at AT&T, general counsel of AT&T and on the board and all that. And they [Sidley] did all the work. [18Ch100+]

---

[13]Though some downstate respondents minimize the importance of board service on business generation:

> [Our business relationship] will probably be just as firm because I go play golf with you or our kids play Little League together. It's different in a big city. But I think down here, everyone—I shouldn't say "everybody knows everybody." But it's not that important. Personal relationships, certainly, are important in cementing that. But being on their board is not. [63DSS<10]

[14] Though the plan may sometimes backfire:

> More and more, I think, there are some corporate boards who have a reluctance to send their corporate work to one of their directors because of just the blatant favoritism that it shows. So I don't know whether it, now, it's going to start becoming more of a disadvantage than an advantage. I don't really have a feel for that. [59Ch50–99]

Moreover, as a downstate attorney now well into his seventies observes, board service can also be used to solidify the relationship between client and firm, thereby minimizing competition from other law firms.[15]

> The development of my practice developed with also serving on boards. . . . I can see where maybe I'm sort of a Neanderthal lawyer at this point. . . . I have found—and in my own mind I justify it—that the firm has profited by it. Because I've been able to retain all of the legal work and be so specifically identified with that company, that nobody even tries to tread on it. [54DSL20–49]

Many companies and nonprofit organizations themselves also like to have lawyers on their boards because of the potential for obtaining free legal advice.

> The feeling fifteen, twenty years ago was that it solidifies the relationship. I think the feeling now more is that they want you on them because they feel that they can get a—quote-unquote—"free legal opinion." [68DSM10–19]

> We represent a lot of banks and they tend to like their lawyers to serve on their boards—usually, it turns out, because they don't want to have to pay $250 an hour to have a lawyer attend their meetings. [43Ch20–49]

Client management may also like to have their lawyer on the board because it gives them a natural ally, someone who they feel will be sympathetic to their position and who, if necessary, can be manipulated by the implicit threat of losing business from the aggrieved client—precisely one of the reasons why conflicts of interest figure into this relationship in the first place.

> I had a terrible experience. A client of mine in the mortgage business . . . organized a property development company . . . —a subsidiary of a subsidiary. And they insisted that I be on their board. And I told them I really didn't want to and explained why. It's all very friendly. And I said to the guy, "I really don't want to vote 'no' when you've got something you want to do. And yet, I'm not going to vote 'yes' if I think it's wrong." Well, they started going into dreadful construction projects—residential, primarily, and some office. And I kept voting "no." And I was almost shunned because I wasn't a team player. . . . I don't think you should be there. What are you going to do? You know, it's easy—as a lawyer—to tell them this has this risk and that risk and the other risk. But, as a businessman, you've got to vote. And, if you vote—particularly in close situations—if you vote against management, they don't really like that. [80Ch10–19]

---

[15] Though, again, some disagree:

> Well, first you have to ask, what do boards do? Boards are for strategic planning and business decision making. Now it is important for a lawyer to understand the industry that he represents. But you don't need to serve on a board to get that kind of knowledge. With respect to relationships, relationships can be cemented in many ways—you can go out to lunch with your clients, to sporting events, dinner. I don't buy the argument. You don't need that extent of hands-on experience. I think those arguments are just rationalizations. [99Ch<10]

Others are attracted to board service because of the directors' fees and the access to centers of status, power, and influence. And many others serve for more public-spirited or altruistic motives:

> We also have many attorneys who serve on not-for-profit corporations. One of the philosophies of this firm is that we owe a commitment to the community. And one way of fulfilling that is providing people who will serve on not-for-profit boards. We're on the board of United Way. We're on the board of [name of organization], which is a rehabilitative service for disabled persons. We have two persons who serve on the board of [name of organization], the local community mental health center and an allied organization. We're on the board of the YWCA, [name of another nonprofit]. There's a lot of that that goes on. And, again, in some instances, those not-for-profits have need for legal services and we have represented them. . . . We recognize that you may . . . have to turn down some business because of that. But, on balance, you're probably going to get more, because you're going to be forming relationships, not only with that organization but with the leadership of that organization, other board members. . . . If you're lucky, they kind of like you and develop some confidence in your judgment and abilities. And they end up becoming clients of yours. So, that's a good way to network for obtaining more business, frankly. [87DSS10–19]

And, whatever their ideology or motives, many individuals, whose personal values and commitment to social change first attracted them to the practice of law, naturally gravitate to public service on various charitable and philanthropic boards as well.

Because the unit of analysis in this study is the firm and not the individual, my finding that more than four-fifths of the firms have at least one lawyer serving as a director on some kind of board is not a terribly illuminating indicator of the extent of board service. Still, the data suggest clear variation among the firms in their participation in corporate and community organizations. Part of that difference reflects opportunity structures. Lawyers in transactional firms, with both more longstanding relationships with clients and greater business acumen, are more frequently tapped for corporate board service than are those practicing in specialty or litigation firms.

> In this firm we don't have a lot of partners sitting on corporate boards or stuff like that. People may be on their church board. I know a couple of people have done that. Our kids used to go to some preschool thing and I was on the board of that. We're just pikers, we're not on those Fortune 500 [laughter] company boards, you know? . . . We're strictly a trial firm. . . . So, we . . . don't tend to really have long-term relationships with clients, where we do their corporate stuff and their tax stuff and things like that. . . . that ends up putting you on the board of somebody. [24Ch50–99]

Attorneys in firms that tend to represent major corporations and financial institutions may not have the wealth, social connections, or pedigree necessary to serve on the board of these Fortune 500 companies.

Moreover, the age structure and work ethic of a firm may afford few attorneys the discretionary time for service of any kind.

> No one here has a life outside of this firm. It's almost true. . . . But we don't have anybody who serves as a director or a trustee of anything except crummy little nonprofits—like somebody serving on the board of their Montessori School or something. . . . The unfortunate truth is, most of the people here work too hard to have a lot of [. . .] I mean, I don't want us to sound like a total sweat shop. . . . One of the things we don't have is, we don't have very many old partners. Like our oldest partner is about fifty-two. So we don't have people who are in states of semi-retirement, where they have a lot of outside interests. [44Ch20–49]

As these respondents suggest, there are clearly generational patterns in board service. Some variation reflects increasing autonomy and leisure time that often accompanies seniority, of counsel status, or retirement. Some reflects increasing visibility, reputation, wealth, social connection, and presumed wisdom and experience that tend to correlate with age and make older lawyers more attractive to organizational boards. But as the elderly respondent who called himself a "Neanderthal" implied, generational differences are not mere reflections of maturation or life course. Unlike his younger colleagues, he had been serving on client boards since the earliest days of his practice. Generational or cohort differences also mirror the growing trend among law firms in the last decade to shy away from board service altogether. Virtually none of the respondents indicated that their firms have increased their commitment to board service—especially in the for-profit sector—in the last decade. Many firms have been cutting back significantly on directorships, and a few have eliminated them across the board.

> There are policies in terms of, for example, boards. Although—as I say—"Is it etched in stone?" No. There are exceptions, but we clearly discourage board membership. And whereas it was commonplace maybe five years ago, I think at this point in time there may be three. . . . I'm saying there are three situations where . . . we made an exception, . . . where maybe ten years ago there would have been three hundred or something. [58Ch50–99]

> We will not allow lawyers in the firm to be members of boards of directors of our clients or of any for-profit companies at all. The policy goes back a couple of years. We had a phase-in period, where everyone was on notice that they were no longer allowed to run for reelection or reappointment to any boards. They could serve out their terms, but had to phase themselves off the board. In the past, lawyers who served on boards were required to turn their directors' fees over to the firm. Once this transition period away from board membership was instituted, lawyers were required to keep those board fees—an effort to try to limit our liability. We also insisted that lawyers make sure that the companies provided D&O [directors and officers liability] coverage during this interim period. There was one lawyer in the law firm who had a very, very lucrative insurance client and who served on its board of directors. He absolutely refused to get off the board and left

> the firm. Now that the transition is over, none of our lawyers serve on boards. [52DSL20–49]

This last respondent alludes to the most significant incentive to abolish board service: fear of liability. In the last decade, especially with the massive failures of savings and loan institutions, regulators and victims realized that law firms have deep pockets into which they could dip.

> In the last few years, we've represented several banks in major litigation where they have been sued. And who has been sued? The members of the board. And I know it's made a few of our partners who sit on boards of banks real uneasy—like, I think the next time around we may not sit on the board. Has there been a conscious decision to resign a board position with a bank due to potential exposure of being sued? Not that I'm aware of. But are we cognizant of that fact? You betcha. You know, it's real scary when we're walking a tightrope. And I don't know if the guys are going out of their way to necessarily jump on sitting on a board. Because we've gotten some new banks in as clients. But there's been no move to get on the board of directors or anything, simply because of that. [64DSS10–19]

Malpractice insurers were even quicker to appreciate the potential liability. Some began to cancel or refused to renew policies; others instituted exclusions of coverage, leaving firms bare for claims that resulted from board service; some raised premiums; some increased their oversight and created burdensome recordkeeping and disclosure requirements; and others pressured firms to withdraw from corporate boards. Firms responded.

> And I can tell you—categorically—that none of us sit on any client's boards because of the liability issue. . . . we were having difficulty finding malpractice insurance a couple of years ago. [laughter] We noticed that, on every application, they asked that question. And we learned from reading [laughter] the application, that the malpractice insurance carriers didn't approve of that behavior. And so, at that point, we formulated a policy and we said, "No more. We're not going to [. . .] We're not [. . .]" I mean, there wasn't a lot of it anyway. But everybody resigned from the couple of positions they might have had with their clients on a board. [77Ch10–19]

> We discourage board involvement. Again, that's primarily because of our malpractice carriers. Most of the available malpractice carriers will not cover you for matters if any partner is a member of the executive committee of a board or an officer that's sort of "operational" control. And it's pretty hard for a lawyer who gets on a board not to get very involved. I mean, they generally are strong members of boards. And the malpractice area's so difficult today that we've said no to a lot of people who wanted to go on boards. . . . even philanthropic, if we do pro bono work for them, the carriers won't cover it—which really is stupid. But there's too many cases out there. [18Ch100+]

Though much allure of board membership has been shattered by fears about liability, concern about conflicts of interest plays a significant role as well. Conflicts arise where the duties to or interests of a client conflict with those of the organizations on whose boards lawyers serve and to which they also have fiduciary obligations. These conflicts can develop regardless of whether the organization is a client and regardless of whether the boards are of for-profit or not-for-profit organizations:

> Let's assume a client of yours is being discussed in a loan situation and you have knowledge of information that [snicker] is not good to the bank. Now, you're acting as a director. What can you do? How do you handle it? Well, first of all, you never vote on it. But you've got the second point: if a board of directors is working well—I mean in the larger banks they do it through loan committees. Those board members who are serving on the loan committees, they're on the overall board. Part of the purpose is for them to bring information that management has been unable to develop—for whatever reason. If I'm sitting there as a lawyer and I know that, well, why the businesses go sour. Small business—one of the reasons they go sour is marital problems. They don't have any focus on it. Let's assume I have just finished a conference with the wife of a very large borrower. And she's telling me that hubby's a transvestite and is going to come out of the closet and everything's going south quickly. And you know, bingo. And I go into a board meeting. What can I do? I have wrestled with that. And what you really get down to is that you've got to say that you asked that they go back and do some further checking because you believe there's some information which you are not willing to discuss which may have an adverse effect on them. Now, some people could argue that that's too much right there and then. I don't think so. But, I mean, that's the kind of issue. [53DSL20–49]

> This kind of conflict is one we have a bunch of. We're all members . . . of various boards. . . . [Colleague 2] is a member of the board of governors of the major hospital in town. These kinds of conflicts, to me, are getting to be more troubling than some of the others. I've got two calls to make today: "Do we want to take matters that might become adverse to the hospital?" . . . The hospital is not a client. . . . I have a new client—newish client—that I've been working on real hard for a couple of years and doing very well with him. And one of the things one of the principals of this company wants me to do is to take a matter that's potentially adverse to one of the doctors at the hospital. . . . I'm talking to the partner who is on the hospital board about how we want to handle that. . . . my view of it is that we have agreed in other cases in the office to allow a matter adverse to the hospital in a contract negotiation with a doctor, based upon the fact that we don't represent the hospital and that our partner board member will recuse himself from those matters. I don't see why we can't do that here. And I'm going to be irritated if my partners take a different view just depending on whose client happens to be being gored. [70DSS10–19]

In situations in which board members also provide legal counsel to the organization, conflicts of interest become more tangled and problematic. First, conflicts of interest can arise from the incompatibility between the lawyer's role as client advocate and counselor and as board member.

> It's just absolutely a conflict of interest for a lawyer to serve on a board. For example, maybe a nonprofit contemplates dipping into its endowment. The legal opinion on this would be whether the company can dip into its endowment and how it could do so. But the director's responsibility is instead to ask, "Should the company dip into its endowment?" And these are inconsistent positions. It's an absolute conflict of interest; it's simply not possible to play both of those roles. [52DSL20–49]

Moreover, the traditional who-is-the-client question—management, the officers and directors, or the shareholders—faced by corporate counsel under normal circumstances becomes far more convoluted when lawyers wear several hats. Their constituency when they wear their lawyer hat (management, officers, or directors) may be different from their constituency (shareholders) when they wear their director's hat. Here they face yet another systemic conflict of interest.

> Because they're now asserting that there are conflicts. . . . you were officer for a bank or you were officer for corporation and you gave advice to the officers and directors. And now it's turning out that the officers or direc [. . .] You know, quote, unquote, "Who were your clients?" Were your clients the company, or were your clients the officers or directors? [10Ch100+]

Second, board members face conflicts from the incompatibility between the interests of their firm and the interests of the organization they serve:

> [There] was a panel for the ABA where [they] discussed this very problem about a year ago. . . . It had to do with conflicts of lawyers who serve on the board of corporations and then recommend their own firm to handle the case. . . . But it's quite interesting. Because in those situations, you have a lawyer that wants, would like to get the business to his own firm. And in many cases—up till the present, where they now are more conscious of conflicts—people take these jobs . . . so they can sit with the board and know what's going on. If they hear of a good case, why, it goes to their firm. And [they] had a big panel discussion as to whether or not that is ethical—where they are feeding cases to their own firm. And it may actually influence their attitude toward whether they want to recommend a settlement, they want to recommend a certain course of conduct. They see a juicy five-year lawsuit coming. It gets a little hard, particularly in a firm with three hundred lawyers and things are tough. [60Ch20–49]

Several respondents explained that they resolve these tensions by continuing to serve on the board but insisting on wearing only one hat, that of board member. When legal questions arise, lawyer-directors instruct the board to seek outside counsel.

> The most difficult conflict of interest problem that there is to figure out is the ones that we have now, which is, can you serve on the board of directors of a non-

for-profit corporation and still represent the corporation? That's the hot issue of the time. And the answer is no. . . . We require not-for-profits to send a letter acknowledging that the lawyer that's on their not-for-profit board will not be required to give legal advice and will not be acting as a lawyer and will not be acting as an agent for the firm. [75DSL20–49]

The problem, though, is maintaining that boundary between lawyer and director and refusing to cross the line when the inevitable trivial legal question arises at a board meeting.

Our policy is not to sit on for-profit boards. We have a lawyer who sits on the board of a local college. The firm serves as part-time lawyers for this college. In the course of a board meeting, someone asked his opinion as a lawyer about something in the bylaws. He answered the question. When I got wind of it, I was angry. I told him, "Either you quit the board or respond when asked such questions that that is something for their attorneys to decide. You cannot serve in the capacity as a lawyer." [71DSL10–19]

So firms develop their own policies and practices. And, not unexpectedly, they vary considerably. About two-fifths of the firms in the sample had policies about board service. Those that barred or discouraged service on for-profit or client boards were more likely to have policies (65 percent and 48 percent of them, respectively) than were those whose lawyers freely served as directors (39 percent of them) or had few such opportunities (0 percent). Because policies deal with procedures for disclosing or getting approval for board service more often than with bans or restrictions, they can be found even in firms that freely permit board membership. Many respondents concede that these policies are in flux.

At this point, I do not think we would accept a board membership where we represented the client. I think you will find—in your survey and so forth—that that's still very commonly done. . . . Now, beyond that, we talk about it a lot. But, gennnnnerally, depending on the prominence of the board, we take the board appointments—even though it might cause trouble. I don't know. I will tell you, in the last year or two I've really have sort of a "hell with all of them" attitude. I'm very tempted to just resign from all boards. People are pumping you for free advice. That's what it's all about. It causes us all kinds of these maneuvering problems that we have to worry about, and so on and so forth. So, yeah, I don't know. I doubt [. . .] It's probably one of those feelings I have that I'd really like to do, but I'll never do it. [laugh] [70DSS10–19]

Overall, 31 percent of the firms permitted or, on rare occasions, even encouraged lawyers to serve on client boards.

There's at least one person who is very visibly willing and eager and has very successfully gone on several boards of our clients. And he's not discouraged from doing so. In fact, he's encouraged to do so. What steps have been taken with

> respect to liability and so forth? I don't know. I think, probably, he just reads the company the riot act to have extensive directors' and officers' liability insurance, and makes sure that, in that capacity, he's covered by the company, and keeps a pretty tight distinction between his work as a director and that as a lawyer, and tries to keep the law firm out of it. Now, whether or not we have to pay an extra premium on our [malpractice insurance] because we have one of our senior partners on a very visible [. . .] on one or two boards [. . .] They may be doing that, but whatever is happening because of the increased risk, we've faced up to it. Because I know people have and continue to serve on corporate boards of our clients. [39Ch50–99]

> We don't have any policies about it. I think the only boards that anybody is on around here are situations where we represent that client on a regular basis. So, you kind of avoid or—I suppose—you create conflicts there, I don't know. But I would think you avoid the conflict by being on the board of a client—I would think. [73CC10–19]

A little more than a quarter of the firms absolutely barred their lawyers from serving, and 42 percent discouraged these activities but allowed exceptions: grandfathering in long-standing board service for important clients, allowing lawyers to serve on boards of companies owned by their families, serving when a great deal of business is at stake, or looking the other way at the activities of of counsels or senior partners. Many respondents explained that they could cool out unhappy clients by agreeing to attend board meetings—as lawyers, not directors—at no or reduced fees.

Medium-sized firms, employing fifty to ninety-nine lawyers, were least likely (6 percent) to absolutely bar their members from board service and most likely to permit it without discouragement (62 percent). Large firms were next in line with relative proportions of 16 and 38 percent. The proportions for smaller firms were 33 and 20 percent, respectively—a striking difference from the medium-sized firms. There are probably several explanations for why medium-sized firms—jumping ahead of their larger counterparts—break the pattern of increasing permissiveness with firm size. One may be the impact of the malpractice carrier that insures the largest firms. Differences in clientele offer another explanation. Large law firms typically represent huge corporations, which draw a particular class of directors and are less likely to pressure or even desire their lawyers to serve on their boards; moreover, these large law firms may be one of a sizable number of other firms also called on to handle their legal business, not all of whom can serve as directors. Medium-sized law firms, on the other hand, are more likely to have exclusive and long-term relationships with smaller companies. It is more likely that these entrepreneurs might want their lawyers on their boards and more difficult for the latter to refuse.

Few respondents commented on board service for for-profit companies that are not also clients. A handful of firms, though, while barring their partners from serving on client boards, will permit directorships on other for-profits.

> We don't do it [serve on boards of clients]. We just don't do it. One of our partners is on the board of directors of a major bank here in Chicago. And we don't

represent that bank—although I'd love to. But it's not worth it. He's not about to give up his directorship. And we wouldn't ask him to. One of our partners is on a board of directors of a company that was his client. But he didn't go on the board until the company was no longer his client. And it was his client at a different law firm. And we don't do any work for the client. [104Ch10–19]

Roughly half the respondents—in firms of all sizes and locations—report that their colleagues serve on boards of not-for-profit organizations. Indeed, as one respondent noted earlier, many firms feel an obligation to give something back to their community and actively encourage their members to serve. And only one or two noted the risk even of eleemosynary service.

> Nonprofit boards could be okay. But lots of nonprofit organizations, like hospitals and universities, are really businesses. And they behave like businesses, like cut-throat businesses. I don't want lawyers serving in that capacity either. [52DSL20–49]

Though some will provide pro bono representation to the organizations on whose boards they sit, many draw the line at paid work.

> For example, one of our partners sits on the board of a hospital in his community. And we were approached—after he was on the board—to do the work for that client. And we said, "We can't do it. As long as [colleague] is on the board, we don't feel comfortable with that. It doesn't look good. It's not good practice. We shouldn't do it." And so we've turned that away. The hope is that—having dealt with that client in that manner—that once [colleague]'s term is up—and he's not going to run again or agree to be appointed again—they may come to us. We'll see. [82Ch10–19]

Curiously, the large downstate cities, whose firms are least likely to allow their lawyers to serve on client boards, are most likely (77 percent) to have lawyers serving on not-for-profit boards. Large firms employing more than one hundred attorneys are next in line (62 percent). (Keep in mind that this figure represents the percentage of firms, not the percentage of lawyers!)

FINANCIAL INTERESTS

Most lay conceptions of conflict of interest revolve around financial interests—situations in which parties violate their fiduciary duties in favor of private pecuniary gain. Curiously, the financial interests embedded in conflict of interest—aside from the obvious one, that lawyers seek to attract and keep business—came up infrequently in the interviews. In part, the inattention reflects the fact that firm finances are proprietary; in part, financial interests tend to be somewhat awkward to talk about, and both respondents and I were uncomfortable dwelling on them. But financial interests received little comment mostly because they are ubiquitous.

Fees

No matter how lawyers fund their practice—including out of their own pockets, as Lawrence Lexman did—conflicts of interest necessarily follow (Ross 1996; Kritzer 1996; Kritzer et al. 1984).[16] Those paid per hour have an incentive to overprepare, protract their services, or do unnecessary work. Those who are on a salary that does not reflect caseload, who are paid a preset fee, or who estimate the fee up front and agree not to exceed it by a given amount have an incentive to shirk. Those funded by contingency fees, whose compensation reflects a fixed percentage of civil damage awards or settlements, allocate effort where it is likely to lead to greatest or most immediate reward, neglecting those with small injuries or those that are costly to prove. Even pro bono work creates conflicts. With no fee forthcoming and a nonpaying client, firms often assign their least experienced lawyers to the case. Moreover, these lawyers have even greater incentive to shirk and not worry about ingratiating the client than where fees are preset. Sometimes worse, attorneys may take the pro bono case because they are ideologically invested in the cause and actually commit considerable resources to the engagement. But in their ideological fervor, they lose sight of the client's interest—for example, refusing to settle the case because they hope to establish a precedent at trial, thereby risking that the client will lose and get nothing.

So attorneys are damned if they do and damned if they don't. Compensation arrangements of all kinds necessarily pit the interests of the client against those of the lawyer, though perhaps in different ways and at different junctures in the representation.[17] There is no way around it. The ethical rules, therefore, simply instruct that lawyers' fees be "reasonable" and based on informed consent (American Bar Association 1983, Rule 1.5a).

Most firms adopt compensation schemes that reflect the markets they serve; incentive structures; risks; or the preferences, power, and financial wherewithal of their clientele, not the threat of conflict of interest. The systemic intrinsic conflicts embedded in these fee arrangements received little comment in the interviews. Rather, respondents reflected on what appears above the surface—typically either what they perceive as the ethical compromises made by lawyers who adopt compensation schemes different from their own or circumstances in which their adver-

[16]As the legal marketplace has become more competitive in the last decade and as clients have exerted greater influence on fee arrangements, attorneys have begun to experiment with alternatives to the traditional billable hour. For an overview, see Reed 1989 and the American Bar Association, Section of Business Law and the Center for Continuing Legal Education 1996.

[17]When clients are powerful repeat-players; take a more active role in setting, monitoring, and limiting fees; and threaten that they will take their ongoing business to another firm if not satisfied, the inherent conflicts of interest may not be troubling. Indeed, the whole movement to fashion alternative fees, a response to pressures from large repeat-playing institutional clients, is an indicator of an attempt to regulate or balance these conflicts. But many clients do not partake of these reforms. They are inexperienced, unsophisticated, not knowledgeable about what is a reasonable fee, and—as one-shotters—have few implicit sanctions available to keep their lawyers in line. Here the conflicts can be quite worrisome.

saries tried to exploit their own fee arrangements, thereby entangling them in potential conflicts of interest. Much remains below the surface.

Case settlement represents one juncture at which fee-based conflicts often surface. Critics of hourly billing observe that lawyers will delay settlement of a case until they have accrued sufficient fee income.

> I've had some dealings with some [larger town about forty miles away] attorneys that, quite honestly, I've never been able to understand it. But they say that they settle the case by the weight of the file. When the file reaches a certain thickness, so that you can justify the fee that you're going to bill, that they will do it in that fashion. They won't consider or talk about settlements prior to that time. [126DSS<10]

Critics of contingency fees observe that lawyers will settle a case rather than go to trial when they need the immediate income.

> A law firm needs to pay the rent, so it sells a case for one hundred thousand dollars instead of two hundred thousand dollars. [6Ch100+]

A contingency fee lawyer reflects on this temptation as well as on how defense lawyers try to exploit it for the advantage of their own client:

> I left [my former firm] when . . . I had a lot of money in the bank that I used to bankroll the creation of the new law firm. And I had two cases that I thought were going to go to trial right away. Well, as circumstances would have it, neither one of those cases went to trial right away. They both got continued. And, in part, they got continued because the defense people came to me and said, "Well, we'll settle this case with you today. Otherwise, for these valid reasons, we have to get a continuance anyway." But the today money was short money—. . . less money than the people were entitled to. And they said, "Well, [L names himself], you're just starting your own business. You could use the dough, da da da. Why don't you take the settlement?" And I refused to do that. And I'm very proud of that. And I never once took less money than I should have on a case. Because I believe that, whatever the results are, they ought to be for the right reasons. And those are the wrong reasons—your own pecuniary gain. And I think that's what we, as plaintiff lawyers, ought to be all about. And that's what we try to live by around here. . . . I mean, I got one verdict where I turned down seven and a half million dollars. That's a lot of money. And I'll wager you that, if I pulled out ten members of the plaintiff's bar, half or more might have taken that dough. I knew it wasn't the right number. And it might have been a quick killing for me to get in and get out and take whatever money I got out of it out of it. It wasn't the right result. And it was clearly the wrong reason to do it just because it was quick and expedient and easy. . . . I have another friend in the defense bar. He says, "You know, a lot of plaintiffs," he says, "including you," he says, "a lot of these guys, they miss the boat on the business side of this." And I said, "What do you mean?" And he said, "Well, you could take your inventory and turn it over, man, in two years. Overnight. And

> you'd make a lot of money." And you know what? He's right. I'd sell an awful lot of cases short to do that. And that's why I suppose this is still a profession and not a business. . . . 'Cause it's an easy business decision to say, "Oh God, that's seven and a half million bucks. That's a lot of money. Geez, look at what we can make." Well, that's business. That's, to me, that's not professional. Because the uncontradicted medical testimony was that the net money left over wouldn't be enough to pay out what [my client's] future cost in medical care would be. [92Ch10–19]

And, certainly, the opposite can occur as well. The lawyer can afford to wait out the anticipated large award from trial (from which he or she will accrue roughly a third). But the dying client needs the money now and would prefer a much smaller settlement, from which he can directly benefit, than a windfall for his estate.[18]

A second theme, touched on in discussions of "who is the client?" in chapter 4, concerns who pays the fee. When fees are so high that clients cannot afford to go it alone, they aggregate, sharing fees and creating conflicts for their lawyer if their interests ultimately diverge. That chapter also described triangular relationships in which fees are paid not by the client but by a third party, often an insurance company, family member, or employer. Here the conflicts arise between the divergent interests of the fee payer and the client and because of the temptation for lawyers to be more responsive to the former than the latter. Recall the numerous insurance defense examples as well as one in which a criminal defense attorney accepted payment from the mother of the accused and didn't put her on the stand as a beneficial witness to offer testimony that would incriminate her, resulting in the conviction of his client.

But who pays the fee not only distorts or at least tests attorney loyalties. It can also affect lawyers' own pocketbooks and thereby create conflicting interests between their nonpaying clients and themselves. The tension is greatest in insurance defense work, where the insurance company and not the client allots fees for their defense. Recall from chapter 4 the complaints of the downstate lawyer about cost-cutting insurance company bureaucrats who audit lawyers' bills and restrict or refuse to authorize expenditures necessary for a proper defense. Certainly, impartial observers might dispute whether the red-penciled items are all truly necessary to a proper defense. And certainly much of how this respondent characterized insurance company auditors could be said of some paying clients as well. The difference is that penny-pinching paying clients themselves undertake the risk that frugality might undermine their case. Insureds do not. Their lawyers are confronted with the choice between mounting a proper defense, partly financed out of the law firm's

[18]Lawyer and client operate in different temporal worlds; their needs for short-term and long-term compensation differ. Moreover, because the client does not contribute to the legal costs, the difference between a settlement and award after trial is simply the time value of money. For the lawyer, on the other hand, settlements require much less work to achieve than verdicts do. One-third of a slightly higher award after trial may not begin to cover the lawyer's expenses of bringing suit. Whereas the difference for the client between a $100,000 settlement and $200,000 award is roughly $67,000, it is only $33,000 for the lawyer, probably not enough to cover litigation costs. The client is probably better off going to trial; the lawyer is better off settling the case.

bank account, and the less vigorous defense for which insurers will pay. Their own financial interests directly collide with those of their client.

A more perilous collision occurs when, as was described in chapter 4, the law firm owns the insurance company obliged to provide a defense for its insureds.

> There are substandard [insurance] companies in this state. And by the way they practice law, you know that there are problems—where the law firm that's supposed to be representing the insureds, the principals of those law firms also have stockholder interest in the insurance company. I don't feel that a law firm should have a stockholder interest in an insurance company that is assigning to them cases to represent insureds. [105Ch<10]

Disinterestedness is difficult to sustain when lawyers have a financial stake in the case. Though some argue that this scenario best aligns the interests of lawyer and client (when the client wins big, so does the lawyer), the tensions in contingency fee cases remind us that aligned interests are not identical interests. One respondent noted that contingency fee arrangements are not restricted to litigation. A variation is found increasingly in the fee structure of some kinds of transactional work. Again, the lawyer's obligations to a client can diverge from the lawyer's own self-interest:

> I think that there's an inherent conflict with respect to contingent fee matters, which is not often addressed, which is . . . the contingent fee transactional matter, . . . where your payment is dependent upon whether or not the deal makes or not. And that's a very common kind of situation with syndication work or with certain kinds of corporate transactional work or development work, where the lawyer gets, quote, "a piece of the deal," or his fee is dependent upon the making of the transaction. And I think there's an inherent conflict there. . . . it's not per se a conflict of interest. But the question is, is the lawyer really able to put forth his best effort for the client when he knows that, if he kills the deal or suggests problems with the deal, he won't get paid? [10Ch100+]

A similar tension—though one step removed—arises in real estate transactions in which brokers will not get their commission if the deal is killed. When the broker refers a large number of real estate cases to the lawyer, the lawyer is torn between loyalty to the client and financial self-interest in the steady stream of business from the broker, which may be jeopardized if the lawyer advises the client against buying the property, thereby killing a big deal.

> I almost always insist that my client come into the office and meet with me before the closing—unless it is an emergency or something. But you see lawyers running from closing to closing without doing anything. The problem is that a particular lawyer gets fed all his cases from a particular real estate broker. If the deal gets killed, the broker doesn't get his commission. Do you think that's a conflict? It's a conflict if the lawyer is not doing the job he is paid to do. Once I take the client, I'm his. If I feel I can't be there for him fully, I don't take the case. When a lawyer

> is in the broker's debt, there's a conflict. If he feels compelled to shade his practice, there's a problem. [115Ch<10]

The potential for conflicts is not limited to cases referred by third parties. Attorneys who refer cases to another firm because they are conflicted out, overloaded, or lack the expertise to handle the matter also face problematic financial incentives. Recall the example earlier in this chapter of the solo practitioner and criminal defense lawyer who shared offices with other criminal defense lawyers. Concerned about whether his office mates would be able to contribute their share of the rent (for which he would otherwise be responsible), this respondent noted that when asked to represent more than one codefendant, he would refer the others to one of his office mates. Being paid referral fees or finder's fees has the same effect.[19] When financial self-interest affects a lawyer's judgment about where to refer a client, conflict of interest threatens, especially when clients could be better served by a firm that does not pay referral fees. Many respondents noted that although the practice of paying referral fees is common elsewhere—especially downstate—it makes them uncomfortable.

> Because I get real troubled by—this is not about conflicts—but referral fees, for example. . . . I actually had someone call me and ask for a finder's fee. [L laughs] What? But they call me and say, "I want to refer a case to you. Do you pay referral fees?" [L laughs] And I say, "No. I don't pay 'em and I don't take 'em." But I don't care what the—the Canons of Ethics say you can do it, if you advise your client and if you share the fee based on the time spent on the case—I think they stink. I think there's something that stinks about them. And . . . sometimes I'm like sort of surprised at people's comfort level with things that I wouldn't feel comfortable doing. I don't care if the Canons of Ethics permit it or not. I'm not willing to do it. [118Ch<10]

Others draw the line on accepting referral fees only when they are referring cases because they are conflicted out.

> I do a lot of workers' compensation petitioner's work. And the first thing I always ask the person—before they explain anything about how they got hurt—is who they work for. And if they name somebody that we represent, I immediately tell them, "Don't go any further; I can't represent you." And I give them the name and number of some other lawyer. Then also, of course, if we refer the case out to somebody because of a conflict, we cannot and do not take a referral fee back. [73CC10–19]

---

[19]The Illinois Rules of Professional Conduct allow lawyers to pay referral fees as long as payment is disclosed to the client and the referring lawyer assumes the same responsibility for performance of the legal services as would a partner of the lawyer to whom the matter was referred (Illinois Supreme Court Rules 1990, Rule 1.5g; Illinois State Bar Association 1995). The rationale for the rule is to encourage lawyers to channel complex cases to attorneys with greatest expertise or resources to undertake the matter.

Investments

Lawyers may have a financial stake in a case because it somehow collides with their private investments or business interests. As noted in the examples regarding contingent fee transactions, a conflict can arise when lawyers participate in the ventures of their clients. Conflicts also occur when outside businesses in which they or their families have equity have disputes or transactions with their clients. They can even arise when lawyers passively hold securities in companies that are represented by the firm or that have adverse interests with clients represented by the firm. Lawyers in the sample do all these things.

Investing with clients. The classic scenario in which lawyers find themselves in business with their clients arises when a fledgling operation, with little money to pay the necessary legal fees associated with securing patents, financing, or incorporation, offers the lawyer an ownership interest in the business in lieu of fees.

> When I first started practicing law, I was aware that it was not an uncommon experience for an attorney—who was, say, actively involved in business creation, development of corporation—that, in lieu of fees, to receive an ownership interest in the business, shares of stock. And when I first started practicing law, I think there were a few limited instances in which this took place. But we quickly found that 99 percent of the businesses never amounted to anything. They usually failed. We never got any fees. And so we stopped the practice. . . . So, basically, our policy—at the present time—is, in lieu of fees, we will not take an ownership interest. [88CC10–19]

Many respondents describe these opportunities, which were especially common early in their careers. Some refused, as the lawyer just quoted now does, because the chance of success seemed remote.

> Somebody did that in 1964 when I first started. Came in . . . and said, "I want to sell band instrument shelving. But I can't get this going out. I want you to do the groundwork and I'll give you"—I forgot what percentage thirty years ago. And someone else came in and said, "We'll give you a sixty-fourth of an oil well, if you'll fill out all this stuff." They left within five minutes. I never saw them again. [laughter] [127DSS<10]

Some refused because their ethical scruples dictated against participation.

> I regret that I have never undertaken that. I really do. Because here we have [gives the call letters of a television station]. . . . And I had a client coming in long before the present owner . . . bought it, back in the infancy, when I first started. "Let's get in together because Conrad Hilton is alive and he will back us money-wise. And why don't you come on in and do this." . . . It didn't take too much money, 'cause we could get it someplace else. . . . Like an idiot, I said no. . . . No, that was insane, but I haven't done that. I haven't gone in with anyone [. . .] For example, I've done

> patent work. I refuse to take my fee out in a percent or something of that sort. . . . And I think that, as I say, that it's maybe a mistake, but I'm not too unhappy about it. I'm jealous [laughs] of someone who did just what I didn't do. . . . It was a wrong thing to do. [110DSM<10]

Some reluctantly agreed because their social ties to the client made it difficult to do otherwise.

> A guy from my hometown—a little town down by [a town about thirty miles away], Illinois—and he's gotten a number of patents. And he came to me and wondered if I could help him get the patents and he would give me a percentage of the patents. And I said, "[Inventor], I don't want that." He said, "No, no." He said, "You should, because [. . .]" he said, "but I'm not going to pay for legal work." So it's been a bad deal, really. But . . . I've got 10 to 20 percent of his patents that probably aren't worth anything. But if one of them would ever hit, why, I suppose I might have a problem. In which I'll just give it back to him if that's a problem with him. I don't think it will be. He's the kind of a guy who feels very strongly that I'm entitled to it. [100DSS10–19]

And others—typically older colleagues of the respondents—participated and became very wealthy as a result.

> Years ago, we were asked to help form two banks. Now each of the banks are part of big systems. We put in our money, the same as everyone else: $24,000 in one and $10,000, eventually increasing to $50,000, in the other. The $50,000 investment has appreciated to $4,000,000 plus stock; the $24,000 investment to $700,000 plus stock. That is the good news; it's a tremendous benefit. [90Ch20–49]

With mature business clients that can afford the fees, this sort of quid pro quo is less common. That is not to say that lawyers do not participate in their ventures:

> The big firms are packed with lawyers who have equity participations in their clients' deals. [104Ch10–19]

> Coventures between lawyers and clients occur fairly frequently [here]. It happens all the time. [31Ch50–99]

A second scenario in which lawyers find themselves in business with clients arises when the latter, after fully paying their legal fees, offer their attorneys an opportunity to invest in the venture.

> I don't invest with clients—with one exception. I have a fella I was in World War II with, who's an industrial real estate broker-developer. And I have invested with him. But in all of those, I never got a free ride. I put up my percentage of the capital. I also got paid. In other words, I never got a piece for services. And that wasn't really my doing so much as it was his. . . . That's him up there [points to a photo-

> graph on the credenza]. That's the way they did it. There was often a broker, a builder, a lawyer, an accountant, and so forth. And everybody put in his dough, including the developer. Nobody got a free ride. And everybody got fees. The broker got fees; the accountant got fees; I got fees. And they've been marvelous. Of course, this started a hundred years ago when the real estate boom was on. [80Ch10–19]

Frequently, this investment opportunity arises when lawyers have been enlisted to secure financing for the deal:

> Because we deal with clients who need access to capital markets, and from time to time, we may very well arrange for either investment of capital or debt. From time to time, we will, the firm may take a position. [58Ch50–99]

> One of the distinctive features, probably one of the controversial features, of this law firm is that we're fairly entrepreneurial. We have investments in a large number of our clients. Our clients come to us to help them find ways to complete transactions, to complete acquisitions, to buy businesses. And often a piece of the financing puzzle will be an investment partnership comprised of lawyers of [this firm]. In the late 1980s, in particular, those investment partnership opportunities occurred often enough that we developed policies that would permit even senior associates to participate. Because part of the firm culture was, this was a desirable thing to do—not only to evidence support for a client, but support for your fellow lawyers in terms of what they were doing for a particular client—and frankly made good economic sense in many instances. There was recognition of the conflict problems and sensitivity to that. Recognition as well that other lawyers might criticize us for what we were doing. But, in the end, we all came to the conclusion that it was in our best interest and our clients' best interests, more importantly, that we continue to pursue those sorts of activities. [pilot interview #3]

Although these lawyers opted to provide "a piece of the financing puzzle," because they believe that there is money to be made, some participate in a more limited way to demonstrate their good faith in their client:

> I bought a hundred shares—mostly to show my support—not because I really expect to get any money for it. [51Ch20–49]

Not everyone partakes of business ventures with clients, though. Many respondents explained that they did not invest in client enterprises because the nature of their practice yielded few opportunities:

> I've been asked to loan money to clients, but that's as close as it comes. [laughter] And the investment was, "Hey, can you loan me a thousand bucks?" [84CC<10]

> I've had clients on occasion ask me if I want to get involved in dealing dope with 'em. That's about it. And I obviously decline that opportunity. [91DSL<10]

Some had no money to invest or they have no taste for it:

> S: With your patent work, you must be on the ground floor of potentially incredibly lucrative newly emerging technologies.
>
> L: Newly emerging technologies are what we work with every day. It's no big deal. Investment is not encouraged, nor is it very common. . . . These issues are too ethereal. We are trying to make a living as lawyers, not as investors. And [sarcastically] somehow we're still able to put bread on the table. [42Ch20–49]

And others considered the ventures too risky:

> We . . . have opportunities. Real estate developers will often ask us to participate in the transaction. . . . I have never done it, but probably less for ethical reasons and more because I am not much of a risk taker. And having set up and seen so many of these real estate ventures, I see how vulnerable they are to failure. I am too averse to risk. I'd like to think, though, that my ethics would prevail (if the deal was not a risky one). I know that lawyers have gotten very rich by investing with clients. But I believe that such activity clouds one's judgment. Plenty do it. Maybe they are better at it than I am. But I know that it would cloud my judgment. [99Ch<10]

But, as this last respondent suggests, many attorneys forgo the opportunity because it is laden with ethical difficulties.[20] Lawyers with a financial stake in a client face a profound conflict between their interests and those of their client.

> I tell them that I don't want my judgment impaired. I don't want my pursuit of pecuniary gain to be a pitfall, getting in the way of doing what is in the best interest on my client. [99Ch<10]

> . . . there's also a distortion of advice because you're so intimate. The lawyer has such a big stake in the company that, humans just being what they are, closes his eyes to reality. [5Ch100+]

Can attorneys truly give objective legal advice when they stand to lose or gain a great deal of money? Again, like in contingency fee arrangements, their interest tends to be akin to the client's. When one does well, so does the other. But because they have different aversions to risk, different temporal orientations to the short- or long-term, different preferences for profit or growth, their interests will frequently diverge. Can lawyers truly maintain their objectivity, can they champion the interests of their clients, when those interests are adverse to their own?

[20]The *Model Rules of Professional Conduct* do not forbid or seemingly even discourage lawyers from having financial interests in their clients. They simply require that "the terms on which the lawyer acquires the interest are fair and reasonable," that they are disclosed to the client in writing, and that the client is given the opportunity to consult with another lawyer before the client consents in writing (American Bar Association 1983, Rule 1.8a).

> I mean, it's been our philosophy here we don't invest with our clients—in any regard—for the obvious reasons. My interest may be adverse to yours. We're not going to go to war over it. But "Let's sell [. . .] let's not sell." . . . You can't represent somebody objectively if you have an interest other than as a lawyer. You can't. I don't care how strong or wonderful you are, you cannot do it—period! There will be a conflict at some point in life. . . . Well, you can't invite those things. You just don't do those things. [83Ch10–19]

Other respondents suggest as well that investing with clients can undermine and, indeed, threaten relationships with them.

> . . . there are potential dangers involved in investing with the clients. And the Code of Professional Responsibility speaks a lot to that issue. . . . our general philosophy is it's always dangerous to invest with clients. I spent some time in the army. And my management skills, feeble though they be, come from the army. And there's class distinctions in the army. And captains don't drink with sergeants, and sergeants don't drink with corporals. . . . But you have to identify your relationship with a client. And as soon as you move over relationship lines, things get clouded. The relationship changes. And my obligations and your obligations become less clear. And so there's always a potential for misunderstanding. And so we just try to avoid those things. [122CC<10]

And, of course, investing with clients inflames liability risks as well as business and ethical risks.

> And, again, I don't think you'll see this in the future: purchasing stock in a client's corporation, entering into a real estate transaction, owning an apartment or something. . . . Those are other things that attorneys quite often used to do. But it just isn't worth it anymore. . . . Because of the liability. If things go bad, it's so easy to say, "Well, you were supposed to be representing me legally and you were really looking after your own best interest." . . . Even if you weren't, how do you prove the negative? Tough spot to be in. . . . And again, everyone [in the firm] has become so sensitive to it and so forth, I think people pretty much do stay away from them. [72DSM10–19]

Several respondents described serious malpractice suits against their firm when a colleague had a financial interest in a client venture that went sour. Others noted that malpractice insurers abhor investment with clients almost as much as they do board service.

> [Our insurers] were more concerned, it seemed to me, with the ownership issue than they were with the director issue. They did not want to be involved in insuring you if you were going to be representing companies that you owned. [97DSS<10]

> But I wouldn't do that [invest in a client], because that's an exclusion under your errors and omissions policy. [117DSS<10]

> And we have been told by our insurance company that they perceive this to be a problem fraught with difficulty. We never thought it was fraught with difficulty. We always thought we were putting our money in and what's the big deal? Okay? They have raised all sorts of—what we perceive to be—theoretical, hypersensitive possibilities: the deal goes south and the other shareholders of the deal look askance at you, who is both the attorney and another investor. Like I say, I just feel that it's [. . .] well, I feel it's overblown. But they have all sorts of examples where lawsuits have arisen. And, therefore, we have come to a compromise position with our insurance company as to our deductible. . . . We accepted a higher deductible to make them happy, while our work is still insured. [83Ch10–19]

In short, why flirt with conflicts of interest, business and liability risks, and loss of insurance coverage? As one respondent concluded, "There are plenty other places to invest." [47Ch20–49]

As this array of opinions suggests, firms vary considerably in their policies regarding investment with clients. Of the firms that have opportunities to invest with clients (about 70 percent of them), one-third bar attorneys from doing so, a quarter discourage it, and the remainder, roughly two-fifths, permit it. Permissiveness increases with firm size. The median-size firm that bars investments with clients has eight attorneys, those that discourage it employ twenty-eight, and those that permit it, fifty-six. A higher proportion of firms allow lawyers to invest with clients than to serve on boards, though the two policies are correlated. Whereas 59 percent of the firms that allow lawyers to serve on client boards also permit them to invest in clients, this option is true of 22 percent of those that forbid lawyers from serving on boards; 14 percent of the former, compared with 67 percent of the latter, bar client investments.

Many of these firms that allow participation in client ventures do so in a limited way, however. I was taken aback the first time I learned of the practice. I had asked my standard question about whether the firm had policies about investing with clients. The respondent exclaimed, "Oh yes!" Expecting, from the tone in his voice, to hear a sermon about why the firm forbids such risky, misguided behavior, he continued, "Opportunities to invest in a client must be shared with the entire partnership." I later learned from other respondents that their partnership agreements stipulate as much.

> Our policy is that, if any one partner is given an opportunity to invest in client companies, that that opportunity has to be presented to the entire firm on an equal basis. [17Ch100+]

> We actually have a philosophy that a lawyer works seven days a week, twenty-four hours a day for the law firm. All earned income belongs to the firm, even if it comes from sculpting in one's spare time. We believe that all investment opportunities belong to the partnership. [43Ch20–49]

The rationale for such policies appears to be to minimize divisiveness or territoriality in the firm that might arise from the investment windfalls bestowed on select partners.

> Generally speaking, if there are investment opportunities with clients, it's something that's discussed by the partnership and something that's usually made available to any interested partners. We don't want to encourage partners on their own taking a piece of investment interests that we aren't aware of or which could create little fiefdoms within the firm. [108Ch10–19]

> I can remember an instance here in the [this city] community, where one of the attorneys did very, very well with a client that went public. And the rest of the firm had thought that he ought to share with it. And he didn't. And that started the breakup of the firm. [54DSL20–49]

But the effect of such policies may also be to spread and sanitize the investment, perhaps limiting the lawyer's personal stake in the client venture and thereby tempering the self-interest that can compete with client interests. Several respondents did observe that these investment-sharing policies have lessened the incentives for lawyers to participate in client ventures altogether.

> We also have a policy that, if an investment opportunity comes to a partner, he has to offer it to everybody else in the partnership. And that kills lots of deals. 'Cause a company comes up and says, "Hey, George, we would really like to give you ten thousand shares for all your work." Well, George knows that he's only going to get one share. And he usually says, "Now, now, now, don't. Give it to us in a fee premium instead." [18Ch100+]

Insider trading. Investment in clients can precipitate a different kind of conflict of interest as well. Lawyers will typically have considerable inside information about their clients. They know before shareholders or the general public when the client contemplates a merger or acquisition, a major transaction or the demise of an expected one, a new invention or patent, an impending bankruptcy, a forthcoming lawsuit or settlement, and all sorts of other incipient corporate fortunes and misfortunes. When lawyers have an equity interest in the client, the temptations are great to indulge in self-interest, buying or selling stock in advance of the disclosure of good or bad news to protect against personal loss or perhaps to make a killing. Such insider trading represents a conflict of interest in that lawyers put self-interest ahead of the interests of the company's shareholders, to which they also have a fiduciary duty. Lawyers sell their stock knowing that its value is about to plummet, dumping worthless shares on those whose interests they are paid to represent. Because insider trading is no mere ethical trespass but a violation of the law, few lawyers probably indulge in it. Nonetheless, in a large law firm with many publicly traded companies among its clientele, even innocent trading in the securities of a client can—in hindsight—look like insider trading, even if the lawyer-investor has no inside information, even if the investor is a secretary or paralegal in the firm. Many firms, therefore, have policies regarding trading of client securities, generally requiring clearance before anyone in the firm can buy or sell stock.

> Every investment—purchase and sale—gets cleared through a check through the conflict data base. But it's to be sure that there isn't something sensitive going on.

> For the clearly sensitive ones, we have a restricted list—that you simply can't trade in securities in that company. For others, the person or paralegal that's monitoring this will call the lawyers involved and say, "So-and-So wants to buy stock in Sears Roebuck." "I see you've recently been doing a lot of work for Sears. Do you know something that's on the border of being inside information?" . . . And the answer will either be "yes" or "no;" rarely "yes" because that name was supposed to be on the restricted list if we really do have that information. . . . And we've learned that one of the risks here is, to find client securities and maybe buy it and then the client may come in with some super secret thing. The lawyer who owns it wants to sell and they're locked in. I've seen that happen. The companies are in trouble and there's no window to get out. They just go down with the ship. [laughter] [5Ch100+]

Other business interests.

> And you get out to a small town of a thousand people in western Iowa that may have one attorney, and the attorney may have investments with half the town. And that's still true to a large extent. But, certainly, it has changed a lot [elsewhere]. [72DSM10–19]

Many lawyers have business interests with companies that are not necessarily clients of their firm. A Chicago lawyer owns a manufacturing company, as does the family of a downstate attorney. Several respondents own farms, and many others have real estate holdings. One owns a computer service, and the spouse of another owns a restaurant. Families of attorneys in many of the small towns own or have significant holdings in local banks. One solo practitioner took a leave of absence from his law practice to run a business. And another devotes only a portion of his time to his legal practice.

> I don't have a high-volume practice. I have other business interests and investments that are quite lucrative. My law practice doesn't dominate my life by way of either income or time. . . . Income wise, I'd say that I derive about 25 percent of my total income from my law practice. My investments are unrelated to my legal work. [109DSS<10]

So some lawyers are born into financial interests, some marry into them, and others embrace them as a source of pleasure, challenge, or outside income. Others, especially in small towns, are drawn to particular investments—as they were to boards of directors—for the affiliations and social networks they spawn.

> . . . in a small town, you may want to do that particular type of work because it does have a certain prestige attached to it and it may lead to other work. . . . So, I think there's a tendency in that regard to maybe take on business that maybe you shouldn't take on. [laughs] Or get involved in partnerships—not necessarily for the money involved, but for the attachments, the affiliations [. . .] And maybe more so in a small town. Well, I'm sure in the big towns, too, you know. [97DSS<10]

But these outside business entities in which lawyers or their families have a financial stake can develop adverse interests with clients of the firm. They may seek to enter into transactions with firm clients.

> [In this case, the lawyer's family business wants to borrow money from a bank client.] Now two of my best clients are together: my bank and my major corporate client are doing a loan negotiation together. . . . The local bank was willing to do a loan to my client—the bank was also my client—if they could get a . . . Farmers Home Administration loan guarantee. Farmers Home Administration looked at the whole deal—this was during the banking crisis of two or three years ago—and said, "We will do it, but [L names himself] has to resign as director of Client." Well, Client happens to be my family's company [laughter]. My brother is the president, and I'm a stockholder. . . . The family says, "Well, there's just no way you're going to resign from the company as director, and we'll just have to forgo that loan opportunity." The bank says, "Oh, wait a minute, we want to do the loan, can't we work this out?" [97DSS<10]

Or transactions may go sour and disputes develop. Lawyers may find themselves suing businesses that they or their partners own:

> So, for example, we've had instances where we've represented a creditor seeking, for example, to foreclose on a building owned by a partnership. It turned out that a couple of our partners were investors. [26Ch100+]

Or they represent clients being sued by them.

Some of these examples seem incredibly fortuitous. And, indeed, some are. But given the role of social networks in the referral of legal business and the fact that lawyers sometimes invest in areas of their expertise, the collision between private interests and professional ones may not be quite so coincidental. Many of the small-town examples look like conflicts waiting to happen. When lawyers own the local bank, it is likely that other clients will, at some point, have dealings or disputes with the bank. When lawyers own a significant local company, it is likely that that company will have relationships with other clients—with the bank, municipal agencies, the local press, service providers, individuals who are employed by the company, and the like. If lawyers are conflicted out by all these incipient conflicts, they will be unable to establish much of a local legal practice.

SOCIAL AND INTIMATE RELATIONSHIPS

Family Ties

> Gone are the days of the Hollywood movies where my wife would be on one side and I'll be on the other side. That's not going to happen. [64DSS10–19]

Although the spectacle of Katherine Hepburn and Spencer Tracy, the husband and wife sparring across the aisle in a murder trial dramatized in the classic film *Adam's Rib,* made good theater, it does not make good ethics. Bedfellows do not make effective adversaries. The challenges of confidentiality, loyalty, and financial self-interest are often too great. Whereas the plot in *Adam's Rib* may have seemed a bit contrived back in 1949 when the film was released, it is all too realistic today.

At that time, roughly 1 out of every 700 Americans was an attorney, and not even 2 percent of them were female. When I conducted my interviews, the figures were 1 in 290 and 23 percent (Weil 1968, 15; Curran 1995, 7, 8). And because the majority of the entering class of law students are now female, the proportion of female lawyers will increase substantially in the next generation (Neil 2000b). Where the monikers, shingles, and portrait galleries of old-line law firms displayed the long tradition of sons following their fathers into legal practice, today we find husbands and wives, mothers and daughters, brothers and sisters, in-laws of all combinations, ex-spouses, and live-in lovers practicing law together or apart.

> You see it more often with associates who are married to associates of other firms. And then that's fairly common now. The older generation, it's a little bit less likely. There were so few opportunities for women in the practice for so many years that you tend not to see it at the higher partner level. You tend to see it at the younger levels. [9Ch100+]

These trends, however welcome on equal-opportunity grounds, are not good news for legal ethicists. With a greater proportion of our population engaged in legal practice, the odds of intimates and family members colliding in the courtroom increase. More significant, the opening of the legal academy to women has meant that many lawyers meet their spouses in law school, often sharing their lives with partners trained not merely in the same profession but often in the same legal specialty, thereby increasing the likelihood that their professional lives will eventually intersect.

> In the day and age of both genders being in the profession, it is absolutely inevitable that they are going to become spouses. It's inevitable. [6Ch100+]

> It's getting to be more of a problem now with the number of lawyers going up and the number of husband/wife, father/daughter, mother/son/daughter relationships among the profession. I think it's getting to be a more difficult issue. Especially because most firms—including ours—have nepotism policies.[21] So, it's not like you're likely to have husband and wife partners. They would be more likely to be in other firms. And I don't think we have a good way to deal with that right now. But that's a tough one. [27Ch50–99]

My study reflects these trends. Although in a minority of firms—usually small ones populated with older males—the attorneys' family trees had only one lawyer on any of the branches, most respondents could jog their memories and begin to itemize numerous familial-legal networks among their colleagues.

---

[21]Not all firms have nepotism policies. Several respondents commented on the trade-offs between nepotism and conflict of interest, neither of which they welcomed:

> Probably, under those circumstances, nepotism is better. For conflicts purposes, you're probably better off having them in the same firm than having them in another firm. [52DSL20–49]

> We are very familiar with that. We had two in our office where they were husbands here and wives elsewhere, as it happened. And then we had one with husband and wife here. I'm trying to think if there's more. I think there may be more. Oh, oh, we have another one now. Sure, we have another one. We have [colleague]. Sure. We have three. Let's see, how many more? Four. There's a lot of two-lawyer families, as I think about it. Five. If I keep on thinking about it [. . .] Six. [laughter] I'll probably get up to ten. [10Ch100+]

Indeed, the thicket of intimate or relational ties is truly dense in many of the larger firms.

> As a practical matter, that is so common that you can't even begin to deal with it. I would guess that we have a spousal relationship with virtually every major firm in the city of Chicago—probably, every major firm in the United States. [17Ch100+]

Of course, merely having a relative in another firm does not create a conflict of interest. Conflicts arise when relatives or intimates have a financial stake in the opposing side of a case, share confidential information with adversaries, or hold back in head-to-head combat because of loyalties to their adversary. A lawyer doesn't have to have an intimate on the other side to do these things, of course; the previous four chapters have amply demonstrated that. Relational contact simply increases the odds, opportunities, and incentives—or at least clients might feel that way.

> There are some firms around central Illinois where there are relatives in different firms. I don't really know how they handle that. I would think you'd have to walk away from it. I, frankly, wouldn't deem that any different than if you had a relative on the bench. I've never asked anybody, "How do you do that?" My gut reaction would be, you just walk away. Because it seems to me that you can't win. One of you is going to lose the litigation. You don't know which one at the outset. But, whoever it is, that guy's going to have a problem. Because, chances are, his client is going to feel that he's right. And he's going to say, "Well, there has to be some reason I lost here, because I was right." And the easiest way to say is, "Well, I think maybe I lost because he threw the case to his brother or he threw it to his dad or whatever." So, I personally think you'd be pretty foolish to even get into that situation. [68DSM10–19]

The previous section included examples of the businesses or stock holdings of parents, siblings, and spouses that create conflicts of interest for the lawyers in their family tree. But relatives do not have to be capitalists or entrepreneurs to have financial interests likely to create conflicts for lawyers near and dear to them. Legal fees, compensation, and income of other lawyers on the family tree can have the same effect.

> We'll have a lawyer here and that lawyer's spouse gets a plaintiff's case and works at a plaintiff's law firm and brings that case into the plaintiff's law firm under an arrangement where, for example, because it's his or her case, he or she gets half

> the fee, alright? And the suit's filed and we get hired to defend it. . . . Very often, for that new business, [the spouse] will get one-third of one-third or maybe half of one-third. And, if it's a ten-million-dollar case, it's a million and half bucks. And now, when your partner settles that case, he's flipping 750 grand. Now what do you do? Yeah, that happens. [6Ch100+]

Because the spouse (and thereby the couple) stands to gain hundreds of thousands of dollars from a sizable award to the plaintiff, the lawyer in the defense firm may be tempted to subtly influence his colleagues or disclose confidential information to his spouse to increase the probability of plaintiff victory and the size of the reward. The defense-firm respondent who offered this example explains the terms under which his firm could take the case:

> You gotta make disclosure [to the client]. You've got to screen it [i.e., hide the spouse behind a Chinese wall]. You can get consent, but it's a very unhappy lawyer when you tell 'em they cannot have that fee. Now, I've had to tell 'em that. Sometimes you can't do it. . . . There's got to be some other mechanism. It's got to become nonmarital property or something. [6Ch100+]

Given its often considerable size and all-or-nothing quality, a share of a contingent fee represents a most compelling financial incentive. But lawyers are also rewarded by compensation that reflects their rainmaking efforts (the amount of business they bring into the firm) or even a share of partnership income. Spouses that direct legal business to their mate or their mate's firm can expect to benefit indirectly by the increased compensation prospects and job security of their partners. Several other examples offered by respondents had a spouse working as in-house counsel in an insurance company, government agency, or other client with responsibility for referring matters to law firms. As in the case of referral fees, when the prospect of benefiting financially from the referred case gets in the way of sending the client to a lawyer who will best represent its interests, the referring lawyer faces a conflict of interest.

> For example, I know one firm where the wife worked in the insurance company; the husband worked at a law firm that the insurance company gave business to. Now, if she had been in a position to actually assign the work—well, actually she was, but . . . any of the work she assigned did not go to that firm. But her company did. Now, in a sense, that created a problem. Because, under normal circumstances, that firm would have gotten the work from her too. . . . From her standpoint, she didn't like the looks of sending business where her husband was. But usually it works the other way around. I mean, where there's family involved, they work as feeder organizations for one another. [33Ch50–99]

Fortunately, the opportunities for lawyer intimates to line each other's pockets are rather limited. Conflicts of interest that arise from the potential leakage of confidential information among intimates or the impact of competing loyalties to client and loved one are far more common. The interviews included diverse examples, usually involving litigation but not always:

> Actually, we've had this situation where someone here, who was married to somebody at another firm and there was a deal that came up with the other firm. And because of the concern that there would be adverse consequences to his spouse at the other firm, he asked not to work on the matter. Because he deemed it to be so adversarial with the other office that he felt that, at the very least, there might be repercussions. And so we had somebody else work on it. But we've never had a situation where someone has actually been on the other side of an individual spouse in this office. [10Ch100+]

Respondents described adversities pitting fathers against their daughters and sons:

> Well, that actually does come up. We've got an attorney here whose father is a plaintiff's attorney. He does not handle any of the suits against his father's firm. I mean, to me there is a potential for some under-handed dealings—or whatever—which I just want to avoid. I don't think it would happen, but—because I know both the father and the son—but I just wouldn't want it to happen. I wouldn't want to give them the opportunity for it to happen. [102Ch10–19]

Adversities also arose between in-laws, brothers and sisters, an uncle and niece, fiancés, and many, many spouses.

> My [spouse], who does . . . very little practice. [Spouse is] a full-time professor. . . . But [spouse] had a client call [. . .] with a case [spouse] sounded very interested in. And [spouse] started to tell me. And [spouse] got like two sentences in, and I said, "Don't say anything else. You can't take the case and don't ask me why." And it was someone I had interviewed. I had not accepted. But I knew so much of the opposite side. And I said, "Just you can't do it. And I can't tell you why you can't do it." And [spouse] . . . never asked me another question. I can't now remember either what the case was or what happened. I just remember that, at that point, [spouse] said, "Fine." And that was it. . . . Because [spouse] does so little practice that I never have to ask [spouse]. 'Cause I know who all [spouse's] clients are. But if someone new comes to [spouse], before [spouse will] take it, [spouse will] come home and ask me if there's anyone involved that I know. . . . Well, [spouse's] expertise is just in a different area. So that helps. [103Ch<10]

In most of these examples, relatives were also private practitioners, working in firms that were frequently competitors or opposing counsel of the respondent's firm. But family members held varied legal roles that created conflicts of interest for their loved ones. Respondents described relatives who were judges, judicial law clerks, government officials, regulators, criminal justice officials, legal services lawyers, school board members, in-house counsel, secretaries, paralegals, state's attorneys, and public defenders.

L: The only conflict that we had is, we hired the judge's daughter.
S: So that means you can't appear before the judge?
L: That's right.
S: Is that a problem?
L: Yeah. He happens to be our best judge. But other than that, it's not a problem. [107DSL<10]

We had a lawyer here whose wife was the head of enforcement for a federal regulatory agency. I don't know what they talked about at home in bed. I don't want to know. I have no doubt that there were things that were said between them that, were they not married, would never have been spoken. Because they both practiced in the same regulated field. I don't know what you can do about that. . . . She would have not undertaken any case which involved one of our clients. She would have recused herself. [79Ch20–49]

My wife served in a local school board for a period of time—seven years. Obviously, we could not—they went out for bids for legal services—obviously, we could not be involved. But she had been on the board about two years and it ended up they took a strike. One of my partners, as I say, is an expert in labor law in this area. They came to him on the possibility of doing the work. We could find nothing in the conflicts rules under the local government rules. . . . She wouldn't vote on it; the other part of the board does. . . . But, to make the long story short, we went to the local state's attorney—who was a longtime friend—and said, "Do you see any problems in this area of conflicts under the state law, etc.?" And he did a little research and called us back and said "No." But, he said, "You can't do it. It stinks." [53DSL20–49]

My brother is the state's attorney here in town. And I do criminal practice. . . . And I have several pending matters. And before they would let me continue [taking public defender cases] after he was elected, they've got an advisory opinion. . . . They said it was not a legal conflict for [my brother] and I to go into court together. But another kind of interesting twist is, his wife was my secretary. And on the eve of the night that he took office, they came in and said that they have decided that that's a conflict. It's not a conflict for [my brother] and I to go into court together. But it's a conflict for [my brother's wife] to work here. 'Cause she would have access to my files and she would also at night—you know, just in her home life—be able to disclose those to her husband. And so the judges in this circuit decided that that was a conflict. But it didn't matter that [my brother] and I are [siblings]. . . . I just recently gave the position up. And I'm assuming it down in another county now. . . . But I did give it up because—although I feel that I rigorously defended all of my clients and I lost to [my brother] and I won a couple against [my brother]—I was uncomfortable in that position of winning or losing against my own brother. [112DSS<10]

This last example is instructive in a number of ways. First, it reminds us that concern about spilling confidences is not restricted to members of the bar. Indeed, the conflict of interest involving a secretary-wife was judged more problematic than that between two siblings who were litigating directly against each other. Second, the example highlights the difficulties that arise when related lawyers work in small towns. This respondent resolved the problem of butting up against a sibling by branching out to other counties where the potential for conflicts of interest are much lower. Many other downstate respondents I interviewed, facing a similar problem, circumvented it through nepotism; they practiced together—typically as father and son. But other relational pairs—especially husbands and wives—were less likely to practice together than were filial ones. Without the shield of nepotism, intimates had to carefully choreograph their professional lives so that they were not constantly stepping on each other's toes. The example of a Chicago couple that decided to practice downstate is particularly telling.

> L: I mean, that's a big deal. I mean, that was a concern when we moved down here. What are we going to do with your [spouse]? . . . My [spouse] is a judge now. Before [spouse] became a judge, [spouse] was always in government practice. When [spouse] got out of law school, I was still with the . . . court, so [spouse] was with the state's attorney's office. Then, when I went into private practice, it was a conscious decision that [spouse] would remain in the governmental sector. And we made that decision early on, rather than to have both of us in private practice in small firms—especially down here. Because it would just be almost be impossible. So, [spouse] has made a conscious decision to do the public sector–type law. And, with the judiciary, it's not a problem. . . .
>
> S: What happens when someone in the firm brings a case before your spouse as a judge? Does that come up?
>
> L: You can't do it. That's a conflict. . . . [Spouse] will not hear any cases with any member of my firm—regardless. And I don't think [spouse] can. And, even if we got a waiver, we wouldn't do it. [Colleague]'s father, [names the colleague's father], for years—just retired a couple of years ago—was the judge over in [another] County. Same thing. He never heard any of our cases. [64DSS10–19]

If squaring off as prosecution and defense is uncomfortable, if acting as judge and advocate is limiting, the alternatives are not any better. Relatives working in some positions in the public sector may preclude even more business for a private firm. And opting for private practice would be, in the words of the small-town respondent transplanted from Chicago, "almost impossible." In a town with only a couple of private law firms, relatives strategically situated in different firms will be continually representing adverse interests. One downstate firm resolves that probability much like the state's attorney's sibling—geographically.

> Spouses has been a problem. Well, not really a problem. We have a basic policy that we . . . can't have attorneys whose spouses work for law firms that do the same type of work that we do—for which we might have mutual cases or relationships—within, I think, it's like one hundred miles of any office. The reason being, it's difficult for people to go home at night and not talk about their cases. And if

> you're on one side, if you're with another personal injury defense firm or a plaintiff's firm or something and [. . .] And so we've adopted that policy. . . . We did have it happen once with a legal assistant that we had who married a lawyer who was actively engaged in personal injury work here in the city. And we just concluded that that would not be compatible. [45DSL20–49]

Small towns, then, do not provide particularly hospitable soil for family trees filled with lawyers to take root, especially those who choose not to practice together. But I do not want this finding to overshadow the equally compelling one, that these family trees don't do all that well in Chicago either. That the city should support many lawyer families comes as no surprise, of course, nor does the fact that large law firms encounter many of them. More surprising was the number of seemingly coincidental adversities among lawyers—husbands and wives on opposite sides of a deal, fathers-in-law litigating against their daughters-in-law, and so on. To the extent, though, that intimates often share areas of expertise and that firms hire and find clients through social networks, the coincidences are somewhat less remarkable.

In any event, familial relationships increasingly put law firms at risk of conflict of interest. Very few have adopted policies to deal with them. The spousal mileage rule adopted by the downstate firm represents perhaps the most developed policy I encountered in any of the firms in the sample. A few of the large firms have begun to input familial relationships into the data base they use to check for conflicts of interest (see chapter 8), and others ask lawyers to disclose problematic relationships on forms they complete to open a new matter. But mostly, firms put the onus on the lawyers themselves:

> Again, we start, I think, with the attitude that our people are professionals and will follow the rules. The firm has strict guidelines as to confidences of clients and of the firm. And everyone is reminded, on a regular basis, that client confidences are not to be shared inappropriately and, certainly, not outside the firm, including with spouses. We haven't set up a police state. . . . We don't routinely inquire of our attorneys as to what they talk to their spouses about. My wife's a lawyer. She practices in an entirely different area out in the suburbs, and the question just doesn't arise. There are some people here who are married to attorneys in other firms where I suspect we do have clients with opposing interests. But I don't think the state has gone so far as to say that it's a violation of the rules yet. [29Ch100+]

> The pillow-talk problem? . . . There's a lot of that. A lot [of] spouses and their children are all over the country, where that's a theoretical problem. We have no formal way of handling it, and I think we just rely on the good sense of our lawyers not to put themselves in a position where there could be an accusation of a conflict. [5Ch100+]

> S: Are there any procedures or policies about conflicts that may arise among family members?
>
> L: Fight it out at home. [51Ch20–49]

When conflicts arise, firms may inform the client or screen the affected family member with a Chinese wall.

> In the case of spouses who work for other firms, we advise our client that the husband or wife of one of our lawyers is working for the other firm. Usually we will screen the spouse as well. This actually comes up a fair amount; we have several lawyers in the firm with spouses working elsewhere as lawyers. [43Ch20–49]

And when conflicts are repetitive, firms may come to an understanding with those employing the related attorney.

> Lawyers do have spouses in other firms. In those instances, we have a mutual agreement with that firm that the spouses will not handle cases against each other. A couple of times we allowed no cases in our firm that involved the other firm. It's come up a couple of times. There is one lawyer in the firm for which this was an issue. Eventually they got divorced and now things are simple again. [12Ch100+]

Social Ties

Not only do lawyers face intimates and loved ones on the other side of the aisle or table, but they also encounter friends, neighbors, professionals, and organizations with which they have deep personal connections. Taking on matters adverse to the interests of these significant others does not pose intrinsic conflicts of interest. But to the extent to which lawyers are inhibited in vigorously championing the interests of their clients because of concern for hurting or jeopardizing relationships with their adversaries, they face potential conflicts.

> Other times it comes up is where . . . the client is someone that you have some relationship with. Maybe not a real conflict, but it may be someone that you know socially or you just would not feel right. And you've got to be totally free as an advocate to pursue the cause that you are taking on. And if you have some situations which may prevent you from giving it your all, you shouldn't be in that case. And so we follow that line. [60Ch20–49]

> And those aren't really what I call "conflicts." But they're uncomfortable situations where, sometimes, you don't want to get involved in a case because you know somebody, somebody's a friend of your family's or something. And, all of a sudden, . . . you're now involved in a divorce in a situation. And it changes, it affects part of your social life or your life outside the firm. And I think those are almost more difficult than the straight conflict situations—which are real easy. It's really easy to explain to somebody, "I can't represent you, because I'm representing your husband." That's a no-brainer. These other ones are more difficult. They're also more difficult to work around with partners who . . . want to take in cases. [94Ch10–19]

The interviews are filled with examples laced with angst, awkwardness, and ambivalence as respondents recount the instances in which friends and neighbors parade through their caseload. They also recount, as did this last respondent, the tensions that arise when the social connections of one partner means lost business for a colleague. They tell of disputes or transactions involving their friends or neighbors:[22]

> There's a business in another community here that's, oh, it's a relatively large business for down here. And the principals in it are now at odds and they're suing each other. And one of the directors lives across the street from me and is really a good personal friend of my wife. The two of them walk every morning. Now, there's another principal who lives half a mile the other way and is friends with one of the other people up here. Now, that fellow went to the other attorney and said they wanted him to represent them. And he talked to me and we [. . .] I mean, the short of it was that we were just going to represent nobody. 'Cause that was a lose-lose situation. [63DSS<10]

Respondents describe clients and their families who have become close friends over the years:

> . . . the ones that always trouble me—and maybe I'm speaking too personally here—but the one that I told you about when the president of the company is let go? . . . From an ethical point of view, you just can't get involved in it. But from a personal point of view, you struggle with trying to recommend other attorneys to your friend, trying to—because you know of the past history—trying to say, "Now, make sure that when you negotiate your severance package, remind them that you passed up another job opportunity a year ago." And you really can't do those kind of things. And it's a very tough situation. [82Ch10–19]

They tell of family doctors:

> There's another case where, at one point, . . . one of my partners asked me to sit in with him to interview a new case, a divorce case. . . . I determined from what he told me, that this was the ex-wife of my children's pediatrician. I got into an argument with him because I told him I don't want to represent the ex-wife of my pediatrician. I said, "You know, I have a doctor-patient relationship. I don't want to worry about taking my kids in to see this doctor, and I'm representing his ex-wife." And I said, "I'm not going to change my doctor because of a divorce case." He got into a fight with me on that one. . . . I mean, we had another situation where—I don't know what it is with pediatricians—but the same partner wound up representing the son-in-law of my childhood pediatrician. And there was a problem because the pediatrician—as the grandfather—was involved in the case. And he was having problems with our client. And there was a lot going on. And

[22]Previous examples echo the same theme. Recall the attorney (in chapter 4) whose close friends living on Hilton Head asked him to handle their divorce and the lawyer (in chapter 3) who refused to sue the partner in a restaurant because his daughter, a dentist, was a client, a good friend of his wife, and someone he sees socially.

> on one occasion, I had to go cover a court hearing—although I wasn't really doing anything in the case. And the wife—who was our opponent—was someone who we had taken a vacation with them when we were kids together. So, I mean, my conversations with her were pretty friendly. But I felt uncomfortable about the fact that we were in that case—even though he is no longer my doctor. It's just something that sort of bothered me. [94Ch10–19]

They even mentioned houses of worship:

> They were going to sue a synagogue up on the North Shore that many of the members of our firm are involved with. One of their clients was hit by a car on the way home from Yom Kippur services and it was necessary to join the congregation [in the suit]. We said, "I don't think so. I don't think this is the kind of lawsuit—no matter how lucrative it is—that we want to be involved in." It's not a conflict, but . . . when you see "Congregation So-and-So," all of the lights went up around here. All the conflict clearance came back saying, "It's not a conflict, but I really don't think we should be doing that." [79Ch20–49]

It is not a surprise that friends, neighbors, and associates should turn up in lawyers' caseloads. As I noted earlier, law firms cultivate social ties, community service, and organizational membership as a marketing strategy. Moreover, when people develop legal needs, they typically turn to their friends and social networks (Curran 1977).

> One of the problems of practicing in a small town is that everybody went to high school together. Whatever is popping in wanting this piece of advice and that piece of advice. And initially you're flattered by that. Then, after a while, you view it as a real pain in the neck. . . . a whole other dimension of the problem—that I've always told my Chicago friends that I feel they don't suffer under—is that my kids won't go to the grocery store with me because it takes us two hours to get out of the place. . . . I mean, you just don't go any place. I mean, I'm going to go out and play golf this afternoon. I'll spend an hour out there and then some jackass will catch me in the locker room or something like that. [70DSS10–19]

As this last respondent observes, the problem is especially acute in small towns, in which residents have a limited pool of lawyers from which to choose and in which attorneys know most of the residents and endure a fishbowl-like existence.

> I suppose these happen in big towns too—just a different level. But, for a number of years, . . . our mayor was a lady by the name of [names the mayor] who, when I was a little boy, her husband was a senior partner in this law firm. And she always took a very motherly interest in me and we then became good friends. And she was a very politically active person and . . . ended up as mayor of [this town]. And during that period of time, we were the utility counsel. And the city still maintained other general counsel. . . . But, in any matter of any import, she was either on my front porch or I was over there. And we'd sit and talk about it. And that

> sort of thing. . . . And the reason I represent the paper is that the publisher of the paper was a childhood good friend of mine and a wonderful character. And he wasn't always nice to [the mayor] while she was mayor, although his relationship with her wasn't a lot different than mine. . . . We had a big sewer project, a new sewer project—which we were bond counsel—and there was a, I mean, it was a big, high-controversy, high-visible item, okay? And just writing that in the papers, writing editorials about how screwed up the city is on . . . the way it's handling the sewer project—part of which is the way it was handling the financing—and picking on [the mayor]. And my good friend and my good friend were absolutely at each other's throats, not speaking to each other [. . .] So, what do you do with all that? [70DSS10–19]

Living in a fishbowl also means that small-town lawyers must weigh the reputational damage or the likelihood that they will antagonize friends, future clients, or even future jurors by championing the interests of unpopular persons or positions. Often they turn away cases that their urban counterparts would embrace.

> And it's true that a lot of firms will not take . . . plaintiff's work because of what they'll say in the Chamber of Commerce against them or Rotary or Kiwanis Club or the country club or whatever. But they all socialize, "How could you sue So-and-So? He belongs to the club." And I know lawyers—for that very reason and they'd lose business—they wouldn't take it. I understand, I understand that. [67DSM10–19]

The burdens of small-town social connections fall not only on lawyers but on clients as well, who may be unable to secure legal representation when most of the local bar declines their case:

> I don't think it's caused more difficulties, other than sometimes you have to go to several attorneys before you find one [snickers] that has no contacts with it. I just got appointed on a criminal case—and I think he's exaggerating—but he had had a prior contact with the court. And he grew up in this area. And he claims he went through fourteen attorneys before he found one that didn't have a conflict on his first case. . . . It may be more so of a problem for the clients than it is for the attorneys. [112DSS<10]

How do small-town lawyers respond to this constricting web of social ties? A few were lucky to have an associate or of counsel who resided or grew up elsewhere to whom they could refer the awkward cases involving friends and neighbors. (Remember, though, that true conflicts of interest cannot be resolved by passing them along to a colleague.) Others took to the roads.

> S: Do you worry a little bit about—as your practice expands—that you're going to be conflicted out of everything?
>
> L: Um hmm. . . . That's why the attorneys in the smaller towns spread out and go to different surrounding counties. Like I'm trying to expand down into [adja-

> cent county to the east] County and [nearby county to the west] County. And I do a lot of work over in [adjacent county to the north] County, where . . . I don't know anyone. . . . And if two people come in—or a person comes in to me—there's probably a 90 percent chance I don't know them, never heard of them, and don't know the other side either. . . . a gentlemen downstairs, he's an attorney; he's in sole practice. He lives in [a nearby town] and practices here in [this town] and enjoys it because he doesn't have a lot of these conflicts like I do. Where, if he practiced in [the nearby town], it would be similar to me practicing in [this town]. [112DSS<10]

After reflecting on these burdens, another respondent suggested:

> Sometimes you think the perfect situation would be to live one hundred miles away from where you practice. [97DSS<10]

That hundred-mile buffer that the downstate firm imposed between spouses practicing in the same area of law comes up in yet another context.

Many small-town respondents speculated about the unencumbered lives of their Chicago counterparts.

> If I was in a bigger [. . .] if I was in Chicago, this probably would never happen to me. It's very rare in a city the size of Chicago that someone's going to come in and I will have gone to school or recognized the name of the codefendant. I just don't think it happens that often. [112DSS<10]

But, ironically, some Chicago lawyers encountered the same problems that stymied their counterparts practicing in the country.

> I have a personal matter, a personal lawsuit on a promissory note. I'd loaned somebody money and called up a friend of mine in town who's a lawyer and said, "Would you handle this for me? I don't have time and I don't want to be my own lawyer. Simple case. There's a note. One, two, three." "Okay, no problem. Who's the defendant?" He says, "Aw, I can't. I grew up with him. I can't represent [you]." [104Ch10–19]

The pediatrician and synagogue examples previously cited also came from Chicago. Moreover, the urban lawyers who specialize in representing small ethnic communities, some of whose experiences were recounted in earlier chapters, described the same fishbowl-like existence as their rural counterparts.

> When you deal in a small [ethnic] community like I do, and there is a lot of interaction between the people in the community about their personal affairs, people tend to take sides or get upset with you if you're involved in certain types of litigation. . . . I had a [ethnic] will contest case . . . involving several [ethnic] families. And there was about a million dollars at stake. And it was basically three or four [ethnic] lawyers. And I know that everyone in the community that knew about the

case—and that word got out 'cause there was an alleged forgery of a couple wills—I know that there were people that probably didn't come to me 'cause of that case. . . . I remember one of my clients is a beautician that was rear-ended by—it just happened to be—another person [of this ethnicity]. And I went to a function at a church. And someone ran up to me and said, "Why are you suing my cousin? She didn't do anything wrong. Your client hit the brakes." And, honestly, with the number of cases we have, I vaguely knew anything about the case. . . . I'm sure that family will never refer anything to me, thinking that I've sued their cousin. So I have a lot of that, a lot more than your average attorney. [121Ch<10]

Large cities contain social networks defined by religion, ethnicity, class, industry, leisure activities, geography, and the like. Urban lawyers embedded in tight social networks may feel as much intimacy, familiarity, and constraint as those bounded only by rural geography. They too live in small towns. The source of the pediatrician examples, a Chicago lawyer, speculated about small-town life:

L: I guess that's probably something that small-town lawyers are much more used to. There are only so many lawyers and judges to go around.

S: It's sort of funny in a place as big as Chicago that [. . .]

L: It's not big. It really isn't big. . . . It's a very small town, because you have different areas of the city. You have some lawyers who are on the south side, maybe some lawyers on the west side, and then lawyers in the north suburbs. And those areas are really very closed in a lot of ways. There are social circles. And it seems like you get business from certain social circles—people who you know. And the people who you know know the people who you know. And so, in a way, it's like being in a small town. . . . I mean, it doesn't happen all the time, but it does happen enough so that you know it's there. You have to be aware of it. [94Ch10–19]

Lawyers also have social relationships with each other. They are former classmates, close friends, neighbors, tennis partners, cochairs of bar committees; they go to basketball games and the theater together; their families vacation together; they plan the other's estates, handle the other's divorces, and defend each other for malpractice. And some are also repeated adversaries. Most lawyers are able to hold their bonds of friendship at bay in the courtroom or negotiating table. But some social ties can compromise their disinterestedness or at least their client's perception of unequivocal loyalty. A common scenario arises when the lawyer or law firm representing the opposing party is simultaneously a client or cocounsel.

I remember we had a medical negligence case. We were defending, or we represented, an emergency room group that had its insurance company go into liquidation and bankruptcy. And one of the attorneys on . . . our side of the case—we represented the emergency room, he represented the hospital—was a defense lawyer on a very large distressed birth case we had. . . . we were on the plaintiff's side on the other case. So that made it a little difficult to deal with tactical problems, because we didn't want it to affect the other case. Us and he and the other two defense lawyers in the case ended up losing. And the verdict against us was about [many millions of] dollars. And then we settled the other case with this lawyer for three million dollars. I think the fact that we had this existing case with them made everyone think that somehow we were conspiring with him to try to hurt the plaintiff in the large verdict case as much as possible—which wasn't the truth. The plaintiff's lawyers felt like we should be friendly towards them, because we do a lot of plaintiff's work. And I'm sure the defense lawyer thought that we should be friendly to him, because we have to see him on his other case which was set for trial a short time thereafter. So those are very unusual type of conflict situations where we really have to try to walk a very thin line and not do anything that would give anyone grounds to think that there was any impropriety in the way we acted or behaved. [121Ch<10]

This last example suggests another element of lawyers' relationships with one another that tugs at their supposedly undivided loyalty to clients. Relationships among lawyers may be repetitive and serial; sometimes advocates may be on the same side of a dispute and sometimes on opposing sides. As Marc Galanter has so insightfully argued (1974), the incentives, strategies, resources, and outcomes of those who use the legal system for a one-shot matter are profoundly different from those who use it repeatedly. For one thing, he observed, in contrast to one-shotters' concern for the matter at hand, repeat players play for the long run—they may sacrifice a given case to maximize future success. Attorneys who repeatedly oppose each other and negotiate settlements and deals cannot repeatedly cry wolf, make unwarranted accusations, file excessive or inappropriate motions, or burn bridges—even if these actions are in the best interest of their present client—because of their consequences for future clients that face the same adversaries. But, of course, holding back to protect the interests of future clients constitutes a clear conflict of interest. So does trading one case off for another—in the previous example, making a deal with a codefendant in one case in exchange for a generous settlement in an unrelated case—something the respondents deny doing or seeing. Still, the temptation is great.

Insurance companies take the position what we're doing is an economics game. We, statistically, over a period of time, we want to pay the least amount of money possible, if we can. And . . . these are one-shot deals . . . from the client's standpoint. And this creates another conflict, it seems to me. From the lawyer's standpoint, . . . interlawyer relationships are long-term. Sometimes, representing individual clients in divorce cases, things like that, are single deals. The laws of negotiation, the laws of human interaction, are different for long-term relationships than they are for single-deal relationships. So the lawyer says, "I'm going to have fifteen more cases with lawyer A. I can't afford to take an all-or-nothing approach or a hard-ball approach. I got to be in front of Judge Jones fifteen times next year. I can't afford to have him mad at me in his courtroom. Yet on the other hand, the lawyer may decide that, in this particular case, for my client, this is a one-shot all-or-nothing deal. . . . I think it serves my client's interest best in this case to take this position which is extremely hard-ball. But yet, for my long-term relationship with the court and the other lawyers, that's going to hurt my personal

> long-term relationship. So, how does the lawyer deal with that? I guess you just have to deal with it, that the bigger good is the system. The long-term, the whole legal system is here for all of us for a long period of time. And I can't sacrifice that for [. . .] Just because this happens to be a better deal for my client in this particular ca [. . .] And it's my duty, I think then, to try to convince the client that it's his best interest and in everybody's best interest in the long run. [laughs] That's probably a hell of a lot more idealistic than reality. [97DSS<10]

THE STRANGER

When we first met Lawrence Lexman back in chapter 3, he seemed like an odd, even slightly pathetic character with no family, no significant other, no friends, no colleagues, no employees, no affiliations or other social ties, no commitments, no income, no financial interests or worries, no employment history, and no former clients—just a huge trust fund sitting in a savings account and one pro bono client. It should now be clear why Lawrence can be so oblivious to conflicts of interest and why many lawyers probably envy him for reasons beyond his fantastic wealth. This chapter is filled with attorneys who fantasize about practicing a hundred miles away from home and others who live out the fantasy, taking to the roads to escape the dense social networks that are strangling their practice; managing partners who heave a sigh of relief when a colleague divorces; lawyers whose children refuse to go with them to the grocery store and others who get harangued at church; and law firms that fracture because colleagues continually conflict each other out of work. Perhaps the vows of poverty and chastity have been squandered on the clergy. Indeed, one small-town lawyer likens his practice to that of the local minister who "within ten years, needs to move on." [127DSS<10]

Clearly social, familial, financial, collegial, and professional ties, however much they enrich our lives, undermine disinterestedness. The solution is transiency or relational celibacy, to become a "Lexman," a stranger.

The truth, however, is that life as a Lexman cannot sustain a legal practice. Lawyers exist, strangled, constricted, compromised, and enriched by their personal ties and organizational baggage. There are personal, professional, and bureaucratic choices to be made, accompanied by difficult trade-offs, some that foster disinterestedness and others that accelerate conflicts of interest. We now turn to how firms deal with the consequences.

Finding Conflicts

The five previous chapters have mapped out the topography of conflict of interest in varied settings of private legal practice. Though it is impossible to chart a detailed map pinpointing where each land mine is located, conflicts of interest are not buried randomly. As detailed in the chapters, conflicts issue from systemic sources that provide some guidance about which parts of the legal terrain are most hazardous. We know that conflicts of interest arise when firms take on new business; when lawyers represent more than one party or entities such as families or corporations that embody multiple parties; when clients experience change; when disputes or transactions evolve, reach turning points, or encompass additional parties; when cases establish legal precedent or have consequences for other clients situated on the sidelines; when new lawyers or staff join the firm; when lawyers take on outside interests, investments, positions, relationships, commitments; and so on. Armed with these somewhat primitive maps, lawyers may try to avoid the hot spots altogether or attempt to sweep and diffuse the mines before venturing forth into these areas. This chapter addresses the minesweeping process, that is, how firms identify potential conflicts of interest; the next chapter details how firms try to diffuse, avoid, or resolve them.[1]

[1]There is at least one other contemporary empirical study that touches on similar themes. Interested in law firm practices surrounding the use of screens or Chinese walls to cloister

Of course, another option is to ignore the mines altogether; if they detonate, they detonate. These are ethics rules, after all, not nuclear warheads. Codes of ethics have often been maligned as window dressing at best or, at worst, linguistic Trojan horses concealing ulterior motives or hidden agendas (Abel 1981). A long tradition in many professions and walks of life honors ethical norms in the breach. What harm is an ethics slap every now and then? No sense making much ado about nothing.

Surprisingly few law firms take this laissez-faire approach. It turns out that, unlike many ethical infractions, conflicts of interest can cause considerable damage when they detonate. Ethical scruples, reputational concerns, and the risk that conflicts of interest could lead to disciplinary proceedings (Schneyer 1991) induce some firms to reject a laissez-faire approach. But lawyers also face substantial economic consequences for taking the wrong course in the face of clashing interests. Relatively significant forms of economic self-interest provide incentives for regulating the process by which firms take on new interests.

Perhaps the most potent incentive applies in the litigation context, where law firms with demonstrable conflicts of interest can be disqualified from representing their client. The threat of disqualification can impose substantial costs on a law firm and the client it represents. It protracts the litigation and increases its cost, exerts extra pressure on the client to settle the matter rather than defend a disqualification motion or find new legal counsel, and if the lawyers are disqualified, burdens the client to find and prepare a new law firm to represent it. In addition to losing face and fees, disqualified lawyers also risk malpractice claims, disciplinary action, and loss of the client forever.

> I would say—regardless of how prestigious the firm is in this particular city—I can probably say most of the biggest, most prestigious firms have been hit. They've had to disgorge significant fees because of not properly addressing the conflict issue. And if you hold that up to your partners and say, "Hey, are you going to address it now and do the right thing, or do work for a year and then give the fee back?" It isn't worth the risk; it isn't worth the aggravation [. . .] [58Ch50–99]

It is hard to imagine a monetary fine that could rival the lost investment a law firm typically makes in a major piece of litigation or in building a long-term relationship with a client.[2]

---

lateral hires. Lee Pizzimenti (1997) conducted a mail survey in the early 1990s of 156 law firms in four states that employ at least fifty attorneys. Detailed questions pertained not only to the firms' use of screens and their procedures for lateral hiring but to their systems for identifying conflicts of interest as well. Unfortunately, only 20 percent of the firms sampled responded to the study, a selection bias that renders the findings of only marginal value.

[2]In a dramatic example reported widely in the press, the Chicago law firm Winston & Strawn was disqualified over a conflict of interest that arose from lateral hiring after it had logged more than ten thousand litigation hours and eighty-five days deposing forty-four witnesses and after seventy thousand documents had been exchanged in discovery—all or a substantial part of the fee from which it had to eat (Tuite 1993).

Motions for disqualification are asserted when lawyers fail to recognize or respond to an alleged conflict of interest in a litigation context. Many situations, in both litigation and transactional practice, don't go that far. Lawyers will discover an unrecognized conflict, an adversary will bring it to their attention, or circumstances will change after the engagement is already underway—giving rise to new conflicts—whereupon the firm may voluntarily withdraw. The costs to the firm may be substantial here as well. The firm will generally make a financial settlement with the client. Some kinds of fee arrangements that kick in at the conclusion of the representation (i.e., contingent fees) may be especially punishing to a firm that must step out prematurely. And considerable goodwill and client loyalty are undermined when trusted lawyers suddenly abandon their client midstream—particularly when the conflict could have been foreseen.

> Oh yeah, I think the climate has changed. Certainly, when I started practice, if I were to call a friend and say, "Look, we've got a conflict here and I'm sending the client over to you," most lawyers would view that as a one-shot deal. But there aren't many firms in this town anymore that I would be too sanguine about the possibilities [laughs] of not having them knocking on the door trying to cross-sell their whole firm. I mean, that's just, unfortunately, the way it's changed. [18Ch100+]

Conflicts don't need to have actually detonated to have significant economic consequences. Another financial cost accrues to firms when they must turn away lucrative new business because of conflicts of interest created by a matter undertaken in the past. By preparing a simple regulatory filing for AT&T, for example, the firm cannot later represent MCI in a multi-million-dollar dispute with the telephone giant. Citing a $200,000 piece of litigation that had to be turned away because it was adverse to the interests of a client in a $5,000 intellectual property matter, one respondent in the study explained that his firm decided to overhaul its conflicts system because they were declining too many big cases in which the interests of prospective clients conflicted with those of current or former clients of the firm. He unhappily noted that in his own personal experience, he had to turn away six or seven of every ten assignments he wanted to take because of conflicts elsewhere in the firm.

As this respondent's displeasure suggests, the incentive to control these business conflicts is not merely institutional. Most large law firms confer financial reward and power on their business-getters or so-called rainmakers, and tag partnership and compensation decisions to the lawyer's ability to bring in business. Few firms credit attorneys for business they secured that had to be declined because it conflicted with interests represented elsewhere in the firm. As a result, individual lawyers tend to be quite interested in the business contemplated by their colleagues and wary that another's potential bird in the hand does not cost them a flock in a nearby bush. These personal investments in rainmaking, though often a source of dissension within the firm, create another impetus to control firmwide conflicts of interest.

The market for professional liability insurance provides an additional economic incentive for self-regulation.

> When malpractice insurance was a thousand dollars a year, I didn't think about conflicts. [90Ch20–49]

Experience rating plays at least some role in a firm's ability to obtain insurance coverage and in the premiums assessed. Firms implicated in previous conflicts of interest or with lax self-regulatory procedures can find themselves virtually uninsurable. As I described in chapter 7, many firms in the study instituted new policies after they had difficulty finding malpractice insurance. Probably more significant, deductibles for malpractice insurance tend to be high—for example, more than $450,000, on average (at the time of my study), for members of the large-law-firm mutual insurance company ALAS (the Attorneys' Liability Assurance Society).[3] The cost of defending a malpractice claim, therefore, is often borne by the law firm rather than its insurer.

> Malpractice premiums have skyrocketed. Deductibles have become enormous, so that most of the malpractice burden is carried by the law firm up to, you know, the million dollars or the five hundred thousand dollars. So those factors, I think, have made a tremendous change in the landscape. [11Ch100+]

Insurers suggest that conflict-of-interest charges added to a malpractice claim significantly increase both the size of the claim (generally into the multi-million-dollar range) and the likelihood of loss (Attorneys' Liability Assurance Society 1991; Hazard 1990).

Because of the belief that conflicts of interest increase vulnerability to and magnitude of liability, some insurers encourage or assist their insureds in undertaking self-regulatory measures. Many law firms are offered premium discounts by their malpractice insurers if lawyers attend seminars on loss prevention. Other insurers, especially ALAS, provide varied loss prevention services: on-site seminars and workshops; firm audits; conferences; a loss prevention journal; loss prevention personnel to advise attorneys; and resources, data bases, and consulting services to assist firms in developing conflict-of-interest regulatory systems. Some require or strongly "encourage" their insureds to designate loss prevention or risk managers, create special oversight committees, and implement procedures to control potential conflicts of interest. The involvement of professional liability insurers in overseeing and micromanaging firms has become so great that some observers now refer to them as "regulators" (Davis 1996).

Practically all the respondents agreed that sensitivities to conflicts of interest and the incentives to regulate the process by which firms take on new interests had intensified in recent years.[4]

---

[3]Indeed, more than fifty firms affiliated with the mutual have deductibles that exceed $1 million (Attorneys' Liability Assurance Society 1991, 10). Deductibles are much lower for smaller firms, averaging $5,000 in Illinois, according to one insurance executive (Gill 1992).
[4]Although a few small-firm lawyers disagreed. For example:

> To generalize, I think that more lawyers are paying less attention to conflicts and ethical rules than when they started practicing. In part, this is probably a function of economics, and as

> But you go back ten years, probably some of our senior partners at that time couldn't spell "conflict of interest"—at least after lunch [laughter]. [3Ch100+]

> I mean, I could say to you that ten years ago, if you asked me about a conflict, I wouldn't know what the heck you were talking about. I mean, I'd know generally what a conflict was, but it was just something you just never saw. [19Ch50–99]

> I think, if you talk to someone who's been in practice for fifty years and you ask them about conflicts, they would tell you they can't ever be involved in a conflict, because they would never be unfair to anyone. . . . And I think that's just because, up until the last few years, there just was no emphasis on this. Yeah, it was a theoretical possibility. No, you would never sue your own client. But it never went much beyond that. And obviously it's changed quite a lot in the last few years. [28Ch50–99]

> People are much more sensitive now than they used to be. . . . This is an accelerating trend. . . . I can assure you that, ten years ago, there was not someone in this firm spending three hundred hours a year on conflicts. Nor was there someone at the Sidleys and Kirklands [two very large Chicago firms] spending a thousand-plus hours on conflicts. [43Ch20–49]

As elaborated in previous chapters, the demographics of legal practice had changed. Firms were much larger, and more of them had offices situated across the globe; lawyers were more mobile, carrying clients and confidences from firm to firm; clients were less loyal, spreading business across many different law firms; as a result, firms represented far more clients—and interests—than they had in the past.

> When I started practicing law in [the 1950s], Mayer, Brown represented Continental Bank and that was it. They were gonna represent the Continental Bank for the next eighteen centuries, and I would never go over to Continental Bank and say, "Hi, I want to represent you." . . . Now in-house counsel are fat people, because people take them to lunch every day trying to get their business. They take them to hockey games, football games, basketball games. So you get the conflicts because there is no more institutional loyalty. There's specialty shoppers, the bargain shoppers, etc. So everybody's representing everybody else, and you get lots of conflicts. [30Ch100+]

> When I started practicing law [more than twenty-five]-plus years ago, there was tremendous client loyalty. A client came into a firm and—if you didn't screw

---

the market has gotten worse, lawyers have been cutting corners or ignoring their ethical obligations. You see this in two ways. First, I think we have bred law school graduates who are less ethically or morally minded. I look at my class in law school—they were already committing ethical violations while still in law school. I think there's a spiritual malaise among law school graduates. . . . Second, I think the economy has created opportunities for lawyers to take more chances. . . . My perception is that the moral malaise has led to ethical indifference. . . . In the day-to-day tough decisions, people tend to stray. {99Ch<10}

> things up—you probably had a client with you until the day you died or retired. Clients didn't move around, one. Two, lawyers didn't move around very much. It was very unusual, when I started practicing law, for a lawyer to change firms. Today, the clients move all the time. [37Ch50–99]

> We've expanded our client base and clients use more law firms. The same client will use three or four different law firms in different matters.... It used to be that the company, for example, would use this lawyer or this group of lawyers exclusively. Those were their lawyers. Now they'll go to this firm for this and another firm for another matter and another firm for another matter—maybe because they're looking for expertise, maybe because they just want to have multiple lawyers and have them competing with one another to keep the bills down, any number of reasons. But you see the same client being represented by multiple companies. And that means that the number of clients you represent is greater than it used to be. Because you've only got 40 percent of the business of this client that you used to have, but now you've got 10 percent of the business of the client that you didn't have before. And so you have more clients. So, yes, from that standpoint, you run into conflicts more frequently now, because you represent more people. [50DSL20–49]

Because of the recession in the legal market, firms had become more competitive, trying to pick off the most profitable lawyers and clients of the other, and were forced to take cases they might not have in the past. Firms diversified their practice to provide an economic buffer from downturns in particular markets. And changes in substantive law led to an upsurge in multiparty litigation and the opportunity for coparties to make claims for contribution against one another. All these developments increased the vulnerability of law firms to conflicts of interest.

But not only did the incidence and risk of conflicts escalate; so, too, did the possible consequences of becoming entangled in competing interests. The legal recession created not only a buyer's market but also the growth of talented and aggressive legal departments within corporations and a greater assertiveness by corporate clients about the conduct of their outside counsel, including whose interests they would champion and under what conditions (Rosen 1989; Gilson 1990; Galanter and Palay 1991, 49–50).

> I mean, my own sense is that this notion of loyalty is disappearing, if not mostly gone.... I think clients are more and more concluding that these are fungible services. I mean, price competition is rampant these days. It's something that you never thought of years ago. It was like, "Well, who cares if someone is cheaper, it's quality I'm looking for or it's this long-standing relationship in this feeling of confidence and whatever." Because now I think clients are very attuned to the fact that they are the gorilla in the relationship these days and that they can really dictate much more than they ever thought they could or ever tried to before.... They really are influencing and changing the relationship. And that also includes less willingness to waive a conflict or to work with someone to resolve a problem. [24Ch50–99]

The explosion of business litigation in the 1970s and 1980s, as corporations seized litigation as a strategy of economic warfare, sparked the growth of powerful litigation departments in large law firms (Nelson 1990; Galanter and Palay 1991; Garth 1993; Dezalay and Garth 1996). Supported by aggressive corporate inside counsel, competing law firm litigators devised, marketed, and pursued high-stakes "scorched earth" or "Rambo-like" tactics (Garth 1993). Among the weapons in their litigation arsenals, motions to disqualify law firms tainted by conflicts of interest proved attractive.

> I see the role of conflicts taking on a mean, nasty, ugly component. Because it has been used more and more, despite what people say, as a tactical weapon. And every disqualification decision you pick up, there's the mandatory rubric about the use of disqualifications as a tactic. And it is. And it's used, from my experience, in lots and lots of cases, especially by large, sophisticated corporations, as a tactic. And it's just another tactic and it's needless, stupid, wasteful. [36Ch100+]

> Frivolous litigation has begun to be less of an issue, and high-stakes litigation has become more of an issue. I believe that conflicts will play a more important part in litigation in the future, because the stakes will be higher and because the cases you will see are serious cases. No one can afford to litigate recreationally—it's too expensive. And so, when the stakes go up, then I think the precision, the technical precision at which the conflict rules apply will become acute. And people will not turn blind eyes to the conflict situations that they used to. Because too much is at stake. [27Ch50–99]

As I described in chapter 6, combative parties also used conflicts as a sword, by placing business, holding beauty contests, or sharing confidences with law firms with specialized expertise in order to conflict them out from upcoming litigation.

> Because very easily, in Chicago, you can get a large multinational that can pick off the fifteen largest law firms in Chicago just like [snaps fingers]—give him a little thing here, a little thing there. And the middle-level companies, they can't get a law firm. Or they can pick off every patent law firm in the city of Chicago. Give them this one, give them that one. And you have someone who needs to hire a boutique law firm with specialized knowledge, and all of your good patent law firms are tied up, because this firm has conflicted them out. And it's a question of "All these firms are this company's lawyers? All at once?" [16Ch100+]

Moreover, attorneys began to break the ban against suing one another.[5] Plaintiffs' lawyers brought large malpractice cases against their brethren. And government agencies, recognizing the deep pockets of law firms, coupled with their complicity

---

[5]According to one malpractice expert, between 1975 and 1992 there were ten times as many reported legal malpractice decisions in Illinois as there were in the history of the state before 1975 (Gill 1992). See especially Ramos (1996), who argues that, at $4 billion a year, the cost to insurers of legal malpractice even exceeds that of medical malpractice.

or at least facilitative role in financial debacles—especially failures of savings and loans—also began suing law firms (Gill 1992). This heightened exposure increased the cost of liability insurance as well as the incentives to reduce insurance costs by implementing self-regulatory practices.

Meanwhile, as lawyers became more vulnerable to the claims, grievances, and inflexibility of increasingly aggressive clients, the law regarding professional responsibility began to change, provoking a closer look at how law firms responded to potential conflicts of interest. A critical conflict-of-interest case, especially for Chicago lawyers, broke in the late 1970s.[6] In 1978, the large Chicago law firm of Kirkland & Ellis was disqualified from representing Westinghouse Electric Corporation in an antitrust suit in which Westinghouse accused oil companies and uranium producers of operating an international cartel that conspired to rig prices and markets for uranium. At the same time that the Chicago office of the firm was bringing this suit on behalf of Westinghouse, its branch office in Washington, D.C., had been retained by the American Petroleum Institute (API) to lobby against legislative proposals to break up the oil companies. Kirkland & Ellis lawyers had interviewed and surveyed API members, amassing confidential data about their market share and pricing practices. Ironically, on the same day these Washington lawyers issued a report celebrating competition in the uranium industry, their colleagues in Chicago had filed the antitrust suit, naming three API members, among others, as defendants. The three brought the motion to disqualify Kirkland. When the law firm was forced to step out of the case, it had been paid roughly half of the more than $5 million in legal fees already expended.

The Westinghouse case provided a resounding wake-up call for many lawyers who had assumed that the attorney-client relationship extended to the American Petroleum Institute but not to its individual members.

> S: Have you seen major changes in the landscape with respect to conflicts?
> L: Absolutely. It's like not comparable. People didn't even think about it.
> S: When do you think it really started becoming [. . .] ?
> L: When people started litigating and bringing motions to disqualify. Westinghouse versus Kirkland & Ellis case—which astonished people. I mean, how could you disqualify them? Their Washington office knew about it. Nobody in Chicago knew about it. It's crazy; they lost all this money. They had to disgorge fees. I mean, there's just no question that it was whenever that was. [10Ch100+]

Whatever primitive conflict-of-interest systems firms employed in those days, few, if any, tracked the interests of members of a trade association client. The Westinghouse case came up repeatedly in my interviews, many respondents instinctively pointing or nodding in the direction of the Amoco building, located in the northeast corner of the Loop, in which Kirkland & Ellis resides. Many large-firm respondents credited the Westinghouse decision as the impetus for their own firm to develop more systematic self-regulatory procedures to track conflicts of interest.

---

[6]For a detailed account, see Stewart 1983, 152–200.

> So when that [the Westinghouse case] happened, we were in practice in another firm. But we said, "We don't ever want this to ever happen to us." So we built up systems at the beginning to try to avoid anything like that. [47Ch20–49]

> In this firm and most others, the systematic practice of conflicts checking began around 1980 as a reaction to the Westinghouse case of 1978. This was a very closely watched case and both opinions were carefully studied. . . . The Westinghouse case had the impact of an asteroid. It was a big event. [8Ch100+]

A second significant legal change that helped jump-start the self-regulatory process predated my study by only a few years. In August 1990, the Illinois Supreme Court imposed new Rules of Professional Conduct for Illinois lawyers. Although generally unremarkable, the new code was "revolutionary," in the words of one of its drafters, in that it no longer treated ethical obligations as pertaining solely to individuals, instead holding law firms and their partners responsible for the ethical conduct of their employees. "For the first time," he wrote, "the law firm itself has professional obligations and is subject to professional discipline, and the responsibility of supervising attorneys for the conduct of both legal and nonlegal personnel is clearly articulated" (Overton 1990, 434).

> There is definitely a greater sensitivity at the firm level about conflicts and other ethical issues. Historically, lawyers have been responsible for their own conduct and bore a personal risk for their behavior. But the new Code of Professional Responsibility created for the first time a notion of collective guilt. The risky activities of any one individual may now affect the entire firm. So now it is easier to get lawyers to pay attention to the rules than it was before the Code. Law firms are responsible for the conduct of their members. I am responsible for any associate in the firm. [58Ch50–99]

Moreover, the new rules required all law firm partners to "make reasonable efforts to ensure that the firm has in effect measures giving reasonable assurance that the conduct of all lawyers in the firm conforms to these Rules" (Illinois Supreme Court Rules 1990, Rule 5.1a)

> I think that there was a tremendous push to really make conflicts an issue within this firm—and I think within other firms that I know about—when we had our new Professional Responsibility Rules, Code of Professional Responsibility. Not that there was so many changes. But it gave people like myself—who have been interested in this and concerned with this for some time—an opportunity to re-educate and to say, "Now you've really got to do it." I'm not so sure that the changes were as significant as what I made them seem to be [laughs] in terms of that. Although there were many changes, especially supervision, direct obligations and other things and educational things which were mandated in these new rules, which I think gave everyone who was interested in this a wonderful opportunity to really come down and say, "I want it done this way [knocking on desk] and I've got the imprimatur now of the Bar and the Supreme Court on my side." [11Ch100+]

A substantial number of respondents also noted that the new state code had precipitated a reexamination of how their firm dealt with professional responsibility. Many of their firms instituted educational programs. Some presented one-time dog and pony shows run by law professors, representatives of the Attorney Registration and Disciplinary Commission, the state bar association, or their insurance carrier. Others developed their own in-house lectures or showed videotaped professional responsibility programs. In the absence of any state bar requirements, at least one partnership instituted a firmwide continuing legal education requirement. Others developed semimonthly educational seminars or annual professional responsibility lectures. A few firms published their own ethics rules, and several began circulating relevant articles and summaries of significant ethics opinions to their colleagues. And many firms began reengineering procedures, policies, and oversight in light of their new ethical obligations, in general, and the "collective guilt" about which the first respondent spoke, in particular.

These developments certainly do not exhaust the factors that contributed to a greater awareness of conflicts of interest within the legal profession or that spurred the development of self-regulatory policies and procedures. Case law on professional responsibility and disqualification issues proliferated, providing clearer guidance to law firms.[7] Bar groups debated professional responsibility ad nauseum. Academic law reviews razed many forests pontificating on the finer points. The American Law Institute worked on a restatement of the law governing lawyers. Law students were required to take semester-long ethics courses for the first time. New case books on the subject were published. Legal journalism came into its own, disseminating gossip and exposing greed, improprieties, and embarrassments among those at the pinnacle of the profession. Disqualification motions were often passed along to disciplinary bodies, which began to take a greater interest in conflicts. And a specialized bar developed to deal with the malpractice litigation and disciplinary cases.

Whatever the reasons, by the early 1990s, most lawyers knew how to spell *conflict of interest,* to paraphrase the respondent quoted earlier, even after lunch. And many firms could also tell you where the conflicts were buried.

NEW BUSINESS

Law firms secure new business in a variety of ways. On rare occasions, a prospective client may saunter into the office off the street, like Lawrence Lexman's first client. Some may call the office and arrange an appointment with a receptionist or secretary; others may speak directly to an attorney. Insurance companies may mail in a copy of a civil complaint to a firm to which it regularly refers insurance defense business or instead notify a contact person in the firm by phone. Public defenders may receive case assignments in court, often only minutes before they must repre-

[7]A 1992 update on conflict of interest prepared by the mutual malpractice insurer that represents large firms noted: "Most of the relevant 'law' on conflicts of interest did not exist 10 years ago; indeed, on many of the issues discussed below there was no law, or the issue itself was not even recognized as such" (Attorneys' Liability Assurance Society 1992, iv).

sent their new client. Other cases may be referred by other lawyers—corporate inside counsel or private attorneys who lack expertise in the matter or who were themselves conflicted out of the case—or by physicians, real estate agents, accountants, bail bondsmen, and others who typically interact with citizens with legal problems. Some matters blossom from referrals from other clients; recall the example of the client son begging his attorney to convince his father to write a will or of the spouses in failing marriages directed to specialized boutique firms by their divorced friends. Long-standing clients may bring up a new or related problem to their legal counsel while consulting on an ongoing matter. Or representations may spawn new legal needs as they evolve—a transaction may end in litigation, an environmental pollution case may give rise to an insurance coverage dispute, a hostile takeover may require fashioning golden parachutes. Other cases are born on golf courses, squash courts, or commuter railroads, in supermarkets, churches, or family gatherings, as prospective clients solicit attorneys who are members of their own social networks. And some new business develops from proactive marketing by lawyers themselves.

These diverse pathways through which law firms acquire legal business vary on a number of dimensions. But, of greatest significance to this chapter, they differ in the clarity that a distinct new legal matter has presented and in the opportunities available to lawyers to amass and control information about the prospective case. Both have implications for how easily the firm can regulate the case intake process and avoid detonating conflicts of interest. When matters evolve through ongoing relationships, for example, there may not be a clear juncture or moment at which an overture or question becomes a prospective "case" and self-regulatory procedures become activated. Moreover, because conflict-of-interest rules are predicated on lawyers' obligations to protect client confidences, the process by which firms gather and evaluate information about a prospective case is critical to their exposure to new conflicts. As I documented in chapter 6, a few indiscrete disclosures by a prospective client—uttered unwittingly or even strategically—can cost a firm dearly. When lawyers—or even their secretaries—learn too much, they may acquire fiduciary obligations, even if the firm ultimately declines the representation or the prospective client decides to take the business elsewhere. These divulged confidences may preclude the firm from representing anyone else embroiled in the case—even a long-standing client for which the firm is sole counsel—or from taking an adverse position against the prospective client in unrelated future cases in which the secrets could be used to advantage the opposition.

> In fact there have been times . . . where we would tell . . . both sides, "We can't touch this case." We've had people call in the office and maybe talk to the secretary and give information before they talk to us. And we get this information, and it looks like a lawsuit. But it could involve one of our clients. What I have done is call this individual and said, "We cannot take your case. The information you told to us I will not reveal to the corporate client [. . .] And if anything comes out of your situation—you see another lawyer—and we should happen to get a call from that corporate client, . . . we will not take the case." I've had to do that at times, because I just can't cut people off on the telephone. Or they get a secretary, and

> the secretary isn't really sure of how to handle it. And we just get information, I think, that would be wrong to pass along to the client. That does happen from time to time. And then when you get the call from the corporate client, "This new case came in involving X." Like, I say, [laugh] "Well, we can't handle that." We just say that "This person had contacted our office and we can't talk about the case. Hire a different firm to do it." Sometimes they question it, but that's how we handle it. We have to, have to. [67DSM10–19]

Client Contact

Ironically, although a conflict-of-interest analysis requires amassing rich, detailed information up front about a prospective case and its likely trajectory, the parties implicated and their social networks, and those situated along the sidelines potentially soaked by the ripples emanating from the case, it also requires forgoing or limiting information lest the firm get conflicted out by unwelcome disclosures. It challenges lawyers to negotiate their way through an intricate maze encumbered by a thick pair of blinders and, when legal problems are of some urgency, to do so with a stopwatch running. They typically resolve the conundrum by pursuing an incremental information-gathering strategy and instructing secretaries, receptionists, and others with client contact to do the same. They begin with blinders firmly in place and, as the view comes into clearer focus, gradually readjust the blinders to allow slightly more peripheral vision. They limit their initial conversation to the basic facts and then slowly widen the intelligence web as they develop some confidence that conflicted interests do not lurk nearby. This incremental process creates great inefficiencies in the investigative process when the obstructed vision imposed by blinders misdirects lawyers down blind alleys and dead ends and when lawyers must retrace their steps each time the angle of vision widens.

When lawyers are proactive in searching for business, the difficulties of controlling the intake of information are relatively minor, because they can undertake research long before prospective clients are even aware that they are a target and at risk of divulging confidences that create unwanted fiduciary obligations for the lawyers hoping to woo them. Sophisticated rainmakers, I was told by several respondents, will inquire about prospective clients and their constellation of interests, business partners, competitors, and likely adversaries and search for potential conflicts before they expend much effort or many resources courting them. They postpone the point of contact until they have some confidence that it's relatively safe to learn their secrets.

> We periodically come up with lists of clients we'd like to represent and try to come up with a game plan for "How do we do it?" If I target a company in Chicago, and I'll try to find out everything about that client. And sometimes you'll find out, "Oops, they're a big competitor with our other major client over here in this area." And how likely is it going to be that we're going to be able to represent both? And we back away from things like that, sure. [18Ch100+]

But most client intake is reactive; firms await overtures from prospective clients who are eager to spill their secrets and thereby resolve the legal difficulties or enjoy the opportunities as quickly as possible. Here the investigative process is more fraught with difficulty, as lawyers try to manage and incrementally structure communications to silence or postpone disclosures that might detonate conflicts of interest.

Some attorneys will take basic information over the phone and conduct a preliminary inquiry about potential conflicts before meeting with the prospective client and eliciting greater detail about the matter. They limit themselves to names in the initial conversation: of the prospective client, the adverse parties, the insurers. As an earlier respondent noted, you have to cut people off: "Stop! Don't tell me anything. Let's not get into the facts right now. Give me names and nothing more." Similarly innocuous questions follow: "Who do you work for? If there are any insurers involved, who are they? Who else is likely to become involved in the case? Do you have any cross-claims or counterclaims? Who are your creditors? Does anyone else have a lien on the property? Who referred you to us?"

> L2: But one of our rules are—particularly with the out-of-the-blue calls or anything that we don't know who it is that's calling us; in fact, it's written into our ethics rules—is, if you are contacted for a new matter, find out who they are, find out just generally what they're discussing, and don't commit, don't try to learn the substance of the matter completely. In other words, don't try to get attorney-client communications. Then run the conflicts check first.
>
> L1: One of things you try to ascertain to the maximum extent possible when you get the call is, who is the caller adverse to? . . . Most of our work here is litigation work. So, if it's the defendant in a lawsuit, they know who the plaintiff is. If it's a plaintiff who wants to sue someone, they know who generally they want to sue. So we ask them that in the first initial call. And then we take all that information and run it through the system before they come in to meet with us.
>
> L2: So that we don't learn information in case the person they're planning to sue, particularly, ends up being one of our clients who would want us to represent them in the same matter. So, we have that process to try to prevent learning too much information right off the bat until we found out whether there's a conflict involved. [47Ch20–49]

Whereas some lawyers have difficulty silencing prospective clients who first contact the firm, others experience clients as reluctant to disclose anything over the phone, especially to a receptionist or secretary. These lawyers wait to gather the basic facts in an initial meeting. Some instruct their secretary midway through the meeting to check out the list of names, while the lawyer and prospective client continue their superficial and awkward conversation, waiting for clearance to delve deeper.[8]

---

[8]Not all attorneys have the luxury of this methodical incremental culling process. For example, several downstate respondents in the sample serve as part-time public defenders and do not receive their criminal cases until they are assigned in open court—where they have neither access to their records to check for potential conflicts nor much opportunity for painstaking inquiry and reflection. Given the repeat-playing proclivities of criminals and their dense social networks in these small towns—which I described in earlier chapters—the risk of unwanted conflicts of interest in this setting can be quite high.

A different tension confounds matters that involve coparties hoping to share the cost of representation. Chapter 4 detailed the conflicts of interest that lurk in the representation of multiple parties. Some joint representations are so mired in actual or potential conflicts that most attorneys forgo them; others can be undertaken with appropriate disclosures to the affected clients. The challenge is determining at the outset, when everyone's interests are compatible, whether the prospective matter falls into the former or latter category.

In chapter 4, I described the difficulties that attorneys face in collecting sufficient information to make that precocious judgment. But attorneys face another challenge as well when they try to evaluate whether they can ethically represent more than one coparty. If codefendants immediately begin pointing fingers at one another, lawyers may get an earful that cannot be struck from the record. (Respondents talk about the horse being out of the barn or their inability to unring the bell.) Conferring with more than one party implicated in the case, then, may unearth confidential information that will preclude the firm from representing anyone.

So the incremental investigative process applies to parties as well as facts. Lawyers confer with prospective coparties seriatim, selecting the entity or individual who appears the most desirable for the first interview before moving on to confer with others if nothing suggests adversity among coparties. When the initial interview suggests that the alliance may be shaky or that interests are too adverse to warrant joint representation, the attorney at least has secured what he or she hopes to be the most attractive client (assuming, of course, that that party decides to hire the lawyer).

> Sometimes you have two different doctor defendants. And they're within a group practice, and they're represented by one insurance company. And they're sued, sort of as two guys doing business as partners in a certain group practice. And you find that one had an active role—a primary role—in the care of the patient. And the other one had a subservient role, but there's something about it. And you find out from one doctor, "Well, my other doctor—my partner—really should have done something at that point." So right away, you get a drift that you can't be representing the two of them. So as quickly as possible, you try to keep the guy you've spoken to and not keep the guy that you haven't spoken to. And you notify the carrier there's a conflict there. There may be some finger-pointing there, even among partners. [19Ch50–99]

Other lawyers interview the parties together, examining their interpersonal dynamics, cohesion, and resolve. Then they incrementally elicit innocuous bits of information until they are confident that the alliance will hold. The alternative, of course, is to refuse certain types of joint representation altogether:

> See, you can't even interview all of them. Because, if you interview 'em, then you're conflicted out of all of them. Okay. So what you do is—what I generally do—is say, "Look, let's not discuss the case. What are you charged with and so forth? Now, let's stop right there." And then I might pick out the one I think is an interesting defendant . . . and say, "Okay, I can represent you. But I'm going to

> have to get other counsel [for the rest of you]. And here's a list of people that you can choose from. . . . See, we don't represent multiple defendants, even if there's no conflict at all. [113Ch<10]

Others make judgments based on structural characteristics of the parties—for example, never representing both surgeons and anesthesiologists or never representing potentially responsible parties assigned to different tiers of responsibility in a Superfund site.

In multiparty litigation in which firms can expect to be solicited by a number of coparties or insurance carriers for representation, they often maneuver cautiously and strategically through the process, minimizing contact until they have lined up the most desirable client or clients to represent.

> So, usually, the calls are coming in in close proximity to each other. Or a letter and a call will come in in close proximity—maybe within a week apart or a day apart. It isn't like you've taken on an assignment. I mean, where we really get nailed is when somebody calls in or writes in and we don't know if anybody else is going to call us. I mean, those other seven defendants may be represented by seven other law firms. And if we identify one of the other seven—and know that they're the insured of a certain insurer—we can actually call the insurer and say, "You've been named in this lawsuit. I know it's one of your insureds. I don't know whether you've been served with summonses yet. But if you are, were you thinking of sending it to us? Because we've been asked to take over somebody else's defense." "Well, we'll look into it and call you back. . . . " And they might say, "Well, no, we wouldn't think of you anyway." [laughter] [19Ch50–99]

Similarly, when firms anticipate that they will be approached by multiple parties in a case or that clients are interviewing more than one law firm and the odds of acquiring the prospective representation are low, they may take special care to stay in the dark. Indeed, they may set some ground rules with the prospective client about what each party will disclose and the consequences for the firm if the client subsequently decides to go elsewhere.

> And I've done a memo that sort of covers this, which basically gives guidelines to lawyers as to how to participate in a beauty contest. And it says things like, "Prior to being retained, you still may be—quote—"their lawyer" if they give you confidential information. And the fact that you haven't gotten a retainer doesn't mean that you can't be conflicted out of representing the other side. And that you as a lawyer must understand this and if you want to prevent this from being done, there are certain steps you should take. For example, you should advise the client in the beginning that, before they give you any information—or a potential client—that they should give you no confidential information, that you are not yet their attorney. It may not be covered by the attorney-client privilege. [11Ch100+]

As I described in chapter 6, several respondents shared their concerns about what they perceived to be the latest fashion, in which clients contrive beauty contests or other occasions to disclose confidences for the sole purpose of conflicting out those firms with the greatest expertise or talent from representing their adversaries. Several informants questioned how they could protect themselves from becoming ensnared by such a ploy.

> L: I'm getting a little worried about logistical beauty contests, strategical beauty contests.
>
> S: Oh, to conflict you out, you mean?
>
> L: Yeah. That's beginning to concern me. And whenever we're cold-called on a big case for that purpose, I'm suspicious. I don't want to say I'm cynical yet—I haven't reached that point—but I'm suspicious why we're getting that call. And so I usually make a few calls around to some of my partners and say, "Let me ask you something" and talk to them about it. Because I have found, not in my experience here at the firm, but through my network with other firms, that it's been known to happen. [27Ch50–99]

> And I'm not sure what you can do, except to just try to ask them who referred you. And if they don't have a good answer, if they sound suspicious in answering the question, I guess you can say you don't want to see them. However, that's not even a good way to do it. Because we have plenty of people who come to us and who really don't know who referred us. Because they might have asked somebody who didn't use us, but who remembers that a friend told them that "So-and-So is a good lawyer." . . . So, it's real tough. I mean, I think, for the most part, what most people do in this business is, if somebody calls them, they interview them. And you don't want to turn away a potential client. And if it turns out that you're getting burned, I guess, those are the breaks. There's no good way—that I know—to deal with that issue. [94Ch10–19]

Lawyers must be circumspect, not only in what they learn from and disclose to their would-be client but in how they structure their inquiry. Sharing even the most innocent information with a colleague in order to investigate the potential that a prospective matter may be adverse to the interests of the colleague's client may spill information that will preclude the firm from representing either side.

One respondent suggested the role of firm intermediaries to absorb information gleaned from a prospective client and thereby ensure that an ethical screen that is erected to resolve any conflicts of interest is not inadvertently breached by the mere act of searching for them.

> . . . we had an in-house seminar on this. And I encouraged people to use the three people who take an active role in this area as the middle person and let them, basically, play mediator between the two situations and let the middle person make a judgment whether there's a conflict. Because if the two of you sort it out by yourselves, there is a potential for information to go from the person who perceives that there might be a conflict, communicating what that conflict might be, and then breaking the very Chinese wall that is all that would be necessary to let us to

go forward with the representation. We're a little informal about that. There's no rule in place reminding the lawyers around the office that this is the way they should proceed if they find such a situation. [39Ch50–99]

Another respondent described a related use of a buffer to protect sensitive and especially explosive confidences:

> . . . if someone . . . needs to do a conflicts check on a [top secret deal] and can't say anything about what the deal is and doesn't want anyone to have any way of finding out, they can simply come to a partner of the Litigation Department and have the partner in the Litigation Department put in some names on a conflicts check, and they can tell the partner in the Litigation Department, "I can't even tell you why you're doing this." But you can get back the results. Because the only thing the firm knows is someone in the Litigation Department did this conflicts check, presumably for litigation. [2Ch100+]

These accounts of how firms choreograph convoluted pas de deux with prospective clients to gather sufficient information about a new matter without obtaining confidences that will trigger conflicts of interest should not be overgeneralized. Large firms have established mechanisms to undertake preliminary conflicts checks before meeting with prospective clients or conferring with them in any detail. But it is unclear how often these mechanisms are used. The self-regulatory system requires checks to be complete before a billing number is issued, but it has no way of enforcing preclearance before a lawyer is allowed to confer with a client—whether in the office or on a golf course. The rare firm may hold seminars to encourage lawyers to use middle persons to investigate the potential for conflicts; but even its spokesperson concedes that they have no way of enforcing this procedure. Lawyers and receptionists may be acutely aware that clients should not be allowed to disclose many details over the phone, but their ability or willingness to rudely cut the client off may not match their theoretical commitment to silence. Lawyers in smaller firms may know the risks but face them so rarely that the inefficiencies embedded in the choreography deter them from following the script. And lawyers in firms of all sizes, exposures to risk, and choreographies are often so thrilled to even get a new piece of business that they are reluctant to do anything that will scare the new client off—especially if all that dancing is designed to ensure that some other rainmaker in the firm doesn't get conflicted out of a prospective matter. Though it might be nice to have the judge of the beauty contest sign a waiver that its disclosures are not to be treated as confidential and that the contestant is not precluded from representing someone else if it loses the contest, few contestants insist on the waiver if it means that the judge will respond by barring them from walking down the runway.

In short, firms and lawyers have other priorities that compete with the costly and socially awkward process of meeting new clients obstructed by blinders and enforcing incremental secrecy. As the managing partner of a collar county firm conceded:

> Even though, on an ongoing basis, we . . . try to be conscientious about our conflicts, it's not something that absorbs [. . .] That isn't, really, the first question that comes in your mind. The first question is "What kind of a problem is it? Is this a kind of legal problem that our office can handle?" Making certain that the person gets in to the right attorney within the office, within their specialization. And then, as that person develops the information, then one can see whether there is some potential conflict. But it's not the real big, burning question that I think is in everybody's mind when someone comes in. Maybe it should be, but [. . .] . . . If I were to label the particular problems of this office, and I were to label them, say, one to twenty-five in terms of the concerns from an administrative standpoint, it would be towards the bottom. That isn't to say we're unconcerned about it, it's just that, on a daily basis, there are other concerns—from an administrative standpoint—that occur with greater frequency. [88CC10–19]

Still, the tensions that gave rise to the intricate choreography do exist, and the costs of freestyle moves or improvisation can be very high.

Forms

Once lawyers have determined that they would like to represent the prospective client, most firms require that they complete forms that initiate the process of assigning a docket or billing number to the case, necessary for lawyers to bill their time, run the copy machine, and acquire a host of other resources essential to undertaking a new matter. Withholding a billing number provides a potent incentive for lawyers to complete the forms and shepherd them through the administrative apparatus quickly.

> The control over me is: I can record my time, but it doesn't go anywhere, because I don't have a billing number. So I've got sheets of paper piling up in my office that are of no value to me. So I have a financial incentive to get this thing registered. [16Ch100+]

Typically, lawyers take notes as they interview prospective clients, and then they or their secretaries later transfer the information onto the appropriate forms. In some firms, forms appear as macros on all personal computers so that lawyers or, more often, their secretaries can complete the form on the computer screen and immediately transmit the data to the relevant administrative departments within the firm. Most forms, though, are still printed on paper, sometimes with multicolored copies that are circulated to various departments or committees within the firm.

These forms are called some variation or combination of New Client, New Business, New Matter, New File, New Case, Intake, Client Contact, Conflicts, Potential Conflicts, Daily Conflicts, or Conflict Clearance Form/Sheet/Report/Memo/Request/Packet, or they are referred to by the color of paper on which they are printed. As the names suggest, the forms are often used for more than mere billing or bookkeeping purposes; they are also used for evaluating the desirability and conflict-of-interest potential of a new matter. Forms range in length from one page to eight or more. Over the years, they tend to put on weight as committees, administrators, or insurers seek more and more data for the deliberative process. Eventually, though, the forms reach a tipping point beyond which harried staff provide incomplete or inaccurate information or refuse to fill them out altogether, after which they slim down.

Figure 8.1 presents a generic new matter form, a composite of all the forms shared by the respondents, their descriptions of their firm's intake procedure, and "The 'Perfect' Client Intake Form" devised by the large firm mutual malpractice insurer ALAS (Attorneys' Liability Assurance Society 1992). The figure simply lists types of data elicited by various forms; it does not spell out specific questions or provide space and format for responding to them. Each topic is preceded by one of three kinds of bullets. The arrows denote data that virtually all new matter forms will elicit: client name, matter, and administrative information (staffing, billing, scheduling). The large round bullets signal additional questions, found on most intake forms, regarding characteristics of the prospective client; affiliated and adverse parties; family trees; insurers; and other legal counsel involved in the case. These more exhaustive forms also typically require a sign-off by the lawyer in charge of the new matter and sometimes by a member of an oversight committee as well. The small round bullets mark information elicited on the most comprehensive intake forms, typically used by the largest law firms, those with a diversified general practice, and those that are members of ALAS. These questions target themes identified repeatedly in the previous five chapters as significant but more subtle sources of conflict of interest: the social networks in which clients are embedded and their prior or ongoing relationships with the firm; related parties with an indirect interest in the matter; how the matter was referred to the firm; and so on. Only a handful of firms in the sample actually elicit information on every theme listed in figure 8.1.

Although the adoption of a given type of new matter form generally reflects firm size, caseload, and practice, it also foretells the kind of conflict-of-interest regulatory system adopted by the firm. Note that the cursory forms, bulleted by arrows, do not even bother to record the identity of adverse parties and therefore lack the single most important piece of information necessary to identify potential conflicts of interest. Of course, self-regulatory systems may secure that information in some other way, but the length of intake forms and the types of data they collect betray much about the self-regulatory system of a law firm.

Ferreting Out Conflicts of Interest

So how do firms identify whether prospective matters contain interests that are adverse to those of past, present, or desirable future clients? Several species of law firm, distinguishable by how they respond to the possibility that new business will detonate conflicts of interest, roam the Illinois landscape.

Ostriches. The most endangered species is the ostrich—law firms that do nothing, that bury their heads in the sand, hopeful that conflicts of interest will not arise. Lawyers in these firms learn of conflicts only after they have detonated, usually when a client tells them. The following exchange with the name partner of a downstate

- ➪ name and address of the prospective client and contact person
- type of client (individual, corporation, partnership, fiduciary, association, government agency)
- principle business of the client
- ➪ description of the matter and area of law
- copy of the litigation complaint
- whether the litigation client is a plaintiff, defendant, third party, or creditor
- whether client is a new or existing client of the firm or a declined client
- if a former or existing client, the legal services currently or previously performed by the firm
- prior names used by the prospective client
- commonly used abbreviations (e.g., AT&T, 3M)
- parents, subsidiaries, divisions, affiliates, and joint venturers of corporate clients
- whether firm has ever represented affiliates of prospective client
- principals, directors, officers, and principal shareholders of corporate clients and of their parents
- all general or limited partners in a partnership
- all members of an association
- all beneficiaries of a fiduciary
- name of spouse and employer or business affiliation of individual clients
- names of any other related parties to which the firm should not be adverse
- adverse parties (including corporate affiliates and partners)
- other parties that might have an interest in the matter (e.g., officers, employees, major customers, suppliers, competitors)
- relationship between the proposed client and any other existing client
- potential conflicts of interest (including issue and positional conflicts)
- why the prospective client sought this law firm and who referred it
- whether and why the client is switching law firms
- other counsel involved in the matter
- whether a third party (e.g., an insurance company) is paying for the representation
- whether lawyers have a relationship other than that of attorney/client (e.g., officer, director, or partner of a client; business transaction with a client; investment in client's securities; acting as a broker in assisting client to secure outside funds or business partners)
- whether any immediate family member of a firm attorney has an ownership interest in or is an officer, director, or employee of the prospective client
- ➪ assorted scheduling, staffing, fee, and billing information
- signatures of the partner in charge of the prospective matter and of a member of the relevant oversight committee

Fig. 8.1. Generic New Matter Form

firm—which specializes in bringing personal injury suits on behalf of plaintiffs and on collections matters—illuminates the ostrich response to conflicts of interest:

S: Would you describe, in the intake of new matters, what process lawyers in the firm go through to evaluate whether there are potential conflicts of interest?

L: We don't. All right? The only thing that happens is, first of all, we have a list of doctors, for instance, that we will not sue—not because of any conflict, but because they're our personal doctors or friends or they have some business connection with one or the other of us. But, other than that, *we have no way of finding conflicts.* What happens is that, as far as the injury end of it is concerned, it would be very unusual for a conflict to occur. As a matter of fact, I don't know how one could occur in the personal injury work, because we don't defend anybody. And, obviously, one plaintiff is not going to be suing another plaintiff. . . . I guess we have had situations where a defendant came in as a plaintiff and was going to sue somebody, and we have discovered that we might represent somebody who's a prospective defendant. . . . But that's by just happenstance that we would discover that. *There isn't any procedure that we have.* The only other area of conflict—and it's one that does arise from time to time—is we have a Commercial Department in this firm. . . . And they are suing people to collect debts and bills in commercial matters and things of that sort. . . . Let's say I have a railroad client, a guy hurt on the railroad, and he owes a hospital bill or owes a grocer or something. The Commercial Department . . . might have that claim against him. And when they send the letter or notice to him that they're representing So-and-So, well, he obviously would know that it's on my letterhead and know that it's my firm and *he would bring it to my attention. And we would resolve the matter. We would have to withdraw from one or the other representations. But we don't have any procedure for discovering that.*

S: So the people in the Commercial Department wouldn't, for example, go through the list of clients or the list of ongoing matters just to make sure that [. . .]

L: No, they would not. . . . it would be such hard work. They handle, they have a large volume of cases. . . . And they're not big cases at all. They have a very large volume of work. And if they had to go through our other client lists each time they took a commercial matter, it would be impossible for them to do. [65DSM20–49, my emphasis]

This ostrich firm is rather large, by downstate standards; it employs twenty-odd lawyers and is located in a medium-sized city. I conducted the interview roughly midway through the interviewing process and was, frankly, stunned by a response I had never heard before—even in much smaller and more specialized firms. Representing powerless, unsophisticated clients who were often disabled by serious accidents, the respondent probably assumed that they wouldn't recognize a conflict of interest if it hit them over the head or wouldn't cause much trouble even if they did. I met few, if any, other lawyers less risk averse or as certain that implementing a few precautions would be "impossible." Indeed, only 2 percent of the firms in the sample were ostriches.

Elephants

> We have clients who come in from twenty, twenty-five years ago and say, "I'm [. . .] " and we can say their name. They're amazed that we remember them at all. And I guess that's just part of being an attorney, for one thing. They claim that attorneys remember, or else they wouldn't be attorneys. [127DSS<10]

The elephant is a somewhat less endangered species than the ostrich and is found in 15 percent of the sample firms, especially the smaller ones. Elephants never forget. They know their clients and assert that they would know immediately if a potential new matter was likely to trigger a conflict of interest. Most elephants explain that, because of the limited size, age, or clientele of their firm, it is easy to keep track of their diverse interests.

> . . . given the size of my practice, it's not difficult for me to identify a conflict as soon as I hear the name, because I remember all my clients. Many of these files that I have open stay open for a year or two. . . . Some years go by when I don't have more than maybe a dozen new files open during the year. . . . And as far as keeping track of those things, I keep track of them in my mind. . . . I mean I just remember what I've done. And, with respect to the . . . the criminal defense practice, . . . there are few enough criminals in town that they—it's like a revolving door—they keep coming back through the system. And you can remember who you have and who you haven't represented. . . . This town's just small enough and the workload is such that we can remember, you know, you remember people. [91DSL<10]

So elephants simply run through a mental checklist before taking on a new case.

> I know the names of the people that I have worked with over the past ten years. And a name will either strike a chord of recognition, or it will be a new and different name. So, the first check is just mentally, sort of, going through what I have done before, thinking about whether it might be a conflict. [85DSM<10]

Herds. No matter how unforgetful the elephant is, intelligence systems based on memory and personal knowledge break down as firms grow. To identify a conflict of interest, lawyers must recall not only all their own clients and potential clients, their family trees, and assorted interests, but those of their colleagues as well. They need to know about the clients that colleagues have or had, and if they want to prevent conflicts that might foreclose future business, they also need to know about clients their colleagues hope to represent. More than half the elephants in the sample, therefore, function as herds. These firms ask that lawyers consult with one another before taking on a new client or matter. In smaller firms, lawyers typically confer face-to-face. In the smallest firms, colleagues often meet every day—even those working in different branch offices—to discuss new cases or consult with each other before taking on a new engagement. As the name partner of a Chicago firm describes:

> Well, we have [about ten] lawyers. Five associates. With the five associates, maybe there's two or three clients that they've brought in. All the other clients are clients

> that come in from the partners. And there's no better microchip than your brain. And with a firm our size, intuitively I know right away whether we've got a conflict. But we always ask, 'cause we have to ask. . . . And we talk to each other. And if there are a sufficient number of parties, or principals, or shareholders, or employees, or people, or related parties that are all people you have to check for a conflict—we'll write a memo. But, for the most part, just walk around and say, ". . . Who are we representing here? Who owns them? Who do they own?" You know, all the questions you have to ask. . . . It's just not that big. We're not like a personal injury firm might have a thousand cases. If [our firm has] a hundred, that's a lot. [104Ch10–19]

In somewhat larger firms, usually with fewer than twenty-five attorneys, partners and associates will meet once a week to discuss new cases and unearth potential conflicts of interests about which colleagues are aware:

> . . . in addition to having a pretty close partnership relationship—I mean, we're all on the same floor and we see each other all the time and we discuss over the cases. In addition to finding it out through direct discussion, the firm also—weekly—goes over new clients with a view toward finding out potential conflicts. We have a weekly meeting. And at that time, we will describe the new clients that have come in. And if there is any potential conflict, the attorneys know immediately to speak up and to say that. . . . the very first thing that we do in that meeting is . . . our billing clerk reads the names of the files that have been opened this past week. And it's the responsibility of the attorney who opened it to—if there's something new or novel about the case or some help that they want—is to mention the details of the case and the question as to whether or not, in our mind, there's a conflict. [54DSL20–49]

In still larger firms, colleagues consult impersonally. Some firms place in their reception area a checklist or clipboard of new matter forms that lawyers must peruse and sign off on as they come and go:

> We have no committee; we have no real centralized management. We really have no system of supervision of conflicts. What we do is we have a form—a New Matter Conflict of Interest form. . . . Every time there's a new matter, the lawyer . . . is responsible for filling that out or having his secretary fill it out. And then it sits at the reception desk. And the receptionist polices—only to the extent of being sure everybody initials it. If there is a conflict, if anybody says "yes," it usually gets to me. Just because I'm a senior. But we have no real structure. If everybody says "no," then it just stays in the file. . . . Well, I guess the initiative for doing this was not really our own need—as we saw it—but our malpractice carrier insisted on it. It's fine. It's not terribly burdensome. [80Ch10–19]

Most other firms adopting an impersonal collegial system for ferreting out conflicts circulate case-specific memoranda:

L: We're pretty informal about all this, and maybe we should be more systematic then we are. But what we do is have people circulate a memo to the firm on all new clients, and more recently, we've been trying to get people to do that as to new matters for existing clients. We do not have a computerized system. We don't try to have names automatically checked against a computerized index. We, of course, have a client and matter index and I think people, probably fairly routinely, consult that. But I think we depend most on circulating memos.

S: So, say a new client with a new matter approaches a partner in the firm?

L: . . . there will be a conflict memo circulated. And it says, "We've been asked to represent So-and-So. Here are the other people involved. Here's what the matter involves." And then, depending on whether any negative response is heard from anybody in the firm—any reason to raise a flag about it—then the attorney involved will send a memo to me . . . [21Ch50–99]

Or they circulate copies of new matter forms:

> . . . the first page of every new matter sheet that we have within the firm is circulated to all attorneys—with certain exceptions where they're highly confidential. . . . We are trying to figure out a way to better computerize this whole operation. But right now, it's just a stack of papers goes around every week and everybody gets it. And it's amazing, people do look at it. . . . A lot of people have interest in what other people in the firm are doing professionally. They are interested in who's developing business; what matters they're handling. And they also know that's a very good way to check for conflicts. So we get calls from people regularly inquiring about the new matter sheets. So we know it works. It's one of the better things that works around here. [chuckle] . . . I can't imagine not doing it. [1Ch100+]

Or they regularly circulate firm newsletters:

> But attached to the daily memo . . . is a listing of all the new files that have been opened. And all attorneys are supposed to read that and look to see if there's anything that jumps out at them. There are those, I'm sure, who never look at it. But . . . we have caught a number of the ones that would have slipped through the cracks—the John Jones who owns the Ford Motor Company—getting picked up by somebody who looks through that and calls and says, "Why are we suing my client?" or "What's going on? Why is my client here? Why am I not named?" So that is a fallback. [11Ch100+]

These communiques are circulated firmwide, listing new matters contemplated in all the branch offices.

Some larger firms go even more high-tech, with e-mail messages blaring across lawyers' computer screens or oral messages clogging their voice mail boxes throughout the day as potential new cases arise.

L2: The other kind of technical innovation that has come up in the past few years is voice mail. And one of the effects of voice mail—which drives some of the people around here nuts—is that you can leave a voice mail message for everybody in the firm. . . . "I have been asked by Joe Smith to bring a lawsuit against John Jones. If anyone knows of any reason why we should not undertake that representation, please call me by noon tomorrow at extension blank, blank, blank, blank." . . . I regard it as another step of protection. It's not a primary thing that we rely on, although sometimes it can be much, much more efficient and ferret out the conflict much . . . quicker. . . . And then again—as I said—we publish it in the daily memo. And you can be sure if [I] open a case, saying, "John Smith vs. well-known franchiser," I'm going to get a phone call from [colleague] or somebody else [another colleague] or somebody else in that group within two minutes.

L1: "What are we doing against a franchiser? Even if it isn't a client of ours?" [11Ch100+]

Attorneys are expected to check their electronic or telephonic messages, newsletters, or memoranda and communicate with colleagues when they discover a potential conflict. Most firms leave it to lawyers' discretion to respond, though some require that all partners sign off on a matter—even if they are out of the office or away on vacation—before a billing number is assigned and work on the case can begin.

> The sheet is circulated to all attorneys and paralegals in the firm as well as the Accounting Section, the Litigation Dockets Section, the Probate/Estate Dockets Section, and eventually we will add Filing Section—though I don't expect that to add much. The form has four boxes, one of which each of these individuals must check off: (1) No known conflict. (2) No known conflict, but relationships exist (familial or personal relationships between attorneys and parties, officer, director, family member). (3) No known conflict, but a review is required because of potential client relations or public relations ramification (examples include positional conflicts such as a lawsuit against an industry in which the firm has lots of clients). If this box is checked, the matter is referred to the managing partner for review. (4) Potential conflict. If this box is checked, the matter is referred to me. . . . Everyone who is sent a copy of this form must fill it out. I guess that's the advantage of a smaller firm. My secretary has a preprinted form with everyone's name on it, and as she gets the completed form, she checks off their name. When someone has not returned the form, there is an automatic procedure to recontact them. . . . They are expected to call in if they will be out for two or three days. When everyone has returned their responses, the secretary signs a form certifying that she received all of the responses. [43Ch20–49]

Even in voluntary systems, lawyers have some incentive to review the list. Many lawyers jealously track the rainmaking efforts of their colleagues; others want to ensure that the firm does not take a case that might preclude them from bringing in future business or that might antagonize a treasured client. Because lawyers' compensation usually reflects—at least in part—the amount of business they bring into the firm, they are more conscientious in reviewing these lists of prospective matters than one might expect. Herds provide one of the best means of identifying the more invisible adversities of interest—such as positional conflicts—that affect clients or prospective clients who are not directly involved in a new matter.

Firm size is related to the depth and extensiveness of communication through the herd. Lawyers in the largest firms are both least likely to know about the client load and prospects of their colleagues and most easily inundated by the sheer volume of information. As a result, colleagues in the largest firms tend to distribute less detailed information to each other and to do so less frequently than those in somewhat smaller firms. The largest firms (median size, 69) generally circulate lists of new matters and parties, whereas somewhat smaller firms (median size, 37) send memos summarizing a prospective case or copies of the new matter forms. The smallest firms (median size, 3) do not bother circularizing each other at all. The relationship between firm size and the frequency with which new matter lists, forms, or memos are disseminated tends to be curvilinear. Only the smallest firms (median size, 15) distribute materials less often than once a week (usually once a month); the largest firms (median size, 207) do so once a week; and somewhat smaller firms (median size, 74) do so more than once a week, usually daily. Firms that circulate case-specific memoranda or forms do so continually as they arise.

That communication through the herd is burdensome is duly noted by many respondents.

> And I know a lot of firms . . . all the partners are given a list of the clients that have taken in new matters on. . . . Actually, that isn't all that productive of information. We don't need to do that in order to uncover conflicts. It might be an added protection. But . . . to send that to every lawyer—and we have [fifty to one hundred] lawyers here—to send every new matter for them to pore over would be very time consuming and wasteful, I think. And I don't think it would get us that much information. And I think we can do it without doing that. [13Ch50–99]

But most find the yield well worth the cost. Indeed, the partners in one relatively large, newly formed law firm intentionally eschewed the methods of identifying conflicts of interest that they had relied on in the past in favor of circulating intraoffice memoranda.

Lawyers in the majority of firms function as herds, systematically consulting each other about potential conflicts before taking on new engagements. But, unlike the elephants, most of the herds rely on more than their memories. The problem with elephants or herds of elephants is that they sometimes do forget, especially aging or active elephants with a great deal on their minds. Suggesting that memory capacity—at least in a general practice—is rather limited, a young solo practitioner explained why he had recently developed a system of records to identify conflicts of interest:

> Well, I've only been in practice now for—in sole practice by myself—for two and a half years. So I am still able to know, when somebody comes in, whether I'm going to have a conflict, because I recognize the parties. But it is getting to the

> point where I'm forgetting what I did two years ago. And I may forget names and faces. [112DSS<10]

Moreover, however complete and accessible the overflowing memory banks may be, this firm resource disappears when elephants retire or die or move to another herd.

> We went through a merger in late [recent year]. And two attorneys that practice in [a neighboring city]—and specialize in labor and employment law matters—merged with us. We weren't as systematic or as methodical in going through a conflict check before that merger. Because, quite frankly, at that time, every attorney—darn near; we're still small enough—really had a good handle on who the clients of the firm were. Well, once that merger took place, and we did wind up suing one of their clients. And then we implemented a better system. [72DSM10–19]

Just because the institutional memory is lost doesn't mean the conflicts of interest desist. And keeping track of the herds and ensuring that each member has had an opportunity to comment becomes a laborious process as members multiply.

Squirrels. Many lawyers now supplement individual and institutional memories with vast storehouses of detritus from prior cases that they methodically collect and squirrel away. The vast majority of law firms in the sample hail from the squirrel family, accumulating and consulting records as a mechanism for ferreting out conflicts of interest. The subspecies *common squirrel,* found in 29 percent of the firms overall, generally stockpiles paper records as well as other detritus developed for purposes other than the social control of conflict of interest; the *cyber squirrel* (55 percent of the firms) amasses electronic records created specifically for this purpose. Some squirrels examine their stash only when their memories and those of the pack fail. But many routinely consult their records before taking on a new engagement, especially the cyber squirrels (83 percent compared with 38 percent of the common squirrels). Squirrels are more solidary than elephants are—almost two-thirds confer among themselves before taking on a new case, compared to a bit more than half the elephants—though their communication is half as likely to be face-to-face (20 percent versus 40 percent).

The most primitive of the common squirrels simply compile a paper or electronic client list that lawyers, secretaries, or receptionists may consult to ensure that the adverse party in a prospective matter is not already a client of the firm. Others scrutinize paper or computerized mailing lists as well as time and billing or accounting records, which generally offer only the most superficial information from which to make inferences about the potential for adverse interests.

> . . . some lawyers just go straight to our thick book of billing and matter numbers that lists all our clients alphabetically and just start looking for the names. And, in certain ways, that's best [of the various methods to identify conflicts of interest]. Now, the risk is that you'll miss someone who's described in their business name and not their individual name and then you're going to sue them individually or

> vice versa—that we represent John Smith and his wife, but there's no listing in our book for the Smith Electric Company. And yet clearly Smith is going to be upset if we sue his company. And yet the system is organized enough by matter and submatter and by client and matter number and alphabetically, and you can do a sort and all kinds of things, that it's a fairly accurate way to do the check. . . . It's a thick book and it just lists all the client and matters going back for some time. . . . Usually, the book is only used for someone to look up a matter number before they punch numbers into the—what's that called?—photocopy machine. That's the principal purpose of the book. But it serves also the purpose of figuring out who we represent. [39Ch50–99]

Though this practice is most common in small law firms, one of the largest firms in the sample uses essentially the same system:

> In every office we have a list of our clients on microfiche and it's updated. It's two weeks old. It's never less current than two weeks. And we are automating it. . . . We keep central registration of clients. So I have a new client that comes in to me; knocks on the door and sits down and talks to me. He says, "[my name], I'd like to bring you something." . . . So the moment the client comes in, we sit down and we begin to talk. And I get a feel for the other parties involved. I'll call my secretary in and give her a note, "Please get the conflict data on [. . .]" And the client has said, "I'm going to buy a farm from John Jones—farmer living out in DeKalb County." I'll put down "Farmer Jones." "And I've got a loan lined up with the First National Bank of Chicago; I'd like you to help me with them." I write down "First National Bank of Chicago." And while we're talking, I'll tell him, "Well, I'm going . . . to have my secretary check." . . . So my secretary will run out and check. She'll go out. . . . She starts on the microfiche, finds a listing for "J. Jones" and sees that it's registered, say, for [my colleague]—lawyer next door. Well, [colleague]'s out for the moment. So I'll then have her check the fee history upstairs. . . . I get the information. I see that we have a registration for "J. Jones" and that we have fees. In the current year, we've received a thousand dollars in fees. And I'll be doing the same thing for the First National Bank of Chicago. Okay. And I see we've got some current fees. . . . I can tell the client, "We'll continue on with our discussion. . . . But I'm going to have to check with my partner [names colleague]—as soon as he comes in—to see." [16Ch100+]

Unfortunately, client lists, photocopy machine codes, mailing lists, and billing and accounting records provide little or no information about the nature of prior representations, nor do they disclose the array of parties implicated in a particular case. It is no wonder that this big Chicago firm is about to get automated. The notion that its hundreds of lawyers, in numerous branch offices, must continually locate one another to gather a few facts about a prior case—even to rule out nonexistent conflicts of interest—is staggering.

A bit more than two-fifths of the common squirrels, therefore, go beyond this incidental stash generated by ongoing engagements, consulting paper records specifically developed to assess potential conflicts. They warehouse versions of their new matter forms, often recorded on index cards, which are scanned before a new case is opened.

> When a new case is brought into the firm, we keep a list of all existing clients of the firm as well as . . . a five- or six-part form that we fill out. One of the forms goes in an adverse party docketing system, where we list all parties that have ever been adverse to us in the docketing system. Another part goes into a docketing system of existing clients. So it's relatively easy to know whether there's a conflict on any one of our files. . . . It's not computerized. It's simply kept on what are little index-sized cards . . . [121Ch<10]

Most firms retain these index cards long after a case is closed. Some file the cards of opened or closed cases separately; others differentiate between clients and adverse parties, as did the firm in the previous example. I visited one firm that allocates a special room for what it calls the "wheels." The room houses nine massive Rolodex-like devices. Each card is color coded to represent the lawyer on the case and then alphabetized by client or party name. Information contained on the cards allows the checker to quickly identify the lawyer on the case and the file numbers and location of the records. The firm's name partner explained that the wheels are used as a backup for what is generally an elephant system of conflict identification. Though it is up to the discretion of the lawyer to consult the wheels, many other squirrels routinely consult their records before opening a new case.

Cyber squirrels. As firms age, grow, and branch out into multiple offices and as litigation and transactions become more complex, the storage and retrieval of index cards can become quite cumbersome. In response to the logjam, larger and more technologically sophisticated firms have abandoned these paper trails—at least for contemporary matters—and undertaken electronic surveillance. Cyber squirrels develop specialized conflicts data bases containing a storehouse of information about each case and devise artificial intelligence algorithms to scan for indicators of potential trouble.

Common squirrels evolve into the cyber subspecies under a variety of circumstances. Some turn to electronic data bases with rapid firm growth and diversification, which taxes institutional memories and impedes manual recordkeeping across multiple offices. One solo practitioner adopted a data base after hiring an associate and suffering embarrassment when his colleague inadvertently sent collection notices to two valued clients. Others went electronic as litigation became more complex and rendered manual methods too burdensome. The managing partner of a smallish downstate firm, in the process of cyber revolution, expressed disbelief and dismay when he learned that it took secretaries forty-five minutes to open a new matter through their conventional manual system. Several firms developed more elaborate systems when they discovered that the firm had been conflicted out of lucrative business by small matters undertaken by others in the firm. Other firms made the transition when their malpractice insurers dangled the carrot of reduced premiums if they automated their recordkeeping systems.[9] Still others evolved unwittingly as they upgraded their office technology and found conflicts-checking software built into their new computerized time and billing, calendaring, or docketing programs.

> We're just updating everything. Just like . . . all the secretaries have PCs. And they used to have Selectrics. . . . And it's the same thing. You didn't have the computerized conflict programs until a couple of years ago. We didn't have that. We had just file boards and file cards. Now we've got the electronic. [50DSL20–49]

And a few of the cyber squirrels evolved directly from elephants or herds of elephants, skipping the intermediate step of sifting through reams of paper to identify conflicts. Indeed, some younger firms in the sample utilized computerized conflicts screening from their inception, often importing systems from firms they left.

Cyber squirrels comprise a little more than half the firms in the sample. But their representation in the animal kingdom is likely to rise. Undoubtedly, some elephants and common squirrels that I interviewed are now cyber squirrels as well. At the time of the interview, more than a fifth of the firms were in the process of transition. Some were already cyber squirrels, upgrading their existing computer conflicts checking software or hardware. Others, like the huge Chicago firm utilizing microfiched records, were negotiating between manual and automated systems—between historical records, stashed in index card files or dusty file rooms, and contemporary records, often stored in different computer files and electronic recordkeeping systems. Indeed, one firm in the sample had just shut down its computer conflicts screening system and returned to tried-and-true manual checking after the computer was flagging virtually everything as a potential conflict:

> L2: Right now, the firm's unfortunately at a manual stage. They've been trying to implement a computer stage where they can screen these. But they have individuals that go through thousands and thousands of cards, and they just search manually for the names of all the parties that are listed on the sheet. . . . we've been having some difficulty getting this whole system computerized. I think half the problem is that lawyers' minds think one way and administrative computer people think another, and it's hard to mesh those two mentalities. . . . They just read things a lot different than I do. They're like, "Well, that's in the claimant section of the computer classification." And I'm like, "Who do we represent, who's the party in interest?" And we just were not relating [. . .]
>
> L1: About six months ago when we first got it computerized [. . .] . . . Well, what's funny is that they did it without ever talking to the lawyers. So what happened was, all of a sudden, they went computer. And I went ballistic, okay?

[9]Small firm insurers are more concerned that firms get scheduling and calendaring software—which lessens the probability that lawyers will miss court appearances or allow statutes of limitations to lapse—than the conflicts screening software that often comes along in the package. Large firm insurers explicitly encourage acquiring conflicts software, and indeed, some assist their insureds in developing these systems.

> Because every case in the whole office was kicking out as a conflict, okay? Because they had done so thorough a job that I must have had a hundred a week, . . . 150 a week, okay? . . . So then what happened was . . . we were so swamped in information that we had to basically shut the thing down and go back. See, the mechanical system never was broken. It wasn't busted. It was workin' and it always has worked. . . . Well, it took time. . . . But we had never had a conflict problem in identifying the conflicts until we had the computer to help us. [laughter] Then every case ended up being kicked out for a decision by [L2] or I. And we're looking at these things and none of them are conflicts. But they're saying they are, so we got to look at 'em. . . . and then you go, "Well, this isn't a conflict." But it took ten minutes to figure this out, to go through all this junk that they give you. [6Ch100+]

The largest of the cyber squirrels have been computerized for several decades. Many others have built conflicts data bases in the past few years. Ironically, those going electronic most recently have by and large the most primitive conflicts systems. They frequently utilize an off-the-rack software package available for conflict-of-interest screening, often linked to billing or docket software. Most of these data bases are constructed by inputting data recorded on new matter forms, typically limited to the more superficial information summarized in figure 8.1 regarding the parties directly involved in the case.

With few exceptions, these data bases begin with the purchase of the new software. Because of significant cost and delay, only a couple smaller firms made the considerable investment entailed in entering data from cases that had opened before the software was on-line.

> The problem with the data base is, when do you start? I think we decided to go back four years in inputting data of prior cases into the data base. We had to locate off-storage files. We hired college people over the summer to review all files and abstract the relevant information. . . . It was a huge job. I continually complained to my colleagues in charge of this about how long it was taking. It was a great frustration. Now that we have input the prior files, we are in the process of completing the input of current files. The data base is reasonably reliable. But it would be worthless if we just started with current files. You need at least five years of files to get any kind of depth. [57Ch20–49][10]

As this respondent observes, computer conflicts screening is generally worthless for the first few years after the software purchase. Most firms, cognizant of this limitation, couple computer surveillance with traditional manual scrutiny of index cards on older matters.

[10]Another respondent in a downstate firm estimated that it will be necessary to hire one or more temporary employees for six to eight months to accomplish data entry of closed cases—an estimate that may, based on the experience of larger firms, be too optimistic. Several respondents told me that they intend to backdate their data bases but haven't yet found the time or resources to do so.

Because these data bases tend to be so lean and the artificial intelligence embedded in off-the-rack software somewhat dim-witted (searching only for literal matches), the screening process is relatively quick and easy. Most respondents in smaller firms noted that it takes anywhere from ninety seconds to ten minutes to a few hours to a day, depending on the complexity of the case, the availability of the staff who run the software, and the power and competing demands on the computer hardware. Because most cyber squirrels still couple electronic and manual surveillance with collegial feedback, few new matters are opened quickly. Firms allow anywhere from forty-eight hours to a week for colleagues to respond to messages regarding prospective matters or for partners or committees to meet and sign off on new cases.

The older cyber squirrels are generally found in larger firms, which faced the challenge of limited memories and unwieldy paper trails much earlier than the smaller firms. Their electronic systems date back to the 1970s and 1980s (some following on the heels of the Westinghouse decision), and many have gone through several refinements as firms encountered the systems' limitations. Unlike the smaller firms that unwittingly inherited off-the-rack conflicts software with their other data management systems, many larger firms spent years searching for the most congenial conflicts system, often hiring programmers to develop or customize existing software for their needs.

These systems tend to use more detailed and comprehensive data bases that incorporate more of the items listed in figure 8.1 as well as complex algorithms that search for more than literal name matches. Some firms have purchased or subscribe to data bases from Standard & Poors, Dun & Bradstreet, or other sources, including one developed by ALAS (Siegel 1994) to incorporate up-to-date information on corporate families and affiliates in their conflicts searches. Some systems use a Boolean or so-called Lexis search engine, with which most lawyers are familiar, in the hope that eventually lawyers can do their own conflicts checking.[11] Because these data bases are larger—with more entries and more data per entry—and the artificial intelligence more complex, searches take longer and often require the expertise of specialists. Respondents in these larger firms talk about the turnaround from conflicts searches in terms of hours and days rather than minutes.

Staff. Squirrels create, collect, and examine their detritus in a number of ways. In most firms with manual records, the task is performed by the secretaries of attorneys who hope to bring in a new piece of business. Although a fifth of the firms in the sample that utilize electronic conflicts data bases also delegate responsibility for data input and computer screening to these lawyers or their secretaries, most rely on outside parties. Half delegate these responsibilities to existing administrative personnel. The remainder employ anywhere from one to as many as eight specialists or paralegals who do little else but input data and formulate and execute conflicts searches.

[11] Lexis, an on-line data base of legal cases, opinions, articles, government regulations, listings of practicing lawyers, and much more, allows the user to search on multiple criteria and to specify relationships between search terms ("and," "or," "not," "within x number of words," etc.).

Not surprisingly, staff allocations for conflicts screening reflect economies of scale. Both specialization itself and the size of the specialist group generally mirror firm size. The median-size firm utilizing specialists or conflicts "gurus" (as one respondent called them) employed 287 attorneys, compared with a median size of 41 lawyers working in firms that delegated conflicts screening to administrative personnel and 13 lawyers that left the task to lawyers or their secretaries. On average, firms employed one specialist for every hundred lawyers or so.

Legal Towers. The most elaborate systems devised by mature cyber squirrels use supple and creative artificial intelligence to drive the analysis. A firm I will call "Legal Towers" provides an example. Situated in a soaring high-rise overlooking Chicago's Loop, this general practice firm employs more than 250 attorneys in several offices across the country. At Legal Towers, an electronic surveillance system coexisting with herds of elephants is administered by a specialized conflicts analysis staff of roughly five nonlawyers.

Attorneys hoping to bring in new business complete new matter forms that contain virtually all information enumerated in figure 8.1. The completed form is sent to the conflicts analysis staff, and a description of the case and parties involved is published in a weekly report of potential new matters that is circulated to all lawyers in the firm. Colleagues are expected to call immediately if anything suggests a problem. The conflict analysis staff enter the information on the form into a conflicts data base.

In addition to collecting the information disclosed on new matter forms, the data base includes:

- information regarding nonclients and nonmatters (where attorneys were consulted about a potential case, but the firm declined the representation or the client went elsewhere)
- annual reports of officer or director appointments (even for charities or nonprofit organizations) and significant ownership interests of firm attorneys and their spouses
- all subsequent changes or new developments in clients (e.g., mergers or acquisitions) or matters (e.g., additional parties joining the litigation) that arise after the case is underway
- memoranda that list all former clients (and adverse parties) of lawyers hired laterally from other law firms or government positions[12]
- a log of prior searches on a given entry in the past six months so that attorneys can learn if a particular entity is in play
- a list of parties that require special consideration

When Legal Towers developed this data base more than ten years ago, attorneys realized that information from closed cases was as essential to conflicts screening as that regarding current matters. But it was difficult to ascertain which

[12]Other cyber squirrels also input lists of cases on which secretaries and paralegals worked in previous jobs.

cases across the firm's long institutional history were relevant and which were not. So all files going back to the beginning of the twentieth century were entered into the data base.[13] It took five years to convert the records to the new system. Firms comparable in size to Legal Towers report anywhere from five thousand to twenty thousand active clients, with as many as one hundred matters open for any given client. And these figures reflect just the number of records, not the number of data points in each record. When we consider the tens or hundreds of thousands of closed cases collected in the data base, we begin to get a sense of the magnitude of the searching process.

Conflicts analysts next formulate a search procedure, listing the names of clients, related parties, adverse parties, and other entities, and they specify the data sources to be consulted beyond the conflicts data base.[14] Initially, the database included information on corporate families and relationships—parents, subsidiaries, joint ventures, and the like. But analysts discovered that these relationships changed too frequently, especially in the turbulent 1980s, leading to significant oversights and errors. So all these relational data were methodically stripped from the data base. Conflicts analysts now go on-line or check published references—*Moody's, Dun & Bradstreet, Standard & Poors, Who Owns Whom, The Directory of Corporate Affiliations, Best's Insurance Directory*—for significant relationships.[15]

Because Legal Towers' conflicts data base, like that of virtually all other firms, is restricted to proper names, analysts sometimes fashion specialized searches that are not identity-driven. For example, particular products of competing clients may create conflicts of interest. Say, analysts wanted to find out whether the firm had ever represented breweries. They would search Standard Industry Codes collected from census data and obtain a list of every brewery in the country. Then they would run a search of all these names against the conflicts data base. In Legal Towers, at least, creative and experienced specialists are required to fashion such searches.

Few cyber squirrels have a single integrated data base that amasses all relevant information necessary to ferret out conflicts of interest. Legal Towers must supplement its data base with reference materials to search on corporate families and products. Other firms have separate data bases for corporate affiliates. Some firms have different data bases for litigation dockets, bankruptcy filings, marketing targets, and so forth, which analysts must search separately. And analysts in a large

[13]In some of the other large firms, data bases go back decades, sometimes to the birth of the firm, though the quality and comprehensiveness of the data on early cases is generally low, in some instances limited to client names.

[14]Analysts here are wary of the trend in some other firms to implement user-friendly software so that attorneys can do their own conflicts searches. They explain that you can't leave this task to the attorneys, noting that it is amazing what attorneys don't bother to tell you if you don't ask them. They may be working on a contracts matter and will give you the name of only one party. Staffers must often use "have-you-died?" memoranda to nudge the lawyers to supply complete information and remind them to complete the necessary forms. Respondents in many firms complained that some of their colleagues—especially the nonlitigators—had at best a tenuous grasp on the concept of conflict of interest.

[15]The conflicts analysis staff try to stay abreast of the business news as well, reading the *New York Times, Wall Street Journal,* and various business periodicals on a regular basis, scouring them for news of mergers or other corporate reorganizations involving firm clients.

number of other firms, as I noted earlier, must manually peruse paper records for cases opened before their firm developed the capacity to screen electronically.

Legal Towers, like many large law firms, has been through several versions of custom-made conflict screening software, all of them far more sophisticated than the latest off-the-rack programs and most still subject to considerable dissatisfaction by their users, a lament I heard frequently during the interviews. These software programs work by identifying matches between the specified list of names of parties implicated in a prospective case and all their occurrences in the data base—all possible spellings and misspellings, abbreviations, acronyms, nicknames, variations, and roots of words. Because false positives (the equivalent of false alarms) are preferable to false negatives (missing true conflicts), programs err in favor of the former. The result, of course, is reams of output involving entities with common or similar names or parts of names ("Smith," "Illinois," "and Sons," "University," "General," "State," "Lincoln") that bear no relationship to the parties touched by a particular matter. And even genuine matches do not necessarily bespeak conflicts of interest. The fact that the firm represented John Doe when he bought a house in 1970 probably does not preclude the firm from defending Mary Roe, whose automobile struck John's decades later. Unfortunately, the artificial intelligence cannot make that sort of determination. So conflicts analysts generate often weighty stacks of so-called hits.

Moreover, because a given matter can involve dozens or hundreds of parties that are repeat players in the legal system—banks, insurance companies, environmental polluters, and the like—the output and amount of searching time can be substantial. The computer scan of a single piece of complex litigation or a massive bankruptcy may take an analyst a full day, the time it takes to complete about twenty-five simple searches. (Checking an individual with an uncommon name will take five seconds.) The output generated by the firm's biggest search, which took two people three weeks full-time to complete, fills an entire file drawer. On routine cases, turnaround is generally about two to three days. Emergency matters—temporary restraining orders, for example—can be turned around even faster.

In most multioffice firms, conflicts searches are sent to the headquarters office, where they are conducted, though in a few firms with centralized, integrated data bases, the searches are run by clerks in the branch office. In a couple of the largest multioffice firms, conflicts analysts are available twenty hours a day or more, seven days a week. Analysts in the largest firms receive anywhere from forty to eighty new matters to review each week. In addition to these full-blown searches, lawyers may request preliminary or preengagement searches before they even agree to talk to a prospective client or before they undertake "marketing" activities to attract new clients. No sense wasting time trying to woo the client only to have to decline their business. Preliminary searches are also input into the data base so that rainmakers who have not yet landed the new client, thereby generating an electronic trail, do not conflict each other out of future business.

> And one of the reasons why we do a preengagement check . . . is that information goes into the system and it's there. And so, if you're doing a preengagement check and you see another preengagement check pop up, where somebody else down the

hall is romancing the major competitor of this client, then that information is captured and is presented. And then we have had those kinds of conversations about "Who do we really want to dance with in this situation?" [36Ch100+]

After completing the conflicts search, analysts send an edited version of the output back to the lawyer responsible for the prospective matter who must evaluate each hit for its conflict potential. The output can be massive—especially if the case involves multiple parties, many of whom have a long trail of prior contacts with the firm. The lawyer analyzes the often inch-thick (or more) stack of paper, weeding out the false positives and then assessing the remaining hits. Evaluation may require examining the accounting data base and billing records to determine whether the parties are current or former clients, pulling the files of prior cases that are identified as hits to analyze the nature and substance of the former representation, but especially consulting with the attorneys responsible for the cases that gave rise to the potential conflict. Chapter 9 describes in greater detail how lawyers evaluate potential conflicts.

An example offered by a member of the Professional Responsibility Committee of another large mature cyber squirrel illustrates the conflicts screening process in action:

> I got a call from [a fast-food restaurant client] a couple of days ago. And they've got a problem. It wasn't an emergency problem, but they wanted to have an answer.... They've got a store out in a particular location. They've had some problems with it; there was an injunction entered against them; they were handling it internally.... The first thing I did was say, "Look, stop. Tell me who is involved." Alright? And they gave me a list of people. Now, amongst those people were two property managers, some owners, a pension fund in the East Coast, a mortgage lender—all of which were involved in this property—as well as a large food company that was also in the shopping center and was seeking to restrain the building because of a restrictive covenant—the building of this [fast-food restaurant client] there.... The first thing I did is say, "Look, I don't recognize any of these as being conflicts in our office. But, before you tell me about the situation, let me do a quick check to see if anything [...] " I then filled out this form.... And I asked my secretary, in this case—although normally, I could take more time—to walk it through. So she took it to the various people. They ran it and they gave a printout immediately, which showed any reference [...] And one of them happened to be [a title company client] and another was [another client]. We had a few matters where we were representing those as well as 150 other matters where there was the word [names a word in the name of the first client—a Chicago street name] in it [laughter] or the word [names a different word in the name of first client—a common collectivity name] in it, which I had to ferret through. But that gets back to the software problem. Listed along with those names were the attorneys who were in charge of those clients. And I called those attorneys. One happened to be a partner who was out of town. But his secretary got in touch with him, and he called me back and said, "Yes, I represented them several years ago. It hasn't gotten out of our code book yet. But I haven't done anything for two years, and certainly nothing in this location, so there couldn't be a conflict (thinking that if it's a former client, but it would relate to that particular

piece of property, it could still be a conflict under substantial relationship)." So then I had called another partner who had represented [the second client]. But, again, he said, "No, those aren't current files. We've never done any work for them on this and certainly not a conflict." So I precleared those conflicts. Then what I did—in order to open up the file, which I did the next day, really—is I ran an official search, sent the file through and did whatever had to be done. And then I put the note in the bulletin and I put a voice mail in, saying, "If anyone knows any reason [. . .] " And then I listed all of these various names. And I got a couple of other calls that weren't in the [printout]. [Name of colleague], one of my zoning partners called up and said, "Gee, we don't represent this company, but I know the principals very well. I think we could get some business from them. How are they involved? And, by the way, they're also the main management agent for [a major discount merchandise company] and all their stores—who we do represent—and we've got a very close working relationship." And then I had to find out specifically, therefore, were they going to be involved? And, as we looked through and sorted through, we realized they had been replaced by [the client with the street name] as the management agent. They weren't even involved any more and they wouldn't be a party to this at all. But we were being overcautious, really, in getting all the names. So those are the kinds of things we do. [11Ch100+]

Oversight

Who decides whether a new matter is tainted by a conflict of interest? Who decides whether the case, though unproblematic at present, is likely to detonate in the future or is likely to commit the firm to championing new interests that might preclude undertaking more desirable business? Who decides whether the engagement should be declined or whether corrective action is necessary? And, unrelated to conflicts, who decides whether this is the sort of case the firm wants to undertake? At Legal Towers, these decisions are made by committees, the last one by a New Business Committee and the rest by a Professional Responsibility Committee. In other firms, they are made by firm administrators, the full partnership, or the interested lawyers themselves.

Figure 8.2 shows the types of oversight structures adopted overall and by firm size.[16] A handful of the very smallest firms cede responsibility over conflicts of interest to the collective. As depicted by the horizontal stripes in the bar on the far left, in 6 percent of the firms (with a median size of four lawyers) all attorneys meet daily or at least weekly to discuss new cases and deal with their potential for provoking conflicts of interest. As I explained earlier, several other firms use partnership meetings (herds) as an extra check that all conflicts have been identified. And, in exceptional circumstances, some partnership meetings become fora for resolving difficult conflicts questions or mediating among contentious colleagues warring over whose

[16]The two firms in the sample that are house counsel to insurance companies have no structure at all (the white bars). They expect the insurance companies to sift out the conflicts of interest before referring matters to their staff lawyers.

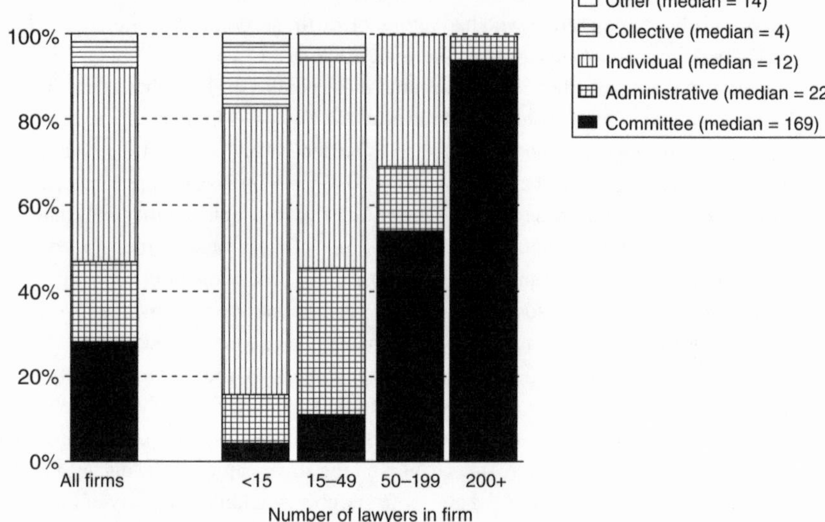

Fig. 8.2. Conflicts Oversight Structure

client will be sacrificed to extinguish an incipient conflict. But few firms—and none with more than twenty attorneys—delegate conflict oversight to the collectivity.

Most firms (45 percent), though especially smaller ones (median size, twelve lawyers), cede responsibility to individual attorneys (vertical stripes). Lawyers who hope to open a new matter are expected to investigate the potential for conflicts of interest—whether through memory, colleagues, records, or data bases—and either resolve those they discover or decline the case altogether. This structural arrangement is certainly more efficient than requiring the collectivity—especially large collectivities—to discuss all new matters. But asking lawyers to police themselves provokes yet another conflict-of-interest problem, because, in most firms, turning away business adversely affects the lawyer's own compensation and may impair his or her relationship with valued clients. Moreover, even disinterested individuals may be unable to appreciate the firmwide opportunity costs imposed by their new case, that their seemingly lucrative $100,000 one-shot matter, for example, will conflict the firm out of a long-term relationship with a client likely to send the firm millions of dollars in legal business. Nor will they necessarily realize that the positions they advocate are likely to undermine the interests of clients in an entirely different practice area of the firm. The problem with individual policing, then, is partly one of incentives but also partly one of omniscience, especially in larger firms. Individuals are less able to calculate these opportunity costs, unlikely to know of client development efforts of colleagues that will be undermined by their new case, oblivious to some positional or issue conflicts the matter is likely to inflame, and rarely privy to the big picture into which this discrete matter fits or doesn't. Larger firms enjoy economies of scale that make it more efficient to locate conflict policing activities in a specialized, centralized structure with better purview of the big picture.

That oversight structures profoundly reflect firm size is dramatically demonstrated in figure 8.2. As firms grow, they tend to forgo communal or individual systems of social control for administrative structures. Note that both the horizontal and vertical bars shrink and then disappear as firms grow; none of the firms with at least 200 lawyers and less than a third of those employing 50 to 199 delegate conflicts responsibility to individuals or the collectivity, a pattern true of more than four-fifths of the smallest firms. In almost a fifth of the firms, ranging in size from 5 to more than 100 lawyers (checkerboard; median size, 22), conflict oversight is delegated to an administrative role. In more than half these firms, managing partners, name partners, or members of the Management or Executive Committee police conflicts; less frequently, this task is delegated to substantive department heads (8 percent, e.g., litigation, bankruptcy, etc.), to a partner responsible for assigning out cases (17 percent), or to some combination of these roles (17 percent). Administrators typically embed their conflicts review in the more general process of approving new clients and matters, judging whether the prospective client is creditworthy, whether the firm has adequate expertise and resources to handle the case, and whether it is the type of case and client the firm wants—themes undoubtedly raised in small-firm collective partnership meetings as well.

Economies of scale and the magnitude of the task in the largest firms justify even greater specialization. Twenty-eight percent of those in the sample—one firm as small as 9 lawyers, though most with hundreds (solid black; median size, 169)—delegate conflicts oversight to specialized committees. About a third of them call these specialized overseers Professional Responsibility/Conduct/Standards/Practice Committees (labeled here "Professional Responsibility"); another third, Conflicts Committees; and about a fifth, Ethics Committees. More than half the firms with Ethics or Professional Responsibility Committees have a separate mechanism for exercising business judgments regarding new matters or clients; this is true of less than a fifth of those firms with Conflicts Committees. Most often, name or managing partners or members of the firm Executive Committee perform this review of new business. In others, it is done by department heads, an assigning or approving partner, or a professional liability partner. And still others use separate New Client or New Business Committees. A final cluster of firms simply combine the review of prospective matters for conflicts or business considerations in a single New Business Committee, reflecting the remainder (14 percent) of the firms with committees overseeing conflicts of interest.[17]

These oversight committees range in size from one to more than ten members. The largest frequently include representatives from the firm's branch offices and major practice areas and may have a special subcommittee to review conflicts of interest, as distinct from other business, ethics, or liability issues. A few also have a paralegal or one or more associates assigned to help with the clerical work and legal research generated by conflicts review. Individuals holding administrative and business develop-

[17]The footprints of malpractice insurers can be seen in committee names and structures. Among the large firms, ALAS members are more likely to police through committees (93 percent versus 77 percent) than through other structural arrangements and are more likely to call their committees Professional Responsibility or New Business Committees than are non-ALAS firms, for which the title Ethics Committee is more popular.

ment or marketing roles are also included in the oversight structure in the hope that they will be better able to identify positional or issue conflicts as well as matters that could preclude future business development elsewhere in the firm. Whatever the committee size, most firms have one or at most two individuals involved in the day-to-day oversight of conflicts issues and do the lion's share of the work.

In the largest of firms (median size, 233), conflicts-like committees have oversight over all new matters. In smaller firms (median size, 97), committees scrutinize only potential conflicts or difficult matters that attorneys choose to refer to them. Overall, committee oversight is optional in half the firms, required only for potential conflicts in a little more than a fifth, and mandatory for all matters in a little more than a quarter. Where oversight is optional or required only for potential conflicts of interest, committees generally meet as needed or once every three or four weeks. Where oversight of all new matters is mandatory, committees generally meet or conduct a conference call every one or two weeks and more frequently, as needed. But committee chairs may be consulted daily on conflicts issues.

Expertise. Lawyers who serve on oversight committees often have special qualities. Because they must command the respect of their colleagues and have sufficient clout to convince a firm gorilla to decline prospective business tainted by a conflict of interest, conflicts czars tend to be relatively senior partners.

> My recommendations to anyone who would do this job is they better start out fairly strong within the firm. You better start out with someone who has a lot of influence within the firm or shouts a lot [laughter] and that somehow has the ability to get people to listen. If you don't do that, it'll be a patronizing situation. I had all sorts of resistance to any form of this and any argument that you could think of was made: "We'll never get any business." I was referred to as the "No Business Committee" rather than the "New Business Committee" [laughter]. [11Ch100+]

Moreover, committee members typically command greater expertise in legal ethics. Several acquired their know-how accidentally, when they became embroiled in a thorny conflict of interest or disqualification case early in their careers and became known as the resident expert and consulted by their colleagues.

> Okay, well, I represented [one of the parties] in the [names case] disqualification case in [. . .] Our consciousness was raised by that. And I guess that's one of the reasons I got stuck with this, is that people thought I knew something after I did that. And so we, I think, got ahead of the curve because of our experience in [that case]. [36Ch100+]

> L: Sometime in the early 1980s I got involved in this role. It was different then. At that point, the firm was a lot smaller. I was sort of recognized as someone who cared about the subject and had acquired some bit of knowledge about it; maybe because I'd gotten disqualified in a former client case and therefore had done some research and knew something about it more than other people. As the firm grew, we had more problems, and so I acquired some knowledge

about it. I tried to get the firm to formalize some procedures in the mid-1980s because I had gotten tired of dealing with conflicts that existed because we were in a conflict problem rather than preventing conflict problems.

S: What was the nature of the procedures in place prior to that?

L: It was "Come to [L] when you get in a wringer." [laughter] . . . At any rate, in the mid-1980s, I started saying we needed formalized procedures. The third time my comment didn't get acted on, I told people that, if they didn't do something, I was going to resign from the Conflicts Committee. That's terrific, except that I was it. And I did resign, and I started telling people that I would only deal with advice about potential conflict problems and how to get out of them. When people came to me with real conflicts, I'd tell them I wouldn't talk to them about it. . . . But it resulted in sufficient pressure to do something. Something got done. So that's how we ended up with this firm procedure. [2Ch100+]

For a substantial number, expertise came at the expense of others; they specialize in professional liability litigation and defend lawyers in other firms for malpractice.

> You have to understand that . . . my department probably has about [large number] pending legal malpractice cases that we're defending right now, okay? And we've been doing that for about [more than 10] years, so we've seen everything that can happen. [6Ch100+]

Several have an abiding interest in legal ethics, have participated in bar association committees, and have taught continuing legal education workshops, seminars, and the like. Many are litigators—almost three-quarters, compared with 42 percent in a random sample of the Chicago bar (Schnorr et al. 1995)—the area of practice in which conflicts of interest tend to be most common and the consequences most costly. Several had considerable experience dealing with conflicts from heading the firm's litigation department, which in many firms serves as a kind of farm team from which conflicts czars are groomed and recruited.

> Well, I've been the head of the Litigation Department for about three or four years. Previously I was a more relatively senior member of the Litigation Department who had a particular interest in the area of the ethical concerns. And probably have been consulted by various people when there was an ethical question for the last fifteen years or longer. Some people called me the conscience of the firm. And so they consulted with me when they had an ethical question. [61Ch20–49]

In many firms, especially the smaller ones, the person with responsibility for conflicts may have no special expertise. Some receive an initiation by fire:

> I will have completed four years on the firm's Executive Committee next October. At no time—not next October, this October—at no time in these four years have I not had a conflict issue in front of me—at no time. The volume for this firm is just simply incredible. There just isn't a day when I don't have something to do with it.

> . . . I'll tell you, it's hard. Professor Hazard [coauthor of *The Law of Lawyering*] is well known. I have here *The Law of Lawyering*. Each of us has these on the shelf. Now that's real nice. But, are we using them? . . . This morning I came in at 7 o'clock and I started to work on a conflicts issue. Here's the matter of "who's the client?" You've got to figure out who's the client before you get to first base. . . . And I'm hoping that Professor Hazard can guide me as to [laughter] who is the client. So, when I first started on the committee, I was relatively new to conflicts. Now I'm not. But I've learned a lot from partners who are quite versed in this. . . . Since we've gotten into it so much, we've learned a lot about it. And we have a significant institutional knowledge regarding conflicts. [16Ch100+]

Others try to stay on top of the literature, citing the prominent case books and professional journals, reviewing ethics opinions, subscribing to the advance sheets.

> L: The rules need amplification by example. If you've read this book [L points to book on his desk on financial accounting standards] or any other technical statutory material, you will see comments to the rules to indicate in what situations the rule is intended to apply and how it should apply. And we don't have that in the area of professional responsibility. And it really takes quite a bit of work to find out. I mean, you have to subscribe to fairly specialized services to even understand how the rules are being used by courts, or else pay attention to it in the advance sheets. And that's not that easy to do. And I think it would help. Because it's part of my responsibility, so, I'm aware of it. I can tell you that partners who I think are terrific lawyers in this firm—and as honest as the day is long, and very ethical—are not anywhere close to as aware of these problems as I am, because they're not forced to deal with it.
>
> S: So, you're the sort of resident expert on . . . ?
>
> L: I hesitate to apply those words to me [laughter] in any context, but I try to keep up with it. And I do that like I do any other reading that I do in this profession. I make it a part of my technical reading. But the opportunities to read about it are far and few between—to be honest with you. There is not that much published in the literature. [27Ch50–99]

One respondent even referred (fondly and with great respect) to a law school ethics professor whose guidance he still follows. And others wing it.

> I've never totally read through the Illinois Code of Professional Responsibility. . . . I became the committee, and when people wanted to have some help, they came to me. But I'm no expert in it. . . . I don't bring anything more to it than judgment—practical business sense and judgment about what's right and what's wrong and what's gray and how can we do it, how can we get around it? I mean not unethically, but ethically, you know. And so far, it's worked; it usually does. [19Ch50–99]

Some respondents suggest that they have no special competence in legal ethics or professional responsibility and indicate that their colleagues are perfectly capable of reaching judgments on their own about whether conflicts of interest threaten a new matter and whether or how they can be resolved. They cite the age and experience of their colleagues, the representation of law professors and former judges on their staff, the fact that their colleagues have defended malpractice cases, serve on bar committees, attend seminars, and the like. One can tease out a rather lively debate among the respondents about whether one needs to be a rocket scientist to deal with conflicts, whether specialized expertise or guidance is necessary, and whether one can trust one's colleagues to abide by the rules. One strand of the argument refers to the sorry state of the literature and lack of practical guidance in the ethics rules.

> But these guys sit around and the Kutak Commission [which produced the *Model Rules of Professional Conduct*] fooled around for years and years and years. And they ducked all the questions where we need guidance. Any fool could have written [Rule] 1.9, 1.7. "Big deal, thanks a lot." But there's absolutely no guidance on parent/subsidiary. . . . You know, "Thanks a bunch, guys!" Because they really haven't dealt with the troublesome issues, where people come to me and want to know answers, and I can't give them answers. And I'm supposed to be up on the rules. I'm up on the rules, and I can tell them that there aren't any answers. . . . And the profession looks to the ABA for this kind of guidance and it's not there. [36Ch100+]

Another strand points to the subtleties in the conflicts rules that often escape those whose area of practice doesn't encounter many conflicts.

> We introduced to them what—I'm sure you're aware of—is this new concept of the unwaivable conflict. And, again, that's not a decision I really want—frankly—maybe some of my real estate partners to make a decision on. Because I don't think they understand it. [11Ch100+]

> More often than not, the attorney can resolve it. But what I've found is that most attorneys have an incomplete understanding of the conflicts rules. And so they don't really have a grasp of what is a conflict and what isn't. You think it would be easy, but it isn't. And so they come to me and just ask for guidance if they're unsure. And they've learned to use me and the other members of the committee as a resource. [7Ch100+]

A third strand questions the scruples or priorities of their colleagues.

> I will tell you that—in all candor—like at any firm, you put fifty lawyers in a room, and they will have varying degrees of sensitivity to what is proper and improper [. . .] . . . I'm sure there is a lawyer in every law firm in America in which they've never seen a conflict of interest come across their door. And those are the ones who you have to sort of keep an eye on and sort of read them the riot act every once in a while and make sure that the firm doesn't find itself in an awkward position. I'll also say there's probably not a law firm in America where that person or persons who fit that bill are near the very top of the food chain. And so then it becomes a little bit harder. [39Ch50–99]

Wherever they come down in this debate, virtually all the respondents cited situations in which they sought outside counsel. Several, especially solo practitioners, called up respected lawyers in other firms when they needed advice.

> You know, honestly, I had never been in that circumstance before. And what I did was, I went over to the law library and tried to see what I could find as far as any research on the issue. There isn't much, as you know. And what I came up with was, I called around to some of my friends who were senior members of the bar. And they said, "Why don't you try this?" And, basically, I winged it. [86CC<10]

A few consulted with a local judge. Several requested an opinion from the Illinois State Bar Association, and one made use of an ethics advisory service offered by a local Chicago law school. Some larger firms would call on the loss prevention counsel of their malpractice insurer. And firms of all sizes have hired outside experts—usually one or two of a handful of nationally known law professors—when they needed advice, needed to validate their judgment, or needed to demonstrate to a client that they took their ethical obligations seriously.

> For the past three years, the firm has had an ethics professor on call who we can consult on the most difficult matters. We ask him to prepare a written opinion which will be filed in the case file. [31Ch50–99]

> But I have some experience litigating conflicts situations, so I have some expertise in the area. And we're smart enough to know to consult with other lawyers outside the firm if we are in doubt. We tell them, "Here are the facts; here is our proposed solution; are we right?" I've even done this once or twice myself on something on which I was working. It's rare that you learn anything you didn't already know. But it's safe. [69Ch20–49]

> Almost always in litigation, where there's a threat of a motion to disqualify or we think there's a good chance one might be filed—whether or not anyone's threatening it—we retain outside counsel, experienced in matters of this kind to advise us, "What should we be doing?" . . . And we want to make sure that that client—in the event that we have to withdraw—feels that we've, nonetheless, we've fully discharged our duty of loyalty to the extent that we can up until the time of withdrawal. And one of the ways that we help ourselves—actually, we really help both clients in this—and say: "We've gone to outside counsel; we're trying to do the right thing; we're trying to follow the ethical rules exactly as they're written." . . . We find generally that clients on both sides are fairly understanding of the—if they're fairly sophisticated at all—they're fairly understanding of that, and give us some time to work it out. [16Ch100+]

Resources. This self-regulatory edifice built of technology, paper, human capital, and bureaucratic procedures does not come cheap. No respondent would even venture to guess the overall cost, and I rarely bothered to ask. An informant at Legal Towers conceded that—given the billable hours of all the attorneys on the firm's New Business and Professional Responsibility Committees, the personnel costs of the five conflicts analysts, the hours lawyers spend reviewing and clearing the conflicts screening output generated for new matters they hope to bring into the firm, the outlay on upgrading computer hardware and software, the hourly fees of on-line data bases and the necessary library resources—conflicts screening on a single matter can cost thousands of dollars (few of which can ultimately be billed directly to the client). Indeed, on a complex case with many coparties, it may cost more to do a conflicts search than the client will be billed in legal fees.[18]

I did ask respondents to estimate how much time they personally devote to the process of evaluating potential conflicts of interest. A few pulled out their time sheets and disclosed precise figures, and others estimated. Most complained that it's taking more and more of their time.

> . . . when I was first responsible for it, it was no more than a couple hours a week. I'd get calls once in a while. And sometimes I'd go weeks without getting calls. And now . . . most of my client work I do between 7:00 and 8:30 or 9:00 in the morning and at nights and weekends. And the day is generally devoted to the firm. So, I mean, it's changed dramatically. [pilot interview #2]

However accurate, these figures are misleading because, in some firms, a single individual performs most of the oversight and in others it is spread more evenly across a number of attorneys. Still, even this partial estimate is telling. Estimates ranged from the informant who said that he would spend more time on conflicts talking to me than he will in the next six months or more to the chair of the Conflicts Committee of a large Chicago firm who devotes fourteen hundred hours per year to these responsibilities.[19]

Overall, about a fifth of the respondents estimated that they spent at least one hour a month, and another fifth, at least one hour a week; an eighth devoted at least an hour a day; and a seventh, more than two hours a day to conflicts. Most of the latter work in large firms or those with mandatory committee oversight of all new business. Seventy-one percent of the respondents serving on committees with mandatory review of all new matters spend at least two hours a day on conflicts of interest, as do half the respondents in firms with 200 attorneys or more. This is true of a fifth of those in firms of 100 to 199 lawyers, 8 percent of those with 50 to 99 lawyers, and none of those with fewer than 50 lawyers. So, although the personnel outlays to oversee or respond to conflicts of interest in large firms can be considerable, this is not so in smaller firms. Respondents in the median firm with fewer than 25 attorneys devote not even an hour a month; in firms of 25 to 49, they spend just an hour a month; and in firms of 50 to 99, more than an hour a week. Of course, these estimates do not include the time of secretaries, billing clerks, and paralegals; administrators who

[18]In that instance, prospective clients may be told that it is not to their benefit to be represented by the firm and that perhaps they would like to be referred to a smaller firm.

[19]A few made estimates of the time commitments of other committee members as well. At least 10 percent of the firms had estimates that exceeded a thousand hours a year. Several respondents suggested that the total was equivalent to one full-time attorney.

approve and assign new matters; other colleagues who also serve on conflicts, ethics, professional responsibility, or new business committees; or firm lawyers who fill out forms, sign off on lists of new matters, wade through computer output, and confer with colleagues before a new case can be opened.

A Taxonomy of Law Firms

The contrast between Legal Towers and the ostrich dramatizes that firms vary in their systems for identifying and evaluating conflicts of interest. Firms can be distinguished by the information technologies they use to ferret out conflicts and by whether they employ specialists to deploy these technologies, whether intelligence systems triangulate by soliciting collective feedback to supplement memories or records, and whether resolutions of potential conflicts are made by lawyers invested in the case or by independent third parties. The classification could be further refined by noting whether third parties are themselves conflicts specialists; whether use of these information technologies, specialists, and third parties is optional or mandatory; the sophistication of the system; and so on.

Table 8.1 classifies firms by the most common and significant variations. The columns distinguish between species. Because information specialists like the conflicts analysts at Legal Towers are only found among cyber squirrels, the last two columns distinguish between cyber squirrels that employ specialists and those that do not. The rows differentiate firms in which lawyers decide on their own or consult third parties about whether a new matter poses a potential conflict and whether they elicit collective feedback from the herd in addition to tapping into their memory or data banks or archives.[20] Percentages on the left of each column are based on column totals; they indicate the distribution of self-regulatory models for a given species. Percentages in parentheses are based on the total sample; they indicate the most frequent combinations in the law firm world. So, for example, although 37 percent of elephants delegate total responsibility for conflicts of interest to invested lawyers, this self-regulatory arrangement represents only 5 percent of the firms of all species in the sample.

The percentages in parentheses along the very bottom of table 8.1 duplicate the distribution of species disclosed earlier in the chapter. As I described previously, we encounter few ostriches or elephants dotting the law firm terrain; five of every six firms are squirrels, and almost two-thirds of the squirrels hail from the cyber subspecies. The largest number of firms by far can be found on the more heavily regulated bottom right corner of the table. One-quarter of the firms in the sample are cyber squirrels eliciting collective feedback and consulting with third parties in evaluating conflicts of interest. And almost half of these also employ specialty staff to help ferret out conflicts.[21] Indeed, most of the activity in table 8.1 is located on

[20]The sample is too small to differentiate between third-party committees and administrators and between firms in which consultation is optional or mandatory.

[21]Still, the Legal Towers model is rare (though more than twice as common as that of the ostrich). Only five firms, 4 percent of the entire sample, have developed the most comprehensive self-regulatory systems, comprised of cyber squirrels soliciting collective feedback and

TABLE 8.1. A TAXONOMY OF FIRMS

	Ostrich	Elephant	Squirrel	Cyber Squirrel	Cyber Squirrel (Special Staff)
Lawyer	100% (2%)	37% (5%)	41% (12%)	8% (3%)	5% (1%)
Collective feedback	0%	42% (6%)	32% (9%)	34% (13%)	0%
Third party	0%	11% (2%)	3% (1%)	24% (9%)	20% (3%)
Collective feedback and third party	0%	11% (2%)	24% (7%)	34% (13%)	75% (12%)
Total	2	19	37	50	20
Percent of total	(2%)	(15%)	(29%)	(39%)	(16%)

Note: Percentage of column is on left; percentage of total is in parentheses.

the diagonal from upper left to lower right. Generally, as species evolve from ostrich to elephant to squirrel to cyber squirrel—from personal to impersonal and from manual to electronic means of retrieving data—they develop a more elaborate self-regulatory system. Column percentages on the libertarian top row decrease with "evolution" (i.e., from left to right), whereas those on the bottom, more heavily regulated rows increase. Still, the evolutionary process is not determinative. Note that even more squirrels than elephants take the libertarian course of ceding responsibility to interested lawyers alone. And firm species does little to predict whether responsible lawyers, operating alone (percentage on the left of the middle three columns of the second row), consult the herd in determining whether a new matter presents a potential conflict of interest.

So how do we explain this taxonomy of firms? It should come as no surprise that firm size plays a powerful role in accounting for the distribution. As firms grow, lawyers cannot function as solitary elephants. Partners need access to institutional memory and a mechanism to learn of the past, present, and future entanglements of their colleagues—whether consulting directly with them or relying on archival records. Larger firms not only have swollen caseloads; their cases also tend to concern more protracted and complex matters involving multiple, often repeat-playing parties—themselves complex organizations continually changing form and structure—each with different stakes in the transaction or litigation. Under these circumstances, ransacking one's memory bank or manually scouring the archives becomes increasingly difficult, as does relying on face-to-face communications among colleagues who often work in different sites and time zones. As firms grow, organizational structures develop specialists to implement the self-regulatory process and adopt forms of cyber surveillance to negotiate the dense and convoluted paper trail.

---

requiring mandatory review by third-party specialists (i.e., conflicts, professional responsibility, new business, or ethics committees) and implemented by a specialized staff. Classification in the bottom right cell of table 8.1 does not require mandatory third-party review, nor are third parties necessarily specialists (they can hold administrative roles, for example). Another nine firms meet all the criteria except *mandatory* committee review.

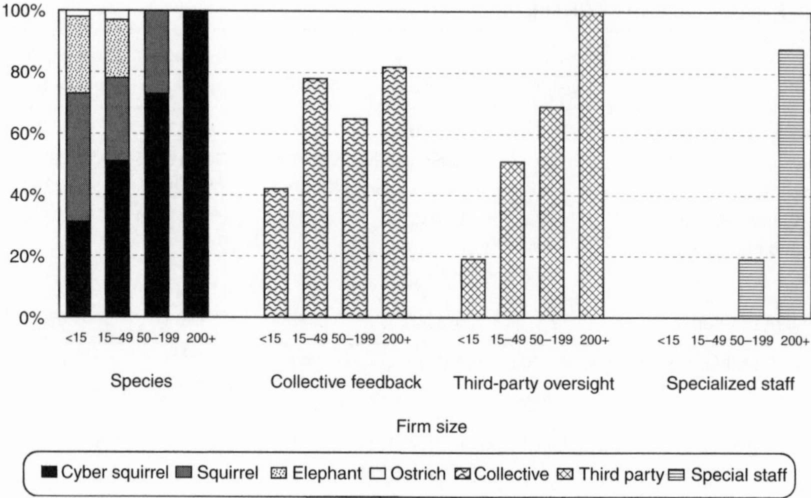

Fig. 8.3. Firm Size

The strong connection between firm size and its self-regulatory system is portrayed in figures 8.3 and 8.4. Figure 8.3 presents simple bivariate relationships between firm size and information technology (i.e., species), collective feedback, third-party oversight, and deployment of specialized staff to implement the self-regulatory process. The figure portrays strong relationships between firm size and species, third-party oversight, and especially use of information specialists, and a somewhat weaker relationship with collective feedback.

The left graph in figure 8.3 confirms that as firms grow, they rely less on personal memories or impersonal records and more on electronic data bases to identify potential conflicts of interest. Squirrels (gray bars) and especially elephants (dotted bars) are found in smaller firms; cyber squirrels (black bars), in larger ones. Indeed, every firm in the sample with more than 200 lawyers is a cyber squirrel. Overall, the median-size elephant has 5 lawyers; squirrel, 13 lawyers; and cyber squirrel, 50 lawyers.[22] Almost two-thirds of elephants, slightly more than half of all squirrels, and only one-fifth of all cyber squirrels employ fewer than 15 attorneys; although a third of the cyber squirrels have more than 100 lawyers, this is true of only 3 percent of the squirrels and none of the elephants.

The next three graphs in figure 8.3 indicate that self-regulation becomes more extensive, comprehensive, and specialized as firms grow. The two middle graphs show that both herds (wavy lines) and especially third-party oversight (cross-hatched) are more likely to be found in larger firms. The median size of the former is 34 attorneys (compared with 12 without collective consultation); the median size of the latter is 60 (compared with 10 without third-party oversight). So, although

[22]Because there are only two ostriches in the sample—of rather disparate size—size estimates are not reliable. Ostriches tend to be small, though not, at least in this sample, as small as elephants.

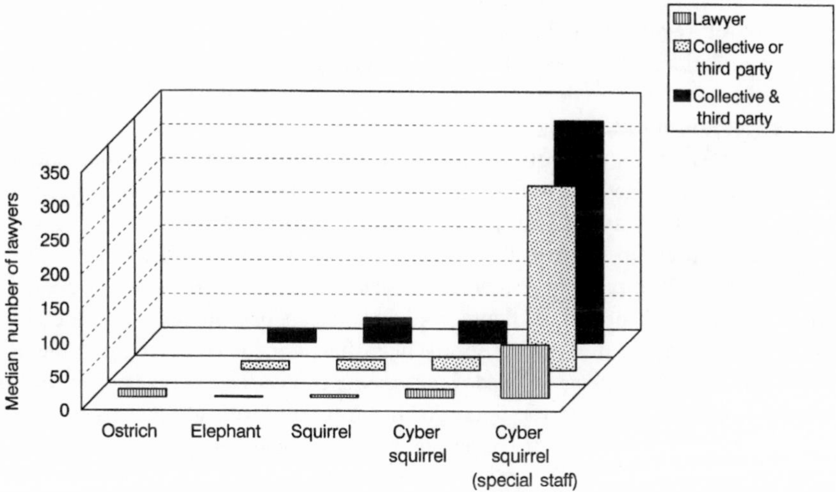

Fig. 8.4. Self-Regulatory System and Median Firm Size

smaller firms are likely to vest responsibility for identifying and resolving conflicts of interest in the lawyers who hope to bring in the business, without any third-party oversight, the majority still require lawyers to canvass colleagues before making these judgments. The far-right graph displays the most dramatic correlation in the figure, that between firm size and specialized staff employed to implement the self-regulatory system (striped bars). Although it is hardly surprising that larger firms are more likely to hire specialists, the magnitude of the difference is stunning: the median size firm with conflicts specialists has 287 attorneys (compared with 16 without them); 90 percent of them employ more than 100 lawyers and none have fewer than 75.

Figure 8.3 demonstrates that as firms grow, they adopt impersonal electronic surveillance of specialized data bases, require consultation among colleagues and third-party oversight, and employ information specialists to facilitate the self-regulatory process. Figure 8.4 pulls these elements of the self-regulatory system together and displays their multivariate relationships. The bars depict median firm size; the taller the bar, the larger the firm.[23] The columns duplicate those from table 8.1; they represent each species, and the last two columns split cyber squirrels into those with and without specialized staff. As we move deeper into the figure, from front to back—from striped, to dotted, to solid bars—self-regulation deepens from responsibility vested in interested lawyers (on the outside edge), to *either* collective consultation or third-party oversight (in the middle), to *both* collective consultation and third-party oversight (in the back). By comparing bars from left to right, we can evaluate differences in firm size by species and by the presence of specialized

[23]Recall from table 8.1 that some of the coordinates in figure 8.4 have very few cases (e.g., there are only two ostriches), especially along the diagonal from deep left to front right.

staff. By comparing bars from front to back, we can assess the relationship between extent of self-regulation and firm size.

The relationship between information technology, or species, and firm size—seen in bivariate form in the left graph in figure 8.3—is not especially impressive in figure 8.4; it is unfortunately obscured somewhat because the huge staff-run cyber squirrels inflate the scale of the y-axis into too-large increments. Still, the relationship is solid, with median firm size increasing consistently from elephant to squirrel to cyber squirrel across each category of regulatory depth.

The relationship between the extensiveness of regulation, reflected in collective feedback, third-party oversight, and specialization, and firm size is more dramatic. As we look deeper in figure 8.4, the median bars increase considerably. Again, staff specialization is most spectacular; these bars on the far right of the figure are so tall that they cast a shadow across the rest of the figure. Those firms in the deepest right corner of the figure, with third-party oversight and triangulated data collection as well as staff specialists, have a median size of 328 attorneys, in contrast with firms in all other columns, which have medians of less than 40. Every firm in the sample with more than 200 lawyers is located in the triangle formed by the three bars in the deep right corner of the figure, 75 percent of them in the extreme corner.[24] As firms grow, then, they are more likely to require colleagues to consult with each other and with third-party overseers and to hire specialized staff to facilitate the process. This pattern reflects, on the one hand, economies of scale in deploying staff and third-party specialists in very large firms, and, on the other hand, the increasing likelihood of conflicts of interest and the difficulties of coordinating large, diverse, dispersed firms that call for more extensive regulation.

Given the strong correlation between firm size and type and depth of self-regulation—which would be even higher if the sample was large enough to sort firms into more homogeneous size categories—there's not much variance left to explain. One can tease out a few crude variables that help account for some of the noise left in figure 8.4.

Part of the correlation between firm size and regulation may be an artifact of firm age. Though conflicts of interest clearly proliferate as firms grow, part of the regulatory challenge arises from the fact that interests do not desist in a quick or predictable fashion. As I noted earlier, firms must keep track of the continually evolving interests of ongoing clients and respect some interests even of former clients. Moreover, as the life spans of firms exceed those of their lawyers, institu-

[24]I will refer to this hatch-market triangle, illustrated here, as the *deep regulatory triangle.*

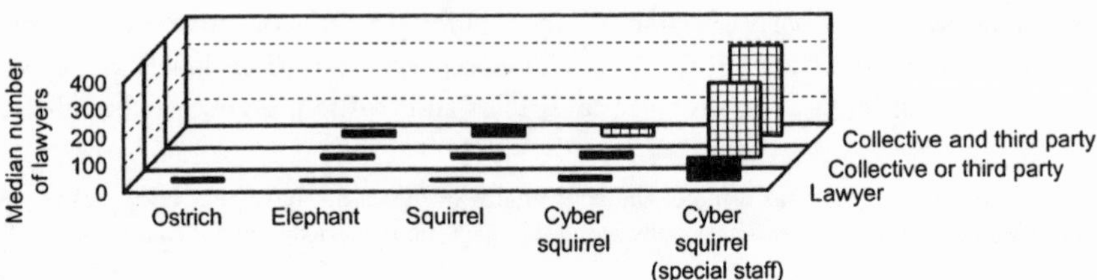

tional memories erode. As law firms age, keeping track of generations of former clients and the interests of the clients of new and departed colleagues strains the brain cells of even the finest elephant.

Indeed, elephant firms on average are fifteen years younger than squirrels, which are twenty-two years younger than cyber squirrels. And, of course, most firms grow as they age. The median size of firms less than twenty-five years old is ten lawyers, compared with twenty-seven for firms twenty-five to seventy-four years old and sixty-nine for firms at least seventy-five years old. In most firms, age and size move together, the self-regulatory system grows with them, and age adds nothing to the relationship between firm size and self-regulation. But the pattern diverges for larger firms. Among the firms with one hundred or more attorneys, 93 percent of those at least seventy-five years old are located in the deep regulatory triangle (cyber squirrels with at least two of the methods of collective feedback, third-party oversight, or specialized staff), compared with 80 percent of those twenty-five to seventy-four years old, but only 8 percent of the substantial number of large firms less than twenty-five years old. Youthfulness then, seems to account for some of the larger firms with more lax self-regulatory systems. Firms may face a chronological tipping point at which they have experienced so much transition, mobility, and change that more extensive intelligence and consultative procedures are needed.

Diversity of practice also affects whether firms develop more extensive systems of self-regulation to ferret out conflicts of interest. As firms diversify, lawyers may know less about the others' business because colleagues with disparate expertise interact infrequently, which necessitates more comprehensive methods to keep everyone apprised of the interests served by partners in the firm. More significant, diversification spawns ongoing relationships with clients because the firm is now staffed to service more of their legal needs. With continuing relationships, client interests do not desist as quickly or predictably, while simultaneously shifting or evolving from matter to matter. As a result, the likelihood that interests of firm clients will collide increases considerably.

Diversification, then, breeds greater vulnerability to conflicts of interest and greater difficulty for self-regulators to stay apprised of the divergent and shifting interests of clients. Firms compensate with greater surveillance and more extensive self-regulation. Controlling for their size, we find that general practices are more likely to be located in the regulatory triangle in the deep right corner of figure 8.4 than are firms offering fewer substantive specialties: all the general practice firms employing one hundred or more lawyers are located in the triangle, compared with two-thirds of those more specialized; for firms with twenty-five to ninety-nine attorneys, the percentages are 56 versus 18, respectively. And at the opposite end of the figure, diversification helps explain whether lawyers in small firms find their memories adequate and reliable for identifying potential conflicts of interest or instead consult their records when a new matter is presented. With diversification, elephants become squirrels. Among general practice firms with no more than ten attorneys, 69 percent are squirrels and 19 percent are elephants, compared with 32 percent and 47 percent, respectively, of their more specialized counterparts.

A related feature of the law firm landscape also accounts for differences among medium to large firms: malpractice insurance carriers. As I noted earlier, the large firm mutual malpractice insurer ALAS has a vigorous loss prevention program, unparalleled among professional liability insurers. Given the amount of oversight exerted and self-regulatory guidance offered, it would come as no surprise if ALAS firms looked somewhat different from their counterparts insured by other malpractice carriers. Indeed, after a few dozen interviews, I could usually guess whether a firm was insured by ALAS by the way my informant described the firm's conflict-of-interest procedures.

Figure 8.5 provides empirical support for my intuitions. The figure differentiates self-regulatory systems adopted by ALAS and non-ALAS firms, controlling for firm size. Firms are distinguished by species and by whether they adopt zero, one, two, or three forms of self-regulation. Because firms must have at least thirty-five to forty lawyers to join ALAS, the figure includes data only for larger firms. Insurance carrier clearly exerts a significant effect, though considerably less so for the megafirms. We find more cyber squirrels pursuing the most exhaustive systems of self-regulation (black and gray bars) among the ALAS firms than among those with different malpractice insurance. The effect is strongest for somewhat smaller firms of fewer than 250 lawyers, where the combined proportion of cyber squirrels pursuing at least two forms of self-regulation (black and gray bars) is more than two and a half times that of non-ALAS firms.

However compelling the empirical and experiential evidence on the impact of insurance carrier on self-regulatory practice may be, one significant caveat must be addressed: the possibility of a selection effect. Law firms do not select their insurers randomly. Just as health insurers providing the best coverage attract the sickest patients, so, too, do their malpractice counterparts attract the riskiest firms. The practice profiles of some large firms—especially boutiques that specialize in insurance defense or intellectual property—place them at lower malpractice risk than general practice firms with securities and banking expertise. As a result, the former can usually find much lower premiums in the private insurance market than they would as a member of ALAS.[25] Similarly, firms that have a less diversified practice or client base or that tend to represent one-shotters may expect fewer conflicts of interest and simultaneously opt for cheaper professional liability insurance *and* invest less in developing an infrastructure to ferret out conflicts of interest. So the relationship between type of insurance and self-regulatory technology may be a spurious one—both artifacts of the firm's practice and client base, on the one hand, and corresponding conflict-of-interest risk, on the other.[26] ALAS membership may serve as a proxy, identifying those firms that

---

[25]Several respondents told me that because of their risk profiles, they paid premiums $2,000 to $3,000 per lawyer lower than those charged by ALAS.

[26]The relationship between ALAS affiliation and extensive self-regulation is not merely an artifact of the proclivity of general practice firms to join ALAS. A strong "ALAS effect" exists even in less diversified firms. Although 50 percent of the ALAS specialty firms of fifty to ninety-nine lawyers are located in the deep right triangle, this is true of 17 percent of those with other insurance; the figures for firms of one hundred plus lawyers are 75 percent and 60 percent, respectively. The ALAS effect is actually slightly higher for the specialized firms than for those with a general practice. So ALAS affiliation exerts an independent effect on surveillance method.

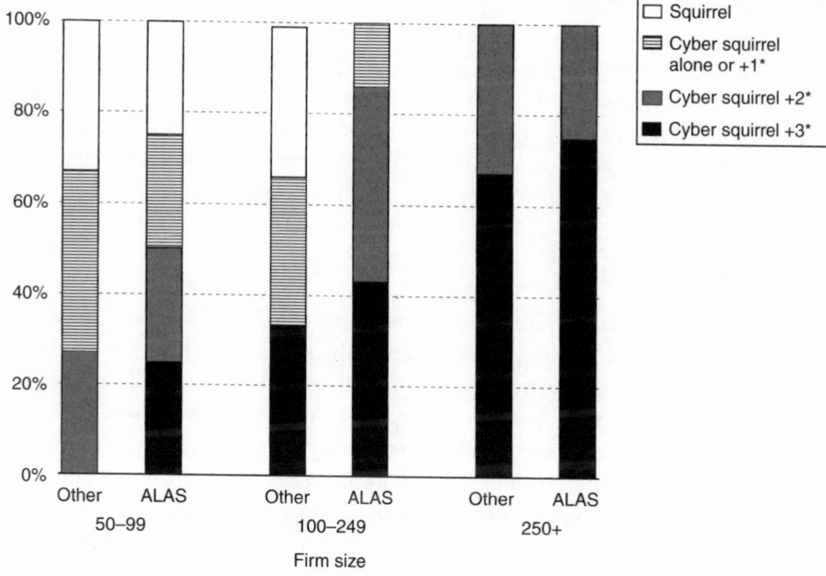

* Plus one or more of the methods of collective feedback, third-party oversight, or specialized staff.

Fig. 8.5. Self-Regulatory System and Insurance

face greater risk and that invest in both better insurance and a more comprehensive regulatory infrastructure, rather than acting as the impetus for that infrastructure. Unfortunately, data to test this hypothesis are not available. Certainly part of the ALAS affect reflects the risks facing its members, but, I suspect, nowhere near all of it.

What about the impact of firm location on intelligence method? Stereotypes might lead us to expect that Chicago firms would be more technologically sophisticated than those downstate. We would be wrong. Among firms of thirty lawyers or fewer (the range of most downstate firms), we find exactly the same proportion of cyber squirrels in Chicago and downstate, despite the fact that the median Chicago firm in this cluster is slightly larger than its downstate counterpart. Indeed, among firms employing fewer than ten attorneys, the downstate firms are almost twice as likely to employ the highest-tech intelligence method—electronic data bases—than are firms located in Chicago. Though, of course, a downstate firm of ten attorneys is likely to have a much more diverse practice profile and more conflicts than its counterpart in Chicago. In fact, its profile will probably look more like that of a Chicago firm five to ten times its size. Even the practice of solo practitioners is much less specialized outside Chicago than in. Once again, then, the risk of encountering conflicts of interest provides a more powerful explanation for intelligence technology than other firm attributes do.

Certainly, a host of other features of the structure, practice, and clientele of a law firm exert an effect on how it identifies conflicts of interest, for example, caseload and the ratio of cases to lawyers; substantive specialties; characteristics of clients, whether one-shotters or repeat players, and the extent to which they have put all their eggs in this basket or patronize other law firms as well; geographic dispersion of firm offices; and the like. Because the sample size is relatively small and the most promising independent variables so profoundly intercorrelated, it would be futile to continue to explore compelling accounts for how firms construct a social and material technology to identify and evaluate conflicts of interest. That there are significant patterns of variation is, however, quite clear.

OTHER CONFLICTS

Although most conflicts of interest in private legal practice arise when firms have the opportunity to take on a new engagement, the previous five chapters attest to alternative trajectories through which conflicts develop. Conflicts blossom "as time goes by," when the client's structure, boundaries, and interests evolve; when new parties join the case; when new evidence emerges; when the case reaches turning points that transform interests and pit allies against each other; when the impact of the case begins to touch clients on the sidelines; and when the outside interests of lawyers and their intimates change. Other conflicts arise as lawyers move from job to job and as law firms hire, fire, and merge.

When the triggering event is expected, apparent, recurrent, and gives rise to a series of routine procedures, it is easier to regulate its potential for detonating conflicts of interest than when it is not. For example, because new matters require the assignment of a billing number against which attorneys can record their time, photocopy documents, make phone calls, and the like, self-regulators can scrutinize potential conflicts before an engagement even begins. This self-regulatory opportunity is more likely, of course, for new matters for new clients than for ongoing clients, because attorneys may be tempted to bypass the bureaucratic procedures and simply allocate their time to the billing number of another engagement for existing clients. When new developments arise in an ongoing case—a client merges with another, or inculpatory evidence is unearthed, for example—the triggering event, about which the attorneys may not be aware, is unexpected and often takes place in an arena far from the firm and its routine procedures. Self-regulators have much less access to these conflict makers than those that occur predictably and regularly under their own noses.

> Now, that kind of case, though, see that kind of case has to be watched all the way, okay? Because as facts develop in the [. . .] There may be no conflict in the beginning and no reason to suspect that there would be, but something can happen in the case that might require a cross-claim. But now, you see, now you're out of the Ethics Committee. Now you're in the individual lawyers' offices. And they have to have enough brains to bring that back. [6Ch100+]

As Time Goes By

None of the other sources of conflict of interest occasion the often elaborate regulatory infrastructure through which new matters must circumnavigate. The majority of firms, for example, have no special procedures or overseers for events and transformations that occur after a case is underway that may reconfigure interests among the parties and may suddenly butt up against those of other firm clients. As one respondent observed, "I don't think there's any bell or whistle that goes off" [17Ch100+] that may trigger a renewed inquiry about potential conflicts of interest. With no policy or process for identifying these downstream conflicts, respondents in these firms hope that clients will inform them or that the conflicts will surface on their own, but they have no way of ensuring that they will.

> I would say we do not have a formal process. The people involved are supposed to recognize that. And we simply do not have any formal process, nor do we have an organized policy for that. I think, normally, we would, again, rely on the fact that the people involved would probably recognize if, all of a sudden, a client is brought in or something changes whereby a client's implicated, and would go to the managing partner. But whether something like that—with our lack of a policy—whether something like that could go unrecognized? Yeah, probably, it probably could. [44Ch20–49]

In other firms, attorneys are expected to fill out an amended form, thereby reopening the matter for conflicts scrutiny when new developments arise. Many large firms have explicit policies recorded in their manuals that require formal updates when cases or clients change course. Some institute an extensive education or indoctrination program to impress upon colleagues the importance of filing new paperwork when the configuration of interests or parties evolves. Some even issue periodic reminders. But, as many respondents concede, there are few incentives to ensure continuing compliance once a billing number has been issued for the case.

> Yes, in theory, every time a new party enters the transaction, you're supposed to add it to the list. Again, since our enforcement mechanism is the ability to open billing numbers, and if you can't open billing numbers, you can't enter your time and you can't do all those things, that's a real stick we have. Once the billing number is open, the stick's gone. And so it's very hard. [28Ch50–99]

And once the matter is off and running, attorneys have many squeakier wheels to grease and higher priorities to address than attending to additional paperwork that is not tied to an instrumental result. More respondents expressed reservations about their ability to stay apprised of conflicts that arise over time than of any other aspect of their system for identifying and avoiding conflicts of interest:

> MP: The updating burden is one which is a problem from time to time. Lawsuits are big and have a lot of parties, and frequently parties get added and lawyers have to be very diligent to update. Transactions can also be the same. You can originally think it's a two-party transaction, and all of a sudden, a new party to the transaction comes in to serve a different function.
>
> L1: We just send a memo around reminding our lawyers to update those things and about the risk of using a miscellaneous or general file for a client and

> putting something in which seems insignificant at the time, but the other name should have been added on a file, but isn't. With all the different ways to do law work and not paperwork, there is that natural human tendency to forget about some of these—what seem like—small details. [5Ch100+]

> It's a fallback. Because the data base—garbage in, garbage out. If people [. . .] I mean, I'm as bad as the next one. If I've got a new matter that's coming in—and it's ABC Company versus XYZ—and nine months later there's a new defendant joined in the suit, I'm not going to go back to the file room or the accounting department and tell them "I've got an additional adverse party," so that when we do our next conflict search it comes up. . . . We have a fairly extensive and expensive software system that we bought with an extensive conflict-of-interest data base capability. . . . It's extremely sophisticated conflict software. But the problem is, I don't think we will get the level of cooperation from the lawyers that we would need to make the software function the way it's supposed to. . . . [sigh] You have to take reality into account. Lawyers hate all of this. They are offended. You have to come back to the real world. The real world is you've got a busy lawyer sitting, drowning in paper at his desk. He or she is not going to fill out the form I want filled out. He or she—90 percent of the time—will not fill out the conflict clearance form. They're going to say, "Secretary, go fill it out, go fill it out." Garbage in, garbage out. . . . So, I don't think it's realistic to expect—realistically—that people will update conflict information as you go. It would be nice, but I'm no better or worse than anybody else—and I don't. I should, but I don't. [79Ch20–49][27]

Because of these difficulties, conflicts regulators try to anticipate future developments even before the case is opened. Or self-regulators attempt to triangulate the process by assigning other staff to monitor alternative sources of information about developing cases or mutating clients. For example, when new parties join litigation down the road or coparties cross-claim or file third-party actions, new documentation is issued by the court—some of it electronically—which can be tracked by nonlawyers in the firm. A few big firms supplement whatever information lawyers supply on changes experienced by their clients by requiring their conflicts department staff to read the business press and continually update the conflicts data base. Others hope that their subscription to an on-line Standard & Poors or Dun & Bradstreet–type data base will supply the missing bells and whistles or at least red flags when corporate families experience birth, death, marriage, divorce, and more temporary dalliances that can ignite conflicts of interests for their lawyers. These efforts are fairly meager, though; none of the respondents suggested that they have developed a computerized process, for example, that automatically issues an alert when an organizational change recorded on the on-line data base pertains to a client, adverse, or affiliated party in an open matter.

Thankfully, many developments in the life course of a case, especially those that arise in litigation, are relatively easy for lawyers to identify. When evidence is

[27]This respondent is the person in his firm delegated to deal with all conflicts of interest.

revealed in discovery that one codefendant is more culpable than the others, when coparties begin to point fingers at one another or balk at a settlement that others favor, counsel can readily see that a conflict of interest is brewing. Other developments occur far away from the courtroom or lawyer's office and are much more resistant to monitoring. Many respondents complained about the difficulty of staying on top of sometimes continual changes in the business operations and organizational structure of clients.

> The biggest conflict problem arises from the growth of clients as they take on new businesses. For example, say we represent a company that makes color TVs. They take on an automobile company. It buys a different color TV company, and we are conflicted out. We represent the world's largest companies; they are buying other companies all the time. . . . The problem is that a single multinational company may make fifty thousand different products. I could hire you to enter every one of these products onto a computer data base. It would take you a month and a half, and by the time you finished, the company would have already bought another seven new companies with still more products. [42Ch20–49]

And still other developments in an engagement may be apparent to the lawyers orchestrating them but are taken for granted because they are compatible with the interests of the client. What may be overlooked, though, is the indirect but adverse impact of these developments as they ripple out to other clients of the firm. Advocates, for example, may find it necessary, as a case evolves, to advance a legal argument or stake out a position that, if successful, would harm a large number of other clients of the firm with no direct standing in the case. When it is apparent at the outset that such a positional conflict is likely, colleagues have an opportunity to alert conflicts overseers or the lawyers involved and perhaps argue that the case be declined. When positions and legal arguments unexpectedly change course well into the engagement, colleagues may have no way of knowing that a positional conflict is about to detonate unless the lawyers involved update and reopen the conflicts process, an occurrence about which I almost never heard. Lawyers seem more likely to take notice when the demographics of a case change—when parties come and go—than when interests or substance evolve.

As a large-firm respondent observed at the opening of chapter 6, "a conflicts search is really only a snapshot and, as time goes forward, things can change." [7Ch100+] Conflicts regulators require motion pictures or at least an ongoing series of snapshots. Unfortunately, some parties pose only once and then move out beyond the camera's range. As a result, conflicts that unpredictably accrete as engagements ebb and flow are most resilient to regulatory intervention. None of the firms have quite managed to overcome this barrier.

Hiring

Recruiting new lawyers represents one of the few regular occasions aside from intaking new matters where firms have the opportunity to regulate the potential that new colleagues will bring conflicts of interest into the firm. Recall from chapter 7 that mobile lawyers can detonate conflicts of interest from both the business they bring and that they leave behind. Traveling cases and clients, just like new matters, may pose direct or indirect adversities of interest with current or former clients of the host firm, or they may arrive conflict-free but preclude taking on lucrative business in the future. Moreover, even on cases they leave behind, if mobile lawyers have actual knowledge of the confidences of a client of their former firm, they are personally barred from taking an adverse position against that client, and correlatively, that knowledge is imputed to all their new colleagues in the second firm, who are also barred.

So, before hiring new lawyers, firms can scrutinize the matters that candidates have worked on in the past and those they hope to bring with them to determine whether the interests of these clients conflict with those of prospective or actual firm clients. Where substantial interests collide, the firm or prospective candidate may decide to end the conversation, they may negotiate over how the conflicts can be resolved and at the expense of whose clients, or they may undertake prophylactic measures to lessen the likelihood that the conflicts carried by the newcomer will infect the rest of the host firm.

Firms respond to this regulatory opportunity much like they do for new matters—as ostriches, elephants, squirrels, and cyber squirrels. Some use computer data bases to check for conflicts; others consult records; some rely on their memories; others do nothing, dealing with the conflicts, if any, after the lateral joins the firm; and some also systematically confer among the herd before bringing in a new attorney. Though the options are the same, the taxonomy is generally more primitive. We find more ostriches and elephants and fewer squirrels and cyber squirrels when new lawyers are recruited than when new matters are evaluated. Because firms hire laterally with far less frequency than they acquire new business, the regulatory apparatus tends to be more ad hoc and far less specialized. Though some of the larger firms have hiring committees, assessment of potential conflicts of interest occasioned by the hire is often addressed elsewhere in the firm—by conflicts or professional responsibility committees, administrators, or staff.

Firms with the most extensive and technologically sophisticated system for regulating the intake of new matters also tend to do more to identify and resolve potential conflicts of interest that arise in lateral hiring. Before conversations with candidates get very far, these firms search their conflicts data base to identify the cases they have with the law firm the lateral hopes to leave; they also issue a memorandum to all partners in the firm asking about any matters or potential matters that involve that firm. (Open adversities between the two firms could possibly disqualify the prospective host, especially if the mobile lawyer had learned of any confidences regarding the client of his or her former firm.)

> A lot of it [conflicts evaluation] goes through prior. I mean, we can easily, we'll know where he's coming from and who he worked for before. I mean that's something that you find out in the first interview or even before then. And the thing we do quickly is pump his prior firms—'cause law firms who represent clients are also on the system too—pump his prior firm through this system to see if we have

matters involving his firm that he may have worked on. And then start clearing them before we ever hire him. [47Ch20–49]

Before a cyber squirrel makes an offer of employment, candidates are asked to supply a list of clients, cases, or occasionally products that they intend to bring with them and that they worked on in the prior firm and will be leaving behind. They also name adverse parties involved in any of these matters and clients they know so much about that the clients might object to the new firm taking a position adverse to them.[28] In some firms, candidates fill out extensive questionnaires that elicit this information; in some, they simply try to reconstruct these lists; and in others, associates or support staff are assigned to probe, record, and research their life histories. Parties that show up in these lists are then checked against the firm's electronic conflicts data base, and hits are evaluated in much the same way as when they arise in the intake of a new matter. These lists are often also circulated to partners of the firm, who are asked to sign off that they see no lurking potential conflicts.

L: But I'll sit down with somebody who wants to come over from a Chicago firm. And I'll say, "Tell me about your cases. Tell me about your work load." And he'll say, "Well, I'm going to, you know, I've got these three cases against company A." And I'll say, "Oops! We represent company A. Not in those lawsuits maybe, but we do a lot of work with them. And that would be a problem." And then they might say, "Well, then I can't leave, because that's my lifeblood." But we do have to examine every one of the clients, . . . including the ones they're going to leave behind. Normally, we will check—it's part of our normal practice—"Does anybody have an adverse relationship with this law firm that this partner is in?" We have electronic mail in our firm, so all our offices are linked. So we can send out a memo to every attorney in the office and get responses back by the end of the day. You know, "Does anybody have an adverse conflict with Sidley & Austin?" And we'll get a list of all the cases where we're opposed. And then we got to find out from this guy, "Well, do you have any contact with any of these clients or matters?" 'Cause even though he's not bringing the matter over, we don't want to get into a situation where Sidley is now, suddenly, moving to disqualify us because we've hired partner A who was there when they had these cases. And that happens a lot. . . . Lots of people go away . . .

S: So, it sounds like a fair number of potential hires don't work out because of conflicts?

L: Oh yeah, 80 percent. Oh yeah, easily 80 percent don't work out. [18Ch100+]

The most rigorous firms follow these procedures for entry-level associates, law students who clerk during the summer, secretaries, and paralegals as well as more seasoned associates or lateral partners who may be importing a great deal of business. More often, firms invoke this elaborate routine when hiring lateral partners

[28]Several respondents noted that it is important to know about affiliated parties as well as simply clients and adverse parties, but none seemed to question candidates about them.

with a substantial book of business, and relax or skip the procedures with more junior associates.

> Certainly, a lateral partner who's bringing business would have to disclose to us his business. In fact, at this firm, he would have to disclose it in intimate detail to pass the threshold. But we don't do that with lateral associates. They certainly talk to us about it; we certainly ask them about it. . . . That's where I said we probably don't do a very good job of it. We, probably, in the exercise of a lot of caution, ought to work those people over a lot harder about what they've worked on. We have some kind of disclosure. But the truth of the matter is, we probably don't do a very good job of it. [44Ch20–49]

Or they review the mobile business for potential conflicts but disregard clients that will remain in the former firm for whom laterals did work and obtained confidences. Or they review litigation matters but not transactional ones.

Even when pursued rigorously, these procedures are not without problems. Lawyers can find it difficult to remember all the matters on which they have worked or acquired confidential information.

> You can't really ask the guy, "Who have you worked on the last seven years." I was hired laterally; I couldn't remember what I did for seven years; I can't even remember what I did last week. [40Ch20–49]

Lateral candidates do not always have access to firm records that would allow them to methodically reconstruct their involvements over their career, and efforts to secure these records may prematurely signal to their firm that they are looking to leave. Because of possible omissions and inaccuracies in these reconstructed client lists, some host firms take the reverse route—exposing candidates to their own roster of clients and asking them to note any potential conflicts.

Even more problematic, client lists are themselves confidential or proprietary. Many informants indicated to me that it was ethically improper to ask candidates to provide them.

> See, I can't ask an associate, "What clients have you worked on?" That would be a breach of ethics for them to disclose it to me. I don't know how to do that. That's a good question. [77Ch10–19]

> Well, that's one of the areas that I'm always uncomfortable with. We probably do things that we shouldn't do. . . . Somebody is brought to us either by a headhunter or calls us or maybe we approach somebody, and we say, "What business are you going to bring over?" We want to make sure we're getting somebody who's not diluting our partnership interest. But we also have to make sure we're not bringing somebody in who's going to have incredible conflicts. That results in partner A in a firm disclosing information to us that probably we're not entitled to. But this goes on throughout [. . .] It's like everybody ignores it. Someday, somebody [. . .] Well, there have been some lawsuits about this, I guess. [18Ch100+]

> The harder question is, if you are—for whatever reason—being solicited by lawyers from another firm who would like to come to work with you. And then it gets to be very difficult because you don't want to sit down and start going over what is proprietary information until and unless everybody understands that that individual's leaving—which makes things very difficult. You can get some sense, but you can't really work it out until afterward. Because it's just not proper, it's not appropriate. It's one of the reasons why [this firm] doesn't go around looking for lots of laterals. [23Ch100+]

Because of these ethical concerns, some recruiters ask for a client "profile" rather than a list or initiate a general discussion of the sorts of work the lateral candidate has done or intends to do.

And, certainly, neither side wants to divulge client lists unless they are fairly certain the hire will go through. So, as a respondent in the last chapter poignantly lamented, by the time firms and candidates recognize that serious conflicts of interest threaten the deal, it may be difficult to unmake it. But the risk of proceeding can be substantial. Mobile lawyers will be forced to leave behind the business that guaranteed a livelihood in the new firm and that attracted the firm to them in the first place. Or their future stream of business will be continually threatened by systemic conflicts between the interests of these new clients and those of ongoing clients of the host firm. Moreover, the host firm faces the risk that it has hired a Typhoid Mary, importing confidences into the firm that will be imputed to all.

Because of these difficulties, much of the self-regulatory activity is delayed until just before the candidate is formally hired, between the time the offer is accepted and the lateral joins the firm, or even after the lateral arrives.[29]

> Well, it's a little hard until somebody is actually in the door to get the conflict resolved. . . . You know, there's fiduciary duties to partners in the other firm. They can't necessarily be going out and negotiating for what the deals would be in the new firm until they're here. . . . Last week, I ran a computer conflicts check and one of the clients the partner was bringing in was adverse to . . . other clients in the firm. We sent him a copy of the relevant matters and without the description; just to show him who the parties were and said to him, "These are the individuals involved. You should get together and talk with the billing attorney [in our firm] and find out what the arrangement is. . . . I mean, you ought to make the assumption that you may not be able to bring this client with you." The primary purpose in our initial screen is to not bring a lateral partner in who subsequently finds out

[29]Timing is critical because, as we will see in the next chapter, prophylactic measures like ethical screens or Chinese walls are valid only if they are erected before the lateral joins the firm. One firm in the sample takes no risks:

> When the new lawyer arrives at the firm, they are immediately placed in a Chinese wall from everything. This may last for several months. Before they are assigned to any new matter or before they can open any new file, an extensive conflicts check will be performed. So the incoming lawyer is gradually released from the Chinese wall. This happens for everyone. [31Ch50–99]

> that his practice has been destroyed from conflicts. Because that's just the worst result for everybody. So we want to make sure that the lateral hire is aware of the conflict in advance. . . . The actual working out of the conflicts does not occur until they are in the firm. [1Ch100+]

Once they join the firm, laterals with mobile business complete new matter forms for each case, which go through a regular conflicts screening process, and new matter memoranda are circulated throughout the firm for feedback on potential conflicts. And, of course, the normal circulation of memoranda eliciting input on prospective new matters developed by stable partners in the firm represents a final strand in the regulatory safety net. Laterals are carefully instructed to review these memoranda for new matters that may be adverse to the interests of clients left behind in their former firm. This step is particularly important, because clients left behind will rarely, if ever, be added to the conflicts data base of the new firm but can nonetheless result in disqualification if the firm takes a matter adverse to their interests. The laterals themselves are probably the only source of information on these clients.

Firms with less rigorous procedures for evaluating lateral hiring prospects relax or skip one or more of the regulatory activities that I have just described. Squirrels simply scrutinize or compare client lists but don't bother to check them against the computer data base (if they have one). Elephants do not consult any records. They tend to have a more general conversation with candidates about the nature of their mutual work rather than an exchange of client lists, and they tell me that they would know right away if any of the prospective candidate's clients had interests that conflicted with a client of the firm. Elephants tend to be smaller firms located in smaller towns. Many explained that not only do they know the caseload of their entire firm but they also know the client base of their competitors. So they can anticipate the kinds of conflicts that might arise when they hire attorneys from particular local firms.

> And generally in a town this size you know what firms represent what companies, etc., I mean, or major individuals in town. You know that this insurance company is a client of this firm, primarily. Or you know that this insurance company sends cases first to this firm, second to this firm, and third to this firm. Or that this major corporation is represented in town by this company. And so you'd know that, say there's a General Motors case. And you know that, for example, [a large local law firm] here in town represents General Motors. So, if we did lateral hire and we got a matter against General Motors, we'd know that they came [. . .] You'd ask them, "Did you ever work on General Motors files?" And they say, "Yeah." "Do you have any familiarity with George Jones, in products liability?" They say, "Yeah." "Okay, so we've got this matter. You know, you can't be involved in this. But I don't want to know anything you know about General Motors. You can't be involved in this file." And we set up a wall. [50DSL20–49]

But, curiously, I found elephants among the very largest firms in the sample as well:

> L: Oh yes, you wouldn't take anybody, you would not bring in a practice group without knowing their clients.
> S: And do you actually go through the computer system with all of their clients? Or how does the evaluation [. . .]
> L: Well, it jumps out. All you've gotta do is look, Susan. I know. . . . If I saw [four Fortune 500 companies in diverse sectors], I'd say forget about it. [30Ch100+]

Ostriches do nothing and instruct newly hired attorneys that they are not to take cases against their former firm or expect that laterals will inform them if any cases in the host firm conflict with cases, clients, or confidences shared in the prior firm.

> You only have a conflict when the guy comes on board and then you go, "Oh my God!" and Chinese wall them out. We're willing to take the risk. Maybe we're a little bit reckless here. [40Ch20–49]

> I don't know that we necessarily address that. One lawyer came with us maybe seven years ago. And we knew he had clients. And I guess it was at least tacitly understood—I don't know that we necessarily articulated it—that we would deal with whatever conflicts came up when they came up, rather than try to create a policy ahead of time. And, as a matter of fact, I don't think we've had problems. [74DSL<10]

> We have clients here that were opponents of clients at the other firm that the associate worked in. I guess I have to rely on the associate to tell me—if he or she is working on a matter which she's worked on the other side of—to tell me that. And then we have to take him or her off that assignment. [77Ch10–19]

This expectation—that newly hired lawyers will inform them if conflicts arise—exists even in host firms that do not function as herds and do not confer with one another about prospective cases. In these firms, laterals have no way to know about potential conflicts in cases to which they are not assigned.

> L: With the individual hires, we don't [check ahead of time]. But it has been a problem in the sense that we've hired a number of people over the last year. We've grown fairly rapidly, and we hire from a lot of the other law firms. So what happens is that, all of a sudden, we find somebody who's been on the other side or for another defendant in a case, on a very large piece of litigation. That happens quite a bit actually. Our feeling on that is we simply make sure that person has nothing to do with that litigation.
> S: How would you know that if [. . .]
> L: Oh, they'll tell you.
> S: So, are lawyers in the firm notified of all new matters, so they can [. . .]

L: No, no. But what [. . .] Yeah, you gotta understand what will happen is somebody comes over. And let's say we've got—I don't know—some big matter. And one of two things happens. First, the person comes in and goes, "Oh, you've got some big matter and I worked on that over there. And it's an interesting case." [laughs] Immediately, we sit down and say, "First of all, we don't talk about it. You don't talk to us about it; we don't talk to you. If you're asked to do anything on this case, you decline and that's it. You're off, you know, stay away from that case totally." The other circumstance is the person doesn't know about it. They get their first assignment, and they say, "Oh, um, oh, I worked on this over [. . .] " We tell people ahead of time: "If you get an assignment when you come in that is a matter that you have worked on at your firm, let us know immediately. Because we don't want you to work on any matters that you worked on."

S: How about . . . where they weren't assigned to the case? They didn't know you were doing the case. And inadvertently—not knowing that—there's a conversation, and then suddenly [. . .]

L: I see. They provide information about the case that we would not normally have. . . . It's never happened. But it could. I could see circumstances where it would happen. [33Ch50–99]

Many firms are ostriches because they never hire laterally or do so only rarely, and when they do, the mobile lawyers rarely travel with significant business or relevant confidences. These firms hire right out of law school or only members of their own families; or their lateral candidates come from another part of the state or from much larger firms with an entirely different client base. So these firms deal with conflicts when they arise—sometimes much to the lawyers' dismay—rather than erecting an anticipatory regulatory structure to avoid them in the first place.

Because the law firms whose lateral hiring practices put them at greatest risk of detonating conflicts of interest are often the same ones at greatest risk of encountering conflicts when taking on new business, the extent and depth of self-regulation in hiring and in business generation tend to be correlated. Practices are correlated as well because some firms rely on their infrastructure of technology, procedures, and personnel to process new matters when they consider a lateral hire. They defer to the staff and committee specialists, computer data bases, and systems for circularizing new matters when they want to identify the conflicts of interest likely to be imported by a new colleague. Still, the regulatory process surrounding lawyer mobility is less rigorous overall. Though we can find the rare elephant—when it comes to intaking new business—that behaves like a squirrel when hiring colleagues, the regulation of hiring in most firms regresses from that developed to address new business.

Again, a caveat is necessary. As I noted before, Illinois is one of only a handful of states that allow conflicts of interest that arise from mergers or lateral hiring to be resolved by shielding the mobile lawyer or lawyers behind a Chinese wall.[30]

[30]More on the use of Chinese walls or ethical screens in chapter 9.

Other states permit this prophylactic device when firms hire government lawyers but not private practitioners who move laterally from another firm, at least not without the consent of all the affected clients. Perhaps the relatively laissez-faire approach toward lateral hiring of many firms in the sample reflects this safety net available to Illinois lawyers. Perhaps few other states house as many ostriches and elephants as does Illinois.

Testing this hypothesis requires multistate data, carefully matched firms, and no other significant variation across states. Unfortunately, I have only limited data, derived from a handful of pilot interviews conducted in large firms located in another Midwestern state that does not permit the use of ethical screens to ameliorate conflicts of interest aroused by private sector lateral hiring. When it came to identifying potential conflicts in hiring, most of these firms were cyber squirrels or at least squirrels, systematically assembling and analyzing—before making an offer—lists of clients and confidences likely to be imported by a mobile lawyer. But these were also large firms, in which more methodical scrutiny occurs even in Illinois. Moreover, the pilot firms described practices no more exhaustive or rigorous than those found in their Illinois large-firm counterparts. Because these pilot interviews do not include smaller firms, where self-regulation would probably be less thorough, and because the number of firms is small, this inquiry is inconclusive. I suspect, though, that differences exist, but not of significant magnitude.

Mergers

> If we try to merge with another firm our size, I'd probably take an early retirement [laughter] rather than wrestle with the potential conflict problems. I mean, they would be massive. [3Ch100+]

As I noted in chapter 7, a substantial number of firms in the sample had flirted with or undertaken mergers or acquisitions of groups of lawyers in the decade prior to the study. In most instances, whales were swallowing goldfish; few of the marriages even approximated the kinds of mega-mergers whose mere contemplation raised the blood pressure of this respondent. So when I asked about the procedures to identify or evaluate conflicts of interest that can arise when two firms or practice groups tie the knot, most responded that they were basically the same as those for lateral hires when the mobile lawyer is bringing a substantial book of business.

But there are some interesting differences. First, the business implications of mergers are far more critical. Although some colleagues are hired laterally solely for their skill and expertise and not their client base, merger partners are attractive only if, as one respondent noted, they are "not diluting our partnership interest." If conflicts of interest that blossom between merging firms dictate that too many clients be jettisoned on either side, the marriage no longer makes economic sense.

> But let's assume that we were thinking of merging with a fifteen-person firm. And they had a certain book of business; they had a sort of a client list. In that instance, we might begin comparing. And they say, "Well, we think we can produce three million dollars a year." We want to be damn sure that, if one million of their

> three million is coming from a certain client, it isn't at odds with some principal interest we have here. Because then they'll come over and their business will suddenly be reduced by one third. . . . We say at three million, it makes sense, at two million it makes no sense—not at what they want to be paid and how much space we have to take on and everything. . . . And so, if there is some built-in conflict right there—we're regularly representing somebody who is adverse to their interests somehow—then you'd make that judgment. . . . But with the lateral hires—individual lawyers or two individual lawyers from an ex-firm that they think they can keep some business—it's less important. They don't bring that kind of business with them. They might say, "Well, we think we can produce three hundred thousand or four hundred thousand." But if you're looking at a big number and you really have a built-in conflict, you'd want to know it right at the beginning. And it would kill the merger. It would be a deal killer. [19Ch50–99]

Surprises that are discovered after the honeymoon, which may be relatively easy to manage in a lateral hire by throwing the mobile lawyer behind a Chinese wall, are often intractable when they involve a mobile firm and can have disastrous consequences for the bottom line of the newly merged partnership. So parties are much more likely to exchange detailed client lists when they contemplate merging than when they consider lateral hiring.

Second, the asymmetries of clout between the host firm and lateral candidate, which allow the former to call the shots, erode with potential mergers. Conflicts are less likely to be resolved in favor of the powerful host, and therefore, the negotiation process becomes more difficult than in lateral hiring, where the host firm holds all the cards. Because client lists are proprietary information, firms will not want to disclose them to a competitor too early in the courtship unless it is quite clear that the marriage will be consummated. So the process of dealing with conflicts aroused by the marriage is often delayed until the eleventh hour, sometimes with disastrous consequences.

> In a hiring situation—from a business point of view—I'm assuming we have all the leverage. We're the acquirer and they're the acquiree. In a merger situation, where you're tending to bring books of business together, that's where it gets more difficult, because the economic leverage tends to be diminished. There's more of an equality of positions of the parties. And neither side wants to give up what it considers to be its vested interest in the economics. Those we typically work through the business side of that deal first, and then go to disclosures on client lists. And we've had two that have just not worked for us when we got that level. And it sort of seems like a waste, but it's the only way to do it. You can't, no one will disclose their client list until they feel relatively confident that the business side of the deal is going to be suitable—if not in detail, at least in general principles. [27Ch50–99]

Third, as the size and diversity of the client base of the suitors increase, conflicts of interest become inevitable.

> I think if you want the deal enough, . . . the conflicts problems do not, generally, run the show. But does it mean that there are difficulties? Yeah, there are difficulties. But I don't think those difficulties were ever not there. . . . And I guess it's only difficult when you're talking about firms getting bigger and firms becoming less dependent on one or two major clients—where they spread out their tentacles more, reaching more people. Then mergers become difficult. Not because people are necessarily more conscious of conflicts in that area—because of the economics, no one is going to go into it when there's a threat of losing the client—but because there are just more conflicts, because the firms' client bases have become greater. Instead of you having five major corporate clients who give you 50 percent of your billings, you may have a hundred clients today, each of whom give you—because no one is counsel to the major corporations on everything anymore. [11Ch100+]

As a result, firms may employ an incremental process for identifying and sorting out conflicts, starting with the most significant and sacrosanct clients and then working their way down when it looks like a marriage might work.

> Well, we generally would exchange a list of the top thirty or top fifty clients, if we're talking about a merger situation, to see if we could highlight obvious conflicts before we got too far down the road. But if there are significant clients, we'll be aware of that typically prior to the time that we engage in any meaningful conversations. [9Ch100+]

Because mergers and acquisitions are even less common than lateral hiring, the procedures for ferreting out conflicts of interest that might undermine the marriage are even more likely to be ad hoc. The fact that suitors will consider possible conflicts of interests that might erupt and will exchange client lists to ferret out potential conflicts does not mean that they will do so systematically. Though we find fewer ostriches under the altar, there are still plenty of elephants.

Outside Interests

Firms do far less to determine whether lawyers' board memberships, investments, financial interests, family or social connections, or other outside interests conflict with those of their clients. A minority of firms try to avoid the problem by barring colleagues from serving on boards or investing with clients. One firm even forbade spouses who practiced in similar areas of law from working within one hundred miles of the firm. But as I noted in chapter 7, lawyers will inevitably take on outside interests, however much firms and malpractice insurers discourage them, and given the social networks of clients, lawyers, and families, adversities of interest can be expected from time to time. The key is to identify these outside interests so that they do not conflict with those of clients and then either find clients more disinterested counsel, require that lawyers divest their interests, or shield lawyers behind an ethical screen.

Firms stay abreast of colleagues' outside interests in a variety of ways. Some require that lawyers get permission before they serve on a board, make an investment, or trade their securities. Aside from limiting colleagues' embrace of outside interests, this policy also provides an opportunity to track them. Some firms or their malpractice insurers require all lawyers to submit an annual list of directorships, board memberships, personal and familial investments, holdings, and other business interests. A couple of the cyber squirrels input these disclosures into their conflicts data base so that the computer would generate a hit, for example, if the adverse party in a lawsuit was partly owned by a firm partner. Data bases do not, however, contain the affiliations of spouses and intimates of firm personnel. Most firms rely on colleagues to inform the relevant parties when these private interests are adverse to those of a current or prospective firm client. Recall from figure 8.1 that the more detailed new matter forms ask whether lawyers have a relationship other than that of attorney/client (e.g., officer, director, or partner of a client; business transaction with a client; investment in client's securities) or whether any immediate family member of a firm attorney has an ownership interest in or is an officer, director, or employee of the prospective client. These new matter forms are likely to elicit the narrow set of conflicts triggered by the outside interests of those filling out the forms. To learn of conflicts of other colleagues in the firm—that a spouse works for the corporation being sued or for the law firm defending the suit, or that a colleague serves on the board of a hospital that is an adverse party in the case—new matter forms need to be circulated throughout the herd and signed off by all lawyers and support staff. When outside interests change in the course of a matter—a partner gets married or takes on a directorship, a family business launches a hostile takeover of a client or adverse party, an associate makes some real estate investments—the odds that affected lawyers will be alerted to the new conflicts are much lower.

BLIND SPOTS

This chapter has documented considerable variation across firms in procedures for ferreting out potential conflicts of interest as well as differences within them in how lawyers identify conflicts that arise from various sources. We have watched packs of cyber squirrels frenetically collecting, storing, retrieving, and cross-checking every imaginable electronic datum about new and existing matters at the same time that their elephant colleagues down the hall simply jar their memory banks when contemplating hiring a new lawyer. Meanwhile, their ostrich counterparts, heads buried in the sand, are entirely oblivious. We have witnessed colleagues who communicate personally or electronically every day—even while on vacation—to ensure that their firm does not trigger a conflict of interest, and lawyers in other firms who do not confer at all. We've seen firms that invest hundreds of thousands of dollars each year in staff specialists and disinterested third-party regulators, while others leave it up to the discretion of the interested lawyer to seek out and resolve potential conflicts of interest; partnerships in which it takes days or weeks to complete these regulatory procedures and begin work on a case; and others in which it takes seconds. The chapter also presented some explanations for how to account for this variability.

But what difference do any of these investments in self-regulation make? Because it appears that firms construct ever more complex, comprehensive, efficient, specialized, triangulated, and universalistic material and social technology to ferret out potential conflicts of interest as the sheer magnitude of conflicts increases, the cyber squirrels have no better track record than do the herds of elephants—maybe even than ostriches. Suppose Legal Towers can expect that one in three new matters will give rise to a possible conflict of interest (a not unrealistic assumption) and that lawyers in the downstate ostrich firm can expect that a client will bring a conflict to their attention in one case in a thousand. And suppose that Legal Towers' regulatory technology fails to identify a conflict of interest a mere one-half of 1 percent of the time (a probably too-optimistic false negative rate that I snatched out of thin air). And, of course, ostrich technology fails 100 percent of the time. Then, after a thousand cases—about six months for Legal Towers and who knows how many more months or even years for the much smaller downstate ostrich—the latter will miss a conflict once and Legal Towers 1.67 times.[31]

So ostriches do not look so bad after all. Of course, if it behaved like an ostrich, a firm like Legal Towers would be out of business—uninsurable, disqualified from most of its cases, virtually all its clients alienated, its profits squandered on massive malpractice awards, its reputation shattered, its partners subject to disciplinary sanctions if not outright disbarment—and so would many other law firms, even smaller ones. It's like the classic example in introductory statistics of the difference between correlation and cause: the fact that there is a strong correlation between the size of a municipal fire department and the number of fires does not mean that firefighters are out setting fires. Resources are invested where risks are high.

The important point, then, is that all these technologies have false negative rates—they miss conflicts—even if we suspect that some are far better than others.

> I think the biggest problem that I've found is not the apparent conflict. It's the one that's hard to find. That's the one that really haunts us. No matter what we do, no matter how much technology we buy, no matter how many people look at sheets, conflicts will occur and there's not much we can do about it. And it's a terrible problem. [1Ch100+]

> Every firm of every size has conflicts that they'd never recognize. It just [. . .] they fall between the cracks innocently. [5Ch100+]

All my informants—though especially the cyber squirrels—acknowledged that their intelligence systems fail and that they do not fail randomly. Their blind spots are systemic. The lesson was conveyed most poignantly in an intellectual property firm.

---

[31]Of course, these figures were snatched from thin air because we don't have a clue about the relative efficacy of the various intelligence-gathering or self-regulatory models, and this research does little to lessen our ignorance. We would need a controlled experiment in which matched firms at similar risk for encountering the same sorts of conflicts of interest were assigned different self-regulatory technologies and procedures, an intriguing and undoubtedly valuable trial that I don't see happening any time soon.

As I waited in the lobby for the interview to begin, the coffee table overflowed with computer and electronics magazines. I eagerly awaited learning how lawyers also trained as scientists and engineers, on the cutting edge of the latest technologies, would structure their intelligence system. I was stunned when I learned the firm was a common squirrel.[32] These lawyers, who are probably more computer savvy than anyone I know, rely on elephants, herds, and occasionally paper records to ferret out potential conflicts of interest. The firm's name partner explained:

> Are you familiar with patent firms? Because there is a huge difference in the kinds of conflicts issues that they face. In a patent firm, you are not interested in the client "name," but in the "product." If you are applying for a patent for a color television, you want to ensure that no one else can produce a color television or get a patent for a color television. You are trying to cover everyone else in the world; they are our enemy. As a result, name searching for conflicts is not very important; rather, product searching is. . . . [The respondent gets up, goes over to his desk and comes back with a filled-out new client form. He shows me the sheet.] The sheet comes in to me first. . . . We don't do computerized conflicts checking. I am a big believer in computers; don't get me wrong. But you can't check products by computer. You can with names. But names do not help. You can't computerize all the kinds of oil extracting processes. It's just very difficult to computerize. [42Ch20–49]

Most data bases—and manual systems as well—operate on the assumption that interests reside in identities, that names betray conflicts of interest. Often they do. And when all the interests can be enumerated and attached to names for a given matter—for example, you have the list of all the coplaintiffs and codefendants in a lawsuit or the name of the buyer and seller and lender in a real estate transaction—a name search through a data base may reliably identify all the adversities of interest. But there are a number of circumstances where this assumption is not true.

The biggest problem, respondents tell me, is that affiliated or related parties are often not known at the outset but are likely to be affected by the outcome of the case. The most common complaint pertains to parents, subsidiaries, holding companies, joint venturers, and other corporate affiliates of named parties. Law firms have difficulty keeping track of these branches on the corporate family tree, many of which are remote or attenuated, hidden by the foliage, and constantly sprouting, growing, and breaking off.

> You can always find something that will not fit because you may not know everybody's subsidiary—and, chances are, never would until someone pointed it out to you. There's a lot of unusual, quirky circumstances that can arise that, unless you . . . had everybody at the outset file some sort of disclosure, saying, "Here's everybody who's related to me in any form or fashion," and then could guarantee that those people were 100 percent accurate. I don't know of any system that could

[32]Indeed, only a third of the firms in the sample that concentrated on intellectual property work were cyber squirrels; the others were common squirrels.

> even hope to identify every conflict at the outset. I think the best you're going to do is get one that will pick out the obvious stuff. [68DSM10–19]

Conflicts have also arisen because data bases have failed to record spouses, heirs, or other significant members of human family trees as well as the names of all the partners of a client; the members of an association client; major investors, stockholders, or others with a significant stake in a corporate client; the business entities tied to an individual client; or coparties, subcontractors, witnesses, experts, or others with a community of interest with the named parties.

> Frankly, I question the total effectiveness of any system, because of the difficulty of identifying related parties. It is possible to identify the direct parties in a matter. The trick is to get the more remote parties. [56Ch20–49]

> The data base cannot possibly be adequate. We are basically a corporate law firm, serving businesses. One can never know all the parties indirectly involved in a matter when a client comes through the door—even if you ask them. Adverse parties can include boards or trustees whose identities you don't know. Matters of this sort will always have unidentified people. You know they have to be out there, but you don't know who they are. [34Ch50–99]

Even if all the relevant parties are named, name searches may have little value. Several practitioners of family law complained about the difficulty of keeping track of female clients who repeatedly remarry and change their surnames. Other surnames, especially in certain ethnic groups, may be too common to be discriminating.

> Computer data bases don't work too well. Seventy percent of Koreans are named Kim, Park, or Lee. So you would need other identifiers. You could use an address, but addresses change a lot—especially when your clientele involves a lot of real estate. [115Ch<10]

And law firms have also gotten into trouble because they failed to record the varying names, nicknames, abbreviations, and acronyms by which a company is identified.

> Well, the computer, of course, simply matches names. And . . . one problem we've had is companies that have different trade names from their real names that do business, and may even have, well, totally different names from their formal name. And when the lawyer who's doing the intake thinks he or she has the right name, they don't. And we've stubbed our toe on that a few times. [36Ch100+]

Not all interested parties can be named, even with diligence. When the case involves creating, exploiting, or restricting zero-sum opportunities, the parties affected are potentially infinite and unknowable. The product or target of opportunity is known, but not the entities who have an interest in seizing it. In the patent example cited earlier in this section, the law firm cannot possibly know which other corporations across the globe are working on developing the same color television technology and will be precluded from marketing their intellectual property by the patent secured for the first client. When a client is bidding on a piece of property or trying to acquire a vulnerable company, the lawyers may not know what other clients are seeking the same opportunity. This blind spot is exacerbated as clients spread more and more of their business to disparate law firms. Their varied counselors cannot possibly know about tantalizing opportunities and business prospects being developed for their client by competing law firms. They cannot protect the interests of a client when they are not privy to all its interests.

Moreover, legal matters do not simply redistribute resources among the parties in contention or lift or levy sanctions. They sometimes create legal precedent, changing the rules that everyone else must play by. The defense of a single client may change the interpretation of a tax rule, raise the standard for deceptive advertising or reasonable care, shorten a statute of limitation, impose new lender liabilities, restrict shareholder's rights, cap damage awards, and the like. Because of the precedential force of case law, if lawyers alter legal doctrine while advancing the interests of one client, they may hurt other clients whose defense requires a radically different interpretation of the law. But, again, a name search or even a search by industry will not necessarily identify the clients whose interests are likely to diverge from those of the prospective client. Most respondents indicated that data bases are useless in identifying such issue or positional conflicts.

Because of these limitations of an artificial intelligence, almost two-thirds of the law firms, as I noted earlier, triangulate their conflicts surveillance procedures by requiring human input as well.

> And, in addition, we have now a computer conflicts check that it's just installed. We went back ten years and put all the matters we had for all of our clients over the last ten years and that system is being refined. But we're now using it. We find it's not entirely reliable. You have to rely on people to look at matters to see if they can develop connections and see potential competitors involved. Where a name may not come up on a computer, they may recognize a relationship. So we find both systems are valuable. . . . it's interesting, you think that a computer conflicts system would be a great solution. And really we find that they are not perfect by any means, simply because, a lot of times, when someone opens up a matter, there may be a certain set of parties involved or they don't necessarily appreciate relationships. You may not list a competitor on a conflicts check and that will only come up by circulating it among attorneys in the firm. They pick up and say, "Hey, wait a minute, if you're going to do this, I've got to talk to this client. Because they're going to be very uncomfortable with this representation." But another lawyer in the firm may not even be aware of that or a competing client. It's very difficult to pick that up. You can't do it through the computer. You've got to do that through a visual check. [1Ch100+]

> We don't have a special computerized conflict data base. I don't trust them. The available programs have a kind of rigidity in what they are able to search for. And besides, the data base is only as good as what you have input. That's all you are likely to know about. I really believe that human and institutional memory is far

better. . . . I like this system [records coupled with colleagues conferring among one another] much better than a computer system. A computer system will give you mechanical reliability, but will the answer be right? Our system will give you the right answer, but the question is how quickly. [43Ch20–49]

The hope is that lawyers are better able to think in abstract terms, to anticipate the implications of a new legal precedent on a whole host of unrelated clients, to know many of the ancillary parties that are likely to be indirectly affected by a given matter. At this stage of the computer revolution, human intelligence is still more supple, more creative, able to fire across unprogrammed but productive neural pathways, and more capable of empathy, of anticipating who will be hurt or offended by a given outcome.

Lawyers pick up the "second generation" conflicts; by that I mean the inferential ones. With respect to binary recognition, both systems pick up potential conflicts equally. The data base is an asset with respect to, one, recall and, two, constant availability; you don't have to worry that someone with relevant information is out of the office. But ultimately, information on the data base goes back to the lawyer, and it is his or her knowledge, analysis, and recall that is essential in evaluating for conflicts. It's not like the system produces a red flag that says "CONFLICT!!!" It's the lawyer's response that is the red flag. You never get that level of understanding with a dumb system. You can't get better information than you put in. Conflicts are about judgments. [57Ch20–49]

If only humans pay attention. And that's the next problem.

I'd like to sit here and tell you that when the conflict clearance form comes around, every partner in this firm puts aside whatever else he or she is working on and scrupulously goes through the whole thing. It doesn't happen. I know it doesn't happen. Because there's conflicts that partner X should catch but doesn't because he's not reading the damn form. I catch it for him, because I know who his clients are as well. It's an imperfect system because people are imperfect. For those who take it seriously, we get a good quality of conflict clearance information. And people take it seriously. For those who—by dint of being crusty or old or just not interested—don't pay attention when they intake a new matter or when they review other peoples' conflicts, you get a lesser quality. [79Ch20–49]

The self-regulatory process is burdensome. Lawyers are busy. They disdain bureaucratic busywork, memos to read, voice mail messages to answer, forms to complete, output to peruse. They have deadlines and trials and motions and depositions and briefs and unhappy clients that command their immediate attention. When their self-interest is threatened by conflicts of interest—they risk losing a lucrative piece of business or antagonizing a valued client—their attention may become riveted. But law firm activity is too diverse and fragmented to activate self-interest on every matter. The environmental attorney may compulsively monitor the Superfund or insurance cases; the intellectual property lawyer, the corporate cases; but both may totally ignore the estate planning or divorce cases. Indeed, respondents with special responsibility over conflicts of interest admitted that even *they* didn't always diligently study the memos. And even though lawyers' inferential reasoning surpasses that of a computer, their memories do not.

> But I certainly don't have a photographic memory, and I doubt that other people do. And I don't even know that they read them. So it might be that if you were working on the matter now, and therefore it was at the front of your conscience [*sic*] that Mr. X, who was the CEO of the Y Corporation, was something you were working on. And—oh my God!—there in the new matters is [this firm] client versus Y Corporation. You put your hands to your forehead and shudder. But the chances that [. . .] that's a possible check, but it's pretty remote that that would hit you. If it was six months ago that the notice of the new matter came out, and you never had dreamed that Mr. X of the Y Corporation was gonna come in to see you, the chances that you would recognize the Y Corporation in that context—the name of the Y Corporation—when X came in is pretty remote, I think. It may be that some people keep those forms and routinely go back and check them when a new matter comes in. I don't. I doubt that they do, but I don't. . . . It's just something that's always scared me. [61Ch20–49]

This discussion has focused largely on the danger of false negatives, of missing true conflicts. But false positives—unfounded hits—are a problem as well. They create inordinate amounts of needless paperwork. They squander attention and goodwill. They burn out lawyers and make them careless and resentful. False positives are even responsible for the social construction of some false negatives when they allow true conflicts of interest to slip through the safety net, drowned out by all the noise the former produce. Earlier in the chapter, I cited the example of a large cyber squirrel that had jettisoned its computer surveillance system altogether, returning to manual scrutiny of index cards, because the sheer number of false positives had inundated the lawyers; other conflicts czars circulate only a portion of the new matters for collegial feedback, concerned that otherwise colleagues will not bother to read and respond at all.

> I think our problem—as many firms' problem—is too much data coming back. The problem is not too little, it's too much. . . . And there are a couple of reasons for that. One is, we have deals with a lot of parties. So, for example, we represent X bank lending money to Y. And it turns out X bank is a member of a group of twenty other banks. And then there's an investment banker or somebody else who's involved. And so what happens is, you get this mass of material that comes back. That's a problem. The other problem is that . . . people, for example, will put down . . . "North American Insurance Company." Well, our conflicts clerk knows that if you enter that exact name, you're limiting your search. And so she may enter "North American." Well, then we'll get "North American Moving Lines" or something like that. That's a problem. . . . I mean, it works, it works fine, but it generates too much garbage, to be honest. [26Ch100+]

What human intelligence offers in suppleness, abstract synthesis, and imagination, then, it lacks in memory, motivation, reliability, universalism, and speed. For this reason, many firms consider their human input more of a safety net, situating their intelligence process in electronic data points unearthed by artificial intelligence. Unfortunately, this reification obscures the fact that the data points are also human constructions.

> The computer data base is superb. It's not perfect, but it's superb. And it picks up virtually every conflict that might arise. It's a really rare instance when the computer would let us down. That's not a fair thing to say. The computer doesn't let us down. [61Ch20–49]

> So, it is an extremely thorough name check. I mean, it is almost impossible to miss it. It'll find a name anywhere in any file in existence. So, it's extremely accurate. . . . And I have a pretty high confidence level that, when I ask them to check a file, the chances are that, if a name doesn't come up, we just haven't been involved in it. Now, that does not mean that you don't get conflicts. There are other ways for conflicts to arise. . . . New things happen in a case and you create as you go along. [13Ch50–99]

> It is, as a matter of fact, a very camouflaged false sense of security to rely on those records. You can't do that. They won't ever get it all. There will be slipups. You can't do it. You've got to talk. [54DSL20–49]

Yet another blind spot, then, concerns the social construction of data, or what several respondents referred to as "garbage in, garbage out."

> The problem with computer screening is that the data base is insufficient. If you have junk in, you will get junk out. I'm sure it's adequate for a simple house closing. But what about a case involving client XYZ? XYZ is a wholly owned subsidiary of ABC. ABC is in a joint venture with DEF. The law firm is suing officers and directors of DEF. There certainly is a direct possibility of conflict. There's nothing out there to disentangle these relationships. [40Ch20–49]

> When we went with the computerized system in '89, I think we were all acutely aware that it has its limitations and that this requires, really, input from all of the attorneys—partners and associates—to work. It's an old garbage in–garbage out sort of process. In fact, it was at about that time that the software companies were touting the advantages of electronic conflicts checking. But we were not convinced of that. In fact, we expanded the requirement that all attorneys—not just partners—review the files being opened on a regular basis. [29Ch100+]

How does a firm ensure that all the necessary information is entered into the data base and then updated as circumstances change? As I noted before, the best enforcement mechanism available to law firms is to withhold issuance of a billing number until the paperwork is complete. But although this strategy increases compliance, it also produces new biases in the data: it gives lawyers an incentive to fill out the forms with minimal or preliminary information rather than waiting until more complete or accurate data become available. It also contributes to the problem that ancillary parties, discovered only as lawyers become more immersed in the case, often fail to get recorded in the data base.

> We've been attempting to find a way to input information that is better than that disclosed on the conflicts sheet. The problem with the sheet is that it includes preliminary information. Once the matter is more well known to the attorney, you tend to get better information. Now, this may take a day or it may take a month. We've been struggling to find a way to capture this information. What we know is that the information in the conflicts sheet that gets input into the data base is less comprehensive than what one obtains after reviewing the file at the end of the matter. As a result, we have been reluctant to merely add the sheet to the data base. We've been waiting to try to find a way to massage it a bit to be more accurate. But the result is that we have fallen way behind. So we've decided to input the information on the conflicts sheets into the data base quickly—just to get caught up—and simply recognize that it is not sufficiently comprehensive. [57Ch20–49]

Moreover, as I have already noted in the section "As Time Goes By," when new developments arise—a new party joins a lawsuit, one defendant files a counterclaim against another, a client merges with another corporation—there is no bureaucratic occasion or incentive to input amended information into the data base, thereby flagging that a conflict of interest is about to detonate. And withholding billing numbers encourages lawyers to do their work off the books, to bypass the docketing process. For example, if lawyers are able to charge their time to an open account—perhaps a related matter for an ongoing client—they can avoid or postpone the paperwork. They're representing ABC Chemical Company on charges of dumping on a site in downstate Illinois, and when the company is named in another Superfund case in Indiana, the lawyers bill their time under the first case rather than opening a new matter. As a result, the names of the other codefendants on the second site (some of whom may be firm clients) never enter the data base and never get flagged as a potentially significant conflict of interest.

> One thing I don't know about is the extent to which people operate outside the system. I'm sure it's . . . possible to do it if you have an existent client. . . . Because you can fold it into an existing matter. It's almost impossible to do it for a new client. Because then you would have to bill them without a number and record your time and that's just sort of completely outside the way the firm operates. But it is possible with an existing client. And I don't know the extent to which that goes on. I think as sort of the trust in the system builds, there's less and less of that where there might have been before. [7Ch100+]

> I mean, you discover a lot of things. We discovered that people were using the same matter number for different deals, for instance, that dealt with the same

> client. But they were reentering . . . they were changing the names of the matters. . . . You know, we had different names for the matter for five different times over ten years. [1Ch100+]

Finally, conversations in which small bits of confidential information are disclosed that do not result in the opening of a new matter—perhaps while a lawyer consults with a potential client who ultimately decides to retain a different firm—are less likely to find their way to the data base.[33]

> I got one [malpractice case that I'm defending] going on right now, where a big firm ran a conflicts check and figured out that they did not have a conflict. Then they subpoenaed some documents from one of the witnesses. And in the documents is a letter from another partner in this big law firm. And what he had done is, he had given some advice as to the subject matter of this case—real fast—never opened the file. [6Ch100+]

In short, intelligence systems are plagued by systemic blind spots that include bad memory, information overload, inadvertence, disinterest, noncompliance, obfuscation, premature closure on data collection, failure to update, inability to anticipate the social networks implicated in a dispute or transaction, difficulty gathering data on nonmatters, and most important, that the search engine—proper names—is sometimes a poor discriminator and often a bad proxy for interests. Some firms have massaged or tinkered with their technologies to shrink the blind spots or make them less opaque. But false negatives are a fact of life.

CONCLUSION

Lawyers have now amassed a list of most—*but not all*—of the interests that are possibly adverse to parties in the prospective engagement. The initial list had lots of problematic hits, but fortunately most of them were false positives that were happily discarded. But a few names remain. And there are those nagging false negatives that they've failed to identify. And then there's the matter of future prospects, lucrative matters out on the horizon that may be conflicted out if they take in this prospective case.

Analysis does not end with a list of hits or potential hits, of course. Attorneys must decide whether they have uncovered an absolute conflict of interest, one that can be overlooked with the consent of the affected clients, or whether they have simply conjured up a remote possibility that might detonate at some point down the road. They might assess the risk that opposing counsel will seek to disqualify the firm, thereby creating delay and additional cost to their client to defend against even an unsuccessful disqualification motion. They will weigh client relations issues that have nothing to do with ethical rules or their professional responsibilities:

---

[33]Though for this very reason, some firms, such as Legal Towers, require attorneys to fill out special forms for nonclients, nonmatters, or declined matters that are then entered into the data base.

whether disclosing an unlikely but conceivable future conflict may drive a prospective client into the arms of another suitor, whether merely asking valued and longstanding clients to waive an insignificant conflict will so anger them that it's preferable to decline the case than even broach the subject. They might weigh the efficacy of prophylactic measures, such as screening tainted lawyers behind Chinese walls to reassure clients of their loyalty and disinterestedness or asking prospective clients to waive future conflicts of interest as a requirement for taking on their case. Often they must deal with heated intrafirm squabbles as one powerful partner refuses to allow his client to be gored in order to resolve a conflict created by someone else in the firm.

Perhaps most difficult, lawyers often try to read the tea leaves about developments down the road that, were they known at the outset, would lead the firm to decline the engagement. What is the likelihood that parties seeking joint representation will have a falling-out and force the firm to withdraw from the case? What is the risk that new parties with whom the firm has fiduciary obligations will join the lawsuit in the future and thereby conflict out the firm? Is this small pittance of business from this Fortune 500 company likely to snowball into a lucrative relationship, or was it placed strategically to conflict out the firm in an upcoming piece of litigation that the Fortune 500 company plans to bring against a major client of the firm? What is the likelihood that the client who readily agrees to waive the conflict at the outset may be less happy when he or she sees the outcome (fearing that the firm somehow held back—or didn't hold back enough—out of loyalty to the other party)? What is the likelihood that taking this matter will preclude the firm from bringing in more lucrative or desirable business in the future by importing a new thicket of interests that must be honored?

These are questions for which there is no artificial intelligence. We consider them in the next chapter.

Diffusing Conflicts

A guy who used to be a partner here told me a story that I always liked. I can't remember what firm he was with at the time, but he was with one of the large Chicago firms. And he walked in with another young partner to the managing partner and said, "You know, I think you better take a look at this; I think we might have a conflict here." And they handed this complaint across the desk to him. He looked at it for a minute, opened up his bottom drawer, and he pulled out a pair of these dime-store eyeglasses that have dollar signs painted on them. And he looked at it for a minute and said, "I don't see any conflict here at all," and handed it back across the desk. [laughter] I think people are more worried about it than they used to be. [44Ch20–49]

ANALYSIS

Few firms today evaluate potential conflicts of interest by blinding themselves to all but their economic implications. When elephants, squirrels, or cyber squirrels identify "hits," or matches between the interests of current or former clients and parties or issues associated with a new matter, lawyers hoping to take on the prospective engagement typically analyze far more than the bottom line. First, they eliminate the false positives, seeming matches that, in fact, reflect unrelated parties with identical or similar names. As I described in the previous chapter, computer surveillance software, developed to minimize false negatives and the possibility that a true conflict will slip through, allows variant or partial names, nicknames, aliases, words with common roots, acronyms, typos, misspellings, foreign spellings, and other mistakes to qualify as hits. As a result, computer searches often generate reams of output. Though tedious, separating the false and true positives is relatively straightforward.

> The worst matters are bankruptcy cases where you're going to now represent a debtor in a bankruptcy case. And you now have to run through the entire list of all creditors, which could be hundreds of names. And, since the computer does a matching by a literal matching, if you put in "John Deere & Company," it's going to pick out everyone whose name has John in it, and are a match, and it's going to spew all that stuff out. And so you'll come out with thousands of matches. And those take a long time to deal with. Just the physical going through and looking through every name, even if, oh yes, you picked up John Henry and John, and you cross them all off, there are lots of them and it takes a long time. So someone will spend several hours going through one of those. [28Ch50–99]

Next, analysts examine the remaining true positives, not all of which denote direct unequivocal adversity. These analysts are always lawyers, though some respondents mused skeptically about whether the task could be delegated to a paralegal. In the vast majority of firms, the initial inquiry is performed by the lawyer hoping to bring in the new matter. Analysts must be part jurist, part fact finder, part sleuth, part historian, part psychologist, and part fortune-teller as they reconstruct prior cases, analyze the relationships, assess the relevant ethical rules, weigh client relations and business considerations, and try to predict the future course of the prospective matter. In deciding whether the firm must decline the new matter or whether and how it might diffuse the conflict and proceed without breaching ethical rules, taking unreasonable risks, impairing relationships with clients or colleagues, or precluding future business opportunities, attorneys revisit themes laid out in chapters 3 through 7:

- Do the hits involve current or former clients? (Recall from chapter 6 that law firms are ethically permitted to take matters adverse to *former* clients as long as these new matters are not substantially related to the prior engagements.)
- What, then, was the nature of the prior engagement?
- How is it different from the work contemplated?
- What confidential information has the firm acquired regarding the current or former client, and who possesses it?
- Is it possible to shield those knowing lawyers behind an ethical screen?
- What is the relationship between the current or former clients and the parties implicated in the prospective case?
- Are these parties corporate affiliates of clients, officers, directors, major shareholders, joint venturers, or family members?
- Can the firm take an adverse position against these related parties?

- What role do current or former clients play in the prospective matter? Are they adversaries or, rather, coplaintiffs, codefendants, creditors, transactional partners, lenders, insurers, competitors, witnesses, experts, legal counsel, victims? Are their interests directly adverse or only potentially or theoretically inconsistent?
- Could smoking guns, uncovered as discovery or investigation proceeds, implicate coparties differently?
- Are allegiances among coparties solid, or are interests likely to diverge as the engagement proceeds?
- Is the advocacy or defense of the new client likely to require that the firm advance positions that will harm other firm clients?
- Is the relationship with the new client likely to lead to further business or to conflict the firm out of representing future clients and taking on more lucrative cases?
- How might the client react to the firm's proposed resolution of the potential conflict? Will it be so angered that it will cut future ties with the firm?
- Which legal rules apply, especially in cases that span multiple jurisdictions with slightly different ethics codes?

In answering these questions, lawyers first study the materials that indicate a hit—be they computer output, manual search results, forms, or voice mail messages from colleagues—which may be sufficient to resolve the question. Some lawyers pull billing records and fee histories to ascertain whether the affected client is a current or former client, an inference made from how recently the client received a statement or whether any bills are still outstanding.

> I will not infrequently ask—and we now have this under computer, too, through our accounting department, through the Records Center—I'll ask for a printout of that two-year-old client or former client, to find out, number one, when was the last bill? When was it paid? And is there any unbilled time at the present time? I can tell by that that it's an inactive client, easily, or a former client, if they paid their last bill two years ago and there's no time that any lawyer in the firm has spent on that client. And that'll back up my feelings after talking to the lawyer on the case. [4Ch100+]

Recall from chapter 8 the example of the big-firm attorney who, while interviewing a prospective client, sent his secretary out to get the fee histories, if any, of the opposing parties. When the secretary discovered that J. Jones had paid a thousand dollars in fees in the current year, the attorney inferred that this adverse party was a current client of the firm. Others may requisition and examine the case files and records of the matters that turned up in the conflicts surveillance process.

> So that's where we get ["Doe"]. We didn't represent [Doe], but here it will also tell you the file number, the case name, . . . the originating attorney, . . . the name party (I think it should say "defendant" or "plaintiff." Yeah, "[Doe]—plaintiff"), and whether or not it's opened or closed—"O" and "C." And that's how we do it.

> And there'll be situations where we'll say, "Geez, I just don't remember that." We have all our files that, if they're not destroyed after a certain period of time, they're all on off-premises storage. So we have an individual . . . an administrative assistant or whatever. And he's in charge of running out there to pull files for us if we need them. They'll kick a file and look at it and go through that file and see if there's a conflict. So that's kind of how we handle it on a typical, routine basis. [64DSS10–19]

And in some instances, lawyers may confer with the affected clients themselves to learn more about their relationships, adversities, interests, preferences, grounds for cross-claims, projections about the future, and the like.

> But we would know right offhand, "Is there, in fact, a potential dispute between those two parties that we're being able to represent? Or, is a defense consistent? Can we, in fact, represent a manufacturer and a distributor under certain circumstances?" And so initially we would know if there is a conflict just because of the factual situation. So we may—right off the bat—say, "No way can we get involved." If, in fact, the facts in and of themselves don't present that conflict, we go to the next step of talking to both of them. We say, "Hey, look, we've been asked to represent. Do you have any problems in our doing this? Do you believe that there may be something that will come in down the line that could [. . .] Because if you perceive that possibility, let's know about it right up front and let's not do it." There's fortunately enough business out there that we don't have to put ourselves in a compromising position. We might have clients saying, "Well, you tell us what kinds of things could come up that we should look for." And then we do it. [76Ch10–19]

These conversations are merely fact-finding missions, used to gather data about the likelihood of a conflict of interest; they are not about the conflicts themselves, negotiations considered later in this chapter.

Relationships among Colleagues

Most frequently, lawyers simply call their colleagues who alerted them to the potential conflict in the first place or who represented the clients that now figure in the hit and whose names appear as the billing attorney on the screening output. Lawyers may call simply to ascertain that the prospective client and the party identified in the hit are one and the same. Or they may contact colleagues to determine whether the case reflected in the hit is closed and whether any ongoing work is being performed for the existing client.

But, typically, they confer with colleagues about the substance of the prior engagement, to establish whether it is substantially related to the prospective matter, and whether the interests of the parties are actually directly adverse.

> In one, we were asked to represent one title company against another. Every law firm in this town—at one time or another—has done some work for or with all of

> the title companies in town. Without going into privileged stuff, there were some issues as to whether we had been asked to work with Title Company A relative to a particular issue. And now, we were being asked to represent Title Company B suing A. We sat down—I got the lawyers involved—we sat down, we talked through it. We reviewed, factually, what we knew, what we didn't know, what we had been engaged to do before, the extent of that representation, the extent of the information provided to us in connection with that representation. We talked about the scope of the engagement for the second client. . . . And we also talked about the effect: we would surely never get any legal work from Title Company A if we sued them. And we talked about that too. That was discussed not just with me and the two lawyers involved, but we discussed it at our Management Committee meeting—weighed the pros and cons of it. [79Ch20–49]

These conversations can be awkward and delicate because, as I described in the previous chapter, lawyers don't want to acquire confidential information from their colleague that will force them to decline a case that might otherwise have been resolved through a Chinese wall or some other means. Cautioning their colleague not to disclose any confidences, they inquire about the rough contours of the prior matter and whether clients shared confidences that could benefit the prospective client.

> You oftentimes will need content. And, therefore, you'll have to go to the attorney who handled the matter to find out the subject matter of what was going on. . . . You'd go in and, without going into details—so you didn't breach confidentiality—you just go in and say, "Sam, I've been approached by XYZ Corporation to represent them in this matter against Z Corporation or Y Corporation. I know you represented them before. What this corporation wants me to represent them in is this type of matter. Does that involve anything that you were, does that relate to anything you represented the other company in before?" And if the answer is "No," "Are you aware of anything [that] would be confidential or a conflict, if I undertook this representation?" If they say "No," then that usually would resolve the matter. [50DSL20–49]

In addition to gathering information on the nature of the prior engagement, lawyers may also ask colleagues about their clients generally, their relationship to the firm, and how they might react if the firm champions interests in the new case that may be incompatible with their own.

> In this kind of potential business conflict situation, the two partners will talk about it. They will try to figure out what to do. Would we really lose the first client by taking the second? Might we even lose the first one by asking about representing the second? The code of ethics is indifferent here; these are not legal issues. They involve business judgment. The two lawyers will spend a lot of time talking about it. They might talk to more experienced lawyers about how to handle it. In other law firms, the Management Committee or its equivalent would make these decisions outright. We don't do it this way. We highly prize not being

> told what to do. Big firms would grind to a halt if they were governed the way we are. They need a more authoritarian governance structure. [69Ch20–49]

> In most firms, the affected colleagues try to resolve the conflict together.

> An obvious conflict comes in. . . . The matter is clearly a conflict with a client of one of my other partners. I would probably tell the new client who has called, "Boy, this is unfortunate. One of my partners represents X, which poses a conflict for your case. Let me talk to him. I'm doubtful that we will be able to take the case, but let me talk to him." I want my partners to know that this income might have been generated to my credit and I am declining it for a colleague. I would not reject a matter without making any noise. For all I know, there may be a creative means to work out this problem. Maybe the other client would agree, if only I worked on the conflicting matter. Maybe it wouldn't mind. Maybe it played only a minor role in the underlying case, while this new client was a mega-player in the case. I wouldn't recognize these options if I didn't bring the issue to the attention of the partner involved. [48Ch20–49]

Sometimes these conversations can become spirited or contentious. Tensions often arise when counsel for the existing client expresses reluctance to jeopardize his or her relationship with the client by alerting it about a problem, asking it to waive the conflict, or even allowing the firm to represent a competitor or champion a contrary position, and presses that the new matter be declined.

> Now, meanwhile, my partner's going berserk. You know, "What are you doing? You're hurting my relationship. Everything." [11Ch100+]

> The most difficult one that I had—and it's the only one in four years that I've taken to the Executive Committee. . . . And, by utter coincidence, it's the only vote I've been—a formal vote—I've been involved in the Executive Committee for four years. . . . And it was a close vote. It was dealing with a trade association, a few of whose members were going to be joined in some litigation—it was in the . . . energy field—joined in some possible litigation in [West Coast], where we had been asked to represent private parties suing certain [members of the trade association]. And we have been general counsel forever for the [trade association]. . . . And we concluded that there was a conflict, because we had—over the course of many years—we had done a fair amount of work for individual members, including some of the target defendants on the West Coast. And when it came to, "Should we ask these members of the association for a consent," we voted not to. . . . The group of lawyers who—on the West Coast—who were urging us to seek consent, were brand new to the firm. . . . So we had the more peculiar business setting of a group of lawyers who had just joined the firm, who felt very strongly, "Gee, how, how could you? We want to prove ourselves in [this firm]. We've got this great opportunity. Just ask for consent. That's the least [. . .]" And we say, "Well, yeah, but you don't understand." "Well, why didn't you tell us that when we joined?" "Well, we didn't know that you were going to have this." So that was a

particularly thorny issue. . . . It wasn't complicated intellectually; it was complicated in the personal relationship. [16Ch100+]

Disputes among colleagues may also erupt when conflicting interests necessitate that the firm represent at most one party and force colleagues to choose between clients.

> And then there is sort of the internal bickering over, well, if you can't represent both sides, can we represent one side? And in most cases the answer is "Yeah, we could do that." Then you go fight about which side it's going to be. And that's very difficult where the parties are both important clients. It may be even worse that we introduced them and so we brought about the transaction and now can't be involved in the transaction. . . . It's not the nature of the conflict itself that's more difficult to deal with. It's really the client relationships and attorney relationships that make those more difficult. [28Ch50–99]

> I think that it can be very divisive and it can be very difficult. Whenever you get in the situation of suggesting to one person that one client is more important than another client, when that other client may be the most significant client to that one partner, it is enormously difficult. [11Ch100+]

Or dissension may flare when the interests even of prospective clients conflict. Colleagues may press to turn away a bird in the hand because its interests conflict with those in the bush—prospective clients they have not yet nabbed, but whose business they hope to attract.

> . . . somebody came to me and said, "You won't believe what happened. I wanted to take on this matter, and Susan's name showed up on the computer, although she's not a client. But she's on somebody's mailing list. And we've never gotten a piece of business from her, and we have no reason to believe we will get a piece. But Partner X thinks we shouldn't take this on—'cause I had to check with Partner X when the conflict showed up—and Partner X says we shouldn't take this on because he/she is confident that, sooner or later, Susan's gonna send this great big piece of business. And here I've got a bird in the hand." [61Ch20–49]

Indeed, conflicts of interest can provide an occasion in which raw disputes about power and control reverberate through law firms.

> I think, frequently, there's a lot of sophistry in this discussion about conflicts, which is really related to who is controlling the revenue streams in the office and that, frequently, we tend to have high-toned discussion about conflict, when we might as well be having low-toned discussion about money. And we tend to throw off onto high-toned conversations about conflicts, what are really struggles over who controls what in the firm. . . . I mean, I openly said that about a year ago. It got everybody all mad. [snicker] But, I mean, I think it's true. I don't want to give you [the] wrong impression. Everybody around here—myself included—would

> probably be more self-righteous about conflicts than is attractive. Okay? I mean, everybody takes the subject very seriously in their own mind. I'm just not sure they always see the dark side of the force. [laughter] [70DSS10–19]

Though few firms in the sample were hopelessly riven by conflicts, several respondents cited instances in their firm or elsewhere in which partners defected because commitments of their colleagues continually forced them to turn away too much business.

> I mean, we have not had situations here—yet—of lawyers actually leaving. . . . We've had instances where we've gotten lawyers who came to us because their prior firms were on opposite sides of issues, and they just couldn't stay. . . . We did lose one client, not that long ago, largely because of a conflict issue. But those lawyers were able to make that up with other business. [26Ch100+]

> L1: But I can conceive of situations where partnerships break up over that kind of issue. I can conceive [. . .]
>
> L2: They have!
>
> L1: . . . of a situation where partners leave because they say, "Look, . . . my major client—which is worth a half-million dollars a year to this firm—is now not going to be our client because we're doing work for another client." . . . I can see a partner saying, "Look, I'm going to go over to Jones Day [very large law firm based in Cleveland, with a branch office in Chicago] or some other firm who doesn't represent this entity and take my five hundred thousand dollars worth of business and other business where I continue to represent that client and be a significant partner in the firm."
>
> L2: And that has happened . . . at major, major firms—Washington offices. [laughs]
>
> L1: I guess, you'll remember that with K&E [Kirkland & Ellis].[1] . . . But we've been fortunate, really, on that. But that's a serious problem. I think that you've gotta just live with that. Those are the rules. [11Ch100+]

Observations about how difficult, painful, divisive, and commonplace are disputes over the resolution of potential conflicts of interest echoed frequently through the interviews, especially through the opulent corridors of large law firms.

> L2: The greatest problem for me, more so than the issues, are the people. Because they want the case and they want their fees and they don't want to give it up, no matter what's at stake. And I'm on the low end of the totem pole, so that's why it's difficult. But the issues are really not difficult at all.

---

[1] In 1983, the Washington and Chicago offices of Kirkland & Ellis—the same firm involved in the late 1970s in the famous Westinghouse conflict-of-interest case cited in the previous chapter—split after a senior partner in the Chicago office became special counsel to Ameritech, a fierce AT&T-affiliated competitor of several significant clients of the firm's Washington branch office.

L1: . . . There are no difficult conflicts. There are painful conflicts. When you have to tell a guy that he can't get—or you have to tell your firm that you can't have—this case, which . . . you anticipate it's going to generate three or four hundred thousand dollars in fees, that is a sad day. But deciding it . . . is not hard. . . . The legal rules aren't that difficult. What's difficult is the pain that is associated with their application sometimes. And you have to come to accept the fact that you're just going to have to say "No." And that may mean that you don't get three hundred thou. But that's life. Tomorrow's another day. [6Ch100+]

Although about a third of the respondents working in firms of fewer than one hundred lawyers described such dissension as at least occasional, this was true of nine-tenths of those in firms of one hundred attorneys or more. Respondents in firms big and small suggested that collegial discord over conflicts is a price of practicing in a large firm.

> Well, you just hear that people don't get along in other firms. You read about it all the time. We get along. People complain about it, I'm sure, but it's life. . . . if you want to practice in a big firm, you take the good and the bad. [2Ch100+]

> It's part of law firm practice. We are not [over fifty] sole practitioners. We're [over fifty] lawyers that have sort of a unified goal. And the unified goal occasionally—it's not a sphere, there's little bumps and dimples in the whole thing—and occasionally you hit those and you just have to convince people that it's for the good of the union. It goes away. It hurts in the short term. [27Ch50–99]

The legacy of compensation. Lawyers, of course, have a personal, proprietary stake in their own clients, which can be threatened when colleagues collide over conflicts of interest.

> Attorneys tend to be very possessive of their clients, I'm sure you probably know. And even in a firm. Most firms, half the guys think of themselves as sole practitioners. And it has more to do with the possessiveness of that client than the compensation itself per se. [72DSM10–19]

> The real problem with it would be that we'd be stepping on someone's ego more than their economic interests, probably. [45DSL20–49]

But economic interests and compensation arrangements in most firms *do* tend to exacerbate the natural hostilities.

> Obviously, no lawyer wants to be told that he can't do something for a potential client. And sometimes you just have to say "No." . . . I would not be surprised that, eventually, we're going to see some situation in which somebody just says, "No, I won't give up on that." And we might eventually wind up with the Management Committee of the firm making a decision on it. But, so far, things have been

> resolved short of civil war. . . . Compensation concerns . . . contribute significantly to the problem. [3Ch100+]

> And the problem also comes up where attorney A has represented the potential defendant and attorney B can't sue 'em. What's the relationship then between A and B at the end of the year, okay? So A is sitting there, "Thank God," and B is sitting there, "You've taken away income from me." [54DSL20–49]

When lawyers must turn down a piece of business because of conflicts elsewhere in the firm, it will most likely be registered in their annual compensation—at least in most firms.

> . . . the report card includes a big category on your business generation. And that's how you get your money. And if you have to lose a five-hundred-thousand-dollar fee because of a conflict, you're going to be, I mean, that's not going to be a real happy situation. [106Ch20–49]

Undoubtedly, many tomes have been filled, hefty consulting fees paid, and friendships shattered over the subject of optimal lawyer compensation schemes.[2] Though I will not exhaustively review them here, the interviews provide a window on the ever-changing drama of how law firms divide their spoils. Commentators refer to the "'Golden Age of the Big Law Firm' when corporate law was prosperous, stable, and untroubled" (Kummel 1996, 379). During this mythic age—which ended sometime in the late 1970s or early 1980s—compensation awards reflected seniority or so-called lockstep systems, in which colleagues hired at the same time advanced the income ladder together regardless of performance. Though the experts now describe lockstep compensation as on the decline (Cotterman 1995, 29; Kummel 1996, 386; Altonji 1996; Coburn 1997), a good number of smaller downstate firms in the sample continue the tradition.

From a conflict-of-interest perspective, seniority-based, lockstep, or "true partnership" compensation systems are indeed "golden," because they extinguish the financial incentives of the lawyer to keep a case at all costs and to undermine the rainmaking efforts of others when they threaten their relationship to a valued client. Respondents in these golden-age firms attributed their relative harmony, at least in part, to the more egalitarian compensation system they have embraced.

> We have a pretty unique compensation system here. And it is not tied to who brought in the client, nor is it tied to who did the work—believe it or not. [snicker] We discuss that from time to time. We have always concluded—thus far—that, in order to eliminate any jealousies, facilitate the transfer of work to the attorney most qualified to do it, and to eliminate some of these potential problems, we expressly do not have a compensation system which is based—in any part—upon whose client it is or who brought in the work—that type of thing. So we don't have that problem. . . . I would think, if we were to look at it strictly

[2]For an overview, see Cotterman 1995.

from, "How does our compensation arrangement impact the handling of conflict situations?" it certainly lessens those problems. It may create tensions in other areas, but not in resolving conflict-of-interest problems. [87DSS10–19]

It doesn't take a sophisticated economist to recognize that the downside of lockstep systems is that they provide incentives for lawyers to shirk or free ride off the efforts of others. Many firms, especially larger ones and those in competitive markets, have therefore developed compensation systems that reflect varied aspects of lawyer performance, typically: expertise, firm leadership or management, mentoring of junior colleagues, collegiality, being a team player, professional and community activities, productivity, billable hours, fees collected, profitability of client portfolios, client relationship building, client retention, development of new business, marketing, and origination or rainmaking. The last ten criteria, of course, exacerbate discord within the firm when conflicts of interest require that someone turn business away or annoy or antagonize an important client in order to resolve a potential conflict.

Firms that run off of business generation, it's a real problem. That's where it's acute. And we have gotten off that model because, in our view, it creates too many problems. If I, to economically survive, if I must bring in that business—at any cost—I will. And if someone says we really can't do that, I'll find a way to do it somehow. And we can't live like that. [27Ch50–99]

How frequently and seriously firms are wracked by discord from conflicts of interest depends in part on their compensation structure but also their social organization, size, internal culture, market, areas of expertise, and so on.

It is a problem every time it arises. And it is exacerbated by our atypical system of partner compensation. . . . our firm compensation is structured with each individual lawyer as an individual profit center. We cannot indulge in the fiction that other firms indulge in that the lawyer who must give up a client due to conflicts won't feel it. Here, if you lost your biggest client, you may not be able to stay. [34Ch50–99]

Under our system, say, if we have a partner in Chicago who wants to represent a particular client—a long-standing, good client—and a party on the other side is a good client of, say, our partner in [another city], one of those partners is going to make less money. And there's no sharing. So, we see some individual economic pressures that our partners will put on our committee, saying "You don't understand. That's a great client of mine. I'm out of business if this [. . .] This client's given me a hundred thousand dollars a year for the last ten years." . . . The partner who "wins," if you will, in Chicago, doesn't have to share anything with the partner who loses in [the other city]. [16Ch100+]

In this firm, compensation is based on a rolling average of the amount of business that a partner brings in over a three-year period. In contingency fee and personal

> injury cases, the amount of money that can come in can be really substantial. Therefore, if a matter like that needs to be turned away, it's likely that compensation will be affected very, very substantially. For lawyers doing transactional kinds of work, losing a case due to conflicts is less likely to have that much impact on compensation. [52DSL20–49]

> Well, one of the things about this law firm and every law firm this size is that, if you really think about economics, you find that it isn't so much a question of how the pie is divided, but, more, how big is the pie? And if a decision as to which of two conflicting clients we're going to represent made a significant difference in how big the pie was, I believe that the lawyer whose client we weren't representing would realize that, in the long run, everyone will be better off economically. Maybe not ethically. [51Ch20–49]

I do not want to create the impression that firms in the sample are roiled by conflicts over conflicts. Most are not.

> I mean, we don't—and I can say this in all candor—there's no scrapping among partners of which assignment we take in. We take in that assignment which we think is in the firm's best interests. I mean, and it's usually related to profitability. And, if partner A got in a case from an occasional client, and partner B gets in a case from a more volume client, it's in the firm's best interests if we can juggle that to take the second case rather than the first. There's no jealousy among lawyers of the fact that "You're dusting off this client who called me." [19Ch50–99]

To mix the respondents' metaphors, most disagreements blow over, everyone's ox eventually gets gored, everything comes out in the wash, and the pie just keeps getting bigger.

> . . . people tend to scream at the end of the year and say, "Well, I would have had X hundred thousand dollars worth of billings had I not been conflicted out of this." We don't take that into account, because everybody's conflicted out of a matter every once in a while, and we figure it comes out in the wash. [1Ch100+]

> We've never had a particular problem with that. I mean, it is fully explored, because we've had some instances in which one particular partner's ox would be gored and he would lose money that he could have otherwise earned—perhaps, in pretty substantial amounts by virtue of that. But we have never had an instance in which anyone has seriously raised a stink about walking away. We've all tended to recognize—in our firm anyway—that, well, that's the luck of the draw. And maybe next time. . . . This month it could be my turn to get my ox gored by the fates and next month it could be the other guy's, and I win. . . . No one has ever taken it as a personal matter. It's just, "What's the best? What can we do here?" . . . As a practical matter, what's going to happen is, they'll have discussed between themselves what happened and then this guy's going to jokingly say, "Yeah, Joe owes me big

> time about this." And we're all going to laugh about it because we recognize that's the way it works. And for a week, a month—whatever it may be—it'll be like, "Yeah, Joe owes me big time" type talk. And then you move on. . . . we've been in business for [over fifty] years. And, for the most part, we've always had a pretty congenial group that has gotten along. So, I think it has a lot to do with the personalities. [68DSM10–19]

But for many medium and large firms, conflicts over conflicts are more routine, disruptive, and divisive. A few firms try to lessen the damage by ensuring that compensation committees are informed when colleagues must turn away significant business to resolve conflicts of interest arising elsewhere in the firm.

> And what we do in our firm is, . . . you get credit for new business that you bring into the firm. We also prepare what we call "declination memos." And if the firm declined the matter because of a conflict of interest or because of a positional conflict or a client-relations problem, we make out a memo and that goes in the attorney's file for year-end compensation. And we take that into account that he had a big matter that he had to turn down because of somebody else's matter. . . . I mean, you'd rather have the business. But on the other hand, if somebody had to turn down a big piece of business because it's adverse to one of our other clients, he ought to get some credit for being asked to take it on. . . . [The policy] helps, but it doesn't help totally. [18Ch100+]

But most respondents concede that it is next to impossible to factor these theoretical possibilities of lost opportunities into precise monetary allocations. Compensation structures can rarely diffuse the inherent conflicts among partners.

> A system to identify and resolve conflicts is going to affect someone's pocketbook in any firm. You need a system that is sensitive to that. . . . Ethical and business conflicts create stresses and strains in the fabric of the firm. They can become so bad that they can cause the firm to break up. When a partner must turn away half or more of his business because of conflicts, he may think, "What do I need this firm for?" One needs to develop a fair system for resolving conflicts if the firm is to dissipate these stresses and strains. [69Ch20–49]

This is one reason that firms develop Conflicts Committees or other governance structures to oversee the acquisition of new business.

Oversight

> I had a full head of hair before I took this role. [43Ch20–49]

Recall from chapter 8 that more than half the firms in the sample (and more than four-fifths of those that employ at least fifty lawyers) have mechanisms by which third parties review the acquisition of new business. Most often (28 percent of the firms), these third parties are specialized Conflicts, Ethics, Professional Responsibility, or

New Business Committees. But administrative positions (managing partners, members of Executive or Management Committees, department heads; almost one-fifth of the firms) or meetings of the full partnership (6 percent of the firms) also provide third-party oversight or feedback. Whatever ethics expertise, business judgment, or sage advice these third parties offer, they also serve as occasional umpires, mediators, judges, or peacekeepers when colleagues cannot resolve conflicts of interest among themselves and as enforcers who ensure that firm interests trump those of individual practitioners.

> There are some times when the conflict has to be resolved by someone who's neutral. Because you just have a situation where one lawyer has one client and another lawyer has a different client and it's sort of a collision. It's more of a business problem, maybe, than a conflicts problem, and then somebody who's neutral, who looks to the firm interest, has to break the tie. . . . One of the main reasons we set up the New Business Committee was that we did have those kinds of problems. Nobody wants to give up business voluntarily. And so we decided it was essential to have sort of a neutral mechanism in place so that we would always have a way of breaking these logjams. And at least it would be perceived as trying to act fairly. Because compensation decisions do depend on the level of business brought in. [7Ch100+]

As I noted earlier, attributes of firm organization, size, substantive expertise, client base, and compensation structure help predict which firms are more likely to turn to enforcers or Solomonic peacemakers. But, whatever the overall amount of discord in a firm, some constellations of colleagues are in greater need of third-party dispute resolution than others. Just as law generally is invoked with greater social distance (Black 1976), third-party oversight is more common in firms where differences over the resolution of conflicts of interest pit partners separated by greater social distance—whether distance is defined physically, geographically, or by substantive specialization, power, age, or gender. For example, when the interests of clients allied with partners of considerably different clout collide, those of the more powerful (i.e., the so-called gorillas) are likely to prevail without outside intervention.

> Those people, obviously, bring all of their baggage into the room. I mean, if one of them is the most senior partner in the firm and another one is the newest partner in the firm, unless the newest partner in the firm says, "This is AT&T that I want to bring in," he's going to lose—if it's a single-matter thing and it's important to the other guy. [44Ch20–49]

> You have to create an atmosphere—and I think we successfully have here—that, when it's a choice between representing Client A and Client B, and Client A is close to a very senior partner in the firm and Client B is close to a new, young partner, that justice is done, that you're not favoring someone because he's the senior partner. . . . We're very strict internally in the firm against favoritism. So we have to talk through these things to get everybody to say, "Now, what is in the best interest of the firm?" And you have to consider the client's best interest too. [5Ch100+]

When disputes erupt among partners in large firms, especially when they cross distant branch offices, colleagues are less able to draw on the social capital of familiarity, reciprocity, and goodwill generally available to intimates to resolve their differences. Committees are often necessary to break the logjam among relative strangers.

> On your facts, if an individual attorney discovers there's a conflict, he will find out that there's a partner or lawyer on the other side. Almost invariably, the first call that's made is to that other lawyer. And if they can work it out, they work it out and we may not hear of it. That doesn't happen that much, because . . . these things usually occur outside a given office. And when it's cross-jurisdictional, . . . cross office borders, almost invariably, our committee is called in to resolve it. Because neither partner wants to necessarily give in. . . . And therefore they need our assistance to help them understand the rules and the role that the firm can play. . . . They are easy [. . .] much easier to resolve [within the office] because we're face to face. . . . If I have a conflict with a client of [office colleague], . . . [colleague] and I are going to go work it out. I'm not going to send it to a committee. . . . If it's a partner—say down in [another city]—and I see that partner once a year; we're good friends, but we're as good a friends as you can be when you see each other once a year. May be a little bit different. Maybe I shouldn't be telling you these things. But I just think that to help you understand the different pressures that are on [this firm] and how you handle them. If it's an environment that's confined to a particular office, it's an environment that's more susceptible to partners working it out in a little bit more civil way. [16Ch100+]

But even where colleagues can resolve differences on their own, firms may prefer third-party dispute resolution so that the interests of the firm as a whole have precedence over those of individuals. Without some centralized control, one matter myopically pursued by an individual practitioner could conflict hundreds of his or her colleagues out of new business and drive away the most significant clients of the firm. With so much at stake, it is not surprising that large firms require third-party oversight and vest it in its most powerful partners.

> . . . the most constructive development that I've seen at this firm has been the development of the New Business Committee screening process. Because, up until then, . . . we didn't really have a centralized mechanism to make sure that the conflicts rules were followed properly or that the business conflicts were resolved in a way that advanced the interest of the firm, as opposed to maybe the most powerful partner. . . . I just wonder how other firms function efficiently, who don't have that sort of process. Because I know how we did before and it was very [. . .] could be acrimonious. [7Ch100+]

> We've thought many times that we won't take a case that involves less than a hundred thousand dollars in fees. But all our, what I call our "little people," would yell and scream and revolt and wouldn't like that. . . . And it happens lots of times. Whenever you've got a conflict, whenever you lose millions of dollars in fees, it's

> because you're getting, collecting five or ten thousand dollars a year from some little person. Okay, that always is the case. It very seldom is that you're giving up millions of dollars of fees because you're collecting millions of dollars from somebody else. It always happens that you've shot yourself. You know, it's a self-inflicted wound. But it's almost unstoppable. . . . And that's why I have to sit as the Supreme Court. Because I'm there to measure the interests of the firm and not the individual interests. And, really, I started to do this because I learned my own lesson. I had a very big case that was offered to me. And one of my partners said she didn't want me to take it because she thought there was a conflict. There was no conflict. It was a client that really produced no business. And I didn't take the matter for millions of dollars in fees. Her client never went anywhere. And then it dawned on me, "Well, this is really stupid." . . . You can't base this upon friendship, collegiality; you have to have somebody who's impartial to sit there and gauge the interests of the firm. [30Ch100+]

So committees and other third parties serve varied functions. They provide dispute resolution services; they balance differences of power; they serve as intermediaries among relative strangers; they serve as the designated "heavy," buffering colleagues and thereby lessening interpersonal hostilities; they represent firm interests and those of powerful clients and partners over those of invested lawyers; they attend to long-term interests, sending away cases that are likely to conflict the firm out of significant future business; they provide ethics expertise; they offer imaginative solutions to seemingly intractable problems; and they serve a self-regulatory function, ensuring that the ethics rules and firm policies are interpreted correctly and followed. Major policy questions or appeals of committee decisions usually go to the firm's managing partner, on to the Management or Executive Committee, and finally to the full partnership. Respondents indicate that such appeals are rare and almost never successful.

In firms in which committees offer expertise and mediation services, lawyers can choose whether to consult with them. When those committees play a self-regulatory function or uphold the interests of the firm over individuals, lawyers are generally required to confer with them. Recall from chapter 8 that committee involvement was optional in half the firms, mandatory for all potential conflicts in a bit more than a fifth, and mandatory for all matters in a bit more than a quarter of the firms. In firms without established third-party overseers, lawyers may assemble ad hoc committees when in need of counsel.

> Well, we don't have any committee. We don't have any compliance officer. Many times—having substantial experience practicing law—you know what the answer is. So you just deal with it. But if you don't, you may well want to consult two or three of your other partners. First of all, it might give you some comfort in the sense that if you talk to three of them, and they all tell you to do the same thing, you haven't made the mistake alone. But it might also be that you feel as though you don't really know the answer to this and that you'd like to get some advice. [51Ch20–49]

DECLINING BUSINESS

Clearly, the easiest way to resolve a conflict of interest is to send away all prospective business that is adverse to the interests of clients of the firm. For a small subset of conflicts, this solution is not only easy but necessary. As I explained in chapter 3, when interests are directly adverse, there is often no alternative. Previous chapters collect examples from diverse settings in which firms, faced with the prospect of litigating against a current or former client (on a matter substantially related to the original matter), decline the new business. As several respondents observed, that's a no-brainer. But these instances of head-to-head adversity represent only a small portion of the declined matters cited throughout the book. The interviews are filled with stories—the ambivalence, disappointment, or anguish often still palpable—of new business turned away where the adversities of interest were far less direct.

Firms declined cases in which they were asked to represent more than one party to a transaction or more than one coplaintiff or codefendant in a lawsuit. They turned away engagements in which another client or former client, represented by a different law firm, was on the other side of a negotiation or transaction or was a coparty on the same side of a dispute. They jettisoned matters in which the adverse party had a social or personal relationship with a lawyer in the firm, was insured by a company that sent business to the firm, was represented by a law firm from which a colleague had been hired laterally, or had a lawyer or major witness who was a client of the firm. They rejected engagements on behalf of parties that were major competitors of important clients. They eschewed litigation on behalf of a client when colleagues in the firm had done the underlying work that led to the dispute. They declined cases in which lawyers or their families served on the boards of or had financial interests in one or more parties. And they turned away seemingly perfectly good cases in which no clashing interests could be found among any of the parties involved.

Respondents explained that firms declined cases because

- they had confidential information about one party that could be used for the benefit of another.
- they risked antagonizing or impairing relations with a valued client or stanching the flow of future business from the client by staying in the case on behalf of another.[3]
- lawyers worried that they might pull some punches or be less vigorous in their advocacy on behalf of the prospective client because of ties or loyalties to other parties in the case—or feared that they would be suspected or accused of doing so.
- they foresaw that the constellation of interests among the parties would most likely shift or that other clients of the firm were likely to join the case.

---

[3]Though sometimes they will keep a case for the very same reason, especially when they fear that the law firm to which the jilted client turns is likely to put moves on the client for a long-term monogamous relationship.

- they suspected that the outcome of the case was likely to harm other clients not directly involved in the matter.
- important clients had given them a general ultimatum about representing this sort of party, taking such cases, or advocating such positions.
- they feared that the engagement would conflict them out of more lucrative future work.

And, on occasion, lawyers will fabricate a conflict of interest or make much of a borderline question as a convenient and benign excuse to decline a case that they don't want for some other reason.

> Sometimes I manufacture a conflict because I don't want to represent somebody. And I can take a little bit of a conflict and—if I think I don't want to handle a case—I'll say to this person that I can't do it because of this conflict. I mean sort of make it more than it really is. If I wanted the case, I could get a waiver for the conflict. [85DSM<10]

Of course, not all firms estimate and weigh the risks similarly. For every respondent who recounted a case that his or her firm had declined because its future trajectory was littered with potential conflicts, several others described identical engagements that their firms had taken, explaining that they deal with the conflicts if and when they arise. Firms have different tolerances or aversion to risk, for one thing. Some need the business more than others. And the fallout of a detonating conflict will be much more toxic for some kinds of firms than others. Nor does a given firm respond to similar matters with comparable risks uniformly. The exercise of discretion reflects criteria such as the sophistication of the client, whether it is a one-shotter or repeat player, the amount of business it directs to the firm, whose client it is, whether it is a routine matter or a so-called bet-the-company case, and so forth.

Virtually every interview in the study contained at least one example, though, in which the firm had declined a prospective matter because it required that the firm champion interests adverse to those of other clients. I wish I could tell you how much business law firms turn away for this reason. Curiously, almost none of them keep track of such things.[4] Some respondents were willing to venture a rough guess, but many were not.[5] And those who did, unfortunately, used different indicators—raw numbers of matters they personally declined or raw numbers of cases

[4]Although sometimes individuals do. A recent profile in the *National Law Journal* described a founding partner of a Chicago law firm (which now employs nearly one hundred attorneys) who left to become a solo litigator. He explained that one reason for his departure was that he was increasingly conflicted out by the transactional work of his colleagues: "In 1991, I began to keep track of how much money I was not able to bring in [due to conflicts] and had to send to other lawyers. By 1996, it grew to almost half a million dollars a year" (Berkman 1997b, A25).

[5]Several noted that colleagues do not need permission to decline matters that pose obvious conflicts, so they had no way of knowing how many conflicts their colleagues declined without informing others in the firm.

turned away by their firm as a whole, proportions of cases declined, numbers of dollars lost, proportions of profits depressed, and so on—and because they didn't always provide a denominator or baseline, it was impossible to convert their estimates into a figure that allowed comparisons across firms. When you learn that a firm declines a few cases a month, it's hard to tell whether the glass is half empty or half full without knowing how many cases are opened each month and whether those lost were likely to generate the same magnitude of revenues as those opened. Other respondents would pick an extreme estimate and then deny that they were anywhere close to it (for example, "it's not zero, but neither is it more than 25 percent" or "I'm not aware of our turning away a million dollars of business because of a conflict"). And others would simply respond, "we turn down business all the time," "not a lot," "very, very, very little," "I'm sure that it's substantial," "can't conceive of it being a lot," "it happens," or "not insignificant and not major."

Respondents themselves questioned the value of these estimates anyway. Several noted that their firm's reputation for advancing certain positions or representing (or avoiding) certain clients or industries is so well known that prospective clients or referral sources know to stay away. So estimates of declined business are artificially low because they don't include the substantial number of matters that firms would have to decline—but never see—if prospective clients did not know to stay away. For many firms, these unseen cases, chilled by visible firm positions, are far more significant than the cases that come through the door and must be sent away because they pose conflicts for the firm.

> You know what? It ain't that much. It really isn't that much. . . . At least the actual sort of legal conflict kind of stuff is not that much. Yeah, what some people say is, "Gee, we're losing a lot that isn't even [. . .] We're not even being considered because of our position on other stuff." . . . So we think we're conflicted out and that we'll never even know it, . . . we'll never be considered. . . . We really have not had a lot of conflicts. . . . we have more of the sort of "presumed" conflict. . . . "What business are we not getting because we're doing all this coverage work?" I mean, that is really the conflict issue for us. And it's amorphous. It's hard. We don't know that, in fact, we've been passed over. We just think we have. [24Ch50–99]

Other respondents noted that when you send clients away because of conflicts, they generally never come back, even when the conflict is over; and it's impossible to estimate that future stream of lost business.

> The biggest factor there would be you probably not only lose that person for this transaction, you probably lose them for everything else they're going to be doing also. And so it's really hard to tell how much business you lose—long range. 'Cause [. . .] say it's just a couple-hundred-dollar case you lose this time. Well, . . . I think clients, in a way, feel betrayed if you send them somewhere else. If you say, "No, we're not going to represent you," they usually don't turn around and come back to you for something else later. And so I think that there's no way of telling how much business you actually do lose, except you lose those people pretty much forever. [116Ch<10]

Others observed that it's difficult to estimate billings forgone; they may turn out to be much less than expected.

> And it's hard to tell. Because you might turn something away that potentially looks great and the lawsuit can settle a month later or a week later. So you're never really sure what you're getting or turning away when you make these decisions. [41Ch50–99]

So I share the following estimates with many grains of salt. They suggest that conflicts of interest are not bankrupting the legal profession but that they can be costly, especially for large law firms. Respondents from two very large firms estimate that, because of conflicts, their firm turns away a third to more than half of all cases; another two large firms are conflicted out of tens of millions of dollars of business annually.[6] A few firms in the thirty-five to one hundred lawyer range decline hundreds of thousands to a few million dollars in fees each year. Respondents from a few other firms of varying size estimate that their firm declines 5 to 10 percent of its prospective business because of conflicts of interest. Even a ten-lawyer firm in a small town loses $100,000 to conflicts each year. Indeed, many of the attorneys practicing in small communities and the positional specialty boutiques declined much higher proportions of cases than did firms of comparable size.

> S: Do you have a sense of how much business you turn away because of these kinds of conflicts questions?
>
> L: No. It would be hard to say. The best answer I could give you is, if I decided to switch and represent [the other side], I am sure I would be very busy immediately. . . . That's probably the best answer for that. That I could go to the other side completely and be busy. [103Ch<10]

And many respondents, even those who observe that their firms are conflicted out of business very rarely, mention the occasional tantalizingly lucrative personal injury plaintiff's case that must be turned away because the firm represents the defendant or the insurer or champions the opposing position in many other cases.

> L2: Great cases—I've turned down just terrific cases—terrific plaintiff's cases—because we have represented the doctor in the past. . . . Oh gosh! We lost a [. . .] I don't want to talk about that. [laughter] . . . Oh, mercy!
>
> L1: It hurts to think about it.
>
> L2: Oh! Just lay-down type of cases involving outrageous conduct. . . . One of our of counsel has represented them. Oh, oh! [absolute anguish amidst laughter] You talk about just being hammered. You know, you just say, "Oh God!" And that's it—goodbye. [54DSL20–49]

---

[6]The managing partner of a Philadelphia law firm of roughly two hundred lawyers observed: "My theory is that of every three phone calls I get, I get to take one on as a client. I've always said that somebody could have a law firm about the size of [this firm] just taking on our conflicted representations" (Berkman 1997a, A16).

Referrals

> When malpractice insurance was a thousand dollars a year, I didn't think about conflicts. Now I farm out cases and worry about the new lawyers keeping a hook on the client. In 1970, I wouldn't have farmed out clients. [90Ch20–49]

Of course, the cost of business turned away can be much greater than the expected revenues generated by the conflicted matter. Clients—angered by the seeming disloyalty of their trusted counselors who refuse to represent them in their hour of need, impressed by the first-rate lawyering of or seduced by the replacement counsel—may never return when the conflict has subsided.

> I don't know a lawyer who doesn't worry about that. [44Ch20–49]

> You hate to do it. We hate to do it. I'm sure there have been times that I've sat here thinking "Is this really a conflict?" And, secondly, "If it is a conflict, can I resolve the conflict by talking to both sides?" I think every lawyer goes through that because of the competition today. It is very heavy, as compared to when I started [over thirty] years ago, I think. And so, yes, you do hesitate before telling the client, "I won't take this business." You're afraid, one, you'll make the client mad . . . and he or she or the institution will go to another firm. You worry, will they try to curry the favor of your client and steal 'em? [laugh] You know. Will they badmouth you? Will they be better than you are—do a better job? Sure, that all goes through our minds. And you make a judgment call. But the call has to be if it's a conflict, it's a conflict. [67DSM10–19]

> And it's often used as a way for somebody else to take your clients. "Don't you realize that he's had a conflict of interest here for twelve years, and he never even told you about it! How can you possibly do business with somebody like that?" . . . Sometimes they [the clients] say, "Gosh, you're right. I'm gonna come to the law firm. I'm gonna come and use you from now on. Thank you for telling me about this awful thing." Or sometimes they say, "That's pretty funny. I'll go tell him you said that." Which is how I know it happens from time to time. [51Ch20–49]

Respondents worry, then, about the new lawyers "keeping a hook on," "pirating," "stealing," or "appropriating" their clients.[7] By directing clients to alternative counsel, some lawyers hope to minimize this risk.

Because the incidence of conflicts of interest is so high for institutional clients and other repeat players, many of them have relationships with a number of alternative law

---

[7]But not all of them:

> When I send somebody to somebody else they owe me. So now they owe me a favor. . . . I'm very happy to send something out. It never hurts. And they're not gonna [. . .] if they can steal my clients, then that's a pretty sad commentary on me. Then I don't have the best law firm in the world—which I think I got. So what do I care? I don't care about sending them someplace else. [30Ch100+]

firms when their first (or second or third) choice is conflicted out. They simply go down their list. But many other clients do not know where to turn, and their lawyers may feel some obligation—or opportunity—to direct them to appropriate counsel when conflicts dictate that they step out of a matter. This referral process is fraught with difficulty. On the one hand, there are ethical concerns. Should lawyers, entangled in conflicting interests, influence or control the client's subsequent choice of representation—directing the client, for example to a law firm that is a less combative adversary? A handful of respondents in firms of all sizes and venues say no.

> I don't per se and we don't per se recommend other firms. Because there really always is that possibility that it may be construed that we're steering . . . one or the other to somebody because of still retaining control. And I think we feel that if we're going to take a step back, we've got to take a step back. So I don't think that we really do steer people one way or the other. [123Ch<10]

These lawyers either refuse to make a referral at all, do so only when the client asks, provide a list of potential candidates rather than a single recommendation, or buffer themselves by referring the client to a lawyer who will refer them to a lawyer.

> I'm not even sure I can send them out to other firms. I think I'll just have to withdraw and say, "I can't give you any advice under any circumstances." Well, for two reasons: . . . One is, there are no other firms I can recommend to do this kind of stuff. And the second is—if I have a conflict—I really can't give any kind of advice, including sending them to another attorney. And I think I just have to leave them high and dry. Which I hate to do, but I don't think I have any choice in the matter. [84CC<10]

> There is a lawyer referral service here, and sometimes we just direct the client to them. In other situations—only because it might be a specialty matter, and by knowledge and experience, we know there are only three or four lawyers who are really doing anything in this area or have the experience necessary to the matter—we'll give the names of everybody who we know is involved. In some specific situations—and again it depends on the dynamics—we will make a specific recommendation for counsel. [49DSL20–49]

> In terms of conflicts, I have these friends getting divorced. And they're both good friends of mine and have stayed both good friends. But I remember the wife calling me up and said, "I don't know what to do. I don't want you to represent me, obviously. And I know you wouldn't. And I don't want you to even refer me to anybody. But could you refer me to someone who could refer me to somebody?" And I did. I called a friend of mine and said, "Refer this woman to somebody who can do her case." And that was five years ago. Naturally, they just wound up the divorce last week. [124Ch<10]

On the other hand, lawyers face a tension between their impulse to find counsel that will not hook the client and their obligation to find good legal representation.

> And we have had—on occasion—to turn things down. And then they say, "Well, where should we go?" And you just think to yourself, well, if I send 'em to a real schmuck—who they'll hate—they'll blame me for sending them to a schmuck who they hate. And if I send 'em to someone really good who does a really good job, then they'll [. . .] But, I mean, I always send 'em to somebody good, actually. [63DSS<10]

> But you're careful who you refer to. You make sure they get quality representation. But you also don't want to refer them to somebody who's quality but you know that they will do everything they can to wine and dine that client and try to keep them. [50DSL20–49]

Lawyers generally resolve the tension in one of several ways. They refer conflicts to friends or office mates. They develop trusting reciprocal relationships with attorneys in other firms and sanction those who abuse their trust:

> Firms are not honorable. But particular individuals are. You know certain individuals will not try to steal your clients. You build up this kind of trust over time. If someone gets burned, it gets known fast. That's the end of the referrals to that individual. [69Ch20–49]

Or they find high-quality counsel that is unable to meet the client's long-term needs. For example, the recommended replacement firm may be too expensive or located out of town:

> It depends on the case. We refer some things to competitors of ours simply because we want the client to get the absolute best representation. And we think these guys are peers and would do as good or better job than we would do—not better, but as good. And we always refer them to somebody that's more expensive than we are. I'm not joking about that. And there's a business reason for that, obviously. There's no use sending them to somebody that's cheaper than we are. That doesn't make us look good. . . . But they're good firms—they're damn good firms. [13Ch50–99]

Even more common, lawyers will refer matters to much smaller firms or specialty boutiques that are unable to service the diverse future legal needs of the client.

> But we have found that we are not a threat when something does get referred to us by a general corporate firm. Because we don't know tax law, we don't know transactional work, we don't do real estate work. And so we're brought in kind of as the "hired gun" on the specialty, and then we're out of the picture. [82Ch10–19]

Indeed, a number of smaller firms in the sample acknowledged that they are more often the beneficiary of other people's conflicts than beset by their own. That's how several new law firms got their start.

> Well, this firm kind of grew up—it's kind of interesting—on receiving conflict business from other large firms. We are a spin-off of [a major Chicago firm]. And one thing that [my colleague] did and did well was allow Kirkland, Sidley, Winston, other big firms, who knew [him] to park a client here on occasion because of a conflict, knowing full well that we would respect the fact that the next issue that arose, it would go back to them when the conflict was removed. We would never make it a point of trying to court that client to stay here. It's just kind of an unwritten rule. And as a result, we got a lot of conflict work as a small firm. And we grew on that conflict work. Because of that, we have similar understandings with partners and former associates who were here, who've gone out to open up their own shop. We've parked some of our conflict work with them, with a similar understanding that they'll do that job and, when the next issue arises, the client comes back here. . . . We respect the fact that, if someone will entrust us with a client for a specific purpose, when we've solved that issue, that client will remain with whoever sent it. [59Ch50–99]

Whatever reciprocal relationships firms develop, stratagems they employ, or sanctions they impose to attract the client back after the conflict has ended, some clients will prefer the new firm.

> That becomes a very one-on-one, personal relationship between, for example, me and the lawyer at the law firm that I would send the client to. But, to be frank, [snicker] you never know. I mean, he's as hungry as I am. And, if the client says to him, "I have been with [L names himself]. [L] did a nice job for me. But I like the job that you did in particular. I mean [L] didn't seem to be interested in me. He seemed to have his practice growing so fast, that he wants to side with this other client that is opposed to me. So, I'd rather stick with you." What can I do? I mean, I can't really blame my colleague to whom I referred. [77Ch10–19]

As one respondent philosophically explained,

> If we refer a client somewhere else—even for one matter—and the client happens to like those lawyers better than us, well, that's life. [94Ch10–19]

But, of course, there's a flip side: some clients will respect their original (conflicted) lawyers even more because of the way they responded to the potential conflict and anxiously return when the conflict has run its course.

> It is very difficult to turn away a very good potential client because you've got a conflict. Again, though, the sense that we have is that, if you deal with the person fairly, they're going to respect that and maybe—somewhere down the road—will come back. It may be that you'll lose them totally. But, if you can put that client in touch with somebody good and they get a good result, they're going to respect you. And, obviously, if they get [a] good result, they're going to like the person that you referred them to. And you may lose that business. But again, that person may have a conflict down the road or that person may not be around. And then it

> may come back. So you do the best you can on that situation. And it is difficult. Because . . . the market right now is terrible. There is so much competition out there. [82Ch10–19]

CONSULTING WITH CLIENTS

Though clients are sometimes kept out of the loop—as they were in the examples in the previous section—frequently lawyers decide whether to accept or decline a new engagement after first consulting the affected clients. It is only necessary to read clients' minds or make a unilateral decision when lawyers fear that the mere asking will betray a confidence or irreparably harm their relationship with the clients, or that clients will tell them what they don't want to hear (and which they will then be obliged to honor). Even casual conversations often yield important data about the risks or possible rifts that could follow a decision to advance an unpopular position or represent a competitor, adversary, or rival; about the likelihood that a conflict or dispute will arise in the future; and about ways to keep clients happy and protected without having to turn away business. These conversations may lead some prospective clients to take their business elsewhere and some attorneys to decline the engagement, others to proceed with the new case or a piece of it, and others to seek formal consent.

Attorneys often confer with clients over matters that are not true conflicts of interest but that may be perceived as a conflict or at least as a significant breach of loyalty. Rarely will the prospective matter be so lucrative or compelling that it is worth undermining a valued long-term relationship with an important client, even if ethically permitted. But some clients may actually welcome having their counselors on the opposite side, or at least not object to it, under certain circumstances. So it might be worth checking out client reactions rather than either automatically declining the new case—on the assumption that it will alienate the ongoing client—or taking on the new matter, because it doesn't technically violate the ethics rules, and later facing the unexpected wrath of a client who feels betrayed.

> I've had situations where one client will be buying a subsidiary of another client. And I will call the second client and say, "Look, we've been asked to represent client A buying your subsidiary. And I know you haven't called me to represent you in the sale, so do you have any objection?" And they will say, "Well, we're doing it in-house." And, most times, good general counsels will say, "I just as soon have you on the other side. 'Cause I know you guys will do a good job. You won't play games like Skadden, Arps or Wachtell, Lipton [two major New York law firms, the first of which has an office in Chicago] will. We want to get the deal done. So go ahead." Sometimes they'll say, "Oops, this is our president's favorite little toy. I think this might be a problem. And if I was using outside counsel, I wouldn't care. But I'd just as soon you guys not be involved, because it's a very visible transaction that may impact on my boss's feeling about you." But that's very rare. Most people, . . . the main thing they want is, they want you to talk to them. They just don't want to be hit. . . . But if you call them and talk them through it, and sometimes, in the middle of the conversation, . . . I can find myself

> saying, "Hey, you know what, Tom? The more I think about this, this isn't worth it to either one of us. I mean, I can hear you saying you agree with it. But the more I think about it, maybe this isn't a good idea." And I'll pull out of it. [18Ch100+]

For example, attorneys may consult with a valued client before taking on an engagement for a major competitor or confer with an insurance company—whose insureds the firm frequently defends—before taking a matter adverse to one of its other insureds, or disclose—as a courtesy to a former client—that the firm has taken a case against the former client on an issue unrelated to the original representation:

> But we have a client in an industry. It's a good client of mine. When I say good client, what I mean is a very close personal friendship with the chairman and owner of the company. And in terms of a revenue generator, it's not huge, but it's regular. And they pay their bills on time. They're nice people. And they're honorable clients. And they're just, they're good clients to have. Now, another one of my partners walked in the door with an opportunity where someone in the same business, but not really a competitor—because the products are different—wants to do a start-up business that would not be in direct competition with my client but would create business issues for my client—directly, not just theoretically. And I said, "Wait a minute. You know, that really might piss them off." And we have yet to work it out. But I've not agreed to take that other client into the firm until I can sit down and have a real heart-to-heart [with my client]. And say, "Okay, this is the deal. Is it a problem?" [104Ch10–19]

> See, sometimes it would be handled informally. What I would say is, "You know what, call up the American Bar Foundation's lawyer and say, 'As a courtesy, I'm telling you right now that we're going to represent Susan Shapiro. And we don't believe our representation of you five years ago on a lease was a conflict. As a courtesy, we're letting you know. I'm not telling you we're going to not file it, but I want you to know that we've [been] asked to undertake the representation.' " That sort of puts the American Bar Foundation on notice that if they want to make a stink about it, they can. . . . usually it puts them in the position where you say, "We're letting you know, but we don't think there's a conflict," they'll say, "It's fine, we don't have a problem with that." [39Ch50–99]

These courtesy disclosures may flush out unanticipated problems or identify situations in which adversaries are likely to make trouble for the firm, even if the source of their animosity falls short of a true conflict of interest. These reactions may persuade the firm to decline the prospective engagement outright or at least disclose the risk to the prospective client that the opposing party may seek to disqualify the firm.

> . . . you should be telling your client, "Hey, listen, we represented client A five years ago. We're not doing anything with him now. We don't think we have any confidential information. But there is a chance that they will disqual [. . .] " If you haven't told your client that and the motion comes in, they're going to be

> madder than a hornet at you. Because then, all of a sudden, they have to decide: "Do I want to spend twenty thousand dollars defending this disqualification motion with [this firm] or should I just go hire Sidley & Austin [one of the largest law firms in Chicago]?" [18Ch100+]

The risk of disqualification is but one of many disclosures that firms may make to prospective clients. Lawyers may disclose the firm's relationships with and loyalties to adverse parties—for example, that the firm derives substantial income from the insurer of the adverse party:

> You know, if I do take it, I will have said to both client and the insurer, "Look, I normally do State Farm's work. I have a lot of other cases here for State Farm. You have to know that. You have to know that there might be a problem from your standpoint. I mean, we're going to represent you, but you have to understand that I have other cases goin' with 'em. And I derive my monies from them." And then—same thing—"Do you want me to take this case against you, State Farm? I mean, I know how you think, etc." [68DSM10–19]

They report that the firm represents or has a relationship with the opposing lawyer on an unrelated case:

> Take an instance where we serve as an expert witness on behalf of another law firm sued for malpractice. Meanwhile, that law firm is representing a party adverse to one of our clients. That is not a conflict. But if we should lose the case and our client finds out about that relationship, they might say that we should have told them. [34Ch50–99]

They disclose that the prospective client's interests are at odds with those of other clients of the firm and positions that the firm is likely to take in the future:

> I have still always maintained that I am hired to advocate a client's position in one case and another client's position in another place. If those two aren't directly opposed, the others are what I call "indirect conflicts" and should not be preventable. Now, do you have a duty to the client, however, to say to that client, you are advocating or may be advocating a different position? . . . That's an entirely different issue. The client, maybe, should be told—and God knows I don't think you do it all the time . . . "Your position that you're asking me to assert here under the antitrust laws may be a position that I will take the opposite view on when I'm representing the plaintiff over here in another suit." I don't think many people do that. [11Ch100+]

Or they acknowledge that one or more members of the law firm have a personal or financial interest in their adversary:

> I was just asked to represent someone adverse to a large company that holds a lot of real estate, commercial real estate that they lease. We represent someone in a

> dispute over the lease. It turns out that one of my partner's wives is an investor in this big real estate company. So, in fact, what I'm doing is suing a company that my partner's wife—and probably, for all practical purposes, my partner—has a very, very small financial interest in. And this is a very, very small lease dispute, . . . probably settled in the ten-thousand-to-thirty-thousand-dollar range. Technically, that's not a conflict of interest. . . . And, basically, I said to my partner, ". . . Do you or your wife have any serious objection to our taking this matter?" And he said, "No, because her holding is so small and they get sued by a million different people for a million different reasons all the time." And then I went to the client and I said, "I don't think this is a conflict and it's not going to affect my representation in any way, but I need to tell you that one of my partners has a small investment in the defendant." Which normally would make a plaintiff pretty nervous but, given the nature of the size of this company, I don't think—and given the dispute at issue—I think my client is confident that I'm not going to take a dive because it's going to affect my partner's financial interests. So that's a situation where . . . a lot of just communicating what might be potential conflict orally, basically, just makes it go away. [39Ch50–99]

These conversations may highlight other risks to the prospective client or clients as well—for example, that, if a particular party later joins the litigation, the firm will have to withdraw; that the unanimity of interests among coparties may erode over time, undermining their continued joint representation; and so on.

> I'm aware of one time where I told two defendants that . . . I felt that we could represent the codefendants, that, depending on what came out in discovery and so on and so forth, that . . . there might develop a point at which there is a conflict between them. And that, if that point occurred and if they were required to get separate representation, I probably could no longer represent either of them, because I would have learned from both of them information and . . . if I stayed on with A, I could use the information that I learned from B against him and so on. And that, if there did come a point where there was a conflict—and I laid out where the potential reasons why a conflict might occur—they would both need to get a new lawyer and that would be very expensive to them. But that, in the meantime, as long as the following things didn't occur, I felt, in good faith, I could represent them both as codefendants. . . and that it was really their choice to make. And I've explained that to them. [39Ch50–99]

Such casual conversations with clients, informally testing the waters, feeling the parties out, and sharing some information are generally adequate when the prospective matter falls short of a true conflict of interest. When attorneys hope to proceed in the face of real conflicts, disclosures alone are not sufficient.

Waivers

> S: Do you have a sense of how much business is being turned away because of conflicts?

L: Relatively little, because we've been pretty successful in getting waivers. . . . I mean, the conflicts of interest are clearly a problem in growing our practice in the future, simply because you gotta go and get waivers. Either that, or you're just not going to go after the work. [26Ch100+]

When lawyers believe that the representation will neither be adversely affected by their obligations to champion the interests of other clients nor adversely affect other cases, and when the clients consent after consultation, the *Model Rules of Professional Conduct* allow firms to represent conflicting interests.

You may recall from chapter 4 a long letter, read by a respondent working in a very small Chicago law firm and addressed to two coworkers who were charging their employer with racial harassment. The letter set out the strengths as well as the risks of representing them jointly, which included issues of confidentiality and the ways in which the coworkers' interests might diverge as the lawsuit evolved, and explained that, should conflicts of interest arise in the future, the attorney would withdraw from representing both of them. The letter asked for the prospective clients' signatures, indicating that they read and understood the letter and agreed to the joint representation. That letter is an example of a conflicts waiver. Figures 9.1 and 9.2 present two generic waiver letters supplied by a large firm, the first a waiver of an actual conflict of interest, the second of a potential conflict. As is common in formal conflicts waivers, the letters disclose

- the nature of the adversity and, where appropriate, why the attorney believes that an actual conflict of interest does not exist.
- the judgment that the representation of one will not adversely affect that of the other.
- how the firm will protect confidential information.
- how a conflict of interest could arise in the future.
- what would happen if a direct adversity developed between the clients or if it was necessary for the firm to withdraw from the matter.

The letters ask that the client consent to the firm's representation of the other party and that the client waive the right to disqualify the firm unless specified future events occur. The letters finally recommend that the client consult with another attorney in deciding whether to give its consent to the conflicts waiver.

L1: . . . we suggest to the client—in the conflict situation—that he may want to have another lawyer look at this before he decides to waive his conflict. And that created a great deal of trouble in our law firm. Because many people said, "Are you kidding? [laughter] We are going to tell our client—who wants to hire us—to go to another lawyer? That lawyer is going to say, 'Then why didn't you hire me? I don't have any conflict.' " [laughter] But anyway, I think it's the way you have to approach it.

L2: And actually—kind of as an amusing aside—our people here have now become used to that. And, in fact, they've become so used to it—the language here says "You may wish to consult with another attorney"—. . . that they will

You have asked us to perform the following services [describe in detail] in connection with [describe the matter and provide a suitable name for the matter – for the purposes of this form letter the term, the "Matter," is used] on behalf of [name of Requesting Client]. As I have discussed with you, we presently represent [name of Conflicted Client] in connection with [give general description of the matters in which we represent the Conflicted Client, providing enough detail so as to convey the nature, extent, and depth of our relationship with the Conflicted Client without disclosing any confidences], and we have represented [name of Conflicted Client] in the past with respect to [give general description of the matters in which we have represented the Conflicted Client, providing enough detail so as to convey the nature, extent, and depth of our relationship with the Conflicted Client without disclosing any confidences].

Since the legal service you are requesting us to perform will be adverse to [name of Conflicted Client], and since our attorneys use their best efforts to obtain favorable results for the clients that they represent, a conflict of interest would arise out of our representation of [name of Requesting Client] with respect to the Matter. While we believe that our continuing representation of [name of Conflicted Client] in the matters described above, and in other matters unrelated to the Matter that [name of Conflicted Client] may refer to us in the future will not adversely affect our relationship with [name of Requesting Client] and, while we believe that our representation of [name of Requesting Client] in the Matter will not adversely affect our relationship with [name of Conflicted Client], we will not proceed with such a dual representation without first obtaining the consent and agreement of both clients. We therefore ask for [name of Requesting Client]'s consent to our continuing representation of [name of Conflicted Client] in the on-going matters described above and in other matters, unrelated to the Matter, that may be referred to us by [name of Conflicted Client] in the future. We are sending a similar letter to [name of Conflicted Client], seeking [his/her/its] consent to our representation of [name of Requesting Client] in the Matter, as well as to our continuing representation of [name of Requesting Client] in other, unrelated matters.

A major concern that arises from dual representation is the possibility that confidential information of one party that is shared with its attorneys may be disclosed to the other party. To prevent this from happening, we have taken and will continue to take a number of internal precautions. First, two distinct teams of attorneys and staff have been established, each to represent one of the clients. During the pendency of the representation, no member of the team representing one party will be allowed to work on any matter involving the other party [or any partner, shareholder, affiliate, etc., of the other party]. Further, no member of the team representing one party will be allowed access to any of the files of the other party. Members of these teams will be prohibited from discussing any aspect of the Matter or any other matter involving the other party with any member of the other team.

We ask that both [name of Requesting Client] and [name of Conflicted Client] agree to these procedures, and that they further agree that they will not seek or accept the disclosure of information about the other party from anyone at our firm. Further, we ask both parties to agree that the disclosure of information to us by the other party will not constitute, or be deemed to be, a waiver of any privilege, and that they will not assert or make any such contention at a later date. We also ask that both parties consent and agree that we will have no obligation to disclose to them any information either obtained by us from the other client, or obtained or learned by us in the course of representing the other client.

Another major concern in dual representation is that, after the attorneys have spent time and effort becoming thoroughly acquainted with a matter, one of the clients may demand that the law firm withdraw from representing the other party, thereby placing the other party in a position where it must incur the time and expense of retaining and educating new counsel. To ensure that this does not occur, we ask that both [name of Requesting Client] and [name of Conflicted Client] agree to the dual representation, and that they both waive any right to disqualify our firm from representing the other party, unless [a specific event that places the clients in a direct conflict] or litigation arises between [name of Requesting Client] and [name of Conflicted Client] with respect to the Matter. [Include any other limitation that the clients may insist upon.] If such a circumstance should occur, we will withdraw from any further representation, including consultation and the rendering of advice, of both parties regarding the Matter, and both parties will be required to obtain new counsel with respect to the matter. You should also be aware that other events may occur in the future which, under the Rules of Professional Conduct, may require us to withdraw from further representation of either or both parties. Should such a situation occur, we will bring it to your attention, and in the exercise of our professional judgment, take such steps as may be necessary or appropriate.

Please indicate your agreement with and consent to the foregoing matters by signing the consent set forth below and returning an executed copy of this letter to my attention. You may wish to consult with another attorney before doing so. If you have any questions, please do not hesitate to call me.

AGREEMENT & CONSENT

The undersigned hereby acknowledges receipt of, approval of, agreement with, and consent to the terms of the foregoing letter, this ________ day of ________, 19__.

[Name of Requesting Client].

By: ________________ Its: ________________

Fig. 9.1. Conflict Waiver and Consent Letter (Actual Conflict of Interest)

send a letter to the general counsel of a major corporation and they will leave that in there. [laughter]

L1: The guy will call up and say, "Are you kidding? I am a lawyer!" [11Ch100+]

The letters reproduced in figures 9.1 and 9.2 are intended to secure the consent of the client ("Requesting Client") hoping to engage the firm in the new mat-

You have asked us to perform the following services [describe in detail] in connection with [describe the matter and provide a suitable name for the matter – for purposes of this form letter the term, the "Matter," is used] on behalf of [name of Requesting Client]. As I have discussed with you, [name of Conflicted Client] is [potentially] involved in the Matter. [State the nature and extent of Conflicted Client's participation in, or connection with, the Matter]. While we do not represent [name of Conflicted Client] with respect to the Matter, we have represented and presently represent [name of Conflicted Client] in connection with certain unrelated matters concerning [give general description of unrelated matters in which we represent or have represented the Conflicted Client, providing enough detail so as to convey the nature, extent, and depth of our relationship with the Conflicted Client without disclosing any confidences.]

You have informed us that: [If the Requesting Client has given you facts or assurances upon which you have based your judgment, in any way, that an actual conflict does not exist, state them here]. Based upon the facts, as you have explained them to us, representation of [name of Requesting Client] with respect to the Matter will not result in a conflict of interest with its representation of [name of Conflicted Client]. However, we would not wish to undertake such a dual representation without both clients being fully aware of it, and agreeing to it. Also, there is always the possibility that a conflict could develop in the future, and it is best to deal with that possibility before it occurs.

For example, [explain the circumstances that could give rise to a foreseeable conflict]. [If the potential conflict would not be waivable, use the following]: Should such a conflict arise, we would withdraw from any further representation, including any consultation or the rendering of advice, of both clients regarding the Matter, and both clients would be required to obtain new counsel with respect to the Matter. [If the potential conflict is waivable, then the agreement of the parties should be stated. Either the same language as the preceding sentence, or the following should be used.] Should such conflict arise, we would represent [name of Requesting Client] with respect to the Matter, and we would decline any representation of [name of Conflicted Client] with respect to the Matter, including any consultation or the rendering of advice. While we believe that our representation of [name of Requesting Client] under those circumstances would not adversely affect our relationship with [name of Conflicted Client] and, while we believe that our representation of [name of Conflicted Client] would not adversely affect our relationship with [name of Requesting Client], we nonetheless seek the agreement and consent of both parties to such representations should such circumstances arise in the future.

You should also be aware that other unforeseen events may occur in the future which may require us to withdraw from any further representation of either or both parties. Should such a situation occur, we will bring it to your attention, and in the exercise of our professional judgment, take such steps as may be necessary or appropriate.

A major concern that arises from dual representation is the possibility that confidential information of one party that is shared with its attorneys may be disclosed to the other party. To prevent this from happening, we have taken and will continue to take a number of internal precautions. First, two distinct teams of attorneys and staff have been established, each to represent one of the clients. During the pendency of the representation of [name of Requesting Client] with respect to the Matter, no member of the team representing one party will be allowed to work on any matter involving the other party [or any partner, shareholder, affiliate, etc., of the other party]. Further, no member of the team representing one party will be allowed access to any of the files of the other party. Members of these teams will be prohibited from discussing any aspect of the Matter or any other matter involving the other party with any member of the other team.

We ask that both [name of Requesting Client] and [name of Conflicted Client] agree to these procedures, and that they further agree that they will not seek or accept the disclosure of information about the other party from anyone at our firm. Further, we ask both parties to agree that the disclosure of information to us by the other party will not constitute, or be deemed to be, a waiver of any privilege, and that they will not assert or make any such contention at a later date. We also ask that both parties consent and agree that we will have no obligation to disclose to them any information either obtained by us from the other client, or obtained or learned by us in the course of representing the other client.

In fairness to [name of Conflicted Client], we must also ask that you agree that, should we undertake the representation of [name of Requesting Client] with respect to the Matter, [name of Requesting Client] will not use or assert that circumstance as a basis for disqualifying, or seeking to disqualify, us from further representation of [name of Conflicted Client] with respect to the on-going matters described above, or with respect to other, unrelated matters that [name of Conflicted Client] may refer to us in the future.

Your signing this letter in the space provided below will indicate that you have read this letter, that you understand its contents, that you confirm the facts that have been related to us, and that you consent to our firm's continued representation of [name of Conflicted Client] and of our firm's representation of [Requesting Client] under the terms and conditions stated in this letter. You may wish to consult with another attorney before signing. If you have any questions, please do not hesitate to call me.

AGREEMENT & CONSENT

The undersigned hereby acknowledges receipt of, approval of, agreement with, and consent to the terms of the foregoing letter, this ________ day of ________, 19__.

[Name of Requesting Client].

By: ________________ Its: ________________

Fig. 9.2. Conflict Waiver and Consent Letter (Potential Conflict of Interest)

ter; there are separate letters for what the forms call the "Conflicted Client," the current or former client of the firm whose interests are or could be adverse in the future to those of the prospective client. These too must be signed before attorneys in the firm can take on the new engagement. These generic consent forms assume that the conflicts involve only two parties. When, as is frequently the case, many more parties have direct or indirect interests in the matter or future matters, the disclosures become even more complex and the number of required waivers quite large.

> And we represented [more than one hundred] clients in a Superfund case. And we did that through a joint defense agreement, requiring a specific waiver from every one of them. It was very cumbersome, . . . took two months to put in place. . . . I think it was worth it, because we convinced ourself we could do it, first of all. And second of all, I think it was appreciated from a business point of view on the other side. I think people really thought we were being as aboveboard as we could possibly be and removed any potential clouds from the situation. I thought it worked okay. I thought it was more trouble than it was worth, to be honest. [27Ch50–99]

Several firms in the sample—generally the larger ones—prepare similar sorts of boilerplate waivers or consent letters, leaving substantial sections blank, in which attorneys specify the substantive issues unique to the specific matter and the interests of the assorted parties.

> We provide to every lawyer in the firm—as part of our manual—a pretty careful outline about how to resolve these simple conflicts and what kind of waivers are required. And we have provided to our partners drafts of the various different kinds of engagement letters and conflict waiver letters. In addition, we have lodged in each office . . . draft engagement letters that we've used in the past. . . . So, if a partner reads the letter in the book and says, "Well, it's close, but it's not quite right," there is an ability for that partner to come talk to us [the Professional Responsibility Committee], see other forms, whatever. [23Ch100+]

Other firms do not, because they worry that lawyers will rely too heavily on the forms and fail to think through the implications of a potential conflict of interest.

> I should, though, say, we do not have a standard form of consent letter. And that's deliberate. And the reason is that I want people to think about what the letter says. And if I give them a form, then they'll fill in the blanks. So I usually try to do a little missionary work and explain to them what the rules are, why there is a conflict, whether it's a [*Model Rules of Professional Conduct* Rule] 1.7(a) situation, a 1.7(b) situation, a 1.9 situation and why those require separate kinds of approaches. And, from time to time, if the people want me to or I think it's appropriate—and it's really a case-by-case situation—then I'll review the consent letter before it goes out. [36Ch100+]

Whether adapted from a boilerplate form or drafted from scratch, these rather complex, formal disclosure documents are the exception more than the rule among respondents in the study. The procedures for disclosing and securing consent to actual or potential conflicts of interest among their firms fall on a continuum, with documents like figures 9.1 and 9.2 on one end and casual conversations on the other. Far more respondents secure consent orally than in writing.[8]

> I don't think they're [written consent] that bad. But people don't like getting things in writing, because they think that . . . then the client really reads it and sees what it all means, and they're not going to want to sign off on it. [18Ch100+]

> L: [Lawyer is effecting a buy-sell agreement on behalf of both sides] I told him very simply. I said, "I will, we will work out a deal. . . . But I'm going to propose terms that you might be able to get a better deal if you went with somebody else." . . . I assume that there are probably some people who today would say that we should have a full written sign-off on all of that.
>
> S: You mean, waivers disclosing [. . .]
>
> L: Yeah. . . . We did not in this case. I have a memo in the file. I trust the people in the deal. Maybe I'm wrong. I don't think so. [53DSL20–49]

Even firms that typically secure written waivers will make exceptions:

> If it's a business transaction and the adversity is an adversity that is [. . .] the other side of a business transaction that's not going to generate any serious liabilities as I look at it, then I might say, "Alright, well, you call, and if you get a consent from both sides, inform me." And I make a note who said it—which lawyer said it—that it was an oral consent. If in litigation in a directly adverse situation, I'm more inclined to require a written consent which I will attach to the screening form before I sign off on it, so we have a record of that. [4Ch100+]

> If they're big people, I wouldn't ask for anything in writing. You know, if they're sophisticated businessmen and so on and so forth, I think that people understand these things and you don't need to get it in writing. On the other hand, if it's, well, let's say, a widow and three children, ages twenty-three, twenty-four and twenty-five, and it's a big trust matter, I might well get it in writing. . . . And we were asked to represent all of them in litigation. . . . So we'd see automatically that there was some conflict. But, if they said, "Oh no, we're all one big one happy family," I might very well ask for something in writing in that situation—while they're still one big happy family. [51Ch20–49]

And even the written "consents" fall short of the formal informed-consent model embodied in figures 9.1 and 9.2. Generally, they take the form of a letter sent to a client reporting on the conversation in which the client orally waived the conflict:

---

[8]Although some states in which these attorneys practice require that conflicts consent waivers be in writing. Moreover, in a very spirited debate, the ABA House of Delegates, as part of its Ethics 2000 process, voted 57 percent to 43 percent—at least in the first round—to require that conflicts waivers be in writing (American Bar Association 2001, Rule 1.7b(4); Commentary Rule 1.7, paragraph 20; I observed the vote count).

> You normally would discuss it with them verbally, of course, first and say, "Well, there's a conflict or potential conflict here because of this historical matter or this circumstance. However, under the Canons, this is waivable, if you choose to do so." And you'll discuss it. And if they'll say, "Yes," then, typically, what we would do is send out a confirming letter. "This will confirm our conversation of yesterday where we discussed that this firm has previously represented this client or been adverse to you. However, as we further discussed, this is a matter you can waive if you want. It is our understanding that, with this knowledge, you want to waive the conflict and have us proceed to represent you," and then go on from there. [50DSL20–49]

Others rely on a few boilerplate sentences embedded in a standard engagement letter:

> We defend workers' compensation claims involving asbestos-related injuries. Let's say we are defending one of the companies that used asbestos in a workers' comp case against them. We might state in the engagement letter to the client that "We also represent one of the asbestos producers. They are not presently a defendant in this case. But there may come a time that they will be. Or there may come a time when they will have a claim against you. We reserve the right to withdraw from our representation of you under these circumstances. You are not objecting that we do so. And we reserve the right to revisit these matters at some point in the future." [38Ch50–99]

Unlike the conflicts letter from chapter 4, clients were not asked to sign or return anything in these examples; a copy of the letter was simply filed away.

Despite their predilection to secure consent informally, many respondents indicate that the "legal climate" and concern about malpractice liability have motivated them to get more in writing than they did in the past.

> A lot of firms don't do that and they don't have written consents. You know, you get adverse to a client . . . and, boy, they start trotting out everything, like, "I didn't know about that you represented them," and all that stuff. The lawyers just say, "Well, here's my time record for this date. And I called you." And the guy says, "I don't remember you ever raising it." Well, it's awfully nice to hand the guy the document and say, "Well, what about the letter that you signed on such-and-such a date; is that not your signature?" But I've seen that, time and time again, when people get—not in our firm—but people get into those kind of situations. And they don't have any record. Yeah, they have internal records that they checked the conflict, but that's a self-serving document, as the courts say. [18Ch100+]

And several respondents indicated that they probably should get waivers in writing but rarely get around to it.

> I haven't done written things, and I should. . . . When the ARDC [Attorney Registration and Disciplinary Commission] complaint is made that . . .—and you don't know when that's going to happen—so, it would be smarter to have that. [85DSM<10]

L: And there are some situations where, on disclosure to the bank and to the other party, they say, "Go ahead." . . .
S: Do you get those in writing?
L: Probably not. I would guess not. It's something we should do. There's a lot of things we should do that we—I'm sure you've found that out in seventy-five law firms that they don't [laughter] get done either. [74DSL<10]

Protecting Confidentiality

Note that both the actual and potential conflict-of-interest waivers depicted in figures 9.1 and 9.2 indicate that in order to ensure confidentiality, the teams of lawyers will be kept absolutely separate during the pendency of the representation. So-called Chinese walls or ethical screens—typically used when lawyers are hired laterally from government or another law firm—will be considered later in the chapter. The arrangements described in these boilerplate waivers are not unlike such screens. They promise to segregate the lawyers, files, and secrets of one client from those of another. Though not required by law nor enjoying any legal protection in this context, these voluntary structures are erected to increase the comfort level of clients asked to consent to conflicts of interest.

> By the way, . . . you should understand that we do set up prophylactic systems on all of our conflicts. Neither the Seventh Circuit nor the Rules have really said that prophylactic systems are—in themselves—sufficient, except in the lateral situation. But we've done that in all situations as an extra guard, number one, and also defensively. Because it's always hard to prove a negative. And it's hard to prove that we didn't transgress, that we didn't cross over these boundaries. And if you have, at least, a system set up in the beginning, I think it helps to show your attempts to prevent any transgressions of confidential information being divulged to someone else. So we lock files, as it were. We say, "No, the files have to be labeled." We say that they have to be kept in a certain area, that no one on this team can have access to any of these files, etc. . . . We tell the client that we will do this, and we do it routinely. [11Ch100+]

> In the firm, we have them all the time, unfortunately—you have to. And it's not only with laterals, it's just where the clients sort of do want you involved, but they don't want that lawyer over here involved. And so, if you can Chinese wall it off to their satisfaction, they'll go along with it. [18Ch100+]

Indeed, in some instances, the clients themselves requested the ethical screens.

> We'll frequently offer a Chinese wall, sometimes where they'll ask for it even if we haven't offered it. . . . With the Chinese wall comes a bunch of things: file security and no cross-communication. . . . Very common. It comes up all the time in what I think of as business conflicts more than ethical conflicts. Clients are concerned about the confidentiality of their information. And they want to make sure that if you're off doing different kind of work for another client, that they have no access and no lawyer has any access. So they take a great deal of comfort from it. [7Ch100+]

Though Chinese walls tend to stand only as long as the problematic matter remains open, they can, in rare instances, become historic landmarks, like the famous Great Wall of China for which they were named. At least one respondent described a screen he expected to be in place permanently in his firm. Recall from chapter 5 the smallish Chicago law firm that represents two very large retail chains:

> One of them we've represented for a number of years; the other came in fairly recently—about two years ago. When that first came in, obviously, we saw a very strong potential conflict, but talked to our contacts at the first retail chain. And they said, "As long as you create a Chinese wall in your firm, we can live with it." And the new client coming in could live with that as well. . . . We basically spelled out how we'd handle the files, the attorneys that would be involved in it. We listed out the cases that we were doing for the first corporation, and made sure that the people that were going to be doing the work for the second corporation had never been involved in it. [82Ch10–19]

Securing Consent

If I were to retell, from beginning to end, the myriad stories that fill the first half of this book and recount the varied ways in which conflicts of interest arise in the practice of law, many of them would conclude with a conflicts waiver or an effort to secure one. But surely this ending would be most repetitious in the retelling of chapter 6, "As Time Goes By," because time often acts as a conflicts catalyst, transforming interests and introducing new ones, rending alliances, and roiling what were initially trivial adversities. Were lawyers able to foresee how their cases and clients would evolve, they would decline many at the outset. But doing so after the passage of time is not so easy. Withdrawing from a matter or ending a relationship after it is well underway risks violating hot-potato rules, not to mention harming a client, undermining valued client relationships, losing substantial revenues, inviting a malpractice suit or disciplinary proceeding, facing embarrassment, and fracturing internal firm harmony. Conflicts waivers sometimes offer a safer alternative.

Some stories in chapter 6 begin with disclosure and consent. In variations on the conflicts waiver reproduced in figure 9.2 or the letter to the two coemployees in chapter 4, lawyers spell out—in advance—the varied ways in which conflicts might detonate down the road and how the firm would respond. Some respondents believe they owe it to their clients to disclose these risks while they can still go elsewhere for legal counsel and, besides, they argue, consent is easier to secure when things are still rosy.

> We do find that the initial waivers are a lot easier to get than those unexpected conflicts that come up later on. They tend to be a lot tougher at that point, because [clients] feel like they've got you over a barrel. And they do. [1Ch100+]

Other stories begin with no waiver at all; lawyers wait for the conflicts to detonate and then turn to disclosure and consent as a way of containing the damage.

> L: . . . you represent a person and that person decides to form a partnership or a corporation and brings in a few investors. And then you begin doing work for

the corporation. And then there's a dispute. And these other people are saying, "You represent the corporation. You represent the partnership. You must do what's best for the corporation. And we, of course, know what's best for the corporation." And it's not what your former client—who's now the president and 50 percent shareholder—wants to be done. . . . I think that's a tremendously difficult problem.

S: And what do you do to protect against being involved in that kind of situation? Or do you just wait till it happens and figure out how to [. . .]?

L: Oh, I wait till it happens and figure out how to deal with it. Because, nine out of ten times, it never happens.

S: And what options do you see available in that situation?

L: If it gets too bad, probably getting out entirely.

S: Would you ever, at the beginning of the creation of this new corporation, make disclosures about, "in the event of a dispute, I will be representing X and not Y?"

L: Probably not. I think that would be very detrimental to my client—who's trying to set this thing up—to say, "Oh, by the way, if you have a dispute with my client later, I'm going to be representing him and not the company." I think that that would be a terrible detriment to my client, because it would be saying, "I think something's going to go wrong." [51Ch20–49]

These respondents argue that disclosing theoretical risks is no way to begin a relationship and, besides, disclosure of what might happen is no disclosure at all.

> I think it's a hell of a way to engage in a relationship with somebody, to say, "By the way, let's get married. But, while we're considering marriage, let's talk about divorce." I think it's an unhealthy relationship. [26Ch100+]

> Let's take the codefendants situation. I go to the codefendant and I say, "Okay, someday maybe I'll decide that I should sue you. Okay? Is that okay?" And he says, "Yeah, that's fine," right? So now a year goes by and I say, "Okay, it's 'D' Day; I decided to do that and . . . here's what I'm going to say about you and here's what I'm going to try to do to you." Now, my first waiver, my first effort at getting a waiver was not one that was made with full disclosure. So he says, "Drop dead." And he's going to win that. Because my first one never had any full disclosures. So, the time that you got to do it is, you got to go in and say, "Hey, this witness just testified that you did it, not my guy. So, now, here's what I'm going to do." And then you lay it out, "Can I?" And he says, "Drop dead." That's full disclosure. [6Ch100+]

And, in other stories, waivers evolve as the stories unfold.

> . . . we have two major clients, one German and the other Japanese [L names them]. We've represented each in a single nonoverlapping area of business. But, over the years, they grew and grew and grew and acquired divisions that duplicated those of the other. We have gone to the two companies and sought waivers and explained that we will only deal with one of them on one area of technology and will represent the other on the other area. [42Ch20–49]

Attorneys typically seek consent from the persons in an organization with whom they have direct contact. Sometimes that person is inside corporate counsel, sometimes a chief executive, executive director, company manager, or claims adjuster.

> More often, it's people, not lawyers, regular businessmen, not lawyers. In big companies it's inside counsel. It depends if they have inside counsel or not. Sometimes it starts off with the businessperson and eventually you get inside counsel. [2Ch100+]

From whom the lawyer secures consent matters. According to most respondents, not all client contacts are equally sophisticated or knowledgeable about technical legal matters or have sufficient authority to give truly informed consent.

> It's easy when I'm dealing with a lawyer. I can simply make the assumption—which I think I'm allowed to make—that this lawyer is as smart as I am, so all I need to do is absolutely tell him minimal facts that disclose the problem. But what do you do when you have a businessman whose main concern is that his lawyer shouldn't take a walk on him? That's purely his concern. "I want you to be my lawyer. I trust you. You know about my business. I have invested in you." And I think that that's a lot of, maybe, part of what goes on. Or maybe it's just, "I trust you; whatever you say is alright." And I think that there's a big factor of that. Otherwise, how could people get these long letters saying, "I called you up and told [you] we're going to represent Jones and you said you don't mind." And I'm sure that's all that happened or maybe they went to lunch, it came up at lunch. [2Ch100+]

> Generally our clients are pretty sophisticated, even the individuals. But the problem is, no one's really a lawyer. And no one understands exactly what you're saying, and even when you write it all down. Well, I wouldn't say no one understands it; that's really not true. But it's rare to find someone who really understands the nuances of what's happening, in terms of what, quote, "an informed waiver" is. [10Ch100+]

So simply having a written signed document in the file may be insufficient, if the client doesn't truly understand what he or she has waived—or have the ultimate authority to do so.

Consent to a conflict of interest is generally solicited by the firm lawyer who has the most contact with the client. Respondents indicate that lawyers do not like to ask for waivers, especially from what figures 9.1 and 9.2 call the "Conflicted Client," the firm client whose interests are adverse to those embedded in the prospective new business. Much tension and discord in law firms is caused by this reluctance to ask for waivers, by resentment toward colleagues who are hoping to bring in new business for putting lawyers in the position of having to (potentially) antagonize valued clients with waiver requests, and by suspicions that colleagues did not try hard enough to get these waivers. That is why many Conflicts/Ethics/Professional Responsibility Committees regulate consent. These committees may decide whether it is in the firm's best interest to solicit a waiver from a valued client in the first place, and, when appropriate, force a recalcitrant colleague to do so.

> There are lots of occasions where somebody has to turn something down. And they'll say, "Gee, it doesn't seem that big of a deal for him to call and ask the client for a waiver." But the Executive Committee makes the decision that . . . that client who we would be adverse to is somebody we've targeted for long-term, big growth, and we just don't want to take the chances of asking them for it. I mean, lots of clients will waive 'em, but they just say, "Okay." You know, it's a question of loyalty: "Well, I'm really not that important to ya. [. . .]" [18Ch100+]

> S: Are there clients that you won't even bother asking for a waiver because you know they'll get so angry?
>
> L: Well, there are some. That's, you know, there are some people who are sensitive to that.
>
> S: You mean, some lawyers that are sensitive?
>
> L: Right, right. Yeah, they're concerned that even asking might prejudice the relationship. But that's, I mean, I guess where [our] committee comes in. I mean, we will say, "No, . . . you do that. This is an obligation you owe to the firm." [24Ch50–99]

Committees will also make the legal judgment about whether a waiver is necessary at all and whether the proposed letter is adequate.

> S: Is it always the case that you will be involved in the development of waivers? Or are there some very routine matters—repetitive kinds of contacts with a particular client—where the lawyer might just go out and take care of the waivers without consulting you?
>
> L: I hope not. No. . . . I had one horrible situation—a corporate matter—where we asked for a waiver. . . . And it shouldn't have been done. . . . There would be instances where . . . somebody will want to say, "Gee, I'll ask for a waiver." My reaction was, "Let's not even ask, because I don't want to get turned down. And I think I have sufficient grounds to say no waiver is needed." [26Ch100+]

> While we wish that the people who got those [waivers] would always come to a member of the Conflicts Committee, they don't always. Whenever we find out about it, we tell them they should have. There are some people who have done these often enough, they write good letters. Most of the people write letters that say, "I called you up and asked. This is to confirm our telephone conversation that you have no objection to our representing the other side of this transaction." And I don't think that fills the bill. [2Ch100+]

In a few firms, committee members actually draft the consent letters themselves.

> Sometimes I will draft [the waivers], when they are complex. On more routine matters, I will review waivers drafted by the attorneys. Sometimes it is quicker for me to draft the waiver in the first place than have to keep reviewing and correcting drafts of a younger or more inexperienced lawyer. [43Ch20–49]

Reliance on Consent

A good number of respondents, especially those in smaller firms, oppose asking clients to waive conflicts of interest, because they don't feel that consent solves the problem:

> I guess you could [get a waiver]. I'm not certain of how valid the waivers are. I mean, ethically, it goes beyond just the waivers. I think, if there is a conflict, there's a conflict. . . . I don't see how you can do it. I mean, it's inherent within the conflict that there's a conflict. And for you to waive it is recognizing its existence. And if they exist, how can you do away with it? It exists. We can't do that. Ethically, we shouldn't represent people who have conflicting interests—or entities. And if they do, the fact that they would waive it doesn't alter the fact that they have potential conflicts. So, it's unfair and unreasonable to represent their adverse interests. [83Ch10–19]

> And then the other problem is, with waivers is, it's almost impossible to fully disclose everything in a waiver. So therefore, the waiver is insufficient. Because, if you sat down and disclosed everything that there was to disclose, no one would sign it: "By the way, I may take your house." [laughter] . . . You can't draft that letter, because it's got to be fully informed waiver. And it's not, because it never can be in really, truly adversary situations. [10Ch100+]

Others eschew waivers because they believe lawyers owe their clients greater loyalty.

> I have an attitude: the lawyer is the client's champion. You must be able to represent it totally. If you have waivers, you are unable to do that. [71DSL10–19]

> I would say that we would hesitate asking for a consent. I mean, it's like saying to somebody "Do you mind if we cut your throat?" I mean, it's a client of yours and you're doing work for them and why should they consent? [4Ch100+]

> Well, you know, the 1980s were so disruptive to the economy that it created enough litigation business to keep our firm busy for the next ten years—as far as I'm concerned. Okay, so I don't have to take every case that walks in the door at the risk of my reputation, by going to clients and saying, "Would you give me a waiver?" And to me it's really as simple as, "How would I feel if my lawyer asked me this?" Would I feel like my lawyer is being a prostitute? Or would I feel like it's a really reasonable, legitimate request that I have to entertain with a clear, objective, open mind? And I have to ask myself what level of consideration does my client owe me on this? You know, my job is first—after I've taken their case—to look after that client's interest. It's not the reverse. . . . I don't want to make the client think that, "Well, if you don't give me this, I'm going to do a bad job on your case. Because I'm mad at you, because you denied me the ability to take on another case." I don't even want them to ever hear a hint of that. 'Cause, number one, it isn't true. But, number two, it'd be very easy for a client to misperceive that kind of request, no matter how sophisticated they are. Because every client's case is important to them. . . . I don't want to

go to a client and say, "Oh, by the way, you know, forget everything I said about how important your case is. I want to represent somebody whose [laughs] interests are actually adverse to you. And do you mind signing this piece of paper that says I can do it?" . . . You know, I don't need that. So that's one reason I would be very, always very reluctant to do that. Because it just looks bad. [104Ch10–19]

Other respondents suggest that lawyers can maintain their duty of loyalty at the same time that they advance positions adverse to their clients. Although the respondents just quoted consider asking clients to waive conflicts practically an act of betrayal, others see it as a source of client respect.

L1: . . . several people have now said to me on several occasions, . . . "You know, I got the strangest call from my client after I sent this letter. He's never seen something like this, and he was amazed at how fair we are and that we're willing to do this. And he says, 'That's the kind of lawyers I want to have.' " There is so much bad press about lawyers, that you send something like this and, even if it appears to be a parade of horribles, after all, he called you because he wants to use you. You start out with that presumption. And, yes, you may scare off somebody. But I think that people generally are very pleased that you are that concerned that you're trying to explain to them why this is necessary and that you're being that fair in telling them all of these things. And, for the most part—although I can't imagine that we haven't lost some business because of it; I'm sure we have—for the most part, I think my partners have realized that they really are respected more—ultimately—by the kind of clients they want to represent.

L2: . . . I would say the same thing. . . . I remember being told by the second senior member in our department, "You send a letter like this to a client, you're going to lose the client. I would never in a million years; it's an insult." And I guess in the, what, two or three years we've had this in effect now, it's routine. And those predictions have proven totally untrue. So the fear has been lost. [11Ch100+]

So, for a good number of—generally larger—firms, soliciting conflicts waivers is quite common.

We always will go to the client for waivers. We don't ever not ask. We just see what they say. [31Ch50–99]

L: Quite frequently, these days, we will instruct the attorney to get written waivers from both clients. And it probably happens at least once a week these days.

R: It's very common.

L: Having an institutional client base, for the most part, we have a reasonable degree of comfort approaching clients regarding a waiver. . . . We wouldn't approach it if we thought it wouldn't affect our ability to adequately represent them. . . . But we use that procedure very often. [3Ch100+]

If you analyze the matters carefully, it's usually possible to get waivers. Ninety percent of conflicts are waivable. You don't have to turn away too much. [43Ch20–49]

What accounts for this exercise of discretion? First of all, economics. The greater the value of the prospective—but conflicted—business, the more likely lawyers will seek consent to the conflicts.

> It's getting to be much more competitive these days. And as the pressure to get business continues to increase and as the competition continues to increase, yeah, we're going to have more efforts to waive conflicts, to get conflict waivers. [24Ch50–99]

Lawyers are less likely to seek consent from clients with adverse interests when they consider the conflict trivial or when they fear that the client will refuse to give consent.

> I think a mundane one would be where we are on the opposite sides on a corporate transaction. For example, we represent a company in doing their securities work, and we now represent another client who wants to buy a piece of real estate from that client. In many cases, I advise my partners—unless there's some sensitivity—let's not even get the waiver. I think, as a courtesy, you tell the first client, "We're representing [. . .]" But I consider that mundane. And we're just not going to go and run around get waivers every time. [26Ch100+]

> There are situations where we get a new matter form in, we spot conflicts all over the place, we think we can get a waiver, and we just say, "Forget it. We're just not going to get involved. We're not going to take this engagement." We will definitely turn down engagements without even consulting with the clients simply because there's too much of a headache. We may know the parties involved. We may know they won't waive it or they'll put such conditions on it that it will adversely impact the client we're trying to bring in. And we just think it's unfair to that client. Frankly, it's an administrative headache. "Forget it. We won't do it." That does come up and we do take that position. That is a less frequent occurrence than trying to work out the conflict and getting a waiver on both sides. [1Ch100+]

> Well, there are some matters that are waivable. And you say, "Well, just don't contact that client," because they would be upset about—even would be affronted—that you even asked them to waive it. So you have to know that too. And that, again, comes with some experience and seniority and knowing the clients. . . . Some clients, you know, fine. . . . You know you can contact them and tell them that, "There's this situation. It's waivable. Will you waive it?" And fine, you can have that conversation on an objective basis. Other clients, you know if you even ask them, they would go off like a rocket. Or . . . you'd hear the silence on the phone, and you know [in stupid voice] "that wasn't a good idea." . . . I would say, "Yes, that's a waivable conflict, but I don't think we want to try to get a waiver. Let's just stay away from it, because it's too sensitive with this client to ask." [50DSL20–49]

> One of the things we discussed was, would we go to client A and ask them if they don't mind if we do the work for client B, even though it's not a conflict? Well, if

> you're going to go to client A and ask them that, you'd better be willing to abide by his answer. Because, if you ask him if he minds and he says, "Yes," and you decide to do the work anyhow, you've got a very unhappy client A. . . . I mean, before I would ask him for a consent I would certainly sound him out to know whether or not I was going to get it. [3Ch100+]

Note that these examples are a mixed bag. In some, respondents, unwilling to ask for consent to the conflict, decline the new matter; in others, they simply fail to ask for a waiver, taking the risk that at some point the client will seek to disqualify the firm for representing adverse interests.

Many lawyers report very high levels of client consent to waive conflicts of interest, perhaps because they know their clients well enough to realize when not to ask for a waiver or because they broach the subject so gingerly that they can back away before the client has a chance to refuse.

> We get 100 percent cooperation from clients. In part, this is because we know when it is inappropriate to ask for them. For example, we represent a large number of companies on an ongoing basis. . . . We do so much for them. We know their records. When there's a real conflict because we have too much knowledge about these entities, we don't even ask for waivers. [12Ch100+]

> Some of them would really question my judgment if I came and asked for a waiver. They would ask, "What kind of 'good drugs' are you on? You know that the answer is 'no.' " And generally I guess right. [38Ch50–99]

> Most clients are willing to waive conflicts. But are they doing it simply because we're telling them it's okay? [40Ch20–49]

This last respondent suggests another reason why attorneys seemingly secure high levels of consent—because they are persuading clients to do so.

> L: First of all, I should tell you that I start out with a premise—and you may not like to hear this; I don't know how you feel about this. But I start out with a premise that there are no conflicts. I have to have it demonstrated to me loud and clear that I've got a conflict. I go right into this with the assumption that I will somehow be able to resolve it and keep the business. That's my theory. . . .
>
> S: . . . So what strategies do you use when you find that you have a conflict?
>
> L: I think, mainly is calling them up and talking reality to them. Say, "Look, there's a technical conflict here. But what's the real practical effect of this? I mean, we're not using information that we got from you in another case against you. We are adverse, but we're really only adverse in whatever the sense is in that particular case." And I try to tell them that it really shouldn't make any difference to them. And, as a matter of fact, it might be better for them to have somebody like us—who they know—on the other side. And so on. And that works a lot of the time. They just say, "Yeah, you're right." [13Ch50–99]

> You tend to encounter recalcitrance at the business level, not at the law [inside counsel] level. The businesspeople will say: "Those animals, those wretched ingrates," for asking for waivers. Some respond at the grudge level. But unless it's a "bet-the-company" case, you can sometimes go to them and say, "Look, somebody's going to take this case. Do you want it to be a bunch of jug heads? Or do you want it to be someone like us?" Some people will respond, "Get out of here!" But sometimes it works. [8Ch100+]

AN OUNCE OF PREVENTION

The first part of this chapter described how lawyers and firms respond when confronted with an actual or potential conflict of interest. But these reactive strategies are costly. They require that committees endlessly deliberate, and result in business being lost, opportunities foreclosed, clients turned or driven away, relationships with clients and among colleagues strained or fractured, debts incurred, and so on. So some firms develop strategies to anticipate and diffuse the potential that conflicts will arise in the first place. These strategies, which generally manipulate firm structure or the temporal dimension of a firm's caseload, were previewed in earlier chapters. Some strategies intervene at the front end, weeding out prospective engagements that are likely to give rise to future conflicts, securing client consent to waive future conflicts in advance, or barricading colleagues behind ethical screens. Others manipulate the back end, taking care to conclude cases or terminate relationships as quickly as possible, thereby transforming current into former clients to whom less onerous conflict-of-interest obligations apply.

Advance Consent

A piece of new business carries both good and bad news. As this book has amply documented, the bad news is that it imports a set of confidences and interests that all members of the firm are obliged to honor for some time to come, often conflicting them out of future opportunities. Indeed, as respondents described, some companies do so strategically, doling out cases to ensure that particular firms cannot oppose them on more significant matters. When firms are large and geographically dispersed, their specialties diverse, and their clients complex with varied legal business that they spread around to many firms, the potential bad news emanating from a one-shot matter often drowns out the good. Lawyers must evaluate whether they are better off declining the business outright rather than being precluded from all the—yet unknown—new matters just on the horizon. If only firms could neutralize these unforeseeable downstream conflicts, thus forging relationships without so much fear of the consequences.

Some lawyers feel they can. They note that some law firms already disclose to prospective clients the risks that conflicts of interest might arise—for example, that the interests of coparties might diverge, that a new party (and client of the firm) might join the litigation, and so on. They disclose how the firm would respond to these emerging conflicts and then ask the clients to waive their right to disqualify the firm if those scenarios materialize. (Such disclosures of potential conflicts of interest were illustrated by figure 9.2.) It is only a small step to seek waivers for future conflicts that might arise *outside* the prospective engagement when new opportunities require that the firm advance interests adverse to those of the original clients.

> But these are the kinds of things that, when you sit down in the very beginning of a relationship, you can work out often. If you don't do it then, it becomes very difficult to work it out. And, again, . . . partners are very sensitive to this. They don't want to lose the business because we're getting too carried away with the conflicts issues. At the same time, people are becoming more and more sensitive, more and more resigned to the fact that this is a good idea and, I think, quite frankly interested in protecting their partners and other clients and future business by trying to get, up front, an understanding of what your role is, what your responsibilities are, what you will and won't do, and what this client does and does not waive in the beginning of the relationship. . . . And in the course of those negotiations with the client—up front—you can learn enough that might even put you in a position of saying, "I don't want to represent this client. It isn't worth it." They don't understand what it means to engage our services to do one tiny little thing. And they don't have an understanding of the fact that we do lots of things for lots of clients and they may be adverse to this client's interests from time to time. And they have to understand what that means. We'll never prejudice their interests because of information that we have. But being forbidden from pursuing matters that may be adverse to that client's interests on behalf of another client is something that we have to think long and hard about—as to whether we're going to do that—when that client walks in the door. [23Ch100+]

In *advance consents* or *advance* or *prospective waivers*, clients agree that they will not seek to disqualify the firm for taking advantage of future opportunities that are adverse to their interests but unrelated to the matter for which they engaged the firm or any of the confidences they shared with their lawyers. Figure 9.3 provides an example of the advance consent language developed by ALAS, the large-firm mutual malpractice insurer.

About a third of the respondents in the study, mostly those in large firms, reflected on the use of advance waivers to minimize the amount of business lost to conflicts of interest. A few had never heard of the concept, and others noted that they probably should consider using them but never had. And more than a third of the respondents who commented on advance consent indicated that their firms did not and would not use this device to limit conflicts of interest. Many felt it undermined attorney-client relationships.

> There's a lot of talk about getting advanced waivers of conflict. But to bring a new client in and say, "We're delighted to help you and here's how wonderful we are. By the way, we want it understood at the outset that we can be unfaithful to you." It's not a very good way to sell yourself in what you hope will be an expanding relationship. [5Ch100+]

> As we have discussed, you are aware that we are a relatively large law firm, and that we represent many other companies and individuals. It is possible that some of our present or future clients will have disputes with [name of this client] during the time that we are representing [name of this client]. Therefore, as a condition to our undertaking this matter for you, you have agreed that this firm may continue to represent or may undertake in the future to represent existing or new clients in any matter that is not substantially related to our work for [name of this client], even if the interests of such clients in those other matters are directly adverse to [name of this client]. We agree, however, that your prospective consent to conflicting representation contained in the preceding sentence shall not apply in any instance where as the result of our representation of [name of this client] we have obtained sensitive, proprietary or other confidential information of a non-public nature that, if known to any such other client of ours, could be used in any such other matter by such client to the material disadvantage of [name of this client].

Fig. 9.3. Sample Advance Consent (Reprinted from Attorney's Liability Assurance Society, Inc., "Selected Conflict of Interest Issues," 1992, 4.)

But almost three-quarters of the respondents in the largest firms indicated that their firms routinely or at least occasionally tried to secure advance consent (only half that proportion of the firms with fewer than one hundred lawyers did so, as did only one downstate firm). Several respondents indicated that they were developing advance-waiver language to use routinely in their engagement letters. They described their use of prospective waivers for one-shot or limited or specialized engagements or for small matters:

> But, on the one-shot deals—where you know they're not coming back—why not? . . . I mean, why take the chance that you're going to be shut out in the future from ever being adverse to them on something that's not a big matter. [18Ch100+]

> When a particular person has tremendous expertise in a specialized area and everyone in the world comes to the firm to use this particular lawyer—parties who would otherwise not come to the firm for more routine legal work—this is an instance where you would get advanced waivers before the firm took on these matters. [32Ch100+]

> With respect to other matters that come in—particularly new clients that will come in with a small matter—most members of the New Business Committee will not permit that matter to be accepted without an acceptable engagement letter anymore. . . . And the engagement letter provides that—if an unrelated matter comes in which is adverse to the interests of this new client, and that new client elects to be represented by other counsel, and no confidential information is involved in our prosecution of the matter against that client—that they give us advance consent to do it. [23Ch100+]

Others use advance waivers when representing only a small branch on a large corporate tree or for competitors or positional conflicts:

> There's one major client that we don't do work for, but we do work—significant work—for several of their subsidiaries. But we did get from the general counsel of this major parent anticipatory consents . . . which says, "Your representation of this subsidiary and this subsidiary will not prevent you, if you have an adversity against the parent, from pursuing it." [4Ch100+]

> Say a new client comes to us for representation. In that instance, we might say to them, "We currently are representing another company in fields that you're in. We want to be able to assure our preexisting client—if we represent you—that we can continue to give them full representation, even in a suit against you." . . . Very seldom do you have that kind of waiver turned down. [14Ch100+]

> You try to arrive at an understanding with the client about what you will and will not do. . . . let's assume you have an insurance company client for whom you're doing some financing work. You may arrive at an understanding with that client that you will not assert against it whether a particular insurance policy that it has issued covers a spill. But you will also work out with that client that that is an issue that you might be asserting against another insurance company, even though it deals with the same language in another policy. [23Ch100+]

Before you draw the conclusion from these reflections that advance waivers play a significant role in ameliorating the risk of conflicts of interest, several caveats are necessary. First, this group is unrepresentative, comprised mostly of large firms for which advance waivers are better suited. Four-fifths of the respondents who commented on advance consent worked in firms with fifty attorneys or more, employing 255 lawyers on average (those that did not, worked in firms with an average of twenty-three attorneys). And almost half were members of ALAS, which, around the time of the study, had circulated information to its members about this prophylactic device. If every firm in the study had been polled about their use of advance consent, probably less than a fifth would indicate that they utilize this device even occasionally, and many more would express unfamiliarity with it altogether.

Second, all respondents commented that it was very difficult to convince their clients to give advance waivers, especially those from whom they were most needed.

> There are some [companies] that appear to have thought-out policies that, . . . as one lawyer told me, "We don't feed the hand that bites us." [2Ch100+]

> This is a huge bone of contention here. We developed, in our standard form of engagement letter, some advanced waiver language. And I don't know the source of it—whether it was an ABA standard form or our malpractice insurer came up with it. We essentially tracked that language in our letters, basically saying that "As a condition of our representing you, if we end up with a conflict in the future, so long as it's not directly related to our current representation, we understand that you will still permit us to be adverse to you in a subsequent representation." So, yes, we have that language. It's probably used, in the exact form that it's written,

> it's probably used in about 30 to 40 percent of our engagement letters. Many lawyers don't feel comfortable doing that. Many clients will not accept it. And so they tend to modify the language. They may soften it a bit. They may request the client to be flexible in dealing with conflicts in the future. We basically require conflicts to be addressed in the engagement letters. The actual advance waiver language doesn't appear in all of them, simply because either the billing attorney doesn't feel comfortable with it or the client will not accept it. . . . Really, the problem where it seems to arise mostly with the very large corporations with large in-house corporate staffs. They tend to really peruse the letters very carefully and they seem to have a problem with it. . . . And we don't use that language with individuals. They don't understand it and they really don't, they can't appreciate what they're waiving and so you just do not use it with individuals. It's limited to corporate clients, and frankly, the clients who tend to use conflicts as a sword rather than a shield are the ones who object. Which tends to defeat the whole purpose of it. [1Ch100+]

Third, even those respondents whose firms used advance consents were dubious about their efficacy, questioning whether clients can give informed consent concerning a future event about which they cannot possibly be fully informed.[9]

> They're worthless as far as this entity is concerned—the reason being that a client cannot prospectively waive that which it does not know about. . . . It can't be, because you don't know what it is. So, you see, I know that it has been suggested and I've even seen letters, proposed letters. They are not used in this firm because I don't believe that they have any efficacy. [6Ch100+]

> We don't and won't use them. We're happy to get a client. I don't know that advanced waivers are ever effective. First of all, you have the hot-potato doctrine;

[9]After I had completed many of these interviews, the American Bar Association Standing Committee on Ethics and Professional Responsibility (1993) issued a formal opinion entitled "Waivers of Future Conflicts of Interest." In a dense, seven-page document, the committee took "a guarded view of prospective waivers," specifying the many risks of such devices (many of them already raised by my own informants) and concluding with the resounding judgment that "it is not ordinarily impermissible to seek such prospective waivers," preferably in writing. Two years later, the American Law Institute's *Restatement of the Law: The Law Governing Lawyers* (1995) included a somewhat more upbeat discussion of "consent to future conflicts" (Ch. 8, 25–26). It noted that "the gains to both lawyer and client from a system of advance consent to defined future conflicts may be substantial" but cautioned that consent would be "ineffective unless the client possesses sophistication in the matter in question and has had the opportunity to receive independent legal advice about the consent." This topic was revisited yet again in the proposed Ethics 2000 revision of the *Model Rules of Professional Conduct,* which addressed the conditions under which it might be appropriate to ask a client to waive conflicts that might arise in the future (American Bar Association 2001, Rule 1.7, Commentary, paragraph 22). This paragraph also generated heated debate by the ABA House of Delegates, reflecting the ambivalence with which many attorneys still view this prophylactic advice. Because of these developments, it is possible that a survey conducted today would find greater familiarity with and more widespread use of advance consent than that found by my study.

> you cannot simply drop a client because they've signed some advanced waiver. Moreover, where there is adversity, the advanced waiver cannot work. And some things simply cannot be consented to. A client could revoke an advanced waiver at some point in the future and no court in the land would rule against them. Clients could argue that there were secrets that could never have been foreseen when they signed the waiver. And it is impossible to argue that there was full, knowing disclosure in such an instance. [34Ch50–99]

This view was more true of those respondents whose firms rejected prospective waivers, two-fifths of whom expressed doubts about whether the waivers would stand up in court if they were challenged, but these sentiments were shared by fully a fifth of respondents whose firms used them. To the latter, the function of advance consents is to increase the level of cooperation when future conflicts do detonate—not to ensure it.

> I tend to view the conflicts language, frankly, to put us in a better position. If a conflict comes up, you can always point to the letter and say, "You agreed to this. When you took it with this understanding, it's unfair for you now to object." If they absolutely object and if they're going to fight it, would we seek to enforce it? I don't know. My gut reaction is probably not. You don't want to get a client involved in a horrible battle over disqualification or conflict issues. You want to make sure that the client's interests are served. If the best thing to do is to withdraw from a representation, maybe that's what you have to do. You don't want to end up in a litigation with another client over . . . your advance waiver language. [1Ch100+]

Besides, as many respondents point out, when the conflict does detonate, it is necessary to go back to the client and fully disclose the new circumstances and ask for continued consent. As the ABA Formal Opinion (American Bar Association Standing Committee on Ethics and Professional Responsibility 1993) decreed, "Even though one might think that the very purpose of a prospective waiver is to eliminate the need to return to the client to secure a 'present' second waiver when what was once an inchoate matter ripens into an immediate conflict, there is no doubt that in many cases that is what will be ethically required." And, of course, the second client whose new business gave rise to the conflict of interest must be informed of the firm's relationship with the client that gave advance consent and give its consent as well.

A Bird in the Hand: Divining the Future

Because of their limited use and uncertain efficacy, advance waivers play at best a modest role in neutralizing future conflicts of interest. Moreover, advance consent, because it applies to future adversities with clients already on board, has little impact on business conflicts with prospective clients. Amalgamated Hospital may promise that it will not disqualify the firm if it sues them on an unrelated matter, but the future plaintiff may be uneasy about the firm's loyalty when vigorous advocacy on its behalf is likely to harm Amalgamated, an important client of the firm.

Moreover, other prospective health care clients may not be as forgiving as Amalgamated when they discover that the firm sometimes sues hospitals. Armed with the advance waiver, the suit against Amalgamated may not have ethical ramifications, but it may have significant business consequences.

Without—and sometimes even with—the insurance policy of advance consent, law firms therefore face the often expensive risk that a new matter will conflict them out of significant future business. Many simply bear the risk. The majority of respondents described a first-come-first-served or bird-in-the-hand policy, in which engagements are taken in the order they come through the door. If these birds in hand ultimately preclude matters lurking "in the bush," so be it. Note how similarly respondents from very dissimilar firms—big and little, located in Chicago, downstate, and the collar counties—describe these policies, their justification, and their consequences.

> We have never turned down business in the expectation that something that may become available in the future would be precluded. We believe in the bird in the hand. The potential of future business is just too ethereal. . . . We take business whenever it comes. [42Ch20–49]

> I don't know that it would be possible or—for that matter—make sense to try to analyze anything and everything that might happen down the trail. You have to pretty much proceed on what is and what is reasonably foreseeable. And if we can foresee a potential problem or a potential conflict, then that might cause us not to become involved initially. But I don't know that we could sit here and say, "Well, if such-and-such happens next year or the year after that, then we want to be in a position to take some things. So we better not take this." You're getting into a real realm of speculation at that point in time. [55DSL20–49]

> But we kind of just handle the matter at the time, and if it turns out later on, so be it. And, unfortunately, [laughter] we've made the wrong decision and we're precluded from representing somebody in the future—which even may have been more lucrative. But we figure that we made our bed, [laughter] now we're going to lie in it and continue on with it. [95CC10–19]

> And we will always defer to the partner who has the business in hand. First in is what counts, and we'll represent that client. And if that means we can't take the other matter, then that's show biz, that's what we do. If there's a way that we can maintain both potential relationships, we'll do that. And that's sometimes possible and sometimes not. [9Ch100+]

These firms do have something in common, though; they predominantly handle litigation, where relationships with clients are more episodic and harder to predict. But even some firms with more ongoing relationships with clients subscribe to first-in policies. As one respondent explained, many valuable relationships begin small. To reject them out of hand in favor of some hypothetical golden egg–laying goose forecloses the opportunity to reap the growing business of a maturing client.

> We generally do not turn down work—in the normal instance—if it's good solid work because something more lucrative might come along later. We sort of take our chances and have always done that. . . . A lot of times you build your relations with a client by taking on, maybe, the less lucrative work. But as they mature and come into other types of problems or what have you, they come to you with that too. And even though client representation has changed—where clients are not as loyal as they used to be and they shop and parcel their work out to diverse firms for various reasons, some of which might be to conflict you out—we still adhere more, maybe, to the older principal that we would like to be full service representation to a client. [41Ch50–99]

But other firms, especially larger ones in which so many colleagues can be conflicted out by the commitments of one, discount the allure of the bird in hand.

> And a lot of firms just say, "Hey, whatever the business is, take it in." Well, that's stupid sometimes. You take in something that's a fifty-thousand fee and it leads to a disqualification on something that could have been millions of dollars worth of business. I mean, you should be thinking about that. But some firms today just have to get whatever they can get. Our firm, we don't—fortunately—we don't have to do that. We can survive without taking on every new matter. [18Ch100+]

As I described in chapter 6, these firms will decline perfectly good cases because of what they suspect or hope that they might one day snare from the bush. But freeing birds in hand goes against the grain; attorneys who are compensated for the business they bring into the firm have few incentives to send it away—unless the hypothetical prospective business is likely to be their own.

> It gets evaluated at the New Business Committee level. That's another reason the committee was set up: to see whether we were foreclosing opportunities by taking on engagements. . . . It's almost invariably the judgment of the people on the committee; . . . It's almost never the lawyer that brings that up. Their interest, really, is in getting the business, even if it's a five-thousand-dollar matter. It's just the nature of lawyers bringing business. [7Ch100+]

These firms implement varied policies, procedures, or structures to wrest discretion away from those who would never liberate the birds they have caught.

The crudest systems involve setting firm policies that exclude wholesale categories of cases, positions, or clients from its caseload. Some firms never take cases against a particular industry or profession or even against any large corporation (unless it is on behalf of an even larger one). Some exclude areas of practice or types of matters that tend to create adversities with prospective clients—consumer bankruptcy, workers' compensation, collections, tax, zoning. And others avoid taking certain positions—insurance coverage on behalf of either insurance companies or insureds, lender liability on behalf of either banks or borrowers, malpractice plaintiffs or defense, and so on.

Other firms systematically analyze the opportunity costs of taking a particular case. On a major multidefendant lawsuit, for example, insurance defense firms may call around to see whether any of its insurance carriers are likely to refer the case of a bigger "fish" before it agrees to represent a minnow.

> Yeah, I've had it happen to me. I can give you examples of where I've been aced out of enormously lucrative matters because I took in stuff from good clients who said, "I want to reserve you on a particular matter." And we turned out not to even get anything as a result of that. They reserved me—nothing happened. Another client called me, said, "Can you take this case for the So-and-So?" I said, "I can't, I took it from somebody else." And he had to get somebody else. And I lost out—on one case I know—a million-dollar fee. That's very sad and I've learned a lesson from that. What I do now is that, if I know that, for instance, if a catastrophe occurs here in Chicago—like a refinery fire or some big deal—I will call the clients that I know are most likely to be involved in those things. And I will say to them, "Do you intend, if you're sued, to call us? Because I want to be sure that I don't take something else from a minor player and not be able to represent you." I did that just the other day, when three suits were filed here against somebody. And I wrote them and I said, "You just got sued yesterday. And I represent people in this field. And I'm going to be contacted by others, I think. And I wanted you to know that. And, if you're going to use us, let me know, so that I won't take in some [. . .] I'd rather represent you." And so on. And they sent me the stuff very shortly thereafter. So that was kind of a preemptive strike. These were people I've been dealing with before, so I can do this. But you can't always do that. And then sometimes you're disappointed. [13Ch50–99]

A few firms include their mailing list or marketing data base in their computerized conflicts search to identify prospective clients whose business the firm has been trying to attract and whose interests are adverse to those of the client hoping to engage the firm. Others create a repository of prospective clients or adversaries for or against whom a matter cannot be taken without consultation.

> We have one other system which we call "the box." . . . The head of Bank X calls me and says, "I'm thinking about acquiring Bank Y. I'll give you a call next week." . . . You then put Bank Y in the box. And then if Bank A calls and says, "I'm thinking about acquiring Bank Y," you then have an issue, which is, which client do you represent that's thinking about acquiring Bank Y? [17Ch100+]

> On the other side of that is a concern about not doing work for potential . . . defendants. There are some kind of people who, from our experience, we know are likely . . . defendants, just because of things we've heard. . . . And we have to say, "Look, we don't want someone to go and represent that company because we think we may sue them one day. . . . You can't represent that company because we're already investigating suing them." Now that's not a real conflict. That's a

> real business conflict. Because sometimes we don't yet know that we have a client to file a lawsuit; we're just looking at the industry. [2Ch100+]

> There are relatively few sacred-cow defendants that we will not sue, hoping that we'll get business from them later on. I'm aware—literally, less than one week ago—of a situation in which one of our bankruptcy lawyers . . . —put out a phone mail to all lawyers—saying, "There is a possibility that we are going to be asked to represent the trustee of the following debtor. They've approached us. Would we be interested? You know, it's in the very initial stages of the discussion. If you get approached by any creditor of the X Corporation, please call me to discuss it before you take on any information from them or indicate that you might be interested." Basically, they were saying, "If we can get this debtor relationship, let's not take on anyone else with respect to this bankruptcy." I'm only aware of that happening very occasionally. [39Ch50–99]

Most commonly, as I described in chapter 8, firms will circulate lists of new matters to all colleagues in the hope that those who have information about prospective clients, adversaries, positions, interests, matters, or opportunities likely to be affected or precluded will come forward and provide input that might result in the decision to decline the new matter.

Firms also adopt structural solutions. As noted before, some firms replaced Ethics or Professional Responsibility Committees with New Business Committees explicitly because they were being conflicted out of too much lucrative business.[10] They needed a mechanism to evaluate new matters for more than ethical conflicts as well as the authority to decline perfectly good matters because of possible long-term business costs. Many firms in the sample require that New Business Committees, managing partners, a member of the Executive Committee, department heads, or designated "officers of the day" sign off on all new matters.

> With respect to future business, we have a strategic five-year plan. We target the types of clients we want. How does the client fit into our strategic plan? . . . We will appoint one or two officers of the day to evaluate all conflicts memos from a strategic vantage point. [pilot interview #7]

Committees and administrative personnel are generally reactive, responding to the prospects and potential costs of each matter as it comes through the door. But the purview of some extends beyond the birds in hand, reflecting prospectively on how to clear the way for targets of opportunity and retrospectively analyzing patterns of lost business that might have been avoided:

> It may be that the firm is trying to move into an area. For example, if we targeted health care as an area that we wanted to build, I wouldn't necessarily want to sue

[10]A few even put the person in charge of marketing or practice development on the committee to ensure that prospective business received adequate consideration.

> a hospital on behalf of a patient or something like that. So those decisions, again, we have long-term strategy plans that we develop as a firm. We have strategy plans, five-year plans for our offices. And so the managing partners and the Executive Committee know those and they work with those. We have a committee in the firm called the Business Development Committee. We have a Planning Committee in the firm. Those committees think about these issues and think about areas that we want to go into or stay out of. [18Ch100+]

> We've also instituted a "second review" policy in which the practice group leader reviews a matter before that business is turned away. This review is mandatory, even if the initiating attorney has no objections to declining the business. A memo must be prepared when business is declined. Who was the client? What was the type of matter? Why was it turned away? It must document that a second review was conducted. This memo must be submitted to the records center. On a monthly basis, the records center collects these memos and submits them to the Conflicts Committee. The committee reviews them to see whether business is being declined that ought not to be or to look for a pattern or problem that can be rectified. [pilot interview #7]

Ethical Screens

As I elaborated in chapter 7, lawyer mobility exacerbates conflict of interest. As attorneys travel through the job market, they accumulate the confidences of and duties owed to each collection of current and former clients they encounter along the way. Career mobility multiplies not only the conflicts of interest faced by these migratory lawyers but also, because of imputed disqualification rules, those of everyone they affiliate with as they move from job to job. They become so-called Typhoid Marys, conflicting out thousands of their colleagues and forcing their new firms to turn away substantial amounts of prospective business tainted by their prior affiliations. As a result, many tainted lawyers become immobile, unattractive to other employers because of the business that their presence in the new firm would preclude.

About two decades ago, the American Bar Association recognized that the imputed disqualification rules deterred from government service able lawyers who feared becoming Typhoid Marys, unable to move from government into lucrative partnerships in private law firms. Law reformers borrowed the concept of the Chinese wall, an institutional mechanism long used in banks, securities, and investment banking firms to segregate departments and ensure that confidential information in one did not find its way into another. The *Model Rules of Professional Conduct* officially greased the revolving door by stipulating that if former government lawyers, judges, or public officials are screened and receive no share of the fees generated by an otherwise tainted matter, conflicts of interest they carry with them into the private sector would not be imputed to their entire firm (American Bar Association 1983, Rules 1.12 and 1.13).

Because, in most firms, the revolving door connects lateral positions in other private law firms more frequently than it does those in the public sector, these provisions for screening former public officials are of only limited value. In only a handful of jurisdictions—Illinois being one—does the prophylactic role of these screening devices, available when attorneys are hired from government positions, also apply when they are recruited from private law firms.[11]

> Lawyers go into government "training programs," then leave to practice on the opposite side. It is only fair that if the courts allow this for government lawyers that they do so for those in private practice as well. [14Ch100+]

Though law firms in all jurisdictions are free to erect what are variously called screening devices, Chinese walls, insulation walls, ethical walls or screens, zones or cones of silence, confidentiality screens, or fire walls, these devices cure conflicts of interest only when the adversities are indirect and the affected clients have given their consent.[12] They serve as barriers for reassuring clients, not for neutralizing conflicts. Illinois lawyers and those in the few other states that extend the provisions for screening government lawyers to migratory private practitioners do not need to secure client consent for conflicts they import into the firm. If the firms build a proper and timely screen, the conflicts of lawyers traveling from other positions are not imputed to their new colleagues.

Firms in the sample varied considerably in the extent to which they made use of screens. Were screening devices as visible as the Great Wall of China, after which some are modeled, I would have seen dozens in place in a few of the firms that I visited and none at all in most of the others. Not surprisingly, none of the firms in the sample with fewer than ten attorneys had ever used a screening device; this was true of a quarter of those with ten to nineteen attorneys, more than four-fifths of those with twenty to forty-nine and virtually all those employing fifty or more lawyers. Although about a fifth of the firms with ten to nineteen attorneys have constructed screens on a number of occasions, this was true of almost half the

[11]Rule 1.10 of the Illinois Rules of Professional Conduct makes an exception to the imputed disqualification rule when "the newly associated lawyer has no information . . . that is material to the matter; or the newly associated lawyer is screened from any participation in the matter" (Illinois Supreme Court Rules 1990). Though controversial (Pizzimenti 1997, 306), the proposed *Restatement of the Law: The Law Governing Lawyers* is compatible with the Illinois regulations, stating that "restrictions imputed from a personally-prohibited lawyer to an affiliated lawyer or firm" can be removed with adequate screening measures (American Law Institute 1995, §204). The ABA Ethics 2000 Commission also recommended a screening provision similar to that in Illinois (American Bar Association 2001, Rule 1.10c). However, after a very contentions debate late in the day, the ABA House of Delegates voted 58 percent to 42 percent to strike the provision (personal observation). Most likely, screening will be revisited again before the Ethics 2000 process is concluded, though whether the vote will change and screening will spread to other jurisdictions is anybody's guess. The rationale for allowing law firms to establish screens to remove imputation occasioned by the mobility of private practitioners is that it gives clients a wider choice of counsel, makes it easier for lawyers to change jobs, and limits the number of costly and disruptive disqualification motions that have become commonplace in the arsenal of hardball litigators.

[12]Some commentators decry the use of the label, "Chinese wall," as ethnically insensitive or politically incorrect (Wolfram 1986, 401; *Peat, Marwick, Mitchell & Co. v. Superior Court,* 200 Cal. App. 3d 272 (Cal. Ct. App. 1988) (Low, J., concurring).

firms with twenty to forty-nine lawyers and roughly three-quarters of those with fifty or more. Indeed, almost half the respondents in firms of one hundred lawyers or more indicated that Chinese walls were common in their firm, with many, sometimes dozens, in place at any one time.

As described in chapter 7, I conducted pilot interviews in the largest law firms (all with more than one hundred attorneys), where Chinese walls would be most common, in another Midwestern state that—like most of the rest of the country—does not permit screens without client consent to resolve the conflicts of interest that arise from lateral hiring. This sample is far too small from which to generalize, but the contrast is telling. The chair of the Professional Standards Committee of the largest firm (which had a branch office in a state that allows screening) told me that most of the firm's lateral hiring occurs in the branch office that allows screening but that the firm as a whole probably uses Chinese walls in a third of the matters in which it seeks client consent to a conflict. The managing partner of a second firm indicated that screening devices are not common but "there are probably Chinese wall situations around here at all times." At the opposite extreme, the chair of the New Client Committee at a nearby firm was barely familiar with the notion of a Chinese wall. What little he knew, he conceded that he learned only hours before our interview when he questioned a colleague who had formerly worked in a Chicago law firm. Moreover, he said, the physical layout of the firm and the ease of access to files would render a wall "farcical." The remaining respondents explained that they erected screens on "a few occasions" or "no more than five times in the history of the firm," and some expressed distaste for the practice.[13] So screening devices appear to be less institutionalized in states that do not allow this prophylactic device to cure conflicts detonated by mergers and lateral hiring.

What does an ethical screen look like?[14] The respondents provided disparate descriptions, usually corresponding to the size of the firm.

S: What does a screen look like in the firm?
L: It's about this big [L gestures]. [laughter] We have a set of forms in which . . . the screened lawyer is notified by the Conflicts Department and our administrative manager that they have been screened from the particular matter or client. . . . And the notice goes to the screened lawyer or lawyers. And the

---

[13]Of course, these "large" firms are half the size, on average, of their counterparts in Chicago. So some of the disinclination to erect screens probably reflects firm size.

[14]Rule 1.10 of the Illinois Rules of Professional Conduct stipulates that:

> (e) . . . a lawyer will be deemed to have been screened from any participation in a matter if:
> (1) the lawyer has been isolated from confidences, secrets, and material knowledge concerning the matter;
> (2) the lawyer has been isolated from all contact with the client or any agent, officer, or employee of the client and any witness for or against the client;
> (3) the lawyer and the firm have been precluded from discussing the matter with each other; and
> (4) the firm has taken affirmative steps to accomplish the forgoing. (Illinois Supreme Court Rules 1990)

See also Pizzimenti 1997.

> screened lawyer must sign an acknowledgment and a pledge to abide by the screen. Then the Conflicts Department sends out a screening memo to all parties and it's put into a data base and then there are periodic reminders that go out. At this point, because of various technical problems, we do not lock files. We do not mark screened files. We're looking at that. [36Ch100+]

> We send out a memo to everyone in the office saying, "Do not discuss whatever case it is with whoever it is." We memo everyone. We indicate that the files for the particular case will be stored in a specific cabinet which is to be locked and that no file is to stay in anyone's office overnight. It must be locked in the cabinet, which is located in a specific spot. But usually the secretary for the lawyers who are working on the matter and the lawyers have the keys to the cabinet. Any interoffice mail regarding those items is to be in a sealed envelope marked "confidential," as opposed to our standard envelope which has a pull-tab on it. [10Ch100+]

Many firms also communicate to attorneys and staff the seriousness with which they regard a breach of these barriers.

> We circulate a memo: "So-and-So has come to us. At their prior firm, they did some work for B. We want to avoid even the appearance of conflicts. This partner is responsible for supervising the files. Don't leave files or records around. Don't ever talk to this individual about the case." We want lawyers to know that this is as serious as talking about a bomb in an airport. [43Ch20–49][15]

> Let me put it to you this way. . . . if we discovered that this person was violating our Chinese wall principles, we'd probably take him out in the street and beat him up and leave him for dead. [51Ch20–49]

The most opaque and seemingly more impenetrable screens, generally found in larger firms, have a mechanism for

- alerting the screened lawyers to their new status, informing them of their obligations, and requiring them to sign a pledge to abide by the screen.
- notifying all their colleagues, file room personnel, and coworkers (even secretaries, messengers, and food service workers) of the screen and cautioning them not to talk to their quarantined colleague about the case.

---

[15]Some lawyers do take the admonition seriously:

> I had an associate come in. I thought the poor guy was going to be in tears. I really thought he was going to cry. "I messed up, I messed up." And what happened, it turned out this guy was an M.D. and he wants to do medical-type work and he got involved in taking a deposition for a partner in a breast implant case and he has been working regularly for another partner in some other kind of medical device case for different client. But this client is also a codefendant in this one and so we had set up a screen and he was flipping through the file and, all of a sudden, he saw the screening memo and he thought that . . . it was the end of the world. [pilot interview #2]

- explaining that all conversations must take place in private locations (and never in hallways, elevators, lunchrooms, etc.).
- restricting access to files.
- segregating, labeling, and locking files.
- reminding colleagues that records and documents must not be left out on their desks, but stored in secure locations.
- placing passwords on affected computer files.
- specifying confidential procedures for interoffice mail.
- naming a party responsible for supervising the screen.
- periodically reminding all personnel of the existence of the screen.[16]

Although screens in some firms are marked by barriers, locks, signs, and passwords and are enforced by assorted border guards, in many others—especially smaller firms—they are more "ephemeral," to quote one respondent, constructed from much simpler blueprints. A few firms simply admonish lawyers not to talk to one another.

> A Chinese wall is "a state of mind." We don't give the screened lawyer access to information and, similarly, he doesn't give you material information. [14Ch100+]

> We just say "Hey, stay away. Stay the hell away from this client. [Case] was at your old office. You worked on it. So forget it." . . . We put something on the file saying, "So-and-So is not going to be involved in this." But people know it. If guys are working on a case, he knows who's working on the case and he shouldn't be talking to anybody about it and he shouldn't read the file. So he doesn't. [20Ch50–99]

Others tell the infected lawyer not to work on the case or assign separate teams of lawyers to work on the conflicting matters.

> What we've done in the past—and what I still do—is that, if an attorney came from a certain firm, they just never work on the files from that firm. . . . But, generally, what we would do if there is a conflict, is just that attorney would not handle—ever handle—any of those files. That would be it. [102Ch10–19]

> We have simply screened off lawyers from cases. And the way we do that is—we work in litigation teams, generally. And if we had such an issue, we would take the case outside of the entire "team sphere" and put it into another team sphere. Because there's very little crossover on the teams. That pretty much would guarantee that that lawyer would be screened off that case. [27Ch50–99]

---

[16]Few of the respondents, even those with heavily fortified ethical walls, spoke about provisions to exclude screened lawyers from their share of the fees accrued from the conflicted matter. Some of the larger and more sophisticated firms construct screens even for support personnel—especially paralegals and secretaries—hired laterally from other law firms. In contrast, some of the independent solo practitioners who share office space, secretaries, computers, phone lines, and file cabinets with other attorneys—who often represent coparties—have no screens in place to protect the confidentiality of their cases.

Virtually all the respondents offered immediate disclaimers that their security could be easily breached by an unscrupulous lawyer.

> . . . we built this enormous edifice and there are times when you wonder what really is going on here. Because you built screens and go through all this. You're really, at the bottom, if the person you hired doesn't have integrity and wants to tell you the secrets that he learned at the other firm, he'll do it anyway. [5Ch100+]

> But do you lock up your files at night? No. Is there a possibility the information could be exchanged through the networks on computers? I think most of the things I do, you got to be a real dull person to raid my computer to find out what the hell I'm doing. I mean, you've got to have a dull life to track what [L names self] is doing. But if in a conflict, that's possible, that's possible to key into our network. And our [. . .] if someone in our [East Coast] office wanted to know what I'm doing—if we have a conflicts situation—Chinese wall won't help. So I think that the computer world is another reason why I'm dubious about them. [16Ch100+]

Still, the risk of inadvertent leaks appears considerably greater in the firms with few border controls or bureaucratic hurdles to enforce secrecy and silence.

But how easy is it to practice law in a firm crisscrossed with barricades—constantly under construction, being moved or torn down—that segregate departments, practice groups, even neighbors? Though most respondents whose firms utilize Chinese walls find them relatively easy to erect and to live with, others note some difficulties. Those in smaller firms comment that screens are difficult to enforce:

> We have a really small firm. This is [less than fifteen] lawyers. We have three thousand square feet here. So I've got—whatever my square footage is—this is a small office. Is a Chinese wall a fiction? I mean, look, if it's a big enough case, then—and you've got a Chinese wall issue—then I've got a problem in a small firm this small. And the problem is—assuming that all the clients think the Chinese wall is wonderful and so on and so forth—how the hell am I going to enforce it? There's no secrets here. Everybody knows what's going on in all the cases. So that would be a problem. [104Ch10–19]

> Of course we could do that [build a screen]. I think I would feel awkward about it, especially if it's going to be a long drawn-out kind of thing. Because there's just too many chances—in a firm like ours—that something is going to be said. You know, the lawyers get together to have a beer—whatever. And you just don't want something said. [76Ch10–19]

> I think that would be pretty unworkable for us. I mean, all of our support staff is centrally located. I simply would walk through the secretarial area and my eyes could see documents that they may be working on. And if that's a problem—and I assume it is—that would make it not feasible for us. [87DSS10–19]

> I can't do that [set up a Chinese wall]. I can't, I can't enforce it. I can't enforce it. I can't be out there worrying about whether she's looking at documents she shouldn't be looking at. I won't place myself in that position. [118Ch<10]

Those in larger firms find that screening devices impede and complicate communication and make access to records and documents sometimes cumbersome and inefficient.

> It would be easier if we were a smaller firm. But, we're a bigger firm and it's harder to wall somebody off from everything. I mean, for instance, we send these [New Business] Sheets out to everybody. . . . How do you say, "Well, don't give that to somebody." . . . How do you limit somebody's access on the computer to documents about that? So it's much more difficult in the age of information, because of the accessibility of things, than it would, you know, the old days, where you'd just sort of block somebody off from everything. And you take as many steps as you can, but who's to say that you've taken all of the steps so that that person doesn't find out anything. . . . I think there are a lot of problems. [1Ch100+]

> Sometimes that's not practical. It's hard to lock a room. It's hard when you've got 200 files for a client and someone's supposed to not have access to them. [2Ch100+]

Other respondents, even those in big firms, found it difficult to adequately staff cases with the necessary expertise when departments are fractured by Chinese walls.[17]

> Sometimes you say, "Well, I'd like to use [. . .] So-and-So's my environmental expert on this matter, but I can't because she's on the other side of the screen." [5Ch100+]

> L: Our biggest problem on that was probably right at the beginning, being sure we had enough people [. . .] You don't want to get all your tax lawyers on one side of the wall. Or your banking lawyers on one side of the wall. You want to leave enough people so you could adequately represent the RTC [Resolution Trust Corporation] and yet you could adequately represent a client.

---

[17]Though others disagree. Clearly it depends on the social organization of expertise in the firm.

> It's not hard. I mean, again, because we're big enough. . . . A perfect example is a recent bankruptcy situation, where . . . one of the attorneys that joined our office from another firm did not work on a particular matter there, but his old office represented the other side of this matter. He's a bankruptcy lawyer. Also, we have another lateral who joined our firm from that same firm who's a business practitioner, okay? We now had a transaction involving that firm and that client, okay? The transaction had started while those two individuals are still at their other firm. So, it's the perfect Chinese wall situation. It wasn't a problem for us, because we have a number of switch players. So we were able to have a different business lawyer and a different bankruptcy lawyer working on the matter. So it wasn't that hard. If we were a smaller operation and the only bankruptcy person we had was that person, then there would have been a significant problem. . . . if you have a conflict and you do a Chinese wall, you have an alternative source for the legal work within the firm. [10Ch100+]

R: Your existing clients, yeah. Yeah, that was probably the hardest part on that one was getting the personnel shifted one way or the other.
L: . . . It can get tricky. Yeah, I mean, we don't have that much turnover. But if you're setting up a wall there that you expect to continue for three or four years, I mean, realistically, you ought to look at scheduled retirements to be sure you don't run down a small area and have nobody left there. [3Ch100+]

Because of these difficulties, a minority of respondents indicated that they try to avoid creating screens or use them mostly to solve conflicts between branch offices of the firm where the impediments and disruptions are less problematic.

> We try to discourage Chinese walls unless we would otherwise lose business. Do a Chinese wall if you have to, but do something else if you are able. They are hard to administer. [pilot interview #7]

> They're very difficult to deal with when they're in the same office. And I'd be very hesitant to really do it in the same office. I mean, it's one thing if my [East Coast] has got a problem. I mean, we're not, it's probably never going to happen that you're going to exchange information. Inside the office—very difficult, very difficult. . . . People are going to lunch and they're talking and you know. I've been at lunch where people will start talking and somebody'll say, "Hey, wait a minute. You know, I'm, I can't hear this." And I'm glad people think about that stuff, but it's [. . .] I'm not so sure it's something that you really should do very often. [18Ch100+]

Small-firm lawyers were particularly likely to disparage Chinese walls—certainly in firms their size and often in much larger firms as well.

> By the way, I do not believe that Chinese walls exist—not in fact, not in fiction. Not even the tooth fairy believes in them. Do you believe? There isn't such a thing. It's all baloney. Once another firm tried to lay this (that they had a Chinese wall) on our office; we wouldn't buy it. Perhaps the notion of a Chinese wall might work under extraordinary circumstances. We're a small operation; you couldn't create an effective Chinese wall here. [90Ch20–49]

At best, they considered screening devices a kind of sophistry that allowed firms to represent adverse interests.

L: We're not like Winston & Strawn [large Chicago law firm] or anything. They probably have a computer program to come up with their conflicts.
S: A lot of the big firms tend to do that kind of thing.
L: Yeah. But they have those Chinese walls, so they can represent both sides. [laughter] [73CC10–19]

At worst, they rejected them out of hand.

> I don't believe, myself, in a China-wall concept. I think it's just a [. . .] it's a big lie. [81Ch10–19]

> S: You smiled at one point when I mentioned Chinese walls. Could you envision a Chinese wall in this firm?
>
> L: No, absolutely not. I [snickers] think Chinese walls are bullshit. . . . I think the whole idea of Chinese wall, especially when you have lawyers talking, it just doesn't work. And the appearance of impropriety should be avoided. You know, I think Chinese walls give me a very strong sense of the appearance of impropriety. Clearly, not in a small firm like this. But, even in a big firm, I think there are pressures that are brought to bear, there are informal talks. It just shouldn't happen. If you're on one side, you should be on that side and not the other. . . . In a small firm, a Chinese wall, everybody would laugh about it. Three lawyers can't have a Chinese wall. You almost live together. Six lawyers: a Chinese wall is not going to happen. . . . I mean, out here, a Chinese wall would have been, "Yeah, I represented the husband. My partner's representing the wife. But don't worry, we won't talk about it." Who are you kidding? [84CC<10]

Other respondents questioned the impenetrability of screening devices as well as the temptations to breach the barrier:

> I'm not a big advocate of that Chinese wall either. I think they have big ears. [105Ch<10]

> You can certainly put your ear to 'em and listen [laughter]—sometimes peek over, right [snicker]? I'm sure that happens all the time. [63DSS<10]

> I don't think it's easy in a large firm to function with a Chinese wall. You're basically asking a firm to be on its honor. There's a temptation there. . . . I kind of like the quote from the one guy that said, "I can resist anything but temptation." I don't want the temptation around. [107DSL<10]

> . . . the judge said, "Set up the China wall, and he's not supposed to talk to anybody about it." . . . And they said, "He's not going to work on the file." Come on! That's what you work with associates and partners with, is to discuss things and bounce things off of them. But I'm not saying that they didn't, but I mean, I think there was strong evidence a impropriety could have existed there. . . . We didn't have any ax to grind with this particular law firm, other than the fact that we felt that, human nature being what it is, there's going to be some communication back and forth. [95CC10–19]

Perhaps most telling, one respondent described his reaction when he learned that the confidences and secrets of his law firm were being protected by barriers equivalent to those of a Chinese wall. It raised his consciousness about the kind of trust in an artificial construct that lawyers routinely ask of their own clients.

> You know, a while ago, I found out that our CPAs—two guys—had joined a large insurance defense firm—a competitor of ours. They moved their practice and all of our files and records right into that law firm. Our files were actually physically located there. These files conveyed virtually everything about our business, our financial condition. When I found out, I said, "No way!" I insisted that they had to move the records out of the firm. They argued that they were all locked up and no one could get to them. But this is a dog-eat-dog world. What if the major law firm client started asking questions about us? I couldn't sleep at night. This experience made me realize how clients must feel when their law firm is representing competitors or parties with adverse interests. [89Ch20–49]

As law reformers continue to debate the ethics and efficacy of extending screening devices to the revolving door between private law firms, Illinois provides an instructive case study.[18] What does the evidence tell us? First, Illinois law firms are not teeming with Chinese walls. They are constructed most frequently where they are most appropriate—in large law firms where conflicts are more common and confidentiality easier to cloister, especially where conflicts span physical, social, or geographic distance within the firm. Screens have not overtaken Illinois law firms because they are administratively costly to maintain and, although they may satisfy ethical requirements, they do not necessarily satisfy clients' expectations of undivided loyalty. Though Illinois lawyers may not be required to secure their clients' consent before erecting a wall, they are unlikely to begin construction if they know that what lies behind the screen may drive away a valued and significant client. Moreover, although Chinese walls may allow Typhoid Marys to travel through the job market, they do not allow them to travel laden down with heavy baggage. They do not permit migratory lawyers to undertake adverse representations shielded by the screen. And that is why, as I described in chapter 7, many prospective lateral hires or mergers wither when lawyers realize that they will have to leave behind significant clients whose interests are adverse to those in the host firm. Ethical walls do not change that fact. They may help to unstick the revolving door; but they do not motorize it.

Do the screens meet the specifications found in the ethics codes and case law?[19] Not always, especially in the smaller firms. Admonitions simply to "stay the hell away" do not live up to the spirit of the rules. Even walls constructed from more

---

[18]Unfortunately, because the efficacy of screening devices was not the central focus of my study, the research was not designed to provide the kind of systematic experimental data that might have informed the debate.

[19]For another perspective, see Pizzimenti (1997), who asked detailed questions about the use of screens in a mail survey of firms with more than fifty lawyers practicing in states that allow screens in lateral hiring between private firms. Though tainted by a very low response rate (20 percent) and a likely selection bias that overrepresents compliant firms mindful of their professional responsibilities, the findings are instructive. The survey concluded that most firms try "to do the right thing" (306), but it also found significant minorities that did not know when screens should be erected or what was required and that did an inadequate job of maintaining them. Indeed the author concluded that she had "real questions regarding the efficacy of screens" (329).

sophisticated blueprints have points of vulnerability, especially with respect to computer networks and firmwide communications. Even more problematic, firms often do not construct screening devices as quickly as necessary because of the lag between the time that the migratory lawyer joins the firm and the time that their tainted baggage is discovered. Some of the most notorious and costly disqualification cases involve firms with the most impenetrable screens, constructed too late.

Whatever the shortcomings of ethical screens, the glass is probably still half full. Because ethical screens in Illinois are routinized and subject to regulation, they are most likely more opaque, more secure, better protected, less vulnerable, and better supervised than those erected in states where screens alone do not solve the imputation problem. In most other states, screens are offered to clients as a way of inducing them to consent to the conflict. They are designed by the affected lawyers and built ad hoc to reassure the clients. Because there are no regulatory standards, each wall can meet different specifications, be constructed from different materials. Because they are devices negotiated by affected attorneys rather than offered by the firm, there is less need to tinker with firmwide information systems—computer networks; voice mail, e-mail, and interoffice mail; communications; and the like—to ensure that screens are not inadvertently breached. In these states, it would be unlikely to find self-regulatory systems as institutionalized and comprehensive as those I have described in this chapter, which are standard in many large Illinois law firms to ensure the integrity of their Chinese walls. Whether Illinois screens are really more impenetrable is, of course, an empirical question. But the economies of scale, the regulatory requirements, and the scrutiny of screening devices by Illinois courts all increase the likelihood that they are. One effect of liberalizing the law may well be that, ironically, clients are better protected and confidentiality even more inviolate.

Still, it is likely that the liberalization of the law will reinforce the double standard encountered many times before in this book. If clients have considerable clout, it may be unnecessary to require that lawyers secure their consent because their lawyers will anticipate their reaction before constructing a screening device. It's those one-shotters we have to worry about. Are their rights and interests being trampled in Illinois? Do they fare better in states in which lawyers must seek their consent? Or do the off-the-rack Illinois screening devices, devised to satisfy even powerful repeat-playing clients, better protect one-shotters than their lawyers do in other states after they have consented to the conflict? Unfortunately, we can only speculate.

Ending Relationships

As firms collect more and more clients, their vulnerability to conflict of interest escalates. And as clients spread their business around to ever larger numbers of law firms, firms seemingly endeavor to do the opposite. All else being equal, the fewer clients, the fewer conflicts.

Lawyers must select their clientele cautiously and wisely because the legacy of a client relationship can be long and littered with enduring obligations. Because of hot-potato rules, attorneys cannot simply dump inconvenient clients whose interests suddenly collide with those of others. And commitments to honor client confidences can continue long after the lawyer-client relationship has ended. The good news, as I explained in chapter 6, is that lawyers' obligations do ease after their representation of the client has concluded. For former clients, the proscription against taking a matter directly adverse to client interests is limited only to new matters that are *substantially related* to those for which the firm originally represented that client. Attorneys can sue their former clients, so long as the lawsuit is unrelated to the original work performed for them.

Though lawyers cannot dump their clients, they can ease the burden of the conflict-of-interest rules by transforming current into former clients. There is nothing that a firm must do to effect this transformation. In time, clients become former clients if the firm performs no further work on their behalf. But legal matters can linger—final details remain incomplete or unattended, awards or settlements are not fully paid or performed, legal bills remain outstanding. And while parties delay or procrastinate, lawyers may be foreclosed from taking matters adverse to their interests. As law firms wait out the natural transformation of client status, conflicts of interest accumulate, some of them involving prospective matters unrelated to the work performed for the not-quite-former-client.

But firms can try to expedite the process or create a paper trail to prove that the party is no longer a client. The firm can send out a final bill and close out its bookkeeping records for the client. It can ship off the case files for permanent offsite storage. It can remove the client from the firm mailing list and terminate all written or telephone communication that may indicate that the party is considered an ongoing client. Or attorneys can be even more direct, sending a letter—variably labeled a *termination, closeout, closure, end-of-representation, disengagement,* or *kiss-off letter*—formally terminating the relationship.

Few law firms pursue this last strategy. Indeed, only one firm—one of those selected for the pilot study—had a policy to officially and speedily end client relationships and a self-regulatory process to ensure that the policy was followed. (None of the firms in the Illinois sample did.)

> As soon as the lawyer is done with a client, the file is finalized and classified as inactive. The client is sent a closeout letter. . . . The letter terminates the present client relationship, reclassifying the client as a former client for conflicts purposes. And the letter allows the firm to tell the client all that it has been able to accomplish for the client and tell it how much the firm appreciates its business and hopes that the client will consider the firm again the next time it needs legal counsel. An annual review is conducted to assess the status of all open matters. If a case has seen no activity for eighteen months, the lawyer must provide an affirmative explanation for why the case should not be closed. As another incentive to encourage lawyers to write closeout letters, the lawyer is not allowed to send the file into storage without a record of a closeout letter. [pilot interview #7]

Though several respondents indicated that this strategy, touted in the law firm practice literature and suggested by some malpractice insurers, was a good one under selected circumstances, many more belittled it.

> Yeah, . . . write a letter of closure. Nobody's going to do it. It's a disaster. How can you say, "Thank you very much. It's been wonderful representing you. Now we no longer represent you." It's exactly what somebody wants to do. [laughter]. . . . I mean, you can write a mealy-mouthed, weasel-worded one which says, "It's been wonderful representing you. That matter is now concluded. We continue to look forward to many other opportunities to serve you." Now, is that a letter of termination or is it not? I don't know. You know, it's a law school concept which has probably been adopted by judges which doesn't really work [laughs]. [10Ch100+]

Most respondents who commented on the strategy of terminating clients observed that it is antithetical to the firm's business interests and flies in the face of human nature, in general, and lawyers' incentives, in particular. Attorneys are constantly scheming to induce clients to refer more business to the firm, not less.

> Termination goes against human nature. If you go up and down the hall and ask the lawyers, they will tell you they have no former clients. They have clients who have not sent any business in three years, but they have no former clients. From time to time, there will be a "situational adjustment"—you see something lurking just ahead and you hurry to send out a kiss-off letter. I did that just recently and am very pleased with myself that I caught it in time and saved us a lot of trouble. Lawyers in general, though, are very reluctant to send out disengagement letters. We have no policy that requires it. [8Ch100+]

> We've discussed it. And I think we passed on it, that we would not ask for termination letters. We have enough trouble trying to write an engagement letter that anyone will accept, anyone in our firm, not less outside. . . . Then a termination letter would be just impossible. And no one would ever agree to send it. Your compensation and your life is based upon your having these clients. And turning around and saying "But you're not my client anymore" as quickly as you could. It's just not going to happen. It just doesn't happen. So, even when a thing's clearly one-shot engagements, you'd never get anybody to send these letters out. And then we would undoubtedly just trip over ourselves by immediately sending them some kind of advertising brochure, and . . . then treating them as if they weren't terminated clients. [28Ch50–99]

Moreover, just because the firm sends out a termination letter does not necessarily mean that the recipient is a former client in the eyes of the law.

A few respondents offered a compromise: to put language in engagement letters that specifies the nature of the attorney-client relationship, the tasks the firm will undertake on behalf of the client, and the conditions under which the engagement will be considered completed. They hoped that engagement letters would have the same transformative effect as termination letters but be less likely to chill future business.

> You know, one of the problems is, do you really want to send a termination letter out? I mean, to protect yourself from potential conflicts in the future, yeah, you

> probably should. But you're always hoping that that person's going to come back to you and say, "I've got this huge deal for you. [laughing] I want you to work on it." If you made a practice to send a termination letter out to everybody that you've worked with, . . . you would just sort of kill your business. . . . we've got a lot of clients who are transactional clients. And when they have transactions, they come to you. And how can you judge, "Well, this is the last transaction they're going to give to me. I'll send them a termination letter." Yeah, you'd probably protect yourselves from conflicts; you may not protect yourself from conflicts. Because they may still argue that you have confidential information that you learned over a period of time, which you're using to their disadvantage. But we don't make a practice of it here. And one of things that . . . we do with the engagement letter is we basically set out in the engagement letter what you're going to do. If you show that you completed that engagement and that there's nothing else dealing with that engagement—you were only retained for that engagement alone. So maybe that's a way out of it rather than sending a termination letter out. [1Ch100+]

A second respondent sprung this idea on his managing partner in the course of our interview.

> L: One of the things that I've been thinking about—I haven't talked to you [addressing MP] about it—is trying to develop an engagement letter which protects the law firm by saying, "We'll do this job and here's what we're doing and we hope there are other things too. But if, after a period of x months, we're not doing any work for you, we reserve the right to consider our relationship terminated." And try to do it in a way where we don't have to say, "It was nice knowing you. You're now a former client and we reserve the right . . . we may sue you tomorrow or next month or next year." We just put it gently in the engagement letter and in a realistic way. Where, if they say, "Yes, that makes sense. Why should we have a permanent lock on that firm if we're not giving them any work?" I haven't seen anybody suggest doing that yet. I don't know why that ought not be explored. It is a difficult area and there was a recent case, that referred to other cases, which gave a lot of people the impression that years can go by, and you haven't done any work for the client, and you consider them a former client, but the judge might say, "You never told them that they're a former client. You lulled them into thinking that. And you can't go ahead and sue them." It's a tough one. [5Ch100+]

Firms have not adopted even this compromise. The strategy of thinning out the roster of current clients by transforming as many as possible to former clients represents a forgone opportunity to lessen the force of the conflict-of-interest rules—or perhaps just a foolish and costly one.

SELF-REGULATORY FAILURES

However sophisticated, comprehensive, and vigilant the reactive and proactive mechanisms are that firms adopt to identify, evaluate, prevent, or diffuse conflicts of interest, some conflicts nonetheless detonate. The firm's intelligence web may fail to identify a conflict, its analysts may conclude erroneously that a conflict does not exist or decide to push the legal envelope, its crystal ball may be a bit too opaque, its gorillas may have the last word, or the firm's financial interests may overwhelm its ethical predilections. Perhaps, through no fault of their own, events out of the lawyers' control suck the firm into a tangle of new conflicts. Or perhaps other lawyers strategically accuse the firm of ersatz conflicts to advance the interests of their own clients in an adversarial contest.

These self-regulatory failures or alleged failures may take several paths. Some may never be discovered, and about others, no one may care or be willing to pay the price of blowing the whistle. The firm may withdraw from the conflicted matter on their own or at the request of the client whose interests they have abridged. In a litigation matter, clients may file a motion to disqualify the firm. In any kind of matter, they may sue the firm for malpractice or report it to bar regulators for disciplinary action. Or aggrieved clients may fire the firm or take their future business elsewhere. Here we consider the more formal outcomes: withdrawal, disqualification motions, malpractice suits, and disciplinary complaints.

We begin with the obvious caveat: this account is based on self-reports. Informants may not be especially comfortable disclosing embarrassing or incriminating information—even off the record and behind the shield of confidentiality—and their disclosures undoubtedly underreport and minimize the seriousness of their firm's self-regulatory failures. Still, no respondent refused to answer my questions (though a couple asked me to turn off my tape recorder), few seemed to squirm or obfuscate, and many came up with ample examples. Indeed, some were quite matter-of-fact about outcomes that, however unwelcome, are inevitable in the practice of law.

Withdrawal

Lawyers are most likely to withdraw from an ongoing representation when they fail to identify a conflict at the outset or, as I elaborated in chapter 6, when changes develop after the case is underway that give rise to new conflicts. Several respondents described mistakes or oversights in which the firm found itself on both sides of a matter, whereupon it gracefully withdrew from one or both matters.

> Example: it was a plaintiff's case that we had several years ago—a fairly serious injury, construction worker that was on a building being built at [gives the intersecting streets in the Loop]. And we ended up filing a lawsuit for him. We named the general contractor and everybody else, the owner—typical Structural Work Act case; you name everybody you know. And about a year into the lawsuit, we were over at depositions and one of the defendant's attorneys—who represented, I think, the general contractor, developer or somebody—commented to the attorney from our firm who was over there on behalf of our plaintiff. He said, "You know," he said, "you guys, you might check and see if you don't have a bit of conflict," he said. In another lawsuit, arising out of the same construction and on the same floor, we had been retained by one of the insurance carriers to represent one of

> the contractors. And we were. And it was a terrible conflict. And somehow we hadn't even become aware of it. That system didn't work very well. And now any one of those lawyers could have moved to disqualify us in both cases. And instead, it was pointed out to us and we had to withdraw—in that client's case—and refer it out, as we should have done before we filed the lawsuit. But we just, it happened. [66Ch20–49]

Perhaps the biggest consumers of the withdrawal response to conflict of interest are the ostriches, which we first met in chapter 8. Because they do nothing to identify potential conflicts of interest before they take on a new engagement, they simply exit when they eventually discover they are representing adverse interests in the same matter. The downstate ostrich firm offered several examples (generally withdrawing from the less lucrative of the two conflicted sides of the dispute):

> Just in the last year, we settled a case where we had a major conflict. . . . I represented a group of people that sued the [company that produces an advertising publication] people. . . . And I took on, I don't know, 200 clients to start with. The [company] had overcharged the people for their advertising space. They had represented that the [this city] [publications] were being distributed in a community east of here—a prosperous community—where, in fact, it wasn't being distributed in that community. And so we had a large number of clients that wanted to sue . . . the [company]. And I took their case. And, oh, I was in the case for a couple of months and had expended sums and everything else, when I learned that the Commercial Department represented the [company] in some relatively small collection matters that had been suing different [publication] advertisers over a period of years. And that was a conflict. So we offered to build the Chinese wall kind of thing and—to let 'em go ahead with it. But we ultimately decided it would be best to withdraw from representing [Company] altogether. And [Company] filed a motion against the firm to disqualify us from representing these other people on the basis that there had been a conflict and we owed the duty of loyalty to them. But we were able to show that we learned absolutely nothing in the representing of [Company] in suing for deadbeats in the [its product] [laugh] that could assist us in any way—had any remote connection to the lawsuit that we were filing on behalf of the other people. So the judge denied their motion to disqualify me on that basis. [65DSM20–49]

Most often, when conflicts detonate after the case is underway, attorneys have made no mistakes or oversights. Many of these downstream conflicts could not have been anticipated by the lawyers and occurred through "no fault of their own." Clients changed or additional parties were implicated in the case and the firm suddenly found itself adverse to its own clients, whereupon it withdrew from the case.

> And we just divested, we just got out of a case because we, after being in it for a year and a half, contemplated filing a third-party action, we retained expert witnesses to disassemble a piece of machinery, did and found out that another of our

> clients made a component part that potentially would have been a direct conflict. So we made a full disclosure and got out. [27Ch50–99]

Some downstream conflicts were conceivable, but the attorneys took the calculated risk that they would not materialize. Others were clearly foreseen and disclosed to the parties, but they chose to proceed nonetheless and deal with the conflicts if or when they developed. This situation was most common when lawyers agreed to jointly represent coparties. When new evidence implicated some parties more than others, when coparties began pointing accusatory fingers at each other, when hostilities began to fracture the alliance, or when transition points in the case exposed incompatible interests among parties, attorneys withdrew from representing some or all of them.

> I do a lot of work in the malpractice area, products liability, that type of thing. Frequently, I'm representing a hospital and a number of doctors. And it will become clear that there's a very real conflict or even a potential conflict developing there. . . . Once you see that—and I think that it's not that difficult to see—you've got to advise the clients right away that there's a very real problem. I can think of one circumstance where, really, the problem was so severe and we'd learned so much, that we really had to get out of the case entirely and send both clients to different firms. That always makes us very unhappy. [laughter] But it will happen very infrequently. Usually what happens is, you see a conflict developing. From our standpoint, it makes sense for us to get that resolved as quickly as possible, so we don't get too far down the road and we have to withdraw from both people. So, if we see anything on the border of a conflict, we try to advise them right away, and say that "We think you should get separate counsel." [33Ch50–99]

In other instances, attorneys agreed to advise a party—short of litigation—in a dispute with another client or with an industry that they typically represented. When litigation became inevitable, they withdrew from the case, as they had forewarned their client.

> The matter I referred out today was a case where there was a problem with an officer of the bank [in which my family has a substantial ownership interest]. . . . And the fellow we were helping—who I felt had been treated a little too harshly by the bank and holding company [. . .] And I had been arguing with the president of the bank and holding company about how they were treating the guy. And that's an adverse relationship. . . . So I referred that out to a local attorney. . . . [The officer] wanted to sue the bank. One of the problems with that one is that I don't want the guy to sue the bank, you know? And on the other hand, I do feel he was unfairly treated. . . . But I made it very clear to him that I was also talking to the bank people involved, and that I did not view any of our conversations as—in that sense—confidential. . . . I made it very, very clear from the beginning—to him—that I was not going to get involved in an adverse situation with the bank. And I was going to—at some point—cut the discussions off. So, I anticipated those things and made it very clear to him. [70DSS10–19]

However much clients might respect their lawyers for withdrawing gracefully when a conflict detonates, they are not necessarily delighted with the prospects of starting over.

> . . . the client that you've been representing has a stake in continuing with your representation because it's more efficient for them to do that. You've acquired a lot of knowledge at their expense. And to pull out would really—in most instances—either prejudice them in that particular case, or it certainly will have cost them a lot of money. [59Ch50–99]

They have invested a lot of time and money in their lawyers. They may have trusted their lawyers and now have to get inexperienced strangers up to speed at the eleventh hour. They perceive that with new, unprepared, less expert counsel, they are now at a relative disadvantage in the case. And they may feel betrayed by their lawyers who failed to forewarn them of the potential conflict or to alert them that it might be necessary to withdraw from the engagement. The sense of betrayal may be magnified if the law firm that dumped them stays in the case on behalf of another party.

The withdrawing firm will generally offer to help the client find and prepare new counsel and to share its records, files, and work product with the new firm. (In situations in which firms are conflicted out because they had access to confidential information concerning the other side, such cooperation—however much irate clients expect it—may be ethically proscribed.)

> But, normally, with a routine, serious conflict, you just have to say, "Stop, halt. Here's the problem. If I push this position, I'm necessarily hurting this position. And that's why I can't do both. What do you people want me to do? I'm coming to ya now so that you can resolve it. If you want me out totally, I'll get out totally. . . . If one of you wants to continue with me, and you can agree upon which one it is and the other one will get another attorney, that's fine—after full disclosure, you know." Or all that's overridden by the idea that sometimes there are those conflicts which you feel "There's no way." It can't be done. They both have to have new attorneys. In which case you just say, "I'm sorry. I wish it could be any way other than this. I will cooperate with both in terms of getting your respective file materials to whomever." . . . Generally, you just say, "Stop." Now, in those cases where you can't even say, "I've got a conflict"—because it would give away that—about all you can do is just sit there and withdraw. Just say, "I'm sorry. I can't do this work anymore. I can't tell you why." [68DSM10–19]

Moreover, the former lawyers will generally eat, refund, or reduce the legal fees incurred.

> And, if we make a mistake on a conflict, we have to swallow the costs; we don't charge the client. They have to go get another firm. But it doesn't cost them any extra money. Because they don't pay us. We blow it on the conflicts check and they point it out to us that there is a conflict and we didn't get it waived, we can't charge them for it. It's our mistake. That's happened. [20Ch50–99]

> Every case I've ever withdrawn on—where I've been paid—I've refunded the money. And when they get that back, they're like, "Hey, he's not such a bad guy after all." Particularly when they go to another attorney and find out what it's really going to cost 'em. [laughter] But seriously, you can't profit off of conflict. And I remember, particularly, one just very vividly. I had a criminal client. He called me because the arresting officer—or an officer who was there—had said, "Hey, you ought to call [L names himself]." So he came in here and we talked. And he retained me. And, geez, we're over there in criminal court. The next thing I know, my client is one of the people—the undercover cop—who's going to testify. And I'm, like, "Hey, judge, [laughter] time out. Wait a minute. We gotta stop this thing." And the judge is looking at me like, "What's up, [L names himself]?" I go, "Geez, I got a major [laughter] conflict here," and he's like, "Oh, you do?" I go, "Believe me, I got a real serious conflict." He goes, "Okay." I just refunded all of his money and said, "You know, God bless you. Get another lawyer [laughter] quick." And that was the end of that. [86CC<10]

Disqualification

If law firms do not withdraw when a conflict of interest arises, their adversaries in litigation may file a motion to disqualify them from the case. This is not an uncommon response. Fifty-four percent of the firms in the sample disclosed to me that they had been subject to a disqualification motion at least once, 59 percent had initiated such a motion at least once, and 38 percent had experienced both. When we consider that some firms rarely engage in litigation and therefore have no opportunity to partake of this process, the finding that only a quarter of the respondents in the sample indicate that they have never been on the giving or receiving end of a disqualification motion is quite striking—especially because this figure is probably an overestimate in that few lawyers boast about filing a disqualification motion or being filed against. Note that these estimates reflect the initiation of the disqualification process; many complaints were resolved long before the court could rule on them because lawyers took some sort of remedial action or withdrew from the allegedly conflicted matter. And, of course, a good number of the motions were ultimately not granted.

> I'm not seeing that many disqualifications being granted. There's lots of motions, not many being granted. Some are. . . . We have been the subject of at least two, three, four motions for disqualification in the last year—our firm. They've all been denied. [27Ch50–99]

Disqualification is generally a big-firm, big-city phenomenon. The median-size firm that had filed and received a disqualification motion was more than five times larger than that with no disqualification experience. Although one in six Chicago firms had neither filed nor received a disqualification motion, this was true of one in two firms located in cities of less than fifty thousand inhabitants. Regional differences remain, even controlling for firm size.

The lawyers' observations shore up the numbers. Respondents from the largest Chicago firms indicated that disqualification motions are common (if somewhat less so than a decade earlier):[20]

> I am often consulted on whether we should try to disqualify people on other cases. And it hasn't happened since last week. [laughter] [36Ch100+]

> L: Well, it's particularly acute for us because, oftentimes, it's very important for a party to get us out of a matter because of our peculiar expertise.
> S: . . . So it's something that's always on your mind?
> L: Yes. [17Ch100+]

Those from their smaller counterparts down the street, however, found the use of disqualification motions infrequent.

> And I don't think we would have one a year where it would go to that kind of a process. It's just not a very common thing for us. [33Ch50–99]

> Disqualification is simply another arrow in your quiver. It comes up in a vast minority of cases. Though every year there is probably one motion pending. [69Ch20–49]

And downstate, the answers to my question about experiences with disqualification seemed to echo practically verbatim—from small towns, to medium-sized communities, to larger cities:

> I don't think I've ever seen one. Read about 'em. But I don't think I've ever seen one. It's not, I know, it's not big downstate. It is in the city. [117DSS<10]

> I don't see it going on at all. . . . Doesn't happen. [65DSM20–49]

> It's a great technique they love to use in Chicago. It's not used as much downstate. [72DSM10–19]

> But I don't think it's all that frequent here in this area. [55DSL20–49]

> We don't see it as much here. I would like to attribute that to the fact that the quality of ethics that's being practiced in this county is such that disqualifications take place at the attorney/client level before they get into the courtroom level. I'm not sure that that's true. I'd like to believe that. [75DSL20–49]

---

[20]The disqualification frenzy reached its peak a few years ago. In pretrial motions, it was commonplace, another tactic. Today, it's not as common as it was. People are being more careful about instituting it only when it's appropriate. [8Ch100+]

As I approached the collar counties within fifty miles of Chicago, the greater influence of Chicago-style practice was apparent. Respondents complained of disqualification motions instigated by Chicago law firms and of the need to resocialize young lawyers trying to emulate their urban counterparts just miles away.

> I've had—I'm going to estimate—five or six attempts to disqualify me in cases. And all of them were brought by Chicago firms. None of them were granted. And I can think of two or three of them—the local judge was outraged by the fact they even brought the motion and thought it was frivolous. . . . I'm absolutely convinced it was done for no purpose than to try to bar me from the case and get me to settle. . . . I think there is an upsurge of it, as compared to what it used to be. . . . And it's changed a lot. But it was a good-ole-boy network where—unless the guy on the other side was an absolute schmuck and everybody knew he was a schmuck—you didn't bring a motion to disqualify. It was ungentlemanly. It's changed a lot. But there's still—to some extent—an idea of you don't mess with a lawyer's livelihood or honor unless there's a good reason for it. [84CC<10]

> I see the young associates wanting to do it, because they read the literature. I mean, it's clearly a violation of the Code of Professional Responsibility to extend litigation or create expense or use something like that for a strategic purpose. . . . I guess the young guys get upset about it and excited about it. . . . And that concerns me. 'Cause they're coming out of law school really thinking it's great to be a litigator. . . . One of the things we have to do here is calm those guys down. I mean, they really think it's great to eat raw meat—with their hands. I don't see it being used. I betcha you do in federal court. I bet you do in the big civil cases downtown. But, you know, we're a suburban law firm. We don't see it being used that much. [122CC<10]

Notice two themes among downstate respondents: First, these sharp practices have been brought into their communities by urban practitioners. Second, disqualification motions are less important as a means to rectify conflicts of interest in smaller communities because lawyers can pick up the phone and resolve their differences; the value of reputation is too precious to jeopardize it by contesting an adversary's claim.[21]

> Well, I'll just take a random sample. In the last ten years, I can think of only two instances in which I've seen a motion to disqualify even filed in a downstate matter. And in each of those instances, it was resolved without any hearing before the

---

[21] Although a large-firm Chicago lawyer has similar concerns:

> . . . I need to have halfway decent relationships with the lawyers in these firms. And if they think I'm one of these jerks who tries to get rid of them all the time, I'm not going to have much of a reputation. I mean, I'm very preachy about that with my lawyers—in terms of litigation strategies and being decent to people on the other side, even if they're not to you. Because it comes back to get you in the end. I mean, you get a reputation of being a jerk, people look for ways to get you. And I think that can happen with conflicts. [18Ch100+]

court. . . . I think it's a combination of two things. One is a less sophisticated approach to conflicts than you may see in Chicago. And the second is the issue that I mentioned earlier—that, for the most part, in downstate Illinois, if you don't have a reputation as dealing squarely on a given issue, you're sunk. . . . It would be a rare instance and it would be a guy who was sort of "outside of the club"—so to speak—who wouldn't call you beforehand and say, "[L], this may not be apparent to you, but here's this issue." And if a guy feels strongly enough to call me up and tell me that issue, then I darn well better look at it pretty carefully. And, in my view, that's what happens. And it's resolved amicably, without a lot of fuss. And you walk away because it isn't worth it to you. You know, if you make $25,000, $40,000 on a given case, if you represent 'em all the way through for several years and there's a lot of depositions and so on like that, that's nothin' compared to the rest of your life. I mean, if you get blackballed by a circumstance which causes you to lose your license—things like that—you're sunk. You know, it isn't worth it. It can't possibly be worth it to you. [68DSM10–19]

This book has been littered with examples of conflicts of interest that led to a motion to disqualify the conflicted firm. For most of the conflicts of interest explored in chapters 3 through 7, respondents offered examples in which their adversaries had sought to disqualify them. And, of course, the shoe is sometimes on the other foot.

Yeah, another thing I've noticed about conflicts of interest is it's almost like there's a special point in your brain where you can understand a conflict of interest. And a lot of lawyers are brain-dead there. And I don't say this to be—totally—to be humorous. But I have had discussions with lawyers. They cannot understand. They cannot perceive. It's almost like asking them to speak German. They cannot perceive the conflict of interest. And it's always fun to go in front of the judge and say, "Judge, he's got a conflict." The lawyer says, "Judge, I don't have a conflict." And the judge says, "You're out of here." It does happen. . . . Haven't you found that in your interviews—that some guys, they're like, "I don't understand what the hell you're talking about?" It's like they're brain-dead on this issue? They don't perceive it. And I really believe they're being honest about it. I don't think a guy goes in front of a judge and gets humiliated by a judge, saying, "I don't see it, Judge," unless he really doesn't see it. Nobody likes abuse. [122CC<10]

The respondents have seemingly encountered more "brain-dead" attorneys than I have. Though many offered examples in which they had filed a motion to disqualify an adversary that were similar to those in which they had themselves been subject to such a motion, the former tended to be a bit more ethically charged, less gray, more black and white. Because many lawyers find the disqualification business somewhat distasteful, they favored examples in which they had little choice but to initiate a motion. The behavior of the other firm was especially egregious:

I brought a motion to disqualify a firm in Texas where, I mean, it seemed to me to be a straightforward sort thing, and I didn't feel that we had much choice in bringing

> it. I gave them a couple of opportunities to get out beforehand. . . . But it was ridiculous. . . . The fellow down in Texas had been with a large firm; had worked on a matter for a particular client about the lease termination. He had represented the client on that lease termination, determining what their rights were to get out of that lease, and what defenses were available and all that sort of thing. He then left that firm and joined a five-person firm of which he was a name partner that was representing the landlord in that very lease dispute. And he then called the general—this was a very large company—he called the general counsel of the large company—who was not involved in the matter, knew nothing about it—and sort of generally asked for a waiver. And the guy said, "Well, okay," not understanding anything about what the issues were or what the matter was or what was involved. And by the time the matter got to us, I just thought that was intolerable. And Texas law doesn't permit Chinese walls anyway. . . . So I asked that firm to withdraw and they refused and we brought a motion to disqualify. I couldn't imagine how they could not withdraw from that. So I didn't bring that as a tactical maneuver. I was flabbergasted that this guy would join a firm that was representing the landlord. And they didn't bring the lawsuit; the landlord didn't bring the action on that lease until after he joined them. And how am I supposed to deal with this? Wouldn't one think that that's a conflict and they couldn't do that? . . . And the local firm in Texas—which is one of the large Texas firms—was uncomfortable bringing the motion to disqualify. Said, "We don't do those sorts of things around here." And, you know, I was in a state of shock. As I say, I didn't think that that was reaching to find a conflict. . . . I thought that was so obvious and elementary. . . . I mean, that was the most obvious and horrible situation I can think of. [9Ch100+]

The confidences possessed by the opposing firm were substantial:

> I filed a disqualification motion where it was clear that the other side had confidential—the lawyers on the other side—had confidential information. And I told them about it in advance of the litigation. . . . They couldn't handle the case without using that information. It was impossible for them to do the job they had to do for the client without using the information. And they ignored it. . . . And, basically, we went to the judge. And I said, "We want to have a conference." And we did it off the record. And I disclosed to the judge. They admitted it. And the judge said, "You guys have got to be crazy. You're going to have a terrible opinion against you." And they had to withdraw. And I didn't do that for a tactical reason. My client just felt like it was going to affect their entire strategy in handling the case because of what the law firm knew. They were always going to be able to anticipate where we were going. They had information that they couldn't erase from their minds. And even though they tried, they said, "We'll do a Chinese wall" and all that, it was impossible. . . . And they were really not happy with me. I think their client was happy with us, actually. Because . . . I think their client was real relieved that at least it happened early on in the case. Actually, it resulted in the case being resolved, too. Because they knew they were going to have to bring in another law firm. And the principal sat down and kind of worked the thing out. [18Ch100+]

The client insisted:

> . . . if lawyers are generally getting unpleasant with each other, I'm convinced it's coming from the clients who insist on that, who now equate competence and results with sort of brash, aggressive, obnoxious, in-your-face kind of litigation. I mean, they think that's what wins and they think that's what constitutes good trial work. And that's garbage, it's just garbage. And you try to tell them that, but [. . .] . . . They don't understand. First they say, "Oh yeah, okay, yeah." Then they write you a nasty letter that says, "If you don't do that, I'll get me a lawyer who will." I mean, nonsense like that. . . . it's that kind of in-house counsel that's going to say, [in exaggerated, vicious tone] "Oh, that lawyer on the other side, get him out of the case because he represented one of our thirteen subsidiaries, twice removed or something." It's become nasty; it's just become real nasty. [24Ch50–99]

Other ethics rules required that they blow the whistle:

> When did I last think of it? Oh, about forty-eight hours ago. I have a case where a plaintiff's attorney filed a lawsuit representing six individuals who were hurt in a car crash. One of the six individuals was the driver of the car. He has filed an amended complaint, dropped the driver of the car as a plaintiff he's representing, saying he no longer represents that party and has named that individual as a defendant—along with my defendant. And I did a memo to the file. And I don't know what I'm going to do. My thought is that attorney has a severe conflict. He can't represent that individual one moment and then the next moment sue that individual. I may move to have that attorney disqualified. Why? Is it because I don't like the attorney or I'm going to gain the upper hand? No. If that attorney stays in that's better for me. Because I'd rather have a guy of his caliber defend those people rather than get somebody who's competent in there. Two, I think I have an ethical obligation to bring that to the attention of the court. So I'll probably—depending on what our law clerks dig up—I'll probably be filing a motion to disqualify. I have brought that to the attorney's attention in a letter saying, "I think you have a problem here." So that's my only time I've ever written—in the ten years I've been down here. . . . See, what scares me is, what if I know that and I don't do anything? Have I violated the Code of Professional Responsibility? I don't know. I'll find out. Well, I'm finding out now. But I think I'm going to bring it to their attention. [64DSS10–19]

Or disqualification afforded a significant tactical advantage:

> I mean, if it's available and would hassle the other side, I wouldn't hesitate to use it. If it's a legitimate problem and it strikes me as a strategy that would benefit my client, then I suppose I'd have to look into using it. And I'm not aware that making the threat is, I'm not aware that it'd be unethical. . . . But the suggestion that, if we can't resolve this case, that we will have to object to your representation on a conflict basis, I'm not aware that there's any ethical problem there. And I would use that, as I would use any other strategy. [81Ch10–19]

Respondents enumerate many ways in which the disqualification process can be used strategically for tactical advantage:

> I think it has been inordinately used as a litigation strategy rather than as a legitimate ethical concern. . . . If you don't have a good case, legally or factually, go after the other lawyer. . . . It's used to distract and undermine, delay, cause unnecessary expense. Some firms have raised it to an art. . . . With certain firms you expect it. [108Ch10–19]

> The issue is whether you can get the lawyer of choice out of this case. . . . there may be only five law firms in the world that I really don't want to litigate against. But if I could get those five law firms out, I would do it. Because they're just nasty and unfair and cheat on discovery. If I could figure out how to not litigate against them, I would do it. Most law firms would, I think, . . . in a lot of situations. . . . A great deal of litigation is to seek an advantage so you can get a good settlement. [2Ch100+]

And it is for these reasons that many respondents find the disqualification process so distasteful.

> I think—if you'll pardon the legal term—I think it's all bullshit. It is a sharp—in the bad sense—tactic that litigators used to use in the same way, today, that litigators use motions for sanctions. I thought it stank then, I think it stinks now. I don't like to make those motions. . . . I think it degrades the profession. When there is a real conflict and a real basis for disqualification—and there are precious few—a good lawyer will walk away on his own. And where there are disputed disqualifications and it's in the gray area, the court's not going to disqualify him anyway. [79Ch20–49]

> We are not shrinking violets if we get jacked around. On the other hand, we do not think it right for it to be used as a standard arrow in our quiver. That is not the way to practice law. [57Ch20–49]

So not all lawyers file motions when they discover that an adversary has a conflict of interest, especially when the advantage is likely trivial. Some don't want to subject their clients to the cost and delay of pursuing a claim. Others would rather litigate against what they perceive to be a more desirable adversary and hope that they can use the ethical breach to their advantage. So they confer with their clients, disclose the likely benefits and risks, and decide together how to proceed.

> Deciding to bring a disqualification motion is really a joint decision by you and your client. Typically it arises at the initiative of the client: "Shoot, I gave them information." We won't know as much as our client will about prior experiences with the other law firm that might give rise to a conflicts problem. If the client is

> offended, if the client believes in his heart that he has been wronged. We might think, "Shoot, this is harmless." We will counsel our client that this won't hurt us here. Even though you think what they did was treasonous, they're not good lawyers; we don't mind having them on the other side. But if the client doesn't want them on the other side, we must represent our client. Typically, only the client knows. Confidential communications are generally made orally, so the client has to tell you about them; you wouldn't know. We must represent their interests. The client is entitled to whatever the test is—which, I guess, is whether the matter is substantially related. In other instances, we might recognize that the opposing law firm has had benefit of confidential communications and the client may not realize it. In that instance, it may be necessary to convince the client to bring a disqualification motion. [48Ch20–49]

> But, obviously, if a client says, "Haven't they got a conflict there?" You owe it to your client to say, "Yes, and if you want, we can move to disqualify them. What good reasons do we have to do this? We think they've hired really a pretty schlocky law firm and why do you want them to get somebody else?" Or, "This is a good law firm. There are other good firms out there. . . . Some day you may want to settle this case. You're going to enrage them. If you don't want to settle this case, fine, but there are a lot of things that you ought to think about before you play that game." . . . If it's a true conflict, that is, your client is really concerned that the lawyer will hurt him because of what he learned while he was representing your client [. . .] The more tenuous ones, you really owe it to the system of justice, I think, to counsel your client to say, "Are we really going to go through this game for a worthwhile end or not?" [5Ch100+]

Similarly, given the considerable cost and delay to their clients, attorneys are often reluctant to contest a disqualification motion leveled against them.

> Usually, unless there's a really incredibly good reason and it's a very, very significant litigation for your client, that if a motion to disqualify is brought, the probability is you're better off resigning. Because your client can't stomach the cost of fighting the disqualification. [10Ch100+]

> Well, part of it, I think, depends on being candid with your clients, saying, "We're in this situation. It's likely to be a long, expensive fight. Do you want us to push it as far as you can? Okay now, would you like to just say, 'We can't wait for this to be resolved. We don't want to pay for it to be resolved?'" Some firms make the mistake of watching out for their own self-interest on this until it's too late and they're totally embarrassed and everyone ends up furious at them, even if they win—that is, their own client—they may fight for a year about disqualification. They may be so upset about it. . . . Lawyers are so competitive these days; they don't want to give anything up. They have to step back and make sure that their client understands the risks of going forward on a conflict battle and is comfortable with what's going on. [5Ch100+]

But perhaps even more important than conferring with clients about how to respond to a disqualification motion, firms must disclose them at the engagement stage—before any time is squandered or funds expended—if they anticipate that such a response is possible.

> So you have to tell the client if you think there's a possibility of a disqualification. You have to tell the client and you have to let him know that, even though you think it's a good case or whatever your evaluation is [. . .] And we've had some clients who say "Well, I hear what you're saying. Roll the dice. See what the judge does. We'll deal with it." Other clients say "Well, we really love you, but we don't want to pay for a disqualification. Have a nice life." And we understand that. But you have to let the client know. Because the worst thing in the world from a client-relations standpoint is to have a disqualification motion presented to you and you haven't told the client that this is likely to happen. And then they want to know, "What the hell is this all about, and why didn't you tell me?" [36Ch100+]

Malpractice Suits

Because some malpractice insurers believe that conflicts of interest increase the likelihood and size of a malpractice award, they have instituted extensive loss prevention programs—described in chapters 2 and 8—to help law firms avoid, identify, or diffuse conflicts of interest. Either their efforts are having a profound impact or their fears are largely unfounded (or the respondents' recollections are incomplete). Respondents in at most 12 percent of the firms in the sample reported one or more malpractice claims alleging conflicts of interest. The demographic characteristics of these firms more or less mirrored those of the overall sample. With the exception of disproportionately fewer small firms of fewer than ten attorneys,[22] those sued and those not were of roughly similar size and location.

The malpractice claims reported were certainly not among the most dramatic examples of conflict of interest unearthed by the study. For example:

> We got into one of those things where it was claimed that we were representing one of the principals who was, in fact, leaving the corporation. Our contact with the corporation came because he joined the corporation. We became counsel to the corporation. He left the corporation. We did work for him. And it was claimed that, because we knew something two years ago with regard to the corporation, we could no longer represent him, because he was now competing with the corporation. [51Ch20–49]

Disciplinary Action

> There are a lot of risks associated with taking on a disqualification motion. And if you lose one, there is—I don't know whether it's automatic—but there certainly is

[22]Probably without pockets deep enough to be attractive to plaintiffs' lawyers.

> a likelihood, substantial likelihood, that an adverse decision will be immediately turned over to the ARDC. And that starts another process. [23Ch100+]

Although several respondents mentioned that successful disqualification motions would be referred to the state disciplinary body, few reported any contact with the Attorney Registration and Disciplinary Commission, or ARDC. Not even one-tenth of the respondents indicated that their firm had been subject to an ARDC complaint concerning a possible conflict of interest. Almost two-thirds of these firms subject to an ARDC complaint were small—comprised of fewer than ten attorneys—and many of the complaints were filed by convicted criminals who were unhappy with their lot. Again, the examples are not especially compelling.

> We do a fair amount of collection work for [a retailer]. Now, someone injured his eye using one of the tools that the retailer sells—[brand of tool]. The plaintiff approached us to sue the retailer. This was so much different than anything we've ever done with them [the retailer]. We asked their permission to take the case. They said no. Moreover, they said that they were going to report us to the ARDC. So we withdrew and sent the case to another firm without taking any fees or making any financial arrangement with the other firm. But the retailer's inside counsel was still indignant. He said that he had reread the Canons and still felt obliged to report our conduct to the ARDC even though we had voluntarily withdrawn from the case. [78CC10–19]

> We had a situation where I was representing a divorce client. And it turned out there was a conflict between the divorce client and a company that was being represented by my partner. He was representing an insurance agency that happened to be owned by the husband of the divorce client. But because the file was opened in the name of the company—because it was a corporation and there was no service being rendered to the individual—we didn't pick that up at the beginning. . . . You know, it's something that nobody was happy about, and it wasn't even recognized at the beginning. Although, it probably should have been by the husband in the case—the opponent—because . . . you'd think he would have known that the law firm who filed an appearance of behalf of his ex-wife was the same law firm that was representing him. But he didn't pick it up until months into the case. . . . I withdrew. . . . he complained to the Bar Association, saying that we didn't do a proper conflicts check, or we didn't have the proper system or something. That's the only occasion that I can think of. . . . It's still pending. I don't think anything should come of it. [94Ch10–19]

In one instance, two lawyers who formerly worked at a firm in the sample had been disbarred for a series of improprieties related to outside investments, some of them with clients. Although the misconduct for which they were disbarred was far more grave than acting on conflicts of interest alone, undoubtedly they committed these misdeeds as well.

In short, the social control of lawyers' conflicts of interest—at least in Illinois—can be found inside law firms themselves, occasionally in the courts, and virtually never in formal disciplinary bodies.

CONCLUSION

One thing should be crystal clear: if self-regulatory systems were structured solely to comply with the ethical rules regarding conflict of interest, this chapter would be five pages long. What inflated this chapter as well as the budgets and time sheets of real lawyers is the fact that ethics are the least of the problem. Conflicts of interest have profound implications for the bottom line, the capacity to take in new business, lawyer compensation, intrafirm harmony, client relations, and the ability to recruit new legal talent or move through the job market. They affect the course of an engagement—protracting and increasing the cost of litigation and sometimes influencing its outcome. They affect the ability of clients to choose and keep their legal representatives. And, rarely, they can subject lawyers to malpractice claims and disciplinary action.

Because these costs of conflicts can be so great, many firms tie themselves up in knots, extracting countless unbillable hours of their most senior partners in an effort to foretell the future and read their clients' minds, consult with and cool out clients, plan for potential contingencies, keep options open, erect structural barriers, construct legal loopholes, create paper trails, manipulate or extinguish lawyer incentives, extract promises, isolate and ignore their most valued colleagues, anticipate and defend against the strategic behavior of their adversaries, even end relationships and jettison business. Firms are variably tangled, of course. Few ostriches or elephants pursue such complex courses. But large firms with diverse practices and repeat-playing clients simply cannot afford to merely comply with the ethics rules. The self-regulatory knots are most intricate where the loyalties are most tangled.

TEN

The Practice of Law and Real Life

Undeniably, law is one of society's most important institutions. The legal system is implicated in our births, deaths, rights, relationships, disputes, jobs, safety, and so on. Roughly three-quarters of American adults have used legal services (Curran 1989, 57–59), and all indirectly subsidize the legal profession through inflated costs of insurance, goods and services, taxes, and the like. At the same time, lawyers comprise far less than one percent of the labor force; their contribution to the gross domestic product is just double that proportion (*National Data Book* 1997, 410; Lum and Yuskavage 1997, 28). A "real world" lives beneath the towering suites and outside the cloistered offices in which legal practitioners ply their trade, where interests also clash and those entangled strive to extricate themselves. It is important to examine this real world for perspective on the conflicts that beset legal practitioners but also to reflect on how our understandings of conflicts of interest in the practice of law might contribute to how others respond to those that snarl their worlds.

In this chapter, we broaden our perspective. We begin with clients, then turn to other fiduciaries and the turbulent markets that have roiled many institutions of trust, not only legal ones. Finally, we reconsider the impact of conflict of interest on the practice of law, the future of the legal profession, indeed, on the future of trust.

CLIENTS

Just as it takes two to tango, it takes at least two to create a conflict of interest. Yet half of the pair, the client, has been noticeably absent from my account so far, at least in the first person. The reason is obvious: I didn't interview clients. Though clients figure centrally in how conflicts of interest arise and especially in how lawyers respond to them, we have seen them through the lenses of their actual or would-be lawyers. As I round out the account in this last chapter and connect it to the real world, clients serve as the bridge.

Of course, there is no such thing as a generic client. Some are corporations or organizations, some individuals, some collections of coparties; some are one-shotters and others repeat players with long-standing ties to a particular lawyer or firm; some are sophisticated in legal matters and others not; a few are fiduciaries bound by similar ethical rules regarding conflicts of interest; and some are themselves lawyers or interface with outside counsel through extensive in-house law departments.

Moreover, how clients view conflicts reflects not only who they are but also what interests are in contention, the circumstances under which the conflict arose, and the kind of relationship they have with the lawyer now entangled in the conflict. Clients respond differently, for example, to a trivial routine conflict than they do to a bet-the-company case; to a conflict triggered by a transaction than by contentious litigation; to a conflict that materialized through no fault of the lawyers than one they could have foreseen.

Furthermore, lawyers often interact with clients over potential conflicts of interest rather than those that have already detonated. For every encounter in which counselors decline, withdraw, or are disqualified from a case because of an actual conflict, in countless others attorneys merely seek a waiver, disclose the risks of downstream conflicts, advise parties to consider separate counsel, or disclose their intention or seek permission to represent a competitor, advance an adverse position, or hire a lawyer from an adversarial firm. Where real conflicts may provoke considerable anger or dismay, the others may receive more positive or at worst indifferent or ambivalent reactions from clients.

So the litany of client reactions reported in this chapter reflects the varied contexts in which conflicts arise, the relationships in tension, what is at stake, and who is ostensibly at fault as well, of course, as the characteristics and experiences of the affected clients. Not surprisingly, then, lawyers report reactions that range across the entire spectrum.

Many clients react negatively to their lawyers' conflicts.

> They're mad. Very mad, very mad. [33Ch50–99]

Some feel betrayed, viewing conflicts as a profound breach of loyalty. They expected their lawyers to champion or protect their interests for all time—even interests that they had never engaged the lawyer to defend—to live and breathe their side, even to eschew clients who have dealings with their enemies.

> Some [clients] don't care at all and recognize the fact that law firms need to make a living, too. Others believe that when they come into a law firm that they, in effect, own you for life. . . . a lot of clients believe that once they become a client, they're a client on all issues, rather than just looking to the law firm to protect that client's interests within the scope of the engagement that was given. . . . Others, particularly some business corporations outside of the financial community, believe that, if you are their lawyer, not only can you not do anything which is directly adverse to their interest, you can't represent competitors, you can't assert in litigation positions which are adverse to the interests of that client. [23Ch100+]

> There are situations in which, if the law firm represents a bank, for example, a client would be enraged if that bank were to loan money to someone who was trying to take them over or buy into them—even if the law firm did not represent the other party or the bank in this particular matter at all. [52DSL20–49]

Respondents described instances in which their own and other firms were blacklisted after taking a position unpopular with a client or industry.

> I remember when Jenner & Block agreed to represent the plaintiff in a punitive damages case which was before the U.S. Supreme Court. They were basically blacklisted by members of the Products Liability Advisory Council, who felt very strongly that punitive damages were unconstitutional. And the fact that Jenner would take a case, basically advocating the constitutionality of it, angered them so that they just said, "Okay, fine, we're not going to give you any more business." [59Ch50–99]

Other clients feel abandoned or betrayed that their lawyer chose someone else over them.

> My toughest conflict situation is the entrepreneur who cannot fathom why you cannot represent him and why you have to have him sign this letter that he cannot understand and doesn't know what it means, and doesn't want you to explain what it means. And says, "Joe Jones . . . has been my lawyer for twenty years. What do you mean, because you represent Prudential, he can't handle this loan that I'm getting from Prudential?" He doesn't want to know about the concept of legal conflicts. He doesn't care about the concept of legal conflicts. [11Ch100+]

Sometimes the reaction to being sent to another firm is less a sense of betrayal than annoyance at the lost investment or the cost of getting the new lawyers up to speed.

> It's when you find yourselves on both sides and you have to get out. And you have to tell the client that the firm must get out of the matter. And the client is angry. They made an investment in you and don't want you out of the case. [14Ch100+]

Other clients react to potential breaches of confidentiality embodied in the rules of professional responsibility and triggered by conflicts of interest.

> I've had clients that have been concerned that, if you represent a competitor, even though the subject matter isn't a conflict in the technical sense, if you learn about their technology, there's a chance that some of the information—through you—will kind of seep through. [41Ch50–99]

And some clients respond negatively simply because they have the power to do so.

> Because now I think clients are very attuned to the fact that they are the gorilla in the relationship these days and that they can really dictate much more than they ever thought they could or ever tried to before. . . . They really are influencing and changing the relationship. And that also includes less willingness to waive a conflict or to work with someone to resolve a problem. [24Ch50–99]

Some, as I described in chapter 5, insist that the firm refrain from taking certain positions. Others, as a blanket policy, refuse to waive conflicts of interest.

> They're being obstinate about consents—and really silly, silly things, where you have two unrelated small matters. . . . they're just bein' jerks. They're just jerkin' you around. And a lot of people now say, "Well, we have a policy"—and this really galls me—"We have a policy that our outside counsel are either for us or against us. And we cannot consent to any adverse representations." Gimme a break! The big problem is that, if this corporation—and this is not just one corporation; I'm talking about a half a dozen of these pompous phone calls I've been on—if these corporations wanna give us all their business, fine. But we're talking about people who have given us one or two little things—maybe ten thousand to twenty thousand dollars in billings—and [we] can't even pay the rent on that. And they expect us to go steady with them for one or two little pieces of business. And that's ludicrous. . . . And I hope that they will get their comeuppance some day. . . . it's becoming fashionable for in-house lawyers not to waive conflicts because they want to exercise more control over their outside counsel. Whether it be major matters or small matters, a lot of them—and I mean a lot—of big companies simply have adopted a no-waiver, no-consent policy. [36Ch100+]

More cynical clients insist that conflicts of interest are not about ethics or loyalty or confidentiality at all but are merely a ploy devised by attorneys to generate more business.

> Say there's three parties, which is your typical mortgagor, mortgagee, and a lender, okay? They don't understand why three guys show up at the closing to handle all this. To them, that is a waste of legal talent. And it is also the case that they feel that the attorneys are gouging. In other words, "I'm going to get my brethren in here and they're going to make some money and I'm going to make some money and we're all going to make some money!" And I have on many an occasion heard them say, "Well, you guys have got a real deal here. You all have each other employed." And if you say, "Well, the reason for that is because everybody ought to

> have their own, so that you know that you're getting representation as to your matter, your issue." It's sort of like, "Right, oh sure, I believe that kind of thing," that they smile, they walk away, and they think, "Okay, well, he's come up with his excuse." [68DSM10–19]

And others just think their lawyers' response to conflicts is absurd.

> Because they'll come to you and they'll say, "You guys are just being ridiculous.... You're 'holier than thou,' and all of the rest of it. Don't give me this junk. We've got a job. You're our lawyers. Do it!" [11Ch100+]

They don't believe that lawyers have ethics and certainly don't want adherence to ethical rules getting in the way of their own legal needs or agendas.

> [Clients] are generally mystified. They've heard too many attorney jokes. They don't believe that lawyers have any scruples. When you say that you can't do something because it violates ethical rules, they are mystified. "Oh, you do have rules?" they will ask. The general public has become so hardened about attorneys. They can't believe that a lawyer wouldn't take every case they could get. [98DSS<10]

> But I don't believe that . . . clients necessarily believe that lawyers have ethics. And if they do, that's fine, as long as those ethics don't get in the way of the client's immediate goals and desires. [75DSL20–49]

But not all clients react with anger, impatience, or cynicism. Some seem to appreciate or even evince greater respect for their lawyers as a result of how they responded to the conflict of interest.

> I think, at least I've found personally, the clients are rather happy that you've disclosed it. And you've been so candid about it, forthright about it, that . . . you've really earned their respect. [123Ch<10]

Even clients furious about the firm's response to a conflict may, in hindsight, feel greater respect for their lawyers for refusing to cave in to their demands.

> And the lender comes back and says, "No, I think this is ridiculous. Why don't you people do it?" And this is a lawyer! And so we said, "We just like to avoid situations like this. We think there's this conflict there and we're questioning whether it can be waived or not. We just don't want to do it. We want to avoid doing it." . . . As I understand now, . . . the lender corporation actually was impressed that we held our ground on it and has sent us some business. Which is also an interesting thing. [11Ch100+]

Or at least they appreciate the lawyer's candor and the fact that the issues were disclosed before they had developed into serious problems.

> They normally appreciate that. Because, if you look at it from their standpoint, typically, you're not dealing with the person who's the president of the corporation. You're dealing with somebody whose paycheck gets paid by the corporation and they don't want anything going wrong with whatever it is that they're handling. They're typically delighted to know that you have this potential problem, so that they can document it—if they have the authority to do it—and say, "Okay, here's what we decided." Or they can take it on up the chain and say, "This firm has asked this question. What should we do?" I have a number of clients who I will tell something to of that nature on a regular basis. And they're always pleased. They haven't taken away any business; they haven't gone anywhere. They're glad. They count on the fact that I'm going to tell 'em that, if I think that there's any sort of problem. [68DSM10–19]

Other clients react positively to their lawyers' conflicts of interest because, as I noted in earlier chapters, that was what attracted them in the first place. In marketing to clients, firms tout their experience in championing both sides of a dispute and their ready access to inside information on how adversaries will fashion their legal case. Some clients buy it. They like that their lawyers are major players in an area of law, that they possess the social capital to grease the right wheels or negotiate more effectively.

> I think most sophisticated clients that hire us know that we do a lot of plaintiffs' and defense work—that we really do a mix. . . . Certainly defendants, like a fairly large Chicago accounting firm—actually national accounting firm—I'm thinking of that hired us in securities litigation, came to us and said, "We're hiring you because you've had so much success representing plaintiffs that we want to hire you because you know this area very well and you know how to fight against the plaintiffs' bar and the plaintiffs' arguments." [39Ch50–99]

And others welcome news of a conflict, assuming that their attorneys will use their connections or draw on client confidences for their own benefit.

> Just because I represent a candy manufacturer doesn't mean I can't represent another candy manufacturer, okay? Sometimes I have wondered about that also, . . . you know, here I represent a candy manufacturer that I might know has some financial weakness and I might represent another candy manufacturer that might, if he knew, might go and take advantage of that financial weakness somehow—in the marketplace or something. I obviously could not advise the second of the information I have of the first. But I've theoretically wondered at times, "What is B, what is the second one, hiring me for? All the knowledge that I come to the table with, or merely answering specific questions that they pose to me?" [81Ch10–19]

Some clients prefer to deal with "their" firm on the opposing side than another, because they believe their firm will be more cooperative, honest, competent, efficient, or less cutthroat than the alternative.

> . . . most transactional clients are pleased to see good lawyers on the other side. Because they think the deal will get done and that it will be papered correctly and that the lawyers won't be fighting and that the lawyers won't be running up big legal bills and so on and so forth. Any good sophisticated businessman is not likely to say, "I don't want you guys on the other side, because you represented me before." [39Ch50–99]

Often implicit in this rationale is the assumption that the client can bank on its relationship with "its" law firm to secure a better deal than they would from a disinterested stranger on the other side (exactly the reason why the firm has a conflict of interest in the first place).

> Well, because of that situation [sibling was elected state's attorney], I initially informed all of my conflicts cases that that was the situation and, . . . if they had a problem with that, I wanted to let them know up front. . . . Generally, the reactions from my clients were favorable. 'Cause they conceived it that I would be either getting them a better deal or that at least I was able to work with this prosecutor on a good working relationship. [112DSS<10]

In some cases, then, conflicts are to be welcomed as golden opportunities to be exploited or indicators of the expertise and stature of the entangled lawyers. And, as I described in chapters 8 and 9, for some clients, conflicts also represent an opportunity for strategic advantage, to be exploited and manipulated in hardball litigation. And other clients don't seem to care one way or another about conflicts of interest faced by their lawyers or those of their adversaries.

> My experience has been that clients are very understanding of those kinds of problems and doesn't seem to really bother them that much. Maybe it's because it's a higher standard than what they're used to. I don't know. [55DSL20–49]

As long as they feel secure that their counselors are loyal and competent, they are not troubled if they sometimes represent adversaries, competitors, or unpopular positions.

> And so I think the client, the business client, is looking for competent counsel. He's looking at somebody who is going to protect him well. And our clients, at least, don't have a perception that our tendency to represent either side is going to sway our aggressiveness and our dedication to them in that particular case. . . . We have a—I think—a sophisticated client base. Small businessmen are very bright, very aggressive, very astute. And, as long as they feel there's loyalty between us and them, they don't care if we're representing a plaintiff in another case against a corporation under the ADA [Americans with Disabilities Act]. They're glad to know we know what ADA is and we've read it and we've tried an ADA case before. [122CC<10]

Conflicts are just part of doing business. If this firm doesn't take the case, someone just as good will.

> . . . if we don't have any special knowledge of the [client], what the hell interest do they have in not agreeing to [a conflicts waiver]? [The prospective client is] going to go to Lord, Bissell and Jenner & Block and Mayer, Brown and Wildman, Harrold [four large Chicago law firms]. And they're going to get—I don't mean to diminish the role of our firm—but they're going to get damn good representation. . . . if you were in Decatur, Illinois [a city in the center of the state with roughly 85,000 residents]—and let's assume there were just a couple of good firms. . . . I got the good one. There's one other good one. If I can block their entry into the case, the defendant's left to pick among some private practitioners who aren't too skilled. Well, then you seek some real advantage there. But that's not true in Chicago or Los Angeles or New York or Cleveland or anywhere else. [19Ch50–99]

Indeed, conflicts are so common for many repeat-playing institutional clients—banks and insurance companies, for example—that they actually have waiver forms that they provide to their conflicted attorneys.

Others overlook conflicts because they want to work with a specific lawyer.

> I think that the insurance companies we represent, they're here because of a certain lawyer who's here. And they want that lawyer. And he's a very good lawyer for them and he's done a lot of good for them. And they're not going to run away so quickly. [94Ch10–19]

And some perhaps don't realize that they should care.

> My recollection of the case involving the cop—the civil rights case—and his wife. . . . I remember that he was like, "Forget it. Who cares? Let's go ahead and file the lawsuit." And his wife was pretty much the same way. She said, "I don't care. As long as you keep my child support coming in"—that kind of thing. . . . It wasn't just that they weren't concerned about the conflict, they weren't even cognizant of it. And I made a point of explaining it over and over again to make sure they understood it. And after I explained it, I sent out a very formal letter explaining all the points, citing the rules and so on. And then I had to remind them to sign it—because they just sort of tossed it away after they read it—and to send it back. So, yeah. In that situation they couldn't care less, as long as they got representation in their case. [84CC<10]

This last example raises a question: how well do clients really understand the notion of conflict of interest, especially in the varied and sometimes subtle ways it develops? Respondents, perhaps reflecting their disparate client base, disagree about the answer. Many observe that clients do not really understand conflicts of interest.

> Most parties don't [understand], or they'll nod their head and say they understand, but I really don't think they do. [116Ch<10]

> "I thought you were my lawyer." "Well, I have done legal work for you. I am the bank's lawyer." "Well, do I need separate counsel?" "Well, there is a potential that

> something may occur in this case. But in the normal case, I suppose maybe you don't. But maybe you want to have another lawyer look at it." "Well, you're preparing it, aren't you? What would I want the other lawyer to look at it?" "Well, you do understand that these are being written for the benefit of the bank." "Well, isn't the bank my friend? Aren't they on the same side as me? Well, I mean, they're lending me money, right?" "Well, yes, they are on the same side of you. They hope you are successful. But at the same time, if you're not successful, they're not on the same side of you." [97DSS<10]

Others indicate that clients do understand conflicts, even individuals.

> Clients that deal with us are businessmen or are executives of companies. So they are acutely aware of things that are adverse to their interests—their economic interests—'cause that's what we deal with. And people who are good businessmen don't need to be lawyers to spot a situation that can be adverse to their economic well-being. [104Ch10–19]

> I think a client understands the idea, "I can't represent you and sue you at the same time." [laughter] I think most clients have a very good gut reaction to what a conflict is. I don't think there's any big trick to identifying a conflict of interest. I think only big Chicago firms make it complicated because they're always trying to avoid them. [73CC10–19]

> Clients all understand the problem. I have never heard of anyone saying, "You know, I keep trying to explain this to my client and he's too dumb to understand." . . . I don't think it's a sophisticated problem. . . . I think an expectation of clients is that lawyers are confidants and that they're loyal. . . . You can't watch television and not know what conflict of interest is. So they understand. [2Ch100+]

Indeed, some clients are so versed in conflicts of interest that they often raise the question themselves when they first contact the firm.

> I would say, probably, on half of the calls that I get for someone seeking my representation, the initial question—if not the first, maybe the second—would I have a conflict? . . . But, again, it depends upon the nature of the practice and how sophisticated the person is in dealing with it. So it really varies. [58Ch50–99]

And, respondents observe, even clients who do not understand conflicts can be educated.

> Yeah, I think there's some learning curve there on the client's side. [15Ch100+]

> That's why I give them all the examples. And those they understand very clearly. They want to feel that my loyalty is totally to them. And that's their right. So if you talk about conflicts of interest in the abstract, that has no meaning to them. But if I talk about, "I don't want to be placed in a position where I'm working for

> one of you, as against the other person's interests." That's very clear. That, that's like basic. That's understood in every kind of human interaction, I think. And there's nothing abstract or obscurely ethical about it, I don't think. [118Ch<10]

As respondents chronicled their varied conflicts of interest and explained how they exercised discretion in each, they commented on specific features of the cast of characters. They described the "sophistication" of the client or prospective client, a linguistic proxy for the client's experience with legal matters in general and litigation in particular. They noted whether the client was a lawyer or represented by an in-house legal department. They observed how much business the client sent to the firm and the density of the relationship—how long it had lasted, how exclusive it was, whether the firm acted as general counsel for the client or only handled a miscellaneous matter here or there, whether the firm provided specialized expertise or serviced a diverse array of legal needs faced by the client—and the strength of the connection between lawyer and client. They evaluated the balance of power in the relationship. Did the firm have specific lawyers or expertise that the client desperately needed, or could the client easily take its business elsewhere? Respondents described whether the party was litigation-prone and especially conflicts-prone (such as insurance companies, asbestos manufacturers, or environmental polluters, for whom conflicts often "roll off their back"). They drew on their experience with similar types of clients. Was this an industry or profession known for thin skins and retribution—medicine, for example? And they shared their own sense of the psychological dispositions, egos, insecurities, and personal histories of the parties. Note that not only are the characteristics of the parties directly involved in the case relevant; so too are those of clients arrayed along the sidelines, witnesses, insurers, and others whose interests may be adversely affected.

In regaling me with their stories, respondents were not merely indulging me with their lay sociology. Social background characteristics are critical in determining how to respond to a potential conflict. On the one hand, it's a matter of ethics: clients cannot give informed consent to waive a conflict if they cannot fully appreciate the issues, costs, risks, and probabilities. Nor is consent freely given if clients do not have the wherewithal to refuse. So there are parties from whom waivers should not even be sought.

On the other hand, it's a matter of business: lawyers do not want to lose valuable clients.

> People are terribly worried about it. . . . I'm very concerned about that, very concerned about upsetting client relationships. Because we're selling service and relationship; we're not selling a product. People don't buy law documents as products. They buy services. And if you tick off your client, you're not selling that service anymore. [10Ch100+]

And losing clients is a function partly of client reaction and partly the client's ease in switching law firms. So lawyers develop intuitive models based on client characteristics and features of the prospective matter and constellation of parties to predict which clients are likely to respond negatively, which positively, and which will be indifferent. Respondents report that reactions are generally more benign from sophisticated repeat-playing clients who are no strangers to conflict of interest, whose relationship with their lawyers is strong and long-standing and built on trust but not so dense or exclusive that clients feel left high and dry when their counselors need to step out of the case, feel betrayed by their lawyer's defense of an adverse or abhorrent position, or are so powerful that they call all the shots in the relationship. Clients who trust their counselors and/or have less to lose react less negatively to their lawyers' conflicts. Here, lawyers may seek a conflicts waiver or represent a competitor or advance an adverse position.

> It varies a good deal by the sophistication of the client and also the nature of our relationship with the client. If a sophisticated client for whom we . . . represent on a casual basis—a deal here, a deal there—. . . they would typically waive conflicts without any trouble. On the other hand, if it's a client for whom you were, day in, day out, representing on hundreds of matters. You represent them in litigation. You know their officers, their directors. You know their business client, how they do business. That's a situation we . . . would feel uncomfortable asking for a waiver. Might not even go to them and ask for a waiver, even though they were not using you on a particular transaction. [17Ch100+]

Unfortunately, this account of the client's perspective on the tango is less than satisfying. First, respondents spoke in generalities. From the jumble of stories, we can abstract few patterns; every rule has compelling exceptions. More significant, the accounts are intrinsically biased. We receive them through the lawyers' antennae. But attorneys are not privy to their clients' true feelings. Though some clients may directly voice their displeasure, others do so through exit. And because some clients engage the firm for a single matter, counselors may not expect repeat business and not realize that its absence is a commentary on their service. Clients unwilling or unable to exit may simply keep their mouths shut, hoping not to aggravate an already uncomfortable relationship. And even when clients honestly share their reactions with their lawyers, the latter may see things—or report them to me—in a more positive light than they were intended.

Moreover, even were lawyers' perceptions and reports and client reactions identical, they reflect a selection bias that overrepresents positive client sentiments. Prospective clients who are troubled by conflicts of interest will eschew law firms with known conflicts—for example, those that work for their competitors or champion adverse positions or represent both plaintiffs and defendants, employees and employers, doctors and patients, and so on. Clients who are attracted to the expertise, inside information, and social capital offered by conflicted law firms will gravitate to them. So conflict-prone firms overrepresent conflicts-seeking or conflicts-tolerant clients. The already abundant collection of negative client reactions to conflicts reported by respondents may be a mere fraction of their real magnitude. In truth, the only way we will know what clients understand and how they respond to their lawyers' conflicts of interest is to systematically ask them. As I argue at the end of this chapter, the future of the legal profession may indeed depend on such data.

A HIGHER STANDARD?

Many clients have themselves been snarled in tangled loyalties—negotiating between the competing interests of patients, constituents, stockholders, clients, family members, and others, not to mention their own interests. Their reaction to the conflicts of interest of their lawyers is undoubtedly refracted through their own experiences and ethical standards. As the respondent quoted in the last section conjectured, his clients are perhaps not bothered by his firm's conflicts because they reflect a higher standard than that to which his clients are accustomed.

But could it be that lawyers' ethical standards or, indeed, even their behavior surpass those of many of the rest of us? The glut of lawyer jokes notwithstanding, the empirical evidence is rather scanty. Anecdotal, journalistic, investigative, theoretical, and normative accounts and surveys of conflict of interest in varied professions, institutions, and fiduciary roles abound. Unfortunately, they suffer from a lack of systematic empirical evidence and the absence of a random representative selection of cases, anecdotes, or examples. In some instances, cases are chosen to expose the most egregious practices, in others the most benign; others analyze whatever data are available, with little reflection on how and why the data were generated, what biases they reflect, and what segments of the profession or industry were excluded.

So holding up this body of "tainted" evidence against the lawyer data presented in this book is unfair and potentially misleading. Just as one would find substantial differences between my interview data and accounts of lawyers' conflicts of interest derived instead from scholarly literature, court cases, government reports, materials from malpractice insurers or professional associations, the trade press, and the mass media, there will be differences between my findings and the accounts of other professions culled from similar public sources. How do we parcel out which of these differences reflects different methodologies and selection biases in the source materials and which can be attributed to true differences in how varied professions encounter and control conflicts of interest?

Though the answer is by no means simple, the exercise is necessary. After completing my journey through the law firm world, I took a side trip across the fiduciary landscape. I visited five institutions: medicine, an arena traditionally compared with law; accounting, which most encroaches on lawyers' turf; psychotherapy, where relationships mirror those between lawyer and client; journalism, which provides a strategic comparison to the others; and—lest the pot call the kettle black—the academy, near and dear to the heart of the author and many readers. For each of these venues of trust, I scoured the most reliable secondary literature I could find, asking what sorts of conflicts of interest arise, whether and how fiduciaries recognize them, how they or others respond to them, and how significant are conflicts in day-to-day practices. Even encumbered by the blinders of a small unrepresentative sample of fiduciaries and limited or anecdotal data, the vistas were revealing. I share a few highlights below.[1]

---

[1]See Shapiro 2002 for the detailed findings and empirical evidence.

Because trust is organized in diverse ways, serves dissimilar kinds of interests, and binds disparate parties and relationships, the sorts of tangled loyalties that issue and the incentives and strategies to untangle them vary from venue to venue, just as they did across legal practices, specialties, and lawyer-client relationships. But, though the conflicts looked a little different across the fiduciary landscape on which I traveled, the foliage was just as dense and snarled by tangled loyalties.

The fiduciaries I studied differ, of course, in the entities whose interests they are obliged to serve. Some, like physicians and often psychotherapists, accountants, and lawyers, serve discernible clients. Others—family or group therapists, academics, and sometimes lawyers—serve more diffuse collectivities—family systems, therapy groups, classes (of students or victims), scholarly disciplines, associations, transactions, deals, or "situations." In contrast, auditors and journalists owe fiduciary obligations to the public (as do doctors, therapists, and lawyers under special circumstances, for example, when their clients risk endangering others).

Despite these fundamental differences, the five institutions also experience similar tensions that create and inflame conflicts of interest. Virtually all the institutions that I examined, including law, have faced increasingly turbulent environments in recent years. Because of deregulation and glutted markets, they have encountered often intense competition, pressure to lower costs, and shrinking profits or, in the case of nonprofit institutions, cutbacks in funding. Many entities—law and accounting firms and news organizations—have responded with sometimes extraordinary growth, swallowing, merging, or affiliating with the competition or other networks or confederations of professionals. The buzzword of *synergy* echoed through many of these institutions, as organizations, often undeterred by antitrust proscriptions, pursued cross-ownership and diversified operations and expertise, internalizing functions previously offered by market competitors. As fiduciary services—audits, hard news, medical or therapeutic services, and education—became less profitable, organizations took on more lucrative ancillary ventures—consulting, "infotainment," forensic expertise, commercial research and development, medical laboratories and home health care companies, and so on—driven by the bottom line rather than by fiduciary principles. With tightened job markets and the instability engendered by organizational failures, downsizing, mergers, takeovers, outsourcing, and the like, individuals faced increasing job mobility. And many professionals and fiduciary organizations watched their self-governance erode as they were purchased or managed by nonprofessionals with little or no substantive expertise—multinational corporations dictating the practices of news organizations; insurance companies and managers setting the protocols of physicians, therapists, and health care institutions; bureaucrats running universities and accounting firms. As these developments unfolded, fiduciaries decried the transformation of their "sacred" professions into businesses attentive only to the bottom line.

These developments, which increase organizational size, diversity, the representation of clients with adverse interests, and job mobility while reducing the autonomy and authority of those accountable to fiduciary principles, profoundly undermine disinterestedness and inflame and accelerate conflicts of interest. When these phenomena merely roiled the legal profession, they were disturbing but also somewhat limited curiosities. When we see that they are deep, shifting fault lines that threaten the entire fiduciary landscape, they become worthy of broad scholarly and regulatory attention. For whatever else these trends portend for our quality of life, they raise very disturbing red flags about the embeddedness and resilience of trust in the social fabric. I will return to this theme at the end of the chapter. Here, let me recount the sorts of conflicts of interest I encountered across the landscape.

Conflicts between Clients

I discovered that the ubiquitous thicket of clashing client interests that pervades the practice of law is less common in many other fiduciary settings. Though patients, principals, or clients occasionally compete for scarce resources or present incompatible interests, usually, when these fiduciaries pursue the interests of one, others are unaffected or they even benefit from the fiduciary's greater expertise, social or political capital, or economies of scale. Psychotherapy is an exception.[2] Therapists, like lawyers, sometimes serve multiple clients—in group, marital, or family therapy—and face the same dilemma that advancing the interests of one may undermine those of another. The problem is particularly acute in family therapy, where the existence of incompatible interests is often what impels family members to seek counseling in the first place. Often, what is good for one member may be harmful, destructive, or countertherapeutic to others. And, as in cases of multiple legal representation, even when families begin counseling with compatible goals, they often diverge in the course of treatment as participants achieve new insight and as deep fissures in the family structure are unearthed. Moreover, in psychotherapy as in law, confidentiality rules and proscriptions from using the secrets of one client to benefit another further strain disinterestedness.

Multiple roles. All five fiduciaries are more likely to become entangled in the conflicting interests of their principals when they play multiple roles. I found many fiduciaries and professionals intentionally, inadvertently, or of necessity bedecked in multiple hats—many more hats than donned by the typical lawyer. One encounters, for example, the physician/instructor/clinical researcher/entrepreneur, the auditor/inside accountant/advocate/tax preparer/consultant, the professor/scientist/scholar/gatekeeper/consultant/entrepreneur/employer/mentor/paramour/forensic expert/administrator, and many others. Some fiduciaries embraced multiple roles as a strategy of attracting and retaining business, of diversifying their portfolio of expertise or services. Physicians referred their patients to service providers they owned. Accountants exploited access to and relationships of trust with their audit clients to market consulting services; their audits identified deficiencies,

[2]In theory, accounting is an exception as well. Accounting firms represent many thousands of corporations with wildly incompatible interests. And like lawyers, auditors have access to confidential client information that could easily be used to benefit one at the expense of another. But the conflicts of interest are finessed away by pronouncing accountants "independent" of their clients, with fiduciary duties to the public.

whereupon they offered to fix them. Media organizations offered "added value" (i.e., favorable editorial content) to their advertisers and coupled news coverage with varied infotainment projects. Fiduciaries of all stripes pursued visible philanthropic activities and served on boards of directors to cultivate social ties with those likely to require their services or know those who do. As trustees slip out of one hat and into another, they are bombarded by competing obligations and incompatible interests that can threaten their disinterestedness.

Others face what they euphemistically call "conflicts of commitment," slighting one set of principals for another. For example, academics, preoccupied with their research or lucrative consulting engagements, neglect their students and procrastinate on professional gatekeeping obligations. Lawyers, psychotherapists, and others who are paid by the hour are able to avoid this conflict; they spend as much time as the client is willing to pay for. Capitated systems, such as managed care or university tuition, in which principals pay a set fee regardless of need or use of resources, invite fiduciaries to neglect their needs or play one principal off against another.

Conflicts between Principals and Fiduciaries

Most conflicts of interest that swirl across the fiduciary landscape on which I traveled arise from the clashing interests of principals and trustees or from the ways in which the latter are compensated. As we saw in chapter 7, all strategies of funding legal services, even doing so pro bono, pose conflicts of interest; they cannot be avoided any more than can the conflicts fueled by the varied systems of compensation I encountered in the five fiduciary institutions. Fee for service, managed care, capitation payments, hourly billing, advertising or underwriting, sponsorship, subscriptions, royalties, contingency fees, and so forth each arouse different, but intrinsic, conflicts of interest. Some lead to overtreatment, others undertreatment, some to shirking, others to bias.

Triangles. When it comes to compensation, lawyers' conflicts look quite different from those of the other institutions. Although, as we saw, limited slices of legal practice—legal aid, public interest law, insurance defense, and the representation of minors—are underwritten by third parties, most legal representations are paid, either directly or as a share of their award if they win, by those whose interests are served. In contrast, third-party payment or triangular relationships are ubiquitous in the other fiduciary arenas surveyed. Virtually all auditing fees are paid by entities from whom accountants are expected to be independent and not by the public they serve. Although, on rare occasions, doctors' or psychotherapists' services are paid from the pocketbooks of their patients and clients, the lions' share of services are covered by third-party government or private insurance companies or by institutions such as public clinics and hospitals, the military, factories, sports teams, and the like. Public consumers help subsidize news media with subscriptions or newsstand prices, though advertisers (from whom journalists, like auditors, are expected to be independent) pay the greatest share, especially for broadcast media. And although student tuition absorbs part of the cost of higher education and although the public subsidizes some university-based science undertaken on its behalf, third parties contribute a significant and increasing share to university balance sheets and faculty pay checks.

Systems of third-party payment create triangles in which the interests of those who foot the bill compete with those of the principals to whom trustees owe complete loyalty. The powerful influence of third parties is exacerbated by the fact that they tend to be repeat players; fiduciaries typically participate in many more triangles with them than with their principals. As a result, they ignore the interests of these third parties at their peril. The exercise of trust within these triangles is captured in the twin cliches: "he who pays the piper calls the tune" and "don't bite the hand that feeds you." The fiduciary landscape is littered with instances in which the interests of those who pay the bill override those of the principals. On orders of managed care companies, patients are denied access to specialists and to expensive drugs and procedures and, in some instances, not even told that such interventions are appropriate or available. News stories promote the business interests of advertisers or underplay their misdeeds or the riskiness of their products. Scientists withhold from publication research reports that question the efficacy of drugs they have been paid by pharmaceutical companies to test or other scholarship that threatens the interests of research sponsors. Audits provide upbeat assessments of problems uncovered by accountants, especially those found in corporations providing lucrative consulting business to the firm. As documented in the longer version of this travelogue (Shapiro 2002), the list is endless. It was not in the examination of the legal profession. Although court opinions and ethics rules neutralize many conflicts inherent in insurance defense law and other kinds of third-party payment for legal services, similar regulations are nonexistent or at best inchoate in the other institutions.

Self-interest. Even more of the tangled underbrush in these five institutions arises from conflicts between the interests of fiduciaries themselves and those of their principals, patients, or clients. Such conflicts are inherent, of course, in the exercise of trust. But I discovered substantial differences across the landscape in the extent to which fiduciaries sought to quiet or immobilize their own interests when they competed with those on whose behalf they acted.

At one extreme are journalists and therapists. Because of the vulnerability of clients, their dependence on the therapist, the potential for transference, and the enormous power imbalance between therapist and client, psychotherapists are far less likely to indulge in the self-interested behavior common in many other fiduciary relationships. Psychotherapeutic ethics discourage or prohibit various kinds of "dual relationships"—which include everything from sexual relationships between therapist and current or former patient to living in the same neighborhood, attending the same church, entering business partnerships together, or supervising the patient's graduate work or employing him or her as a research assistant—social ties that few other fiduciaries would even question, let alone avoid. As I described earlier in this book, lawyers and many others intentionally create, cultivate, and exploit such social ties as a means of soliciting clients and marketing their services.

Just as therapists' dual relationships can undermine their clinical relationship with and fidelity to their clients, the outside roles and interests of journalists threaten their credibility and objectivity to report dispassionately and disinterestedly about their world. Journalists are expected to live a circumscribed, almost monastic life, one unencumbered by ties and commitments, to ensure the public's perception of their disinterestedness. Reporters and editors are forbidden or discouraged from running for political office; campaigning for, advising, or supporting a political candidate; making campaign contributions, indeed, from all political activity short of voting; participating in a demonstration; displaying bumper stickers; affiliating with causes or organizations; taking a public position on a controversial issue; serving in a leadership position in or handling publicity for civic or community organizations; serving on a corporate board; or establishing personal relationships or close friendships with the subjects of their beat. They are admonished about moonlighting or consulting for news sources or about advising, taking freebies from, or getting too friendly with them, because these relationships and rewards threaten the journalist's objectivity in reporting about events affecting these sources. Accountants, too, in a more limited way, are prohibited from having a personal or financial interest in companies they audit—for example, investing in or engaging in a joint venture with a client or traveling through the revolving door into an employment position with the client—although recent scandals have revealed that noncompliance is the norm.[3]

Curiously, academics—who, like journalists and accountants, are thought to be disinterested reporters of the social and natural worlds—face no such normative constraints. And even more curious, neither do those who own news organizations. Both have financial interests and social, political, and ideological commitments in the subjects of their research, scholarship, or news reportage. Some academics consult, testify, write opinion pieces, and mobilize political organizations in their areas of expertise. And while journalists are barred from displaying a simple bumper sticker, their employers are filling the coffers of political candidates and proclaiming their allegiances in the editorial pages of their publications. Moreover, as news organizations seek to monopolize information and entertainment outlets, erecting infotainment conglomerates (cable stations, sports teams, movie studios, theme parks, book publishers) that cross-sell the products of their siblings, they further blur the lines between the messenger and the message. These corporations also own many of the subjects of news coverage—defense contractors, manufacturers, tobacco companies, nuclear power plants, waste management services—which undermines the appearance if not the fact of objective disinterested reporting. It is ironic that the institution most aggressive in its pursuit of synergy as a route to market power also demands the most monastic lifestyle of its employees.

Sporting their many hats, accounting firms and some physicians can be found along the end of the continuum where fiduciaries do little to neutralize self-interests

[3]An investigation by the Securities and Exchange Commission found that approximately 86.5 percent of the partners of PricewaterhouseCoopers, the world's largest accounting firm, had at least one (and usually a handful) of what they called "independence violations"—largely, owning the securities of audit clients. Indeed, all the partners who administer the firm's independence program reported at least one violation (U.S. Securities and Exchange Commission 2000). These findings have sparked a new spate of regulations and enforcement activity.

that clash with those of their clients. Perhaps because managed care has tended to lower their compensation, more and more physicians have embraced entrepreneurial activities—for example, dispensing drugs or medical products and investing in home health care agencies, medical laboratories, pharmacies, x-ray and diagnostic imaging facilities, physical therapy and rehabilitation facilities, ambulatory surgery centers—to which they refer their patients. Some physicians split fees with or accept kickbacks for referrals to specialists and take kickbacks, rebates, gifts, free meals, and paid trips from medical suppliers, laboratories, pharmaceutical companies, or hospitals that admit their patients. And others earn bonuses from the corporations that employ them for staying below a ceiling for referrals, hospitalizations, laboratory tests, or prescriptions. These practices conflict with the interests of patients in two ways: they spawn unnecessary, more expensive, or excess treatment, and they sometimes result in lesser quality care when treatment decisions are based on financial rewards to the physician rather than on quality or efficacy for the patient.

In the quest for greater revenue, accounting firms have also moved into new and more lucrative lines of business that threaten to further undermine their independence and objectivity. These ancillary services include corporate consulting, tax advising, investment banking, quasi-legal services, and outsourcing activities such as internal auditing, among many others. Indeed, some firms use audits as a loss leader to sell their other services to audit clients.

Self-Regulation

Across the fiduciary landscape, I encountered many of the same social control mechanisms mobilized to avoid or respond to conflicts of interest that are found in legal practice. But the five fiduciary institutions vary substantially in the extent to which practitioners are sensitive to conflicts, who takes initiative for social control, which measures are used, to which conflicts they are applied, and what resources are invested.

Some trustees simply eschew conflicts. When the interests affected by fiduciary service are expansive and unpredictable, the easiest way for trustees to ensure disinterestedness is to divest themselves of interests. For every fiduciary clamoring to don yet another hat, I found a counterpart renouncing all but one, decrying so-called dual relationships as an abuse of trust or at best as taboo. The latter fiduciaries abjure social ties and commitments and pursue instead a kind of reclusive, cloistered, monastic life. Journalists often restrict their political expression to that shrouded by the voting booth, avoid friendships or personal relationships with those who populate their beat, and turn away assignments to cover people, organizations, or events in which they have a stake or to which they are somehow linked. Psychotherapists, too, shun connections with their clients away from the office, whether in the classroom, courtroom, bedroom, weight room, neighborhood, or church and refuse to counsel a family member if another is an ongoing client. We can find physicians who decline kickbacks for referrals and refuse entrepreneurial opportunities related to their practice, academics who forgo opportunities to take a financial stake in the subjects of their research, and accountants who will not invest in audit clients or undertake consulting or any other work on their behalf.

Some fiduciaries recuse themselves from participation when their interests are at odds with those of principals. Others turn away prospective clients if interests are likely to collide down the road. And some continue to embrace the conflicts but disclose them. A handful of academic journals, for example, now require that authors disclose any financial interests that might have influenced their judgment about material presented in the article and publish the disclosure in a footnote; the Food and Drug Administration requires the same disclosure by physicians who test new drugs.

Many institutions issue rules about conflicts of interest: they formulate ethics or employment codes that bar sexual relationships, investments, or board service with clients; limit outside activities or the amount of time practitioners can devote to consulting; require permission to take on varied outside roles; seal revolving doors; or require disclosure of the interests and activities of family members. Few of these regulations carry significant sanctions or enforcement resources, however. Others are weakened by institutional commitments to free speech or academic freedom and tenure that make it difficult to terminate employment for noncompliance.

Most of the fiduciaries have also implemented some sort of peer review that indirectly touches on conflict-of-interest issues: quality assurance reviews and ethics committees in hospitals, institutional review boards in the academy, editors in news organizations, peer consultation groups assembled by individual psychotherapists, concurring partner reviews within accounting firms and peer reviews of the firms themselves undertaken by professional associations.

Many organizations adopt structural devices to separate, buffer, or conceal interests. When competing interests are served by different members of an organization, walls are often erected to segregate or barricade them. Newsroom walls are so sacred and inviolate that they have traditionally commanded a capital *W.* The Wall sequestered the business and editorial sides of the newsroom—literally restricting passage and communication across it—so that the interests of owners and advertisers would not affect or interfere with the editorial judgment of journalists, with which stories were and were not told, and with how they were reported. Law and accounting firms build Chinese walls, fire walls, or ethical screens to insulate fiduciaries entrusted with client confidences, secrets, or proprietary information that their colleagues must not learn. Other fiduciaries approximate the wall. Academics undertake blind reviews of manuscripts, concealing identities and affiliations of authors and reviewers, and scientists design double-blind experiments. Of course, many individual fiduciaries of necessity don multiple hats and confront competing interests that cannot be blinded or hidden behind a wall. Psychotherapists may adopt confidentiality rules to ensure that secrets shared by one spouse are kept from another. But no physical device or set of blinders can neutralize the sometimes wrenching tug of competing loyalties when the therapist sees them together in marital counseling.

Besides, many walls are tumbling down in pursuit of synergy. As a publisher who threatened to use a bazooka, if necessary, to demolish the inviolable Wall at his newspaper suggests (Shaw 1998), the synergy movement has no patience for screens and barriers because they impede the very connections and cross-pollination it seeks to foster. And even organizations that do not strive for or celebrate synergy find walls rather cumbersome. As I noted in chapter 9, law firms avoid ethical screens because they fragment and segregate expertise, make it difficult to staff engagements adequately, and impede communication among colleagues on unrelated matters. The impenetrability of walls as devices to segregate and sequester interests has always been suspect, of course. They have "ears," as one of my respondents observed. But they have become increasingly vulnerable in today's competitive environment, because they are viewed in some institutional contexts as archaic barriers that impede diversification, growth, and the construction and exploitation of new opportunities.

Though these varied forms of self-regulation penetrate all six institutions, their structure, reach, extensiveness, intensity, regularity, and priority vary considerably. One striking difference separates law from the others: concern for institutional conflicts. Whatever their commitment to circumventing or ferreting out conflicts of interest, the five institutions concentrate almost exclusively on individual conflicts. Universities strive to ensure that the self-interests of faculty do not undermine their research or teaching; accounting firms, that auditors do not get too close to their clients; news organizations, that journalists do not cover beats in which they have personal, financial, or ideological investments; hospitals, that doctors do not profit at the expense of their patients. But organizations devote little if any attention to the possibility that their own disinterestedness has been compromised—that the promise of external research funds and patent income corrupts their standards for the protection of human subjects or for awarding promotion or tenure, that prospective revenues from consulting undermine the vigilance or objectivity of an audit, that reverence for the bottom line induces them to punish doctors who refer too many patients to specialists, that the drive to attract advertising revenues compromises editorial content.

But law firm self-regulation is virtually always institutional. The rules of imputed disqualification, which attribute the conflicts of interest of any individual attorney to the entire firm, make it so. So while universities, accounting firms, news organizations, hospitals, and HMOs are winking at their own institutional conflicts, law firms every day are engaged in sometimes wrenching debates about how to avoid or resolve their own. While universities give tenure and endowed chairs to their most prolific generators of conflicts of interest, some law firms refuse to hire them, hide them behind ethical screens, turn away much of the business they generate, or encourage them to take their practice elsewhere.

External Social Control

Self-regulation is not the only game in town. Outsiders and third parties also undertake social control in many of these institutions. If the insistent demands of third parties, which undermine the ability of doctors, therapists, accountants, journalists, academics, and others to champion or attend to the interests of their principals, can be silenced, triangular relationships embedded in fiduciary settings are not all bad. Third-party repeat players can sometimes extinguish or regulate conflicts of interest that discrete principals have little clout to control. Medicare, Medicaid, and private insurance companies, for example, have been responsible for cutting medical costs, reducing unnecessary procedures, requiring second opinions, reviewing treatment decisions, prohibiting self-referral to medical facilities owned by referring doctors, and the like—all of which often serve the interests of patients as well as their own.

Some states and the federal government have adopted statutes outlawing certain self-interested activities (though few statutes have teeth and many contain large loopholes). Government agencies—professional licensure organizations, securities and banking agencies (which oversee accountants), and organizations that fund academic research (e.g., the National Science Foundation or National Institutes of Health)—dictate conflict-of-interest rules and can impose disciplinary sanctions, though many defer to the enforcement activities of self-regulatory organizations.

Conflicts of interest can also result in civil liability for malpractice, self-dealing, fraud, negligence, and the like. Insurance companies that pay to defend and resolve this litigation often impose additional self-regulatory procedures on their insureds or, through high deductibles, create incentives for greater self-regulation. And, just as some law firms seek to disqualify their opponents for conflicts, adversaries and competitors in other fiduciary institutions sometimes exact sanctions for conflict of interest as well. Media watchdogs, for example, wield their pens, cameras, and microphones, aggressively reporting on the conflicts of interest and other journalistic misdeeds of the competition.

Although this list of loci and types of internal and external social control seems impressive, it is an artifact of the compressed summary I have provided. It collects the potential responses available across all five institutions, but it does not document the extent to which trustees actually exercise any of these regulatory options. In truth, a traveler has to search to locate these activities across the fiduciary landscape (Shapiro 2002). From institution to institution, the regulatory framework is spotty, piecemeal, often lacking enforcement mechanisms. Some practices receive no regulatory notice at all. As I noted in the previous section, most of the social control activities focus on the conflicts of interest of individual practitioners, not of the organizations themselves. They promote fidelity to the organization, not to patients, clients, or principals (Rodwin 1995, 250). And, of course, entrusting regulation to the very organizations whose financial interests create many of the most significant conflicts their employees face has its own problems. In most settings, conflict-of-interest rules are hortatory, with few resources invested in enforcing them or encouraging compliance. Mostly they require the sensitivity, restraint, and goodwill of the individual fiduciary. In many loci, those qualities seem in short supply.

Aside from third-party payers, whose willingness to write or withhold checks creates substantial clout, few other third parties have sufficient resources or meaningful sanctions to exact compliance. In many professional and trade associations, membership is voluntary, so they have no means of enforcing their ethical standards on nonmembers. State licensure boards do have jurisdiction over all practitioners but tend to expend their limited resources on incompetence, embezzlement, gross misconduct, and other pressing priorities; controlling mere conflicts of interest is a luxury few can afford.

The Practice of Law versus Real Life

The practice of law is not monolithic, of course. Law firms vary significantly in the resources they commit to regulating conflicts of interest. Ostriches look as different from cyber squirrels as accountants do from journalists. Still, on a number of dimensions, the practice of law diverges radically from that of medicine, accounting, psychotherapy, journalism, academic teaching and research, and undoubtedly many other fiduciary institutions. It is not merely that law firms vigilantly attend to institutional conflicts of interest, that they have developed court-sanctioned norms to liberate themselves from the conflicts captured in triangular relationships, that they routinely disclose their conflicts (and sometimes even potential conflicts) to clients through informed consent, and that they have so far resisted the seductions of synergy and unrelenting metastatic growth somewhat better than many other fiduciaries coping with turbulent environments. Law firms contend with conflicts of interest every day, entrusting regulation to their most senior and powerful attorneys. Even in more laissez-faire firms, every new piece of business and lateral hire is scrutinized in some way for its potential to trigger conflicts. Bigger firms buy expensive hardware and software, libraries and data bases; generate daunting paperwork requirements; devote thousands of otherwise billable hours; hire staff specialists to implement systems running twenty-four hours a day and accessible across the globe; turn away millions of dollars worth of new business each year, in some instances as many as half of all prospective matters; restrict the outside activities of their personnel; and inflame considerable intrafirm discord in the name of conflict of interest. Few of the other institutions considered here come close on any of these dimensions.

What accounts for the difference? Many factors, of course. First, the conflicts are different. Typically, conflicts of interest for the other institutions pit the interests of the fiduciary against those of the client or principal, sometimes further mediated by the interests of third parties (i.e., "he who pays the piper"). The most common and significant conflicts of interest faced by lawyers pit the interests of one client against those of another. Arguably, fiduciaries have greater incentive to negotiate the conflicting interests of clients than to choose between self-interest and that of another. And the techniques for ferreting out conflicts will differ when the potentially contentious interests are held by outsiders rather than by trustee and principal. We don't need state-of-the-art computer hardware and artificial intelligence to ascertain that the HMO's interest in reducing costs conflicts with the patient's interest in seeing a specialist. Second, the rules are different. Lawyers face sanctions for honoring the interests of third-party payers over those of their client. Even more significant, as I noted earlier, rules of imputed disqualification—seemingly unique to law—make individual lawyers' conflicts institutional conflicts. Law firms ignore their own institutional conflicts at their peril.

But the chasm that separates lawyers and other fiduciaries was created by many other factors as well. Perhaps most significant, law is normative and frequently adversarial; it provides the stage on which interests collide, contend, and compete and the mechanism by which they are advanced or negotiated. If Hazard (1996, 85) is right, that the function of a profession is to serve the interests of others, then the function of law is to champion the interests of some over those of others. When legal disputes are zero-sum, producing winners and losers, interests are unmistakably in conflict. So too when win-win negotiations "go south," as my respondents would say, when they turn ugly. And because law is normative, producing and altering the rules according to which all members of society must play, interests are often realized at the expense of many, many others. That is why an entire chapter of this book is devoted to conflicts of interest that implicate those on the sidelines with no direct stake in a dispute at all. Physicians and therapists certainly have chapters in their books about the impact on the entire family of a medical diagnosis or therapeutic intervention on behalf of one member. But the impact and ripple effects of lobbying and legal precedent on the interests of "innocent" clients can be considerable. Conflict of interest is not only ubiquitous in law, it is self-evident, even palpable; those whose interests have been abridged often know it and so do their lawyers. This is less true in academia, medicine, psychotherapy, accounting, and journalism.

Moreover, the adversarial nature of law means that someone is often looking over the lawyers' shoulders, and it provides incentives for these outsiders to control law firm conflicts of interest. Litigation adversaries can use conflicts or their appearance for strategic advantage and seek to disqualify the conflicted lawyers, thereby protracting the proceedings and increasing the opponents' cost, denying their choice of counsel, and perhaps inducing them to capitulate or settle. This threat of external social control provides an added impetus to self-regulation, motivating many law firms to identify and disable potential conflicts of interest before they can detonate in full sight of outsiders.

The cost of liability provides another incentive for self-regulation. Law firms and many other fiduciary institutions have deep pockets and may be held liable for injuries that occurred on their watch, especially those exacerbated by conflicts of interest. The financial and reputational costs of defending libel suits provoke many news organizations to implement extra self-scrutiny, even—ironically—to pay first-amendment lawyers to precensor the news (Shapiro 1989). And, of course, the substantial malpractice and other liability faced by doctors, hospitals, auditors, therapists, and universities motivate varied forms of self-regulation in these institutions as well.

This book has demonstrated the role that some legal malpractice insurers play in educating, consciousness raising, counseling, advising, facilitating, or requiring specific self-regulatory measures and practices to minimize the risks of law firm conflicts of interest; the insurers' input was so distinctive that I could often guess after the interview who insured the firm. My examination of the other fiduciary institutions was too superficial to unearth similar insurance practices surrounding conflicts of interest, if they exist at all. Because of the adversarial quality of law and the ubiquity of conflicts of interest, which increase risk and associated liability costs, I would not be surprised if legal malpractice insurers were on the cutting edge and played the most extensive regulatory role. Nor would I be surprised if the greater commitment to self-regulation among law firms is due in part to the influence of those who pay for their negligence.[4]

The role of clients in the struggle over conflicts of interest further distinguishes law from many other fiduciary institutions. Law firm clients are by no means a homogeneous group, nor are their relationships with their lawyers uniform, as Heinz and Laumann (1982) and their progeny have dramatically documented. But a significant subset of clients—especially those of large law firms—are both organizations (typically much larger and commanding far more resources than their outside counsel) and repeat players (both in the sense of bringing continuing legal business and in having repetitive legal problems and therefore a stake in particular bodies of law). Because of their repeat business, many law firms depend financially on a handful of clients in a way that doctors or therapists or universities or news organizations do not. Moreover, unlike patients in an HMO or particular insurance arrangement, law firm clients are not locked in; they have the power to exit when dissatisfied with their lawyers' services or their loyalty. A buyers' market facilitates such exit. And unlike many of those who rely on varied fiduciary services, repeat-playing organizations often match their legal representatives in expertise, sophistication, and savvy. They know when their interests have been abridged and have the knowledge and resources to do something about it.[5]

As we have seen, legal clients care about some conflicts of interest and about the loyalty of their legal representatives. Their feelings matter. The rules of professional responsibility require that law firms secure their consent before taking on conflicted business. They have the right to disqualify from litigation law firms that fail to do so, and they occasionally exercise that right. Some have the muscle to call the shots, even disarming the conflict of interest intrinsic in systems of compensation by dictating law firm billing practices. And they have the power of exit even when lawyers do not violate their technical fiduciary obligations. As many respondents argued, client relations often trump ethics rules. Pleasing powerful clients typically demands higher standards, and failure to do so carries heavier sanctions than those delivered or even contemplated by disciplinary authorities.

In short, the potential business threat of powerful clients provides an added incentive for lawyers to control conflicts of interest. Like lawyers who concentrate on one-shot, unsophisticated clients of limited means, many other fiduciary institutions serving one-shotters do not face this powerful self-regulatory incentive. Galanter (1974) has argued that even one-shotters can boost their clout by collectivizing or securing representation from third-party interest groups. We have certainly seen news organizations threatened by the occasional reader or viewer boy-

[4]As both Davis (1996) and Heimer (1985) have argued, insurers, because of their access to detailed information about risky practices and powerful incentives to induce compliance, can be effective external regulators. They certainly are for some law firms, especially the mutual insurers that lose when their clients face expensive litigation and liability judgments. In contrast, some for-profit liability insurers simply raise their rates when their insureds do not desist from risky practices. The role of liability insurers in controlling conflicts of interest across various institutions and different insurance arrangements certainly warrants systematic research.

[5]See Gilson's argument (1990), reviewed in chapter 1.

cott targeted at their product or their advertisers; doctors and hospitals, by Medicare, Medicaid, or private insurers; accounting firms, by the Securities and Exchange Commission acting on behalf of the public; and universities, by government agencies. But the impact of client preferences on large law firm practices surrounding conflicts of interest has few rivals.

So, although conflict of interest is a matter of honor to some fiduciaries, it is also a matter of economics to many lawyers. Conflicts create real and sometimes substantial costs to legal practitioners: insurance and liability costs, the price of disqualification battles and judgments, loss of fee income when firms must withdraw from a case, being conflicted out of lucrative new business, reduced individual compensation from business lost to a colleague's conflict, driving away or undermining relationships with clients. Lawyers' vigilance is driven, at least in part, by multiple mutually reinforcing economic incentives and self-interests that are not found in many other institutions of trust. Although ignoring or embracing conflicts of interest may be economically rational for many fiduciaries, it often is not for lawyers. And therein lies a big difference.

Finally, unlike many other fiduciaries, including those explored in this chapter, lawyers have traditionally resisted the trend to cede ownership and control of their workplaces to nonprofessionals. Despite considerable controversy and debate, U.S. law firms are still owned by lawyers, controlled by lawyers, and run by lawyers, and their partners and investors are lawyers.[6] My investigation of the other fiduciary institutions documented the difficulties of honoring professional standards when physicians must follow medical protocols set by business executives, when journalists must follow the dictates of greedy stockholders with no reverence for their constitutionally protected public trust, when independent auditors must take orders from the management consultants whose lucrative revenues have tipped the balance of power in their accounting firms, when professors are accountable to elected officials or bureaucrats. Lawyers perhaps better honor their ethical obligations—or at least are free to do so—because they have retained their professional autonomy (Fox 1997).

Lawyers have many more degrees of freedom than some of us with which to resolve conflicts of interest. Some readers undoubtedly envy the lawyers' conflicts. Though lawyers do so very reluctantly, few of us share the luxury of simply walking away, declining to serve those whose interests collide with those of others we serve, or discarding hats that are incompatible with others we wear.

To return to the joke that inaugurated this book, there may be some things that even rats won't do. But there are also some things that lawyers won't do, things that their counterparts strewn across the fiduciary landscape undertake without a second thought. Though it would be nice to say that the difference is one of integrity and honor, it would be more accurate to attribute it to the social structural topography of the landscape. The topography of the legal terrain is not uniform, of course. Because different legal practice settings encounter or attract different clients, cases, conflicts, adversaries, markets for legal services, or insurance coverage, they respond to conflicts

---

[6]At least outside Washington, D.C. Though proposals to allow lawyers to practice in multidisciplinary practice groups may soon change all that.

of interest differently. Still, it would be surprising to find in a random sample of physicians or psychotherapists, of journalists, accountants, or academics—and undoubtedly of politicians, corporate executives, clergy, real estate or stock brokers—as few ostriches as I found among the sample of lawyers.

ALBATROSS OR SALVATION?

> Years ago, it never bothered me that, if there was a family dispute—even a husband and wife dispute—it never bothered me if the two of them came in the office and I tried to resolve it. It never bothered me that two brothers owned a business and they were having troubles within themselves, that I wouldn't pull them into the office and try to knock heads and get the thing resolved. And it might even end up drafting some type of an agreement between the two of them. And I never worried about their not being represented by another attorney. That just didn't even come into my head. This was the job [knocks desk for emphasis] . . . that I had to do. I didn't have a conflict. I was trying to resolve differences between people. . . . And actually—and this may be a matter of conceit—if you were permitted to stay and the consequences weren't so difficult, you probably could have done a better job for everyone if you could remain as that mediator—which we used to be able to do—and resolve it all for everybody and patch things up. And that's becoming very, very difficult to do. . . . But, today, if that came into the office, I'd start to think, "Whose side am I on? And shouldn't that other person be represented?" That, to me, is the biggest difference. In a certain sense, I feel it's extremely unfortunate. I think that I could avoid a lot of the litigation that's going on. But somebody might say, "But maybe at the expense of somebody." And the practice of law is not what I used to envision it to be. . . . And, as far as I'm concerned, that . . . almost creates a turmoil in me in practicing law. And it almost wants you to give it up. Because, in the past, you were always looked at as the family attorney, as the attorney for the business. The kids got in trouble, why, you always were called and you found a way of taking care of this and that and the conflicts and everything else. And you could sit in the shareholder meetings and let 'em holler at each other. And you could make the decision for 'em and everything else and not feel that you were getting into some kind of a conflict. It's difficult now. . . . I think that that's part of my responsibility in having gotten to that point with the family. But, in today's world, it's [. . .] With the concept of the development of some of the conflict of interests, the smartest thing would be just to wash your hands and walk away from it. I have a hard time doing that. [54DSL20–49]

As the reflections of this septuagenarian, whom we first met in chapter 4, remind us, conflicts of interest are continually in flux. Over the course of a generation, an era when other professions seemingly embraced or winked at many of their own conflicts of interest, lawyers, at considerable cost, became more vigilant as they sought to avert, neutralize, and eradicate conflicts and sanction those who failed to do so. But was it worth it? This respondent is not the only one who isn't so sure.

Clients, the intended beneficiaries of these reforms, bear many of their costs. Conflict-of-interest avoidance discourages law firm growth and diversification, thereby limiting economies of scope and scale and increasing the cost of legal representation borne by the client. Discouraging lawyers from acting on behalf of "situations" or families or multiple interests increases the need for multiple lawyers and, thereby, the cost of resolving disputes or facilitating transactions. Sometimes the increased cost results in the denial of legal representation entirely for particular clients. Often the hordes of lawyers required tend to escalate the dispute, inflame adversariness, and reduce the likelihood of a conciliatory resolution. And the proliferation of lawyers also means that less money is left after the legal bills have been paid to clean up toxic wastes or compensate victims. Conflicts also limit clients' choice of lawyers, in some instances forcing the clients' own experienced counselors to decline their cases and in others restricting access to experts who have been conflicted out by the clients' competitors or adversaries. Getting new, pristine, less experienced, unconflicted lawyers up to speed once again increases the cost of legal services and probably reduces the quality of representation. The conflicts rules are often used as a sword to increase strategic advantage, inciting disqualification battles in which accusations of conflict of interest are made purely to achieve instrumental outcomes. Again, these strategic tactics increase the cost of legal representation, contribute to delay in the legal process, and sometimes induce litigants to drop their claims or settle on unfavorable terms. And, surely, even if they are not billed directly, clients are underwriting the expensive edifice of law firm self-regulation elaborated in chapter 8—of computer hardware and software, full-time conflicts analysts, endless committee work undertaken by senior partners, and onerous paperwork requirements. The sentiments of the respondent just quoted—that clients are sometimes ill-served by this version of professional responsibility—were echoed by many lawyers in the study, their ambivalence often laced with anguish.

Perhaps most ironic, this more narrow, legalistic conception of fiduciary loyalty competes with and frequently precludes alternative, extralegal notions of loyalty. Strategies that allow law firms to maneuver through the minefields of their fiduciary obligations often create a formulaic adversariness, a kind of stripping away of social networks and ties of familiarity, a distancing between lawyer and client that collides with lay conceptions of loyalty or a commitment to looking out for what is truly in the best interests of clients. For example:

- always being there for the client, never letting the client down
- keeping costs down by representing multiple parties or serving as an intermediary
- handling the personal problems of corporate clients and their loved ones
- serving on the client's board of directors, maybe even investing in the client's business as an act of good faith

Earlier in this chapter we heard lawyers report their clients' feelings about their firms' response to conflicts of interest. But we don't really know whether clients are better or worse off from the increased vigilance toward conflicts. Nor do we know whether some clients (repeat players, one-shotters, coparties, corporations, individuals) are better off than others, though most likely, some are.

It's not as though lawyers celebrate the new vigilance either. Their complaints have echoed through the chapters of this book. It's expensive and time-consuming. They've had to turn away great cases and great lateral hires and prospective suitors. They haven't been able to move laterally themselves. They have lost valued colleagues who were conflicted out so often that they left the firm. They can't grow their firm. They've had to endure tensions with their clients. They contend with more discord now among colleagues. Law has become just another business. It is no longer fun. The passive voice of the septuagenarian poignantly reflects: "That almost creates a turmoil in me in practicing law. And it almost wants you to give it up."

To make matters worse, lawyers can feel the accounting firms and others breathing down their necks.[7] As conflicts rules stunt the growth of American law firms, competitors across the globe swell with legal personnel. Offering their clients "one-stop-shopping" and "seamless representation" under a diversified "umbrella" of services, accounting firms—or "multidisciplinary professional service firms" (MDPs) as they prefer to call themselves—have gobbled up lawyers, both domestically and internationally, swelling to become the largest de facto "law firms" in many parts of the world (Shapiro 2002). Although the largest law firms in my sample were turning away as many as a third to half of prospective new matters because of conflicts of interest, legal personnel at accounting firms many times their size, with extraordinarily tangled loyalties, were counseling on mergers and acquisitions, intellectual property, taxation, labor law, bankruptcy, corporate finance, licensing, environmental law, corporate compliance and regulation—and providing mediation, litigation support, expert witness assistance, and other law-like services to clients with competing interests, unencumbered by the conflict-of-interest rules that constrain legal practice.

With a diversified array of tens of thousands of professionals to service their clients' every need—including their legal needs—coupled with capital, visibility, brand-name recognition, location, a broad client base, and easy access to top corporate management from their audit and consulting work to cross-market their legal services, multidisciplinary accounting firms are formidable competitors indeed (Bower 1997; Morris 1998a; Rubenstein 1997, 20).[8] But how do lawyers compete when the conflicts rules tightly shackle one hand behind their backs?[9] If

---

[7]And banks, insurance companies, and securities firms are also clamoring to enter the legal services market (American Bar Association, Commission on Multidisciplinary Practice 1999a).

[8]A law firm consultant and chair of the International Bar Association's Standing Committee on Multidisciplinary Practice estimates that the movement of accounting firms into big-ticket litigation "could jeopardize as much as 30 billion dollars in annual fee revenues to U.S. law firms alone" (Bower 1997).

[9]Conflicts rules, of course, are not the only impediments to competition. Other rules of professional responsibility also get in the way—those concerning privileged communications and prohibiting (1) partnerships and fee sharing between lawyers and nonlawyers, (2) nonlawyers' ownership interests in law firms, and (3) third parties from directing lawyers' professional judgment.

the world's largest law firms, in order to match the largest accounting firms, grew by a factor of more than fifteen,[10] if each represented at least a fifth of the largest publicly traded corporations, industrials, and financial institutions,[11] and diversified to offer one-stop legal shopping to all clients, they would be conflicted out of virtually everything and be completely paralyzed.

There are many good reasons to reassess the legal profession's rules of professional responsibility, even if the profession was not threatened by this onslaught of accountants, or what lawyers, with some hyperbole, describe as "a sort of 'Armageddon' for the profession" (Gibeaut 1998, 44). The ethics rules were created when the practice of law looked very different than it does today. In 1983, when the *Model Rules of Professional Conduct* were enacted, the United States had 14 law firms with more than 300 lawyers, the largest of which employed 658 ("The NLJ 250" 1983). Almost twenty years later, these figures are 126 and 2,771 (3,025, according to the firm's latest website), respectively, and the 250th largest firm is roughly twice the size of its counterpart in 1983 ("The NLJ 250" 2000, C3, C16). As I have documented throughout this book, in the past decade and a half, not only have the social organization, economics, and demographics of legal practice been transformed, so, too, have those of clients. They, too, have become much larger and more complex, their operations globalized; many have developed legal sophistication in-house, shifting somewhat the asymmetry between lawyer and client. So, too, has the market for legal services been transformed. And, as a result, so, too, has the relationship between lawyers and clients.

Do the *Model Rules* still properly regulate this changing social organization of legal practice? The conflict-of-interest rules are predicated on lawyers' duties of loyalty and confidentiality. But are confidences threatened in the same way when law firm offices are arrayed across the globe and most colleagues have virtually no contact with one another? Is it still reasonable to impute knowledge—and thereby conflicts—to all members of a firm, regardless of the structure of the firm, the features of the conflict, or the barriers erected or structural artifices created to sequester it? Is loyalty ensured in the same way when the balance of power shifts to the client who increasingly calls the shots? Indeed, how important are the *Model*

---

[10]See "Special Supplement: Annual Survey of National Accounting Firms—2001" (2001) and "A Record Year, In Spite of Everything" (2001). Unfortunately, the available data often compare apples and oranges—that is, domestic versus global, gross versus net revenues, and so on. These figures reflect the fiscal year in which three of the Big 5 accounting firms divested at least part of their consulting operations. A few years earlier, things were even rosier: the Big 5 largest accounting firms employed fifteen times more partners (27,781) and sixty-seven times more professionals (334,482) than the five largest U.S. law firms (with 1,817 partners and 4,957 other lawyers). Moreover, the $43.1 billion annual revenue of the Big 5 accounting firms was more than twice that of the one hundred highest grossing law firms in the United States (Gibeaut 1998, 44; Oster 1998; Morris 1998b).

[11]See *Who Audits America* (2000), 526–28. Though I am unable to find more recent data, in 1991, the Big 6 accounting firms (the sixth largest accounting firm has since merged into one of the Big 5 firms) audited 98 percent of the Fortune 500 industrials, 99 percent of the Fortune 100 largest commercial banks, 97 percent of the largest insurance companies, 97 percent of the Fortune 100 fastest-growing companies, and 92 percent of the top 100 defense contractors (Cook et al. 1992).

Rules at all if law firms comply with a more rigorous set of standards dictated by powerful clients? And ought these more symmetric relationships between lawyers and legally sophisticated clients be shrouded in fiduciary duties at all, especially when they are trumped by de facto rules legislated and enforced by clients? Should parties be allowed to opt out of mandatory fiduciary rules altogether and instead negotiate their own private contracts, as so-called contractarian legal scholars have proposed in the corporate law arena (Easterbrook and Fischel 1983; Butler and Ribstein 1990; Coffee 1988; Brudney 1985; Frankel 1995)?

The looming incursion of MDPs and others into sacred legal monopolies confers weight and urgency to these questions. The threat of competition by unregulated outsiders often incites talk of deregulation in all sorts of markets. One ethics expert predicted that the battle between law and accounting will ultimately be "over whether or not the Model Rules will survive" (Gibeaut 1998, 46). Again, that is probably hyperbole. But the scores of experts and committees assembling along the battle lines will surely give the *Model Rules* a close look.[12]

This study identified some obvious candidates for scrutiny. But before reformers dismantle or relax the rules of imputed disqualification for large, multibranch law firms or those that have erected elaborate screens; before they tinker with the meaning or conditions of adversity; before they redefine who is a client or what is a law firm; before they contrive to turn back the hands of time, which so often exacerbate conflicts; before they give lawyers license to fashion particularized waivers for sophisticated clients or allow them to opt out of their fiduciary duties altogether, it's critical to step back.

An empirical study does not supply ready answers to normative or public policy questions. But, to mix many metaphors, it does keep in perspective both the forest and the trees, examine whether the silent lubricated wheels look at all like the squeaky ones or whether the base of the iceberg looks at all like the tip, and identify the hot spots simmering below the surface. In short, it lends visibility to the unexceptional and mundane that often become transparent in times of crisis and whose neglect often subverts whatever reforms follow. In this regard, the findings of this study are particularly relevant as legal reformers arm for their Armageddon.

---

[12]In recent years, the American Bar Association and many state bar associations have been reviewing their rules of professional conduct in general and in particular evaluating whether ethics rules that bar lawyers from forming partnerships with or sharing legal fees with nonlawyers ought to be relaxed in order to allow lawyers to deliver legal services in multidisciplinary practice groups. As I write this, several commissions have been appointed and many hearings held, testimonies offered, recommendations drafted, reports issued, votes taken, resolutions postponed, and much blood spilled. It would be folly to predict where these debates will ultimately lead. What is clear, though, is that conflict of interest has become their linchpin. Without a relaxation of the conflicts rules, it will be impossible for the massive multidisciplinary practices constructed by the Big 5 accounting firms to practice law in the United States. So far, bar leaders are steadfastly upholding traditional conflicts rules, including those of imputed disqualification: "In connection with the delivery of legal services, all clients of an MDP should be treated as the lawyer's clients for purposes of conflicts of interest and imputation in the same manner as if the MDP were a law firm and all employees, partners, shareholders or the like were lawyers" (American Bar Association, Commission on Multidisciplinary Practice 1999b).

In my extensive travels through Illinois, I learned that conflict of interest provides a panoramic window on the social world of legal practice. My view took in extraordinarily varied terrain that, despite the rhetoric and hyperbole, seems unlikely to be flattened any time soon by some looming glacier of inexorable social change. At the same time that some law firms are ballooning in size, access to on-line libraries and data bases and office management software have made it easier than ever for small firms and solo practitioners to compete and flourish. It's easy to forget that in all of Illinois, there are about seven times more sole practitioners than there are law firms employing two or more attorneys (Carson 1999, 83–84). For every firm that is wildly diversifying, swallowing up specialty firms to offer all things to all clients, new boutique firms are born, concentrating on doing one thing very well. The terrain may tremble from growing numbers of Goliaths bullying or strong-arming their lawyers. But there are still plenty of powerless, unsophisticated clients and necessarily one-shot problems that the legal system will continue to serve.

Dismantling the regulatory structure on behalf of these behemoth firms, Goliath clients, and other assorted squeaky wheels will leave the most vulnerable clients in traditional, asymmetric relationships exposed. The alternative of creating a switchboard of regulatory tracks with varied exemptions and opt-out provisions—for big and little firms, single office and multioffice practice settings, symmetric and asymmetric relationships, one-shotters and repeat-players, sophisticated and unsophisticated clients, powerful and vulnerable clients, single-party and multiparty matters, deals and disputes, and so on—is hardly better. This convoluted ethical maze will give rise to a host of double standards, wide slippery loopholes through which to escape fiduciary obligations, and normative collisions across an uneven playing field when adversaries are playing under very different rules (some, for example, relying on off-the-rack fiduciary duties and others directly dictating their lawyers' moves and obligations). To borrow from Galanter (1974), such changes would most likely provide yet another venue for the "haves" (big firms and powerful clients) to come out ahead. And with everyone playing under different rules and regulations or none at all, the fabric of trust will undoubtedly fray and tatter.

Moreover, dismantling ethical frameworks will require erecting a massive new regulatory structure to determine which parties or matters or firms travel along which tracks. Who decides if clients are sophisticated enough to waive their rights? Surely not the clients or their lawyers. Don't forget that asking a client to consent to a conflict itself poses a conflict of interest; lawyers are surely the only fiduciaries who recommend that their clients consult with an independent attorney before waiving a conflict. Lawyers can neither disinterestedly advise a client about whether to consent to a conflict nor help them negotiate a particularistic contract to specify their own duties to these clients. Ethical laissez-faire, then, is laced with profound conflicts of interest that ironically call for yet more regulation. And, of course, the legal skirmishes incited by the new ethical maze, in which clients or adversaries contest exemptions, allege unfair advantage, or assert deception or breach of contract, are likely to dwarf contemporary battles over motions to disqualify.

But there is another reason to proceed with caution. Disinterestedness may not be such an albatross around the legal profession's neck after all. Lawyers simulating legal practice in multidisciplinary practice firms can promise neither confidentiality nor loyalty to their clients. They do not enjoy privileged communications with clients and may, indeed, be obliged to disclose material legal problems, liabilities, or other confidences of their clients to their auditor colleagues whose ethical obligations require that they be publicly disclosed (Rubenstein 1997, 20). Loyalty is surely even harder to attain, because the accountants, auditors, tax specialists, management consultants, and other professionals employed by MDPs routinely represent scores of competitors and clients with directly adverse interests, providing services intended to advance those interests. Although lawyers who own and manage their own law firms simply reject any new matters that strain their loyalty to ongoing clients, in MDPs, such business-intake decisions are typically made by nonlawyers, driven by different ethical standards and business judgments.[13]

The attraction of one-stop-shopping touted by the MDPs is somewhat tarnished if, in order to protect their legal secrets, clients must use a different firm to audit their books than to handle their legal problems or, to ensure unbridled loyalty, clients must use a different accounting firm to sue a valued client of their auditor. And the attractions of synergy are undermined if multidisciplinary practices must erect fire walls to protect the confidences of clients from colleagues in the practice who may be obliged to disclose these secrets.[14] Because clients can't count on their MDP as they could their law firms to disclose the fact that it represents parties with adverse interests or to refuse to represent adverse parties in the future once it has signed on with a client, prospective clients must undertake an excruciating analysis of whether potential targets of or aggressors in a future hostile takeover, adversaries in future litigation, or parties to a possible deal are represented or likely to be represented by the lawyers, consultants, or auditors of a particular MDP before they sign on as clients. And even if the relationship begins with a clean slate, the likelihood that these fiduciaries will be conflicted out down the road is extraordinarily high, given their huge number of clients, the varied professional services offered under the firm umbrella, and the fact that conflicts of interest do not figure into the intake of new clients or engagements.

However much the lines between the services provided by law and accounting firms have blurred, one bright line remains: that of conflict of interest. Law firms eschew them; accounting firms at best ignore them and at worst embrace them. Law firms are disinterested; accounting firms, uninterested.

Clearly, not all kinds of legal services require such fierce loyalty and absolute confidentiality. Corporations certainly are patronizing the lawyers working at the

---

[13]As Lawrence Fox (1997, A23) implores, "When a client goes to Price Waterhouse's Moscow office for legal services, does the lawyer clear all conflicts? At what level? And even if conflicts are cleared throughout the entire accounting firm, who is making the judgment as to whether conflicts exist? Someone trained in the law—or an MBA who wouldn't know the Model Rules from the Model Code if he or she were hit over the head with them?"

[14]As a former SEC director of enforcement argued: "And even if firewalls could actually be effective in dealing with these conflicts—which we would suggest they cannot—these firewalls would then effectively destroy the information sharing and service enhancements that are put forward as the justification for allowing a single firm to offer these services in the first place" (Walker 1998).

MDPs. But if clients truly never cared about conflicts of interest, my interviewees would have been less anguished and my interviews much shorter. And so would this book. The proof, of course, is in the pudding. Are multinational corporations steering different kinds of legal needs to different kinds of service providers? Are the sensitive and significant bet-the-company cases going to traditional law firms and more routinized legal work to MDPs? The empirical jury is still out on that question, but I doubt that the answer would be a surprise.[15]

As we begin the new millennium, the state of trust is very fragile indeed. As we have seen, the changing social organization of fiduciary services has created structural impediments to disinterestedness. Fiduciary organizations have become too big, too concentrated, too diversified, and too few to ensure that organizations do not take on interests likely to subvert or undermine those of others served. Fierce market competition has ratcheted up self-interested behavior by trustees. The increasing role of third-party payment through insurance, government funding, advertising, or sponsorship has turned dyads of trust into triangular relationships, where third parties other than the principal increasingly call the shots and direct the trustee. Fiduciary organizations are being bought and sold on the financial markets like widgets or pork bellies, owned and administered not by professionals and trustees but by shareholders and managers. Fiduciary and professional judgments are being dictated by bureaucrats beholden to the bottom line rather than by those beholden to ethical obligations of confidentiality, loyalty, and disinterestedness. Law firms, too, struggle against these trends but, it seems, with more success than many of the others.

Perhaps these developments do not herald such a tragedy. As more and more transactions and services bring one repeat player to another, asymmetries of expertise, information, and power begin to balance, and the need for trust diminishes altogether. But it does not disappear. Though disinterested agents may become a luxury few can routinely afford or even find, they will also remain a necessity for the big-ticket items of life.

American lawyers, in their rush to make their practices globally competitive, may be throwing out the baby with the bath water. Far from spurring their demise, disinterestedness may, in fact, be their salvation. It may provide the unique market niche of the legal profession. Perhaps the solution is not to dismantle the self-regulatory structure but to elaborate and celebrate it, to structure the organization of law firms and market for legal services to shore up the conditions of trust. Instead of licensing pockets of laissez-faire that create uneven playing fields and ambiguity and

[15]Although testimony before the ABA Commission on Multidisciplinary Practice indicated that several large multinational corporations have been drawn to MDPs to provide their legal services, others have not. One inside counsel, for example, testified that her corporation does not use MDPs to "provide legal advice." This choice is both a quality issue, "a lack of the best legal minds being attracted to accounting firms," a "dumbing down of the practice of law"; and a reaction to the "disadvantages of lack of strong conflict regulation, lack of confidentiality safeguards and the issue of the preservation of legal privilege." Though MDPs may prove attractive to less sophisticated small and medium-sized companies, she concluded, "the message is buyer beware" (Wall 1998). Of course, the official public testimony of a handful of self-selected clients does not empirical data make.

suspicion about the disinterestedness of legal advocates, perhaps the ethical rules should become less flexible. Such a solution will not disable the ongoing shakeout in legal services, of course. Surely some kinds of routinized low-stakes lawyering will end up being provided by other organizational forms that are cheaper or more efficient. And to survive, some legal practices will have to sell out to them. But the remnants will nourish many a traditional lawyer.

So, rather than a historical throwback or ethical curiosity, conflict of interest and the cultural icon of the lawyer as disinterested hired gun might instead represent an astute marketing strategy. In this brave new world, where others are strangling on their tangled loyalties, law firms may turn out to be last fiduciary bastion where confidences are honored and uncompromising loyalty fiercely defended, the one place where clients always come first, where they can count on their interests being zealously championed above all others. That would certainly be the most perverse lawyer joke of all. And guess who gets the last laugh.

Appendix

Research Methods

THE RESEARCH SITE

Conflict of interest in the practice of law has its own distinctive geography. Jurisdictions vary in their rules of professional responsibility as well as in local legal cultures and practices. Revolving doors through which lawyers traverse between the public and private sectors concentrate in certain areas (especially state capitals and cities such as Washington, D.C., and New York City that provide robust alternative markets of legal employment). Clients array themselves in idiosyncratic geographic patterns as well, concentrating competitors in a circumscribed legal market, demanding particular legal specializations and firm structures to service their needs, and thereby creating distinctive conflicts of interest for local counsel. Urban and rural settings foster different opportunities for conflicts of interest to arise as well (Landon 1988, 1990).

In order to investigate and control for the geography of conflict of interest and the impact of divergent regulatory practices on its expression, research ought to be national in scope and comparative in design. I hope it ultimately will be. But it was necessary to begin somewhere. I chose Illinois. Among its virtues, this research site was the cheapest and easiest to study. The distinguished legacy of research on the Chicago bar (Carlin 1962; Heinz and Laumann 1982; Schnorr et al. 1995; Curran et al. 1985, 1986; Curran and Carson 1991; Carson 1999; Halliday 1987; Nelson 1988) offered a solid base of empirical work on which to build. Moreover, Illinois affords considerable variation in the kinds of structural arrangements from which conflicts of interest arise or are circumvented—the scale, social organization, and competitiveness of legal practice; the market for legal services; economic conditions; firm size; recruitment patterns; legal specializations; kinds of clients; urbanicity; and so forth. At the same time, the texture of legal experience in Chicago is probably less distinctive and idiosyncratic than that of other potential research sites such as New York, Washington, or Los Angeles and therefore affords a more compelling venue to learn about the generic problems of conflict of interest in the private practice of law.

Moreover, many large Chicago firms have branch offices outside the state—typically in Washington, D.C., and New York and often in a large city in the Midwest, West, South, and occasionally Europe or Asia. And many large law firms headquartered elsewhere maintain a Chicago office. So Illinois firms provide a window—albeit a small one—on ethical rules, regulatory practices, and legal cultures—at least of large law firms in big cities—across the nation and world.

Illinois is distinctive in at least three ways, however. First, only a handful of states in the United States allow law firms to set up Chinese walls or screening devices—without securing client consent—to shield conflicts of interest that arise when a lawyer is hired laterally from another private firm; Illinois is one of them. As I elaborated in chapter 9, I explored the implications of this difference by locating pilot research in two other states, one that, like Illinois, allows Chinese walls without consent and another that does not. The pilot data did not give me reason for significant concern.

Second, it is not clear how many other states have adopted rules of professional responsibility like those enacted in Illinois in 1990 that hold law firms and their partners responsible for the ethical conduct of their employees and that subject firms to professional discipline (Overton 1990). Illinois law firms may, therefore, undertake more self-regulation than those in other jurisdictions.

Third, as I noted in chapter 2, more law firms and lawyers in Illinois are covered by a major large-firm mutual malpractice insurer—Attorneys' Liability Assurance Society (ALAS)—than in any other state in the United States or the District of Columbia. Because this insurer actively promotes loss prevention activities—a significant component of which concerns avoiding conflicts of interest—I was concerned that I might discover more firm self-regulatory activity and more homogeneity among ALAS insureds than among others. I also worried that because ALAS members must employ at least forty attorneys, large firm–small firm differences uncovered by the research might be artifacts of patterns of insurance coverage rather than reflections of firm size.

Although I found far more variation among firms in Illinois than between large Illinois firms and their counterparts in the two other Midwestern states in the pilot, further empirical research is necessary to determine how generalizable my findings are to the experiences of the more than six hundred thousand private practitioners who practice outside the state (Carson 1999, 24, 82). Nothing I learned in the course of this research or from observing national conferences on lawyers' professional responsibility or by sharing my findings with attorneys from around the country suggests that my findings do not ring true for lawyers practicing elsewhere.

SAMPLING

I targeted a sample of roughly ten law firms in Chicago and ten outside Chicago comprised of more than one hundred lawyers, fifty to ninety-nine lawyers, twenty to forty-nine lawyers, ten to nineteen lawyers, and one to nine lawyers. Because few law firms outside Chicago have more than twenty lawyers, I compensated with larger numbers of Chicago firms.

There is no single authoritative roster of law firms from which to draw a sample. A number of law firm directories and other sources exists, but none is complete and each embodies different sorts of biases. Moreover, my goal of stratifying the sample by firm size complicated the task immensely, because few sources list firms by size. And those that do, I later learned, rarely do so consistently or accurately.

The more work my research assistant and I did constructing a sample—especially of small law firms—the more imperfections we found in the traditional directories of lawyers and law firms. As a result, the sampling design was arduous, with more and more triangulated sources incorporated over time. Literally hundreds of person-hours were devoted to painstakingly constructing the sample.

I have a twenty-five page memo describing the details of this process, which I am happy to share. What follows here are the highlights. The following sources were used to draw the sample: "The Illinois 100" survey in *Merrill's Illinois Legal Times* (published data on the largest one hundred firms as well as information for firms that fell outside the largest one hundred and that ended up on the cutting-room floor, to which we were generously given access); *Martindale-Hubbell Law Directory* (published volume, CD-ROM version, and LEXIS data base version, each of which is updated at different times and has different features on which to search); *Sullivan's Law Directory for the State of Illinois* (published volume as well as lists of all firms with six to ten or eleven to twenty lawyers, which we purchased); telephone Yellow Pages (for Chicago and various downstate communities); and the *Illinois Legal Directory.*

First, we enumerated, from various triangulated sources, every Illinois firm with more than nine lawyers and used a random numbers table to draw a sample. This procedure was not realistic, however, for the thousands of Illinois law firms with fewer than ten attorneys. For those in Chicago, I drew three samples—one from the *Martindale-Hubbell* volume, one from the *Sullivan's* volume, and one from the Yellow Pages.[1] For the small downstate firms, I opted for a sample of somewhat greater depth rather than breadth—selecting a few representative communities and conducting several interviews in local firms of varied size. I chose one large city, one medium-sized city, and a collar county city from communities already represented in the sample because they were home to a firm with ten or more attorneys. Because few small towns have law firms so large, I randomly selected two small towns. Using *Martindale-Hubbell, Sullivan's,* and the Yellow Pages for each of these five communities, I assembled a population roster of all attorneys, from

[1]Not a single firm selected was listed in all three sources. So utilizing a single directory would have excluded a number of firms and yielded an undoubtedly biased sample.

which I drew a random sample. Because, on statistical odds, a random sample of firms of less than ten lawyers would hover closer to firms of one or two than nine, I stratified the Chicago and downstate samples to include equal numbers of firms of one to two lawyers, three to five lawyers, and six to nine lawyers.

Finally, I added a few extra firms to the sample to satisfy other questions about the social construction of conflict of interest. First, I randomly selected four large law firms headquartered in other states with branch offices in Chicago. Second, when I discovered that all but one of the randomly selected Chicago law firms were located in the Loop, I randomly selected four additional non-Loop firms. Third, in order to assess the potential contamination effect of being insured by ALAS, the malpractice insurer with a vigorous loss-prevention program, I oversampled large firms that were not members of ALAS as well as smaller firms that were to secure a sufficient number of cases for comparison. Finally, to see how conflicts of interest are resolved when a community has but one law firm to serve its diverse legal needs, I randomly selected four towns that had only one law firm or practicing lawyer.

RESPONSE RATE

The response rate in the study was 92 percent. Initially, 23 of the 140 firms sampled refused to participate. Eventually, after dozens of letters and phone calls, my research assistant or I was able to convince almost half of them to do so.

Reasons for nonparticipation were not unexpected. Half said they were too busy. When I asked whether I might interview someone else in the firm, I was rebuffed. The other half of the nonrespondents were divided between those with a personal reason for not participating (the death of a spouse, an imminent retirement), annoyance with me or with the American Bar Association (which they confused with the American Bar Foundation, where I work), or general discomfort ("it's not in the firm's best interest," "we are exercising our freedom of choice,"[2] "this is proprietary information which I don't feel comfortable discussing").

Of course, the problem with these excuses is that they apply equally well to those who *did* participate in the study. It's hard to provide a compelling account for the nonresponders. Could they have more to hide? It's certainly possible, though I was unable to find any negative press coverage for them—although I could for firms that did participate (though the latter was mostly a function of their larger size, thereby warranting media attention). Fortunately, though, the nonrespondents do not look terribly different demographically from the respondents.

INTERVIEWS

I will be the first to admit that I am enamored with survey research. Responses are so much an artifact of how and when the questions are asked and who asked them. At best, they are filtered through the distorted perceptual lenses of the informant;

[2]Probably a snide reference to the American Bar Association's then-recent and controversial position on abortion rights.

at worst, they are self-serving fabrications. Though an astute interviewer may discern some of these distortions and though questions can be framed to minimize them, the task is all the more difficult when the subjects of research are professionals whose expertise lies in information control. If there had been some other way to conduct this inquiry, I would have seized it. The problem is that most of the action in conflict of interest occurs inside law firms—in procedures, conversations, meetings, memoranda, data bases and computer output, disclosures, oral and written waivers, ethical screens, and the like. Conflicts of interest leave few residues that are observable to outside researchers. Those that make their way into the public domain are not only rare, they are exceptional, aberrant, and profoundly unrepresentative of the conflicts lurking within law firms.

By questioning the lawyers on the front lines of the struggle over conflicts of interest—about their own experience as well as what they have learned from their clients and what they have seen in encounters with other firms—I was able to establish the broad outlines of the role of conflicts in the everyday practice of law and how different kinds of law firms respond to them.

Interviewing continued from July 1992 until May 1994. I conducted all the interviews myself. Chapter 2 details how respondents in each firm were selected and describes their characteristics. Respondents were questioned about whether, how, and to what extent conflicts of interest arise in their practice and how their firms identify and resolve potential conflicts when they do. I found that many lawyers tended to offer fuller and more reflective accounts when the conversation was not too regimented. So my questions served more as an interview guide than as a structured agenda. Because of the open-ended quality and complexity of the interviews, it was necessary to conduct them face-to-face. Only four respondents insisted that we do the interview over the phone.

Interviews ranged in length from twenty-five minutes (a phone interview) to two and a half hours; on average, they took an hour and a quarter. To keep the interviews as short as possible and to capture the richness and detail of the responses, most interviews (78 percent) were tape-recorded. Immediately after an interview was completed, I reconstructed a transcript from my detailed notes of those that had not been taped and wrote field notes for all interviews.

The interviews were subsequently transcribed, and a research assistant and then I checked the transcriptions against the tapes, correcting mistakes; filling in the inaudible passages, where possible; and deleting all references that might identify the firm, replacing names with more generic descriptions, and eliminating gendered language. I then thematically coded all the interviews so that they could be analyzed systematically. Research assistants also assembled a demographic data set on the firms (including those that refused to participate in the research), culling materials on the history and age of the firm; its size and growth; numbers and locations of offices; mergers or spin-offs; and areas of specialization.

As the extensive materials quoted throughout the book attest, the respondents were candid, reflective, analytical, insightful, articulate, occasionally self-critical, rarely guarded or combative, and extraordinarily generous. Many were wonderful storytellers and powerful orators. Their examples were rich, complex, and nuanced. Many respondents were clearly troubled by the impact that conflicts of interest had on their practice and seemed to appreciate the opportunity to share their confusion, frustration, and dismay. Others expressed the hope that they would be able to learn from the experiences of others.

Did I get the full story? Undoubtedly not. I certainly heard respondents confess their most embarrassing experiences, worst nightmares, most problematic oversights, disqualification motions lost, and disciplinary sanctions imposed. A few prefaced their more incriminating stories or policies by noting that they were sure glad that the interview was confidential or instructed that this comment was off the record. But lawyers traffic in impression management, in spin control; there is no reason why I should have been spared.

Moreover, because I generally interviewed the person with the most experience with or responsibility for conflicts of interest, the data reflect another sort of bias, which probably overstates the role and importance of conflict of interest in the practice of law. It is unclear, for example, the extent to which young associates think about, know about, or respond to potential conflicts in their work. Some respondents told me that they had colleagues (junior and senior) who wouldn't know a conflict if it was staring them in the face. Moreover, learning about firm conflicts from the conflicts czar is a bit like learning about disputing by looking at Supreme Court cases. Each is a victim of selection bias; the most difficult or serious matters tend to end up there; their purview is unrepresentative of the world that lies beneath. Many conflicts will escape notice of firm experts or regulators—and, therefore, be invisible in my research—because individual lawyers eschewed these conflicts in the first place, privately neutralized them, failed to recognize or disclose them, or successfully concealed them. More research is necessary is see how different the iceberg looks from its tip.

CONFIDENTIALITY

I promised law firms, lawyers, and other informants anonymity and absolute confidentiality. I made this pledge not only to comply with my own code of professional ethics but also to ensure the broadest access, highest response rate, and greatest candor from respondents. This assurance had many more implications than appeared on first blush. I had a lock installed on my office door and obtained locked file cabinets, passwords embedded in my computer and keyboard, and encrypted project-related computer files. I indoctrinated research assistants and transcribers about maintaining secrecy and never leaving papers on their desks or project-related files displayed on their computer monitors when they walked away. I mailed my correspondence personally rather than letting it sit in the out-box in the Foundation to be picked up by mail room couriers and possibly seen by my colleagues. Instead of recycling waste paper from the project, I either shredded it or carried it home to be destroyed with my domestic trash. I began to get an exquisite sense of how it must feel to work behind a Chinese wall. When respondents and colleagues asked where I had been or where I was going, I gave vague, generic answers. When visiting more than one firm in a small town, I would hide out between interviews in a place were I would be unlikely to be seen.

References

Abbott, Andrew. 1988. *The System of Professions: An Essay on the Division of Expert Labor*. Chicago: University of Chicago Press.

Abel, Richard L. 1981. "Why Does the ABA Promulgate Ethical Rules?" *Texas Law Review* 59:639–88.

———. 1989. *American Lawyers.* New York: Oxford University Press.

Acton, Jan Paul, and Lloyd S. Dixon. 1992. *Superfund and Transaction Costs: The Experiences of Insurers and Very Large Industrial Firms.* Santa Monica: Rand Corporation, The Institute for Civil Justice.

Adler, Bill. 1992. *First, Kill All the Lawyers: Legal Proverbs, Epitaphs, Jokes, and Anecdotes.* New York: Citadel Press.

Allen, Michael Patrick. 1974. "The Structure of Interorganizational Elite Cooptation: Interlocking Corporate Directorates." *American Sociological Review* 39:393–406.

Alpern, Wayne O. 1988. "Conflicts of Interest in Cultural Peer Review." *New York Law Journal* (July 22), 5, 26.

Alschuler, Albert W. 1975. "The Defense Attorney's Role in Plea Bargaining." *Yale Law Journal* 84:1179–1314.

Altonji, Joseph B. 1996. "Bonuses and 'Thresholds.'" *Accounting for Law Firms* (September), 4.

American Bar Association. 1969 (amended). *Model Code of Professional Responsibility.* Chicago: American Bar Association.

———. 1983 (amended). *Model Rules of Professional Conduct.* Chicago: American Bar Association.

———. 1986. *In the Spirit of Public Service: A Blueprint for the Rekindling of Lawyer Professionalism.* Chicago: American Bar Association.

American Bar Association, Commission on Evaluation of the Rules of Professional Conduct. 2001. *Report 401: Amendments to Model Rules of Professional Conduct (Ethics 2000) to the House of Delegates* (August 6–7). Chicago: American Bar Association.

American Bar Association, Commission on Multidisciplinary Practice. 1999a. "Background Paper on Multidisciplinary Practice: Issues and Developments." (January). Chicago: American Bar Association. http://www.abanet.org/cpr/multicomreport0199.html.

American Bar Association, Commission on Multidisciplinary Practice. 1999b. "Report to the House of Delegates." (August [released in June]). Chicago: American Bar Association. http://www.abanet.org/cpr/mdpFinalreport.html.

American Bar Association, Section of Business Law and the Center for Continuing Legal Education. 1996. *Saying Goodbye to Hourly Billing? How to Succeed in the New Economic Climate: An ABA Satellite Seminar.* Chicago: American Bar Association.

American Bar Association, Standing Committee on Ethics and Professional Responsibility. 1993. "Formal Opinion 93–372: Waivers of Future Conflicts of Interest." Chicago: American Bar Association (April 16).

———. 1995. "Formal Opinion 95-390: Conflicts of Interest in the Corporate Family Context." Chicago: American Bar Association (January 25).

American Law Institute. 1990–92. *Restatement of the Law: The Law Governing Lawyers.* Tentative Draft nos. 3–5. Philadelphia: The American Law Institute.

———. 1995. *Restatement of the Law: The Law Governing Lawyers.* Preliminary Draft no. 11 (May 18, 1991). Philadelphia: The American Law Institute.

"The AM LAW 100." 1992. *The American Lawyer* (July/August), special pullout report, 1–66.

Andersen, Steven. 1998. "It's Bullish Times for Law Firms: A Decade of Steady Growth for Illinois' 100 Largest." *Illinois Legal Times* (July), 1, 19–25.

Attorney Registration and Disciplinary Commission of the Supreme Court of Illinois. 1994. *Annual Report.* Chicago.

Attorneys' Liability Assurance Society. 1991. *Annual Report.* Hamilton, Bermuda.

———. 1992. "Selected Conflict of Interest Issues." *ALAS Loss Prevention Manual,* Tab II.K. Bellevue, WA: Timeline Publishing Company.

———. 1999. "About Us." http://www.alas.com/about, January 1, 1999.

Barnard, Jayne W. 1988. "Curbing Management Conflicts of Interest—The Search for an Effective Deterrent." *Rutgers Law Review* 40:369–427.

Berkman, Harvey. 1997a. "Sidelined by Client Conflicts." *National Law Journal* (June 2), A1, A16.

———. 1997b. "Two Litigators Who Went Solo." *National Law Journal* (August 18), A1, A25.

Black, Donald J. 1976. *The Behavior of Law.* New York: Academic Press.

Black, Henry Campbell. 1968. *Black's Law Dictionary,* 4th ed. St. Paul: West.

Blumberg, Abraham S. 1967. "The Practice of Law as a Confidence Game: Organizational Cooptation of a Profession." *Law & Society Review* 1:15–39.

Bower, Ward. 1997. "Multidisciplinary Practices—The Future." In *Global Law in Practice,* ed. J. Ross Harper. The Hague: Kluwer Law International.

Brudney, Victor. 1985. "Corporate Governance, Agency Costs, and the Rhetoric of Contract." *Columbia Law Review* 85:1403–44.

Butler, Henry N., and Larry E. Ribstein. 1990. "Opting Out of Fiduciary Duties: A Response to the Anti-Contractarians." *Washington Law Review* 65:1–72.

Carlin, Jerome. 1962. *Lawyers on Their Own: A Study of Individual Practitioners in Chicago.* New Brunswick: Rutgers University Press.

———. 1966. *Lawyers' Ethics: A Survey of the New York City Bar.* New York: Russell Sage Foundation.

———. 1994. *Lawyers on Their Own: The Solo Practitioner in an Urban Setting.* San Francisco: Austin & Winfield.

Carson, Clara N. 1999. *The Lawyer Statistical Report: The U.S. Legal Profession in 1995.* Chicago: American Bar Foundation.

Chanen, Jill Schachner. 1999. "Coverage Goes Out on a Limb: Bull Market Is Allowing Malpractice Insurers to Offer Expanded Policies." *ABA Journal* (September), 18.

Clark, Robert C. 1985. "Agency Costs versus Fiduciary Duties." In *Principals and Agents: The Structure of Business,* ed. John W. Pratt and Richard J. Zeckhauser. Boston: Harvard Business School Press.

Clayton, John. 1970. *The Illinois Fact Book and Historical Almanac, 1673–1968.* Carbondale: Southern Illinois University Press.

Coburn, Jeff. 1997. "Even If It Ain't Broke, You Can Still Fix It; It's Time to Tune-Up Your Partner Compensation System." *Law Firm Partnership & Benefits Report* (February), 1.

Coffee, John C., Jr. 1988. "No Exit?: Opting Out, the Contractual Theory of the Corporation, and the Special Case of Remedies." *Brooklyn Law Review* 53:919–74.

Coleman, James S. 1990. *Foundations of Social Theory.* Cambridge, MA: Harvard University Press.

———. 1991. "Constructed Social Organization." In *Social Theory for a Changing Society,* ed. Pierre Bourdieu and James S. Coleman. Boulder: Westview Press.

Committee on Lawyer Business Ethics. 1998. "Report: Business and Ethics Implications of Alternative Billing Practices: Report on Alternative Billing Arrangements." *The Business Lawyer* 54:175–207.

Cook, J. Michael, Eugene M. Freedman, Ray J. Groves, Jon C. Madonna, Shaun F. O'Malley, and Lawrence A. Weinbach. 1992. "The Liability Crisis in the United States: Impact on the Accounting Profession." *Journal of Accountancy* (November), 18–23.

Cooter, Robert, and Bradley J. Freedman. 1991. "The Fiduciary Relationship: Its Economic Character and Legal Consequences." *New York University Law Review* 66: 1045–75.

Cotterman, James D., ed. 1995. *Compensation Plans for Law Firms,* 2d ed. Chicago: American Bar Association, Section of Law Practice Management.

Cox, James D., and Harry L. Munsinger. 1985. "Bias in the Boardroom: Psychological Foundations and Legal Implications of Corporate Cohesion." *Law and Contemporary Problems* 48:83–135.

Curran, Barbara A. 1977. *The Legal Needs of the Public: The Final Report of a National Survey.* Chicago: American Bar Foundation.

———. 1989. "1989 Survey of the Public's Use of Legal Services." In *Two Nationwide Surveys: 1989 Pilot Assessments of the Unmet Legal Needs of the Poor and of the Public Generally.* Chicago: American Bar Association.

———. 1995. *Women in the Law: A Look at the Numbers.* Chicago: American Bar Association Commission on Women in the Profession.

Curran, Barbara A., and Clara N. Carson. 1991. *Supplement to the Lawyer Statistical Report: The U.S. Legal Profession in 1988.* Chicago: American Bar Foundation.

———. 1994. *The Lawyer Statistical Report: The U.S. Legal Profession in the 1990s.* Chicago: American Bar Foundation.

Curran, Barbara A., with Katherine J. Rosich, Clara N. Carson, and Mark C. Puccetti. 1985. *The Lawyer Statistical Report: A Statistical Profile of the U.S. Legal Profession in the 1980s.* Chicago: American Bar Foundation.

———. 1986. *Supplement to the Lawyer Statistical Report: The U.S. Legal Profession in 1985.* Chicago: American Bar Foundation.

Davis, Anthony E. 1996. "Professional Liability Insurers as Regulators of Law Practice." *Fordham Law Review* 65:209–32.

Dezalay, Yves, and Bryant G. Garth. 1996. *Dealing in Virtue: International Commercial Arbitration and the Construction of a Transnational Legal Order.* Chicago: University of Chicago Press.

Dzienkowski, John S. 1992. "Lawyers as Intermediaries: The Representation of Multiple Clients in the Modern Legal Profession." *University of Illinois Law Review* 1992:741–817.

———. 1993. "Positional Conflicts of Interest." *Texas Law Review* 71:457–540.

Easterbrook, Frank H., and Daniel R. Fischel. 1983. "Voting in Corporate Law." *Journal of Law and Economics* 26:395–427.

Feerick, John, Carol Izumi, Kimberlee Kovach, Lela Love, Robert Soberly, Leonard Riskin, and Edward Sherman. 1995. "Standards of Professional Conduct in Alternative Dispute Resolution." *Journal of Dispute Resolution* 1995:95–128.

Fox, Kelly A. 1995. "The 100 Largest Illinois Law Firms." *Merrill's Illinois Legal Times* (July), 1, 14–16, 18–20, 22.

Fox, Lawrence J. 1993. "Special Corporate Counsel Report: In-House Ethics: The Ethics of Conflicts: Are There Any?" *The American Lawyer* (March), 41, 42, 44, 45, 48–50.

———. 1997. "Accountant Bosses Pose Ethical Threat." *National Law Journal* (October 6), A23.

Frankel, Tamar. 1983. "Fiduciary Law." *California Law Review* 71:795–836.

———. 1995. "Fiduciary Duties as Default Rules." *Oregon Law Review* 74:1209–77.

Freidson, Eliot. 1975. *Doctoring Together: A Study of Professional Social Control.* Chicago: University of Chicago Press.

———. 1986. *Professional Powers: A Study of the Institutionalization of Formal Knowledge.* Chicago: University of Chicago Press.

Galanter, Marc. 1974. "Why the 'Haves' Come Out Ahead: Speculations on the Limits of Legal Change." *Law & Society Review* 9:95–160.

———. 1994. "Predators and Parasites: Lawyer-Bashing and Civil Justice." *Georgia Law Review* 28:633–81.

Galanter, Marc, and Thomas Palay. 1991. *Tournament of Lawyers: The Transformation of the Big Law Firm.* Chicago: University of Chicago Press.

Galanter, Marc, and Joel Rogers. 1991. "The Transformation of American Business Disputing? Some Preliminary Observations." Institute for Legal Studies, Disputes Processing Research Program, working paper DPRP 10-3.

Garth, Bryant G. 1993. "From Civil Litigation to Private Justice: Legal Practice at War with the Profession and Its Values." *Brooklyn Law Review* 59:931–50.

Gibeaut, John. 1998. "Squeeze Play." *ABA Journal* (February), 42–47.

Gill, Donna. 1992. "Targeting Lawyers: Legal Mal in the '90s." *Chicago Lawyer* (September), 18–21, 63–64, 82.

Gilson, Ronald J. 1990. "The Devolution of the Legal Profession: A Demand Side Perspective." *Maryland Law Review* 49:869–916.

Gluckman, Max. 1967. *The Judicial Process among the Barotse of Northern Rhodesia.* Manchester: Manchester University Press.

Gordon, Robert W., and William H. Simon. 1992. "The Redemption of Professionalism." In *Lawyers' Ideals/Lawyers' Practices: Transformation in the American Legal Profession,* ed. Robert L. Nelson, David M. Trubek, and Rayman L. Solomon. Ithaca: Cornell University Press.

Granovetter, Mark. 1985. "Economic Action and Social Structure: The Problem of Embeddedness." *American Journal of Sociology* 91:481–510.

Halliday, Terence C. 1987. *Beyond Monopoly: Lawyers, State Crises, and Professional Empowerment.* Chicago: University of Chicago Press.

Handler, Joel F. 1967. *The Lawyer and His Community: The Practicing Bar in a Middle-Sized City.* Madison: University of Wisconsin Press.

Hazard, Geoffrey C., Jr. 1987. "Triangular Lawyer Relationships: An Exploratory Analysis." *Georgetown Journal of Legal Ethics* 1:15–42.

———. 1990. "Conflicts Are Often Key in Malpractice." *National Law Journal* (September 10), 13–14.

———. 1996. "Conflict of Interest in the Classic Professions." In *Conflicts of Interest in Clinical Practice and Research,* ed. Roy G. Spece, Jr., David S. Shimm, and Allen E. Buchanan. New York: Oxford University Press.

Hazard, Geoffrey C., Jr., and William W. Hodes. 1990. *The Law of Lawyering: A Handbook on the Model Rules of Professional Conduct.* Englewood Cliffs: Prentice Hall.

Heimer, Carol A. 1985. *Reactive Risk and Rational Action: Managing Moral Hazard in Insurance Contracts.* Berkeley: University of California Press.

Heinz, John P., and Edward O. Laumann. 1982. *Chicago Lawyers: The Social Structure of the Bar.* New York: Russell Sage Foundation.

Heinz, John P., and Edward O. Laumann, with Robert L. Nelson and Paul S. Schnorr. 1997. "The Constituencies of Elite Urban Lawyers." *Law & Society Review* 31:441–72.

Hengstler, Gary A. 1993. "Vox Populi: The Public Perception of Lawyers: ABA Poll." *ABA Journal* (September), 60–65.

Howard, Elizabeth, and Lynn Remly. 1995. "Post-Merger Work: Setting Unified Objectives." *New York Law Journal* (March 28), 5–6.

"The Illinois 100." 1992. *Merrill's Illinois Legal Times* (July), 19–28.

Illinois Legal Directory. 1995. Dallas: Legal Directories Publishing Company.

Illinois State Bar Association. 1995. "ISBA Advisory Opinion on Professional Conduct." Opinion no. 94–22: "Referral Fees" (March) Springfield, IL. http://www.illinoisbar.org/courtsbull/EthicsOpinions/94-22.asp.

Illinois State Bar Association Mutual Insurance Company. 1999a. "History of Our Company." http://www.isbamutual.com/history, January 1, 1999.

———. 1999b. "Loss Prevention." http://www.isbamutual.com/prevention, January 1, 1999.

Illinois Supreme Court Rules. 1990. "Article VIII: Illinois Rules of Professional Conduct." Springfield, IL. http://www.state.il.us/court/SupremeCourtRules/Art_VIII/default.htm.

Jensen, Michael C., and William M. Meckling. 1976. "Theory of the Firm: Managerial Behavior, Agency Costs and Ownership Structure." *Journal of Financial Economics* 3:305–60.

Katz, Jack. 1982. *Poor People's Lawyers in Transition.* New Brunswick: Rutgers University Press.

Klein, Chris. 1997. "Poll: Lawyers Not Liked." *National Law Journal* (August 25), A6.

Kneier, Andrew. 1976. *Serving Two Masters: A Common Cause Study of Conflicts of Interest in the Executive Branch.* Washington, DC: Common Cause.

Kritzer, Herbert M. 1996. "Rhetoric and Reality . . . Uses and Abuses . . . Contingencies and Certainties: The American Contingent Fee in Operation." Madison: Institute for Legal Studies.

Kritzer, Herbert M., William L.F. Felstiner, Austin Sarat, and David Trubek. 1984. "The Impact of Fee Arrangement on Lawyer Effort." Madison: University of Wisconsin Law School, Disputes Processing Research Program.

Kummel, William. 1996. "A Market Approach to Law Firm Economics: A New Model for Pricing, Billing, Compensation and Ownership in Corporate Legal Services." *Columbia Business Law Review* 1996:379–421.

Landon, Donald D. 1988. "LaSalle Street and Main Street: The Role of Context in Structuring Law Practice." *Law & Society Review* 22:213–36.

———. 1990. *Country Lawyers: The Impact of Context on Professional Practice.* New York: Praeger.

Larson, Magali Sarfatti. 1977. *The Rise of Professionalism: A Sociological Analysis.* Berkeley: University of California Press.

Law Firms Yellow Book. 1995. New York: Monitor Publishing Company.

Lipset, Seymour Martin, and William Schneider. 1983. *The Confidence Gap: Business, Labor, and Government in the Public Mind.* New York: Free Press.

Lum, Sherlene K.S., and Robert E. Yuskavage. 1997. "Gross Product by Industry, 1947–96." *Survey of Current Business* (November), 20–34.

Mann, Kenneth. 1985. *Defending White-Collar Crime: A Portrait of Attorneys at Work.* New Haven: Yale University Press.

Martindale-Hubbell Law Directory. 1963–95. New Providence, NJ: Reed Publishing.

Martindale-Hubbell Law Directory (CD-ROM). 1995. New Providence, NJ: Reed Publishing.

Menkel-Meadow, Carrie. 1994. "The Future of the Legal Profession: Culture Clash in the Quality of Life in the Law: Changes in the Economics, Diversification and Organization of Lawyering." *Case Western Reserve Law Review* 44:621–63.

_____. 1995. "Ethics and the Settlement of Mass Torts: When the Rules Meet the Road." *Cornell Law Review* 80:1159–1221.

———. 1997. "Ethics in Alternative Dispute Resolution: New Issues, No Answers from the Adversary Conception of Lawyers' Responsibilities." *South Texas Law Review* 38:407–54.

Merrill's Illinois Legal Times. 1995. "Legal Map of Chicago, 1995" (August).

Moe, Terry M. 1984. "The New Economics of Organization." *American Journal of Political Science* 28:739–77.

Morris, John E. 1998a. "King Arthur's March on Europe." *American Lawyer* (June), 48.

———. 1998b. "Too Good To Be True?" *The American Lawyer* (July/August), 5.

National Association for Law Placement. 1994. *Directory of Legal Employers.* New Orleans: National Association for Law Placement.

The National Data Book: Statistical Abstract of the United States, 117th ed. 1997. Washington, DC: U.S. Bureau of the Census.

Neil, Martha. 2000a. "Corporations See Increase in Fees Paid to Law Firms." *Chicago Daily Law Bulletin* (January 18), 1.

———. 2000b. "More Women Than Men May Start Classes in 2000." *Chicago Daily Law Bulletin* (May 5), 3.

Nelson, Robert L. 1988. *Partners with Power: The Social Transformation of the Large Law Firm.* Berkeley: University of California Press.

———. 1994. "The Futures of American Lawyers: A Demographic Profile of a Changing Profession in a Changing Society." *Case Western Reserve Law Review* 44:345–406.

Nelson, Robert L., David M. Trubek, and Rayman L. Solomon, eds. 1992. *Lawyers' Ideals/Lawyers' Practices: Transformation in the American Legal Profession.* Ithaca: Cornell University Press.

Nelson, William E. 1990. "Contract Litigation and the Elite Bar in New York City, 1960–1980." *Emory Law Journal* 39:413–61.

1990 Census Snapshot for All U.S. Places. 1992. Milpitas, CA: Toucan Valley Publications.

"No Surprise: The Public Mistrusts Lawyers." 1993. *National Law Journal* (September 6), 6.

Oster, Patrick. 1998. "The NLJ 250: Annual Survey of the Nation's Largest Law Firms." *National Law Journal* (November 16), C5–C18.

Overton, George W. 1990. "Supervisory Responsibility: A New Ball Game for Law Firms and Lawyers." *Illinois Bar Journal* (September), 434–36.

Papanastasiou, Claire. 1996. "Help Wanted! Finally, There's Some Good News for Lawyers in the Job Market." *Massachusetts Lawyers Weekly* (August 26), B1.

Patton, Paula A. 1996. "Things Are Looking Up—If You're Already In." *National Law Journal* (August 19), C4.

Pierson Graphics. 1988. *Loop and Central Chicago.* Birds.eye.View, 1995 edition. Denver: Pierson Graphics Corp.

Pizzimenti, Lee A. 1997. "Screen Verité: Do Rules about Ethical Screens Reflect the Truth about Real-Life Law Firm Practice?" *University of Miami Law Review* 52:305–64.

Pratt, John W., and Richard J. Zeckhauser, eds. 1985. *Principals and Agents: The Structure of Business.* Boston: Harvard Business School Press.

"Public Confidence in Leaders Hits Low—Lawyers at Bottom." 1997. *National Law Journal* (March 10), A5.

Ramos, Manuel R. 1996. "Legal Malpractice: Reforming Lawyers and Law Professors." *Tulane Law Review* 70:2583–2629.

"A Record Year, In Spite of Everything." 2001. *The American Lawyer* (July), 149–50.

Reed, Richard C., ed. 1989. *Beyond the Billable Hour: An Anthology of Alternative Billing Methods.* Chicago: American Bar Association Section of Economics of Law Practice.

Rodwin, Marc A. 1993. *Medicine, Money and Morals: Physician's Conflicts of Interest.* New York: Oxford University Press.

———. 1995. "Strains in the Fiduciary Metaphor: Divided Physician Loyalties and Obligations in a Changing Health Care System." *American Journal of Law and Medicine* 21:241–57.

Romansic, Lara E. 1998. "Conflict of Interest: Stand By Your Client? Opinion 95–390 and Conflicts of Interest in Corporate Families." *Georgetown Journal of Legal Ethics* 11:307–18.

Rosen, Robert E. 1989. "The Inside Counsel Movement, Professional Judgment and Organizational Representation." *Indiana Law Journal:* 64:479–553.

Rosenthal, Douglas. 1974. *Lawyer and Client: Who's in Charge?* New York: Russell Sage Foundation.

Ross, William G. 1996. *The Honest Hour: The Ethics of Time-Based Billing by Attorneys.* Durham, NC: Carolina Academic Press.

Rubenstein, David. 1997. "Big Six Poised to Enter Legal Market." *Illinois Legal Times* (October), 1, 19–21.

Samborn, Randall. 1993a. "Anti-Lawyer Attitude Up." *National Law Journal* (August 9), 1, 20–24.

———. 1993b. "Tracking Trends." *National Law Journal* (August 9), 20.

Sander, Richard H., and E. Douglass Williams. 1989. "Why Are There So Many Lawyers? Perspectives on a Turbulent Market." *Law & Social Inquiry* 14:431–79.

Sarat, Austin, and William L.F. Felstiner. 1995. *Divorce Lawyers and Their Clients: Power and Meaning in the Legal Process.* New York: Oxford University Press.

Schneyer, Ted. 1991. "Professional Discipline for Law Firms?" *Cornell Law Review* 77:1–46.

Schnorr, Paul, John P. Heinz, Robert L. Nelson, and Edward O. Laumann. 1995. "Changing Patterns of Inequality in the Chicago Bar: 1974–1994." Paper presented at the Law & Society Association Annual Meeting, June 4, Toronto.

Seron, Carroll. 1992. "Managing Entrepreneurial Legal Services: The Transformation of Small-Firm Practice." In *Lawyers' Ideals/Lawyers' Practices: Transformation in the American Legal Profession,* ed. Robert L. Nelson, David M. Trubek, and Rayman L. Solomon. Ithaca: Cornell University Press.

———. 1996. *The Business of Practicing Law: The Work Lives of Solo and Small-Firm Attorneys.* Philadelphia: Temple University Press.

Shapiro, Susan P. 1984. *Wayward Capitalists: Target of the Securities and Exchange Commission.* New Haven: Yale University Press.

———. 1987. "The Social Control of Impersonal Trust." *American Journal of Sociology* 93:623–58.

———. 1989. "Libel Lawyers as Risk Counselors: Pre-Publication and Pre-Broadcast Review and the Social Construction of News." *Law & Policy* 11:281–308.

———. 1990. "Collaring the Crime, Not the Criminal: Reconsidering the Concept of White-Collar Crime." *American Sociological Review* 55:346–65.

———. 1999. "The Roads Not Taken: An Unorthodox Journey across the Landscape of the Legal Profession." American Bar Foundation, working paper 9909.

———. 2002. "Bushwhacking the Ethical High Road: Conflict of Interest in the Practice of Law and Real Life." American Bar Foundation, working paper 2101.

Shaw, David. 1998. "Breaching the Wall: A Revolution in American Newspapers. Cooperation within *Times* Viewed with Trepidation; Publisher Says Interdepartmental Initiative Will Foster Journalistic Success, but Many in Newsroom Fear Intrusion." *Los Angeles Times* (March 30), A21.

Siegel, Matt. 1994. "The Next Step in Conflicts Checks." *American Lawyer* (November), 110–12.

Slater, Courtenay M., and George E. Hall, eds. 1995. *1995 County and City Extra: Annual Metro, City and County Data Book.* Lanham, MD: Bernan Press.

Smigel, Erwin Orson. 1964. *The Wall Street Lawyer: Professional Organization Man?* New York: The Free Press of Glencoe.

Spangler, Eve. 1986. *Lawyers for Hire: Salaried Professionals at Work.* New Haven: Yale University Press.

"Special Supplement: Annual Survey of National Accounting Firms—2001." 2001. *Public Accounting Report,* S1.

Spillenger, Clyde. 1996. "Elusive Advocate: Reconsidering Brandeis as People's Lawyer." *Yale Law Journal* 105:1445–1535.

Stewart, James B. 1983. *The Partners: Inside America's Most Powerful Law Firms.* New York: Simon and Schuster.

Stone, Harlan F. 1934. "The Public Influence of the Bar." *Harvard Law Review* 48:1–14.

Suchman, Mark C. 1994. *On Advice of Counsel: Law Firms and Venture Capital Funds as Information Intermediaries in the Structuration of Silicon Valley.* Ph.D. diss., Stanford University.

Sullivan's Law Directory. 1992. Barrington, IL: Law Bulletin Publishing.

"The NLJ 250: A Special 5-Year Report on the Dramatic Growth of the Nation's Largest Law Firms." 1983. *National Law Journal,* a Special Anniversary Section (September 19), 1–19.

"The NLJ 250." 2000. *National Law Journal* (December 4), C1–C17.

Tuite, Cornelia Honchar. 1992. "Lawyers Called to the Stand May Witness Their Own Dismissal." *Chicago Daily Law Bulletin* (February 7), 5.

———. 1993. "Occasionally, Newly Hired Lawyers Can 'Rob' a Firm of Business." *Chicago Daily Law Bulletin* (December 3), 6.

Twentieth Century Fund. 1980. *Abuse on Wall Street: Conflicts of Interest in the Securities Markets.* Westport, CT: Quorum.

U.S. Securities and Exchange Commission. 2000. "Independent Consultant Finds Widespread Independence Violations at PricewaterhouseCoopers." Press release, January 6.

Useem, Michael. 1979. "The Social Organization of the American Business Elite and Participation of Corporation Directors in the Governance of American Institutions." *American Sociological Review* 44:553–72.

Van Hoy, Jerry. 1997. *Franchise Law Firms and the Transformation of Personal Legal Services.* Westport, CT: Quorum.

Walker, Richard H. 1998. "Auditor Independence—The Issues." Symposium on the CPA and Independence, sponsored by the New York State Society of CPAs and the CPA Journal, December 17. http://www.sec.gov/news/speech/speecharchive/1998/spch246.txt.

Wall, M. Elizabeth. 1998. "Summary of Testimony of M. Elizabeth Wall before the Multidisciplinary Practice Commission." November 12, Washington, DC. http://www.abanet.org/cpr/wall1198.html.

Weidlich, Thom. 1993. "Law Firm Mergers Dwindle." *National Law Journal* (April 19), 1, 27.

Weil, Fred B. 1968. *The 1967 Lawyer Statistical Report.* Chicago: American Bar Foundation.

Weinrib, Ernest J. 1975. "The Fiduciary Obligation." *University of Toronto Law Journal* 25:1–22.

Weisenhaus, Doreen. 1991. "The NLJ 250: Annual Survey of the Nation's Largest Law Firms." *National Law Journal* (September 30), S5, S6, S13–S31.

Welles, Chris. 1980. "Nonprofit Institutions." In *Abuse on Wall Street: Conflicts of Interest in the Securities Markets,* Report to the Twentieth Century Fund. Westport, CT: Quorum.

Whitfield, Robert. 1996. "Few Benefits from Present Law Firm M&A Process." *Illinois Legal Times* (July), 8.

Who Audits America. 2000. Menlo Park, CA: Data Financial Press.

Wilkins, David B., and G. Mitu Gulati. 1996. "Why Are There So Few Black Lawyers in Corporate Law Firms? An Institutional Analysis." *California Law Review* 84: 493–618.

Williamson, Oliver. 1975. *Markets and Hierarchies.* New York: Free Press.

Wolfram, Charles W. 1986. *Modern Legal Ethics.* St. Paul, MN: West.

Wunnicke, Brooke. 1989. "The Eternal Triangle: Standards of Ethical Representation by the Insurance Defense Lawyer." *For the Defense* 31(2):7–16.

CASES

Flatt v. Superior Court, 885 P.2d 950 (Cal. 1994).

Peat, Marwick, Mitchell & Co. v. Superior Court, 200 Cal. App. 3d 272 (Cal. Ct. App. 1988).

Picker Int'l, Inc. v. Varian Assocs., Inc., 670 F. Supp. 1363 (N.D. Ohio 1987), *aff'd,* 869 F.2d 578 (Fed. Cir. 1989).

Truck Ins. Exch. v. Fireman's Fund Ins. Co., 6 Cal App. 4th 1050 (Cal Ct. App. 1992).

Index

CONFLICTS, BY HAPPENSTANCE, SERVED AS A PATHWAY BACK TO MYSELF.(?)

OVER THE LAST 5 YRS I HAVE HAD THE OPPORTUNITY TO GAIN EXPERIE[NCE] & UNDERSTANDING IN A SOMEWHAT PECULIAR & OFTEN OVERLOOKED FIELD. THE PRACTICE OF LAW FINDS ITSELF IN A UNIQUE POSITION

- THE LAWYER/CLIENT RELATIONSHIP CREATES A SPECIAL ETHICAL & LEGAL BOND. CONFIDENCES MUST BE GUARDED & INTERESTS MUST BE PROTECTED & ADVANCED. THE LAWYER & THE FIRM, GENERALLY SPEAKING, ARE BOUND TO ACTIVELY .... BLAH BLAH

KEYS - FOCUS ON 'SPECIALNESS' OF LEGAL PROFESSION
- FOCUS ON UBIQUITY OF CONFLICTS
  - ↳ INTERNALLY FOR ~~EACH~~ NATURAL PERSON (INDIV.)
  - ↳ AMONGST ORGANIZATIONS & EVERY FACE[T] OF LI[FE]
- FOCUS ON MORASS OF INTERESTS IN MODERN LIFE
  - ↳ CORPORATE RELATIONSHIPS
  - ↳ INCREASED PERSONAL RESPONSIBILITY / ROLES
  - ↳ POLITICAL (527's, ETC...)
  - ↳ GLOBALIZATION (PRODUCTION / INVESTMENT / ETC...)

THE DIFFICULTY OF KNOWING WHETHER AN ACTION WILL FURTHER YOUR OWN INTERESTS
IN KNOWING THE ORIGIN OF IDEAS & PRODUCTS
OF KNOWING THE DESTINATION OF PROFITS

TRANSPARENCY & AWARENESS (ACTIVELY GUARDING AGAINST)

- FOCUS ON EFFORTS W/IN CONFLICTS
  - PAPER
    - OPEN SOURCE
    - OFFSHORE
    - SPECIALIZATION

POTENTIALLY MIRRORING LARGER SCALE SOLUTIONS.

FEW ARENAS - POLITICAL, BUSINESS, PERSONAL
HAVE DEVELOPED THE SENSITIVITY TO CONFLICTS
OF INTEREST THAT THE LEGAL PROFESSION HAS.

& THIS SENSITIVITY, THIS ABILITY TO DISCOVER & MANAGE
CONFLICT, TO LAY BARE THE WEB OF RELATIONS,

&